D0742360

MANAGING PRODUCT INNOVATION

ADVANCES IN BUSINESS MARKETING & PURCHASING

Series Editor: Arch G. Woodside

Recent Volumes:

ADVANCES IN BUSINESS MARKETING & PURCHASING
VOLUME 13

MANAGING PRODUCT INNOVATION

EDITED BY

ARCH G. WOODSIDE

*Wallace E. Carroll School of Management, Boston College,
Massachusetts, USA*

2005

ELSEVIER
JAI

Amsterdam – Boston – Heidelberg – London – New York – Oxford
Paris – San Diego – San Francisco – Singapore – Sydney – Tokyo

ELSEVIER B.V.	ELSEVIER Inc.	**ELSEVIER Ltd**	ELSEVIER Ltd
Radarweg 29	525 B Street, Suite 1900	**The Boulevard, Langford**	84 Theobalds Road
P.O. Box 211	San Diego	**Lane, Kidlington**	London
1000 AE Amsterdam	CA 92101-4495	**Oxford OX5 1GB**	WC1X 8RR
The Netherlands	USA	**UK**	UK

© 2005 Elsevier Ltd. All rights reserved.

This work is protected under copyright by Elsevier Ltd, and the following terms and conditions apply to its use:

Photocopying
Single photocopies of single chapters may be made for personal use as allowed by national copyright laws. Permission of the Publisher and payment of a fee is required for all other photocopying, including multiple or systematic copying, copying for advertising or promotional purposes, resale, and all forms of document delivery. Special rates are available for educational institutions that wish to make photocopies for non-profit educational classroom use.

Permissions may be sought directly from Elsevier's Rights Department in Oxford, UK; phone: (+44) 1865 843830, fax: (+44) 1865 853333, e-mail: permissions@elsevier.com. Requests may also be completed on-line via the Elsevier homepage (http://www.elsevier.com/locate/permissions).

In the USA, users may clear permissions and make payments through the Copyright Clearance Center, Inc., 222 Rosewood Drive, Danvers, MA 01923, USA; phone: (+1) (978) 7508400, fax: (+1) (978) 7504744, and in the UK through the Copyright Licensing Agency Rapid Clearance Service (CLARCS), 90 Tottenham Court Road, London W1P 0LP, UK; phone: (+44) 20 7631 5555; fax: (+44) 20 7631 5500. Other countries may have a local reprographic rights agency for payments.

Derivative Works
Tables of contents may be reproduced for internal circulation, but permission of the Publisher is required for external resale or distribution of such material. Permission of the Publisher is required for all other derivative works, including compilations and translations.

Electronic Storage or Usage
Permission of the Publisher is required to store or use electronically any material contained in this work, including any chapter or part of a chapter.

Except as outlined above, no part of this work may be reproduced, stored in a retrieval system or transmitted in any form or by any means, electronic, mechanical, photocopying, recording or otherwise, without prior written permission of the Publisher. Address permissions requests to: Elsevier's Rights Department, at the fax and e-mail addresses noted above.

Notice
No responsibility is assumed by the Publisher for any injury and/or damage to persons or property as a matter of products liability, negligence or otherwise, or from any use or operation of any methods, products, instructions or ideas contained in the material herein. Because of rapid advances in the medical sciences, in particular, independent verification of diagnoses and drug dosages should be made.

First edition 2005

British Library Cataloguing in Publication Data
A catalogue record is available from the British Library.

ISBN: 0-7623-1159-2
ISSN: 1069-0964 (Series)

⊗ The paper used in this publication meets the requirements of ANSI/NISO Z39.48-1992 (Permanence of Paper). Printed in The Netherlands.

Working together to grow libraries in developing countries

www.elsevier.com | www.bookaid.org | www.sabre.org

ELSEVIER   BOOK AID International   Sabre Foundation

CONTENTS

v

LIST OF CONTRIBUTORS

Fredrik von Corswant	Department of Operations Management and Work Organization, School of Technology Management and Economics, Chalmers University of Technology, Göteborg, Sweden
Magnar Forbord	Centre for Rural Research, Norwegian University of Science and Technology, Trondheim, Norway
Ricardo Madureira	University of Vaasa, Faculty of Business Studies, Department of Marketing, Finland
Paul Matthyssens	Department of Management (University of Antwerp) and Erasmus University, Rotterdam
Hans Mühlbacher	University of Innsbruck, Austria
Günter Specht	Technical University Darmstadt, Germany
Petri Suomala	Tampere University of Technology, Cost Management Center, Finland
Koen Vandenbempt	University of Antwerp, Faculty of Applied Economics – Department of Management, Belgium
Clas Wahlbin	Jönköping University, Sweden
Arch G. Woodside	Boston College, Department of Marketing, Carroll School, USA

EDITORIAL BOARD

Per Andersson
*Stockholm School of
Economics*

J. Scott Armstrong
*Wharton, University of
Pennsylvania*

George J. Avlonitis
*Athens University of Economics
and Business*

Joseph F. Hair
*Ourso School, Louisiana State
University*

Wesley J. Johnston
Georgia State University

J. David Lichtenthal
*Baruch College, City University of
New York*

Peter W. Liesch
University of Queensland

Kristian Möller
*Helsinki School of Economics and
Business Administration*

Hans Mühlbacher
*University of Innsbruck,
Austria*

James A. Narus
*Babcock Graduate School, Wake
Forest University*

Jagdish N. Sheth
*Goizueta School of Business,
Emory University*

Lars Silver
Uppsala University

Günter Specht
*Technical University Darmstadt,
Germany*

Robert J. Thomas
Georgetown University

Jan B. Vollering
Rotterdam School of Management

David T. Wilson
*Smeal College of Business,
Pennsylvania State University*

Jerry Wind
*Wharton University of
Pennsylvania*

Arch G. Woodside
Carroll School, Boston College

Eunsang Yoon
*University of Massachusetts at
Lowell*

PREFACE

The dominating theme in Volume 13 is managing new product development (NPD) processes. Historical research on firm-level innovation behavior results in the following main conclusion: firm-level decisions focusing on innovations are critical, difficult, and often result in failure to act. While acceptance is widespread among executives that firms must innovate radically as well as incrementally, success by firms mostly nurtures inertia and eventual failure rather than search and adoption of new superior technologies. What does it take to craft and maintain successful radical NPD programs? Volume 13 provides worthwhile answers on the specific actions executives can adopt to achieve successful radical NPD programs.

Related to managing new NPD processes successfully and additional strategic marketing issues, the following few words summarize the wisdom that Volume 13 elaborates upon:

- Leverage interfirm relationships
- Pay attention to products that can be co-created by interfirm networks
- Think and act globally via personal contacts
- Evaluate NPD performance using a life cycle perspective
- Identify upstream as well as direct influences on NPD performance.

Volume 13 includes six papers. The volume follows prior practice in presenting the papers in alphabetical order by name of the lead author.

LEVERAGING RELATIONSHIPS: ORGANIZING INTERACTIVE NEW PRODUCT DEVELOPMENT

In the first paper, Fredrik von Corswant offers a firm level theory of interfirm network relationships for blending resources effectively for NPD. Thick descriptions of NPD processes in three case studies in the transportation vehicle industries illustrate the theory. A key conclusion: modular product development may entail a modular organization with regard to teams and interactions between business units including entire enterprises.

PAYING ATTENTION TO PRODUCTS THAT CAN BE CO-CREATED BY INTERFIRM NETWORKS

Both products and interfirm relationships can grow old and die. In the second paper, Magnar Forbord describes how a seemingly old and tired product can be transformed using the same network relationship theory introduced in the first paper. A key conclusion: a series of micro tactical breakthroughs are implemented by cooperating executives working in an interfirm network of relationships; a new product champion must become a network champion.

THINKING AND ACTING GLOBALLY VIA PERSONAL CONTACTS

In the third paper, Ricardo Madureira applies the industrial network approach to describe how multinational firms coordinate the implementation of strategy globally. As an example, the paper empirically focuses on Portuguese sales subsidiaries of Finnish multinational corporations. A key conclusion: executives operating cross-nationally benefit from awareness and training in multiple interpersonal roles – thinking and acting globally requires adaptability in interpersonal communications. Madureira illustrates nuances that must be learned for developing such adaptability.

EVALUATING NPD PERFORMANCE THROUGH THE LIFE CYCLE

In the fourth paper, Petri Suomala evaluates NPD performance across entire life cycles for six B2B environments. This paper advances NPD evaluation research beyond the traditional view of whether or not a product gains sales volume and profitability. Key conclusions in this paper include the following points. Profitability, to a great extent, depends not only on the physical product but increasingly also on after-sales business and service function. Life cycle costing is one of the means that can be applied to grasp the cumulative effects of products and product life cycles.

OVERCOMING BARRIERS TO STRATEGIC INNOVATION IN INDUSTRIAL MARKETS

In the fifth paper Vandenbempt and Matthyssens bridge the gap between the strategy literature and the business-to-business marketing literature by applying a multilevel methodology. The paper gives insight on how firms may overcome barriers to strategic innovation. It addresses the following questions:

(1) Which barriers withhold managers from adapting their competitive strategy and improving their overall market position?
(2) What strategies overcome these barriers and what is the impact of these strategies on the management of relationships?
(3) How can a network perspective enable managers to overcome barriers to strategic innovation?

IDENTIFYING UPSTREAM AS WELL AS DIRECT INFLUENCES ON NPD PERFORMANCE

In the final paper, Woodside, Specht, Mühlbacher and Wahlbin advance a system dynamics view for evaluating NPD performance. The paper is unique in examining both highly successful and not-so-successful product introductions among high-tech Austrian, German, and Swedish firms. A key conclusion: multiple paths lead to high versus low NPD success – the presence or absence of any one "key success factor" is not want is critical – it's the alternative interactive paths of factors that lead to success or failure.

A NOTE OF GRATITUDE AND A DEDICATION

The success of the Advances in Business Marketing and Purchasing series is due in large part to the sharing of substantial expertise by members of the Editorial Board. Each paper published in the ABM&P series completes two to five rounds of double-blind reviews – and given the objective of publishing more in-depth papers than found in a journal format – the resulting reviews require longer hours and greater toil. On behalf of the authors and readers of the ABM&P series, Volume 13 is dedicated to the members of the ABM&P Editorial Board. Thank you for your efforts, insights, and very useful suggestions for improving the contents as well as the styles of the papers.

Arch G. Woodside
Editor

ORGANIZING INTERACTIVE PRODUCT DEVELOPMENT

Fredrik von Corswant

ABSTRACT

This paper deals with the organizing of interactive product development. Developing products in interaction between firms may provide benefits in terms of specialization, increased innovation, and possibilities to perform development activities in parallel. However, the differentiation of product development among a number of firms also implies that various dependencies *need to be dealt with across firm boundaries. How dependencies may be dealt with across firms is related to how product development is organized. The purpose of the paper is to explore dependencies and how interactive product development may be organized with regard to these dependencies.*

The analytical framework is based on the industrial network approach, and deals with the development of products in terms of adaptation and combination of heterogeneous resources. *There are dependencies between resources, that is, they are* embedded, *implying that no resource can be developed in isolation. The characteristics of and dependencies related to four main categories of resources* (products, production facilities, business units *and* business relationships) *provide a basis for analyzing the organizing of interactive product development.*

Three in-depth case studies are used to explore the organizing of interactive product development with regard to dependencies. The first two cases are based on the development of the electrical system and the seats for Volvo's

Managing Product Innovation
Advances in Business Marketing and Purchasing, Volume 13, 1–209
Copyright © 2005 by Elsevier Ltd.
All rights of reproduction in any form reserved
ISSN: 1069-0964/doi:10.1016/S1069-0964(04)13001-9

large car platform (P2), performed in interaction with Delphi and Lear respectively. The third case is based on the interaction between Scania and Dayco/DFC Tech for the development of various pipes and hoses for a new truck model.

The analysis is focused on what *different dependencies the firms considered and dealt with, and* how *product development was organized with regard to these dependencies. It is concluded that there is a* complex *and* dynamic *pattern of dependencies that reaches far beyond the developed product as well as beyond individual business units. To deal with these dependencies, development may be organized in* teams *where several business units are represented. This enables* interaction *between different business units' resource collections, which is important for resource adaptation as well as for innovation. The* delimiting *and* relating *functions of the team boundary are elaborated upon and it is argued that also teams may be regarded as actors. It is also concluded that a modular product structure may entail a modular organization with regard to the teams, though, interaction between business units and teams is needed. A strong connection between the technical structure and the organizational structure is identified and it is concluded that policies regarding the technical structure (e.g. concerning "carry-over") cannot be separated from the management of the organizational structure (e.g. the supplier structure). The organizing of product development is in itself a complex and dynamic task that needs to be subject to interaction between business units.*

1. INTRODUCTION

When you and I met, the meeting was over very shortly, it was nothing. Now it is growing something as we remember it. But still we know very little about it. What it will be when I remember it as I lie down to die, what it makes in me all my days till then – that is the real meeting. The other is only the beginning of it.

C. S. Lewis, Out of the Silent Planet (1938).

This paper deals with the organizing of interactive product development. This phenomenon has received an increasing interest in the past decades, not least regarding the automotive industry (see e.g. Kamath & Liker, 1994; Lamming, 1993; Womack et al., 1990). Auto manufacturers seek new organizational forms for interacting with suppliers in product development to cope with rapid technology development and to reduce production cost (e.g. von Corswant & Fredriksson, 2002). Involving suppliers in product development implies that product development activities are divided between different firms. With such *differentiation* also follows a need for *integration*, i.e. a need to coordinate development activities that are carried out by different firms. The need for integration is related to *dependencies* between different development activities. Due to dependencies, a change of the design of a specific component may influence several other components, as well as various other resources. By exploring what dependencies need to be considered and dealt with, an improved understanding regarding the organizing of interactive product development can be achieved.

The dependencies that need to be considered and dealt with when organizing product development stretch across several firm boundaries. The analysis therefore requires a framework that, in addition to dyadic relationships, can be used for analyzing interaction between a number of different firms. An analytical framework based on the Industrial Network Approach (e.g. Axelsson & Easton, 1992; Håkansson & Snehota, 1995) has been developed. In particular, there is a focus on the resource-layer in the network model, and the framework provides a basis for analyzing dependencies related to the four resource categories *products*, *production facilities*, *business units*, and *business relationships* (Håkansson & Waluszewski, 2002). These resource categories provide a basis for exploring the organizing of interactive product development.

The empirical material originates in three longitudinal in-depth case studies conducted within the automotive industry (both cars and trucks, see Section 4). The first two cases are focused on the development of components for the electrical system and the seats for Volvo's large car platform in interaction with Delphi and Lear respectively. The third case is focused on the development of pipes and hoses for a new truck model, performed in interaction between Scania and DFC Tech.

Based on the theoretical framework and the three cases, an analysis is performed regarding the characteristics of and dependencies related to the four resource categories products, production facilities, business units, and business relationships. The analysis is then concerned with how interactive product development was organized in the different cases with regard to the dependencies between resources. In other words, this paper explores *what* dependencies between resources had to be considered and dealt with and *how* interactive product development may be organized with regard to these dependencies.

1.1. Structure of the Paper

The structure of the paper is illustrated in Fig. 1.

In this first section follows an industrial background to interaction with suppliers in automotive product development is provided. Then, a theoretical background is provided in terms of differentiation and integration. This also includes an

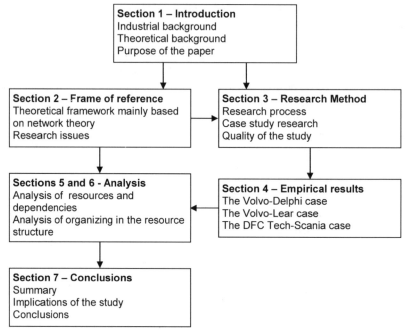

Fig. 1. The Structure of the Paper.

interorganizational perspective on organizing. The problem at hand is discussed in relation to previous research and, by the end of this section, the purpose of the paper is formulated.

In Section 2, a theoretical framework for organizing interactive product development is developed, based on the Industrial Network Approach. The framework is mainly focused on resources, and a model for interactive development of products, production facilities, business units, and business relationships provides an important basis for the analysis. The section ends with the identification of three research issues.

In Section 3, the research process is outlined, including descriptions of the different research projects behind this paper. The methods used are described and discussed, and various methodological considerations are reflected upon.

In Section 4, empirical data from the three case studies is described. First, a description of the new car platform and Volvo's supplier relationships is provided. This is followed by descriptions of the development performed in Volvo's relationships with Delphi and Lear respectively. Then, the development of various pipes and hoses in interaction between DFC Tech and Scania is described.

With the theoretical framework outlined in Section 2 as a basis, an analysis of the empirical data is performed in Section 5 concerning characteristics of and dependencies between resources (i.e. *what* needs to be organized).

In Section 6, the analysis is focused on *how* interactive product development was organized with regard to dependencies between resources. In particular, the analysis is focused on how interactive development is organized in relationships and development teams to create and deal with dependencies.

Then a brief summary of the paper is provided, implications of the study are discussed, and conclusions are drawn.

1.2. Background and Problem Description

Auto manufacturers have always to some extent been dependent on suppliers. Already at the beginning of the 20th century, the pioneering automakers relied on suppliers for product development. Hochfelder and Helper (1996) describe this with the following words: "Despite the legends of lone heroic inventors tinkering with their first automobiles under primitive backyard conditions, the first automobile builders relied on an existing network of supplier firms skilled at producing precision components for bicycles and carriages." No single auto manufacturer was able to alone develop all the technology needed for a functioning automobile. As noted by Womack et al. (1990, p. 24), "[m]ost parts and much of the vehicle's design came from small machine shops. The system was coordinated by an owner/entrepreneur in direct contact with everyone involved – customers, employers, and suppliers." In some cases, even the complete car was delivered from suppliers, requiring the auto manufacturer only to label and sell the vehicle. However, as production volumes increased and automakers grew larger and became increasingly vertically integrated, the suppliers' role in product development was steadily reduced (Hochfelder & Helper, 1996). Many suppliers were acquired by auto manufacturers, or ended up producing components on the basis of drawings and specifications provided by auto manufacturers (e.g. Chandler, 1962; Lamming, 1993; Womack et al., 1990).

Then, during the last decades of the 20th century, the suppliers' role in product development has come into focus again, mainly as it was revealed as an important factor behind the challenging competitiveness of Japanese auto manufacturers (Bidault et al., 1998; Hochfelder & Helper, 1996). In a situation with tough competition, auto manufacturers are seeking ways to reduce development and production costs (e.g. Lamming, 1990; Womack et al., 1990). In addition, product specialization, rapid development of new technologies and shorter product life cycles have led to a focus on reducing time to market (e.g. Millson et al., 1992; Smith & Reinertsen, 1992; Wheelwright & Clark, 1992).

What role, then, does supplier involvement play in such a situation? It seems that the most important benefits associated with product development collaboration are reduced development time in combination with reduced costs and improved product performance and quality (Bidault et al., 1998; Clark, 1989; Dyer, 1996; Littler et al., 1995; Wasti & Liker, 1997; Wynstra & ten Pierick, 2000).

Clark (1989) found that planning and administration of product development could be done faster and more efficiently within the network established between the customer firm and their suppliers than within the customer firm only. Even a modest share of development performed by suppliers was found to shorten development time considerably. According to Bidault et al. (1998), timesavings can be contributed to parallel development work and a reduction of rework. Further, early availability of prototypes and early identification of problems save time (Bonaccorsi & Lipparini, 1994). For example, Dyer (1996) identified that since 1989 Chrysler had reduced the time it takes to develop a new vehicle by more than 40%. Supplier involvement was regarded as an essential factor behind this reduction.

Further, collaboration with other firms in development is often seen as a way to access new technologies (Lambe & Spekman, 1997), to improve innovation (Bidault & Cummings, 1994; Chesbrough & Teece, 1996; Teece, 1989) and to increase specialization (Axelsson, 1987; Brusoni & Prencipe, 2001; Sanchez & Mahoney, 1996). Considering suppliers' experience and knowledge is important since decisions made already in the early phases of product development can have a significant impact on product performance and cost (Ragatz et al., 1997). Further, Clark (1989) found that supplier collaboration allows the customer to use more specifically designed parts in their products, thereby improving product performance. At the same time, involving suppliers may imply that suppliers' existing component designs can be reused, thereby contributing to component standardization (Bonaccorsi & Lipparini, 1994). Another aspect of product performance is that with collaboration the product can be better adapted to manufacturing and assembly processes (Bidault et al., 1998; Burt, 1989; Wasti & Liker, 1997).

Hence, auto manufacturers relied on suppliers for product development already in the early days of the automobile era. Later, vertical integration reduced the suppliers' role in product development. However, tough cost requirements combined with rapid technology development has led to a renewed interest for collaboration with suppliers. This shift from viewing product development mainly as an internal matter to also incorporating other firms, influences the organizing of product development. Various issues related to supplier relationships and collaboration with suppliers in product development have been covered during the past two decades in a growing amount of research. This is further elaborated in the following sections.

1.2.1. Division of Product Development Activities Between Firms

A fundamental problem that arises when suppliers are involved in product development is how development activities should be divided between firms (i.e. between the auto manufacturer and the respective suppliers). It seems that this issue can be related to the overall design of the product. By dividing the product into smaller product elements, the development work can be divided between firms.

In studies of Japanese car manufacturers, Clark (1989) and Clark and Fujimoto (1991) among others, have found that components and systems are often divided into three main categories; supplier proprietary parts, black box parts and detail controlled parts. Supplier proprietary parts are standard components where the supplier assumes full responsibility for the development. These are often referred to as standard or "off-the-shelf" parts. Detail controlled parts, on the other hand, are entirely developed by the auto manufacturer, and the supplier is responsible for process engineering and production. Hence, both these product categories imply a division of work, though, only to the extent that either the customer or the supplier performs the development.

However, for the third category, black box parts, development work is divided between the auto manufacturer and the suppliers. The auto manufacturer typically provides cost and performance requirements, exterior shapes, interface details and other basic design information based on the total vehicle planning. This is then used as an input to the supplier's development process. According to Clark and Fujimoto, black box parts enable auto manufacturers to utilize suppliers' development capabilities while retaining control of basic design (cf. "product architecture"; Ulrich & Eppinger, 1995) and total vehicle integrity. However, Lamming (1993) argues that the term black box is not fully adequate since it is also necessary to distinguish "gray box" parts. These are black box parts where the auto manufacturer has more influence on the internal functioning of the parts. Hence, black (or gray) box implies that the supplier performs a certain share of the development activities, though specifications regarding technical and geometrical interfaces and functions are provided by the customer.

Modularization as a way to decompose the product has received increasing interest in the past decades. This implies that standardized interfaces are defined between components (Brusoni & Prencipe, 2001). Thereby, a high degree of independence between component designs can be achieved (Sanchez & Mahoney, 1996). According to Baldwin and Clark (1997), this implies that a complex product can be built "*from smaller subsystems that can be designed independently yet function together as a whole*" (ibid., p. 84). Further, by modularizing the product, the development of "loosely coupled" modules can be divided between different organizations (Sanchez & Mahoney, 1996). According to Gadde and Jellbo (2002), there is a clear connection between increasing modularization and outsourcing, both in manufacturing and in product development. Benefits with modularization include, among other things, improved innovation and learning (Sanchez & Mahoney, 1996), scale economies because of specialization (Gadde & Jellbo, 2002), increased product performance, and improved possibilities to create product variety (Ulrich, 1995).

However, product modularization, and thus the division of product development activities among firms, may be done in many different ways. It seems that there is often a focus on modularization with regard to production (e.g. to facilitate pre-assembly) and, thus, physical component interfaces. However, Ulrich (1995) discusses modularization with regard to production as well as product design, and Baldwin and Clark (2000) also discuss "modularity in use." Considering different perspectives (e.g. "design," "production" or "use") results in different modular product architectures (Persson, 2003). Hubka and Eder (1988) suggest twelve different bases for classifying technical systems. Among these twelve are function, action principle, degree of complexity, manufacturing similarity, difficulty of designing, production location, degree of standardization, degree of novelty, and type of production. Even if the authors do not relate this classification of technical systems to the division of development work between firms, it shows that products, and thus product development work, may be divided according to many different principles.

Thus far, the division of development activities between firms has been related to the decomposition of the product. It is, however, also important to note that activities may be divided between organizational units according to various other principles such as similarity of purpose, process, clientele, or place (Scott, 1998). In addition to the product dimension, Browning (2001) suggests that the organizing of product development can be based on, for instance, groups of people and their interactions, or activities and information flow (cf. information-processing perspective on organization; e.g. Allen, 1979). Others have suggested that activities can be divided between firms based on what products and competencies are regarded as "core" to the firm (e.g. Prahalad & Hamel, 1990; Venkatesan, 1992).

1.2.2. Different Types of Customer-Supplier Relationships
Relationships are often regarded as a means for coordinating the development of products between firms and much research has been devoted to studying product development relationships, within the car industry as well as in other industries. Regarding customer-supplier relationships, several researchers have identified large differences between U.S. (and European) auto manufacturers and Japanese auto manufacturers (e.g. Bensaou & Venkatraman, 1995; Clark, 1989; Clark & Fujimoto, 1991; Dyer, 1996; Helper & Sako, 1995; Kamath & Liker, 1994; Lamming, 1993; Nishiguchi, 1994; Wasti & Liker, 1997).

The picture seems to be that U.S. (and European) auto manufacturers traditionally have applied strategies focused on short-term contracts, "arms-length" relationships and several suppliers for the same part. A tendering process aiming at lowering the part price is used and a number of suppliers compete for a specific contract. In most cases, suppliers receive drawings from the customer firm that is responsible for product development. "The fundamental assumption in this environment is that trading partners are interchangeable and that they will take advantage if they become too important" (Spekman et al., 1998, p. 631).

In contrast, Japanese relationships are often referred to as "partnerships" implying close collaboration, frequent communication, knowledge sharing, mutual dependency, and a long-term focus on the relationship. The customer firm cultivates suppliers' development capabilities and helps them to solve problems, while suppliers are committed to build development capability and provide the customer with new product solutions.

In much literature (often inspired by studies of the Japanese car industry) a close relationship, or "partnership," seems to be the desirable form of relationship with suppliers (Bidault et al., 1998; Ramsay, 1996). However, as noted by Cooper et al. (1997), this type of relationship requires a large degree of managerial attention, which precludes it from being the norm in business-to-business relationships.

Regarding product development, several attempts have been made to distinguish between different types of supplier relations. Based on experiences from the Japanese auto industry, Kamath and Liker (1994) distinguish between four different "supplier roles" in product development (see Fig. 2; a similar approach is presented by Asanuma, 1989). These roles imply fundamentally different division of development activities during product development. However, as noted

	Supplier roles			
	Partner	Mature	Child	Contractual
Design responsibility	Supplier	Supplier	Joint	Customer
Product complexity	Entire subsystem	Complex assembly	Simple assembly	Simple parts
Specifications provided	Concept	Critical specifications	Detailed specifications	Complete design
Supplier's influence on specifications	Collaborate	Negotiate	Present capabilities	None
Stage of supplier's involvement	Pre-concept	Concept	Post-concept	Prototyping
Component-testing responsibility	Complete	Major	Moderate	Minor
Supplier's techno-logical capabilities	Autonomous	High	Medium	Low

Fig. 2. Supplier Roles in Product Development (Kamath & Liker, 1994).

by Kamath and Liker, suppliers may play different roles in different customer relationships.

Partner suppliers are responsible for entire subsystems (such as seats and air-conditioning) and they often participate in the planning of a new car model even before the concept stage. The partner supplier and the customer jointly determine the specifications of the subsystem. Like partners, suppliers in the mature role are responsible for complex assemblies, but they have less influence on design. While the supplier performs the development, the customer provides critical specifications for performance, interfaces and space constraints. Both partner and mature suppliers do their own testing. For suppliers in the child role, detailed specifications are provided by the customer while the supplier works out the details of the design and builds testing prototypes. Contractual suppliers manufacture parts, usually standard parts or commodities, entirely designed by the customer.

Models such as this one that differentiate suppliers (see also Asanuma, 1989; Clark, 1989; Lamming, 1993) have, however, been criticized for being static and inflexible in assuming that a supplier should be involved in the same way in different development projects (see Wynstra & ten Pierick, 2000). These authors argue that this type of model often focuses more on suppliers' potential contributions than the actual *need* for such contributions. Further, these models only provide guidelines for the extent and timing of involvement, while explicit advice regarding differentiation, coordination and communication is missing. Therefore, with inspiration from Kraljic's (1983) portfolio approach, Wynstra and ten Pierick (2000) suggest an alternative model referred to as the "Supplier Involvement Portfolio." Based on "degree of development responsibility" and "development risk" it distinguishes between specific development *situations* rather than generalized supplier roles.

1.2.3. Involving Suppliers in the Development Team

Most authors seem to suggest that suppliers should be involved during the early phases of product development (e.g. Bidault et al., 1998; Clark, 1989; Dyer, 1996). Thereby, suppliers will have the possibility to influence the design already at the concept stage. That is before many important design decisions are made that will influence the suppliers' abilities to develop and later produce the products. Early involvement, however, also implies that a high degree of uncertainty and equivocality need to be handled in the relationship. As a consequence, there is a need for close interaction (von Corswant et al., 2001; Wynstra & ten Pierick, 2000). Several authors have emphasized, for instance, direct cross-functional interfirm communication, shared education and training, commitment, alignment of development processes and conflict resolution techniques for joint problem solving to be significant for efficient coordination between collaborating firms (see e.g. Evans & Jukes, 2000; Littler et al., 1995; Mohr & Spekman, 1994; Ragatz et al., 1997; von Corswant & Tunälv, 2002). Then, a relevant question is what organizational means can be used to achieve efficient coordination between firms that collaborate in product development.

Usually, when suppliers are involved in product development, they are either directly managed by one of the customer's functional disciplines (e.g. purchasing), or they are involved in the project team (Lakemond, 2001). In cases where product development work can be clearly divided between different firms, for instance when product development activities have been defined as "black box" assignments, the first of these coordination forms may be applied. However, as argued by Karlsson et al. (1998), changes in specifications are unavoidable in any engineering project and, therefore, specifications cannot be regarded as a "fixed" document. Instead, the authors emphasize that *"there is a need for very frequent information exchange for mutual adaptation and evolution of interfacing components"* (ibid., p. 542).

Therefore, to ensure efficient coordination and communication, cross-functional teams may be established where different functions as well as suppliers are represented (Dyer, 1996; Kamath & Liker, 1994; O'Neal, 1993). According to Nishiguchi (1994), such a team may consist of planning, design, product and process engineers from the customer (often reinforced with quality and purchasing managers) as well as engineers from different suppliers (see Fig. 3). However, as noted by Dowlatshahi (1998) not all tasks require the same degree

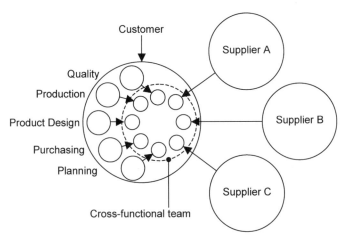

Fig. 3. A Cross-functional Development Team with Representatives from Different Suppliers.

of functional representation. Therefore, the team structure may change as the need for coordination between functional areas, as well as between suppliers, changes over time. The cross-functional team with its supplier representatives is often compiled for a specific development project. According to Hobday (1998), a project exists to "communicate design and architectural knowledge and to combine the distinctive resources, know how and skills of many suppliers" (ibid., p. 703). Hence, the important thing is not just to gather technical expertise from a number of disciplines, but also to ensure that this expertise is applied and integrated (Evans & Jukes, 2000). The project (and, thus, the development team) is, for instance, responsible for realizing the product, for coordinating decisions across firms, for enabling involvement of external actors and for allocating technical and financial resources (Hobday, 1998). For large development projects, such as the development of a new car model, a number of parallel development teams may be used, each with responsibility for a specific development area (see e.g. Dyer, 1996).

The engineers that suppliers position at their customers' facilities are often referred to as "resident engineers" (Nishiguchi, 1994; Twigg & Slack, 1998). According to Twigg (1997), the use of resident engineers (or "guest engineers") has traditionally received little attention in literature and research, but it is not a new phenomenon as it was used in Japan already in the 1950s (reference to Nishiguchi, 1994). However, as the interest in supplier collaboration in product development has increased, so has the interest in the use of resident engineers.

Dyer (1994) provides several examples of how resident engineers are used for product development coordination in the Japanese car industry and he states that "[w]hen the suppliers' engineers have desks in the same room as the automaker's engineers, it is easy to coordinate activities. Direct interaction is also a more efficient way to communicate complex, dynamic information during the development of new vehicle models. [. . .] In fact individual employees from different companies, working together over time, develop specialized knowledge and information – and a shared language – that allow them to communicate effectively and increase the ability of all parties to catch errors" (ibid., p. 175). Greater efficiency, faster product development cycles and products that are more reliable are positive results of this emphasis on communication.

Although suppliers are deeply involved already at an early stage, resident engineers from two competing suppliers can be involved simultaneously to see who can come up with the better design (Dyer & Ouchi, 1993; Kamath & Liker, 1994). Hence, resident engineers can be used also before the final selection of supplier (Twigg, 1997). While the resident engineers predominantly are involved in a particular project, (Japanese) suppliers also have "dedicated teams." These teams of product development engineers are always positioned at the customer, irrespective of specific product development projects (Nishiguchi, 1994).

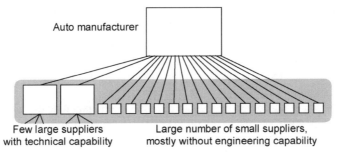

Fig. 4. U.S. and European Supplier Structure (Clark & Fujimoto, 1991).

1.2.4. Supplier Structures

The type of supplier relationships that emerge between the customer and the supplier seems to be reflected also in the industrial structure. According to Clark and Fujimoto (1991), the short-term arms-length relationships can be related to a broad supplier base with a large number of suppliers that to a limited extent participate in product development (see Fig. 4).

In contrast to this, Japanese auto manufacturers have emphasized a tiered structure based on fewer long-term relationships instead (e.g. Lamming, 1990, 1993). First-tier suppliers provide the auto manufacturer with sub-assembled units (e.g. complete seats or instrument panels) based on components from lower-tier suppliers (see Fig. 5). This tier structure simplifies communication between customers and suppliers as "first-tier suppliers coordinate the activities of the

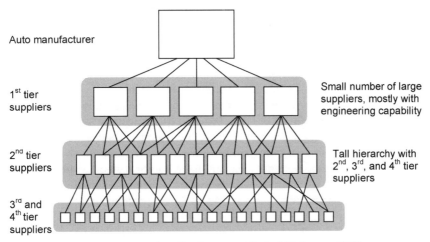

Fig. 5. Japanese Supplier Structure (Clark & Fujimoto, 1991).

second tier and so on down the hierarchy, allowing customers to focus scarce communication resources on the top tier" (Kamath & Liker, 1994). The auto manufacturer guarantees a long-term relation with the suppliers but demands that they take a significant responsibility in return. This mutual dependence between suppliers and auto manufacturers motivates close coordination and communication (Clark & Fujimoto, 1991).

With inspiration from Japan, U.S. and European auto manufacturers have begun to restructure their supply bases during the last decades, shifting from a large number of direct supplier relationships to a few close relationships (Bidault et al., 1998; Womack et al., 1990). However, the Japanese structure is still different in that Japanese auto manufacturers own large shares of equity in their largest suppliers (Dyer, 1996; Lamming, 1993). Further, it should be noted that not all Japanese first-tier suppliers are regarded as partners: "In fact, [Japanese auto manufacturers] typically regard only a handful as partners and assign more limited roles to the rest. [. . .] Only an elite corps of about a dozen first-tier suppliers enjoy full-blown partnership with their customers" (Kamath & Liker, 1994).

The increased focus on structuring the supplier base and creating long-term supplier relationships has resulted in stronger horizontal as well as vertical relationships (Lamming, 1990). The increased focus on vertical relationships is often referred to in terms of supply chain management (e.g. Harland, 1996; Harland et al., 1999; Hayes & Wheelwright, 1984; Spekman et al., 1998). This implies that not only the supplier found closest to the auto manufacturer, but rather a number of interrelated suppliers, all involved in the chain of production operations resulting in the purchased product, are concerned (Ellram, 1991). In other words, a firm's linkages are extended upstream and/or downstream the value chain (Spekman et al., 1998). According to Lamming (1990, p. 656), the "process of delegation, from assembler to first-level supplier, of much of the responsibility for such things as R&D, quality assurance and just-in-time supply, will mean that vertical relationships will need to be stronger at all levels throughout the supply chain." In Fig. 6, a supply chain is illustrated as an example.

What is performed by each one of these suppliers and how this contributes to the value of the end product is of major concern. By focusing on the value-adding activities only, trying to eliminate waste, cost savings can be achieved throughout the supply chain. This is also referred to as value stream management (see Hines et al., 2000) and is an important ingredient in the lean production philosophy (see

Fig. 6.   An Example of a Supply Chain with Different Tier-level Suppliers.

Womack & Jones, 1996). Hence, supply chain management implies co-ordination of a number of vertically interconnected relationships. However, to single out a particular supply chain from a larger context may imply an oversimplification of reality. Different supply chains cross and merge and, as argued by von Corswant (2000a), a particular supplier is often part of several supply chains where it has different positions or roles.

Further, when for example a new car model is developed, several different suppliers are involved at the same time (e.g. Kamath & Liker, 1994). Some suppliers have a direct relationship with the auto manufacturer while others are found at lower tier levels. The need for coordination implies that a number of different relationships, vertical as well as horizontal, need to be considered simultaneously. This structure of firms is often referred to as a (supplier) *network* (e.g. Bonaccorsi & Lipparini, 1994; Clark, 1989; Harland, 1996; Harland et al., 1999; Norén et al., 1995; Wasti & Liker, 1997). In many studies, the "supplier network" seems to be placed on an equal footing with the tier structure presented above. However, according to Lamming (1993), some relationships may be important although the supplier cannot be attributed a certain position in the tier structure. For example, the supply route of materials may be indirect while product development is handled in a direct relationship between the supplier and the customer. According to von Corswant (2000a), supplier relationships are arranged mainly in relation to assembly sequence when regarding production (cf. the supply chain), while various other interdependencies between components and, thus, other relationships need to be considered when regarding product development. Hence, different supply chains (or rather networks) can be identified for different business processes (Lambert & Cooper, 2000). However, Harland (1996) emphasizes the importance of integrating across supply chain levels and argues that existing partnership/relationship research does not adequately recognize the significance of the network context. Lambert and Cooper (2000) argue that the "supply chain" should not be regarded as a chain of businesses with one-to-one, business-to-business, relationships but rather as a network of multiple businesses and relationships.

Hence, from this background description it is evident that product development that was earlier performed within auto manufacturers' organizational boundaries is increasingly being divided between different firms instead. This, in turn, influences the form of relationship between firms as well as the larger industrial structure. A few more or less practically oriented reasons for this division of activities have been brought up. However, a more profound theoretical approach to organizing product development across firm boundaries is also needed. It is relevant to ask why activities are divided between different organizational units and what implications such differentiation has for the organizing of product development across firms.

In the following sections, this is further elaborated in terms of differentiation and integration.

1.2.5. Differentiation of Product Development Activities

Differentiation here refers to the division of activities, which are needed to accomplish a certain task, between different organizational units. Most theory on differentiation concerns division of activities *within* a firm, though, some basic principles can also be applied for the division of product development activities *between* firms.

According to Scott (1998), differentiation is one of the most difficult and critical decisions facing an organization, and organizational theorists have for a long time been concerned with finding ways to differentiate and group activities in such a way as to minimize the total cost of carrying out all the activities. Early examples are "scientific management" as proposed by Taylor (e.g. 1911) and the "administrative management theory" (see March & Simon, 1958). Then, what are the potential benefits with differentiation and how can they be related to product development that is performed across firm boundaries?

According to Galbraith (1967), differentiation permits specialization of organizational function. Specialization, in turn, permits the application of scientific or engineering knowledge. Thereby, differentiation contributes to rationalization and routinization of a field of action. Smith (1776) mainly focuses on the productivity gains that an increased degree of specialization can bring about. He derives these gains to three fundamental factors increasing the productivity: "... first, to the increase of dexterity in every particular workman; secondly, to the saving of the time which is commonly lost in passing from one species of work to another; and lastly, to the invention of a great number of machines which facilitate and abridge labour, and enable one man to do the work of many" (ibid., p. 7). Hence, Smith views division of labor, or specialization, mainly as a means to support the application of technology or rationalized procedures to increase the scale of work organizations (Scott, 1998).

Further, specialization implies sharing of common resources (Mintzberg, 1983). Therefore, activities that require the same resources may enable economies of scale (Richardson, 1972), and the degree to which resources can be used in a specialized manner can be related to the scale of operations (Mintzberg, 1983; Penrose, 1959).

Other researchers, such as Lawrence and Lorsch (1967b) and Thompson (1967) have considered differentiation as a way to cope with a complex and changing environment. Lawrence and Lorsch (1967b, p. 3) define differentiation as "*the state of segmentation of the organizational system into subsystems, each of which tends to develop particular attributes in relation to the requirements posed by its relevant external environment.*" Then, as the organization has been differentiated into basic subsystems, the environment is segmented into related sectors (ibid.). This implies that each organizational subsystem, created by organizational differentiation, can be adapted to a particular part of the organization's environment. In other words, differentiation can be regarded as a means to handle uncertainty of an organization's environment (Dessler, 1980). However, as argued by Galbraith (1977), differentiation may also contribute to uncertainty since the need for information processing between differentiated units increases.

The view presented by Thompson (1967) is somewhat different from Lawrence and Lorsch's. Thompson regards differentiation as a means for protecting the technological core (a closed rational system) from variation and uncertainty in the environment. By differentiating the organization into input, technological and output units, the technological core can be surrounded by input and output units. The input and output units then handle all interaction with the organization's environment. Thereby, the influence of the environment on the technological core can be reduced. Thompson refers to this as buffering.

The benefits with differentiation presented this far seem to be relevant not only for repetitive manufacturing activities, but also for innovation. According to Loasby (1998), differentiation in the form of division of labor is important for developing knowledge and creating new capabilities. In addition, specialization implies that the whole group need not deal with the whole problem, instead different parts of the problem can be assigned to different specialists (March & Simon, 1958). Further, also the perspective on differentiation as a means for adapting an organization to its environment may be relevant for innovation and technical development as different parts of an organization may be focused on developing different technologies. Hence, differentiation can be regarded as a structural response to technical complexity (Scott, 1998).

Further, differentiation may facilitate parallel performance of activities (e.g. von Hippel, 1990). According to March and Simon (1958), the mode of subdivision influences to what extent activities can be performed simultaneously: "The more detailed the factorization of the problem, the more simultaneous activity is possible." Simultaneous performance of activities can have great impact on lead-time, for example in product development (see O'Neal, 1993; Womack et al., 1990; see Fig. 7). Simultaneous design (Rothwell & Whiston, 1990) and concurrent engineering (O'Neal, 1993) are terms frequently used for describing the parallel development work performed in differentiated organizational units.

Hence, a number of potential benefits associated with differentiation can be identified. However, differentiation also implies certain requirements regarding the organizing of activities. This is an issue that we now turn to.

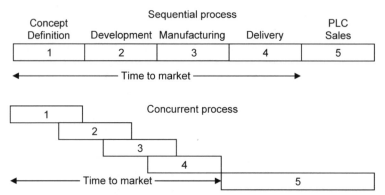

Fig. 7.   Time Advantage of Parallel Development Activities (O'Neal, 1993).

1.2.6. Differentiation and the Related Need for Integration

Differentiation implies that activities are divided and grouped within different organizational units. Thereby the benefits described above can be realized. However, the problem is that this grouping encourages strong coordination *within* units while it complicates coordination between units (Mintzberg, 1983). As activities are differentiated between a number of specialized organizational units, considerable interdependencies may be created between these units (March & Simon, 1958). Interdependence refers to the extent to which activities are interrelated so that changes in the state of one element affect the state of other elements (Scott, 1998).

Due to interdependencies, differentiation creates a need for integration. Lawrence and Lorsch (1967b, p. 4) define integration as "the process of achieving unity of effort among the various subsystems in the accomplishment of the organization's task." According to Lawrence and Lorsch, there is generally a trade-off between differentiation and integration, implying two essentially antagonistic states where one can be obtained only at the expense of the other. However, their empirical studies showed that the high-performing organizations had both a high degree of differentiation and a high degree of integration. They found that integrative devices would emerge in organizations with environments that require high differentiation and integration simultaneously (ibid.).

Then it is relevant to ask how integration can be achieved between differentiated organizational units. When referring to the literature on integration the term *coordination* occurs frequently. It is apparently closely related to integration. In many cases, integration and coordination seem to be given a similar meaning. It is, however, necessary to be more precise on how the terms integration and coordination relate to each other. Integration can be illustrated by the boundaries between differentiated organizational units, to some extent, being blurred. Thus, although these units are "separated" (through differentiation), there is a certain degree of unity of effort (compare with Lawrence and Lorsch's definition quoted above) between the activities performed within each unit. Coordination can then be defined as the actions taken to achieve this unity of effort. Hence, coordination is considered a *means* for reaching a certain degree of integration.

It should, however, be noted that coordination has somewhat different meanings in economic and organization theory respectively. Within neo-classical economic theory (e.g. Coase, 1937; Williamson, 1985) coordination is focused on the division of activities (allocation of resources) based on the functioning of the price mechanism. Within organization theory, on the other hand, coordination is mainly related to the characteristics of differentiated activities and their interdependencies. As will be illustrated later on, Richardson (1972) presents a model unifying the two perspectives on coordination. First, however, an intraorganizational perspective on coordination will be elaborated in more detail. We then turn to coordination of activities between firms.

1.2.7. Organizing to Achieve Integration with Regard to Dependencies
As mentioned above, differentiation creates a need for integration and, thus, coordination. Furthermore, the need for coordination is related to what interdependencies exist between differentiated organizational units. The greater interdependence, the more resources must be devoted to coordination (Scott, 1998).

With different terminologies but similar underlying concepts, several researchers have addressed the issue of interdependencies in technical development (see e.g. Clark & Fujimoto, 1991; Eppinger et al., 1994). Thompson (1967) has provided a conceptualization of dependencies based on the following three categories: *pooled*, *sequential* and *reciprocal* dependencies (see Fig. 8). When there is a pooled interdependence, the work performed is interrelated only in the sense that each element or process contributes to the overall goal. Sequential interdependence exists when some activities must be performed in (specific) sequences. Reciprocal interdependence implies that activities relate to each other as both inputs and outputs.

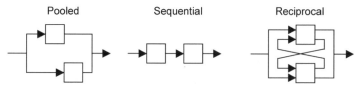

Fig. 8. Pooled, Sequential and Reciprocal Activities (Adapted from Eppinger et al., 1994).

Based on March and Simon's (1958) categorization of coordination mechanisms, Thompson (1967) suggests that pooled activities are coordinated through standardization (i.e. routines and rules), while sequential activities are coordinated through planning, and reciprocal activities are coordinated through mutual adjustment (coordination that involves transmission of new information). According to Thompson, the choice of coordination form is mainly dependent on the need for communication and decision-making. Efficient communication increases the tolerance for interdependencies (March & Simon, 1958).

The interdependencies that exist between activities, and the related need for coordination, affect the way activities are differentiated and grouped together. According to early administrative theorists (see March & Simon, 1958, pp. 22–32), activities should be grouped so as to combine homogenous or related activities within the same organizational unit. However, as noted by March and Simon, there are often several different and competing bases for determining homogeneity (cf. Section 1.2.1).

According to Thompson (1967), organizations seek to group activities according to their degree of interdependence since it is related to the cost of coordination. Mutual adjustment is the most costly coordination form and therefore reciprocal activities are placed in the same or closely adjacent units. Sequential tasks that can be coordinated to a lower cost by schedules are placed in less closely adjacent units. Rules are least costly and therefore tasks inhibiting pooled interdependence are placed in the least closely adjacent units. In short, Thompson argues that organizations attempt to group tasks so as to minimize coordination costs (Scott, 1998).

Hence, differentiation creates a need for integration caused by different forms of interdependencies between organizational units. The interdependencies occurring in technical development are often reciprocal. That is due to the "unprogrammed" characteristics of innovation requiring problem solving containing a great deal of randomness (March & Simon, 1958). Hence, according to Thompson (1967), advanced coordination is needed. A relevant question is then what coordination mechanisms may be used to achieve the needed integration.

The classical formalized bureaucracy where most communication flows vertically in the hierarchy (e.g. Weber, 1946), and where a top manager serves as the primary communication link, results in functional activities occurring sequentially and the developing product is "thrown over the wall" from one functional department to the next (Wheelwright & Clark, 1992; Womack & Jones, 1996). Several researchers have therefore pointed to the need for mechanisms handling lateral coordination between different organizational functions or departments. However, where product designs are stable, customer requirements are well defined, interfaces between functions are clear and life-cycles and lead-times are long, functional groups may develop new products effectively with a modest amount of coordination (Wheelwright & Clark, 1992, p. 175). A brief review of coordination mechanisms is provided here.

The "liaison relationship" (Rubenstein, 1957; Scott, 1998) implies that individuals are assigned to communicate directly with their counterparts in other departments, but they have no formal authority to make decisions that aim at resolving interfunctional conflicts (Mintzberg, 1983; Olson et al., 1995). A related coordination mechanism is labeled "integrator" or "integrating manager" (Lawrence & Lorsch, 1967a). Product manager, brand manager, project leader and program coordinator are examples of this kind of management position. In differentiated firms that face rapid technological change, it might even be suitable to create "integrating departments" (ibid.).

According to Mintzberg (1983), a "temporary task force" may be formed to accomplish a particular task and then disband. The interacting members represent various functions and interact directly. Another increasingly common form of coordination between functions is the "cross-functional team" (see e.g. Wheelwright & Clark, 1992). These teams can either be established for a certain development project or be permanented (Lorsch & Lawrence, 1965). According to Olson et al. (1995), cross-functional teams provide participative decision-making, consensual conflict resolution, and open communication processes.

To maintain the primacy of the functional structure while efforts are made to coordinate the activities performed by the different departments is common for the coordination mechanisms presented this far. However, when coordination is achieved by imposing a "matrix organization," activities are structured according to a product or market focus as well as a by function (Olson et al., 1995). In other words, "the organization avoids choosing one basis of grouping over another; instead it chooses both" (Mintzberg, 1983, p. 86). Thus, a matrix structure implies that the principle of unity of command is abandoned as a dual authority structure is set up. Functional managers and project team managers are equally and jointly responsible for the same decisions, thereby creating a delicate balance of power.

Hence, the fundamental problem addressed here is that differentiation of development activities between organizational units creates a need for integration and thus coordination. The need for coordination can be related to what interdependencies exist between the organizational units. To handle interdependencies between organizational units, different coordination mechanisms may be used. This far, we have mainly been focusing on coordination *within* firms, though, the present paper focuses on product development performed *across* firm boundaries. Lawrence and Lorsch (1967b), Thompson (1967) (and other theories referred thus far) do not explicitly consider relationships between organizations (Doz & Prahalad, 1991). It is therefore relevant to ask how activities may be coordinated between organizations. This is dealt with in the following section.

1.2.8. An Interorganizational Perspective on Coordination

Economists have for a long time been occupied with explaining how activities are divided and coordinated between firms. In classical economic theory, perfectly competitive markets are assumed to ensure optimum resource allocation among numerous competing firms. Coase (1937), however, argued that there is a cost for using the price mechanism, referred to as *transaction cost*. Transactions that are associated with high transaction costs on the market will be coordinated within a firm instead. In this way, Coase's theory explains why some activities are coordinated within firms and other activities are coordinated via the market place.

Coase's transaction cost approach was later revived and extended by Williamson (e.g. 1975, 1979, 1985). He also introduced intermediate governance forms, though, the core of Coase and Williamson's arguments is that activities are coordinated either within firms (hierarchy) or via the market, depending on the costs associated with each transaction. The transaction cost model has been applied in various different studies, though, the model has also been criticized since it fails to provide answers to several important questions related to the organization of activities within and between firms. For example, Doz and Prahalad (1991) argue that "[t]he usefulness of transaction cost analysis for research on management processes is limited by [. . .] its primary focus on single transactions as units of analysis." With the single transaction as the unit of analysis, the model is less suitable for analyzing a course of events over time. In other words, it does not consider historical or future aspects of the transaction. In addition, with the transaction as the unit of analysis follows a focus on the dyad between two firms. This implies that the model is less useful for answering questions concerning multiple (i.e. more than two) firms and the relationships between them (see Johanson & Mattsson, 1987). The focus on the single transaction also limits the potential for analysis of dependencies between firms. Further, even if intermediate governance forms were introduced in the model, a focus on opportunistic behavior and reduced transaction costs implies that the model is less useful for addressing issues related to cooperative value creation, resource utilization and relationships between firms (see e.g. Uzzi, 1997). This is also related to the social dimension of relationships not being considered (Granovetter, 1985).

Within transaction cost economics, intermediate forms of coordination (e.g. relationships) are generally regarded as market imperfections and can be found on a continuum somewhere between the two extremes of market and hierarchy (see e.g. Eccles, 1981). However, other authors have questioned this view, arguing that a relationship is neither an imperfection, nor an intermediate form between markets and hierarchies (e.g. Blois, 1971; Powell, 1990; Richardson, 1972). In his article from 1972, Richardson argues that cooperation between firms can be superior to coordination by direction (hierarchy) or coordination via the market. He states that "[t]he dichotomy between firm and market, between directed and spontaneous co-ordination, is misleading; it ignores the institutional fact of co-operation and assumes away the distinct method of co-ordination that this can provide." According to Richardson, also highly interdependent activities can favorably be coordinated through cooperation between firms (i.e. relationship), and not only within the firm as proposed by the transaction cost approach. Richardson thereby challenges the whole notion of a firm/market dichotomy (Penrose, 1959, p. xvi). The view on relationships presented by Richardson can be related to "quasi-integration," defined by Blois (1971) as situations "where some firms are gaining the advantage of vertical integration without assuming the risks of rigidity of ownership" (ibid., p. 253).

During the past two decades or so, relationships have increasingly attracted researchers' attention as an alternative form of coordination between firms. The relationship concept, as it has been described this far, mainly refers to the economic dimensions of collaboration between firms. There is, however, a steadily increasing amount of research on different aspects of relationships. For example, marketing relationships (e.g. Ford et al., 1998) and purchasing (i.e. supplier) relationships (e.g. Clark, 1989; Gadde & Håkansson, 2001; Gadde & Snehota, 2000; Lamming, 1993) have received much attention. Relationships have also been studied in relation to learning and knowledge creation (Doz, 1996; Hamel, 1991; Inkpen, 1996; Powell, 1998), cultural aspects (Palmer, 2000), politics (see Mizruchi & Schwartz, 1987), and there are studies regarding the development of relationships over time (Ring & Van de Ven, 1994; Spekman et al., 1996).

Granovetter (1985) has emphasized the importance of social relationships, arguing that "there is evidence all around us of the extent to which business relations are mixed up with social ones" (ibid., p. 495). According to Granovetter, economic action is, to a certain extent, embedded in structures of social relations. He thereby criticizes the atomistic and "undersocialized" view held by classical and neo-classical economists that neglect social relations and treat them, if at all, as "a frictional drag that impedes competitive markets" (ibid., p. 484). The concept of embeddedness (see also Section 2.2.3) and its effects on organizational and economic outcomes have been further investigated by, among others, Uzzi (1997). He concludes, in line with Granovetter's arguments, that "the critical transactions on which firms depend most are embedded in networks of social relationships that produce positive and unique outcomes that are difficult to imitate via other means" (ibid., p. 64).

An aspect of relationships, that is of particular interest in this paper, concerns technical development. Relationships are, at least implicitly, dealt with in studies of technological systems. Hughes (1983) has studied "inertia" within large technological systems, involving several organizations that are bound together by technological interdependence. Freeman (1995) has studied the "National System of Innovation" and its relation to the development of internal R&D in organizations. He addresses the importance of relationships by stating that "many improvements to *products* and to services came from interaction with the market and with related firms, such as sub-contractors, suppliers of materials and services" (ibid., p. 10). Other researchers have focused their research on when and for what type of technologies that relationships are needed. For example, Doz and Hamel (1997) argue that patents, licensing rights and technology transfer agreements may be coordinated between firms by means of the market, while relationships are needed for sharing and coordinating complex and embedded technologies. According to Chesbrough and Teece (1996), relationships are needed as they enable firms to "direct the path of future systemic innovation." Whether a technology should be developed through a relationship or acquired by other means (e.g. merger or acquisition) depends, according to Lambe and Spekman (1997), on the degree of technology acquisition urgency and industry uncertainty. In situations of major product innovation (the authors refer to Foster's S-curve) the combination of urgency and uncertainty makes relationship a feasible choice.

Thus, there are many different conceptualizations of relationship coordination (i.e. economic, social, technical, etc.). In some cases these are linked as, for example, Granovetter (1985) binds together economic and social aspects of relationships. However, independent of focus, most conceptualizations of relationships seem to have one thing in common; that relationships give possibilities to achieve certain advantages that are not possible with the market and hierarchy as the only forms of coordination. Hence, we can conclude that relationship seems to be an important and widely spread organizational form of coordination between firms, and a complement to the traditional coordination forms of markets and hierarchies.

To summarize, technical development is to a large extent performed across firm boundaries, not least within the auto industry. This form of differentiation of product development activities between firms may relate with certain benefits. However, with differentiation also follows an increasing need for integration and coordination. Various forms of coordination mechanisms as well as relationships have been discussed as means for dealing with this problem. How this problem is approached also needs to be related to what perspectives are applied regarding organizing and product development respectively. This is discussed in more detail in next section.

1.3. Problem Discussion and Perspective Selection

The view of the firm and how it relates to its environment, or rather to other firms, is fundamental when analyzing technical development performed across firm boundaries. In this section, different perspectives on organizing and technical development are discussed. Based on this discussion, a theoretical perspective is chosen that will constitute a basis for the development of a theoretical framework.

There is a significant amount of (organization) theory available regarding various aspects of differentiation and integration. A considerable share of this theory (e.g. Lawrence & Lorsch, 1967b; March & Simon, 1958; Thompson, 1967) views the firm as an organizational entity whose internal structure needs to be adapted to the environment, or to conditions determined by the market. Hence, the firm is the unit of analysis and there is a focus on *intra*organizational issues (though, environmental conditions are considered). These theories on organizing are useful for this paper, though, there is a need for widening the perspective and consider the firm's relations to specific counterparts.

An interorganizational perspective is also needed when regarding technical development. Much research has been devoted to issues concerning the individual firm's development organization and efficiency (e.g. Allen, 1986; Tushman & O'Reilly, 1997; Wheelwright & Clark, 1992). Based on external (market) requirements the firm innovates and develops new products. Applying a perspective on technical development where the firm is the unit of analysis can be useful for studies that are mainly concerned with intraorganizational issues. For the present paper, however, a perspective is needed that can deal with situations where technical development is mainly carried out in *interaction* among several firms.

According to Mizruchi and Schwartz (1987), a perspective on the organizing of technical development is needed that takes "a fully structural view, in which an organization is viewed as interacting with its environment – molding it as well as being molded by it" (ibid., p. 3). The relationship view (discussed in Section 1.2.8) implies that instead of being surrounded by a "faceless environment" or a "market," the firm is connected with a highly specific external organizational structure. This perspective opens up for studies investigating the relationship between two firms, i.e. a dyad. For instance, numerous studies have been focused on relationships between auto manufacturers and suppliers or "strategic alliances" between firms (e.g. Dyer, 1994; Kamath & Liker, 1994; Lambe & Spekman, 1997). Further, as inter-firm collaboration has received increasing interest, the importance of considering connected relationships has been noticed.

According to Cook and Emerson (1978, p. 725), "[t]wo exchange relations are *connected* to the degree that exchange in one relation is contingent upon exchange (or non-exchange) in the other relation." This implies that, for example, what a supplier develops in collaboration with a specific customer may influence, or be influenced by, what is developed in relationships with other customers. Hence, when studying organizing across firm boundaries let us consider various other relationships in addition to the focal relationship. Thereby, the dyad needs to be connected to a larger organizational structure. The "supply chain" referred to in Section 1.2.4 implies that additional vertical relations are included. Further, "networks" include relationships within chains but also across chains. According to Cook and Emerson, a network can be defined as "a set of two or more connected exchange relations" (ibid., p. 725).

The term "relationship" is, however, given somewhat different meanings in different research. In turn, depending on what issues are investigated, this influences the view on technical development and how it is performed across firm boundaries. In many studies, technical development seems to be treated as a phenomenon that is performed internally within the respective firms involved in a relationship (see e.g. Sanchez & Mahoney, 1996). Then, technical development across firm boundaries is mainly an issue of dividing development work between the firms in the most efficient way (cf. "black box" design described in Section 1.2.1). Further, studies concerning relationships between firms often take the perspective of one of the firms involved in the relationship. For example, studies of supplier collaboration in product development often take a customer's perspective on the relationship (e.g. Kamath & Liker, 1994). In studies concerned with a specific firm's relations with other firms, this may be a relevant perspective. With this perspective on the relationship, the focal firm is often (implicitly) assumed to be the active part that actively selects its counterparts, while the counterpart in the relationship is seen more as a "passive resource." In other words, relationships with other firms are considered while the focal firm is still the unit of analysis. The present paper is, however, concerned with technical development performed *within* as well as *between* firms. Thereby, a somewhat different view of relationships is needed where the *interaction* between both firms involved in a relationship is considered. An interactive perspective implies that the relationship can contribute with additional values that none of the collaborating firms could create alone (cf. "team effects"; Alchian & Demsetz, 1972).

Further, depending on research focus, relationships between firms can be viewed differently with regard to the time dimension. For instance, transaction cost economics (e.g. Coase, 1937; Williamson, 1985) is mainly concerned with single transactions between firms that are rather independent from other transactions in the same or other relations. This model can be used for discussing choices between governance modes (i.e. market or hierarchy), but it is less useful for studying continuous and long-term interaction between firms. In other cases, relationships are treated as an organizational solution that can be applied when needed and then be "dissolved" (e.g. Lambe & Spekman, 1997). A relationship can, however, also be viewed as a resource that the interacting firms make investments in. This implies that the durability and substance of the relationship is important for the firms' possibilities to economize on previous investments. By viewing a relationship as a resource that is developed over time as a result of repeated interaction between firms, the additional values referred to above can be explained and understood.

Considering technical development as a process that is performed in interaction between various firms also has implications for how the developed product is viewed. For example, the final use of the product may not be known since it will be combined with other products that have not yet been developed. In addition, some product concept may be available, though, the technologies needed to realize the product may remain to be developed. Further, products and technologies are continuously developed in interaction between different firms that have different previous experiences and needs, as well as different relationships with other firms. This makes it difficult to anticipate what path technical development will follow. Therefore, the product cannot be treated as "given," and the development process may be far from "linear" or "sequential" and, thus, cannot be planned in detail.

Taken together, this implies that an approach to organizing technical development across firm boundaries is needed, that provides an interactive perspective and that can handle multiple interdependencies between several different firms. Therefore, the industrial network approach (e.g. Håkansson, 1987; Håkansson & Snehota, 1995) has been chosen as a theoretical perspective for this paper. By applying a network approach, an understanding for the organizing of interactive product development that goes beyond the individual firm and the dyad can be achieved. Before further developing the Industrial Network Approach, the purpose of the paper is presented.

1.4. Purpose of the Paper

Differentiation of product development between firms implies a need for integration and, due to various forms of dependencies between product development activities, there is a need for coordination of activities performed by different firms. This raises questions regarding how interactive product development can be organized with respect to various dependencies. Therefore, the following purpose has been formulated:

The purpose of this paper is to explore dependencies and how interactive product development may be organized with regard to these dependencies.

2. FRAME OF REFERENCE

In this section, an interactive approach to technical development across firm boundaries is presented. First, a network perspective on organizing is presented, mainly with focus on the Industrial Network Approach. In the following sections the resource dimension of the network model, which is central for technical development, is further elaborated and a framework for analyzing dependencies between resources is developed. Finally, research issues are identified.

2.1. Networks and the Industrial Network Approach

As the traditionally dominant governance modes markets and hierarchies have been questioned (see e.g. Richardson, 1972) and complemented with different intermediate or hybrid concepts, the network as a way to organize economic activity has gained increasing interest. It has been argued that the network form of organization lies on a continuum somewhere between markets and hierarchies. This has, however, been criticized by e.g. Powell (1990) who argues that the network is "neither a market transaction nor a hierarchical governance structure, but a separate, different mode of exchange, one with its own logic" (ibid., p. 301). As expressed by (Scott, 1998), the network form of organizing industrial activities is more reciprocal and egalitarian than hierarchies, while connections between firms are more enduring and diffuse than in markets.

An approach to conceptualizing the network form of organizing that has gained much interest is often referred to as the Industrial Network Approach. It has its theoretical origins in social exchange theory (e.g. Blau, 1964; Emerson, 1962) and organization theory (e.g. Alchian & Demsetz, 1972; Cyert & March, 1963; Thompson, 1967). Important inspiration came from the open system theory that developed during the 1960s. Instead of the neoclassical focus on individual organizations with clear boundaries, the open system theory entailed a shift towards *interaction* between the components of a system. The shift from the neoclassical market-based model opened up for a different view of the firm and its interaction with other firms.

Another important origin of the Industrial Network Approach is a number of empirical studies performed in the 1960s and 1970s. For example, Johanson (1966) found that long-term relationships were established between firms on international steel markets. This allowed for adaptations of the involved firms' organizations, processes and products. Based on this and other empirical studies, Håkansson (1982) emphasizes a number of factors that largely had been neglected in previous studies, but were found to be important in industrial markets. In contrast to the classical market model, both buyers and sellers are active participants in the market and, frequently, they develop long-term relationships. Instead of focusing on single business transactions, these relationships tend to involve a complex pattern of interaction between and within the participating firms. Therefore, it is emphasized that also previous transactions are important for the development of a relationship, including infrequent transactions. Further, the adaptations made within and between the involved firms tend to lead to an institutionalization of the relationship, implying certain roles for how work is to be divided between firms. These adaptations seldom come about without friction and, thus, relationships involve both conflict and cooperation.

In order to theoretically conceptualize *networks* of firms it is necessary to capture interdependencies between different relationships and the context in which these relationships are embedded. With various empirical studies as an important source of inspiration, a theoretical model was developed based on the three components *activities, resources* and *actors* (see Håkansson, 1987, with references Hägg & Johanson, 1982; Håkansson, 1982; Håkansson & Johanson, 1984; Hammarkvist et al., 1982; Mattsson, 1985) as an important basis for the development of the model. See also Håkansson and Johanson (1992). The developed model is here referred to as the Network Model (see Fig. 9) and it is briefly described below.

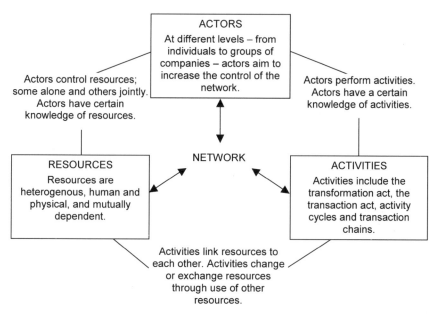

Fig. 9. The Network Model (Håkansson, 1987).

Actors are defined as those who, alone or jointly, control resources and/or perform activities. Actors can be individuals or firms, as well as groups of individuals or groups of firms, depending on the level of analysis. Actors have intentions and goals and strive to increase their control, but they do not act in isolation. Since actors control resources and perform activities that in different ways are connected to other actors, their possibilities to act (as well as react and interact) are circumscribed by relationships to these other actors. At the same time, these relationships are developed through exchange processes, thereby giving access to other actors' resources. As a consequence, each actor is embedded in a network of relationships with other actors.

Actors control different combinations of resources and activities and they engage in different relationships. As a consequence, actors develop differential knowledge about activities, resources and other actors in the network. Therefore, every actor is regarded as unique. This uniqueness also implies that actors are tied to investments in specific resources. To make changes therefore becomes a matter of finding new ways of combining existing resources.

Activities are performed by actors who activate resources. That is done in order to combine and develop other resources. Some activities, for example the assembly of separate components into a common product, even connect different activity chains. Thereby, a network of activities is created.

Actors strive to improve efficiency by reducing the amount of resources used for performing certain activities. However, as activities are dependent in different ways, the efficiency of one actor is related to the performance of other actors in the network. Therefore, actors adapt to each other over time and learn how to perform and coordinate activities in a more efficient way. Strong interdependencies are created between actors that bring about stability. However, the activity network will always be imperfect, since its efficiency can always be improved by changing the existing activity structure. In other words, there will never be an optimal activity network.

Resources consist of physical, financial or human assets. In other words, resources may be either material (e.g. machinery and materials) or immaterial (e.g. knowledge and labor). In the network model even relationships are regarded as resources. A resource can be controlled either by a single actor by means of a hierarchy or jointly by several actors by means of relationships. What is of importance to actors is not ownership, but the ability to access a resource when it is needed, i.e. through some form of control.

With this conceptualization of industrial networks as point of departure, the resource layer is further developed in next section to provide a basis for the analysis of technical development across firm boundaries.

2.2. Technical Development – Resource Interaction and Adaptation

As has been described above the interplay between actors, activities and resources is essential for relationships and, hence, interaction between firms. Although all three layers are important also when considering technical development, innovation and development tend to be focused on resources (Håkansson & Snehota, 1995, p. 134). Further, the need for integration and, thus, organizing relates to what dependencies need to be considered. Dependencies can be analyzed in terms of ties between different resources. Following from this, an understanding of the resource dimension can provide important insights to the organization of technical development across firm boundaries.

Traditionally, economizing on (given) resources and the related allocation of resources (mainly by means of the price mechanism) has interested economists (see e.g. Coase, 1937). This view of resources implies that the control of (scarce) resources can provide firms with an advantage. However, this traditional view of resources has been criticized. Instead of regarding resources as "given," Penrose (1959) argues that it should be seen as a relative concept, implying that the value of a particular resource is related to its use. Hence, more important than the resource as such is the "services" (i.e. activities) it can provide. Increasing knowledge about the resource increases the services it can contribute with. The work by Penrose is mainly focused on the growth of the firm, but her thoughts regarding resources and how they are used and developed have provided an important basis for the development of alternative approaches. Besides the Industrial Network Approach, Penrose's work has influenced, for example, what is usually referred to as the Resource-Based Perspective of the firm (see e.g. Barney, 1991; Nelson & Winter, 1982). The Resource-Based Perspective (RBP) refers to resource heterogeneity for explaining firms' competitive position. According to Foss (1998), the overall objective that informs the RBP is "to account for the creation, maintenance and renewal of competitive advantage in terms of the resource side of firms" (ibid., p. 135). Resource heterogeneity leads to efficiency differences and thereby specific competitive advantages for the firm. In other words, firms are heterogeneous in terms of competitive power due to heterogeneous resources. Further, RBP draws on basic economic equilibrium price theory (ibid.) and, hence, the focus on competitive advantage implies that there is little interest for cooperative arrangements between firms (Ring, 1996). In addition, Foss (1998) points to the difficulties of handling dynamics and evolutionary factors (e.g. new resource creation) within RBP.

Within the industrial network approach cooperation and interaction between firms is essential. Although Penrose (1959) is mainly focusing the growth of a single firm, her theory on resources has provided fruitful inspiration for the development of theory on interorganizational relationships. In the foreword to the third edition (1995) Penrose also discusses, for example, business networks. In the following sections, the resource dimension is elaborated in more detail, with a focus on how it is perceived within the Industrial Network Approach.

2.2.1. Value of Resources – Resource Combination and Adaptation

All firms need access to resources – tangible as well as intangible resources. According to Penrose (1959), a firm can be viewed as *"a collection of resources."* Every firm has a unique resource collection. At a certain point in time, a firm's resource collection may be considered "given." However, if seen over a longer period of time, the resource base is continually developing (Gadde & Håkansson, 2001).

Fundamental to this development is that resources are always used in combination with other resources (Håkansson & Snehota, 1995). That is because "no resources [. . .] are of much use by themselves; any effective use for them is always viewed in terms of possible combinations with other resources" (Penrose, 1959, p. 86). This is illustrated by Rosenberg (1982) who argues that the benefits from an innovation (i.e. a form of resource) often comes about first when it is combined with complementary technologies: "many innovations have had to await the development of appropriate metallurgical inputs with highly specific performance characteristics. The compound steam engine had to await cheap, high-quality steel. Higher pressures (and therefore greater fuel economy) in power generation required high-strength, heat-resistant alloy steels. Hard alloy steels, in turn, were of limited usefulness until appropriate new machine tooling methods were developed for working them" (ibid., p. 61).

Hence, the resource concept is relative – the value of a resource is related to its combination with other resources. Therefore, as firms are always seeking to improve the efficiency of resource utilization, they try to combine resources in new ways. Then, what is required of an element to qualify as a resource? Not just any element can be used in combination with other resources. According to Håkansson and Snehota (1995), an element can be considered a resource only if there is known use for it: "Various elements, tangible or intangible, material or symbolic, can be considered as resources when use can be made of them. No element without known use is a resource and the value of resources lies, of course, in their use potential" (ibid., p. 132).

Following from this, elements that do not have known use cannot be considered resources. However, as identified by Holmen (2001), value seems to be related to both: (1) known use; and (2) perceived use potential. A resource is an element with known use, though, there may also be an additional use potential, which has not yet been explored. This implies that elements that have no known use, and therefore cannot be considered resources, may have a use potential and can thus become resources in the future.

Håkansson and Snehota (1995, p. 132) distinguish between two sides of the "double-faced nature of resources": the provision side and the use side. The provider of a resource gives it certain features that can, but need not be, used by the user. There is a relationship between the provider and the user or, in other words, a resource can be regarded as a relation between its provision and use. The interaction between provider and user implies that different features can be adapted and developed in relation to other resources. This relation, i.e. how provided features are used is, in turn, dependent on the knowledge of resources among providers and users. Knowledge is crucial for the use and combination of resources: "increases in knowledge can always increase the range or amount of services available from any resource" (Penrose, 1959, p. 76). Firms have certain knowledge about resources and this knowledge is further developed as they get experiences from combining resources in new ways. For example, developing a new product implies that existing products, knowledge, experience and equipment are combined in new ways. The combining of resources introduces dynamics and innovation and, therefore, it is fundamental to the development of new knowledge. However, full knowledge about resources can never be achieved (ibid.).

The potential use of a resource changes over time as new knowledge is developed and new resource combinations are made possible. Further, the resource itself may be adapted in a way that increases its value in relation to other resources. Håkansson and Snehota (1995, p. 133) state, "resources are not entities given once and for all but variables." Thus, the number of possible combinations in which a single resource can be used appears infinite (Holmen, 2001). However, as argued by Holmen, "resource versatility" is bounded due to combination potential and modification potential. Although the number of possible resource combinations is (theoretically) infinite, the features of a specific resource will not be useful in any possible combination. Further, a focal resource can be de-composed into sub-resources to the extent that the modification potential equals the issue of combination potential. An interesting point made by Holmen, based on this reasoning, is that a focal resource should never be treated as "given" as sub-resources may be detached and used for new combinations.

2.2.2. Resource Heterogeneity

This far, it has been argued that the value of a resource is related to its use in relation to other resources. This is the basis for an important assumption, namely that the need for combining resources, and thus to achieve innovation, is attributable to resources being *heterogeneous*. This means that the value of a particular resource is dependent on how and with which other resources it is combined. According to Penrose (1959), a resource can be viewed as a bundle of potential services and ". . . exactly the same resource when used for different purposes or in different ways and in combination with different types or amounts of other resources provides a different service or set of services" (ibid., p. 25).

When discussing the characteristics of markets, Snehota (1990) illustrates heterogeneity of resources in the following way: "A seller may enter a market with an apparently homogenous supply of resource elements; but the exchange is driven by the heterogeneity of the demand side. Apparently homogenous supplies are attached different values, are heterogeneous, from the users' perspective. [. . .] [V]alues in exchange are given by its content, its meaning to the parties, and not simply by the characteristics of the object of an exchange transaction" (ibid., p. 97). Hence, it is not the resource per se, but rather the possible combinations with other resources (i.e. the users' resources) that determine its value.

Alchian and Demsetz (1972) have used heterogeneity of resources to explain the existence of firms. They argue that what they denote "team production" is present when: (1) several types of resources are used; and (2) the product is not a sum of separable outputs of each cooperating resource. Hence, the combination of heterogeneous resources is important for the output of team production: "Efficient production with heterogeneous resources is a result not of having *better* resources but in *knowing more accurately* the relative productive performance of these resources" (ibid., p. 793). As resources are assumed heterogeneous, team production implies that it is difficult to define and measure the contribution to the output of individual resources. The authors argue that the firm as a governance form therefore can make more efficient use of heterogeneous resource combinations than the market. In this way, Alchian and Demsetz use heterogeneity for explaining the existence of firms: ". . . the firm is a specialized surrogate for a market for team use of inputs; it provides superior (i.e. cheaper) collection and collation of knowledge about heterogeneous resources" (ibid., p. 794).

Although he does not explicitly make use of the term "heterogeneity," the arguments proposed by Richardson (1972) bear similarities with the arguments presented above. Richardson argues that when activities of two different firms are closely complementary, a need for coordination arises that cannot be handled by means of a market. This need for coordination is created as firms specialize in a limited number of activities in order to utilize their resources in the best possible way. The more specialized the more integrated a firm is with its counterparts. Therefore, as Forsgren et al. (1995, p. 29) conclude, "specialization may be a factor which elicits a heterogenization at company level." Interdependence both creates and is a result of heterogeneity – interdependence and heterogeneity are mutually reinforcing (Easton, 1992).

Resources are multidimensional and it is difficult, in many cases impossible, for a firm to determine which qualities are, and will be, important for the firm (Forsgren et al., 1995). Thus, this view of resources is very different from classical economic theory, where resources are often assumed homogenous, implying that the value of a resource is independent of the other resources with which it is combined. The distinction between homogenous and heterogeneous resources is crucial and, according to Penrose (1959), it is heterogeneity that gives each firm its unique character.

2.2.3. Possibilities and Limitations to the Development of Resources

Thus far, it has been argued that the value of a specific resource is dependent on how it is combined with other resources. Further, resource combination is important for innovation, though, as new combinations are searched for adaptation of resources may be needed. When resources are adapted and combined with other resources, they are also tied up in the larger resource structure. The resource becomes embedded (see e.g. Halinen & Törnroos, 1998). This has consequences for how the resource can be used in new combinations with other resources. As a resource becomes increasingly embedded in the resource structure, it may also become more difficult to change (see e.g. Rosenberg, 1982). Embeddedness at times facilitates and at times derails exchange (Uzzi, 1997) and, as argued by Halinen and Törnroos (1998), embeddedness is useful for describing and explaining network dynamics. The present paper is concerned with how resources can be adapted and combined across firm boundaries, to achieve technical development. By considering how resources are embedded in larger resource structures, the limits to as well as opportunities for technical development can be described and explained. Therefore, the concept of embeddedness is now elaborated in more detail.

2.2.3.1. Resource embeddedness.

Embeddedness is a term that is far from restricted to resources. It is a concept that has been increasingly used for understanding economic organization, in particular how social structure affects economic life (Uzzi, 1997). In this meaning, the concept of embeddedness can be traced to Polanyi's (1944) *The Great Transformation*, and it has been further developed by, among others, Marx, Weber, Schumpeter and Parsons (see Dacin et al., 1999; Uzzi, 1997). As classical economic theory does not consider the effects of social relations, or even regards it as a source of inefficiency, the embeddedness concept provides alternative explanations to economic behavior (Uzzi, 1997). The importance of social relationships and embeddedness to economic behavior is accepted by most organization theorists and it is an important assumption for researchers interested in business networks.

Among contemporary theorists, Granovetter (1985) has provided important inspiration for the conceptualization of embeddedness within the Industrial Network Approach. According to Dacin et al. (1999), Granovetter presents embeddedness as the contextualization of economic activity in on-going patterns of social relations. He criticizes classical and neoclassical economic theory for applying an undersocialized conception of human action where individual actors are socially atomized – a prerequisite to perfect competition (with reference to Smith, 1776). However, Granovetter also rejects oversocialized accounts of economic action where the internalization of behavioral patterns also leads to atomization and where social relations are assumed to only have peripheral effects on behavior (1985). Instead, actors' attempts at purposive action are "embedded in concrete, ongoing systems of social relations" (ibid., p. 487). Further, " '[e]mbeddedness' refers to the fact that economic action and outcomes, like all social action and outcomes, are affected by actors' dyadic (pairwise) relations *and* by the structure of the overall network of relations" (Granovetter, 1992, p. 33). Granovetter distinguishes between relational and structural aspects of embeddedness, aspects that roughly can be "translated" to relationships and networks within the Industrial Network Approach. The structural aspect of embeddedness is particularly emphasized as it is easy to slip into "dyadic atomization," that is, to focus on dyads only.

Thus far, the conceptualization of embeddedness has mainly been focused on the social and economical aspects of relations and structures. In general, the social aspects of embeddedness can be found in the actor layer within the Industrial Network Approach (Holmen & Pedersen, 1999). However, from a resource perspective and, in particular, when regarding product development, technical embeddedness is of particular interest. As has been argued earlier, the value of a resource is dependent on which other resources it is combined with. Hence, the value of an investment made by a firm in a certain technology is dependent on how it relates to other existing technologies. Furthermore, as firms engage in relationships with other firms, the value of an investment will be dependent on the technologies of other firms as well. Thereby, each technology is embedded into a larger set of complementary technologies (Ford et al., 1998; Rosenberg, 1982). In complex technical systems where a large number of technologies are combined, for example a car or a paper mill, the technical embeddedness stretches far across firm boundaries. Therefore, no firm can decide on the development and adaptation of these technologies in isolation. The dependencies that exist between firms and the logic that different firms act upon are embedded in each others (Wedin, 2001).

Embeddedness is required for (efficiently) utilizing and economizing on resources but, at the same time, it limits the possibilities of change. The difficulty to impose change has been recognized within different fields of research. Within social science and organization theory, the term *inertia* is frequently used to illustrate that organizations cannot easily change their structural features as the environment changes. When the environment is fairly stable, inertia is associated with reliability and accountability, but as environmental uncertainty increases, inertia becomes a liability rather than an asset (Scott, 1998). Inertia has been used also within the Industrial Network Approach regarding the establishment of new relationships between customers and suppliers (see Ford et al., 1998). Within the field of applied economics, von Hippel's (1994) term *stickiness* is frequently applied in a similar meaning.

Drawing on the results of an empirical study of the development of high quality printing paper, Håkansson and Waluszewski (2002) use the (physical) term *friction* to illustrate how embeddedness affects the possibilities to change resources. Friction is used to illustrate the stabilizing force that makes it difficult to move resources in relation to each other due to their interaction and embeddedness. In this respect, friction is used in a similar way as inertia. However, friction also implies that the changing force that is applied to an embedded resource will be distributed to other elements in the resource constellation. As there are always resource features that are not used or that can be used in different ways, this will cause connections between some resources to break up, thereby enabling new combinations. In this way, friction is stabilizing at the same time as it has a de-stabilizing effect (see Fig. 10).

Two important aspects of friction are *heaviness* and *variety* (Håkansson & Waluszewski, 2001). Heaviness is closely related to what Ford et al. (1998) refer to as *fixed* resources. Variety refers to the difficulties to predict the effects of friction,

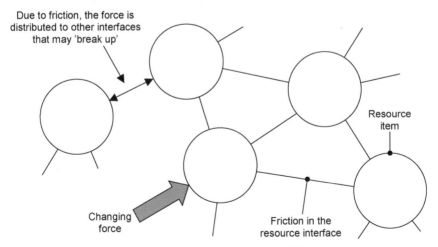

Fig. 10. The Impact of Friction on Embedded Resources.

as the outcome of a change is dependent on a complex pattern of relationships between more or less embedded resources. For example, the change of a resource may cause different effects depending on its related context or a variety of resource combinations may produce the same output.

2.2.3.2. Embeddedness and the time dimension. An important aspect of embeddedness is the time dimension. What has happened in the past is memorized in present structures and relations and therefore need to be considered: "It is [. . .] important to avoid what might be called 'temporal reductionism': treating relations and structures as if they had no history that shapes the present situation" (Granovetter, 1992, p. 34). A classical and frequently cited example of the importance of history to the present situation is the development of the QWERTY keyboard. It achieved its original design due to technical restrictions in the mechanical typewriter with the "up-stroke typebar mechanism." As noted by David (1985) an interplay between technical interrelatedness, economies of scale and quasi-irreversibility of investment "locked in" the QWERTY design, even though the technical obstacles had later been overcome. "Even the very radical leap to personal computer technology carried with it the old and the familiar: the QWERTY keyboard" (Utterback, 1994, p. 18).

Path-dependence is a term largely developed by economists concerned with the evolution of technology and institutions (Araujo & Harrison, 2002). It is frequently used for explaining how the eventual outcome of a sequence of economic changes can be exerted by temporally remote events (David, 1985). However, no parallel should be drawn between path-dependence and historical determinism (Håkansson & Lundgren, 1997). As formulated by Tilly (1994), path-dependence is the idea: (1) that the order in which things happen affects how they happen; (2) that the trajectory of change up to a certain point itself constrains the trajectory beyond that point; and (3) that choices made at a particular moment eliminate whole ranges of possibilities from later choices.

The *sequence* of events is of importance when considering what has happened in the past. Antonelli (1997) makes a distinction between past-dependence and path-dependence. Past-dependence only considers the state at a certain point in time, while path-dependence takes into consideration the consequences of events at each point in time. Another important aspect of path-dependence is that both systematic and unpredictable processes are merged in the same trajectory of events (Araujo & Harrison, 2002).

2.2.4. Resources and Relationships in the Network Model
Firms have resources, but only part of the resources needed to perform activities are owned by the firm. An important part of a firm's total resource base is to be

found beyond the boundary of the firm (Gadde & Håkansson, 2001). A firm is dependent upon other firms' resources, which it may access via different business relationships. At the same time, following the same logic, the firm is a provider of resources to other firms. Hence, relationships allow resources controlled by one firm to be combined with resources controlled by other firms. In other words, a relationship connects the resources of two firms. Thereby, activities can be performed that would not have been possible to perform within one of the firms alone.

Relationships with other firms are important for the development of knowledge about resources and, as stated by Håkansson and Snehota (1995, p. 137) "a company can, in interaction with others, learn how and for what purpose different resource elements can be used." Knowledge of resources is important as it can help to "increase the range or amount of services available from any resource" (Penrose, 1959, p. 76). The combination of resources often comes about in business relationships, where resource confrontation is frequent. Therefore, technical development performed across firm boundaries is important for increasing the knowledge of resources and, therefore, for innovation (see Gadde & Håkansson, 2001).

As a relationship develops, the resources become increasingly oriented towards each other through adjustments and, as a consequence, the resource ties grow stronger. The firms become increasingly interdependent. As this development goes on new uses for resources are discovered and, consequently, new resource combinations are likely to arise. Over time, the two firms may become tightly tied together and the boundary between them therefore becomes increasingly blurred.

Resources are often tied to several other resources owned by the same firm or resources owned by other firms. This implies that different resource ties are connected, forming an aggregated structure referred to as a resource *constellation* (Håkansson & Snehota, 1995). The resource ties, that a firm develops with other firms within the resource constellation, affects what the firm can and cannot do. Moreover, the multiple ties in the resource constellation imply that the value of a specific resource is dependent on which other resources it is *indirectly* tied to. Hence, the change of a resource controlled by a third party may have consequences for a firm's perceived value of a specific resource.

Thus far, we have seen that relationships are important elements in the network structure. However, what is a relationship? According to Håkansson and Snehota (1995, p. 25), a relationship is "mutually oriented interaction between two reciprocally committed parties." However, the authors stress that it is necessary to look at the elements being connected in a relationship and the effects of these connections. Therefore, they distinguish between what they denote the function and substance of business relationships. Function addresses who is affected by the relationships, while substance addresses what is affected.

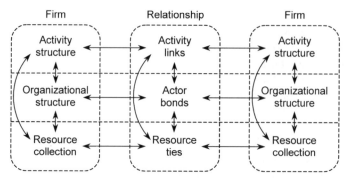

Fig. 11. The Substance of Relationships (Adapted from Håkansson & Snehota, 1995).

Regarding substance, the authors identify three different layers to exist in business relationships; an activity layer, a resource layer, and an actor layer (see Fig. 11). Hence, this conceptualization of a business relationship largely builds upon the dimensions presented above as basic building blocks in the Network model. The activity links, resource ties and actor bonds all affect the outcome of the relationship in different ways. The activity layer can be related to productivity, the resource layer to innovativity and the actor layer to identity (Dubois, 1994), though, it is important to consider that these layers are interrelated.

According to Håkansson and Snehota (1995), a relationship can be characterized by the relative importance of the three layers. Activity links, resource ties and actor bonds play different roles in different relationships. In some relationships, the actor bonds play an utterly important role while the activity links are few and not very well developed. In other relationships, it may be the other way round. This implies that each relationship is unique. Further, there are always possibilities to develop a relationship as new interconnections, within as well as between any of the three layers, are created. This interplay between substance layers is a driving force in the development of business relationships. Hence, the three substance layers are not independent of each other.

Three different functions of a relationship are distinguished. A relationship influences and is influenced by the individual actors, by the dyad between actors, and by the network. As a relationship can be a resource in itself that can be exploited (e.g. combined with other relationships) by the actors involved in the relationship. Hence, actors use the relationship in different resource combinations and therefore the relationship affects individual actors differently. Further, the relationship will have effects for the dyad between the actors as they together can perform activities and utilize resources in a way that none of them could accomplish in isolation. Each relationship is embedded in a larger network of relationships.

Hence, the relationship is, directly or indirectly, connected to other relationships: "Any relationship is because of its substance a constituent element of the wider network in which relationships are interconnected" (ibid., p. 40). The network function therefore reflects the interdependence of individual and collective action.

To summarize, the three substance layers (activity links, resource ties and actor bonds) constitute the content and characteristics of a relationship. The relationship has a function for each of the two involved actors, as well as for the dyad between them and for other third parties that are indirectly connected with the relationship. Hence, the function regards what is affected by the relationship. A change in the substance layers affects the network structure, i.e. the function of the relationship, just as any change in the network affects the substance of relationships. Hence, substance and function are interrelated.

As relationships are connected, activity links, resource ties and actor bonds are connected, directly or indirectly, to the links, ties and bonds of other relationships. This forms an aggregate network structure that is "an organized web of conscious and goal-seeking actors; it is also an organized pattern of activities as well as an organized constellation of resources" (ibid., p. 40).

2.3. A Framework for Analysis of Dependencies Between Resources

In this section, a framework for analysis of the organizing of interactive product development will be developed. By analyzing resources and dependencies between resources (i.e. *what* needs to be organized), an understanding of the organizing of interactive product development (i.e. *how* these dependencies can be dealt with) can be achieved. Therefore, a framework is needed that can support the identification of dependencies between various categories of resources. For this purpose, the resource dimension of the Industrial Network Approach will be further developed based on a model presented by Håkansson and Waluszewski (2002).

As products and other resources interact, they become increasingly embedded into each other, which may influence the possible use of the resources in other combinations. To create an understanding of this interactive resource development, that is essential to understanding technical development, it is necessary to consider how different types of resources relate to and influence each other. Håkansson and Waluszewski (2002) have developed a model based on four different resource categories: Products, production facilities, business units and business relationships (see Fig. 12). Together these four categories represent the resource constellation in a business network.

Products are physical items or services that are developed and produced through the interaction between different resource elements. A product may be exchanged

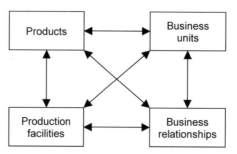

Fig. 12.   Four Categories of Resources in a Business Network (Håkansson & Waluszewski, 2002).

between two firms and it can be used in combination with other resources to produce other products. The heterogeneity of resources implies that a product cannot be treated as "given." The traditional view of economic exchange assumes that the product is given, implying that the customer can choose to buy it from one of many suppliers. However, empirical studies show that products can seldom be regarded as given. Products are rather developed and adapted in interaction between seller and buyer (Håkansson & Waluszewski, 2002). Each product has its unique features in relation to other resources. These features will be a result of how the product is embedded with both the provider's and the user's other resources. To provide a value for the user the product must have features that can be combined with the user's other resources. At the same time, the product features must also be related to the provider's other resources. Hence, the interaction between provider and user in this way creates "imprints" on the product. At the same time, the interaction between provider and user creates "imprints" on the different resources with which the product interacts.

Since a product is embedded with other resources, changes in these other resources may affect the features of the product and, thus, its value. Hence, although the product itself remains unchanged, its value may change over time. Changes in other resources may imply that the product loses some value, but it may as well create opportunities to use the product's features in new ways or even in new combinations with other resources. Consequently, the value of a product can be different for the provider and the user.

If a product is assumed to have known use, it can be regarded as a resource. This implies that the product can have a value (only) when used in combination with other products. As a product is combined with other products, it becomes part of a product structure. This product structure may be referred to as a product as well, but on a higher level of aggregation. Further, the products with which a product is

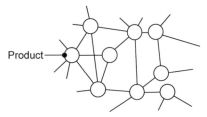

Fig. 13. As a Product is Combined with Other Products, it Becomes Embedded in a Larger Product Structure.

combined also have interfaces to other products. Hence, when combining a product with other product elements, it becomes embedded into a larger product structure (see Fig. 13).

Thus far, product elements have been combined to form larger structures that have also been referred to as products. It is, however, useful to make some distinction between products at different levels of aggregation. Therefore, a delimitation of the seemingly endless product structure presented above is needed. However, the embeddedness of any product will make it impossible to focus that product without considering its connections to the larger resource structure. Though, for analytical reasons, it will be useful to define a boundary between the product in focus and the wider product/resource structure. Where this boundary is drawn must be related to the type of product studied and the level of analysis. The product that is distinguished by this boundary will be referred to as a complete product (cf. the term "end-product" used by Dubois, 1994).

A complete product may be divided into a number of smaller product elements that will be referred to as *components*. Each component fulfils some function that contributes to the overall function of the complete product. Components can be identified at different levels of aggregation. A component may be a single physical part (e.g. a screw, a nut or a spring) or a number of assembled physical parts (e.g. a hatch lock, an alternator, a brake caliper or even an engine).

There are many terms available for describing components at different levels of aggregation (see e.g. Hubka & Eder, 1988; Ulrich & Eppinger, 1995), though stringent definitions of the terms used are rare. Terms such as component, sub-assembly, part, chunk, sub-module, module, system etc are frequently used, though they are seldom distinctively defined and there seem to be great overlaps in the meaning of different terms.

Hence, component is a general term for the smaller building blocks that together form a complete product. From the definition follows that one component may be made up of a number of smaller components and, therefore, exactly what is defined as a component needs to be related to the level of analysis (cf. the definition of a complete product above). According to Hubka and Eder (1988, p. 81), a component "may be defined in terms of any of the levels of complexity [...] The definition depends on the complexity of the system being considered."

As components are combined with other components, they become connected via interfaces that affect how a particular component is embedded in the product structure. In other words, there are dependencies between components. The interfaces have different characteristics and, depending on purpose (e.g. to regard functionality, degree of complexity, or manufacturing), it may be useful to classify technical products according to similarities and relationships (cf. dependencies) between its components (ibid., p. 93). A product fulfils one or several functions and it needs to be physically realized and, consequently, there seem to be two general categories of interfaces between components, namely *physical* and *functional* (Holmqvist, 2001; Hubka & Eder, 1988; Jellbo, 1998; Pahl & Beitz, 1996; Ulrich & Eppinger, 1995). Two components attached to each other imply a physical interface. For example, they may be bolted, welded, glued or riveted together. A functional interface exists when two components work together to provide one or several functions. For example, there is a functional interface between the brake pedal and the brake pads in a car. Further, two components may be geometrically adapted to each other to fit within limited space constraints. This type of interface will be referred to as a *spatial* interface (Hubka & Eder, 1988; Sanchez, 2000). Even if there is no direct physical interface between components, heat, magnetic fields, or vibrations may be transferred from one component to another. This will be referred to as an *environmental* interface (Sanchez, 2000). Spatial and environmental interfaces may be regarded as special forms of physical and functional interfaces.

Production facilities are, like products, often of a physical nature. Products are both used (input material, machines, equipment etc.) and produced in production facilities. Hence, a production facility is a resource that transforms products into other products. This implies interaction between the product and the production facility to achieve efficient utilization of these resources. Due to this interaction, the product and the production facility become embedded into each other.

Further, the output from one production facility is often further processed in other facilities. Therefore, firms in many cases recognize that resources can be utilized more efficiently if different production facilities are related and adapted to each other. One firm might change its production facility to fit the production facility of a counterpart. For example, the use of a certain production technique in one facility may enable a particular production process in another facility. As another example, the need for keeping products in stock can be reduced by adapting the flow of material between facilities. This interaction is important to find and exploit latent features of production facilities. Consequently, production facilities may become important parts of the relationship between the firms. Hence, production facilities become embedded with other facilities.

This embeddedness, in combination with large capital investments, often implies that production facilities are regarded as "heavy" resources. Investments in equipment and knowledge make it difficult to impose changes, creating "lock-in" effects that reduce flexibility. This will have effects on the possibilities to adapt facilities to each other as well as it will affect the interaction between products and facilities. In less capital-intensive industries, product design may be less restricted by existing production facilities. In some cases a production facility may even be developed based upon a certain product, though interfaces to other existing production facilities still need to be considered.

Business units reach beyond being a combination of products and production facilities. Except physical resources, business units incorporate social features related to, for example, knowledge, experience, capabilities, routines and traditions. In this sense, business units, production facilities and products can be regarded as complementary and interrelated resource elements. However, while products and production facilities are activated by actors, business units are active and they strive to improve and develop their position within the network. In the present study, the analyses of business units are mainly focused on issues related to the production and the development of products, i.e. activity structures and resource structures. Various other issues that are generally attributed to business units such as strategies, capital structure, and ownership structure are considered only when relevant for the analyses and are therefore not explicitly analyzed.

Through interaction, the features of one business unit become embedded with the features of other business units. For example, knowledge in one business unit is developed through interaction with other business units. This interaction also contributes to develop a business unit's knowledge and skills regarding how to work with other business units. This includes, for example, experiences of involved people and knowledge of how facilities have been used earlier. The embeddedness may help, but also constrain, a business unit's possibilities to change its position within the network.

Business relationships (or just "relationships") can be regarded as resources since actors can use relationships to develop and utilize resources controlled by themselves or other actors. With this perspective, as resources are embedded with other resources and development comes about through interaction, actors cannot disregard the importance of relationships. For example, a business unit that wants to change its position in the network may utilize some of its relationships with other business units. At the same time, other relationships may restrict changes.

Relationships can be said to be embedded "by definition" as they form connections between different resource elements. It is, however, also important to consider how relationships, and other resources, are embedded due to connections between different relationships. This implies that what happens in one relationship may affect other relationships. Hence, actors must not only consider their own relationships with other actors, but also how relationships between other actors develop over time.

A relationship is a resource that is often developed over long periods of time. Therefore, relationships can be said to reflect the time dimension as experiences from the past are connected with future expectations. Just as with other types of resources, there may be features of a relationship that have not yet been discovered or developed and that may increase the value of the relationship as a resource in the future.

Hence, the four categories of resources (products, production facilities, business units and business relationships) identified by Håkansson and Waluszewski (2002) together represent the resource constellation in a business network. With this view, it is evident that different resource units within each category are related to each other. For example, a production unit is related to other production units. It is, however, important to consider connections between the different resource categories as well. For example, two business units can be related through a business relationship and together they develop a certain product. This product, in turn, may have an interface to another product that is produced in a production facility operated by another business unit that is dependent on other business relationships. In this way, different resource elements become directly or indirectly related to each other.

2.4. Research Issues

With the theory presented thus far as a basis, three research issues have been identified concerning:

- The interaction between the technical structure (products and production facilities) and the organizational structure (business units and relationships).
- The organizing of product development with regard to dependencies between resources, in particular with regard to dependencies between components in the developed product.
- The function of teams – where different business units are represented – for the organizing of interactive product development.

3. RESEARCH METHOD

Many similarities can be identified between writing this paper and the product development projects I have been studying. Even though I knew from the beginning that my research was supposed to result in this paper (a Ph.D. thesis) and it was rather clear what the subject of the paper should be, the content has evolved over time. Hence, the outcome could not be regarded as "given," neither from the beginning nor during the research process. In fact, this paper is the result of a process that has been far from linear. The many different research activities leading to this paper did not follow a planned sequence, even though the final structure of the paper may give that impression. Instead, due to opportunities that could not be identified *ex ante* and dependencies that had to be dealt with in different ways, the different sections, and even single words, have developed in a highly non-linear and iterative process. This, however, does not mean that the process has not been guided and managed in different ways. The present paper is the result of an interactive process of combining and adapting theory and empirical data, based on the ideas, the knowledge, the experience, and the perspectives of myself as well as of others, in combination with different tools and models. Just like the content of the paper, the "research resources" in terms of theory and empirical data as well as the network of actors, were not "given" from the beginning. Over time, these "resources" have developed in different directions. I have certainly influenced that development, though it could not be fully anticipated. In this section, considerations and different paths that finally led to this paper are described in more detail.

3.1. The Research Process

The research and the results that are accounted for in this paper have evolved over time as interplay between theory and empirical evidence. The empirical data emanates from four different studies: (1) The Autoliv study; (2) The PICS study; (3) The Volvo study; and (4) The DFC Tech study. Figure 14 illustrates the four

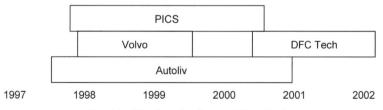

Fig. 14.   The Four Studies on a Time Scale.

studies on a time scale. Originally, I intended to include empirical data from all four studies. It soon became evident, however, that this would result in a scope too broad for the paper. I therefore decided to narrow the focus, in favor of more depth, by delimiting the empirical material. Therefore, the empirical material that has been included in the present paper mainly originates from the Volvo and the DFC Tech studies. Still, the PICS study (see e.g. von Corswant, 2000a, b) and the Autoliv study have been crucial for the development of research questions as well as the interpretation of results and, hence, for my understanding of interactive product development. With the four studies as a basis, the research process is now described in more detail, including the use of different theoretical approaches.

3.1.1. The Autoliv Study

The first study started in the summer of 1997 together with Autoliv Sweden AB (Autoliv), a large producer of safety products for the automotive industry. Less than a year earlier, Autoliv had initiated a supplier association. involving ten of their most important Swedish component suppliers. These suppliers would all qualify as small and medium sized enterprises (SME:s), although some of them belonged to larger corporations (three of the suppliers were subsidiaries within the Autoliv group). The purpose of the supplier association was to strengthen the relationships between Autoliv and these ten suppliers and, thereby, create means for jointly improving operative performance (e.g. quality, delivery performance and product cost). By cooperating with Autoliv and the ten firms in the supplier association I was able to study several SME:s that all belonged to the same supplier network.

Initially, the study aimed at investigating how knowledge can be transferred from universities to SME:s. However, my research focus soon turned into studying how the firms in the supplier association developed their operative performance and why. The suppliers in the association had a common customer (i.e. Autoliv), though, they also had relations with other firms (e.g. other customers) that affected their behavior. I soon realized that these firms' relationships with Autoliv could not be studied as isolated entities and, hence, an interorganizational perspective was needed. At that time, however, I was not familiar with the Industrial Network Approach and I tried to apply various other models and theories concerned with supplier development and collaboration.

I first studied how the firms in the association developed over time regarding, for example quality and delivery performance, but I realized that I would need to focus my research. One issue that had frequently been discussed within the supplier association and that seemed to be important for these firms' development was product development. The increasing focus on suppliers actively participating in product development seemed interesting and I decided to study this phenomenon in more detail.

As I reviewed existing research concerned with supplier collaboration in product development, it became evident that most research took a customer (often car manufacturer) perspective (e.g. Dyer, 1996; Kamath & Liker, 1994). Although dyadic relationships involve two parties, the (small) supplier firms' perspective was seldom regarded in any detail. At the same time, I saw from my studies of Autoliv's supplier association that the suppliers found it difficult to participate in product development due to scarce resources and lack of previous experience. Hence, there was a need for also taking a supplier perspective on collaborative product development.

As mentioned above, there was an ambition to initiate a collaborative product development project among the firms in the supplier association. Although this was discussed several times, it was never really carried through. Still, the insight into these firms' situation and the experiences and problems that they shared have been valuable to this paper. It certainly helped to gain an understanding of the perspective of (small) supplier firms. The study was ended in December 2000.

3.1.2. The PICS Study

In parallel with the Autoliv study, a survey called PICS (Profit Impact from Change Strategy) was initiated after the summer of 1997. It aimed at investigating production and product development performance among different categories of Swedish automotive suppliers. PICS inherited its name from an earlier survey (see Tunälv, 1996) focusing on change strategies among Swedish automotive suppliers. In this later version of PICS (see von Corswant, 2000b), however, many questions were changed. Largely based on the experiences from the Autoliv study, the focus was re-directed towards suppliers' product development activities.

The supply chain model had gained much interest (see Section 1.2.4) and seemed to enable a division of supplier firms into different categories based on their relations to suppliers and customers. The supply chain was therefore assumed a suitable model for categorizing suppliers. This would enable an analysis of differences between categories along the supply chain regarding, for example, product development activities and the suppliers' relationships to their own suppliers and customers. Respondents were therefore asked to estimate their firm's position in the supply chain (see Fig. 15) based on how their annual sales were distributed among the different firm categories.

However, profound analyses of the data indicated that the supply chain might not be a suitable model for distinguishing between suppliers when regarding product development (see von Corswant, 2000a). For instance, some suppliers that manufacture fairly simple components for the automotive industry were found to develop advanced products within other lines of business. These results were interesting since it was shown that while the supply chain model is based on

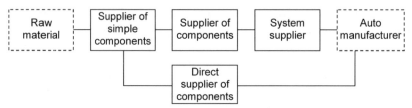

Fig. 15. The Supply Chain Model Used for Categorizing Firms. *Note:* Categories marked with dotted lines included for reference only.

(sequential) production flows, the results indicated other *patterns* of relationships between firms when regarding product development. This generated questions regarding, for example, what such patterns look like, how they develop and how they can be studied. This, in turn, increased my interest for studying *interaction* between collaborating firms. In this way, the findings from the PICS study generated questions that underpinned the interactive approach to product development that has been used for the analyses in this paper.

3.1.3. The Volvo Study

Shortly after the preparations for the PICS survey had started, another study was initiated in co-operation with Volvo Car Corporation (Volvo). Volvo had been working together with a number of different suppliers for the development of the new P2 platform and the first car model, the Volvo S80, would be introduced within less than a year.

The Volvo study aimed at exploring particular aspects that need to be considered in collaborative product development projects, i.e. critical success factors. Therefore, detailed information regarding different development projects and the involved firms was needed. It was also considered important to set the studied development projects into a larger context, which called for a case study approach (regarding the use of case studies, see Section 3.3). However, the development of the P2 platform was a large development project, requiring delimitations. At the same time, different development projects might give different perspectives on collaborative development (e.g. due to different types of technologies being developed). Therefore, in co-operation with Volvo representatives, five different development projects were selected for the study. These projects covered five different development areas (interior, exterior, engine, chassis and the electrical system). In each project, Volvo collaborated with one or several suppliers. With the five projects all involving Volvo, the study was conducted as a case study with five embedded cases (Yin, 1994).

Before the collection of empirical data began, a literature survey was conducted in order to find out what different aspects of supplier collaboration had been identified by other researchers. As argued earlier, supplier collaboration is often studied based a dyadic perspective. This certainly influenced my own approach to the problem at hand. However, at this time, I did not question this perspective on collaboration. Consequently, the study was mainly focused on dyadic relationships, though, it soon turned out to be important also to consider other, related relationships. In parallel with the literature study, documents and records regarding Volvo's product strategies, Volvo's product development organization and other information regarding the P2 project were studied.

Initially, 24 semi-structured interviews were conducted regarding the five relationships. The respondents were people with different positions in the five development projects, including representatives from the suppliers. A majority of the respondents were project leaders, development engineers, quality engineers and pre-production engineers. When the individual interviews were finished, group interviews were conducted for four of the five development projects, based on affinity-diagrams (see e.g. Bergman & Klefsjö, 1994).

To check that the collected data corresponded to the respondents' view, and to give feedback, a synthesis of the results so far was presented during a seminar. The respondents as well as other people interested in this issue were invited to participate. The seminar showed that some complementary data collection was needed mainly concerning product development, but also issues related to purchasing. Therefore, an additional 12 interviews were conducted mainly with managers within Volvo's product development and purchasing organizations.

The initial analysis of empirical data was mainly based on the theoretical frame provided by the literature survey performed in the beginning of the study. As a result, a number of aspects that need to be considered when collaborating with suppliers in product development could be identified (see von Corswant & Tunälv, 2002). Thereby, the aim of the study was fulfilled. A report was written for Volvo and the study formally ended in the summer of 1998. However, already when collecting the data, it had been evident that it was difficult to focus the study on isolated development projects and relationships since they were obviously interconnected in different ways. For instance, technical component interfaces also connected different projects that caused problems in one project to "spill over" to other projects. Due to the dyadic perspective of the studied theory, this kind of dynamics was difficult to cope with from an analytical point of view. Although the original aim of the study had been fulfilled and it had formally been ended, I was frustrated by not being able to better explain the complexity that had been revealed in the study. It was necessary to further develop my theoretical frame, but I did not know how or in what direction. However, although I lacked a "research strategy" for explaining this complexity, it had profoundly influenced the collection of empirical data. In addition to focusing on the specific development projects, I also collected much "contextual data" concerning how the projects and the involved firms related to other projects and firms. Much of this data was never really used for the initial analysis referred to above, though, later it should prove to be a valuable resource.

About one year later, in the fall of 1999, I attended a doctoral course on network theory at Uppsala University. Until then, I had been searching for alternative models and theories for understanding and explaining collaborative product development. The study of Autoliv's supplier association had made me search for theories involving more than two collaborating firms. I also searched for alternatives to the supply chain model that had been applied in the PICS study. In addition, I was looking for some theory that could help to explain the "complexity" that I had found in the Volvo study. In many respects, this course should prove to be a turning point for my research, to have an impact on the Volvo study, the later DFC Tech study, as well as on this thesis. During the course, we were assigned the task to analyze a case based on the Industrial Network Approach. My colleague Peter Fredriksson (who studied production and assembly of modules for the Volvo S80) and I chose to analyze both development and production of the Volvo S80. With this "new" tool, the empirical data from the Volvo study could be analyzed from a different perspective. Now the "extra" contextual data that had been collected proved to be useful. By analyzing relationships between different activities, resources as well as actors, an understanding was provided for the complex patterns of interrelatedness that had been identified earlier but could not then be explained. This also contributed to the generation of new questions regarding, for instance, combination and development of resources in interaction between the involved actors.

The results of the analyses were also presented and discussed at different seminars and conferences, which helped to further develop the reasoning (see also von Corswant et al., 2001). In addition, representatives for Volvo and the suppliers provided feedback on the case descriptions. Later, to provide more detail for the analyses in this paper, six complementary interviews were conducted with people that had been involved in Volvo's relationships with Lear and Delphi respectively.

Hence, in this study, the relationships between Volvo and five (later reduced to two) suppliers were studied. The underlying theoretical model implied a dyadic view of the relationships. However, the way data had been collected enabled the use of a different tool for the analysis, i.e. a network approach. Thereby, the empirical findings could be analyzed and explained in a different way.

3.1.4. The DFC Tech Study

In December 1999, contacts were established with the automotive supplier Dayco Sweden AB (Dayco). Shortly before that, Dayco had established a joint venture (called DFC Tech) together with a consultancy firm to perform product development in collaboration with their customers. Within short, DFC Tech became involved in a product development project with the truck manufacturer Scania (the case is described in detail in Section 4.4). It was considered an opportunity to study product development collaboration from a supplier's perspective and the DFC Tech study started in February 2000. This was the fourth and last study and (together with the Autoliv study) it complements the customer perspective of the Volvo study.

Mainly based on the experiences from the Volvo study, but also from the PICS study and the Autoliv study, it was regarded necessary to not only apply a dyadic focus on relationships. Therefore, in addition to a focal relationship, I also wanted to include other, connected, relationships in the study. This implied that a network perspective could be applied for the analyses. The relationship between DFC Tech and Scania was chosen as the focal relationship. I focused my interest on this relationship, but I also tried to understand how it influenced, as well as it was influenced by, other relationships. This was done mainly from DFC Tech's (and Dayco's) perspective. However, to understand how the relationship developed and why, it was regarded important to also include Scania's perspective. Hence, with the relationship between DFC Tech and Scania in focus, the study was expanded in different directions to also include more "contextual" aspects. Because of this approach, the research was conducted as a case study.

Already when I started this study, the Industrial Network Approach had a great influence on me. The network perspective not only implied that multiple relationships were considered. As described above, the network analyses of the Volvo study had provided a different perspective that helped me to interpret the empirical data in a different way (e.g. regarding dependencies between resources). In addition, a picture of this paper began to emerge where the resource dimension and different forms of dependencies came to play an important role. Consequently, from start the study was focused on dependencies between different resources and how this was reflected in the organization of the collaborative development work.

The data collection was mainly based on semi-structured interviews, but also other sources such as CAD-models, company records and various documents (e.g. service manuals) were used. I started by interviewing a few "key persons" that had been identified from the very beginning. Then other interviewees were identified as the project went on. In total, 12 interviews were conducted. However, when writing case descriptions and performing data analyses, some missing information could be identified. Therefore, three complementary interviews were carried out with people who had been involved in the project. Further, representatives from both Scania and DFC Tech read the case descriptions and provided feedback.

During the whole project, I had a continual contact with the managing director of DFC Tech, also after the project with Scania was halted. We have had many fruitful and interesting discussions regarding DFC Tech's, as well as Dayco's, future. These discussions gave opportunities to discuss my view of DFC Tech and their relationship with Scania, as well as other (potential) customers. We also discussed the analyses of the case from different perspectives, and the combination of his empirical experiences with my theoretical (network) approach resulted in new knowledge as well as new questions. For instance, at several occasions DFC Tech's role in the relationship with Scania was discussed. This generated questions about what value was created and for whom, how product development should be organized between DFC Tech and Dayco and so on.

3.1.5. Some Reflections Upon Important Choices

How empirical data and theory has been used can be traced back to different choices made throughout the research process. I have chosen a theoretical perspective, what empirical data to include in the paper and so on. Some choices may be regarded as "informed" ones, while some choices I may not even have been aware of. In hindsight, I have questioned some choices that I have made. However, at the same time, each choice must be viewed from a perspective reflecting the conditions when the particular choice was made. This not only includes "external" conditions, but also my own perspective, knowledge, and experience. It is also important to consider that in many cases there has been no freedom of choice, since choices are always constrained to different extents by different circumstances. Further, different choices are interrelated, which makes it even more difficult to foresee the consequences of a particular choice. Still, it is necessary to make choices.

In most cases, the possibilities to freely choose firms to collaborate with in a study are limited. Different factors such as timing of studies with product development projects and financing conditions have had an impact on the choices. In addition to this, it should be borne in mind that not only the researcher, but also the firms make the choice to participate in a study or not. Further, it can be questioned whether the selection of firms is really a matter of choice (at least not an "informed" one) since it is impossible to know beforehand what will be found. Instead of making the "right" choice from the beginning, it is important that the chosen research approach enables the research to take different directions depending on what empirical data is found and how it corresponds with existing theory. Further, the selection of firms has also influenced, as well as it has been influenced by, the choice of research methods and theoretical perspectives. The initial dyadic perspective on relationships had consequences for how the Volvo study was designed. At the same time, the research method (i.e. case study) allowed me to collect empirical data that later contributed to challenge my choice of theoretical perspective in favor of the network approach.

Also writing this paper has implied making various choices that to different extents have been constrained by my earlier choices regarding research method, theoretical perspective and so on. One such choice has concerned what empirical data to include in the paper. As evident from the description above, I have chosen to include data from the Volvo study and the DFC Tech study only. This choice was made because these two studies address issues that I found to be relevant for the paper as a whole. Hence, I chose a more narrow scope of the paper instead of a broad one. Still, the data that was not explicitly included has been crucial for my ability to write the paper.

Moreover, a comparison between the research process described above and the paper reveals differences in structure. The research process has been characterized by interaction between empirical data and theory, while the paper has a more deductive structure. In the paper, existing theory is used for formulating a problem and, then, additional theory is presented as a basis for analysis of the empirical data. Although this may not give a fair picture of the research process per se, I have chosen this structure for the paper since it enabled a focus on a specific problem that could be elucidated with a selection of empirical data (as argued above some form of selection was necessary).

3.2. Research Context

My research context has certainly influenced my view of the world and how I have chosen to interpret it in my research. Such contextual aspects include my personal interest for technical products as well as my academic background in engineering. This interest has certainly contributed to direct my research towards studying the development of complex products based on fairly advanced technologies. Such influences affect the research in different ways. In fact, all interpretations, selections, choices, and analyses that lie behind my findings and conclusions reflect my own view of the studied reality and how it has been presented for me or, as expressed by Silverman (2001, p. 287) *"all data are mediated by our own reasoning as well as that of participants."* My own perspective has certainly influenced my interpretations of empirical observations, but it has also helped me to see things that other researchers, with other research contexts, would have missed. Total objectivity in the search for scientific knowledge is impossible. I have strived, however, to attain an awareness of various sources of influence on my own frame of reference, which can help to make "informed" choices.

An important source of influence is the research context here at Chalmers University of Technology. My research has been conducted at the Department of Operations Management and Work Organization. The department has a long tradition of longitudinal in-depth case studies, based on close relationships with industry, though, surveys and other research approaches can be found as well. This "heritage" is to some extent reflected in my choice of research method, i.e. to conduct case studies. Further, a large share of the research at the department has traditionally been conducted in cooperation with the automotive industry (but also other industries such as white goods and electronics), which became an important foundation for my own relationships with firms within the automotive industry.

In the beginning of my research process, this research tradition had great influence on me, and I actively tried to develop my own frame of reference based on operations management theory. However, unlike most other research that had been conducted at the department, I chose to focus my research on what happens not mainly *within* a firm but in interaction *between* firms. As described earlier, this implied difficulties to explain certain phenomena and I started looking for alternative theoretical models and approaches. This resulted in my participation in the doctoral course on the Industrial Network Approach at Uppsala University. This showed to be the beginning of a very important "extension" of my research context that has had a great influence on my research. My interest in the Industrial Network Approach led to contacts with several different researchers within the IMP Group (see e.g. Gadde & Håkansson, 2001), among them colleagues at the department for Industrial Marketing, the neighboring department at Chalmers. I also participated in different seminars and conferences, which helped to develop my own understanding for this line of theory. In this respect the academic dimension of my research context reaches far beyond my "home" department and Chalmers.

My relation to industry is also an important part of my research context. The close relations with many of the studied firms have provided an insight into the empirical world that would otherwise not have been achieved. Being on site, participating in meetings and discussions, has in many cases given me more than interviews could provide per se. For instance, at Volvo I received my own access card that gave me possibilities to be working in their environment and to talk with many different people that I otherwise would not have got in touch with. This, of course, helped to develop my view of the empirical context, as well as influenced the formulation of research questions and so forth. At the same time, however, it is important to consider that this closeness to certain parts of the empirical world may have influenced my collection of empirical data. There is a risk that some data has been "favored" because it is more easy to access, or relations with certain people may have influenced how I have chosen to interpret data. In addition, the closeness may imply that respondents and other people in the studied firms change their views of me as a researcher, which may influence what information they contribute with. I tried to deal with these issues already when collecting the data by, for instance, relying on various different sources of information and checking data with respondents (these issues are discussed in more detail in Section 3.4). Hence, the closeness to the empirical world has been a fruitful source of information for me and, at the same time, I have tried to deal with the potential influence of the research context on my empirical data.

3.3. The Use of Case Studies

For both the Volvo study and the DFC Tech study I needed a research method that could be used for describing and analyzing complex settings with multiple and interrelated variables. The product being developed had to be related to other products, but also to other types of resources such as production equipment. Further, several different firms were involved which, in turn, had connections to other firms. Taken together, there were a number of dependencies between the studied phenomenon and its context.

Therefore, to create an understanding for how products are developed, it is necessary to also include parts of the context (Leonard-Barton, 1990). As argued by Halinen and Törnroos (1998), ". . . the key to simple and powerful models lies in an awareness of the broader and more complex reality from which the models are drawn." Pettigrew (1990) emphasizes the importance of "contextualism," implying that the analysis should draw on phenomena at both vertical and horizontal levels of analysis, and the interconnections between those levels through time. In other words, this implies that higher and lower levels of analysis as well as sequential interconnectedness among phenomena in historical, present and future time need to be considered. According to Yin (1994), *case studies* are suitable for studying a phenomenon in its real-life context, especially when the boundaries between phenomenon and context are not evident.

Case studies are typically focused on *how* and *why* questions (Meredith, 1998; Voss et al., 2002; Yin, 1994) and the evidence may be qualitative, quantitative or both (Eisenhardt, 1989). According to Eisenhardt, the case study approach is especially appropriate in new topic areas. In traditional positivistic research, the case study has often been regarded as a preliminary stage to the "real" study, e.g. to explore relevant variables that can be tested by quantitative methods. However, as argued by Yin (1994), case studies are far from exploratory only – case studies may also be descriptive or explanatory.

For both the Volvo study and the DFC Tech study, the use of a case study approach can be traced back to the type of research question behind these studies.

In essence, I wanted to investigate *how* interactive product development works in order to understand *how* it is organized. Interactive product development involves, by definition, several different actors. In addition, as described above, different forms of dependencies are created, between actors as well as between resources and activities that need to be considered. This implied, as argued above, a need for a research approach that could handle a complex setting with many different variables, including the interconnections between the studied phenomenon and its context. Therefore, a case study was considered an appropriate approach for the problem at hand. In fact, there are few alternatives to case studies when in-depth empirical data that is related to its real-life context is needed.

The possibility to test and, in particular, create new theory from case studies is frequently emphasized (e.g. Dubois & Gadde, 2002; Eisenhardt, 1989; McCutcheon & Meredith, 1993; Meredith, 1998; Voss et al., 2002). According to Ragin (1992, p. 225), a case is most often "... an intermediate product in the effort to link ideas and evidence. A case is not inherently one thing or another, but a way station in the process of producing empirical social science." However, perspectives on how theory is created from empirical data differ. With inspiration from Glaser and Strauss (1967), Eisenhardt (1989) proposes an inductive approach, arguing that ideally case research should begin with no theory under consideration and no hypotheses to test. For instance, thinking about specific relationships between variables should be avoided. The building of theory can start only after at least some initial empirical input. This is considered important since otherwise the findings may be biased and limited by preordinated theoretical perspectives or propositions. However, Eisenhardt admits that it is *"impossible to achieve this ideal of a clean theoretical slate."*

Contrary to this, Melnyk and Handfield (1998) propose a deductive approach labeled "theory driven empirical research." The authors emphasize that the researcher should start with a theory before the collection of empirical data begins. The theory will provide a structure for the collected data, which also makes it possible to interpret data and convert it into "information." Further, it is argued that the theory helps to direct research by identifying unclear, incomplete or paradoxical areas within current theories. However, the theory is not static. Rather, it is viewed essentially as "work-in-progress," being developed as the researcher interacts with the empirical data. According to Yin (1994, p. 27), theory development is an essential part of the design phase for case studies: "the relevant field contacts depend upon an understanding – or theory – of what is being studied."

When looking back at my own research process, it is difficult to say that I have followed either a deductive or an inductive research strategy when using case studies for collecting empirical data and developing theory. For instance, the Volvo study began with a survey of existing research and, in that sense, it may be regarded as deductive. However, as described earlier, the empirical experiences from the Autoliv study had much influence on how the Volvo study was designed and conducted. Thereby, there was also a strong inductive influence. Further, although I had roughly defined a focus of the paper at an early stage of the research process, the formulation of the research problems as well as the use of theory were influenced by my experiences from the empirical world. Hence, the empirical data has been shaped by research problems and theory and vice versa. Therefore, as argued above, although the paper may seem to be deductive in character, there has been much inductive influence. It is therefore difficult to say if I have pursued an inductive or a deductive research strategy.

Systematic combining (see Dubois & Gadde, 2002) is an abductive approach where the theoretical framework, the empirical fieldwork and the case analysis evolve simultaneously. The theoretical framework plays an important role, though, it is neither tight and pre-structured nor loose and emergent as in the deductive and inductive approaches respectively. Instead, the authors suggest a tight and evolving theoretical framework that shapes the researcher's view of the empirical world, at the same time as the framework is continuously being shaped by empirical observations. This process bears resemblance with what Ragin (1992, p. 218) refers to as "casing": ". . . ideas and evidence are mutually dependent; we transform evidence into results with the aid of ideas, and we make sense of theoretical ideas and elaborate them by linking them to empirical evidence." For instance, the framework, initially developed for the Volvo study influenced how I interpreted my empirical observations. However, as the dyadic perspective on relationships did not help to explain the complexity identified in the empirical material, a development of the theoretical framework was needed. This, in turn, led to new perspectives on my empirical data. In a similar way, I searched for empirical evidence in the PICS study regarding the supply chain, and I discovered things that contributed to a generation of new questions. This, in turn, led to a developed search for new empirical material in the other studies. Hence, my cases have evolved by alternately developing and combining theory and empirical data. However, the process has not been systematic in the sense that it was planned from the beginning. I have at several times followed various "side-tracks" that have later been abandoned, though, also these "side-tracks" have been valuable for the collection of empirical data as well as the development of my theoretical framework.

3.4. Sources of Data and Credibility of the Study

Several different sources may be used for data collection. According to Leonard-Barton (1990) a case study can be seen as the "history of a past or current phenomenon, drawn from multiple sources of evidence. It can include data from direct observation and systematic interviewing as well as from public and private archives. In fact, any fact relevant to the stream of events describing the phenomenon is a potential datum in a case study, since context is important." Yin (1994) refers to documents, artifacts, interviews, direct observations, and participant-observations as important sources of information and he emphasizes that this ability to deal with a variety of different data sources is a unique strength for case studies.

Interviews have been an important source of empirical data for my own research. To some extent, it was possible to plan in advance who to interview. By using, for example, organization charts potential interviewees could be identified. However, the process of systematic combining described above contributed to the generation of new questions, which made it impossible to identify all interviewees from start. Instead, as the theoretical framework and empirical analyses developed, additional interviewees were identified that might add valuable information.

In addition to interviews, the other sources mentioned above (i.e. documents, artifacts and observation) have been used to different extents. For instance, documents describing development processes and product strategies as well as minutes from meetings provided valuable information that in many respects complemented, and provided a basis for, the interviews. Further, the importance of observation should not be under-estimated. "Being there" implied that I got many impressions that complemented what I had learned from interviews and documents. For instance, I was offered a desk at Volvo's product development department, which enabled me to sit there (and not only at my office at the university) and work with my research. During my research, I have also visited a number of different car and truck assembly plants as well as various suppliers' plants for production of components. By observing how production equipment is used, what plant layout is applied and how products are assembled, I learned much that can be related to product development. To this, I also want to add that discussions with colleagues that conducted research on similar issues or in the same industries provided important insight that complemented the direct collection of empirical data. As mentioned earlier, my colleague Peter Fredriksson studied Volvo's production system and our discussions have been valuable for my understanding of, for instance, the link between product development and production. Hence, different sources of data have been important in different ways. In particular, the *combined* use of different sources has been valuable, especially for investigating abstract and complex issues such as dependencies.

Then, how can the credibility of data be evaluated? The systematic combining of empirical data and theory makes these "heterogeneous resources" inseparable (Dubois & Gadde, 2002). Therefore, credibility of data has to be ensured throughout the "casing" process. Lincoln and Guba (1985) suggest a concept referred to as "trustworthiness," focusing on how a researcher can "persuade his or her audiences (including self) that the findings of an inquiry are worth paying attention to, worth taking account of" (ibid., p. 290). To establish the credibility of research the following activities are emphasized.

Prolonged engagement and persistent observation emphasize the importance of spending an adequate amount of time in the empirical field to build trust, gain a sufficient understanding of the "culture" and identify the most relevant aspects of the studied phenomenon. When conducting my different studies I have spent a lot of time at various firms conducting interviews and collecting information, but also participating in meetings and discussions and studying various production plants.

Triangulation techniques imply crosschecking of data using different sources of information. As described earlier, several different data sources, including interviews, company records, CAD-models, artifacts and minutes have been used throughout the research process. Triangulation is further elaborated below.

Peer debriefing implies that the research is exposed to a "devil's advocate" with the purpose of "exploring aspects of the inquiry that might otherwise remain only implicit within the inquirer's mind" (ibid., p. 308). At several different occasions such as workshops, seminars and conferences, my research has been exposed to different people who have provided feedback and questioned my thoughts and ideas. In addition, the present paper has been "debriefed" by an appointed peer.

Negative case analysis can be regarded as a "process of revising hypotheses in hindsight" (ibid., p. 309). This is done until the hypothesis "accounts for all known cases without exception" (ibid., p. 309). I have not developed and tested any hypotheses in this paper, though, my research questions have continuously been "revised in hindsight" in interplay with my findings from the different cases.

Referential adequacy implies that part of the empirical data is archived for the purpose of later recall and analysis. Each of the four studies has been conducted over a fairly long period of time, often in parallel with other studies. Therefore, even if I had no clear "strategy" for this, data collected in one study has been left "untouched" for some time while working with another study. Then, the data has been recalled and analyzed over again.

Member checks involve asking members of the empirical setting to check data and provide feedback regarding case descriptions, interpretations and conclusions. This has been done continuously throughout the research process. By asking individual informants to read case descriptions as well as arranging various seminars and workshops, I have at several occasions received feedback regarding the empirical data and my interpretations of it. For instance, I held a seminar at Volvo where respondents and other people were invited. This type of data verification has also been important as it often contributed to the creation of new questions.

Hence, various activities have been undertaken to ensure and improve the credibility of the empirical data. Among the activities that have been described and commented above, only negative case analysis was "left out" since the purpose of this paper is not to test and verify hypotheses. Further, it is relevant to elaborate upon the use of triangulation.

As argued above, the use of several different sources of data (triangulation) provided possibilities for checking the collected data. However, it is not only relevant to ask how data was checked, but also what can be achieved by checking the data. As noted by Tashakkori and Teddlie (1998), triangulation presumes that there is a single reality that can be triangulated. Following the reasoning above regarding influences of my own perspectives on research, it can also be assumed that different interviewees have different perspectives on a particular issue (e.g. Eisenhardt, 1989). As argued by Silverman (2001) one should avoid treating a single actor's point of view as an explanation. Denzin and Lincoln (1994, in Tashakkori & Teddlie, 1998, p. 91) refer to a crystal as an illustration of different perspectives: "Crystals are prisms that reflect and refract, creating ever-changing images and pictures of reality. Crystallization deconstructs the traditional idea of validity, for now there can be no single, or triangulated, truth." Hence, "checking" data cannot be done to find "the truth," but it may be a way to contrast and compare different perspectives on a particular issue or phenomenon. According to Dubois and Gadde (2002), this can be used for discovery rather than verification: ". . . in systematic combining the emphasis on verification, i.e. checking the accuracy of data, is not the main issue. Rather, multiple sources may contribute to revealing aspects unknown to the researcher, i.e. to discover new dimensions of the research problem."

3.5. Analytical Generalization

This paper presents three different cases. A relevant question is how the results from the analysis of these cases can be generalized. The case study results are applicable also to other firms within the automotive industry, that have established similar inter-firm relationships, that use similar technologies, and that produce more or less the same products with similar production equipment. Thus, the cases, the findings, and the conclusions can be interesting per se, though, according to Dubois and Gadde (2002), case studies have to rely on analytical inference. By developing theory from a case study, the findings can be extended to other settings where the conditions appear to be similar in critical respects (McCutcheon & Meredith, 1993). As expressed by Eisenhardt (1989, p. 547) "the specifics of data produce the generalizations of theory." Therefore, the goal for this study should be to develop theory in order to enable generalization. This is what Yin (1994) refers to as "analytical generalization."

As described above, theories and empirical data have been combined in a continuous process. In this way, my view of the empirical world and my interpretation of data have been influenced by my theoretical framework. At the same time, this interactive process has implied that the framework has been influenced by the empirical findings. The theoretical framework has continuously been developed by adding and subtracting various theories. Moreover, and this is important for the analytical generalization, the empirical findings have influenced the theoretical framework in the sense that I have been able to develop these theories. Hence, the results can be generalized in terms of "theoretical imprints" rather than transferring of the empirical findings per se to other settings.

> Though this be madness, yet there is method in it.
>
> William Shakespeare

4. EMPIRICAL RESULTS

The empirical results originate from three longitudinal in-depth case studies. The first two cases relate to the development of the new P2 platform at the car manufacturer Volvo (developed prior to Ford's acquisition of Volvo). These two cases describe Volvo's product development collaboration with Delphi and Lear respectively. Delphi and Lear are both large system suppliers to the automotive industry. The case describing the relationship with Delphi is focused on the development of various components for the electrical system. The case describing Volvo's relationship with Lear is focused on the development of seats. Before the cases are described, a background to the development of the new platform, Volvo's supplier relationships, the product structure, and the organization for product development collaboration is provided. Then, the cases are described in a way that captures both technical and organizational issues related to the collaboration between the respective firms.

The third case focuses on the product development collaboration between the supplier DFC Tech and the truck manufacturer Scania. DFC Tech mainly develops pipes and hoses for engine compartment installations and the case focuses on the development of various components for a new truck model. In the first part of the case a background to DFC Tech is provided. Then, similar to the two first cases, the collaboration between DFC Tech and Scania is described considering both technical and organizational issues. This third case is, however, somewhat different from the first two cases. Apart from the first two cases, the product development collaboration is mainly described from a supplier's perspective. Furthermore, the products studied in this third case have a much lower degree of complexity (in terms of number of interdependent components; cf. Simon, 1962) compared to the products developed for Volvo.

In all three cases, the developed products play a central role and, by using numerous examples, different aspects of organizing are related to technical issues concerning the development of the products. The empirical data for all three cases mainly originates from interviews with people involved in the studied relationships, but also from company records, documents etc (for more details, see Section 3).

4.1. The Development of Volvo's New P2 Platform

In the summer 1998, Volvo introduced the S80 as the first car model based on the new P2 platform. Later the V70, the S60 and the XC90 followed (see Fig. 16). When this study was performed, however, the development of the XC90 had not started and is therefore not considered here.

It was necessary for Volvo to replace the Volvo P80 (i.e. the 850 model) that had been introduced in 1991 (with a "face-lift" in 1996). Therefore, the new platform was of utmost importance for Volvo's future. Only four years earlier, in December 1993, the cooperation between Volvo and Renault had been terminated. Volvo and Renault had been working on a common platform and Volvo had invested a considerable amount of development resources into that project. However, when it was decided that the two should no longer continue the cooperation, Volvo was facing a tough situation. Volvo was forced to develop a new platform in short time,

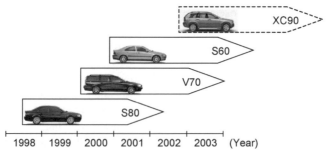

Fig. 16. The Different Models Based on the P2 Platform. Start of Arrows Indicates Time for Market Introduction.

but only fractions of the development performed together with Renault could be re-used. Therefore, it was necessary to invest large amounts of money in new technology development, though, resources were scarce. At that time, Volvo was the smallest freestanding car manufacturer in the world. Therefore, Volvo needed to find new ways of organizing the development and production of cars.

With inspiration from other car manufacturers, such as Chrysler that had recently made a turnaround, Volvo decided to develop a new way of working regarding product and process development, which also had implications for their relations with suppliers. Increased cooperation with suppliers in production as well as product development made it possible to develop and produce new car models in shorter time and at a lower cost than before.

4.1.1. Volvo's Supplier Relations – A Historical Perspective
The first car with the Volvo brand was manufactured in 1927 and ever since then Volvo has, to varying extents, cooperated with suppliers in different settings. Just like most other car manufacturers, Volvo had during the 1970s and 1980s a large number of suppliers that mainly delivered various components that were being assembled in Volvo's assembly plant. Sub-assemblies, such as rear axles, engines and seats, were mainly produced in plants owned by Volvo, based on fairly "simple" components manufactured by different suppliers. In the beginning of the 1980s, about 65% of the unit cost of a new car was purchased from suppliers.

At that time, a large share of the product development was performed internally at Volvo. Then, based on detailed drawings, suppliers were invited to participate in a tendering process. The suppliers were given the possibility to provide feedback that could help to improve produceability and thereby reduce production costs. The possibilities to change the product design at that stage were, however, limited. Therefore, most suppliers' contributions resulted in minor changes only.

Although a large share of the development of a new car model was performed internally at Volvo, there were also suppliers that developed their own products. For example, Volvo has for a long time had a relationship with Autoliv, a leading supplier of safety products for the automotive industry. This relationship has developed over long time with product development as an important driving force. Volvo's tough demands regarding safety have been important for Autoliv's focus on product development. In many cases, Volvo has also provided important financial support for the development of products that Autoliv has been able to sell also to other customers. At the same time, Autoliv's relationships with other auto manufacturers have been important for innovation, but also for reaching higher production volumes and thereby lower product prices. Autoliv has often developed new products in collaboration with Volvo who gets exclusive rights to use the product for a limited period of time, often one to two years. Then, after that period, Autoliv can sell the products also to other auto manufacturers, which means possibilities to benefit from scale economies and, hence, lower product prices.

Hence, for many decades, Volvo has performed a major part of the product development internally, but it should be remembered that relationships with certain suppliers have also played an important role for product development (see e.g. Axelsson, 1987). Respondents at Volvo also emphasized that this tradition of collaboration with suppliers has facilitated a change towards closer and more formal collaboration with suppliers in product development.

4.1.2. Changed Supplier Relationships

When the cooperation with Renault was terminated, Volvo was forced to develop and produce car models of their own. Increasing customer demands, new legislation and rapid technology development made it difficult for Volvo to keep on performing a major part of the product development internally. In addition, it was necessary to radically reduce development time for new car models, especially since about two years of development time had already been lost because of the termination of the cooperation with Renault. Volvo was facing a situation where more development resources were needed. At the same time, in order to shorten lead-times, more development activities needed to be performed in parallel.

At this time, many firms had chosen to outsource production activities, but also product development, to an increasing extent. Further, the American auto manufacturer Chrysler had made a successful turnaround that was attributed to a different way of working in product development, including cross-functional teams and a long-term orientation of close collaboration with suppliers (for more details, see e.g. Dyer, 1996). In addition, different studies of Japanese auto manufacturers had shown potential benefits with more supplier involvement in product development (see Section 1.2). After having performed a pre-study, including a study of Chrysler's product development organization, Volvo decided to change their organization by establishing cross-functional teams, where also suppliers were represented.

This new situation led to questions regarding, for example, how to develop an organization based on cross-functional teams, within what development areas it was feasible to collaborate with suppliers, with which suppliers, and so on. Based on the experiences from Chrysler, it seemed that the division of development work between different development teams, but also between Volvo and different suppliers, would be facilitated by dividing the car into a number of smaller building blocks, i.e. some form of modularization.

4.1.3. Dividing the Car into Modules

How to divide the car into different modules could, however, not be decided solely from a development perspective because the module design would also influence other functional areas such as production. It was regarded as important to focus production-related issues, and Volvo therefore tried to adapt the products to the production process to a larger extent than before. Consequently, the definition of modules was strongly influenced by different issues related to production while, for example, issues related to product development and service had less influence.

Volvo aimed at creating module interfaces that would facilitate pre-assembly of modules in parallel with the assembly line, at the same time as these interfaces should facilitate the assembly of the complete modules on the assembly line. Pre-assembly was regarded important since it would enable assembly activities to be moved away from the main assembly line (for example to suppliers' plants). This, in turn, would free up floor space and enable a shorter assembly line (principally illustrated in Fig. 17). This was important to consider since Volvo intended to use their existing assembly plants (Torslanda in Sweden and Ghent in Belgium) where floor space was limited. In addition, pre-assembly gives possibilities to perform certain tests regarding functionality and quality before the module is assembled into the car. This would also contribute to faster production start-up, leading to reduced time to introduction of a new car model.

Furthermore, product customization implies that a large number of variants of each module must be handled in production. There are, for instance, about 1,200

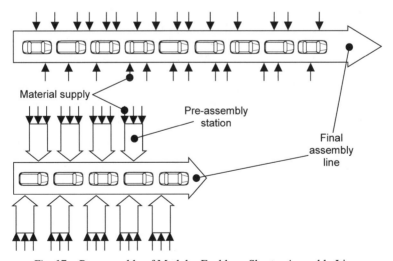

Fig. 17. Pre-assembly of Modules Enables a Shorter Assembly Line.

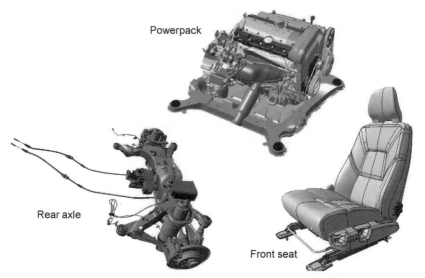

Fig. 18.   Examples of Different Modules. *Note:* Pictures used with permission from Volvo
Car Corporation.

different variants of front seats. To buffer different module variants along the
assembly line would, however, demand too much floor space and be too costly.
Therefore, the ability to pre-assemble customer-specific modules in parallel with
the main assembly line was important to consider, when dividing the car into
modules. Further, the conditions for pre-assembly of modules had consequences
for the module suppliers. Due to the large number of variants, module suppliers
must assemble modules based on customer orders. These modules are then
delivered to Volvo in sequence, i.e. the same sequence that individual cars appear
on the assembly line. Due to the short time window between order and delivery
this, in turn, made it necessary for the module suppliers to establish local Module
Assembly Units (MAU:s) close to Volvo's assembly plant (for more details, see
Fredriksson, 2002; von Corswant et al., 2001).

In total, the car was divided into about 20 different modules (see Fig. 18),
for instance seats, cockpit (instrument panel with instruments, audio equipment,
climate control etc), power pack (mainly engine, gearbox and subframe) and "soft
nose" (front bumper with grille and fog lights).

4.1.4. The Selection of Suppliers for Collaboration
Then, which suppliers should be selected as module suppliers for the new platform?
Some of the suppliers that Volvo already had an established relationship with

were considered. It was, however, clear that also some new supplier relationships would be needed since most of Volvo's existing suppliers lacked the capacity to both develop and produce the more complex modules that were now considered. However, the restructuring of the automotive industry had resulted in the emergence of a few "new" global actors such as Lear, Visteon and Delphi that could be potential suppliers to Volvo.

The selection of module suppliers was largely based on experiences from former collaboration with suppliers in different forms, though, few suppliers had been involved to this extent in product development before. The experiences that Volvo had concerning supplier evaluation mainly concerned production issues. However, in this situation, the suppliers' abilities to participate in and actively run product development projects were also important criteria. To enable some kind of comparison between suppliers, Volvo tried in different ways to structure information regarding the different suppliers and grade them according to certain criteria. For example, issues such as company profile (e.g. ownership structure and line of business), management (e.g. strategies and management support systems), quality, environmental issues, aftermarket, logistics, purchasing were evaluated. In addition, an evaluation was made concerning the different suppliers' abilities to run development projects, to develop new technologies and if they had the required capacity in terms of personnel and equipment (e.g. CAD and equipment for prototyping and testing).

Another issue that was regarded important was the suppliers' relationships with other auto manufacturers. Volvo aimed at establishing relationships with suppliers that already had been involved in product development projects with other auto manufacturers. Preferably, it should be auto manufacturers within the "premium" segment, for example Mercedes or BMW that face similar customer requirements etc as Volvo does. Volvo saw possibilities to learn from these suppliers' experiences, which could help to avoid repeating other auto manufacturers' mistakes. The risk for information "leakages" from Volvo to other auto manufacturers via the suppliers was regarded to be insignificant. On the contrary, Volvo was prepared to share their experiences with other auto manufacturers in exchange for the learning opportunities that Volvo could benefit from through the supplier relationships.

In reality, there were often only a few alternative suppliers to choose between. Even if there are a large number of suppliers within the automotive industry, only a few suppliers within each development area fulfilled Volvo's requirements, mainly regarding product development and production capabilities. In fact, the suppliers' ability to provide Volvo with new technology and low product cost outweighed many other requirements.

The evaluation process finally resulted in the selection of 13 module suppliers that would take an extensive responsibility for the development and production of modules for the P2 platform. In addition to these 13 "external" suppliers there were also a few module "suppliers" owned by Volvo. Furthermore, a number of other suppliers were also involved in the development of various systems and components.

4.1.5. The Organizing of Product Development in Module Teams

An important aim with the new platform was to enable the use of the same technologies and product designs for several car models. One respondent expressed this as "an important issue was to work on more common and parallel product development – to think about the third product while we were developing the first one." At the same time, each car model should be unique in certain dimensions (e.g. regarding size and available features). This focus on a common platform implied a strong need for coordination between different car projects. Even if the different models should be unique in some respects, there was a focus on a high degree of common components to achieve scale economies. Further, different models would be assembled on the same assembly line, implying tough demands on coordination of production processes. Currently, the plant in Torslanda (Sweden) assembles the S80 and the V70 (and the XC90) and the plant in Ghent (Belgium) assembles the S60 and the V70. Therefore, the focus on "process-driven product development" described above was important.

Even if much was common for the different car models, it was necessary to divide such a big development project into several smaller projects. Therefore, the development of each car model (the S80, the V70, the S60 and later the XC90) was treated as an individual project. This was also necessary since not all models were developed simultaneously. By shifting the development projects in time (with some overlap), the use of development resources could be "smoothened."

However, from earlier experiences of dividing development work into different projects in this way Volvo had learned that it might be difficult to achieve the desired commonality. There was the risk of the different projects diverging, leading to insufficient communication and coordination between the projects. Therefore, an organization was needed where all car projects could be held together at the same time as each model was being developed in an individual project. To handle this situation, cross-functional teams were created.

These cross-functional teams, referred to as module teams, became a cornerstone in Volvo's product development organization. In total, there were thirteen (later merged to 12) different module teams. The smallest module team had about 50 members, while the largest had about 250. This includes about 80 persons representing about 35 different suppliers at Volvo's site. Mainly based on how the modules had been defined, teams were created which were responsible for the development of the respective modules. Some details that were difficult to attribute

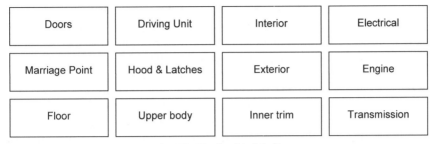

Doors	Driving Unit	Interior	Electrical
Marriage Point	Hood & Latches	Exterior	Engine
Floor	Upper body	Inner trim	Transmission

Fig. 19. The Twelve Module Teams.

to a particular module were gathered in a separate module team ("inner trim"). The different module teams are illustrated in Fig. 19.

Each module team had representatives from different functional areas such as product development, pre-production, production, aftermarket, purchasing and design. Depending on what specific competencies that were needed at different times, the composition of the team varied over time. In order to improve the communication between team members, they were co-located in Volvo's development department in office landscapes. As mentioned earlier, the module teams also had supplier representatives from different functional areas. In this way, the suppliers could take an active role in the development activities and thereby influence the design of the products that they would later produce.

Since each module team was responsible for a specific development area, i.e. a module, that in turn had connections (e.g. physical and/or functional interfaces) to other development areas, there was also a need for coordination *between* different module teams. Such issues were often solved through direct communication between members of affected teams. In addition, different forms of formal meetings were held, often on a weekly basis, where issues concerning several different teams could be discussed.

4.2. The Relationship Between Volvo and Delphi

For the development of the electrical system, and different related applications, relationships were established between Volvo and a number of different suppliers. Among them was Delphi, a large global supplier within the automotive industry. Delphi was the supplier that had the most extensive collaboration with Volvo regarding development of components for the electrical system and it is the relationship between Volvo and Delphi that is in focus in this case.

Then, what made Delphi interested in collaboration with such a small "niche" manufacturer as Volvo? As mentioned above, Volvo was known for the development of new technology. In addition, Volvo had a good reputation regarding relationships with suppliers. Delphi regarded it as positive to collaborate with a smaller auto manufacturer, since this would not make Delphi just one of many suppliers. Further, Delphi regarded Volvo's "new" way of organizing the development work in module teams as interesting. In particular, Delphi regarded the fact that Volvo largely aimed at running the development projects and solve problems *together* with the suppliers as interesting. Moreover, the electrical system required development of new advanced technology and, therefore, the collaboration with Volvo was regarded as a prestigious project for the recently "spun off" Delphi.

Delphi became involved already during the pre-study phase, which was relatively early compared to when Volvo involved other suppliers. Even if there had been a dialogue with potential suppliers long before the pre-study, Delphi was among the first suppliers to start the development work for the new platform. Both Delphi and Volvo saw this as an advantage since it would give Delphi more time for development. In addition, Delphi was given better possibilities to influence the product design since fewer design parameters had been frozen that early.

4.2.1. Multiplex – The New Technology for the Electrical System

Volvo had decided to develop an electrical system for the new platform based on so called "multiplex technology." This technology enabled, among other things, more advanced functions, but it also had consequences for how the collaboration with suppliers in product development was organized.

Multiplex is a common expression for serial exchange of information between different electronic units and systems. Hence, the multiplex system can be regarded as an electronic network that links different applications (such as climate control or mobile phone). In their new multiplex system, Volvo intended to incorporate nearly all functionality that could be related to the electrical system.

Contrary to traditional electrical systems, the multiplex technology enabled integration of several functions in the same control unit. It also made it possible to gather the information flow, which had earlier demanded several different cables, into one (twisted pair) cable – a data bus. For example, this enables the same speed signal to be used as input for a number of different applications, such as the engine management system, the ABS system, the audio system, the windscreen wipers, the gearbox, the instrument and the navigation system. Thereby, the multiplex technology enables an increased functionality without the need to increase the number of cables. The amount of cables in the P2-models is about the same as in the predecessor (1300 meters), but the number of functions has been increased by about 30%.

On an overarching level, the electrical system can be divided into two main parts; a distribution system and a signal system. The distribution has many system similarities with a traditional electrical system and its main task is to *distribute* electricity to different electrical applications in the car. Hence, the distribution system includes, for example, cable harnesses, connectors, relays, fuses and various boxes for electronic components. Also the physical cables used for signals can be seen as part of the distribution system since they are assembled in the same cable harnesses.

The signal system is based on the multiplex technology and it handles the *communication* between different applications. The signal system can be divided into a physical and a logical structure (Andersson et al., 1995). All hardware and software constitute the physical structure, while functions and sub-functions constitute the functional structure. A function can be used by the car user, for example ABS brakes or climate control. Sub-functions are necessary to realize functions. For example, the sub-function calculating the speed is necessary to realize the ABS function. The physical structure can be regarded as a "mirror" of the logical structure. The physical structure is built up as a network mainly consisting of nodes and gateways that are connected with a bus (see Fig. 20).

Each application that uses the electrical system is represented by a node. The different nodes in a Volvo S80 are illustrated in Fig. 21 (e.g. SAS = Steering Angle Sensor; DDM = Driver Door Module). However, not all applications in the car need to exchange information. Further, some applications exchange more information than others do. Therefore, the network is divided into network segments that are connected with gateways. Further, by separating certain applications through creating sub-networks, the need for information exchange is reduced and the performance of the system as a whole can be improved. Audio equipment and mobile phone are examples of applications that may be realized in sub-networks.

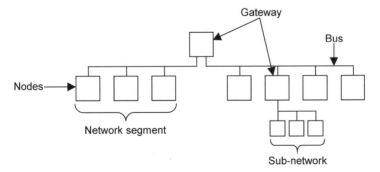

Fig. 20. The Physical Structure of a Multiplex System.

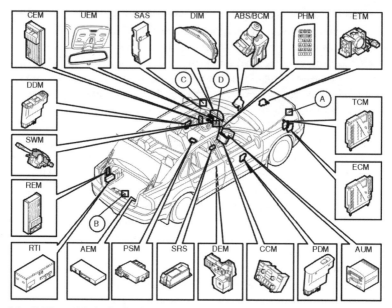

Fig. 21. Different Nodes in the CAN-System. Nodes A-D are Slave Nodes. *Note:* Picture
used with permission from Volvo Car Corporation.

In each node there is a CPU (Central Processing Unit) that registers values from
different sensors (e.g. temperature or speed) and compares these values with a
local register. This is to judge whether a message should be sent on the bus or not.
Each message that will be sent on the bus is assigned an identifier. Each identifier is
unique and contains information regarding the content and priority of the message.
For example, messages concerning the brake system must have priority over the
windscreen wipers.

To make the electrical system work, there is also a need for different types
of software. While the applications are controlled by certain software, the
communication between applications is based on two different protocols. A low-
level protocol (CAN) controls how data is sent on the bus and a high-level protocol
(Volcano) links CAN with the application software (i.e. a form of "driver"). This
configuration implies that a standardized interface is created to the suppliers that
develop different applications. Further, the high-level protocol (Volcano) enables
functionality of one application to be transferred to another application. Hence, the
communication between different applications is mainly dependent on software
and not on hardware, which facilitates system updates and the addition of new

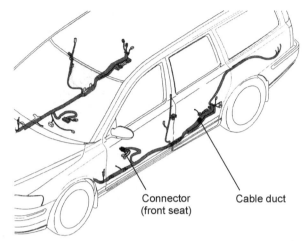

Connector
(front seat)

Cable duct

Fig. 22. Two Cable Harnesses in the V70 Driving Compartment. *Note:* Picture used with permission from Volvo Car Corporation.

nodes. Information from a specific node can be accessed in all other nodes, which creates possibilities to add functionality without adding physical components.

Thus, the development of the new electrical system implied a new way of designing and linking different applications. However, even though an existing CAN protocol was used as a basis, this standard was modified in various ways. Therefore, much development work was required regarding both hardware and software to get a functioning system.

4.2.2. Delphi's Role in the Development of the Electrical System

Delphi received an extensive responsibility for the development of the distribution system, but also for important parts of the signal system. Delphi's development responsibility for the distribution system included several different cable harnesses and related details such as cable ducts (see example in Fig. 22), boxes for electronics, connectors, fuses and relays.

Further, Delphi was assigned the development of two central parts of the signal system; the CEM (Central Electronic Module) and the REM (Rear Electronic Module; see Fig. 23). The CEM is a gateway between the engine compartment and the rest of the car where certain key functions such as electronic immobilizer, central locking system, alarm and light controls have been gathered. Further, all diagnostics data is gathered in the CEM. The REM is a node that, among other things, takes care of the rear lights and controls the inclination sensor (for the alarm). For Delphi, this implied development of hardware (e.g. circuit boards,

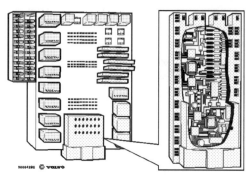

Fig. 23. The Rear Electronic Module (REM). *Note:* Picture used with permission from
Volvo Car Corporation.

integrated circuits, plastic boxes and connectors) as well as certain software
development.

4.2.3. Delphi's Product Development Organization

Delphi, that is an American corporation, has development and production in
several different places, including Europe. Those of Delphi's product development
units that were primarily involved in the collaboration with Volvo are located
in Germany and Spain. In Germany, Delphi has two different units with both
product development and production that were involved in the development of
components for Volvo. One of them (here referred to as Delphi Germany) was
responsible for development and production of parts to the distribution system, for
example cable ducts, connectors and electronics boxes. Hence, their development
was focused on mechanical design, mainly incorporating plastic details. The other
unit is Megamos, a subsidiary of Delphi with about 200 employees. Megamos
developed both electronic hardware and software, mainly for the CEM and the
REM. They were also assigned the production of these parts. Even if Megamos
had a direct relationship with Volvo, with their own representatives in the module
team, the "commercial" part of the relationship was handled by Delphi Germany.
The production of cable harnesses was located to Delphi's unit in Spain. Since
the production of cable harnesses is difficult to automate, and therefore demands
a high proportion of manual work, the production was located to Spain, where
wages are lower than in the northern parts of Europe. In Spain, Delphi had some
resources for developing cable harnesses, including development of prototypes
and specific production equipment.

Delphi's "mother" organization is located in the U.S. where Delphi has located
some advanced engineering to support different units within Delphi. While the

contacts between Delphi's organization in the U.S. and Volvo were limited, Volvo appreciated this large organization "standing behind" those of Delphi's units that Volvo collaborated with. In some cases, Delphi Germany received engineering support from the U.S. that helped them solve certain problems. In a similar way, Megamos sometimes received support from other units within Delphi and so on.

To make the collaboration with Volvo work, it was necessary for representatives from Delphi to be present in Volvo's module team. Therefore, Delphi needed to establish some form of local office close to Volvo. At that time, Delphi had no business unit in Sweden, though, Delphi Germany had for many years had ESMA as a representative. ESMA is a Swedish firm acting as an intermediary between suppliers and customers in the manufacturing industry. This relationship resulted in Delphi assigning ESMA the task to establish and organize a local office for product development support close to Volvo. The office was staffed with people from ESMA as well as with engineers from Delphi's different European units. Delphi regarded it to be important that knowledge was built up over time within this organization and, therefore, few consultants were involved. Both Delphi and Volvo regarded it to be important that issues related to production were considered already in the early phases of product development. Therefore, also representatives from Delphi's different production units were present. In total, about 30 persons worked at the local office.

In parallel with the development of the parts to the electrical system, Delphi was building a new module assembly unit (MAU) for cable harnesses (mainly for creating customer specific variants and sequencing material) close to Volvo's Torslanda plant in Gothenburg, Sweden (a similar MAU was built close to Volvo's plant in Ghent, Belgium). Later, with the production start at hand, Delphi took over the local Gothenburg office and it was co-located with the MAU.

The business units that were the main actors with direct connections to the relationship between Volvo and Delphi are illustrated in Fig. 24. Even if Volvo generally takes specific costs (e.g. for specific production tools), Delphi's role in product development and later in production implied comprehensive investments in the relationship with Volvo. For example, the relationship implied specific investments such as the local development office, the module assembly units (in Gothenburg and Ghent), investments in the Spanish plant, and expansion of Megamos' production plant in Germany. In the following sections, the relationship between Volvo and Delphi is described in more detail. Further, the description includes how the relationship between Volvo and Delphi influenced, and was influenced by, relationships with other suppliers. This implies that more business units are added to this picture.

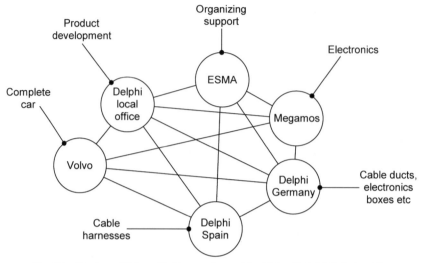

Fig. 24.   Business Units with Connections to the Volvo-Delphi Relationship.

4.2.4. *Organizing the Collaboration – The Module Team*

The establishment of the development office in Gothenburg gave the closeness to Volvo that was needed for Delphi to be able to actively participate in the module team. This team was one of the largest module teams. The number of members varied over time, but about 150 persons were involved when the different car projects were run in parallel. Out of these 150, about 20 were representatives from several different suppliers that had their own desk in Volvo's office landscape (engineers working at the suppliers' development departments or in their local offices close to Volvo have not been included in this figure). About one third of the members in the module team were consultants that were assigned either by Volvo or by the different suppliers. Most consultants were product design engineers, though, some of them were also assigned as leaders for different development projects.

Delphi, that was one of the suppliers that was most deeply involved in the development of the electrical system, had members in the module team on a daily basis. In total, Delphi had about 10 (sometimes up to 20) members in the module team. There were, for example, design engineers, project leaders, production engineers, pre-production engineers and quality engineers. However, the composition of representatives from Delphi varied over time according to what specific competencies were needed. Some of Delphi's representatives were working "full time" at Volvo, while others spent part time at the local office or in their respective home organizations. Volvo emphasized that Delphi's representatives were present in the team most of the time. However, both Volvo and Delphi also thought it was important that they did not spend all their time at Volvo. It was considered a risk that they would "lose contact" with their respective "home organizations," implying that it would be less meaningful having these representatives at Volvo.

Volvo had some previous experience from cross-functional work, but collaboration with suppliers in this form was rather new. In many cases, both Delphi and Volvo found it difficult to agree on how to divide development work between them. Certain things, that both of them thought the other would do, were not done at all. In other cases, coordination mistakes caused unnecessary double-work. As a result, the project lost pace. However, these problems mainly occurred initially. As both parties knew each other better, and as their communication behavior and working routines were adapted, these problems were overcome and the project gained pace. With reference to these coordination problems, respondents from both Volvo and Delphi emphasized the importance of careful documentation of communication and decisions. This was regarded particularly important since both Delphi and Volvo are large organizations with many people involved.

Other initial "struggle" in this relationship concerned the adaptation of Delphi's product development competences to Volvo's specific needs. The engineers that Delphi took from Germany and Spain contributed to increase the competence in the team regarding issues related to product technologies and production. At the same time, it was necessary for Delphi to quickly learn more about Volvo's way of working, including the development process (implications of different toll gates etc) and Volvo's different support systems (e.g. for handling drawings). Therefore, as a solution, Delphi recruited people from Volvo that already had this knowledge. Volvo was positive to this and regarded it to be a better solution than increasing the number of consultants. However, this also implied a risk that Delphi's competence regarding product technologies and production would be too similar to Volvo's own competence. Volvo had chosen to collaborate with Delphi not only to get access to more product development resources, but also to access specific competence that Volvo did not have in its own organization. For instance, one important issue was technical competence regarding Delphi's production system. Over time, though, Volvo perceived that Delphi managed to find a balance between knowledge that was specific for Delphi and knowledge that was needed to collaborate with Volvo.

Several respondents emphasized that even if a large share of the coordination between Volvo and Delphi could be performed within the module team, it was important that both parties had a clear picture of each other's respective line and project organizations. This would help to clarify how responsibilities and authorities were divided *within* but also *between* the respective organizations.

Therefore, knowledge about each other's organizations was regarded important since it could facilitate finding "communication partners" within the other party's organization. Hence, even if a large part of the development work could be coordinated within the module team, direct contacts between people in the respective organizations were in many cases necessary.

Already when the collaboration between Volvo and Delphi was initiated, it was clear that Delphi's development responsibility would reach further than just performing "black box" development. The multiplex technology was a new area for both parties and it was important, as far as possible, to make use of their respective development capabilities. Therefore, the aim was to also develop product specifications and project goals in collaboration between the two parties. This was done with reference to the specific properties (e.g. response time for a certain signal) that the electrical system must fulfill, i.e. on a rather high level. However, it turned out to be difficult to agree on at which level this specification should be decomposed. While Volvo often preferred to use the properties as specifications, Delphi often wanted information that was more detailed. There were different reasons for these different views. One explanation that was brought forward was that, in order to understand and make use of the properties as specifications, profound knowledge about different other parts of the car was necessary since the electrical system interacts with these parts in different ways. It was, however, more difficult for Delphi, being an external party, to achieve this comprehensive view that existed more "naturally" within Volvo.

Furthermore, the demands for certain properties and functions were changed as other parts of the car developed. This affected, for example, how Volvo prioritized between cost and performance of the electrical system. Hence, the conditions for the specifications changed over time and, consequently, it was difficult for Volvo to give a detailed picture during the early phases of what they wanted Delphi to develop. Taken together, this implied that it was necessary to let the specifications and job-split evolve over time. It was therefore emphasized that frequent meetings were important so that specifications could be "adjusted" according to how the project goals changed.

Issues regarding, for example, distribution of resources or time schedules that needed coordination between different module teams were often discussed at so-called Design Review Meetings (DRM). For these meetings people from different functional areas and supplier representatives participated. This also included people from other module teams. For example, the cable ducts developed by Delphi have physical interfaces with the car floor. Therefore, changes of the car body design sometimes also required changes of cable harnesses and cable ducts. This created a need for coordination across module teams, which was facilitated by Delphi's participation in the meeting.

4.2.5. The Development Work and Relationships with Other Business Units

Also some of Delphi's component suppliers participated in the development work, sometimes implying direct contacts with Volvo. Rieselmann, one of Delphi's German suppliers of plastic components, would manufacture cable ducts for Delphi. Although Delphi had the main responsibility for the development work, also Rieselmann sent engineers to Volvo to participate in the development work. Thereby, Rieselmann could influence and improve the design of the cable ducts, mainly from a production point of view. Hence, a direct contact was established between Delphi's component supplier Rieselmann and Volvo.

In other cases, Volvo had old relationships with certain component suppliers that Volvo wanted to keep. For example, Volvo had traditionally purchased certain connectors from the Japanese supplier Yasaki, one of Delphi's competitors. Volvo had good experiences from using these connectors and since they were already used in Volvo's current models, Volvo wanted to use them also for the new platform. This was important to Volvo, in particular in order to keep down the number of variants in the production system as well as on the aftermarket. Therefore, even though Delphi had their own connectors that they wanted to use, Volvo in several cases decided that Delphi should buy connectors from Yasaki.

Nolato is a Swedish supplier of, among other things, plastic components. Nolato had delivered plastic details for Volvo's previous models, implying that a relationship already existed between Nolato and Volvo. Then, when Volvo found that the development of production tools for an electronics box took too long time at Delphi Germany, Volvo decided that Nolato should take over the development of the tools since they were able to perform the work faster and at a lower cost. Thereby, a relationship was established between Nolato and Delphi (the local development office), since Delphi still had the responsibility for developing the electronics box. However, later Volvo decided to buy the electronics box directly from Nolato which, of course, created frustration at Delphi. In this case, Volvo bypassed Delphi and used their direct relationship with Nolato.

In addition to Delphi, also a number of other suppliers were involved in the development of parts related to the electrical system. As mentioned earlier, Maisa was assigned the development of the cable harness for the engine compartment (including some related components) and Motorola developed components for the node electronics. Further, Melco was assigned the development of nodes related to "infotainment," for example radio, loudspeakers, antennas and navigation systems. Alps is another important supplier that was assigned the development of, for instance, the climate control node, the door nodes, the headliner node and nodes related to the steering function. In addition to these, Volvo collaborated in product development with, for example, Yasaki (instrument cluster), Bosch (airbag sensors), Donelli (headliner electronics) and Autoliv (mobile phone and

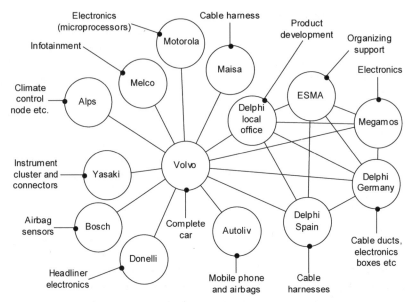

Fig. 25. Various Business Units Involved in the Development of the Electrical System.

airbags). Even if these suppliers respective roles in product development varied, they all had a direct relationship with Volvo. In addition, most of them also had representatives in the module team at Volvo. In Fig. 25, the network around the Volvo-Delphi relationship is illustrated, including the suppliers mentioned in this section.

The multiplex system implied fairly standardized interfaces between different applications. This enabled the development of different parts of a specific application to be divided between different suppliers. For example, Autoliv developed the mobile phone, while a unit within Volvo developed its software. The development of hardware and software for the climate control was divided between Alps and Volvo in a similar way. These possibilities to divide development between different suppliers was regarded an advantage since it might be difficult to find a single supplier that can develop both the physical parts and the software. For example, developing the mobile phone requires knowledge of plastic molding, styling, electronic components as well as advanced software. Hence, even if Delphi was involved in different ways for developing both hardware and software for the electrical system, relatively clear interfaces could be defined between the distribution system, the signal system and the software. This facilitated, or rather reduced, the need for coordination between suppliers.

This however, did not mean that the component solutions of the different suppliers were totally "decoupled." In some cases, problems occurred in one part of the system that then "spilled over" to other parts. This often had consequences for several different suppliers' design solutions. For example, such a problem was detected during the production start of the Volvo V70. At a late stage, EMC-related interference and noise had been detected in the radio system (see e.g. Bauer, 2000, pp. 890–896 for more details on EMC). Although Delphi had not been involved in the development of the radio system, these problems significantly influenced Delphi. The problem was that the radio antenna picked up high-frequency oscillations in the signal system. Even if interference had been suppressed in the CAN-bus, narrow-band spikes occurred in the CAN-system. In some nodes, there are microprocessors, working with high frequencies, which may generate high-frequency oscillations. Then, under certain circumstances, some cables may function as antennas that transfer the oscillation to the radio system. Since these problems were detected at a late stage, there was not enough time for changing the circuit board from where the problem emanated. Such a change would involve new design of the circuit board, in turn causing changes of production tools etc. Such a re-design would therefore take several months.

Instead, it was decided that the problem should be solved by adding suppression capacitors to the cable harness. This, of course, had consequences for Delphi. This change implied that more space was needed for the cable harness, which in turn required design changes of some cable ducts. Even if this only implied a smaller change of the geometry, changes of the production tools used for molding plastic components were required. Further, the assembly tables used in Delphi's plant in Spain, where the cable harnesses are produced, had to be changed and some testing equipment had to be complemented. As a result, this caused delays for the proofing of drawings and deliveries of cable harnesses. Hence, in this case, Delphi was affected by problems that originated in a part of the electrical system that they had not developed. To test these components beforehand to avoid these high-frequency oscillations would, however, have been difficult since this problem was caused by a complex interplay between different parts of the electrical system and its different applications.

4.3. The Relationship Between Volvo and Lear

Volvo has a long tradition of development and production of seats. Seats are important for, among other things, comfort and safety, and have for long time been regarded a key area within Volvo. However, Volvo had problems with their plant producing seats (located in Bengtsfors, Sweden) and in 1992 it was sold to the American automotive supplier Lear Corporation (Lear). This implied that Lear took on the current products, e.g. seats for the S/V70 models. Later, Volvo decided to also collaborate with a supplier for the development and production of seats for the new P2 platform. Since a relationship between Volvo and Lear already existed, Volvo decided to continue the collaboration with Lear for the new platform. In addition to seats, Lear was also involved in the development of plastic frames for instrument panels, door panels and some other plastic details for Volvo. This case, however, mainly focuses on the development and production of seats.

Lear is a global supplier to the automotive industry. In 1997, the year before the S80 was introduced, Lear had an annual turnover around $7.3bn and 50.000 employees. After an acquisition of Delphi's seat division Lear had become the largest producer of seats with 173 production plants worldwide. Hence, Lear was larger than Volvo Car Corporation (Volvo), though not as large as Delphi.

Lear's ownership of Volvo's former seat plant in Bengtsfors (approx. 170 km north-east of Gothenburg) implied that when the product development collaboration for the P2 platform was initiated, Volvo and Lear had already been working together for a while. However, these experiences mostly concerned production related issues, even though Lear had hitherto contributed with some product design improvements on the products that they had taken over. Hence, the "real" product development collaboration between Volvo and Lear started with the development of seats for the P2 platform.

Lear and Volvo collaborated on the development of front seats (driver and passenger seat) and rear seats. A front seat (see Fig. 26) can be divided into five main parts; a chassis (for height and length adjustment) a seat cushion frame, a backrest frame (including headrest), foam and upholstery. For the front seats, many

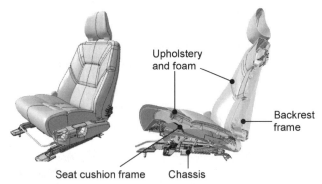

Fig. 26. Volvo S80 Front Seat. *Note:* Pictures used with permission from Volvo Car Corporation.

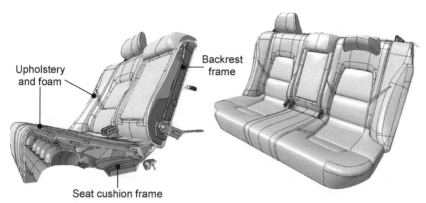

Upholstery and foam

Backrest frame

Seat cushion frame

Fig. 27. Volvo S80 Rear Seat. *Note:* Pictures used with permission from Volvo Car Corporation.

details were carried over from the S/V70 models to the P2 platform. Similar seat frames (seat cushion frame and backrest frame) were used while new foam and upholsteries were developed. In addition, a new larger side airbag was introduced (that also protects the car passengers' heads) and the sliding rails were lengthened. These product design changes were carried through mainly for the S80 and similar design solutions were later used also for the V70 and S60 front seats.

While the front seats are similar for the different models (nearly the same for S60 and V70), there are larger differences between the different rear seats. A rear seat consists of four main parts; a seat cushion frame, a backrest frame (including headrests), foam and upholstery (see Fig. 27). The backrest frame includes locks, which are vital for keeping the foldable backrest in its upright position. In addition, the V70 backrest frame has an integrated luggage net. While the rear seats for the S80 and the S60 (saloons) have a similar product design, the rear seat for the V70 (estate) is different since it must be able to take much higher loads. The car body design of the V70 does not allow any centrally placed fastening for the backrest. Still, the backrest frame (which is divided into two halves) must cope with forces from seatbelts as well as from luggage that is placed behind the backrest. Therefore, the development of the rear seat for the V70 was a more complex task than developing the rear seats for the other two models.

4.3.1. Lear's Product Development Organization

In Trollhättan (80 km north of Gothenburg), Lear had built up a product development unit adjacent to the plant where Lear produces seats for Saab. When the product development collaboration with Volvo for the P2 models started, Lear had about 5–6 engineers devoted for the project in Trollhättan. About a year later, the number of engineers had increased to about 30. Hence, Lear went through a sharp build-up of development capabilities in a fairly short time.

As mentioned earlier, Volvo saw a potential benefit with supplier collaboration regarding the possibilities to learn from suppliers' experiences that had been gained in relationships with other auto manufacturers. However, according to Volvo, the development units that Lear built up in Trollhättan for Volvo and Saab respectively were fairly autonomous. In 1996, Lear implemented a "platform organization" with different teams dedicated to particular auto manufacturers. Each team was responsible for time plans, technical solutions as well as cost for a particular product project (e.g. the P2 platform). According to Lear, this organization gave a better customer focus since specific resources were dedicated to each customer. Volvo, however, remarked that the transfer of knowledge and experiences between these different development units at Lear was limited. According to Volvo, there was no collaboration between the teams developing for Volvo and Saab respectively. Further, as mentioned above, Lear was also involved in the development of plastic frames for instrument panels, door panels and some other plastic details for Volvo. However, even if they had the same customer (i.e. Volvo) these different development projects were performed separately with little or no connection between them.

The rapid build-up of Lear's product development capabilities made it difficult for Lear to find and employ the needed engineers and project leaders. Few people were interested in moving from Lear's U.S. or German operations to Trollhättan in Sweden and it was difficult to find all the needed competencies locally. Consequently, a large share of the people working in the development projects were consultants. Lear had an ambition that no more than 40% should be consultants, but this could not always be fulfilled. This made it necessary for Lear to use consultants not only for engineering tasks, but also in some cases as project leaders. According to Volvo, the large share of consultants caused delays in the projects since it was difficult to get continuity as consultants were often replaced. Further, to smoothen differences regarding the need for development resources in different development projects, Lear had a "resource pool" of engineers. This provided flexibility, but Volvo often felt that they did not get people with skills that were specific enough. One respondent at Volvo expressed this as "*a Catia engineer could one day be working with an instrument panel and the other day with packing a rear seat and that does not provide a good enough result.*" Instead, Volvo wanted engineers that worked within the same development area for longer periods of time since this was regarded important for the learning over time. Hence, Lear had difficulties to rapidly build up the product development capability needed for the collaboration with Volvo.

4.3.2. The Module Team at Volvo

Most development of interior details had been divided between three different module teams; "interior," "cockpit" and "interior trim." Module team cockpit mainly developed details related to the instrument panel (plastic frame, glove compartment, nozzles etc) while interior trim developed the headliner, the carpets for the luggage compartment, and various plastic panels. Module team interior developed the seats as well as the tunnel console, the carpets, the seatbelts and various surface materials.

Module team interior had about 20–30 members coming from Volvo (varying over time). When including supplier representatives, the team had 40–50 members in total. In general, the composition of the module team followed the same principles as for other module teams with representatives from different functional areas as well as suppliers. The members of the team were in varying constellations and at various times co-located at Volvo's product development department. Further, module team interior was divided into five sub-teams, each one being responsible for the development areas mentioned above (see Fig. 28). In addition, there was a team with responsibility for geometry assurance (each module team had a sub-team with responsibility for geometry assurance). Hence, not only seats but also other interior details (e.g. tunnel console and carpets) were developed within the same module team, which facilitated coordination concerning these details. For example, the seats have physical interfaces to the tunnel console that need to be considered.

Meetings' were held in the team on a weekly basis (often during a whole day), involving representatives from Lear and Volvo as well as other suppliers. Lear was generally represented by a project leader and 4–5 development engineers that were working with a specific seat. From Volvo, people within concerned functional areas were called to participate in the meetings. During these meetings the progress in the project was checked in relation to the time plan and budget, which led to discussions about what actions needed to be taken and when. Based on current design solutions, Volvo told Lear how they wanted to change

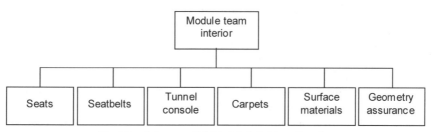

Fig. 28. Sub-teams Within Module Team Interior.

the design in order to fulfill Volvo's needs. In addition, these meetings were important for briefing Lear about changes in other projects that could influence the products developed by Lear. In turn, Lear could tell Volvo if they might not be able to handle a certain demand and suggest an alternative solution. Several respondents at Volvo emphasized that the supplier must flag for potential problems in this way as early as possible. However, in many cases Volvo experienced that Lear waited too long before revealing problems, implying that the problem became even more serious. There were also weekly meetings involving the module team leader and the sub-team leaders, though not the suppliers. At these meetings, project plans, budgets and, for instance, different suppliers' offers were discussed.

The seats also have interfaces to other development areas, which implied a need for coordination with other module teams. For instance, coordination was needed with the team developing the electrical system (e.g. for electrical seat adjustment, electrical heating and airbag electronics). Further, the seats have several interfaces to the car body. Both the seat cushion and the backrest of the rear seat have complex geometrical interfaces to the car body. Further, it may seem that a front seat has a rather simple interface to the car body (i.e. principally four screws). However, the seat frame with its transversal steel pipes is crucial for crash protection (especially side impact). Therefore, the interplay (and thus the interfaces) between the car body and seat must be fine-tuned, among other things based on the results of various crash tests. Hence, changes in body design had implications for the seat design and vice versa. These interfaces required frequent coordination since in particular the car body is dependent on expensive production tools that cannot easily be changed. When coordination was needed between module teams, meetings were arranged where representatives from affected teams were invited, or as expressed by one respondent at Volvo: ". . . depending on where the biggest problem was, the team developing the car body called for the team developing the seats or vice versa, but there were no regular meetings between the teams developing the seats and the car body respectively." Since Lear had the main responsibility for the development of seats, Volvo wanted Lear to also handle the coordination related to the car body. However, this showed to be difficult for Lear and, therefore, most of this coordination was handled by Volvo.

Another area that required frequent coordination with seat development was styling. Styling is concerned with the car as a whole and cannot easily be limited to certain parts of it. Therefore, styling had no formal role in any specific module team. Instead, the styling was coordinated directly between module team interior and the styling department. Meetings were held at the styling department on a weekly basis where members from the module team, including Lear, participated. Thereby, styling features regarding color, surface structures and so on were coordinated between the styling department and module team interior as well as between different affected module teams.

4.3.3. Division of Development Activities

Most of the time Lear had representatives working in the team at Volvo. However, a majority of these representatives were consultants, a fact that sometimes made it difficult for them to make decisions on behalf of Lear. Therefore, even though Lear had resident engineers in the team, the project was largely managed from Trollhättan. According to respondents at Volvo, the resident engineers often did not have the required formal authority in the project and could therefore not be the kind of "speaking partner" that Volvo wanted. Consequently, much of the coordination between Lear and Volvo had to be taken care of during the weekly meetings described above.

While Volvo's idea with the module teams was to develop products in close collaboration with suppliers, Lear's way of organizing favored more division of the development job between the two parties. This division, in turn, created a lack of continuous coordination between Volvo and Lear in the module team. Therefore, to compensate for this, a well defined "job split" between the two parties was needed. However, according to Lear, it was often not clear how the development work should be split up and, as a result, some development activities were not performed as planned. In some cases, for example, product designs were not tested and verified in time since both Volvo and Lear thought the other party would perform the tests.

Related to the need for a job split, Lear also emphasized the importance of clear product specifications (e.g. regarding interfaces and functionality). Lear remarked that Volvo interfered too often in the detailed product design and argued that better product specifications would enable Lear to perform more "black box" development. However, continuously changing design requirements (e.g. related to interfaces and packing) for the seats made it difficult for Volvo to provide this kind of detailed specifications. The development of the seats is highly dependent on, for example, changes of other interior products, the car body or changes regarding design and styling. This was one important reason for Volvo's more interactive development approach.

Hence, Volvo and Lear had somewhat different views regarding the organizing of development work. Even if Lear had representatives in the module team at Volvo, this increased the demands on direct contacts between Volvo and Lear's respective organizations. Therefore, instead of coordinating the development work mainly within the module team (i.e. the forum designed to handle coordination between the organizations), much coordination also had to be performed directly between Volvo's representatives in the module team and Lear's development organization (principally illustrated in Fig. 29).

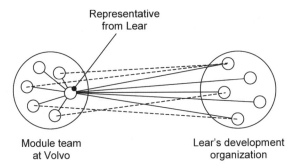

Fig. 29. Coordination of Development Work Between Volvo and Lear.

4.3.4. Relationships with Other Firms – Component Suppliers

Since Lear was working with building up their product development capabilities, some development work that had been assigned to Lear was transferred to Lear's component suppliers. In this way, Lear strived to benefit from these suppliers' development capabilities in a similar way that Volvo relied on suppliers for development. This "extended" collaboration provided Lear with more development resources as well as feedback (e.g. regarding production issues) from their component suppliers, but it also contributed to increase the complexity of the relationship between Lear and Volvo. This was further complicated by the fact that Volvo in many cases decided which suppliers Lear should collaborate with.

Lear's reliance on suppliers for product development sometimes implied that Volvo found it difficult to know what was going on in the different development projects. When product development activities had been located at a supplier, Lear's role was more of a coordinator. Even though Volvo intended to let Lear take an extensive responsibility for development, Volvo did not have the required confidence in Lear's capabilities. To some extent, this could be attributed to Volvo's traditional role, where Volvo had a detailed control also over component development. The lack of confidence was, however, also explained by the fact that Lear was often not able to present the concepts and product designs that Volvo expected. This made Volvo regard Lear as a "filter" between Volvo and the component suppliers at the same time as Lear acted as a "system integrator."

One such example was Lear's relationship with the German supplier Ieper that was responsible for the development and production of the luggage net for the V70 rear seat (see Fig. 30). The luggage net is integrated with the backrest and can be pulled up to stop luggage from reaching the passenger compartment in case of a crash. This makes the luggage net a crucial safety component. When the production of the V70 started, it turned out that Lear had problems to deliver seats as ordered by Volvo. This caused many problems for Volvo and it was urgent to

Luggage net

Fig. 30. The Luggage Net on the V70 Rear Seat. *Note:* Picture used with permission from Volvo Car Corporation.

solve the problem. When Volvo and Lear tried to locate the problem together, it was traced to the luggage net. The investigation showed that Ieper had to discard a large share (about 40%) of the produced luggage nets since there was a problem with the locking mechanism. In addition, a considerable share (10–20%) of the luggage nets that actually reached Lear had to be discarded for the same reason. As a result, Lear was not able to produce the quantities of rear seats required by Volvo. At first, Volvo thought there was a problem in Ieper's production process, but it showed to be the design of the locking mechanism that was not robust enough. The locking mechanism often fell apart during the assembly of the luggage net, thereby causing the delivery problems. Lear that together with Ieper was responsible for this component had tried to change the design, but the problems remained. According to Volvo, the problem had occurred because the chosen product design had not been tested enough before production start. It had been possible to produce the luggage net in small series, but when production volumes increased, the problem became visible. Volvo had not been involved in the detailed design of the locking mechanism since Lear was responsible for designing components for the rear seat. However, the urgent situation forced Volvo to "dictate" design changes to reach a working product design.

A similar situation occurred regarding the rear seat locks for the V70 (see Fig. 31). This is also a crucial component for safety since, in a crash situation, it must handle strong forces from seatbelts and luggage to keep the backrest frame in its upright position. In this case, Lear collaborated with the German supplier Witte, a producer of many different kinds of locks for the automotive industry. However, Witte did not manage to come up with a product design that fulfilled Volvo's demands, which caused problems. According to one respondent at Volvo, "... it is always tricky to design locks that don't rattle and that can stand the forces in a crash." In addition, the design task was a difficult one since

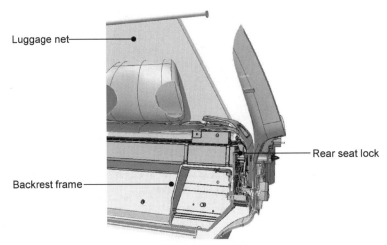

Luggage net

Rear seat lock

Backrest frame

Fig. 31.   Rear Seat Lock in the V70 Rear Seat. *Note:* Picture used with permission from
Volvo Car Corporation.

Volvo wanted a special lock design, allowing the seat backrest to be locked in
two different positions. To solve the problems, engineers from Volvo and Lear
went to Witte on several occasions where they carefully studied the details in
the locks to identify what caused the problems. Hence, even though Witte was
supposed to develop the complete locks, Volvo and Lear "dictated" different design
changes. In both these cases, however, Volvo emphasized that Lear was involved
too. One respondent expressed this as: *"We did not want to 'cheat' them [Lear] by
establishing direct contacts with suppliers without letting them know, that would
have been devastating."* However, in some other cases especially where Volvo
already had an established relationship with a component supplier, Lear perceived
that Volvo went direct to the supplier without involving Lear. In such cases, the
supplier then got different instructions from Volvo and Lear respectively, which
made it difficult to coordinate the development work.

Hence, at several occasions, Volvo interfered with Lear's relationships with component suppliers. However, as mentioned above, in most cases Volvo had influenced
which component supplier Lear should collaborate with. This, in turn, affected the
outcome of the development project in different ways. A typical example is the
development of the backrest frame for the V70. Traditionally, the backrest frame
had been made by steel, but to save weight Volvo decided to make it in aluminum
instead. Already during the concept phase, Volvo had established development
collaboration with the Norwegian aluminum supplier Hydro. Based on a special
alloy, a concept for the backrest frame had been developed. This would make the
backrest frame strong enough and still lighter than if it had been made from steel.

Hence, there was a working concept that also Lear, that would be responsible for the seat as a whole, had accepted. However, when the development project was about to start, Volvo hesitated. The backrest frame is essential for safety and, according to Volvo's policies, it is then important that Volvo selects a well-known supplier. Volvo had, however, no previous experience from working with Hydro. Therefore, although the project team at Volvo found that the collaboration with Hydro worked well, it was decided that Autoliv should develop the backrest frame instead.

As described above, Volvo had been collaborating with Autoliv for many years and, in addition to the backrest frame, Autoliv was involved in the development of several other components such as front seat frames, front seat chassis, airbags and seatbelts. Hence, Autoliv was an important supplier that was already represented in the module team. As expressed by one respondent at Volvo: "*Autoliv was a key player, of equal importance as Lear.*"

This change, however, caused much trouble in the project. Changing supplier at this point in time implied that Autoliv in short time had to come up with a new concept that matched the existing concept's cost and performance. This, however, showed to be a difficult task and it turned out that it was hard to find a new design that could stand the crash tests. Consequently, much time was lost in the project. This, in turn, caused problems for Lear that was responsible for the integration of the backrest frame with the other parts of the rear seat. Further, it turned out that the final design of the backrest frame became heavier and more expensive than the first concept. It also showed to be difficult to produce, which initially caused quality problems.

When serious problems arose in the different projects, special "task forces" were compiled to solve the problems as quickly as possible. These task forces included representatives from Volvo as well as from involved suppliers. For example, such a task force was used for solving problems with the electrically adjustable front seats. When the production of the Volvo S80 started, quality audits soon revealed that some electrically adjustable seats made too much noise. In addition, there were problems with an unacceptable play. The problems were traced back to the seat chassis (see Fig. 32) that had been developed by the German supplier Brose (only the manual chassis are developed by Autoliv). The electrical motors equipped with small worm gears caused the noise and the play could be traced to different moving parts in the chassis. However, these problems could not be solved only by fine-tuning Brose's production and, hence, some re-design was required. In this situation, a task force was compiled where Volvo, Lear, Brose and Autoliv were involved (Autoliv had developed the seat cushion frame that has an interface to the seat chassis).

Volvo gathered the task force for meetings that aimed at finding alternative design solutions. Based on their own ideas as well as the suggestions that came up during the meetings, Brose re-designed the chassis and then the new designs were

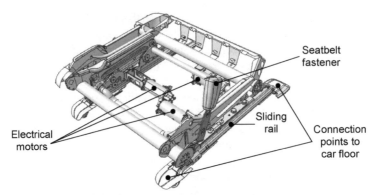

Fig. 32. A Seat Chassis for an Electrically Maneuvered Seat. *Note:* Picture used with permission from Volvo Car Corporation.

tested. Quite a lot of effort was put into solving this problem and, during certain periods, the task force met every day. In addition, direct links were established between Volvo, Brose and Lear, enabling videoconferences. Even though this could have been regarded as Brose's problem, this example illustrates that the interactive collaboration in the task force, involving several suppliers, helped to quickly reach a working design solution.

However, although the problems with noise and play were solved, this example also illustrates how design changes may lead to "consecutive" problems. To eliminate some of the play in the chassis, the electrical motors were turned a little bit. There was enough space underneath the seat for this, and it seemed to be working well. However, after this design change had been approved, it was revealed that in a certain seat position, the motor could damage one of the air ducts placed on the car floor. Therefore, also the air duct had to be re-designed. This, in turn, implied that the already completed tools for molding the air duct had to be changed, which was rather costly. Hence, when re-designing the chassis, enough attention had not been paid to the interfaces to other components and, as the interface was changed, new problems were created. One respondent at Volvo expressed this (when a similar problem occurred in another context) in the following way: "*Generally, for every interface that was changed we got problems. Problems always occurred in the interfaces. [. . .] I cannot remember a single interface that was problem-free [. . .] – it speaks for itself . . .*"

To summarize, the business units that have been mentioned above and the relationships between them are illustrated in Fig. 33. Hence, in addition to Lear that had the main responsibility for the development of the complete seats, several other business units were involved in the development work. As illustrated above

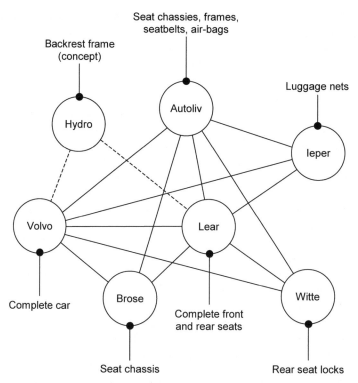

Fig. 33. Business Units with Connections to the Volvo-Lear Relationship.

and in the figure, it was necessary to establish relationships between not only Lear and the other business units involved, but also directly between several of these business units. For instance, the luggage nets developed by Ieper and the rear seat locks developed by Witte have interfaces to the backrest frame developed by Autoliv that required coordination. Hence, even if Lear was supposed to act as the "spider in the net," not all activities were coordinated by Lear.

4.4. The DFC Tech Case

This case describes the development collaboration between DFC Tech and the truck manufacturer Scania. DFC Tech was established in March 2000 as a joint venture between the Swedish supplier Dayco Sweden AB (Dayco) and the engineering consultancy firm Fasitet to facilitate product development collaboration between

Dayco and their customers. Shortly after the establishment, DFC Tech became involved in the development of pipes and hoses for a new truck model at Scania. In the following sections Dayco's products, the establishment of DFC Tech and the collaboration with Scania is described in more detail.

4.4.1. Dayco's Products

Dayco is a Swedish supplier to the automotive industry with an annual turnover of MSEK270 and about 270 employees (fiscal year 2001). When this study was conducted, Dayco (i.e. Dayco Sweden AB) was part of Mark IV Automotive, a group mainly supplying the automotive industry with hoses, drive belts, pulleys, air intake components as well as small gasoline engines and continuous vehicle transmissions (CVT).

Dayco provides pipes and hoses for the automotive industry, with a focus on engine compartment related air and fluid distribution in cars, trucks and buses. This includes engine cooling, oil, fuel, air, brake, heat/ventilation/AC and power steering systems. Dayco's ambition is to provide all necessary connections regarding air and fluid distribution between these systems (see Fig. 34). Dayco's customers are the large Swedish auto manufacturers Volvo Trucks, Scania, Volvo Cars and Saab Automobile.

Dayco produces pipes in two different plants in Sweden. The plant in Varberg produces pipes for cars and the plant in Ulricehamn produces pipes for trucks and buses. Since pipe dimensions and production volumes (and, consequently, the production equipment) differ for cars in comparison with trucks and buses, one plant has been dedicated to each of these product segments.

In most cases, Dayco buy standard dimension steel (or aluminum) pipes, which are machined in different ways. For example, Dayco cuts, bends, and end-forms the pipes to obtain the desired geometrical shape. Most of these activities are

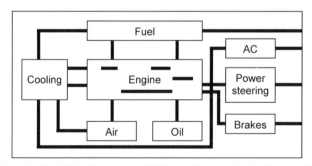

Fig. 34. Dayco's "Role" in Connecting Different Systems in the Engine Compartment (Dayco Automotive AB, 2002).

performed in numerically controlled machines where pipe length, bending radii etc can be pre-programmed. Then, different components such as flanges, fasteners, consoles and couplings are, for instance, pressed or welded on to the pipes. In most cases, these components are purchased from component suppliers. In cases where painting and surface treatment is needed, other firms perform this before the pipes are delivered to the customer. Further, Dayco aims at providing total solutions, incorporating all necessary connections for air and fluid distribution. This implies that also other components, such as hoses and valves, may be part of the sub-assemblies that Dayco delivers. These components are also purchased from component suppliers. Hence, Dayco produces pipes internally, while hoses and other related components are purchased from suppliers.

4.4.2. The Development of Pipes and Hoses
Hence, the products that Dayco provides connect different components such as AC compressors, radiators or oil filters. In other words, the pipes and hoses can be seen as the "interface" between these other components. Consequently, moving or changing the design of these other components often require a changed pipe or hose design. Therefore, auto manufacturers often await a "frozen" design of these other components before designing pipes and hoses. However, even after these other component designs have formally been "frozen," late design changes often cause additional changes of pipes and hoses. Therefore, pipes and hoses must constitute a "flexible link" between other components.

The late design of pipes and hoses makes it difficult for Dayco as a supplier to influence the design. This is important since, for example, the choice of pipe diameter and bending radius affects how a specific pipe can be produced. Too small a radius or too little distance between two bends may require more expensive production tools. Even if there are tables available for this kind of design parameters, it may be difficult for an engineer at an auto manufacturer to perform a design that fits Dayco's specific production equipment.

Seen from Dayco's point of view, the late design of pipes and hoses that is performed with no particular supplier in mind makes it more difficult to build a long-term relationship with customers, i.e. auto manufacturers. Auto manufacturers may find this suitable (at least in a short-term perspective) as it facilitates switching between suppliers. However, Dayco emphasized long-term relationships since it enabled more specific investments in production facilities and product development that in the long run could provide lower product costs.

4.4.3. The Establishment of DFC Tech
In the late 1990s, however, Dayco experienced that auto manufacturers generally increased their demands on the capabilities of their suppliers' product development,

wanting them to take an even more active role in product development. Dayco therefore saw a possibility to become involved at an early phase of the customers' product development process, before most other design solutions had been "frozen." Thereby, Dayco saw possibilities to develop pipes and hoses that were better adapted to their existing products and production equipment and, which would reduce the product cost. At that time, Dayco had four engineers working with product development in different forms, though, to take a step towards a total design responsibility more resources were needed.

A solution to the problem was presented as Dayco got an opportunity to establish a joint venture with Fasitet, a Swedish consultancy firm. Fasitet is located in Gothenburg and mainly provides Swedish auto manufacturers with development engineers. Although Fasitet has not specialized in any particular area, they have long experience from product development in the automotive industry. No former relationship existed between Dayco and Fasitet, but a joint venture seemed to be beneficial for both of them. While Fasitet had long experience from product development in the automotive industry, Dayco could provide specific knowledge regarding pipes and hoses. This suited Fasitet that for some time had been looking for some development area to specialize within.

A joint venture was established in March 2000 and it was called DFC Tech (DFC stands for Dayco Fasitet Connection). Initially, Dayco owned 70% and Fasitet owned 30% of the shares in DFC Tech. DFC Tech was located in Fasitet's office in the central parts of Gothenburg, thereby providing Dayco with a product development "platform" not far from Volvo Cars and Volvo Trucks that both are important customers of Dayco's.

DFC Tech's business idea is to be the product development link between Dayco and the customer. For example, DFC Tech can take on complete development projects including pre-studies, development of product concepts, design and prototyping. All these activities, especially prototyping, are performed mainly in collaboration with Dayco's production plants (see Fig. 35). Different issues related to production can thereby be considered continuously, which helps to reduce production costs and improve product quality. In addition, DFC Tech could collaborate with other firms within Mark IV Automotive regarding, for instance, product development and prototyping.

With DFC Tech, Dayco saw possibilities to sell product development capacity to the customers at similar conditions as the pure consultancy firms. In addition, performing the product development in a separate company enables DFC Tech to take assignments from other suppliers than Dayco. At the same time, there are no guarantees that Dayco will finally receive the production order. However, since DFC Tech can influence the design and adapt it to Dayco's specific conditions

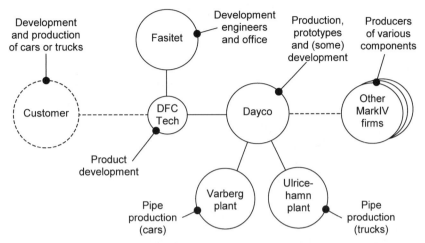

Fig. 35. Different Business Units and Their Main Roles in Relation to DFC Tech.

(e.g. regarding production equipment, standard dimensions etc) Dayco will have better chances to also receive the production order.

4.4.4. DFC Tech and the Collaboration with Scania

Traditionally, Scania has performed a major part of the product development "in-house." However, When Scania started the development of a new truck model (here referred to as project "Alpha"), also suppliers played an important role in product development. DFC Tech was involved in the development work almost from the start of project Alpha. Scania regarded supplier collaboration important since suppliers could contribute with fresh ideas and knowledge, potentially resulting in better design solutions. In particular, Scania was interested in the suppliers' combined knowledge of product development and component production. In addition, Scania saw possibilities to benefit from what suppliers had learned from relationships with other customers. Further, Scania's resources for the project were limited and therefore the suppliers' development resources were regarded valuable to Scania. This was also the case for pipes and hoses in the engine compartment, i.e. the type of products developed by DFC Tech. Scania regarded these products to be important, as they consciously wanted to avoid problems with leakages etc. In addition, Scania saw possibilities to reduce the cost for this type of products. Therefore, Scania emphasized that a supplier developing pipes and hoses should be involved early in the development process. After some comparisons with other potential suppliers, DFC Tech was selected as a development partner for pipes and hoses for the engine compartment in project Alpha. Based on preliminary design specifications DFC Tech assumed the responsibility for the task as a fixed-price assignment.

4.4.5. The Products Developed by DFC Tech

DFC Tech was assigned the responsibility for developing a number of different pipes and hoses in the engine compartment. To keep the product cost down, DFC Tech wanted to use steel pipes as far as possible. However, to compensate for movements and vibrations, mainly between the engine and components mounted on the chassis, different types of hoses or bellows of rubber or silicone were used in combination with steel (or aluminum) pipes. The different pipes and hoses are schematically illustrated in Fig. 36.

In addition to pipes and hoses, DFC Tech also developed different consoles for fastening the pipes. These consoles were regarded as rather easy to design. In addition, they frequently had to be changed due to changed pipe and hose design. Therefore, in the early phases of the project, no detailed design was done. Instead, "dummies" were designed to indicate that the space was needed for a console. Scania also required some form of console to be designed to make cost and weight estimations for the truck as a whole more accurate.

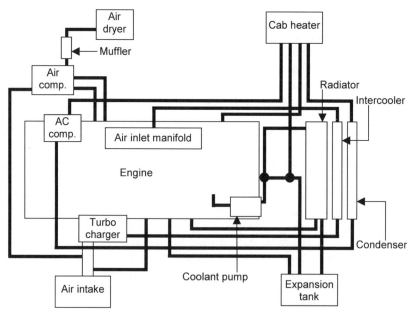

Fig. 36. Pipes and Hoses Developed by DFC Tech (Illustrated as Bold Lines).

Further, DFC Tech also equipped all pipes and hoses with suitable couplings, flanges, clamps etc. For these components, DFC Tech collaborated with a firm based in Stockholm called IFE (Ingeniörsfirma Fritz Egnell) that has specialized in this type of components for pipes and hoses. IFE is mainly a sales agent for different suppliers such as Rasmussen and Oetiker, two German suppliers of clamps and couplings. However, IFE also performs flow calculations and some product design for their customers. DFC Tech only used standard components to keep costs down and reduce the need for product design, though, it was nevertheless important to choose the "right" components. Based on the requirements that had to be fulfilled for a particular pipe or hose, for example regarding pressure, temperature and assembly time, IFE could help DFC Tech to find suitable components for different connections.

In addition to the products developed by DFC Tech as described above, there were other pipes and hoses in the truck that DFC Tech did not develop. For instance, DFC Tech was not involved in the development of pipes and hoses for the brake system (except the connection between the air compressor and the air dryer) or the power steering system. Scania's experience from supplier collaboration was limited and, therefore, they did not want to give DFC Tech the full responsibility for all pipes and hoses. Even if taking responsibility also for these other systems might have provided better possibilities for DFC Tech to coordinate all pipes and hose design, this division was not a problem since the different systems work rather independently of each other.

4.4.6. The Team and the Development Work at Scania

For project Alpha, Scania had compiled a cross-functional team where also a few suppliers were represented (see Fig. 37). As mentioned above, due to Scania's modular product architecture many components from existing models could be re-used for the new model and therefore did not have to be (re-)designed.

A project manager was responsible for the whole team. In addition, there were two technical project managers for chassis and power train respectively. In addition to chassis and power train design (constituting about half the amount of people in the team) there were representatives from purchasing, technical marketing, sales marketing, quality and production and logistics. There were also business controllers and representatives with responsibility for geometry assurance, strength calculations and coordination of Catia (i.e. CAD) models and related information. Most of these team members came from Scania's Swedish organization, though, most functions also had representatives from Scania's operations in Latin America.

In addition to the team members from Scania, three suppliers had representatives in the team. One supplier, here referred to as "Cool" (fictive name), was responsible for developing and integrating the radiator, the intercooler and the condenser and

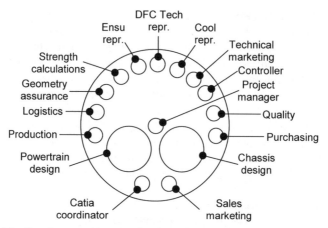

Fig. 37. The Development Team at Scania (Schematic Picture Only). *Note:* Does not reflect position or number of people in the team.

an engine supplier (here referred to as "Ensu," a fictive name) was responsible for developing the engine (based on an existing engine design). Cool had their own development center from where their development activities were controlled. A representative was present in the team at Scania for one or two weeks and then spent two weeks at the home site. Ensu had two representatives in the team who spent about half their time at Scania and half the time in their home organization. The third supplier was DFC Tech that had a full-time representative in the team. In addition, DFC Tech collaborated with Exacuo, a one-man firm (run by a former engineer at Volvo Cars) with profound experience of pipe and hose development within the automotive industry. The engineer from Exacuo (here regarded as a representative for DFC Tech) participated in the team on a part-time basis, visiting Scania a couple of times per week.

Other suppliers were more indirectly involved in the development work, especially in cases where components used for current models could be carried over to the new truck model. For instance, the same air dryer would be used for the new truck. This implied no design changes, though, the challenge was the positioning of these components. One of DFC Tech's representatives expressed this as "Scania tried to use the same AC compressor, air dryer and other components that had been used before. But the position was not 'given.' These details were moved around. The interfaces are often kept while a new pipe and hose design is needed." The positioning was a task that Scania chose to manage internally and, hence, the coordination regarding these carry-over components was handled by Scania's engineers.

In total, there were about 50 people in the team. This includes the above mentioned supplier representatives, but not other engineers that were working at the respective suppliers' home sites. Nor does this include the development activities that were performed in Scania's line organization. Further, about half the team was consultants.

All members of the team were co-located in the same office space to facilitate communication and coordination between different functional domains and development areas. According to DFC Tech's representatives, the development work in the team went incredibly smoothly as there was frequent communication between team members: "Our components crossed different interfaces, both the engine and the frame, which implied that it was necessary to have contact with all the other people [in the team]. That made me feel that the network was really big and it gave DFC Tech a good position. We could provide others with advice, for instance when designing a flange or a pipe, even if we were not responsible for that particular component." It was also stressed that the project management had authority to make decisions and that the relatively small team, resulting in small distances between people, facilitated the communication. The respondents at Scania shared this view: "It works really well. People are discussing interfaces and the communication goes directly between the suppliers and not necessarily through Scania. This works much due to the organization. The *whole team is co-located in one place.*"

However, sometimes when, for instance, Cool's engineers had been working at their home site for a couple of weeks and came back to the team, there was an "accumulated" need for coordination. Although many problems could be solved via telephone and email in the meantime, sometimes larger "clashes" were detected first when they came back to the team. A representative for DFC Tech expressed this in the following way: "The first day back at Scania they often told me about certain design changes. Sometimes it worked out well and sometimes their changes destroyed three weeks of my work ... Then we had to discuss this, sometimes together with the project manager. [. . .] In many cases there were no problems, but when the big intercooler pipes were involved it could create problems. One could work for a long time to find a solution and, if a large design change was carried through, it might be very difficult to find an alternative solution – one had to turn the available space inside out to see where the pipe could be drawn. But it could not be drawn just any way because there must be consoles etc. There were lots of compromises."

Meetings were held on a regular basis. For some meetings all people involved in the teamwork were called while other meetings concerned people from Scania only or people involved in a particular development area (e.g. power train) only. Maybe the design meetings held every Tuesday afternoon were the most important ones for DFC Tech. All design engineers in the team were called to these meetings where, for instance, the possibilities to "freeze" a particular product design were discussed. Further, these meetings aimed at checking the interplay between different components and, thereby, to minimize the number of "clashes."

In-between the formal meetings there were different meetings gathering a few people that were involved in a particular problem or issue. For instance, even if there seemed to be some free space it might be a good idea to check with some other engineers first what they planned to do next. DFC Tech's representative at Scania explained, "... *more and more time was spent in meetings. And the more I was there the more I became involved. [...] There were more and more meetings towards the end of the project, because there was an increasing need for eliminating clashes*." Hence, it was important to keep an eye on the "environment" and what other engineers were working with.

4.4.7. DFC Tech's Participation in Project Alpha

When DFC Tech was involved in project Alpha it had been going on for over a year. Cool and Ensu had been involved about six months earlier, but when DFC Tech was involved the project was still in the concept phase. In practice, this implied that concepts existed for a few components that DFC Tech was particularly dependent on such as the engine, the radiator, the condenser, the intercooler and the frame. However, neither position nor a final design existed for these components. Hence, there was still much room for changes and there are plenty of examples of how different compromises were worked out between the involved firms.

4.4.7.1. The intercooler pipe.

One such example is the intercooler pipe that goes between the turbo charger and the intercooler. The turbo charger was originally placed on the upper part of the engine and the air outlet (where the intercooler pipe is connected) was placed on its upper side. This implied that the pipe had to be connected to the turbo charger from above. Therefore, the pipe went from the turbo charger to the intercooler underneath the cab floor. To begin with, this solution seemed to work well, although the available space was very limited. However, it later turned out that there was a risk for a collision between the cab and the intercooler pipe. In extreme situations, the suspended cab could move downwards and come too close to the pipe. However, in the meantime, many other components had been added around the rather big intercooler pipe, which made it difficult to find an alternative way for it underneath the cab floor.

In this situation, DFC Tech had to interact with the department responsible for cab development. One solution was to hollow out parts of the insulation under the cab floor and thereby create more space. This, however, would imply more

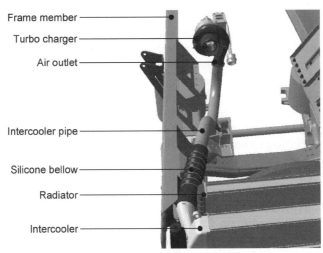

Frame member

Turbo charger

Air outlet

Intercooler pipe

Silicone bellow

Radiator

Intercooler

Fig. 38. The Turbo Charger was Turned 180 Degrees to Enable a New Intercooler Pipe Design. *Note:* Picture used with permission from Scania.

noise, thereby affecting the driving comfort in the cab. Instead, it was necessary to find a totally new way for the intercooler pipe. After negotiations with Ensu, it was agreed that the turbo charger would be turned 180 degrees so that the outlet pointed downwards instead (see Fig. 38). Hence, in this way, the intercooler pipe was moved away from the cab floor. This, however, also implied that the other connections on the turbo (e.g. for exhaust pipes and lubrication pipes) were moved. It was also necessary to design a shield underneath the intercooler pipe for protecting it from flying stones. Further, the intercooler pipe's new position implied that a rather expensive (forged) pipe knee on the turbo could be eliminated. Instead, the intercooler pipe was collared so that it could be connected directly to the turbo charger using a standard coupling.

In the other end, the intercooler pipe (i.e. a silicone bellow, see Fig. 38) was connected to the intercooler developed by Cool. Based on existing designs, Cool had chosen a connection with 76mm diameter on the intercooler. This, however, is not a standard metric dimension (76mm corresponds to 3 inches). Therefore, DFC Tech strived to change this to a metric standard dimension that would make the pipe less expensive. In addition, flow calculations showed that the pipe diameter could be reduced, which further helped to reduce cost and weight. This change did not cause any big problems for Cool, since no production tools had yet been produced, only prototypes. However, there was certain deadlines that affected what could be changed or not. One of DFC Tech's representatives expressed that "Scania had to 'freeze' the design at a particular date, and then it would not be possible to change certain details. One by one, different designs were frozen. In this case, however, the matter was left open for a rather long time because we needed the flexibility. Therefore, there was a very close collaboration between DFC Tech and Cool."

To compensate for vibrations and movements between the turbo (i.e. the engine) and the intercooler a bellow was needed. To stand the hot air from the turbo, the bellow had to be made from silicone. For the design of this and other bellows (and pre-formed hoses), DFC Tech collaborated with the German hose supplier Phoenix Automotive (Phoenix) and their subsidiary Mündener Gummiwerke (MGW). Scania had collaborated with Phoenix earlier and Phoenix had been approved according to Scania's quality standards. Therefore, Scania and DFC Tech had agreed to choose Phoenix as a development partner for hoses.

Based on requirements regarding temperature, air pressure, movement in different directions and so on, Phoenix could help DFC Tech to design a suitable bellow (e.g. regarding selection of material, thickness and number of folds). Since the bellow was more expensive than steel pipe, it was important to make it as short as possible. In addition, DFC Tech tried to use metric standard dimensions, which was facilitated as the pipe diameter was changed. Phoenix and MGW also provided important information regarding how to design the bellow so that the production cost could be reduced. For instance, a bellow with "smooth" folds can be made by vulcanizing rubber on a fabric that has been thread on a "horn" with a particular shape, while more advanced designs required more expensive tools (e.g. for molding). The clamps for fastening the bellow were chosen in collaboration with IFE.

Hence, the development of the intercooler pipe shows how DFC Tech had to collaborate also with the department for cab development in the line organization. In addition, it shows how the interaction between DFC Tech and Cool resulted in a lighter and less expensive pipe design as well as how the interaction with Phoenix contributed to develop a well-adapted solution for the silicone bellow.

4.4.7.2. The radiator connections. The design of the radiator connections provides illustrative examples of how different departments within Scania, as well as DFC Tech and Cool, collaborated in the development team. The radiator reduces the coolant temperature and, hence, prevents the engine from getting over-heated. It is placed in front of the engine, which implies that it may be necessary to remove it when repairing certain other components. One of Scania's representatives in the team was responsible for adapting the truck for the aftermarket, i.e. service and maintenance. A frequent communication with repair shops in different countries enabled experiences from repairing existing truck models to be fed back to the design team. In addition, new ideas and design solutions could be "tested"

Fig. 39. A Quick Connector Used for the Radiator. *Note:* Picture by courtesy of
Norma/Rasmussen GmbH.

regarding repair and maintenance before they were implemented. Based on this
kind of information, it had been decided that the radiator should be equipped with
quick connectors (see Fig. 39) to make it easier to remove it. Further, the use of
quick connectors implied that no clamps were needed. This, in turn, would help
to facilitate assembly and reduce assembly time. In addition, the risk for leakages
was reduced. Hence, this design solution affected both production and aftermarket.

Standard quick connectors from IFE were used and, since both Cool and DFC
Tech had been involved at an early stage, there were no problems associated with
implementing these connectors. For instance, this did not really affect Cool since
each radiator has a specific design and, hence, specific tools are used. The tool is
designed for a specific connector, but at that point in time, tools had not yet been
produced.

However, in order to facilitate the "docking" of the radiator, it was decided that
also part of the cable harness should have quick connectors. As explained by a
DFC Tech representative, this in turn affected the pipe and hose design: "There
was a cable duct that should be 'docked' and this system implied that we had to
find compromises for the cables all the time – we [DFC Tech's representative and
Scania's cable design engineer] shared lots of problems. At the same time as we
wanted to draw our pipes and hoses in a similar way as we drew the cables, some
of our pipes were rather hot and could therefore not be drawn too close to cables
and plastic cable ducts."

Hence, the cross-functional collaboration in the team helped to find a design
for the radiator connections that also fulfilled production and maintenance
requirements. It also shows how involving suppliers at an early stage may facilitate
implementation of a new product design.

4.4.7.3. The use of prototypes in the development work. Physical prototypes played an important role in the development work, both for testing a single component as well as for understanding its interplay with other components. Prototypes were built at different "prototype levels" aiming at certain deadlines in the project. Hence, prototypes were important for confirming that a certain level of development had been reached. In this way, prototypes were an important means for project coordination.

Since DFC Tech had no facilities of their own for producing prototypes, they mainly relied on Dayco's production plants for prototype production. When a new prototype was needed, a CAD model was sent to an engineer at Dayco in Varberg who opened the file and converted the information into certain bending coordinates. These coordinates were then sent to the plant in Ulricehamn where a few pieces of the needed prototype were produced and then sent to DFC Tech's representative at Scania. In total, this process only took a few days. It was important that DFC Tech could get hold of new prototypes quickly since new pipe designs were often required due to other design changes, often carried through close to project deadlines. In a similar way, Phoenix and MGW provided DFC Tech with hose prototypes.

DFC Tech often participated in meetings held at a chassis workshop at Scania where prototype trucks were built. Then, all participants at the meeting gathered around the prototype truck and different problems (e.g. "clashes") were discussed. In this way, also DFC Tech's physical prototypes could be tested in relation to its "environment." These prototype meetings were particularly important for finding suitable positions for pipe consoles. It was easy to see where a console could be placed or if a pipe had to be given a different shape to better fit existing or possible consoles. Therefore, according to a representative from DFC Tech, the prototype was an important complement to the electronic CAD models: "Such things [i.e. positioning of consoles] were much easier to see in the physical environment than in the Catia environment. In the Catia environment, you cannot include everything and if you do so, you get blinded. [. . .] Not until everything else is put in place is it possible to see where to put a console." The prototype truck also made it easier to see if different pipes and cables could be fastened using the same console. This was important to reduce cost but also, for instance, to reduce the need for making holes in the frame members.

Further, prototypes were an important means for adapting the product design to the production system. Experienced senior operators, that could provide much valuable feedback to the design engineers regarding assembly, assembled the prototype trucks. It was generally regarded important that the design engineers frequently went to those who assembled the prototype trucks to confirm that a design solution was adapted to certain production requirements. A representative from DFC Tech said, ". . . we had a very good contact with those who built the trucks. They were professionals among assembly operators with a lot of knowledge and experience. Especially the design engineers that had been in this business for 20–25 years had a very frequent communication with these skilled assembly operators and together they solved complex problems smoothly."

The prototypes were also used for different kinds of tests. When running the prototype vehicles different problems with, for example, leakages and vibrations could be detected. DFC Tech also had the possibility to test prototypes in shake rigs at Dayco in Varberg that were specially made for testing fatigue etc in pipes. These tests could show if there was a risk for pipe cracks, requiring a re-design (e.g. an increased bending radius).

4.4.7.4. DFC tech and the relation to Dayco. As mentioned above, DFC Tech relied on Dayco for the prototypes. Thereby the production engineers at Dayco also had possibilities to provide DFC Tech with feedback regarding the adaptation of the pipe design to Dayco's production system. Further, to adapt the pipe design for production, DFC Tech's representatives at Scania had tables showing what standard tools were available for bending the pipes. Still, however, the direct contact between DFC Tech and Dayco's production plants was important. If, for example, a "double bend" was needed to avoid a "clash" with another component it was necessary to check with the production engineers if this was technically possible to produce.

Further, in many cases, DFC Tech sent a CAD model to Dayco for testing the design in a special "bending simulator." This is a software used for simulating the production process using specific tools and equipment. In addition to information regarding whether a pipe design can be produced or not, the software provides data about production cycle times etc. This information was useful for the discussions in the team at Scania as it enabled more detailed comparisons between alternative pipe designs.

Dayco also performed some of the design work needed for project Alpha. While DFC Tech's full-time representative in the team focused on the communication with Scania and the other suppliers (e.g. design of pipes and hoses and their interplay with other components), an engineer at Dayco took care of different details needed for the finished drawings (e.g. tolerances). The finished drawings were then sent to DFC Tech's representative who saved them in Scania's system so that the component could get a higher status in the system. The engineer at Dayco was also involved in, for example, upgrading the design of currently produced products. Thereby, this connection with Dayco also provided an important link between DFC Tech and Dayco's production units. As remarked by one respondent at Scania: "It is valuable that the engineer who performs the design also knows the person who will bend the pipe."

4.4.8. Summary of the Case

In different ways, this case shows how close collaboration between several different firms in the development team facilitated the development of pipes and hoses for the new truck model. Although DFC Tech had the main responsibility for developing the pipes and hoses and related components, the frequent communication and interaction with Scania and the other suppliers in the team was crucial for achieving the results. To summarize, the most important firms in the network that evolved around the relationship between DFC Tech and Scania are illustrated in Fig. 40.

Regarding the results of the development work in project Alpha, representatives from Scania as well as DFC Tech expressed that the close collaboration between the involved firms certainly contributed to reducing development time, product cost and weight. As described above, pipes and hoses is often a neglected area. However, the attention on pipes and hoses in this project, combined with the interactive work in the team, in several cases helped to reduce the unit cost by up to 40–50% compared to the "normal" unit cost for similar components.

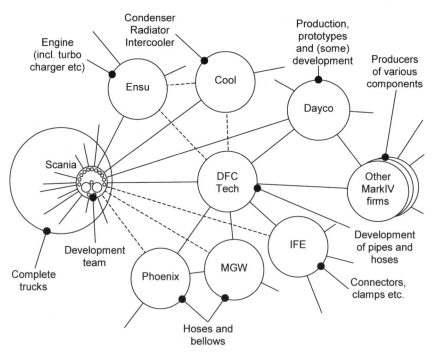

Fig. 40. The Network Around the Relationship Between DFC Tech and Scania.

5. ANALYSIS – RESOURCES AND DEPENDENCIES

This paper is concerned with the organizing of interactive product development. The overall purpose is to explore dependencies and how interactive product development may be organized with regard to these dependencies. By analyzing dependencies related to products and other resources, i.e. *what* needs to be organized, an understanding for *how* interactive product development may be organized can be achieved. This first part of the analysis is focused on the features of different resources and the dependencies between these resources. Next part of the analysis is focused on the organizing of product development in the resource structure.

With the empirical data presented in Section 4 as a basis, the three research issues identified in Section 2.4 are explored and elaborated upon in the analysis. The first part of the analysis is structured in the following way.

- In Section 5.1, the analysis is focused on products, the components within specific products, and how these components are related through various (technical) dependencies.
- In Section 5.2, production facilities are analyzed. Requirements regarding the utilization of production equipment, as well as dependencies between production facilities are analyzed. Also dependencies between production facilities/equipment and products are analyzed.
- In Section 5.3, business units are analyzed as resources. In addition, dependencies between business units and different business units' requirements regarding the utilization of different resources are analyzed.
- In Section 5.4, business relationships are analyzed as resources. In addition, Dependencies within relationships as well as between several different relationships are analyzed with regard to the other three resource categories.
- In Section 5.5, the results of the analysis in terms of dependencies between different resources are summarized.

The second part of the analysis is presented in Section 6. This analysis is focused on the organizing of interactive product development with regard to *how* dependencies between resources can be dealt with. That section has been divided into two main parts. In Section 6.1, the analysis is focused on how dependencies may be dealt with within as well as between business relationships. In Section 6.2, the use of development teams is analyzed.

Finally, Section 7 contains a concluding discussion where implications of the study are discussed in relation to previous research and conclusions are drawn. Now, we turn to the analysis of resources and dependencies, starting with "products."

5.1. Products

When the P2 platform was developed, each one of the new car models had to fulfill various different performance criteria regarding "handling" (i.e. how the car feels to drive), comfort, styling and design, quality, safety, environment, weight, cost and so forth. For trucks, there are similar requirements, though, since it is a commercial vehicle, some requirements are given different "weights" compared with those of a car. For instance, performance criteria such as reliability, fuel consumption and maintenance are crucial for a truck. Both the car and the truck consist of a large number of components and the interplay between the components influences the performance of the car or the truck. Therefore, each individual component, as well as how it relates to other components, is crucial to fulfill various performance criteria. In this section, the analysis is focused on various dependencies between components that need to be considered during product development.

5.1.1. Dependencies Between Components Related to Pipes and Hoses

The main function of the pipes and hoses developed for Scania was to enable a certain flow of gas or liquid, at certain pressures and temperatures and without leakages, between different components in the engine compartment. This function was realized by combining various components such as steel pipes, clamps, couplings, rubber hoses, fasteners, and bellows into a complete pipe. Bellows were thread on to steel pipes and fastened with clamps, and specific couplings were designed to be welded onto steel pipes and so on. Thus, these components are connected to each other through various physical interfaces. Further, the design of each component, and the interfaces between components, influence the function of the pipe as a whole (e.g. in terms of flow), implying various functional dependencies between the components.

In most cases, standard components were used for clamps and couplings. This implied that the interfaces to these components had to be regarded as "given." Other components, such as steel pipes and bellows, were specifically designed. However, the steel pipes were developed based on standard dimensions. This mainly implied that the pipe diameter and thickness were regarded as "given" within certain intervals (i.e. available standard dimensions), while the pipes could be bent to nearly any geometrical shape. In other words, certain *features* of the pipes were regarded as "given," while other features could be modified. The "given" pipe diameter also implied that certain features (mainly the diameter) of the bellows, that were thread onto the steel pipes, had to be regarded as "given." This implied that there were dependencies between specific features of these connected components.

The complete pipes and hoses, in turn, connect different components in the engine compartment and, thereby, provide different systems with specific

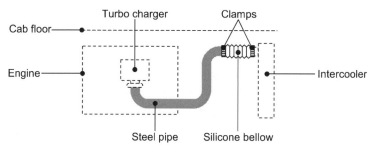

Fig. 41. The Intercooler Pipe and Related Components in the Engine Compartment.

functionality. The expansion tank is one component in the engine cooling system and, since Scania chose to use an existing design, the hose connections on the expansion tank had to be regarded as "given." A closer examination of the intercooler pipe shows that it has direct physical interfaces to the turbo charger and the intercooler respectively (see Fig. 41). The primary function of the intercooler system is to reduce the air temperature before the air goes into the engine. The intercooler pipe is, however, only one of a number of components in the intercooler system (other components are the turbo charger, the intercooler, the air inlet manifold and another pipe between the intercooler and the air inlet manifold). These components are needed to provide cooled air to the engine, implying various functional dependencies between these components and the intercooler pipe. Moreover, the intercooler pipe is warmed up by the hot air flowing through it. Therefore, to avoid damaging cables and plastic components in the engine compartment, enough space must be left between the intercooler pipe and components that are sensible to heat. Thus, there were also spatial dependencies between components.

When the development of the intercooler pipe started, the connection on the intercooler had already been designed. This implied that also the diameter of the intercooler pipe could be regarded as "given." Further, an existing turbo charger design was used, which implied that its connection to the intercooler pipe was "given." It was also known that the pipe would have to stand a certain temperature and handle a certain air pressure and flow. Further, some preliminary data regarding the geometrical space was available. The engine and the intercooler had been placed on the truck frame and the cab floor had been positioned in relation to these components. Hence, several interfaces to components in the engine compartment were more or less "given" from start.

When developing the intercooler pipe, it soon turned out that the motions of the suspended cab implied a risk for clashes with the pipe and there was a risk that the heat from the intercooler pipe would damage the cab floor insulation. Thus, there was a spatial (environmental) dependence between the pipe and the cab floor that had not been foreseen. An adaptation of the cab floor insulation could help, though, this might have a negative influence on the noise-level in the cab. Hence, also functional dependencies between components in the cab had to be considered.

Therefore, alternative designs were required. The pipe diameter had initially been regarded as "given," but it turned out that it could be reduced without affecting the airflow negatively. However, even if the pipe diameter was reduced and the connection on the turbo charger was adapted with a special forged pipe knee there was not enough space available. Therefore, the turbo charger was re-designed by turning it 180 degrees. To do this, however, various physical and functional dependencies between the turbo charger and the air intake as well as the lubrication pipe had to be considered. Hence, the re-design of the pipe implied that various different dependencies had to be considered, and dependencies that were initially regarded as "given" had to be reconsidered.

Moreover, there were frequent changes of components to which the pipes and hoses had various physical, functional, or spatial interfaces. Since the pipes and hoses connect several different components, almost any such change implied a need for a changed pipe and/or hose design. Changing the position of the expansion tank, moving the pipe connection on the intercooler, moving the air compressor, or changing a cross member in the frame implied that the "pattern" of dependencies related to the pipes changed. Thus, a certain dynamics had to be considered.

5.1.2. Dependencies Between Components Related to the Seats

To realize a front seat, a number of components such as a chassis, a seat cushion frame, a backrest frame (including headrest), foam, and upholstery are joined by various physical interfaces. Each one of these components, in turn, consists of a number of even smaller components joined by various physical interfaces. The seat chassis, for instance, consists of sliding rails and various other components needed for the positioning of the seat. This realization of a seat implies that various functions related to, for instance, driving comfort and safety can be provided.

The case showed that the side airbag that is integrated in the backrest of the front seat has an interface to the seat upholstery. The geometrical space needed for the airbag implies a physical dependence to the upholstery. At the same time, a functional dependence is created between the airbag and the upholstery since the textiles (or leather) must come apart at a particular seam when the airbag inflates. Thus, when developing a specific interface, both physical and functional dependencies between components may have to be considered.

Further, several moving parts are required in the seat chassis to enable adjustment of the seat into different positions. To avoid clashes between components, this implies that various spatial dependencies need to be considered. Therefore, when developing the seat as a whole, as well as various moving components in the seat chassis, an "envelope" was specified, within which these components were allowed to move. Thereby, spatial dependencies between components were easier to consider.

The physical interfaces between various moving components (mainly in the seat chassis) are essential for avoiding play. However, the design and position of the electrical motors and the interfaces between various components in the electrically maneuvered seat chassis initially caused trouble in terms of play and noise. Even a small play in the chassis can imply that the top of the backrest can be moved several centimeters, which is not acceptable. Thereby, the case illustrates how physical interfaces between a few components in the seat chassis affected the functionality of the seat as a whole.

When developing the rear seat for the Volvo V70, both the rear seatbelts and the rear seat locks were integrated with the backrest. This implies that, these components have physical and functional interfaces to the backrest frame, though, there is no direct physical interface between them. Therefore, moving the position of the seatbelts may not influence the position of the rear seat locks. There is, however, a direct functional dependence between these components since moving the seatbelts may influence the forces exerted on the rear seat locks, see Fig. 42. Thus, a specific component may have different types of interfaces that are interrelated, to various other components.

The dependencies between the upholstery and the airbag described above are related to specific properties of the seam and the fabric (or leather). At the same time, the function of the airbag and the physical space needed for the airbag is independent of, for instance, the color of the upholstery. Thus, the side airbag has dependencies not to the upholstery per se but to specific features of it. Further, the backrest frame for the V70 was made by aluminum (instead of steel), mainly

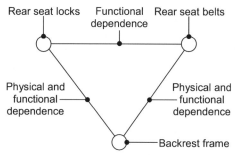

Fig. 42. Dependencies Between the Rear Seat Belts, the Backrest Frame and the Rear Seat Locks.

because that implied possibilities to reduce the weight. In this way, a specific feature of this material was utilized while other features of aluminum, such as resistance to corrosion, were not utilized. Aluminum is also less resistant to fatigue than steel, though, this feature was of less importance in this specific case.

All components in a seat are assembled into a delimited physical unit and there are only a few direct physical interfaces between the seat and the rest of the car (four screws joining the seat chassis and the car floor and a few cable connectors). However, the clash between the electrical motor and the air duct illustrates that developing a seat also implies that several other physical (or rather spatial) interfaces are created between the seat and other components, and need to be considered too.

Further, the integration of a side airbag in the front seat backrest implies that functional dependencies are created between the seat and several other safety-related components in the car such as the airbag control system, other airbags, and the seatbelts. In addition, functional dependencies are created between various components in the seat frame and the car body to provide safety in terms of side impact protection. Various plastic seat components as well as the upholstery also need to be matched with other interior details regarding, for instance, surface structures and colors. Thus, styling and design implies dependencies between seat components and other interior components. There are also dependencies between the seat and the steering wheel, the pedals and the instrument panel related to comfort and handling. Furthermore, when developing the seats, problems were detected where specific vibrations from the engine were transmitted to the seat frame. Hence, various physical, functional, spatial, and environmental dependencies, which reach far beyond the seat's physical interfaces, need to be considered (see Fig. 43).

When developing the front seats for the P2 platform, the basic design used in the previous models (the S/V70) was "carried over" to the new platform. This implied that the need for new development was reduced, though, it also implied dependencies to the seats used in the previous models. In addition, many seat components would be used in several different seat variants as well as across the different car models on the platform. This implied dependencies between car models as well as between different variants of specific components.

5.1.3. Dependencies Between Components Related to the Electrical System
When considering the electrical system developed for Volvo, components such as nodes and gateways are placed at different positions in the car (often close to specific applications). This implies that these components have no direct physical interfaces to one another, though, they are physically connected, mainly by various cable harnesses. These cable harnesses, in turn, consist of a number of physically

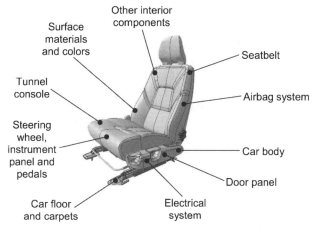

Surface materials and colors

Other interior components

Seatbelt

Tunnel console

Airbag system

Steering wheel, instrument panel and pedals

Car body

Door panel

Car floor and carpets

Electrical system

Fig. 43. Examples of Dependencies Between a Seat and Other Components in the Car.
Note: Picture used with permission from Volvo Car Corporation.

connected components. At the end of the cables, there are connectors, and cable ducts keep the cables together. While some cables supply components with electrical power, other cables (e.g. data bus cables) are needed for the transmission of signal information between components. The nodes and gateways such as the CEM and the REM, in turn, consist of a number of plastic components, relays, fuses, circuit boards, integrated circuits, electronic components and so on that have different physical interfaces. Also in this case various spatial dependencies between components had to be considered due to potential heat transfer and interference between components.

The high degree of customization of the complete car implies that there are numerous possible variants of the complete cable harnesses. It is, however, not possible to design and produce a specific cable harness for each individual car. Instead, the cable harnesses are produced according to certain predetermined configuration levels. This, however, implies that a car that does not have all options included in a certain configuration level may be equipped with more cables than necessary. In other words, the need for standardizing the cable harnesses implies that certain features of these components may not be utilized in each individual car.

A component such as a speed sensor has a simple physical interface (i.e. a connector) to the electrical system. Since a speed sensor is used for various different functions, however, there are numerous functional dependencies between the speed sensor and other components in the electrical system. Further, functional dependencies are created between the engine management system and the brake system to provide the anti-spin function. There are also functional dependencies between the mobile telephone, the road and traffic information system and the audio system. If the seat can be regarded as a physically delimited unit, this case illustrates that developing the electrical system rather implies dealing with and creating a complex pattern of functional dependencies, involving nearly all electronic components and applications in the car.

This complexity could, however, be reduced by standardizing the communication interface (i.e. the communication protocols) between various electronic components. At the same time, the problems with noise and interference illustrate that even if interfaces are standardized, not all dependencies between components can be anticipated.

The use of multiplex technology also implies that new functionality may be added to the car, without re-design of any physical components. By implementing changes in the software code, existing components can be used in new ways and in new combinations. Thus, new features can be added, even after the design of physical components has been completed.

Further, physical interfaces between the cable harness and the car body implied that a change of the car body design required a change of the cable harness and the cable duct. Hence, even if the exact physical location of components related to the electrical system may be of less importance for its functionality, its many physical interfaces to other parts of the car influence the (physical) design of the components in the electrical system.

5.1.4. Summary

In all three cases, numerous physical, functional, spatial, and environmental dependencies between components were found that need to be considered when developing a product. As will be illustrated further on, these different categories of dependencies (in particular physical and functional dependencies) also influence how resources within the other three resource categories relate to each other, i.e. these product-related dependencies have implications for the organizing of interactive product development. Further, various combinations of these product-related dependencies often need to be considered, and some dependencies are created or appear in the development process. While some dependencies influence the design of a few components only, other dependencies influence numerous different components that often have no direct physical interfaces. In addition, the "pattern" of dependencies that needs to be considered changes as the product design evolves. Even some interfaces between components that were initially regarded as "given," non-existing, or non-important had to be (re-) considered and/or changed. Even this brief analysis of the studied products has revealed complex patterns of (technical) dependencies between components that need to be considered when developing a product. However, the product being developed also has to be related to various other resources. This, among other things, is analyzed in the following sections.

5.2. Production Facilities

In this section, the analysis is focused on the second category in the resource model, production facilities. First, production facilities are analyzed mainly in terms of investments and requirements for utilizing these investments. Then, the analysis is extended and dependencies to other production facilities as well as to products are considered.

5.2.1. The Production Facility as a Resource

5.2.1.1. Investments in production resources. When regarding a production facility as a resource, investments that have been made in various production resources need to be considered. Dayco has two production facilities for producing pipes. One is dedicated to producing truck components and the other to producing components for cars. In addition to the buildings, investments have been made in different production-related equipment such as bending machines, welds, forklifts, and so on. At different points in time, worn-out machines have been replaced by new ones and old but functioning equipment has been upgraded. For instance, older bending machines have been complemented with systems for numerical control. Investments have also been made in MRP-systems, systems for quality control, and vast knowledge and experience has been built up over time regarding how to run machines, plan production and so on. Part of the production equipment has been used over long periods of time, often several decades. However, some investments in equipment, such as product specific tools and jigs, have been made for specific products and, therefore, such equipment has been in use for more limited time periods. When more production capacity has been needed, investments in additional production equipment have been made.

When regarding the assembly of cars, the building of Volvo's Torslanda plant began in 1960 and, in addition to investments in different assembly lines, various investments have been made in the buildings, the paint shop, the body shop and so on at different points in time. For producing the different P2 models, large investments were needed in the assembly shop to enable assembly of complete modules, to increase the degree of automation, and to improve ergonomics. Even if future models had been considered when investments were made in the body shop for the 850 and S/V70 models, the P2 models required additional investments. However, when regarding the paint shop, existing equipment could largely be re-used. Much time and money was also dedicated to educating the work force. Further, when the Volvo S80 was introduced in 1998, Volvo continued to assemble the S70 for about two years in the same plant. This implied that the new assembly line for the P2 models had to be adapted to space and logistics requirements set by the S70 assembly line. Even if the S70 assembly line was later removed, these adaptations left "imprints" on the layout of the P2 assembly line.

Delphi has several different production facilities that are used for the production of cable harnesses and components for the electrical system. Even if previously made investments in these facilities could be further utilized, the P2 models required additional investments in Megamos and Delphi's respective plants to reach the required production volumes of electronic circuits and cable harnesses. Some of these investments, such as the assembly tables used for cable harnesses, were made for specific products while other investments, such as equipment for cutting cables, can be utilized for many different products. Delphi as well as Lear (after deciding to move the seat assembly from Bengtsfors to Torslanda) established new assembly plants (MAU:s) adjacent to Volvo. Even if this implied some freedom to create new production layouts, hire new staff, build up new control systems, and make investments in production equipment, the design of these facilities did not start with a "blank paper." Lear, for instance, utilized an already existing building and they tried to move some staff and equipment from the plant in Bengtsfors to the new facility.

Thus, production facilities are seldom built up "from scratch." Instead, different investments have been made at different points in time and with different time-scope (see Fig. 44). At each point in time (t) there are a number of production resources that still need to be utilized over some period of time to economize on previously made investments (illustrated by the shaded areas). To utilize this equipment over its full lifetime, however, investments in additional production equipment are required. Thereby, the time-perspective is further extended into the future and a specific investment also influences what can be done in the future. The result is a complex pattern of embedded production resources. This, in turn, influences how these production resources can be adapted and, therefore, production facilities in many cases can be regarded as "heavy" resources. Consequently, other resources may have to be adapted to the existing resource structure in a specific production facility.

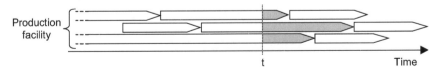

Fig. 44.   Investments in a Production Facility at Different Points in Time.

5.2.1.2. Requirements for the utilization of production resources. In order to utilize a specific production facility and its production equipment in an efficient way, various requirements need to be considered. While an almost infinite number of different requirements can be identified, the (brief) analysis in this section is focused on production equipment and technology, the work force, and various support systems (i.e. what is often categorized as "machine," "man" and "method"; see e.g. Imai, 1986, p. 237), as well as how these resources interact.

Both steel and aluminum pipes can be manufactured in Dayco's production facilities, though, existing production equipment cannot be used for producing plastic pipes. Production of plastic pipes would imply comprehensive investments in new production equipment, such as molding machines. Thus, from the point of view of Dayco's production facilities, the selection of a production technology (material) that is adapted to existing production equipment is essential. In a similar way, the production equipment at Phoenix and MGW influence what materials and geometries can be provided for hoses and bellows, and Megamos' production equipment influences what type of soldering can be performed on the circuit boards. Moreover, the production equipment in the respective production facilities imply restrictions in terms of what volumes can be produced, with what quality, and at what speed (e.g. influencing delivery time). Thus, requirements in terms of both production technology and capability of the production equipment need to be considered.

Further, how to bend a specific pipe to achieve a desired geometry can be simulated in computers, but the outcome is also highly dependent on the machine operator's knowledge and experience. The production and assembly of cable harnesses require much manual work and is therefore highly dependent on the (often tacit) knowledge held by different people in the work force. Specific knowledge regarding production technologies, how to handle production equipment, quality assurance, production planning and so on is essential for the utilization of the various production equipment in a production facility. Further, the assembly of cable harnesses requires a lot of manual work and so does the final assembly of the complete car. Furthermore, the use of pre-assembly stations at Volvo's final assembly plant implies that the workload here can be reduced compared with the workload of the main line. Thereby, better working conditions can be achieved for skilled senior workers. Therefore, the size of the workforce, abilities of individual operators as well as how work can be divided between various different tasks need to be considered.

The production facilities that have been studied in the cases also have a number of different support systems and routines for controlling and monitoring the production operations. There are, for instance, support systems for material handling, production planning and quality assurance. These systems aim at increasing the utilization of different production resources, though, they also have certain limitations that need to be considered. For instance, the number of different product components that can be handled may be limited, which implies that the possibilities to handle large numbers of product variants are limited. Further, systems for production control may be designed according to different basic principles (e.g. "push" or "pull") which has implications for the facility layout, production sequence, the need for buffering material, batch sizes, set-up times and so on. Therefore, it may be difficult to implement Just-In-Time in a production facility, if this is not supported by different systems used for material planning, quality control and logistics. Thus, different support systems influence how production resources can be utilized.

Furthermore, the cases illustrate that the utilization of resources in a production facility is dependent on how various resources are related to each other, for instance in terms of assembly sequence. In Volvo and Scania's respective assembly plants, the positioning of assembly stations along the line determines the assembly sequence and, to utilize available resources, it is essential to find a suitable balance between stations in terms of staffing, work load and cycle times. Placing several assembly stations with high workloads and long cycle times in a row may cause balancing losses. Further, the design and sequence of assembly activities influence the need for staffing as well as various ergonomic conditions. It also influences material supply along the line, which needs to be related to, for instance, availability of handling equipment and floor space.

Hence, various requirements need to be considered in order to ensure efficient utilization of production facilities. While such requirements can be related to any particular production equipment, it is also important to consider how this production equipment is utilized in combination with other resources in a production facility. Moreover, the production equipment (and the interdependencies between different equipment) needs to be related to products. This is done in the following sections.

5.2.2. Production Facilities and Products

5.2.2.1. One facility, several different products. In this section, implications related to the fact that a specific production facility often produces several different products are analyzed. As described above, the S80 and the S70 were produced in parallel in Volvo's Torslanda plant for about two years. Now the S70 has been phased out and the plant is not only used for assembly of the S80, but also for the new V70 and the XC90 (the S60 is assembled in the plant in Ghent, together with the V70). However, when the production of the S80 started, a decision had not yet been taken regarding the production of the XC90. This implied that additional investments were later required in Volvo's assembly plant to enable the assembly of the XC90. Also Scania assembles several different models in the same production facilities. By combining different chassis, axles, engines, gearboxes, cabs and so on, a large number of different models and variants can be obtained. By producing different models on the same final assembly line, the total production volume on the line is increased which enables a higher degree of utilization of the production facility's resources. However, different models and variants require different amounts of work. It is, for instance, not possible to assemble a large number of full spec cars in a row. This implies that the mix of products needs to be adapted to how the assembly line is balanced.

One of Dayco's two plants has been dedicated to truck components (i.e. large pipe dimensions) and produces several different pipes related to air and fluid distribution, as well as other components such as consoles for splashguards. Also Delphi's different facilities produce various different products. In addition to the various cable harnesses produced for Volvo, the facility in Spain produces cable harnesses for other car manufacturers. The production volume of a specific product is in most cases too small to motivate the required investments in production equipment. Therefore, the possibilities to switch between different products, i.e. altering the product mix, is also important for reaching a high level of utilization of the production equipment. Thus, from these production facilities' point of view, it is important not to be dependent on the production of a single product.

Further, Volvo started production of the different P2-models during a five-year period (S80 in 1998 – XC90 in 2002). Thus, the different products that are produced in parallel in the production facilities have often been introduced at different points in time (t_i), see Fig. 45. Further, different products are produced during different periods of time (t_p). Moreover, the time-scope of the products often does not coincide with the time-scope for the production equipment needed for producing it. In this way, a complex pattern of dependencies between products and production facilities is created over time.

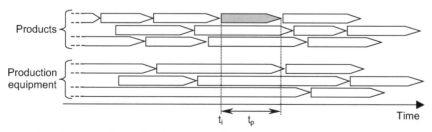

Fig. 45. Time Dependencies Between Production Resources and pProducts.

5.2.2.2. Adaptation of products and production equipment. As shown above, there is some degree of flexibility in Dayco's production facilities regarding product materials since both steel and aluminum pipes can be produced. However, the flexibility in this dimension is still limited since, for example, plastic pipes would require investments in equipment for injection molding, which is a totally different production technology. When it comes to the shape of the steel pipe there is a relatively high degree of flexibility, i.e. many different physical geometries can be produced without additional investments in production equipment. By considering different basic requirements when designing a new steel pipe, for example regarding pipe diameter and bending radii, the pipe can be produced with existing (standard) tools. This case illustrates that Dayco's facilities can be regarded as "heavy" with regard to the investments made in a specific production technology. While this resource heaviness may require far-reaching adaptations of some product features (e.g. choice of material), it has less influence on other product features (such as the shape of the pipe).

All clamps and nearly all couplings used for the pipes and hoses developed for Scania and many connectors used for the electrical system developed for Volvo are standard components. By using standard components, existing production equipment can be used. Thereby, the use of standard components may be regarded as an adaptation of the component design to existing production equipment. However, complex products with high demands on product performance and design, such as cars and trucks, put high demands on the interplay between components. Therefore, in many cases, it was not possible to use standard components. In all three cases, it was necessary to develop components with specific designs for specific needs, such as bellows, bent pipes, seat frames, rear seat locks, electronic circuits, and cable ducts. The pipes could be produced with existing production equipment, and the bellows only required limited investments in specific production equipment.

However, various plastic components developed for the electrical system and the seats have a specific design that requires unique molds. The molds are relatively expensive, implying a need for high production volumes to pay off this investment. This also means that once the product design has been "frozen" and the mold has been finished it is costly to change the component design. In other words, the mold can be considered as a more or less "fixed" resource. In a similar way, various other components that are stamped, casted, deep drawn, and so on require investments in specific production equipment.

Further, a plastic component must be designed with proper draft angles so that it can easily be ejected from the mold cavity. Other requirements concern the injection speed and the ability to evenly fill the mold with plastic material. A complex or poorly designed component may require several injection holes, which increases the cost for manufacturing the mold. It may also result in longer production cycle times. The same applies for components with advanced geometries requiring integration of certain moving parts in the mold. In addition, both size and geometry of the component will affect the possibilities to produce more than one component in one molding cycle, thereby affecting production cycle time and cost. In addition, the selection of plastic material will affect the ability to fill the mold as well as the risk of shrinkage. Thus, even if the component design is specific, and mainly determines the design of the mold, the plastic component also needs to be adapted to certain requirements determined by the mold.

Even if a mold is developed for a specific plastic component, the injection-molding machine can be used also for producing other plastic components by switching to other molds. Thus, while the mold is specifically designed for the plastic component, the injection-molding machine can be regarded as standard production equipment. This implies a certain degree of flexibility in this particular dimension, though there are also dependencies between the mold and the injection-molding machine. The size and geometry of the component that can be produced will, to some extent, be dependent on the injection-molding machine since that is related to, among other things, what molding pressure can be achieved. This, in turn, implies restrictions on product design. Thus, utilizing standard production equipment such as a molding machine provides some flexibility since different plastic components can be produced (with different molds). Still, however, a number of specific requirements related to the molding machine need to be considered when developing the product.

5.2.2.3. Production sequence and product design. In Fig. 46, different production steps for a pipe are illustrated. In each of these production steps, different production equipment is utilized. The pipe must be bent before the fasteners are welded onto it, since they would cause problems in the bending machine and

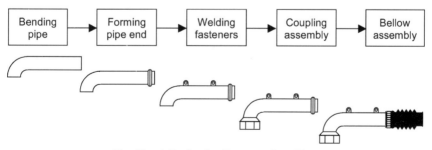

Fig. 46. A Production Sequence for a Pipe.

the bellow cannot be assembled before the end of the pipe has been formed. Thus, physical interfaces between components create dependencies between different production equipment. Also the sequence of production activities largely depends on the design of individual components and the (physical) interfaces between them.

When assembling a front seat, the side airbag must be assembled to the seat frame before the upholstery is put on. The design of the cable harnesses influences in what sequence cables, connectors and cable ducts are assembled to a complete cable harness and so on. Hence, also in the other cases, the development of components and interfaces implied dependencies between various production equipment.

As shown above, designing a pipe implies creating various physical (and spatial) dependencies to other components in the truck. These dependencies influence at what station on the final assembly line the pipe can be assembled and with what tools. In a similar way, physical interfaces between the cable harnesses and other components in the car make it necessary to first assemble cable harnesses and then the floor carpets in the car. Then, among other things, seats may be assembled into the car. Consequently, these requirements regarding sequence influence the layout of the assembly plant. Further, when designing the coolant pipes, the demands for fast and simple assembly required that the pipes were equipped with quick connectors. In a similar way, there were design requirements related to the assembly of seats and cable harnesses into the car. Hence, the cases illustrate how the product design influenced assembly, though, also requirements related to assembly influenced the product design.

Dependencies between products and production sequence seem to be primarily related to physical interfaces between components. However, the pre-assembly of modules enables Volvo to test certain functions before the module is assembled in the car. Thus, also functional dependencies between components need to be considered with regard to production sequence and plant layout.

Further, some components that are assembled on Volvo's final assembly line require more space than others do and to provide enough space for the supplied material, several large components cannot be assembled at subsequent stations. Hence, product interfaces, and thus the assembly sequence, are related to the need for floor space and material supply along the assembly line. In addition, these influences the extent components can, or need to be, pre-assembled. This also influences the plant layout as well as various other issues such as the need for specific handling equipment.

5.2.3. Dependencies Between Production Facilities
Pipes and hoses that are produced in Dayco's plants are assembled into the truck in Scania's assembly plant. Further, the seats and cable harnesses that are

produced and assembled in Lear and Delphi's respective plants are assembled into the car in Volvo's assembly plant and so forth. In this section, the analysis is focused on what dependencies this may create between these production facilities.

5.2.3.1. Dependencies related to produced quantities and time. What pipes are produced in Dayco's production facility is related to Scania's production and assembly of trucks. Therefore, coordination between Dayco and Scania's respective plants in terms of quantity and time for delivery is required. Dayco have tried to reduce set-up times and thereby adapt their production equipment to the smaller batch sizes required by Scania. However, in some cases Dayco have better possibilities to utilize their production capacity if larger batches are produced and then partitioned into several smaller deliveries to Scania. Thus, in this way, ordered quantities can be matched with available production capacity, which can increase the utilization of production resources.

Further, modules are delivered from different MAU:s to Volvo's assembly plant. This also implies dependencies between these MAU:s and Volvo's assembly plant in terms of quantity and delivery time. However, since the modules are delivered in sequence, the production activities in the MAU:s are also dependent on the sequence in which Volvo assemble the cars. Furthermore, there are only a few hours between the order reaching a MAU and the delivery of complete modules at Volvo's assembly line. For modules that are assembled at the start of the assembly line, there are only 4 hours from order to delivery. Towards the end of the line, the corresponding figure is about 12 hours. This implies strong time-dependencies between the MAU:s and Volvo's assembly line. The differences in time from order to delivery (4–12 hours) imply that different MAU:s face very different requirements. The strong time-dependence also puts high demands on the transport and logistics between the MAU:s and Volvo's assembly plant. Due to the strong dependencies between these facilities in terms of quantity and time, a disturbance in a specific MAU (for example related to inferior quality) quickly results in disturbances in Volvo's assembly plant as well as in other MAU:s. Thus, what production activities are performed in one production facility are heavily dependent on production activities performed in other facilities. Moreover, Delphi and Lear's respective MAU:s produce modules for delivery to only one other facility (i.e. Volvo's assembly plant). From the individual MAU's point of view, this implies that the possibilities to influence the product mix and thereby the utilization of production resources is very limited. Instead, the MAU is highly dependent on the production volumes in Volvo's assembly plant and the mix between different product variants.

5.2.3.2. Adaptations between production facilities. In addition to dependencies between facilities in terms of produced quantity and delivery time, the cases illustrate how various adaptations between production facilities are necessary. The transport of complete modules requires special racks to keep the modules in the right sequence and protect them from being damaged during the transport. These racks need to be mutually adapted, for example in terms of size, to requirements set by the MAU:s, by Volvo's assembly plant as well as by the equipment used for transporting them. The sequenced deliveries of modules have also required far-reaching adaptations of the MAU:s in terms of, for instance, plant layout, staffing, and production planning. To ensure on-time deliveries with approved quality, several specific routines have been developed between the different MAU:s and Volvo's assembly plant regarding, for instance, quality assessment. It is important to "calibrate" how quality is measured and to ensure that workers at Volvo and the different MAU:s respectively "speak the same language" to avoid misunderstandings.

In addition, the localization of the MAU:s close to Volvo's assembly plant can be regarded as an adaptation to requirements set by Volvo's assembly plant. If it were not for the short time between order and delivery of modules, the MAU:s could have been located elsewhere. The specific adaptations to Volvo's assembly plant imply strong mutual dependencies between the MAU:s and Volvo's assembly plant. The more adaptations between these production facilities, the stronger the dependencies become between them.

When regarding Dayco's production plants, the adaptations to Scania have not been that radical, though there have been some adaptations of, for instance, the quality control system and routines for deliveries. Even if these adaptations have been performed for a specific auto manufacturer's assembly plant, the cases illustrate that such adaptations often imply developments of certain features that also other production facilities can benefit from. Adapting routines for quality assurance for a specific production facility may imply that also other facilities can benefit from improved quality.

Further, in order to handle the coordination of orders and deliveries between production facilities, different forms of EDI (Electronic Data Interchange) solutions had been implemented in the different cases. With these data links, coordination between production facilities regarding orders, deliveries, quality assessment, invoicing and so on can be dealt with electronically. This reduces the need for manual administrative work, but also requires investments in specific electronic connections between facilities.

Thus, there are various dependencies between production facilities related to the matching of plans, the adaptation of routines and processes as well as different technical adaptations. Such adaptations may improve the possibilities to utilize the production equipment in the respective facilities, but it may also reduce flexibility regarding possibilities to combine different production facilities. It is also relevant to consider how dependencies between production facilities can be related to products and product design. This is elaborated in more detail in next section.

5.2.3.3. Dependencies between production facilities related to product design.
While mainly steel pipes are produced in Dayco's production facility, other components needed for assembly of a complete pipe such as bellows, hoses, and couplings, are produced in other facilities. The decision to use bellows to compensate for the engine vibrations entailed dependencies between Phoenix and Dayco's respective production facilities. In addition, the hot air in the intercooler pipe and the hot coolant in the coolant pipe required silicone bellows, implying dependencies to MGW's production facility. Hence, specific product requirements in combination with interfaces between components entailed specific dependencies between production facilities.

Also components for the seats and the electrical system are produced in various different production facilities. As mentioned above, the side airbag needs to be assembled on the seat frame before the upholstery is put on. In this way, the component interfaces imply that dependencies are created between Autoliv's facility that produces the side airbag and Lear's seat assembly plant. This case also illustrates how the physical component interfaces, and thus the assembly sequence, result in dependencies between the facilities producing the luggage net, the rear seats and the complete car. Moreover, if there is an incident with, for instance, a side airbag (e.g. it inflates accidentally) Volvo requires that individual components, such as the gas generator, can be traced all the way back to its origin. This makes it possible to trace other individual cars that have side airbags containing components with similar faults. This, in turn, requires a special system for identifying individual components (e.g. using bar codes), which entails dependencies between facilities that produce and assemble the cars, the seats, the side airbag module and its various components.

The development of specific component designs also implied that specific production tools had to be developed. Different plastic components on the seats, the bellows used for the pipes and various plastic components in the electrical system required specific production tools. In most cases, these tools are produced in special production facilities and then delivered to the facility where the component will be produced. These deliveries may not be frequently recurring, though, this illustrates that the output from one production facility may be used as a production resource in another facility. Hence, there are other dependencies between production facilities than those related to what sequence a specific product is produced and assembled in.

In all three cases, various alternative production techniques as well as possible production facilities were continuously considered during the development work. The designs of steel pipes, bellows, and other components were continuously checked with the production facilities that would produce these components and assemble them into the truck. In a similar way, the development of components for the seats and the electrical system was continuously related to several different production facilities producing rear seat locks, air bags, electrically maneuvered chassis, cable harnesses, plastic components and so on. Hence, even if this analysis has illustrated that component interfaces in various ways influence how production facilities relate to each other, also specific production facilities and their relations to other facilities influenced the design of and the interfaces between components. Further, alternative component designs and production techniques, such as the use of a flexible steel pipe instead of a bellow or the use of two-component molding for integrating a gasket in a plastic detail, were continuously considered. This, in turn, implied that neither component design, nor dependencies between production facilities could be regarded as "given" when developing the different products.

5.2.4. A Network of Production Facilities

Thus far, the analysis has been focused on single production facilities as well as dependencies between specific production facilities. However, as shown above, Dayco as well as Delphi's production facilities produce several different products that are delivered to several other suppliers' plants as well as different auto manufacturers' final assembly plants. Further, Scania and Volvo's respective assembly plants, Dayco's production facilities, the MAU:s, Delphi's various plants and so on are dependent on deliveries from several different suppliers' production facilities. As mentioned in the case, Volvo has about 175 direct suppliers to their plants assembling the different P2 models.

Further, since Dayco has limited possibilities to paint pipes in their own facilities, painting is performed in another supplier's production facility. This in some cases implies that pipes that are produced in Dayco's facility are sent to this other facility for painting and then sent back again for assembly with other components before it is sent to an auto manufacturer's assembly plant. In this way, the production process for a complete pipe is divided between different production facilities. Thus, from a specific production facility's point of view, the dependencies identified thus far need to be dealt with in relation to several different production facilities. This results in a complex pattern of dependencies between production facilities (see Fig. 47) that needs to be considered in order to enable efficient utilization of various production resources.

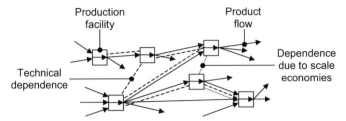

Fig. 47. Dependencies Between Production Facilities.

5.3. Summary

In this section, the analysis has been focused on production facilities. Various conditions for efficient resource utilization have been analyzed, mainly from a production facility's point of view.

The analysis illustrated how investments made in production facilities at different points in time and with different time scope, in combination with the production of different products that are introduced at different points in time and with different lifetimes, result in a complex pattern of dependencies between different resources. New products need to be matched with previous and future investments in production equipment as well as with other products in terms of technical adaptations, available production capacity, production flow and plant layout, the work force's knowledge and abilities and so forth. Thus, there are numerous requirements and dependencies related to various production resources, and the interplay between these resources, that need to be considered. How production resources can be utilized is also closely related to the products that are produced in a specific facility, not least with respect to product design. Moreover, different components needed for a complete product are produced in different facilities, at the same time as most facilities produce several different components (products). This implies dependencies between production facilities related to matching of plans, adaptations of processes, routines and internal structures as well as various technical adaptations. As a result, there is a complex network of production facilities that need to be taken into consideration when developing products.

5.3.1. Business Units

Volvo, Delphi, Lear, DFC Tech, Dayco, and Scania can be referred to as business units. Within some of these business units, several smaller business units can be identified. Megamos is, for instance, part of Delphi. This means that business units can be identified at different "levels" of aggregation. Whether it is part of another business unit or not, each one of these business units consists of a set of resources that gives it specific features and that the business unit strives to economize on. In this section, the analysis is focused on business units' resources, dependencies between business units, and business units' demands regarding the development of products.

5.3.2. Knowledge, Experience, Routines and Traditions

Volvo, Scania, Dayco, Delphi, Lear and most other business units mentioned in the cases are focused on developing and/or producing various products. This means a strong focus on the resource categories products and production facilities, which have been covered in previous sections of this analysis. These resources are important to business units, though, a business unit is more than a set of products and production facilities.

Volvo has for many years been developing and producing various components as well as complete cars and, over time, an immense amount of knowledge and experience has been accumulated. Volvo has knowledge and experience regarding, for instance, numerous product technologies, legal restrictions, marketing, sales, car assembly, logistics, distribution and quality assurance. Similarly, Dayco, Scania and the other business units have knowledge and experience that is related to the development, production, and sales of pipes and hoses, trucks, and so on. Since this knowledge and experience is related to various heterogeneous resources within the respective business units, no business unit has exactly the same knowledge as any other business unit, i.e. each business unit is unique.

When developing the intercooler pipe, the backrest frame for the V70 rear seat, or designing the final assembly line for the P2 models, various resources were confronted, adapted and combined by different individuals within different business units. To perform this development of resources, these individuals utilized existing knowledge and experience and, at the same time, they gained experience that could be utilized for developing other resources. Knowledge and experience is largely held in a tacit form by individuals, implying that business units are dependent on these individuals to get access to and utilize their knowledge and experience. Delphi, for instance, chose to employ people at the local development office that had been working at Volvo and therefore had specific knowledge regarding Volvo's development process. However, part of the knowledge that can be found within Scania, Volvo, and the other business units has been made explicit in documents and databases that contain drawings, product information, production quality data or that describe various technologies. Further, Volvo uses "white books" to capture and make explicit the knowledge and experience that has been created in specific development projects. In this way, different individuals' experiences may, to some extent, be transferred to future projects.

Further, Volvo has for a long time been involved in product development collaboration with Autoliv and Bosch, as well as they have been collaborating with numerous other suppliers, other auto manufacturers, distributors, and so forth. This implies that knowledge and experience has been built up within Volvo regarding other business units' resources such as products, production technologies, and specific knowledge. In a similar way, Dayco has knowledge regarding, for instance, surface treatment, production of rubber hoses, and assembly of cars and trucks, that is, various technologies utilized by Dayco's suppliers and customers. Thus, *within* a specific business unit, there is knowledge and experience that "reach beyond" the boundary of that business unit. Moreover, this implies that within Volvo, Dayco, and the other business units, knowledge has been developed regarding how to interact with other business units. Even if Dayco is mainly focused on production, they have had a few development engineers mainly working with customer specific adaptations of Dayco and Mark IV's different products. Dayco have also provided various customers with prototypes during product development. Thereby, Dayco have acquired experience regarding collaboration in product development that could be utilized for the collaboration with DFC Tech and Scania.

Thus, in addition to products and production facilities (including buildings, computers, testing equipment and other "physical" resources), business units have other resources, mainly in terms of knowledge, experience, routines and traditions. Dayco and the other business units have made considerable investments in products and production facilities. By utilizing their knowledge, experience and various routines and traditions, they can develop strategies and intentions for how to develop and further improve the utilization of these resources. Dayco, for instance, saw possibilities to improve the utilization of their existing production facilities by becoming more actively involved in the development of new products (and therefore established DFC Tech).

5.3.3. Dependencies Between Business Units
As business units interact with other business units, their respective resource collections are confronted. This implies that various forms of dependencies and tensions between these business units need to be considered.

Dayco utilizes several different technologies for cutting, bending, end forming, welding, and assembling pipes, hoses and other components. Even if adaptations have been made to Dayco's other resources, these technologies have largely been developed by other business units than Dayco. Different suppliers of production equipment are, for example, important for the development of (new) production technologies. These equipment suppliers, however, often perform this development in interaction with various customers such as Dayco. Thus, Dayco is dependent on interfaces with various equipment suppliers for getting access to new production technologies. Further, the multiplex technology played an important role for Volvo's new electrical system. Even if Volvo built up an extensive competence regarding multiplex, important knowledge regarding this technology was found within several other business units such as Megamos, Motorola, and Volvo Technical Development. None of these business units would have been able to develop the multiplex technology on their own. Instead, the development was enabled by the combining of these different business units' competencies, knowledge, experience and other resources. Thus, a specific business unit is dependent on different technologies that can be accessed through interaction with various other business units. This implies that dependencies are created between business units that have complementary knowledge about specific technologies. Furthermore, this "overlap" implies that there is seldom a one-to-one relationship between business units and technologies.

As mentioned above, Volvo have been collaborating with Autoliv, Bosch as well as with various component suppliers for a long time. Further, Dayco have been producing pipes for Scania for several years. Through this interaction, different individuals within these different business units have got to know each other. Thus, various social bonds have been developed between these business units. The discussions at Volvo regarding which suppliers to collaborate with for the development of the P2 platform were certainly influenced by such social bonds to certain suppliers.

Further, special contracts were established between Volvo and Delphi, Volvo and Lear, as well as between Dayco and Scania regarding the collaboration between these respective business units. It proved, however, to be difficult to make any detailed specifications in these contracts regarding the content and outcome of the collaboration. Therefore, at several different points, adjustments of the contracts were needed. The contracts mainly implied economical and legal dependencies between these business units.

Product development collaboration implies that interfaces are created between different business units' processes and routines for product development. DFC Tech had not yet made any large investments in developing their own routines for product development and could therefore relatively soon start working according to Scania's routines and systems. When regarding the interfaces between Volvo, Delphi and Lear's respective development processes and routines, it soon turned out that various adaptations were necessary. However, while Volvo were concerned with all suppliers following the same routines for development (e.g. regarding development "gates"), each one of these suppliers also had to consider what effects different adaptations of their routines and processes would have on their relationships with other auto manufacturers.

Further, as DFC Tech had recently been established, they did not have a "complete" collection of resources to rely upon. However, by combining various resources from, among others, Dayco, Fasitet, and IFE, it was possible to rather quickly develop the resource collection that was needed to collaborate with Scania and other auto manufacturers. In addition to financial resources, these different business units contributed with knowledge and experience, and DFC Tech got access to, for instance, Dayco's routines for quality assurance. Thus, DFC Tech could combine other business units' resources and, thereby, create a resource collection "of their own." At the same time, this resulted in dependencies to these other business units that influenced how DFC Tech could develop and utilize these resources.

Further, from Scania's point of view, it was regarded as risky to assign an extensive development responsibility to the relatively small and recently established business unit called DFC Tech. However, DFC Tech was owned by Dayco that, in turn, was owned by the even larger corporation Mark IV. This ownership structure was important to convince Scania that backup resources were available in case DFC Tech would not make it all the way through on their own. Similarly, Delphi is part of Delphi Corporation, which made Volvo more confident both regarding Delphi's financial strength and regarding the possibilities to access knowledge and technologies. Thus, these suppliers' ownership structure influenced the interfaces to their respective customers.

Even if Volvo at an early stage decided to develop the multiplex technology for the electrical system, it was from the beginning difficult to foresee what other business units that had to be involved. The need for developing specific features of the multiplex technology as well as what applications should be developed influenced what other business units Volvo had to interact with. Further, for some of the pipes used in the engine compartment, Scania considered using plastic materials instead of steel or aluminum. However, changing to a plastic material would imply that these pipes could not be produced by Dayco (see Section 5.2.1). Instead, Scania would have to purchase these pipes from some other supplier. Thus, what interfaces are created between business units and how these interfaces develop may be difficult to foresee.

Hence, each business unit is concerned with utilizing its own resources in the most efficient way, though, also various dependencies to other business units concerning financial and legal issues, access to technologies and so forth need to be considered. The cases also illustrate that different business units have different intentions and demands regarding how to utilize their respective resource collections, which may result in tensions between business units. This is further elaborated upon in next section.

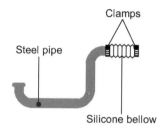

Fig. 48. The Complete Intercooler Pipe.

5.3.3.1. Product development and the demands of different business units. Product development implies adaptation and combination of different business units' resources. In this section, the analysis is focused on dependencies and tensions between business units mainly related to the adaptation and combination of products and production facilities.

5.3.3.2. The development of pipes and hoses. DFC Tech (and Dayco) assumed responsibility from Scania for developing the intercooler pipe between the turbo charger and the intercooler. The pipe consists of a steel pipe, a silicone bellow, and two clamps (see Fig. 48).

From Scania's point of view, product performance in terms of the functionality of the pipe in concert with the engine, the turbo charger, and the intercooler is of major concern, since that will influence the overall performance of the complete truck. Reliability is also of utmost importance for Scania since defect intercooler pipes may cause unplanned stops for their customers. In addition, this may cause considerable warranty costs as well as loss of "goodwill." In order to utilize the resources in the assembly plants in an efficient way at the same time as tied up capital (stock levels) is kept low, Scania is also concerned with the pipe being delivered to the assembly plant on time, in relatively small batches, and with approved quality. Based on previous experience from interaction with Dayco's production facility, Scania considered this possible to achieve. The efficient use of resources in the assembly plant also requires that the pipe is easy to assemble into the truck. Further, an important part of Scania's business is service and maintenance of sold trucks. Therefore, Scania also requires that the pipe is easy to replace or repair. In addition, the pipe must be purchased at a low cost. Thus, Scania wants an intercooler pipe that fulfils a number of specific requirements (see Fig. 49).

DFC Tech and Dayco, on the other hand, have specific knowledge and experience regarding what has an impact on cost and performance. To achieve a low cost, a steel

Scania's demands

DFC Tech and Dayco's demands

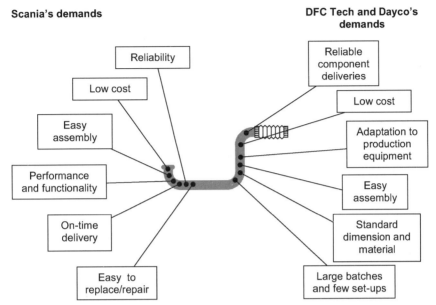

Fig. 49.   Scania and DFC Tech/Dayco's Demands on the Intercooler Pipe.

pipe design is required that is adapted to standard pipe dimensions and standard material quality. Further, if the type of steel pipe is the same as is used for producing pipes for Dayco's other customers, Dayco's purchasing volume increases and the price can be further reduced. Dayco is also concerned that the pipe, with respect to dimension and shape, as far as possible can be produced with existing production equipment.

Further, Dayco need reliable deliveries of bellows and clamps from MGW and IFE respectively and it must be easy to assemble the complete pipe. Flexible delivery times to Scania's assembly plants and few set-ups also improve Dayco's possibilities to utilize the production equipment and thereby reduce cost. When regarding the performance of the pipe in terms of air pressure, flow and so on, DFC Tech and Dayco had valuable resources in their own experience from developing similar products for other customers. DFC Tech and Dayco could also utilize knowledge and experience from other actors, such as Exacuo.

Thus, DFC Tech/Dayco and Scania were both concerned about reaching a low cost and a well functioning component design. However, with respect to their respective resource collections, which they want to utilize as efficiently as possible, the analysis shows that they had different demands on this specific component that could not always be matched. This, in turn, implied tensions between these business units, which required different forms of compromises. However, Scania had realized the potential benefits of also considering DFC Tech and Dayco's demands regarding pipe design. A respondent at Scania expressed this in the following words: *"We want to collaborate with DFC Tech and Dayco because, for them a pipe is something more than just a bar with a hole in it."*

5.3.3.3. The development of components for the electrical system. When regarding the electrical system it was, from Volvo's point of view, important to ensure that there was enough space available (i.e. packing) for the different components in the electrical system as well as for other components in the car. Further, among other things, Volvo were concerned about the assembly of the cable harnesses into the car since that influences assembly cycle times and assembly sequence and, thus, the utilization of resources in Volvo's assembly plants.

Also Delphi had specific requirements regarding the design of the cable harnesses since that influences the division of (manual) work and utilization of resources between Delphi's plant in Spain and the MAU respectively. Delphi wanted a large share of the production and assembly activities to be performed in the plant in Spain, since wages are lower there. In addition, similar products are produced there for other car manufacturers, implying possibilities to benefit from scale economies. Further, the design of the cable harnesses influenced what assembly tables, i.e. specific equipment, that had to be developed for performing the assembly activities in Spain.

Delphi also wanted to use their own series of connectors for the cable harnesses since that would simplify development (e.g. due to previous experience from using these connectors) and imply increased utilization of Delphi's production facilities. However, from Volvo's point of view it was more beneficial to use connectors from Yasaki since Volvo already used their connectors in other car models. Thereby, Volvo could reduce the number of different products for the aftermarket. When regarding plastic components such as the cable ducts, Delphi did not have the needed resources internally and therefore chose to collaborate with Rieselmann. From Delphi's point of view, this implied that they did not have to make additional investments in production capacity for these plastic components. Instead, investments in knowledge, experience and routines related to previous interaction with Rieselmann could be utilized.

The electrical system is characterized by a complex pattern of (functional) dependencies between various components. Further, these components (or applications) were developed by several different business units. The multiplex technology, however, provided standardized interfaces (i.e. the CAN and Volcano protocols) between the different applications and the signal system. This helped to reduce the number of dependencies that had to be dealt with between

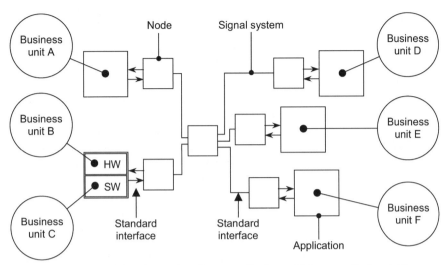

Fig. 50. The Need for Interaction Between Business Units was Reduced Due to Standardized Interfaces Between Nodes and Applications.

applications and, thus, between the different suppliers of these applications (see Fig. 50). From these suppliers' point of view, the limited need for interaction was regarded as positive since they in many cases regarded each other as competitors.

Further, as illustrated in Fig. 50, either the supplier of an application could develop both hardware (HW) and software (SW), or this could be divided between different business units (e.g. *B* and *C*). Dividing the development of the mobile phone between a business unit within Volvo (SW) and Autoliv (HW) implied that Volvo was less dependent on finding a single supplier that could take care of both these areas. In a similar way, the airbags were developed by Autoliv while algorithms for the airbag control system were developed by Bosch. Thus, also clear interfaces between hardware and software in the nodes contributed to reducing the dependencies stretching across business units.

However, the standardized interface did not eliminate all dependencies since, for instance, a specific application may be dependent on information that is provided by another application. Further, problems occurred with interference and noise in the audio system, due to high-frequency oscillations, that could not be foreseen. This type of problem may come about as interplay between the frequencies used in a circuit and the length of a particular cable. From Volvo's perspective it was important to solve this problem quickly since it had been discovered during start of production, thereby influencing several different activities in the assembly plant. There was, however, not enough time to re-design the circuit board from where the problem had emanated. Instead, it was decided that suppression capacitors should be integrated in the cable harness. From Delphi's perspective, however, this change caused some trouble since this implied that their plastic molds used for producing cable ducts had to be changed. This change also involved Rieselmann that produces the cable ducts as well as the tool supplier. In addition, the assembly tables used in Delphi's assembly plant in Spain had to be modified. These changes, in turn, implied that Delphi for some time had difficulties to assemble cable harnesses and deliver them on time to Volvo's assembly plant. However, even if the taken measure caused problems for Delphi, this was regarded a best compromise to avoid other types of delays in Volvo's assembly plant.

Hence, this case illustrates how standard interfaces between components may reduce dependencies between business units. Further, not all dependencies, that actually had to be dealt with between the different business units, could be foreseen. This, in turn, implied product design modifications that had different implications for different business units' possibilities to utilize their respective (production) resources.

5.3.3.4. The development of seats. Volvo, Lear as well as Autoliv were all deeply involved in the development of the seats for the new platform. While Lear assumed responsibility for the complete seats, Autoliv developed several key components such as side airbags and seat frames. Volvo were concerned about reaching a seat design that matched the design of other interior components and that fulfilled various requirements related to driving comfort and safety. Further, from Volvo's perspective it was regarded as important that the seats could be delivered to the assembly plant in the right sequence and at the right time and that they could be easily assembled into the car. These are key factors for Volvo's possibilities to adapt, combine and utilize various resources in the assembly plant.

From Lear's point of view, it was important with a seat design that is easy to assemble in the MAU. Further, due to the many different variants of complete seats, Lear was also concerned about using the same components for several different variants to simplify assembly and reduce stock levels. Since the seats for the P2 platform had much in common with the seats used in previous models (the S/V70), Lear could also utilize the knowledge and experience they had gained from assembling these seats. Lear were also concerned about at what assembly station in Volvo's final assembly plant the seats were going to be assembled into the car since this affects the time available from order to delivery of a complete seat.

Volvo, Lear and Autoliv were concerned about reaching a side airbag design that fulfils its desired function in interplay with, among other things, the seam in the upholstery. Autoliv were also concerned about the possibilities to efficiently produce and assemble the different components into a complete side airbag. Several components such as bags and gas generators are produced by different business units within Autoliv. Therefore, Autoliv were concerned about utilizing knowledge, experience and production resources from these business units for the development and production of the side airbags for Volvo. Autoliv were also concerned about the possibilities to utilize their existing relationships with various components suppliers, and they wanted to use the same components as for other car manufacturers to enable scale economies in production. Examples of requirements of the three business units regarding a front seat are illustrated in Fig. 51.

As Volvo, Lear, and Autoliv as well as other suppliers such as Brose assumed responsibility for developing different components in the seats, various physical and functional dependencies between these components implied dependencies between these business units. Further, as evident from the analyses in earlier sections, safety requirements create dependencies that "cut through" many different parts of the car. Therefore, various (functional) dependencies related to safety implied dependencies to Delphi (electrical system), Autoliv (airbags and seatbelts), Bosch (airbag control system), and other business units developing components related to safety. Furthermore, dependencies related to styling and design (e.g. matching of colors and surface structures) as well as spatial dependencies to other interior components implied dependencies to, for instance, Lear (door panels and instrument panel) and Becker (tunnel console). During the development of the new platform, new market trends and changed fashion

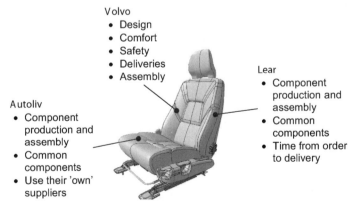

Fig. 51. Examples of Volvo, Lear and Autoliv's Respective Requirements on a Front Seat.

also called for various adjustments of interior colors, surface materials and surface structures. Due to various dependencies related to products, production facilities, and other resources, also a minor change of the textiles for the upholstery affected Lear, the textile manufacturer, their yarn supplier and so on. Hence, the development of the seats also illustrates how dependencies related to more overarching product features such as styling and safety implied dependencies between various other business units than those directly involved in the development of seats.

5.3.4. Summary

In addition to resources such as products and production facilities, business units have knowledge and experience regarding how to develop and utilize these resources. Business units also have knowledge and experience regarding other business units' resources as well as how to interact with these other business units. This implies that the knowledge and experience within a business unit "reach beyond" the boundary of the business unit. Further, due to resource heterogeneity, each business unit's knowledge and experience is unique. The development and utilization of various resources is also supported by various routines, traditions and processes.

The analysis also illustrates various dependencies between business units in terms of shared technologies, social bonds, legal and economical issues, processes, routines, and ownership. These dependencies often involve several different business units, implying that an adaptation of a resource between two business units may influence a third business unit. Further, as different components are developed and produced by different business units, dependencies related to products and production facilities result in dependencies between business units. However, standardized interfaces between products may contribute, to some degree, to reduce such dependencies between business units. At the same time, dependencies related to more overarching product features, such as safety, may imply dependencies stretching across several different business units. Like many other dependencies that have been identified between resources, dependencies between business units may be difficult to foresee and change over time, i.e. they cannot be regarded as "given."

Further, business units have specific requirements regarding the development of products, which can be related to their concern about efficient utilization (e.g. concerning scale economies) of their respective resource collections. Different business units' requirements may be combined, but in many cases conflicting requirements result in tensions between business units that call for various forms of compromises. Such compromises can be dealt with within business relationships, a resource category that is analyzed in next section.

5.4. Business Relationships

Business relationships are established between business units. In this section, the analysis is focused on relationships as resources and different features of relationships are identified. Then, dependencies between relationships are analyzed with respect to the products developed in the relationships.

5.4.1. History and "Size" of the Relationships Used in the Development Projects

When developing the electrical system for the new platform Volvo did not have all the knowledge and development resources required to perform this development alone. Therefore, relationships with different suppliers were utilized. The relationship between Volvo and Bosch had been going on for many years and these business units had much previous experience from working together. Further, Volvo had been working with Autoliv (for the development of electronics) for previous models, implying that there was some experience to fall back on. Volvo also had relationships with various component suppliers, such as Yasaki, that they wanted to continue to utilize. At the same time, new relationships with, for instance, Delphi were established for the development of the P2 platform. In this case, however, ESMA had been working with both Delphi and Volvo and initially acted as a link between them.

When regarding the seats, Volvo had traditionally performed most development internally. However, the development of airbags had for many years been performed in interaction with Autoliv, implying that there was an already established relationship. Further, Lear had taken over Volvo's seat assembly plant, which implied that the relationship with Lear had been going on for a few years when the development of the P2 platform started. Up until then, this relationship had mainly been focused on issues related to production (including minor modifications of the product design), though, for the new platform also product development was performed within the relationship.

Traditionally, Scania had developed most pipes and hoses internally. However, there had been a relationship going on between Scania and Dayco for many years. Even if Dayco had been involved in some product development, this relationship had mainly been concerned with production issues. However, for the development of the new truck model, Scania decided to complement the existing relationship with Dayco by also establishing a relationship DFC Tech, mainly focused on product development. In this way, Scania saw possibilities to, among other things, achieve pipe and hose designs that were better adapted for Dayco's production and, thus, less expensive to produce.

Thus, when the development projects started, there were already several different relationships that had been going on for some time that could be utilized. In other words, there was an established structure of relationships. At the same time, several "new" relationships were established for the specific development projects. In some cases, these new relationships were complementary to and, in other cases conflicting with, the established structure of relationships. Further, in some cases the business units involved in a relationship had already been working together for some time within areas other than product development, such as production. This implied that even if product development was new for the relationship, there was some experience from collaboration that could be utilized.

Further, roughly 30 people were working at Delphi's local office or in the module team at Volvo, i.e. they were directly involved in the relationship between Volvo and Delphi. If other people in Delphi's different business units as well as employees at Volvo that worked with the components for the electrical system are included, the number increases further. At the same time, only three people were directly involved from DFC Tech in the relationship between DFC Tech and Scania. A few more people were involved on part-time basis for making prototypes, performing production simulations etc. at Dayco. Thus, the relationships were very different in terms of how many people they involved, which is closely related to the scope of the different development projects. Developing advanced electronics, such as the CEM and the REM, put high demands on the relationship between Volvo and Delphi (Megamos). At the same time, the relationship between DFC Tech and IFE was mainly focused on finding suitable standard components for the pipes, with limited possibilities for development of specific components. Hence, there were large differences regarding what was dealt with in different relationships. In next section, the content of these relationships is elaborated upon in more detail in terms of relationship features.

5.4.2. Relationship Features
Within the relationship between DFC Tech and Scania, DFC Tech had representatives with knowledge and experience regarding how to design and produce pipes and hoses. At the same time, Scania's representatives in the relationship had knowledge regarding the functioning of the complete truck, truck assembly, customer needs and aftermarket requirements. In the relationship between Volvo and Delphi, Volvo's representatives had knowledge regarding, for instance, the interaction between the electrical system and other components in the car, and requirements related to the assembly of the complete car. They also had experience from developing electrical systems for previous car models. Delphi's representatives contributed with knowledge and experience regarding various technologies used in the components for the electrical system and the production of these components. In addition, the representatives in the respective relationships had knowledge and experience regarding where to find specific knowledge within

their respective business units as well as within a larger network of actors, such as other auto manufacturers and suppliers.

Further, the interactive development of components implied that DFC Tech, Delphi and Lear acquired specific knowledge regarding, for instance, Scania and Volvo's other products and specific requirements regarding their production facilities. Each time DFC Tech participated in the meetings at Scania's pre-production plant, they learned more about Scania's requirements regarding assembly and service of the truck. At the same time, the interactive development implied that Scania and Volvo developed their knowledge regarding, for instance, requirements for scale economies and component assembly in the respective suppliers' production facilities. Scania and Volvo also learned more about their respective suppliers' own supplier relationships.

Thus, the representatives in the relationships contributed with knowledge and experience originating from their respective business units. Thereby, the combined knowledge within the respective relationships was different from the knowledge held within any of the involved business units. Further, the interaction required for developing a specific component also implied that each business unit developed its knowledge about the counterpart's resources. The development of (counterpart-specific) knowledge can be regarded as investments in the relationship, which may be utilized also for future development projects.

Other features of the relationships include the many specific adaptations and technical connections related to products, production facilities, and business units that have been covered in the previous parts of this analysis. It was shown that the far-reaching adaptations of routines, production equipment as well as the location of the MAU:s have resulted in strong dependencies between Volvo's assembly plants and the MAU:s. At the same time, these adaptations can be seen as investments in specific features of the relationship between Volvo and the suppliers that can be utilized for producing current as well as future car models.

Further, before the P2 platform was introduced, Volvo had a large number of suppliers for various components. Many of these suppliers had been delivering components to Volvo for many years and there were established routines for, among other things, quality assurance, packaging and transport of components, and invoicing. This implied that Volvo knew what machine capability, quality, delivery times and so on that they could expect from these suppliers. In addition, many people at Volvo and at these suppliers respectively knew each other well since many years. Thus, various features of these relationships had been developed over time in terms of technical adaptations, knowledge, routines and also social bonds.

For the development of the rear seat locks and the luggage net for the V70 rear seat, Lear established direct relationships with Witte and Ieper respectively. However, it turned out that Witte and Lear had difficulties to come up with a design

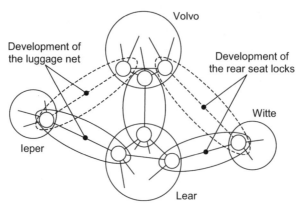

Fig. 52.   Volvo Also Established Direct Development Relationships with Ieper and Witte.

of the rear seat locks that fulfilled Volvo's safety requirements. Further, Ieper and Lear had problems with the design of the locking mechanism for the luggage net. Volvo therefore regarded it to be necessary to interfere in the development work (see Fig. 52). Thereby, part of the development for the rear seat locks and the luggage net was performed in the relationships between Volvo-Witte and Volvo-Ieper respectively, although this had not been "planned" from the beginning. Even if Volvo already had relationships with Witte and Ieper, this implied that complementary features had to be developed within these relationships with regard to product development.

Further, the backrest frame for the V70 rear seat was first developed in the relationship between Volvo and Hydro. Then, Volvo decided that this component should be developed in the relationship with Autoliv instead. This, however, implied that much of the investments that had already been made in the relationship with Hydro could not be utilized. Consequently, much time was lost in the development project, which influenced the development performed in the relationship between Volvo and Autoliv. Hence, these examples illustrate that the use of a specific relationship and the features within it may change quite rapidly. This, in turn, may have consequences for the utilization of previously made investments in the particular relationship, as well as for other relationships.

5.4.3. Dependencies Between Relationships

In all three cases, several different relationships were utilized for the development of products. It is, therefore, relevant to ask what this implied in terms of dependencies between relationships.

When developing the backrest frame for the Volvo V70 rear seat, there were various dependencies related to the assembly of the rear seat, component sharing between seats for the different car models, and the interplay between the seats and other components in the car that involved resources represented in the relationship between Volvo and Lear. At the same time, Autoliv developed and would later produce various components for the rear seat, among them the backrest frame. This implied that dependencies influencing, for instance, safety requirements, weight, and production cost affected the relationship between Volvo and Autoliv. Since the backrest frame is a key component in the rear seat, there were also a number of dependencies between Autoliv and Lear. As illustrated in the analysis in Section 5.1.2 there were, for instance, various functional and physical interfaces between the rear seat locks, the seatbelts, and the backrest frame. However, numerous dependencies that involved both Lear and Autoliv also required that Volvo be involved. Therefore, as resources were confronted, adapted and combined within the respective relationships, dependencies were also created *between* these relationships, see Fig. 53 (illustrated as arrows).

In the relationship between Volvo and Delphi, the situation was somewhat different. In addition to Delphi, Volvo had established relationships with a number of different business units for the development of various different nodes and applications. As was shown earlier in this analysis, there are numerous (functional) dependencies between these components. However, the multiplex technology with the standardized communication protocols, contributed to reduce the impact of dependencies between applications and, thus, between various relationships.

In a similar way, clearly defined interfaces in Scania's modularized product structure also contributed to reduce the number of dependencies between different relationships. At the same time, however, the use of standardized

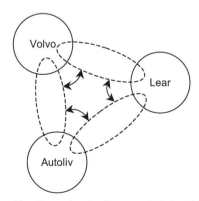

Fig. 53. Dependencies Between Relationships.

components across several different models implied that also relatively small design changes (such as changing the design of the expansion tank) would influence Scania's relationships with different component suppliers. Moreover, even if some components were standardized and interfaces were clearly defined, pipes and hoses are generally regarded as "flexible links" between other components. This implied that almost any design change carried through in one relationship influenced the components developed in the relationship between DFC Tech and Scania.

The development of the steel pipe for the intercooler pipe involved several different relationships, see Fig. 54. Further, as illustrated in the figure, different features of the pipe were developed in different relationships. In the relationship between DFC Tech and MGW the end form and diameter of the pipe were adapted to the silicone bellow. In the relationship with Dayco, the shape of the pipe and the selection of pipe diameter (dimension) were adapted to requirements set by Dayco's production facilities, and so forth. A change of, for instance, the pipe diameter influenced all relationships illustrated in

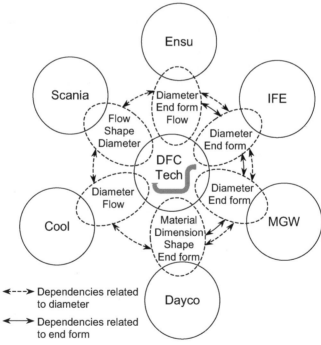

Fig. 54. Examples of Dependencies Between Relationships Related to Features of the Steel Pipe.

Fig. 54 in different ways. Thus, there were dependencies between all these relationships. At the same time, however, changing the shape of the pipe mainly influenced DFC Tech's relationships with Scania and Dayco. Thus, dependencies between relationships were related to specific component features. While some adaptations of a component may influence several relationships, adaptations of other features may involve one or a few relationships only. However, the flow through the pipe is also dependent on the shape of the pipe. Such dependencies between component features imply additional dependencies between relationships.

Further, when establishing development relationships with different suppliers, both Volvo and Scania were concerned that they, through these relationships, would get access to knowledge and experience that the suppliers had gained in relationships with other auto manufacturers. For instance, the pipes and hoses that were developed in the relationship between DFC Tech and Scania could be improved by avoiding mistakes made in other relationships. In this way, what was performed in one relationship was dependent on knowledge and experience developed in other relationships. However, when regarding the relationship between Volvo and Lear, Volvo found this kind of knowledge sharing between Lear's different customer relationships to be missing since Lear had different development teams that were dedicated to particular auto manufacturers.

The pipes that were developed in the relationship between DFC Tech and Scania would probably later be produced by Dayco. Then, the cost for producing these pipes was dependent on what other pipes would be produced in the same facility, and to what extent the same basic material and production equipment could be utilized. Therefore, when developing the pipes for Scania, pipe dimension, material, required machine operations and so forth for pipes produced in the relationship with, for instance, Volvo Trucks, also had to be considered. Thus, there were dependencies between these relationships related to scale economies in production. When regarding connectors for the electrical system, Volvo required that Delphi used Yasaki's connectors because that would provide Volvo with scale economies on the aftermarket. Thus, there were dependencies between what was developed in the relationship between Volvo and Delphi and what was exchanged in the relationship between Volvo and Yasaki.

As argued above, the relationship between DFC Tech and IFE mostly concerned standard components such as couplings and clamps. Therefore, the possibilities for development of specific component designs within this relationship were limited. Instead, the challenge was to find suitable components within a wide range of standard components. Here, IFE played an important role since they had established relationships with several important producers of standard components such as Rasmussen and Oetiker, see Fig. 55. This implied that through the

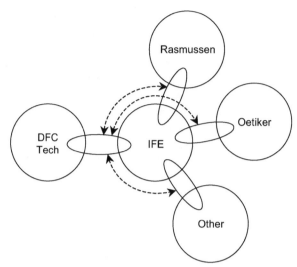

Fig. 55. Dependencies Between Relationships Between DFC Tech, IFE, and Various
Suppliers of Standard Components.

relationship with IFE, DFC Tech could get access to (standard) components
from many different producers. Hence, even if the standard components could
not be adapted within the relationship between DFC Tech and IFE (as standard
components they were regarded as "given"), the relationship implied a connection
to other relationships.

Thus, dependencies between products, production facilities and business units,
in terms of scale economies, knowledge and so on, imply dependencies between
relationships.

5.4.4. Summary

The analysis shows that in relationships that had been going on for some time,
various features had been developed in terms of knowledge and experience,
adaptations of products and production equipment, adaptations of routines, as
well as social bonds between individuals. In the recently established relationships,
such features had to be developed during the studied development projects. The
relationship features could be utilized and further developed during the studied (and
future) development projects. Thus, these features can be regarded as investments
in the relationship that may be utilized for adaptation and combination of resources
in the future. As such, features of a relationship change over time.

The features of relationships seem to be similar to those of business units and, just like a business unit, the relationship relates a number of different resource items. However, the knowledge found within a relationship is a combination of knowledge held within the interacting business units. Therefore, this knowledge is different from the knowledge found within each one of these business units. In a similar way, routines, products, and other resources and features found within relationships are combinations of the business units' resources. While relationships can be regarded as combinations of business units' resources, it can be argued that business units are functions of their relationships (cf. Dubois, 1994).

The analysis also illustrated various forms of dependencies between different relationships. Various technical dependencies between components developed in different relationships implied dependencies between these relationships. Further, what was developed in one relationship was dependent on specific features (e.g. experience) that had been developed in other relationships. There were also dependencies between relationships related to the possibilities to achieve scale economies in production.

5.5. Summary of the Analysis

Based on the resource model described in the analytical framework, the analysis has here been focused on the four resource categories products, production facilities, business units, and business relationships. The analysis has explored various forms of dependencies between resources (within and across these categories), as well as different requirements that need to be fulfilled to enable efficient utilization of these resources or specific features of them.

When regarding products, numerous physical, functional, spatial, and environmental dependencies were identified between different components. These different types of dependencies were found to be only partially overlapping, and some dependencies influence many different parts of the complete product. Further, dependencies related to the matching of plans, and various technical adaptations were identified between production facilities. Dependencies between production facilities were also found to be closely related to product design and dependencies between products. Regarding business units, dependencies related to knowledge, experience, routines, and traditions were identified between business units, in addition to various economical and legal dependencies. As different business units control different products and production facilities, also dependencies related to these resource categories imply dependencies between business units. Moreover, business units may have different requirements regarding how to develop and utilize specific resources, which imply tensions between these business units that call for various forms of compromises. Further, business relationships are established between business units and, as resources are adapted and combined, specific features of business relationships are developed in terms of, for instance, knowledge, routines, technical adaptations, and social bonds. Various dependencies between relationships were identified that could be attributed to, among other things, technical adaptations of products and production facilities, to the utilization of common knowledge, and to scale economies in production.

The result of this analysis is a complex and multifaceted pattern of dependencies between resources. Dependencies related to the four resource categories are principally illustrated in Fig. 56. Each resource item (and their specific resource features) is embedded in larger resource collections. While different resources need to be confronted, adapted and combined in order to develop a specific product, this resource development must also be related to an existing resource structure (cf. resource constellation; see Section ?). This means that a specific dependence is not just the result of the combination of two resource items, it is the result of the combination of two resource collections. Therefore, when developing a new product, far more resources than the developed product per se need to be considered. Failing to do so may have far-reaching consequences regarding the possibilities to embed the developed product into, and to efficiently utilize, other resources in the existing resource structure.

While some dependencies are crucial for a particular resource combination, others can be eliminated or neglected. Further, as resources are adapted and

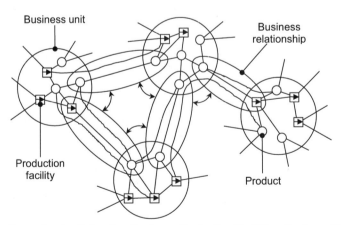

Fig. 56. Dependencies Related to Products, Production Facilities, Business Units, and Business Relationships.

combined during the development process, various new dependencies are created. Some of these dependencies may not be foreseen which, in turn, may have consequences for how (other) resources can be adapted and combined. This implies that neither resources or resource features, nor dependencies between resources, can be regarded as "given." Thus, it is a *dynamic*, and to some extent unpredictable, pattern of dependencies that needs to be considered when developing a new product.

With this complex and dynamic pattern of dependencies between embedded resources as a point of departure, it is relevant to ask *how* these dependencies may be dealt with. Therefore, in next section, the analysis is focused on the *organizing* of product development.

6. ANALYSIS – ORGANIZING IN THE RESOURCE STRUCTURE

While the previous analysis was focused on *what* needed to be organized in terms of dependencies, the analysis in this section focuses on *how* product development was organized in the three cases to deal with dependencies across business units. This section has been divided into two main parts. In the first part (Section 6.1), relationships are in focus and development in a single relationship as well as in several different relationships is analyzed. In the second part (Section 6.2), the analysis deals with the use of development teams for interactive product development.

6.1. Organizing Interactive Development in Relationships

In the three cases, several different relationships between business units were developed and utilized. These relationships were an important means for dealing with various dependencies related to products and production facilities (i.e. the technical structure), as well as various other forms of dependencies and tensions between business units. First, single relationships are analyzed (Section 6.1.1) and then, in Section 6.1.2, the analysis is focused on various aspects of dealing with dependencies in several different relationships.

6.1.1. Dealing with Dependencies in a Single Relationship

6.1.1.1. Utilizing relationship features. The relationship between Volvo and Lear was important for dealing with dependencies related to the development of the seats for the new platform. However, the relationship between Volvo and Lear had recently been established. This implied that, in addition to developing the seats, there was also a need for adapting and combining other resources in terms of knowledge regarding safety requirements, routines for testing and verifying the product design, and making adaptations of interfaces between production facilities.

In contrast, the relationship between Volvo and Autoliv (that was also important for seat development) had been going on for several years. The relationship had a long "track record" of completed development projects and there was an ongoing exchange in production. This implied that Autoliv knew from the beginning what type of safety requirements had to be fulfilled and they were familiar with Volvo's development process. At the same time, Volvo had knowledge regarding what type of product development could be performed by Autoliv and regarding their abilities to deliver components with approved quality on time. Thus, various features in terms of knowledge, routines and so on, that had been developed over time within the relationship between Volvo and Autoliv, could be utilized for the development of the seats for the P2 platform.

Further, the relationship between Volvo and Delphi was established for the development of the electrical system for the P2 platform. This implied that there were no previous "investments" in specific relationship features to fall back on. Therefore, in the beginning of the project much time was devoted to develop various routines for the collaboration, agree on how to divide the development work between Volvo and Delphi, decide what CAD-system to use and so forth. Even if these adaptations implied that some time was "lost" in the beginning of the project, Volvo also regarded it to be beneficial to establish a new relationship since this could be an important source of new ideas. Thus, even if some initial investments were required, Volvo also regarded the new relationship with Delphi to be important for the possibilities to try out new resource combinations.

6.1.1.2. Interactive product development in a relationship. Then, how are dependencies dealt with within a relationship? For the development of pipes and hoses for Scania, DFC Tech had formed a small group of people that had the main responsibility for the development work. These people had experience from developing the type of components that were developed in the relationship with Scania. They also had knowledge about various dependencies between these components and DFC Tech and Dayco's other resources, such as the production facilities. At the same time, the people from Scania had previous experience from truck development. They also had knowledge regarding various dependencies to resources within Scania, such as assembly plants, that they could relate to the components developed in the relationship with DFC Tech. Thus, people from DFC Tech and Scania respectively acted as *representatives* for these business units' resource collections in the relationship. In a similar way, Delphi and Lear had representatives for the development of various components in their respective relationships with Volvo.

When Delphi and Lear became involved in the development of the electrical system and the seats respectively, most development activities concerned concept development. However, as the development projects went on, more and more development activities were focused on production, logistics and so on. This, in turn, implied that other representatives with knowledge about these resources had to be involved in the relationships. Due to DFC Tech's small organization, (nearly) the same people represented DFC Tech throughout the project, though, the representatives from Scania with whom they interacted changed over time. Hence, as the development work went on and various components were adapted and combined also the relationships between the business units had to be adapted in terms of what resources were represented in the relationship.

When developing the intercooler pipe, the interface between the turbo charger and the intercooler pipe required interaction between Ensu and DFC Tech/Dayco (see Fig. 57). Among other things, they had to agree on a suitable physical connection between these components. Within the relationship, the representatives for the engine/turbo charger (Ensu) and the intercooler pipe (DFC Tech) worked with trying out different design solutions based on their knowledge about the components, including various dependencies to other resources in their respective business units. However, changing the interface between the turbo charger and the intercooler pipe influenced the end form of the steel pipe and, thus, how the steel pipe would be produced. Therefore, DFC Tech's representative had to interact with Dayco's production facility regarding various production-related issues. Then, the work with combining the pipe and the turbo charger could be taken one step further within the relationship. It turned out, however, that also the connection on the turbo charger would have to be slightly modified. The same turbo charger was used for different customers and, therefore, Ensu's representative had to deal with adaptations of the turbo charger in interaction with different units within

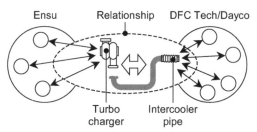

Fig. 57. Interaction Between Resources Through the Relationship Between DFC Tech/Dayco and Ensu.

Ensu's organization. However, when certain changes of the turbo charger could not be carried through due to dependencies to specific production equipment, other alternative solutions had to be worked out within the relationship. This, in turn, resulted in additional changes of the steel pipe end form that had to be dealt with in interaction between DFC Tech's representative and Dayco's production facility. In this way, various compromises were worked out between the components within the relationship as well as between the respective components and other resources within the respective business units.

Thus, part of the development in terms of resource adaptation and combination was performed (by the representatives) within the relationship, while part of the development was performed between the relationship and other resources in the respective business units. In this way the relationship facilitated dealing with dependencies between resources within different business units, i.e. compromises went "back and forth" between the business units. Due to the many dependencies between the specific components and other resources, more than just the components had to be represented in the relationship. However, in case resources not represented in the relationship played a crucial role for the development of the product, representatives for these resources could be involved in the relationship as well. In this way, the relationship was continuously developed, functioning as a flexible link between the two business units.

Further, when developing injection-molded plastic components for, for instance the seats, the ability of the component to come loose from the mold was important for Lear and their suppliers, though, Volvo had no specific interest in this particular feature of the plastic material. Therefore, this issue could be dealt with within Lear, or in interaction between Lear and their suppliers of plastic components. However, deformation of the same plastic component due to changed temperature, concerned both Volvo and Lear. This feature of the plastic material is related to the perceived quality of the seat (fit between components) as well as the production of the specific component and, therefore, such issues had to be dealt with within the relationship between Volvo and Lear. Another feature of the plastic material is that it may cause "squeak" (i.e. noise) in contact with other (plastic) materials. This is something that Volvo is concerned about, while it does not influence the production of the plastic component and, therefore, Lear would not have to be concerned about it. However, this particular feature is related to the selection of plastic material used for the component. It is therefore related to the production of the plastic component and, therefore, this feature may need to be dealt with within the relationship anyway. Thus, when developing components in a relationship, some *features* of that component may require interaction within the relationship, while other features of the same component may not need to be dealt with in the relationship.

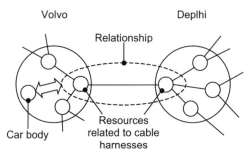

Volvo   Deplhi

Relationship

Resources
Car body   related to cable
harnesses

Fig. 58. Dealing with Dependencies Between the Volvo-Delphi Relationship and the Unit Developing the Car Body.

6.1.1.3. The relationship as a "heavy" resource. Above, it was shown that investments in particular relationship features might facilitate adaptation of resources within the relationship. A great part of the development of the cable harnesses was performed within the relationship between Volvo and Delphi. As the development work went on, and various resources were confronted and combined, a product design evolved that was adapted to Delphi and Volvo's respective resource collections. For instance, the design of the cable ducts had been adapted to interfaces with the car body as well as the design of the molds. However, when the car body design was changed also the design of the cable harnesses, and thus the cable ducts, had to be changed. Since Volvo was actively involved in the development of both cable harnesses and the car body, the dependencies between the car body and the cable harnesses could have been dealt with within Volvo only. However, both Volvo and Delphi had already made considerable "investments" in the existing harness designs. In addition, specific knowledge, routines, social bonds between representatives, and other features had developed in the relationship. Therefore, dependencies between the cable harnesses and the car body were dealt with between this *relationship* (i.e. representatives from Volvo *and* Delphi) and the unit within Volvo that developed the car body (see Fig. 58).

Thus, how a relationship is utilized to deal with dependencies is related to what "investments" have been made in the relationship and the resources developed within it. This case shows that as resources are adapted and combined within a relationship, i.e. investments are made in the relationship, features are developed that may imply that the relationship itself is regarded as a "heavy" resource, which requires that other "outside" resources are adapted to it.

6.1.1.4. Summary. The analysis in this section has been focused on how dependencies between resources may be dealt with in a relationship. Various relationship features, which have been developed over time, can be utilized in current development projects. However, even if new relationships did not have such features to fall back on, the establishment of new relationships was considered important to access certain resources and improve innovation. Further, the interacting business units have representatives within the relationship, who deal with various dependencies. The representatives confront, adapt and combine the different business units' resources (or specific resource features) within the relationship, but also relate them to other resources "outside" the relationship. Thereby, compromises go "back and forth" between the two business units' resource collections. Furthermore, as resources are adapted and combined within a relationship, the relationship itself may be regarded as a "heavy" resource.

6.1.2. Dealing with Dependencies in Different Relationships

Thus far, the analysis has been focused on a single relationship. However, as illustrated above, the interactive development of products involved more than two business units. Therefore, in this section, the organizing of interactive development is analyzed with respect to several different business units and relationships.

6.1.2.1. Organizing in an existing relationship structure. When the development of the P2 platform started, Volvo already had relationships with several different (component) suppliers. In many cases, these relationships had developed over a long period of time. This implied that there was an existing resource structure with different relationships and business units, but also different products and production facilities. However, for the development of the P2 platform, relationships were also established between Volvo and several (larger) module suppliers such as Delphi and Lear. These suppliers assumed responsibility for developing various components and integrating them into modules. Delphi and Lear, in turn, also had relationships with several component suppliers.

Just like Volvo, the module suppliers had made investments in terms of resource adaptations in their relationships with component suppliers and, therefore, they wanted to utilize these relationships. The module suppliers developed components together with component suppliers, though, various other issues related to purchasing of the components, legal responsibilities, quality assurance and delivery precision were often dealt with directly between Volvo and their component suppliers. Therefore, Volvo were concerned about utilizing their own existing relationships with component suppliers. Consequently, Volvo in many cases decided what component suppliers Delphi, Lear and the other module suppliers should collaborate with. For instance, Volvo required that Lear collaborated with

Witte and Ieper for the development of the rear seat locks and the luggage net respectively. When regarding the seat frames, Volvo required that Lear collaborated with Autoliv since these components were closely related to safety requirements.

This way of organizing the development of modules and components with regard to the existing resource structure implied that some of the module suppliers' relationships with component suppliers became "redundant" (see Fig. 59). However, the module suppliers also utilized these "redundant" relationships in interaction with other auto manufacturers. Thereby, Volvo's requirements to use other than these component suppliers may have implied that some scale economies in component production were lost.

Moreover, this restructuring implied that Delphi, Lear and the other module suppliers in many cases had to establish new relationships with Volvo's existing component suppliers. Consequently, there was no earlier experience to fall back on. This may have been one explanation why Lear's relationships with Witte and Ieper had difficulties providing the desired outcome. Also Scania had some requirements regarding which component suppliers DFC Tech should collaborate with. Scania already had a relationship with Phoenix/MGW that they wanted to utilize and therefore wanted DFC Tech to establish a direct relationship with them. It turned out that this new relationship functioned well without large adaptations, which

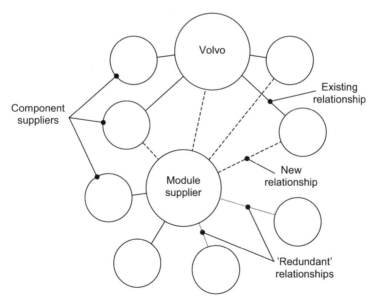

Fig. 59.   The Module Suppliers (e.g. Delphi and Lear) Established New Relationships with Volvo's Existing Component Suppliers.

implied possibilities to confront and combine resources related to pipes and bellows in new ways. Thereby, the relationship with MGW became important for DFC Tech's interaction with Scania and the other suppliers. In other cases, for example regarding Delphi and Yasaki, the suppliers were competitors, which hampered the development of a close relationship between them.

Thus, the organizing of the interactive product development projects required some degree of restructuring of the existing resource structure. While this implied possibilities to try out new resource combinations as new relationships were established, it also meant that features developed in other relationships could not be utilized (to their full potential). This also implied that economies of scale and learning were achieved in some relationships, but lost in others.

6.1.2.2. The relationship "integrator". Then, what role did DFC Tech, Delphi and Lear have in relation to their own (component) suppliers? When developing pipes and hoses, various dependencies had to be dealt with between DFC Tech, Scania, Cool and Ensu. Further, DFC Tech established relationships with MGW for the development of silicone bellows. The bellow has dependencies to (the connection on) the intercooler, which imply dependencies between MGW and Cool. Moreover, considering the complex pattern of dependencies between components that were identified earlier in this analysis, numerous dependencies would have to be dealt with between a large number of business units and relationships. However, most dependencies related to components in the pipes were actually dealt with by DFC Tech. Even if there was an interface between components developed by MGW and Cool, related dependencies were mainly dealt with between DFC Tech and Cool (see Fig. 60). DFC Tech, in turn, dealt with these dependencies in the relation with MGW. Thus, DFC Tech functioned as an "integrator" between different relationships (cf. "systems integrators"; Brusoni et al., 2001), which reduced the need for dealing with dependencies (and establishing relationships) between all involved business units.

In a similar way, Ensu and Cool functioned as "integrators" for a number of suppliers involved in the development of components to the engine and to the intercooler/radiator/condenser respectively. Also the local development center that Delphi established close to Volvo functioned as an "integrator" for Delphi's different business units and suppliers (e.g. Megamos and Delphi Germany, and Rieselmann). Thereby, the number of relationships that Volvo were directly involved in could be reduced. Thus, the "integrator" role implies fewer relationships and, thereby, more manageable development projects.

However, as illustrated in the Volvo-Lear case, the supplier's "integrator" role also implied long lead-times for decision making and "filtering" of information. Thus, as the number of relationships was reduced, there was also less efficient

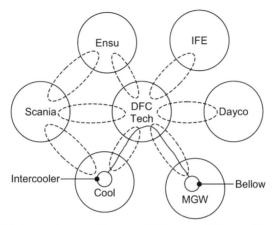

Fig. 60. DFC Tech acted as an "Integrator" Between Different Business Units and Relationships.

integration between business units. It may, however, also be argued that this "clustering" of relationships implies that each business unit can focus their development activities on specific parts of the resource structure and, thereby, achieve benefits in terms of specialization.

When developing the rear seat for the V70, Lear was regarded as an "integrator" with respect to, for instance, the relationships with Ieper and Witte. However, as illustrated above, the complex development task and the many problems that occurred implied that Volvo found it necessary to interact directly with Ieper and Witte. When regarding the rear seat locks, they had to be adapted to Volvo's safety requirements to pass the crash tests and Volvo found it difficult to deal with these issues indirectly via Lear. Thus, "integrators" help to reduce the need for direct interaction between all involved business units. It may, however, for instance due to unanticipated dependencies in the technical structure, be necessary to make "shortcuts" in terms of direct relationships between business units to facilitate more efficient interaction.

6.1.2.3. Interactive product development in multiple relationships. Thus far, the analysis has been concerned with the structuring of business units and relationships. Then, a relevant question is how this structure was utilized for the development of products. Previous parts of the analysis has illustrated that different business units have different requirements regarding the utilization of their respective resource collections. This implies dependencies and tensions between these business units, which may be dealt with in relationships. In addition, it was shown that what

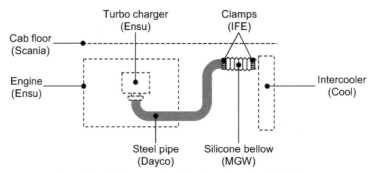

Fig. 61. The Intercooler Pipe Developed by DFC Tech.

is performed in one relationship may also influence other relationships. The development of the intercooler pipe (see Fig. 61) can illustrate how products are developed under such conditions.

When DFC Tech was involved in the development project at Scania, the engine and the intercooler had already been positioned on the frame members. This implied that the interfaces to the turbo charger and the intercooler and other design parameters concerning the physical space available were initially regarded as "given." With this as a starting point, DFC Tech began to develop a steel pipe. This was done in interaction with Scania to ensure that it could be assembled in the truck, and with Dayco to get prototypes and adapt the pipe to the production equipment. In addition, a silicone bellow was needed, which required interaction with MGW. To design the bellow, DFC Tech had to interact with Ensu to, among other things, gather data regarding engine vibrations and air temperature. DFC Tech also interacted with IFE to find suitable clamps for the bellow. The bellow, in turn, had an interface to the intercooler, which required interaction with Cool.

When it turned out that the pipe came too close to the cab floor DFC Tech interacted with Scania's department for cab development, but it was not possible to re-design the insulation on the cab floor. An alternative solution was to reduce the pipe diameter. This required interaction with Dayco to find a suitable pipe dimension and get new prototypes. This also required interaction with Ensu and Cool regarding airflow and the possibilities to change the connections on the turbo charger and the intercooler. In addition, the bellow had to be re-designed, which required interaction with MGW and IFE. Still, however, there was not enough space. Through interaction between Scania, Ensu and DFC Tech, it was decided that the turbo charger should be turned 180 degrees. This also implied that a forged pipe knee could be eliminated, which required interaction with Ensu to find a new connection between the pipe and the turbo charger. This also required interaction with Dayco, since the end-form of the pipe was changed. Further, this required interaction with Scania regarding clearance to the frame and the cross members, the positioning of fasteners as well as the possibilities to assemble the pipe into the complete truck. The new shape of the pipe also required interaction with Dayco concerning new prototypes and various production-related issues.

Thus, various dependencies between components, production facilities and business units imply that even minor changes of a specific component require interaction in several different relationships. Even if it was not explicitly included in the above description, the development of the intercooler pipe also required adaptation of resources in relationships with Ensu and Cool's respective suppliers. However, from DFC Tech's perspective, Ensu and Cool acted as "integrators" with regard to these suppliers, which implied that DFC Tech dealt with these resource adaptations with Ensu and Cool (and not directly with their respective suppliers). DFC Tech were involved in the development of several different components and, for each one of these components, it would be possible to "map" similar patterns of interaction between business units.

Furthermore, the cases illustrate that interactive product development is a highly iterative process. Different business units' resources are confronted, adapted and combined in the relationships and, when some conditions change, new adaptations and resource combinations are tried out. Thus, adaptations "go back and forth" within and between relationships. When regarding the other cases, similar patterns of interaction can be seen between Volvo, Lear, Autoliv, Brose and the other suppliers involved in the development of seats. Also when regarding the components developed in interaction between Volvo and Delphi there was frequent interaction between several different business units. However, as illustrated earlier in this analysis, the fairly standardized interfaces between different applications reduced the need for interaction between suppliers of different applications.

When regarding the steel pipe used for the intercooler pipe, it can be seen that different features of the pipe were developed in different relationships (see Fig. 62). In the relationship between DFC Tech and MGW the end form and the diameter of the pipe were adapted to the silicone bellow. In the relationship with Dayco, the shape of the pipe and the selection of pipe diameter (dimension) were adapted to requirements set by Dayco's production facilities, and so forth. A change of the pipe diameter influenced all relationships illustrated in Fig. 62 in different ways, while changing the shape of the pipe mainly influenced DFC Tech's relationships with Scania and Dayco. Thus, what dependencies had to be dealt with within and between different relationships was related to specific component features. While adaptations of some component features may influence several relationships, adaptations of other features may influence a single relationship only, and still some features may be dealt with internally. However, the case with the steel pipe

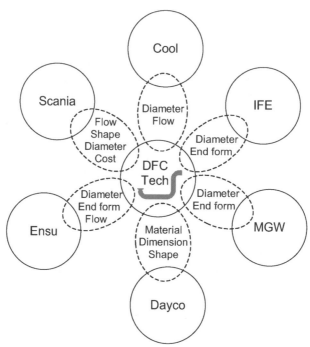

Fig. 62. DFC Tech Dealt with Different Features of the Steel Pipe in Different Relationships.

also illustrates how several different features such as shape, pipe dimension, and end form may influence another feature, such as the flow through the pipe. Such dependencies between component features implied additional dependencies that had to be dealt with in different relationships.

Furthermore, when developing the intercooler pipe, certain features such as the pipe diameter and the end form towards the bellow were (temporarily) "frozen" and could therefore be regarded as "given." This, in turn, implied that the need for interaction with MGW and IFE (regarding the bellow and the clamp respectively) was reduced, at least for a while. Meanwhile, the interaction with other business units regarding other features such as the shape of the pipe could be intensified. Also interfaces to other components such as the turbo charger were temporarily "frozen" in order to reduce the number of different design parameters that had to be dealt with in different relationships.

When developing the front seats, many spatial dependencies between the seat and other interior components had to be dealt with in interaction between several

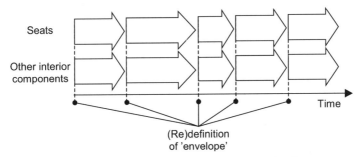

Fig. 63. Parallel Development of Seats and Other Interior Components.

different business units. However, a geometrical space (an "envelope") within which the seat was allowed to move was defined. Then, as the design of the seats and the other interior components evolved, this "envelope" was successively redefined (narrowed). In this way, interfaces between the seats and other interior components were temporarily "frozen." This implied that development activities were parallelized (see Fig. 63) and that the need for interaction with other business units, developing other interior components, was reduced.

Also the different components for the electrical system had numerous dependencies to other components that could not be dealt with simultaneously. Therefore, when developing, for instance, the cable harnesses various features and interfaces to other components such as the number of cables in a branch of a specific harness and the car body design were temporarily regarded as "given." This implied that cable ducts could be developed without requiring continuous interaction with the unit within Volvo that developed the car body. However, when the car body design had to be changed, this interface could no longer be regarded as "given" and interaction with the unit developing the car body was required.

Thus, specific component features or interfaces between components were successively "frozen," which implied that they could be regarded as "given" for some time. Thereby, the complexity in terms of number of different dependencies that had to be dealt with, and thus the need for simultaneous interaction in several different relationships, could be reduced. This also facilitated parallel development of different components. However, regarding interfaces or features as "given" for some time implies, that resources cannot be mutually adapted. Then, adaptations and combinations of other resources that are carried through during this period of time may influence how the "given" resource can be adapted and combined later on, when it has been "unfrozen." Thereby, the "freezing" of interfaces also imply a certain degree of sequencing of the resource adaptation and combination.

6.1.2.4. Suppliers involved in multiple relationships. Thus far, the analysis regarding the organizing of interactive development has been focused on the development of various components for Scania's new truck model and Volvo's new car platform in several different relationships. However, in addition to the relationships with Volvo and Scania that were focused in the cases, Delphi, Lear and DFC Tech/Dayco respectively were involved in relationships with other auto manufacturers. As illustrated in Section 5, there may be dependencies between such relationships, for instance in terms of economies of learning and scale in development and production. Then, a relevant question is how such dependencies between relationships were dealt with by Delphi, Lear, and DFC Tech.

DFC Tech/Dayco also developed and/or produced pipes for Volvo Trucks and Volvo Cars (see Fig. 64). The case illustrates how dependencies between these relationships were sometimes dealt with directly between DFC Tech/Dayco's representatives working with the respective auto manufacturers, though, there were no formal routines for this. Further, the components developed for Scania and Volvo Trucks respectively would be produced in the same production facility, which required some coordination between these relationships to ensure scale economies in production. Even if these issues were not dealt with directly between DFC Tech/Dayco's representatives in the respective relationships, they had to relate their component designs to (nearly) the same production equipment. Thereby, even if the representatives for this production facility were not working within the relationships, they functioned indirectly as coordinators between these relationships. Furthermore, the engineer from Exacuo that acted as a representative for DFC Tech in the relationship with Scania was also involved in development projects at Volvo Cars. This facilitated the sharing of knowledge and experience

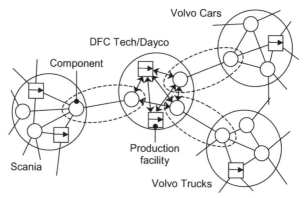

Fig. 64. Coordination Between Different Customer Relationships at DFC Tech/Dayco.

regarding the development of pipes and hoses between the relationships with Scania and Volvo Cars.

Also Delphi utilized the same production facilities for producing components to several different auto manufacturers. Apart from DFC Tech, Delphi had representatives from their different production facilities (as well as other functional areas) in different customer relationships. Their role was to both relate component designs to production equipment and to coordinate production-related issues between different customer relationships. This implied, for instance, that when designing the cable harnesses for Volvo, Delphi could contribute with their experience regarding harness assembly that they had developed in relationships with other auto manufacturers. Further, in some cases, the same people represented Delphi in different relationships, which facilitated the sharing of knowledge and experience between relationships.

When regarding Lear, the situation was different. The seat assembly plant that Lear had taken over from Volvo assembled seats for Volvo only. This implied that when developing the seats for the P2 platform there was limited need for interaction between Lear's different customer relationships regarding the utilization of this plant. Further, Volvo in many cases decided what component suppliers Lear should collaborate with. This made it difficult for Lear to coordinate component production for Volvo's seats with component production for seats produced for other auto manufacturers. Furthermore, in addition to Volvo, Lear's development unit in Trollhättan also developed seats for Saab Automobile. However, the seat development for Volvo and Saab respectively was divided between two different teams, which implied that the possibilities to share knowledge and experience regarding seat design between these relationships were limited.

Thus, interactive product development not only requires coordination between the different suppliers involved in a specific development project, it also requires coordination and interaction between each supplier's different customer relationships. By learning from other customer relationships, component design, the utilization of production equipment, as well as various routines and methods used within the relationships could be improved. However, the potential for coordination and learning between customer relationships is related to how each supplier has organized its different relationships with regard to each other.

6.1.2.5. Summary. In this section, the analysis has been focused on how dependencies can be dealt with in relationships. While the first part of this section was focused on a single relationship (summarized in Section 6.1.1), this second part focused on development involving several different relationships. The cases illustrate that the development projects implied some reorganization of the existing structure of relationships. Consequently, it was difficult to utilize features that had previously been developed in some relationships. However, the establishment of new relationships also implied possibilities to try out new resource combinations. Thus, the reorganization implied that the requirements for and possibilities to utilize the existing resource structure were changed.

The cases illustrated that the product development required interaction in several different relationships, also for making minor adaptations of a single component. Resource adaptations made in one relationship had to be tested against resources developed in other relationships. In this way, adaptations went "back and forth" within and between several different relationships. Numerous iterations were required to reach a working component design.

Further, the suppliers involved in the development projects functioned as "integrators" between different relationships. Thereby, there was no need for establishing relationships between all business units involved. This helped to reduce the complexity of the pattern of relationships and may also have enabled benefits in terms of specialization. At the same time, however, this in some cases implied less efficient integration between business units.

Different features of a specific resource may be developed in different relationships. By "freezing" some specific feature, the number of different relationships that need to be handled simultaneously may be reduced. However, dependencies between different resource features may require interaction between several relationships anyway. Also interfaces between components were "frozen," which reduced the complexity of the pattern of dependencies that had to be dealt with. This implied that development could be parallelized, though, it also entailed that specific dependencies were dealt with in a certain sequence, i.e. the "freezing" of interfaces encumbered the mutual adaptation of resources (for a while).

Furthermore, the cases illustrate that suppliers that are involved in a development project with a specific auto manufacturer may also have development relationships with other auto manufacturers (and suppliers). These relationships may be important for economies of learning and scale and some coordination between these relationships is needed. As production facilities in many cases were important "common resources" for these relationships, representatives from production functioned as integrators between these relationships.

In all, this analysis has illustrated that the interactive development influenced, and was influenced by, several different business units and relationships. To deal with dependencies in an efficient way, within and across these different relationships, additional forms for organizing of the interactive development were needed. This is elaborated in more detail in next section.

6.2. Organizing Interactive Development in Teams

For the development of the new platform, Volvo established twelve development teams, referred to as module teams. Within some of these module teams, several "sub-teams" were established. At Scania, a single development team was established for the development of the new truck model. In this section, the analysis focuses on the designed of these teams and how they were utilized for dealing with dependencies between various resources.

6.2.1. The Product Structure and the Formation of Development Teams

The division of product development activities between different business units may be performed in many different ways, see Section 1.2.1. In this section, the analysis is focused on the formation of the development teams in interaction with the product structure as well as other resources.

6.2.1.1. Modules and development teams at volvo. When developing the P2 platform, it was considered necessary to divide the development work between different development teams. The decomposition of the complete car into a number of modules facilitated the formation of teams that assumed responsibility for developing one or (in some cases) several modules.

When regarding a front seat, a complex pattern of physical, functional, and spatial dependencies were identified between its different components (see Section 5.2). The seam in the upholstery must come apart when the airbag inflates, there must be no clashes between the moving parts in the seat chassis, and there must be no play in the chassis since it will propagate throughout the seat. In the rear seat, various physical and functional dependencies related to the backrest frame, the seatbelts, the rear seat locks and the luggage nets were identified. When regarding the electrical system, various physical and functional dependencies were identified between its different components. When Volvo divided the car into modules, the aim was to group components so that such "strong" dependencies were contained within modules while there were weak dependencies between modules (see Fig. 65). Then, organizing the development of specific modules in specific module teams would imply that the "strong" dependencies could be dealt with within the teams.

However, as illustrated above, both the seats and the electrical system also have numerous "strong" dependencies to other components in the car. For instance, dependencies related to safety "cut through" the seats, and the cable harnesses have various physical dependencies to the car body. Many of these dependencies are difficult to anticipate and can therefore not be considered when defining the modules.

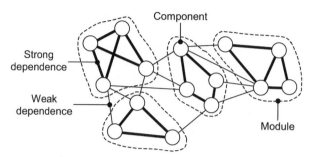

Fig. 65. Defining Modules Based on Dependencies Between Components.

Further, Volvo was concerned that the modules could be developed and produced in interaction with different suppliers. Over time, these suppliers had developed resource collections of their own, for instance in terms of knowledge, routines, technologies, and production facilities. In addition, the suppliers had developed relationships with different auto manufacturers for which they developed and produced specific components and, in some cases, Volvo already had relationships with suppliers that they wanted to utilize. Thus, in addition to the dependencies between components in the product (i.e. the car) the existing structure of business units, relationships and production facilities was considered when defining the modules. By defining modules that in some respects were similar to those developed and produced by these suppliers for other auto manufacturers, economies of learning and scale could be achieved in development and production. Consequently, the complexity of the overall pattern of dependencies between different resources made the decomposition of the car into modules and the formation of module teams, a difficult task.

Therefore, various compromises in terms of prioritizations between different dependencies were necessary. As described in the case, Volvo regarded "process-driven product development" to be important. Consequently, the definition of modules was largely based on dependencies related to production. This implied that mainly physical dependencies between components were considered. From this perspective, a front seat is a "perfect" module, since the only physical interfaces between the seat and other parts of the car are the four screws in the car floor and a few cable connectors. However, when regarding the electrical system, the nodes and applications were placed at many different positions in the car and related mainly by functional dependencies. However, it was considered important to deal with these dependencies within the same module team. Therefore, the complete electrical system was regarded as a module during development, i.e. largely based on functional dependencies. In production, mainly the cable harnesses were treated as modules, while various nodes were included in other modules. Thus, both physical and functional dependencies between components influenced the formation of the development teams.

The compromises between different types of dependencies implied that certain issues were prioritized. However, even if modules in this case were defined with a focus on production-related issues, Volvo considered it important that as many different dependencies as possible related to a specific module could be dealt with within each module team. Therefore, representatives from product development, production, logistics, purchasing and quality were present in each team. Thus, the teams were made cross-functional. Thereby, various different dependencies related to different organizational areas (departments) could be considered. However, styling and design were not represented in the module teams, even though many modules contained "styled" components. As was illustrated in Section 5, issues related to styling and design (e.g. color matching, surface materials, and surface structures) need to be coordinated across several modules. Volvo therefore chose to let the department for styling and design deal with these issues for the complete car, in interaction with different module teams.

Further, in order to enable dependencies to different suppliers' resources to be dealt with, also suppliers were represented in the teams. Both Lear and Delphi had representatives in the respective module teams from product development as well as production and other areas such as quality and logistics (some of them part-time). Thus, the teams were cross-functional also with respect to the suppliers. However, as has been illustrated in Section 6.1.1, what functions were represented in the teams was related to what dependencies had to be dealt with at different points in time and therefore varied over time. Moreover, the development of plastic components for the cable harnesses (e.g. cable ducts) required frequent interaction with Rieselmann, the supplier that would produce these plastic components. Therefore, also Rieselmann had a representative in the module team at Volvo at a few occasions. Thus, also the composition of business units represented in the team could be adapted to what specific dependencies had to be dealt with.

Thus, various dependencies related to several different components, production facilities, business units and business relationships influenced the definition of modules as well as the formation of the module teams (i.e. what resources were represented in the respective teams). However, the compromises regarding what dependencies should be considered when defining the modules also implied that certain dependencies could not be dealt with within the module teams. When regarding, for instance, the front seat, there were also several important dependencies between the front seat and other components (e.g. related to safety), which had to be dealt with across team boundaries. Thus, the definition of modules and the formation of teams, and thereby what dependencies could be dealt with in the teams and not, can be described as a matter of how to prioritize among various dependencies.

6.2.1.2. Modules and the development team at Scania. Also Scania had to consider how to form the team with regard to the modular product structure. As described in the case, Scania have for a long time systematically worked with standardizing components and defining groups of components that have clear interfaces to surrounding components, i.e. modules. The new truck model was a complement to the existing model range (the 4-series) and the (existing) product architecture implied that various product designs could be "carried over" to the new truck model. The existing modular product architecture also facilitated the development since many interfaces between components had been "tried out" before. Scania's previous experience from using these interfaces implied that many (but far from all) dependencies between components were known from the beginning. Consequently, the need for new development was reduced. Thereby, the development of the complete truck, and thus many "strong" dependencies between modules and components, could be dealt with within a single development team.

Using a single team implied that Scania did not have to divide the product development activities between several different teams. However, Scania's existing product architecture implied dependencies to other truck models that share the same modules and components (see Fig. 66). For instance, the expansion tank that was used in the new truck was the same as is used in other truck models. It was therefore difficult to change the existing design since, for Scania, this commonality between models implied fewer components and possibilities to

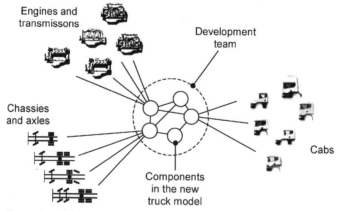

Fig. 66. Examples of Existing Product Designs that may Influence the Development of the New Truck Model in the Development Team.

benefit from scale economies in component production. Thus, component sharing between truck models implied dependencies to various other resources, including different suppliers' production facilities.

While the new truck was developed within the team, the other truck models in the existing program had mainly been developed within different functional areas in Scania's line organization. Even if there were representatives from the line organization in the team, dependencies to existing components in many cases had to be dealt with between the development team and other parts of Scania's organization. Hence, even if Scania used a single team, not all dependencies related to the development of the new truck model could be dealt with within that team.

With project "Alpha," Scania also wanted to try out a development organization that facilitated communication between different development areas and functions as well as it facilitated interaction with suppliers in product development. A major part of the representatives in the team came from different product development areas in Scania's development organization, such as chassis and powertrain. There were, however, also representatives from production, quality, logistics, aftermarket, marketing, and purchasing. Thus, also Scania's development team was cross-functional. In addition, there were representatives from the three suppliers DFC Tech, Ensu and Cool. While Scania had a cross-functional representation in the team, DFC Tech had very limited resources. Therefore, they only had representatives for product development in the team at Scania, and relied on frequent contacts with different functions within Dayco to ensure that various dependencies related to production, quality, logistics and so on were considered. This cross-functional team implied that (nearly) all development activities could be performed within the same team and, to facilitate coordination within the team, the members were co-located in the same office landscape.

Thus, the existing product architecture enabled "carry-over" of various component designs, which implied a rather limited scope of the development project. This, in turn, implied that the new truck model could be developed within a single cross-functional team. However, the case also illustrates that the existing product architecture implied dependencies to other components and products, as well as other business units' resources, which could not be dealt with within the team. In other words, the existing product architecture also implied "lock-in" effects.

Hence, both Volvo and Scania formed cross-functional teams, also involving representatives from different suppliers. To reduce the need for coordination across ("outside") the teams, they tried to gather "strong" dependencies within the team boundaries. The teams were formed with regard to Volvo and Scania's respective (modular) product structures, though also dependencies to production facilities, other business units, and relationships had to be considered. Thus, there was an

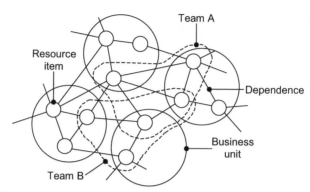

Fig. 67. What Dependencies are Considered Influences the Formation of the Team Boundary.

interplay between the (technical) resource structure and the organizing of the interactive product development.

Further, the different and competing bases for determining what dependencies to consider when defining modules and forming teams, implied that various compromises were necessary. What dependencies were considered when forming the development teams influenced the team boundary in terms of which business units and what resources were represented. This is illustrated in Fig. 67. Moreover, dynamics in the pattern of dependencies implied that the composition of the teams in terms of members representing various resources changed over time.

6.2.2. Dealing with Dependencies Between Several Business Units

The analysis in Section 6.1 illustrated that some dependencies were dealt with within relationships, while other dependencies had to be dealt with between relationships. In this section, the analysis is focused on the use of development teams for dealing with dependencies between several business units and relationships.

For the development of the new truck model, Scania utilized the relationships with DFC Tech, Ensu and Cool. These relationships made it possible to deal with dependencies between Scania and each one of these three suppliers. However, as illustrated in Section 6.1.1, dependencies between the steel pipe and the turbo charger had to be dealt with between DFC Tech and Ensu. Without the development team at Scania, this would have to be dealt with between the relationships Scania-DFC Tech and Scania-Ensu, or be coordinated via Scania, see Fig. 68. However, the representatives from DFC Tech and Ensu were brought together in the team at Scania, which facilitated "negotiations" regarding various adaptations of their

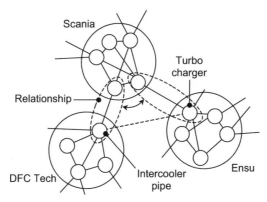

Fig. 68. Dependencies Between the Intercooler Pipe and the Turbo Charger.

respective components. When needed, the representatives could also relate certain design changes to various other resources, such as production facilities, within their respective business units. In this way, the development team enabled a direct connection between DFC Tech and Ensu that resembles a development relationship. This, in turn, helped to reduce the need for Scania to deal with dependencies between these suppliers' components.

Further, when DFC Tech tried to avoid the clash between the intercooler pipe and the cab floor, first by reducing the pipe diameter and then by re-designing the whole pipe, this influenced Ensu, Cool as well as Scania, that is, all four business units represented in the development team. The pipe diameter, as well as various functional requirements (e.g. regarding air flow) related to the intercooler pipe, had to be dealt with in interaction between DFC Tech, Ensu and Cool. Also Scania was involved since they developed the cab. At Scania, they were also concerned about a pipe that was easy to assemble. Then, within the team at Scania, DFC Tech, Cool and Ensu could quickly confront various resources and try out alternative design solutions for the pipe. At the same time, each one of them had possibilities to relate these design solutions to their respective business units' resource collections, thereby reducing some friction. Thus, the development team implied that more than two different business units' resource collections could be confronted at the same time. The development team thereby functioned as an integrator between several different relationships, i.e. dependencies within and between relationships could be dealt with in the team (see Fig. 69). This also implied that the development work could be more parallelized, which helped to reduce the development time.

Moreover, together with the other representatives in the team, DFC Tech managed to develop product designs that would otherwise not have been possible.

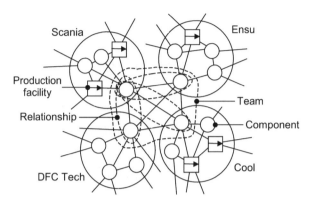

Fig. 69.   The Development Team at Scania.

If DFC Tech had not been represented in the team and if pipes and hoses had been developed during the last phases of the project (i.e. the traditional way) it would not have been possible to turn the turbo charger 180 degrees to enable an alternative pipe design. Thus, the simultaneous confrontation and adaptation of different business units' resources facilitated experimentation with resource interfaces and features which, in turn, resulted in better and less expensive product designs. In other words, the confrontation of resources facilitated innovation.

Further, both Lear and Autoliv were represented in the module team at Volvo developing the seats. This implied that the seat frames developed and produced by Autoliv could be adapted to requirements set by Autoliv's production plant and to Volvo's requirements regarding safety. At the same time, the possibilities to assemble the complete seat in Lear's MAU were considered. Thus, the co-location of Volvo, Lear and Autoliv implied that the dependencies between their respective relationships could be dealt with in the module team. However, both Lear and Autoliv are suppliers of various seat components, which means they are competitors. Therefore, at several times Volvo had to take an active part in the coordination regarding dependencies that could have been dealt with directly between Lear and Autoliv within the team.

Also several suppliers of components for the electrical system were competitors and they were sometimes reluctant to interact, especially regarding sensitive technology development. In this case, however, this was not a big problem since the standardized interfaces between components reduced the need for dealing with dependencies between different suppliers within the team. However, the problem with interference and noise in the audio system influenced components developed by several different suppliers. In this situation, Volvo discussed different solutions with different suppliers and it was decided that Delphi had to re-design the cable harnesses. Thus, several suppliers were involved in the module team, though, a major part of the coordination was performed not directly between the suppliers but through Volvo.

Furthermore, even if there are standardized interfaces between many components (applications) in the electrical system, similar technologies are used in several different applications. This implied that suppliers of different applications sometimes ran into similar problems. Then, the closeness to Volvo's as well as other suppliers' representatives in the team implied that experiences could be shared between business units, which implied more rapid problem solving. In addition, DFC Tech's participation in the team at Scania helped DFC Tech to more quickly adapt to and learn to use Scania's systems for handling drawings as well as following Scania's development process. Further, at both Volvo and Scania, meetings were held within the teams on a regular basis where time plans, the status of other related development projects, and project budgets were discussed. Thus, in addition to facilitating the development of specific components, the development teams were also important for the sharing of knowledge and experience between business units as well as for coordinating the development projects.

Thus far, this analysis has illustrated how the development teams functioned as integrators between different relationships. It is, however, relevant to make a distinction between the development teams that were established for specific development projects and the relationships that were part of the existing resource structure. For instance, contracts and legal issues were often dealt with directly between business units, within the relationships but "outside" the development teams. Large changes of the industrial structure, such as Lear's decision to move the assembly of seats from Bengtsfors to Torslanda, were dealt with at top management level and, thus, not in the teams dedicated to product development. Further, Dayco, Lear, Autoliv and several other business units already delivered components to Scania and Volvo respectively when the studied product development projects started. This implied that these business units frequently interacted with Volvo and Scania's assembly plants regarding product quality, matching of plans, delivery dates and so on. These parts of the relationships between these business units were represented in the development teams only if they could contribute to the development of the specific products that were focused on in the respective teams. Further, Autoliv assumed responsibility for the development of all airbags in the complete car implying that the relationship between Volvo and Autoliv was "split up" between different module teams (mainly the module team "driving unit" and the seat sub-team within module team "interior"). Furthermore, in addition to the development of components for the P2 platform, Autoliv and Lear were involved in different projects focusing on various upgrades of existing models, implying that there was more than one development project going on in a specific relationship.

Thus, mainly those parts of a relationship that were related to the development of specific components were represented in the development teams. Many other issues and dependencies were dealt with "outside" the team, but within the respective relationships.

Moreover, as illustrated in Section 6.1.2, DFC Tech as well as Lear and Delphi acted as integrators of the components that they assumed the development responsibility for. This was necessary since Witte, Ieper, IFE, MGW, and many other component suppliers (e.g. the supplier of the air dryer and the AC compressor to Scania) were not represented in the development teams. It was not possible to involve all these suppliers in the development teams, simply because there would have been too high a degree of complexity. Therefore, dependencies related to these suppliers' resource collections were dealt with in relationships with these suppliers, but "outside" the development teams (see Fig. 70).

Thus, as illustrated by the analysis in this section, the interactive development involving various different business units also required that dependencies between different relationships could be created and dealt with in an efficient way. Therefore, development teams were established as a complementary form of organizing interactive product development. While a relationship mainly connects two business units, several different business units may be represented within a development team. However, relationships are often developed over long periods

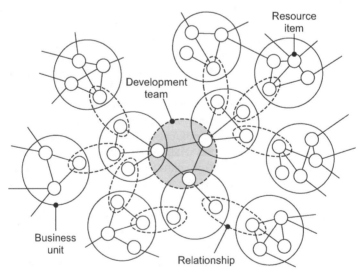

Fig. 70. The Business Units Represented in the Team Act As Integrators with Regard to Other Business Units not Represented in the Team.

of time while a development team can be established for a single development project and then be "dissolved." Moreover, many dependencies are dealt with between business units, within the relationship, but "outside" the development team. Thereby, the development team functions as a complementary organizing unit, which integrates different relationships and deals with specific dependencies between business units that are relevant for the development of a specific product.

6.2.3. Dealing with Dependencies in Different Teams

When developing the P2 platform, it was not considered possible to gather all development activities within a single team. The development of a complex product such as a car (or even several car models on the same platform) would require an extremely large team in terms of what different resources (and thus members) would need to be represented in the team. Therefore, Volvo considered it necessary to divide the development work between a number of smaller module teams.

In each module team, a number of representatives, with knowledge regarding specific resources within their respective business units, developed a specific module (or several modules). The composition of represented business units was different in different teams, though, Autoliv was represented in more than one team and Volvo was represented in all module teams. Thereby, the modules developed in the respective teams were related to different but partly overlapping resource contexts. A structure with three different teams is illustrated in Fig. 71.

This enabled some degree of specialization within the teams. However, as illustrated in previous analyses regarding the seats and the components for the electrical system, there were also numerous dependencies between modules. Consequently, the differentiation of product development among a number of teams also implied a need for coordination between teams. This coordination was performed by project managers with responsibility for the complete car(s), or through interaction between the teams. Thus, in addition to the resource collections of the business units represented in each team, the teams also needed to relate "their" module to the development performed in other teams.

As illustrated by the development of the seats and the components for the electrical system, it was, however, not possible to continuously adapt a specific module to changes in all other modules. Nor was it desirable, since continuous adaptation with regard to all possible dependencies would have increased the complexity that had to be dealt with, and thereby taken away the effect of differentiation of the development between different teams. Therefore, as exemplified above, when developing the seats an "envelope" was defined that reduced the need for dealing with interfaces to other interior components developed by other teams. In this way, interfaces to components developed within other teams could temporarily be regarded as "given." However, as illustrated by the redesign

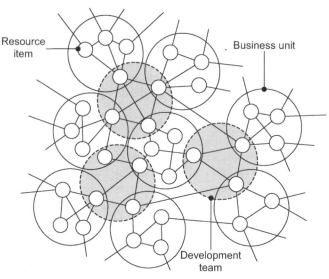

Fig. 71. Development in Different Development Teams.

of the electrical motor in the seat chassis that interfered with the air duct, certain "non-reversible" adaptations that have been made within a specific team may have consequences for components developed in other teams. Thus, "freezing" may imply "discontinuous" adaptation of resources developed in different teams, which may result in considerable friction between teams (as well as between teams and other resources in the existing resource structure).

Further, the electrical system, the seats as well as most other modules in the car contain different plastic components. Some of these plastic components may be produced with similar (or even the same) production equipment. However, these components were developed in several different module teams involving different suppliers. Thus, the division of development between different development teams also implied that it was more difficult to coordinate the utilization of different suppliers' production resources. This, in turn, influenced the possibilities to achieve scale economies in component production. This was one reason why Volvo sometimes decided which component suppliers the module suppliers should collaborate with. However, as illustrated above, this also implied a risk that scale economies were lost since the module suppliers utilized specific component suppliers in relationships with other auto manufacturers.

Hence, the Volvo-cases illustrate how the differentiation of development work among several teams enabled some specialization within teams, but also required coordination between teams. Although the product had been decomposed into modules, there were various dependencies related to physical components as well as to other resources that had to be dealt with between teams. While "freezing" of such dependencies reduced the complexity of the development task, this also implied a risk that the modules developed in different teams could not be combined. Further, as each team was composed by representatives from different business units, the developed modules could be adapted to and embedded in an existing resource structure (e.g. suppliers' production facilities). However, when regarding the complete car, also interaction and coordination between development teams was crucial to achieve a well-integrated product design and production structure.

6.2.4. Two Functions of the Development Team Boundary

While some dependencies were dealt with between resources represented within a specific team, other dependencies were dealt with between the team and other resources in the existing resource structure. This can be further elaborated by considering the team boundary as having two principally important functions, a *delimiting* and a *relating* function.

6.2.4.1. The delimiting function of the team boundary. Within Volvo and Scania's respective development teams, there were representatives with knowledge regarding specific resources that were needed for developing a specific module and the truck respectively. This implied, for instance, that representatives from Scania, DFC Tech, Ensu, and Cool could confront and adapt their respective resources within the team. By defining the team boundary, the development work in the team could be *delimited* from various other resources. This was necessary since the ability of the team to simultaneously deal with a large number of dependencies was limited. Thus, gathering specific resources and dependencies within the development team implied that the team members could focus on the development of a specific product or module, see Fig. 72.

When the problems with noise and play in the electrically maneuvered seat chassis were detected, representatives for Volvo, Lear, Autoliv, and Brose formed a "task force" within the development team to find a solution. By adapting and combining various resources represented by these business units, the problem could be solved fairly quickly within the development team. However, it later turned out that the electrical motor that had been moved in order to solve the problem interfered with an air duct that had to be re-designed. Thus, delimiting a task within the team may imply efficient adaptation of represented resources, though, there is also a risk that interfaces to other resources are not considered (cf. differentiation).

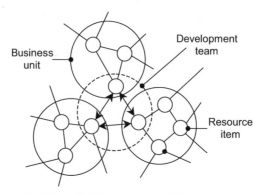

Fig. 72. The Delimiting Function of the Team Boundary.

While the team boundary defines (and delimits) what dependencies are dealt with within the team, it does not "protect" the team from external influence. Nor does it hinder adaptations and combinations of resources performed within the team to influence other resources "outside" the team. Therefore, the relating function of the team boundary is also important to consider.

6.2.4.2. The relating function of the team boundary. When developing the pipes at Scania, DFC Tech could perform much development work within the team in interaction with representatives from Scania and the other suppliers. It was, however, also important that the design solutions tried out within the team were related to production facilities and other resources within DFC Tech, Dayco, Scania, Phoenix/MGW, IFE, Ensu and Cool. Also the development of seats and components for the electrical system was performed within specific module teams. However, the developed components had to be related to various resources within the represented business units as well as to resources developed in other module teams. In other words, the development in a team cannot be performed in isolation. It must be done with regard to other resources. The resources represented in the team are all part of larger resource collections. Therefore, independently of what dependencies are considered when determining the team boundary, what is developed in the team will always need to be related to resources not represented in the team (cf. integration). This makes the *relating* function of the team boundary important (see Fig. 73).

When developing an individual component such as the silicone bellow used for the intercooler pipe, it was related to MGW's production facility that was not represented in the team. However, the team organization also implied that adaptations of the bellow and the production equipment could be related to

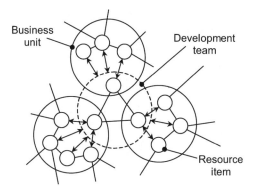

Fig. 73. The Relating Function of the Team Boundary.

the complete intercooler pipe and even the (nearly) complete truck. Similarly, when developing specific components for the seats, adaptations between these components and other resources "outside" the team could be related to the complete seat. Thus, by determining a team boundary, a resource item represented in the team becomes part of a whole set of resources. As illustrated in Fig. 73, this implies that, in addition to relating individual resource items (arrows crossing the team boundary), this whole *set* of resources represented in the team can be related to resources "outside" the team (arrows pointing at the team boundary).

This is an important function of the team boundary since it allows individual representatives to focus on the development of specific components while also the whole product/module (i.e. *combinations* of represented resources) can be related to different resource collections "outside" the team. This implies that dependencies can be dealt with not only in relation to specific components but also in relation to the whole product developed by the team.

6.2.5. Summary of the Analysis

This part of the analysis has been focused on *how* product development was organized in order to deal with dependencies in interaction between business units. Dependencies between business units can be dealt with within relationships and, as dependencies stretch beyond a single relationship, the development may require interaction between several different business units and relationships (the analyses regarding relationships have been summarized by the end of Sections 6.1.1 and 6.1.2). In order to deal with dependencies within and across several different relationships, the interactive product development was organized in cross-functional teams where different business units were represented. While the relationships in many cases had been developed over a long period of time, the teams mainly functioned as a complementary organizational unit that was established for specific development projects.

The cases illustrate how the formation of the development teams was influenced by the decomposition of the respective products into smaller building blocks, in these cases modules. The intention was to group "strong" dependencies within teams. However, when defining the modules this had to be done with regard to dependencies in the product as well as with regard to dependencies related to production facilities, business units, and relationships. This complex pattern of dependencies implied that various compromises were necessary when defining the modules and forming the teams. Therefore, while some dependencies could be dealt with within the teams, other dependencies required interaction across the team boundaries.

Further, the use of a "well-established" product architecture implied that many "known" module interfaces could be re-used, thereby reducing the scope of the development project. At the same time, however, this also implied "lock in" in terms of various strong dependencies to the existing resource structure, requiring interaction across the team boundary.

However, the need for interaction across team boundaries could be reduced by temporarily "freezing" certain interfaces. Thereby, these interfaces were regarded as "given," which implied that the complexity of the pattern of dependencies dealt with within the team was reduced. At the same time, however, regarding interfaces as "given" implied a risk that actual changes in these interfaces were not considered. This, in turn, may result in considerable friction between the product developed in the team and other resources "outside" the team.

Even if various compromises were necessary when regarding what dependencies could be dealt with within the teams, this was to some extent "compensated for" by making the teams cross-functional. Even if the products were decomposed mainly with regard to physical dependencies and requirements related to production, the involvement of representatives from several different functional areas implied that also various other dependencies could be dealt with within the teams. Further, the involvement of representatives from different suppliers in the teams implied that dependencies related to several different business units' resource collections could be dealt with within the team. Thereby, the team also facilitated the interaction between different relationships. This implied that dependencies between different suppliers' resources could be dealt with within the team, without requiring involvement of the auto manufacturer. The team organization enabled simultaneous confrontation and adaptation of several different business units' resources, thereby contributing to shorter development time and innovation. However, to keep complexity at a manageable level, not all business units involved in the development of components for a specific module could be represented in the respective teams. Instead, the represented business units acted as "integrators" with regard to these other business units.

Further, two important functions of the team boundary were identified; the delimiting and the relating function. The delimiting function is important to enable a focus within the team on the development task at hand. The relating function is important for the adaptation of resources represented in the team to the existing resource structure. The relating function implies that not only individual resource items, but also the whole set of resources developed within the team, may be related to the existing resource structure.

In next section, the organizing of interactive product development in teams is elaborated in more detail and related to previous research.

7. IMPLICATIONS AND CONCLUSIONS

Section 7 provides a brief summary of the paper. Section 7.1 discusses implications of the study are discussed. Section 7.2 offers conclusions.

7.1. Summary of the Paper

As a point of departure for this paper, the increasing interest for developing new products in interaction between several different firms was highlighted. In particular, the involvement of suppliers in product development within the automotive industry provided a background for studying the organizing of interactive product development.

As a theoretical point of departure, the division of development activities between different firms was approached in terms of *differentiation*. Based on existing organization theory it was argued that, by differentiating activities among different organizational units, various benefits may be achieved. In particular, the possibility to achieve *specialization* is of importance, as it provides possibilities to achieve economies of learning and scale. In addition, differentiation enables parallelization of product development activities, which may contribute to reduce the development time. Benefits of differentiation in terms of possibilities to adapt the organization to a more or less anonymous "environment" have, however, been of less importance as the present study deals with interaction with specific counterparts.

At the same time, however, differentiation implies an increased need for *integration*, i.e. to achieve unity of effort among organizational units. *Coordination* was defined as the actions taken to achieve this unity of effort. The need for coordination was attributed to *dependencies* between development activities that have been differentiated between organizational units. Dependence refers to the extent to which activities are interrelated so that changes in the state of one element affect the state of other elements. By analyzing what dependencies need to be dealt with between organizational units, an improved understanding of the need for coordination and, thus, requirements regarding the organizing of interactive product development, can be achieved. This led to the purpose of the paper that has been to explore dependencies and how interactive product development may be organized with regard to these dependencies.

The study of dependencies and how these dependencies relate to the organizing of interactive product development required a theoretical framework that could deal with multiple organizational units. From existing research, it could be seen that various forms of *relationships* may function as an organizational means for dealing with product development between firms. An important starting point, however, was that interactive development involves several firms that are connected through multiple relationships. Therefore, a theoretical framework was developed based on the Industrial Network Approach. The concern with products and product development implied a focus on the *resource* layer and product development was approached in terms of *adaptation* and *combination* of resources. Following from the assumption that resources are *heterogeneous*, the value of a specific resource depends on which other resources it is combined with. Further, resources are *embedded*. This implies that no resource can be adapted and combined in isolation since dependencies to other resources also need to be considered. Based on a model for interactive development of resources, the framework was further developed for analyzing characteristics of and dependencies related to *products*, *production facilities*, *business units*, and *business relationships*.

The empirical data originated from three longitudinal case studies focusing: (1) the development of components for the electrical system; and (2) the development of seats for Volvo's P2 platform; and (3) the development of various pipes and hoses for a new truck model at Scania. Based on the formulation of the purpose of the paper, the analysis of the empirical data was divided into two main parts. The first part focused on the characteristics of different resources and explored *what* dependencies related to these resources that needed to be considered. The second part of the analysis focuses on *how* interactive product development was organized with regard to dependencies. This part of the analysis was divided into two sections focused on relationships and development teams respectively.

7.2. Implications of the Study

In this section, some important implications regarding resource-related dependencies and the organizing of interactive product development are discussed.

7.2.1. The Product Structure and the Organizing of Product Development
The present study has illustrated how the decomposition of the product into smaller product elements and the organizing of product development are interrelated. It is, however, relevant to question the view put forward in the current literature and further elaborate upon the relation between (product-related) dependencies and the organizing of product development.

When regarding the organizing of product development, dependencies between resources were taken as a starting point. A basic assumption is that the greater the interdependence, the more resources are needed for coordination (Scott, 1998). Following Thompson's (1967) arguments, development activities should be grouped according to their degree of interdependence with highly interdependent, i.e. reciprocal, activities in the same or closely adjacent units in order to reduce the need for coordination between organizational units. In a similar way, von Hippel (1990) argues that development tasks should be partitioned so that highly interdependent tasks are unified within the same task boundary, thereby reducing the need for problem-solving across task boundaries. These ideas follow Simon's (1962) arguments of "near decomposability," implying that "intra-component linkages" are generally stronger than "intercomponent linkages" (ibid., p. 477). A related concept is the "loosely coupled system" (Orton & Weick, 1990), where elements are regarded to be coupled (interdependent), but where they also preserve some degree of independence. Thus, there seems to be an agreement regarding the importance of unifying strong dependencies within organizational units in order to reduce the need for coordination between these units.

When regarding products, modularization is often regarded as a way to decompose a product into smaller and more manageable building blocks (i.e. modules) by clearly defining standardized interfaces. In modules, the *"structural elements are powerfully connected among themselves and relatively weakly connected to elements in other units"* (Baldwin & Clark, 2000). Following Ulrich's (1995) definition, a modular architecture implies a one-to-one mapping of functions to physical components. Then, a relevant question is what relation can be identified between such a decomposition of the product and the organizing of product development.

Most researchers that have investigated the development of modular products (e.g. Brusoni et al., 2001; Langlois & Robertson, 1992; Sanchez & Mahoney, 1996) have assumed that the development of individual modules is mainly performed *within* (specialized) firms. According to Sanchez and Mahoney (1996), the standardized interfaces between modules provide a form of "embedded coordination." Thereby, the modular product architecture enables each organizational unit participating in the development of a product to "function autonomously and concurrently" (cf. "black box" development). Sanchez and Mahoney argue that the creation of a modular product architecture enables creation

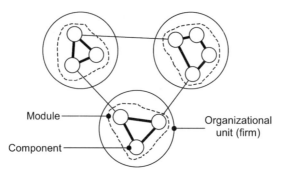

Fig. 74. A Modular Product and a Modular Organization.

of a modular organization structure. This is illustrated in Fig. 74. This, they argue, provides a means to *"quickly link together the resources and capabilities of many organizations"* (ibid., p. 68). These arguments correspond with what Robertson and Langlois (1995) refer to as the "conventional view." This implies that "autonomous innovation" (a change in one part of the system does not affect the rest of the system) can be performed in decentralized networks, while systemic innovation (a change in one part of the system necessitates corresponding change in other parts of the system) calls for internalization within firms.

In the cases studied, the complete products were decomposed into modules and components. However, these modules and components were not developed within single business units. Instead, the development was performed in *interaction* between several business units, implying that it was neither internalized within specific firms nor "autonomous." In addition, this interactive development was organized in development teams, i.e. organizational units involving representatives from several different business units. Thus, there was no one-to-one relationship between a modular product architecture and a modular organization as depicted in Fig. 74. Still, however, the decomposition of the product into smaller building blocks was important for the organizing of product development and the possibilities to benefit from specialization. It is therefore relevant to further elaborate upon the relation between product modularization and the organizing of product development.

7.2.2. Confrontation, Adaptation, and Combination Resources
It seems to be a common view that modularization (based on the logics of differentiation) provides possibilities for specialization (see e.g. Sanchez & Mahoney, 1996; Ulrich & Tung, 1991), though, this often aims at specialization within a specific organizational unit (firm). At the same time, product development

implies combination and adaptation of resources and, due to resource heterogeneity and embeddedness of resources into different contexts, the confrontation between *different* business unit's resources is important for innovation. Thus, development of a module within a specific business unit may provide specialization, but then the possibilities for confrontation with other business units' resources and, thus innovation, are limited.

In the present study, the decomposition of the complete product into smaller building blocks enabled development to be focused on "nearly decoupled" groups of components, or modules. Thereby, some degree of specialization could be achieved. However, even if a group of components could be decoupled into a module, this module was not developed within a single business unit, but in interaction between different business units. Hence, the outcome was the result of interaction, enabling compromises between several different business units' resources, which also contributed to innovation (see Fig. 75).

The differentiation of development between business units implied that the development teams played an important role. By defining a team boundary that coincides with the module boundary, different business units' resources may be confronted, adapted, and combined within the team, which facilitates innovation. Two important functions of the development team boundary were identified; the *delimiting* function and the *relating* function. The team boundary implies that the developed module can be delimited from other products, production facilities and relationships, thereby enabling a certain degree of specialization within the team. This may be done by temporarily "freezing" certain dependencies, i.e. regarding them as "given." At the same time, the team boundary is important for relating the module to resources "outside" the team, which enables embedding of the module into the existing resource structure, as well as it may improve innovation.

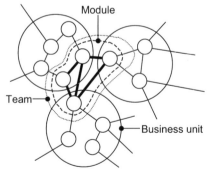

Fig. 75. Development of a "Nearly Decoupled" Module in Interaction Between Business Units.

7.2.3. Dependencies Between "Nearly Decoupled" Modules

As was described above, modularization implies that a product is decomposed so that strong dependencies are kept within modules and weak dependencies are found between modules. According to Sanchez and Mahoney (1996), the structure of standardized module interfaces, i.e. the product architecture, implies an "information structure" that "*coordinates the loosely coupled activities of component developers*" (ibid., p. 66). However, even if a product has been "nearly decomposed" and dependencies between modules are weak, these dependencies are not negligible (Simon, 1962). The present study illustrates that even if interfaces were standardized, not all dependencies could be "captured" within modules. This implied that a certain amount of interaction was required to deal with dependencies between modules. Thereby, it can be argued, in accordance with Brusoni and Prencipe (2001), that the information structure that was provided by the standardized interfaces (i.e. the product architecture) was not sufficient for dealing with the loose couplings between modules and, thus, not sufficient for coordinating the development activities.

This far, modules have been regarded as more or less decoupled building blocks. However, from the analysis it can be seen that far from all components may be aligned to form a fully modular product structure. In a complex product, where interaction between numerous components is required to provide a large number of different functions, it may be difficult to define "nearly decoupled" modules (cf. Ulrich & Tung, 1991). However, also when regarding less complex components, several (strong) dependencies to other components that need to be considered were found.

Based on the present study, it can also be argued that it may be necessary to abandon the principle of a one-to-one relationship between function and physical module. That is, since the patterns of functional and physical dependencies between components are different and only partly overlapping. In other words, each physical component implements more than one function (cf. Gadde & Jellbo, 2002) and vice versa. Instead, modules may be defined based on physical dependencies only (see Baldwin & Clark, 2000, p. 63 footnote; Ulrich & Tung, 1991) and, in other cases, on functional dependencies (i.e. a system) or certain combinations of physical and functional dependencies. It may be argued that this is not a "true" modular product architecture, though, if all dependencies between components are considered, it is (practically) impossible to define modules according to the principle of a one-to-one relationship between function and physical module. According to Ulrich (1995), most products embody hybrid modular-integral architectures.

Moreover, modules cannot only be based on dependencies between physical components. Also dependencies related to resource categories other than products need to be considered. Defining a module based on, for instance, various physical dependencies between components can make the module well adapted for pre-assembly in a particular production facility. At the same time, however, this module may not at all be suitable from the perspective of service and maintenance of the complete product (cf. Persson, 2003). Further, since the development of modules requires interaction among different business units, relationships between these business units as well as their specific resource collections need to be considered. By adapting the definition of modules to different business units' (e.g. suppliers) existing knowledge, routines, products, production equipment and so forth, these business units' possibilities to benefit from economies of learning and scale may be improved.

This discussion illustrates that far from all dependencies can be "encapsulated" within (nearly) decoupled modules. Independent of how a module is defined, there will be dependencies related to other modules or other resources that persist in "sticking out." As noted by Gadde and Jellbo (2002), the subdivision of a "whole" into its parts can be done in many different ways. Therefore, the grouping of components and the definition of modules is always a question of various compromises.

7.2.4. Changing Interfaces

It is generally argued that the product architecture, defining the design rules for individual modules, should be specified before commencing the development of these modules (Baldwin & Clark, 1997; Sanchez & Mahoney, 1996). However, the present study illustrates that far from all dependencies can be anticipated. As individual modules are being developed, new dependencies are created (some of them incidentally), some characteristics of the dependencies are changed, and some dependencies are eliminated. Thus, the pattern of dependencies is continuously changing. An important implication of this is that the modular product architecture cannot be defined before development begins and then be regarded as "given." Consequently, it may not be possible to separate development at the architectural and modular levels respectively.

Therefore, as noted by von Hippel (1990), task partitioning and, thus, the specification of module interfaces, may be improved as the project unfolds with respect to the evolving pattern of dependencies. According to Karlsson et al. (1998), design specifications cannot be regarded as fixed. Specifications should instead be regarded as an "*open arena for technical adjustments*" (ibid., p. 547). Even if it is not desirable to change module interface specifications, it may be necessary. Such changes, in turn, imply that the conditions, under which different modules are developed, change. Consequently, the development organization also needs to be adapted. This implies continuously changing team boundaries and, thus, changes regarding what resources are represented in a specific team. In addition, changing module interfaces requires interaction between different teams developing different modules.

7.2.5. Knowledge Related to the Developed Module
According to Sanchez and Mahoney (1996), a modular product implies that development can be performed by a dedicated organizational unit (e.g. a supplier), which also embodies all the knowledge needed for the development and production of the module. However, the present study has illustrated that modules are developed in interaction between business units. This implies that the knowledge required for developing a specific module reaches beyond single business units. Further, due to various dependencies, the development of a specific module also requires knowledge regarding other modules, other products, as well as other resources, such as production facilities and relationships. Using Loasby's (1999) terms, the relevant knowledge may be "direct," meaning that it is possessed by those developing the specific module, or "indirect," meaning that they know how and where the required knowledge can be accessed. Hence, as various dependencies reach beyond a specific module, also the knowledge regarding various resources must reach beyond that module (see Fig. 75). This means that there is no one-to-one relationship between product modularization and knowledge modularization (cf. Brusoni & Prencipe, 2001).

7.2.6. The Decomposition of the Product and the Organizing of Development
An important starting point for this discussion was the question regarding the interrelationship between the decomposition of a product into modules and the organizing of product development. The general view seems to be that product development should be internalized within firms and, by decomposing the product into (nearly) independent modules, these modules can be developed within different firms. With this principle as a basis, Sanchez and Mahoney (1996) have argued that modular products enable modular organizations. However, as illustrated by the present study, it was neither possible to group all (strong) dependencies within (nearly) decoupled modules, nor were these modules developed within individual business units. Consequently, interaction was required between modules as well as between business units.

This could lead us to a conclusion similar to that of Brusoni and Prencipe (2001) and Brusoni et al. (2001), who state that there is no one-to-one relationship between product architecture and organizational architecture. According to Langlois (2002), the organization "arises as a non-modular response to the fact of, or the need for, interactions between the modules" (ibid., p. 32). However, even if not all dependencies could be "encapsulated," the basic principle of grouping strong or reciprocal dependencies within the same organizational unit was still

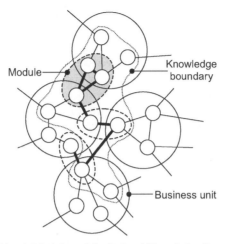

Fig. 76. A Module and the Related Knowledge Boundary.

found to be valid in the present study. It is, however, relevant to ask within what organizational unit these dependencies were grouped. The answer is that, even if strong dependencies had to be dealt with across business units, dependencies were, as far as possible, grouped within *development teams* (see Fig. 76).

As argued above, the organizing of product development in teams has important implications for innovation and the possibilities to make adaptations of resources controlled by several different business units. An important feature of this way of organizing product development is that the team boundaries, which dependencies are grouped within, are *different* from the firm boundaries. Therefore, while most other researchers concerned with the differentiation of product development activities have been focusing on the firm boundary, an important implication of the present study is that other organizational boundaries, such as the team boundary, may sometimes be more important to consider.

It may be argued that the "multiple team" organization illustrated in Fig. 76 is modular, as it corresponds to the modular structure of the product. However, as argued above, dependencies also reach beyond the teams. In addition, the direct and indirect knowledge that is related to the resources represented in a team reaches far beyond the boundaries of that team. Following the arguments of Brusoni et al. (2001), this implies that the team organization cannot be regarded as modular. However, by considering the two functions of the development team boundary, the following distinction can be made. The delimiting function of the team boundary enables a focus on dependencies dealt with within the team. Thereby, certain benefits associated with a differentiated (modular) organizational structure, such as specialization and parallelization of activities may be achieved. At the same time, the relating function of the team boundary implies that what is developed within the team can be related to resources "outside" the team, thereby enabling benefits associated with an integrated development organization.

Thus, an important feature of the team is that the team boundary is different from the firm boundary. Still, the decomposition of the product into modules is of importance for the organizing of interactive product development in teams. It is argued that the development of different modules in different teams may imply a modular organizational structure. Development is, however, not isolated within these teams, but performed in interaction with the existing resource structure.

7.2.7. The Team Boundary and the Organizing of Product Development

When considering interactive product development, the team boundary is important for delimiting the developed product from, and relating it to, the existing resource structure. The utilization of the delimiting and relating functions of the team boundary has important implications for product development.

In a team where the delimiting function is "weak," the resources that are adapted and combined within the team are continuously influenced by the existing resource structure. This may imply that the team mainly functions as a forum for finding compromises between resources controlled by different business units. It is likely that a product is developed that is well adapted to the existing resource structure since the (potential) friction between resources is continuously dealt with within the team. There is, however, a risk that the developed product becomes an "insipid compromise."

If, instead, development activities are delimited from the existing resource structure and individual resource items, as well as the complete product/ module developed within the team, are continuously related to the existing resource structure the outcome might be different. This implies that a product can be developed that has some distinct characteristics and is well integrated, with respect to the interplay between its different components, but also with respect to the existing resource structure.

Thus, the delimiting and relating functions of the team boundary give teams different characteristics. In this latter case, where the product/module developed in the team is delimited from, but also related to, the larger resource structure, representatives in the team may not only represent their individual business units' resources, but also the whole product/module developed within the team. An important implication of this is that not only business units or firms, but also *teams*, can be regarded and function as *actors*. The team itself may be regarded as an actor by the business units represented in the team, by other business units not represented in the team, as well as by other teams. However, such an "actor team" implies that business units need to deal with yet another actor, something that might be regarded as a problem by other actors that are not involved in the team.

Even if teams that function as actors may not be desirable in all cases and from all perspectives, *both* the delimiting and relating functions may be important for the team. In Section 6.2.4, the delimiting and relating functions of the team boundary were related to differentiation and integration respectively. In line with Lawrence and Lorsch's (1967b) findings regarding this pair of variables, it can be argued that there need not be a trade-off between the delimiting and relating functions where one can be obtained only at the expense of the other.

Further, the relating function of the team boundary may be regarded as an *alternative* to the "information structure" that, according to Sanchez and Mahoney (1996), can be obtained with a stable product architecture where module interfaces have been fully specified prior to development of individual modules. While organizing development based on such a static structure (cf. Brusoni & Prencipe, 2001) does not consider the need for interaction between teams developing different modules, the relating function of the team boundary allows for continuous confrontation and adaptation of modules developed within different teams. This is particularly important with regard to the dependencies that may not be grouped within a specific team. As argued above, in this way the relating function of the team boundary may contribute to improved innovation. In addition, by continuously relating various resources, the organizing of product development may not be static and predetermined, but rather an on-going process.

Furthermore, the relating function is important for the creation of knowledge and experience regarding the technical structure (products and production facilities). This knowledge and experience is embedded into the organizational structure (business units and relationships) and may be utilized in future development projects. Preserving the technical structure, e.g. in terms of product architecture or product platforms, may enable benefits such as "carry-over" and "commonality" (e.g. Johnson & Bröms, 2000; Meyer & Lehnerd, 1997; Ulrich, 1995) and many firms set tough targets regarding such benefits. At the same time, it is often regarded as possible to frequently and freely change relationships (with suppliers) in the organizational structure (cf. Fine, 1998; Lambe & Spekman, 1997; Sanchez & Mahoney, 1996). The present study, however, illustrates that what can be achieved in the technical structure is closely related to the utilization of what has been built into the organizational structure (business units and relationships). In this way, the technical and organizational structures are closely related, implying that extensive organizational restructuring may limit the possibilities to achieve "carry-over" and "commonality" in the technical structure. The utilization of what is embedded into the resource structure is further elaborated upon in next section.

7.2.8. Implications for the Organizing of Projects that are Dispersed in Time
The resources that are adapted and combined in a development project are part of, and need to be related to, an existing resource structure. Thereby, this existing resource structure influences the product design, as well as the organizing of product development. In other words, no development project starts with a "blank paper." However, apart from the outcome (i.e. the developed product), every development project also leaves "imprints" in the existing resource structure. In this section, such "imprints" are elaborated upon. The discussion has this far been concerned with the organizing of teams in a "single" project, but it is also relevant to consider implications of such "imprints" for the organizing of development projects that are dispersed in time.

It has been argued that the decomposition of the product into smaller product elements, e.g. through modularization, is important for the division of development work between organizational units. Depending on how the product is decomposed, different knowledge and experience is created during the development project regarding specific interfaces and the interaction between different components. This knowledge and experience can be utilized also for development of products in the future and, thus, be regarded as "imprints" in the existing resource structure.

Further, the design of, and interfaces between, individual components in a product influence what adaptations and investments are needed regarding specific production equipment, in what sequence it can be utilized, as well as how different production facilities are connected to each other. However, investments in production facilities often have a longer lifecycle than the developed product. In addition, a specific production facility often produces several different products, with different time scope, which are also influenced by the developed product (e.g. in terms of scale economies). Thereby, the design of individual components changes, and thus leave "imprints" in, the structure of production resources that reach far beyond the time scope of the developed product.

When developing a product in interaction between business units, existing relationships can be utilized. However, the product architecture, the need for specific knowledge, and the need for specific production technologies may imply that it is also necessary to establish new relationships. Then, as the development project goes on, knowledge, routines, and social bonds, are developed and various production facilities and products are adapted and combined within the relationships. When the development project is finished, there will still be considerable "substance" in these relationships, implying that "imprints" are left in the existing structure of business units and relationships.

Thus, as resources are adapted and combined, the existing resource structure is changed. Thereby, any development project leaves a variety of "imprints," with different extensions in time, in the existing structure of products, production facilities, business units and relationships; cf. Thompson (1967) who argues that resources are more or less enduring, more or less mobile, more or less disposable.

When regarding implications of these "imprints" for a new development project, it can be seen that the utilization of the same product architecture (or at least certain interfaces) for other products enables component commonality and/or "carry-over." This also implies that the investments made in specific production facilities can be utilized for larger production series. Consequently, there may be scale economies in design and production. Further, specific features of existing relationships, developed during the last development project, may be utilized also in the new project. The continuation of relationships over a longer period of time enables, for instance, adaptations of knowledge and routines as well as the development of social bonds between business units. However, using an existing product architecture may also require that various interfaces be regarded as "given" in the new development project, which may hamper innovation. Therefore, there may be a need for compromises between product "newness" (requiring changes in the product architecture) and scale economies (requiring that product design and interfaces are kept the same). Further, considerable investments in a specific relationship may imply "lock-in" with regard to a specific business unit. Thereby, the possibilities to chose which counterparts to involve in a new development project, and thus what resource combinations that can be tried out, may be limited. Hence, the "imprints" from the last project may be utilized for the new project, but such "imprints" also have implications in terms of "lock-in." The degree of product "newness" and the amount of "carry-over" to the new project influences the pattern of dependencies that needs to be dealt with and, thus, the organizing of the new project, i.e. the formation of teams.

Furthermore, although there may be considerable "imprints" and investments made in an earlier project that need to be utilized, the existing resource structure is comprised by a large *network* of actors. These actors continuously confront, adapt, and combine various resources in order to improve the utilization of their respective resource collections. Thereby, these actors also leave various "imprints" in the resource structure. This introduces dynamics, implying that the existing resource structure cannot be regarded as "given" between projects that are dispersed in time. This, in turn, implies that conditions for utilizing an existing product architecture and requirements for scale economies in production change between projects. Therefore, in order to deal with various "new" dependencies that have emerged since the last project was carried through, the organizing of the project team(s) may have to be modified for the new project.

Moreover, when organizing a development project, a fundamental question is what dependencies need to be considered and dealt with. However, as illustrated above, the complex and dynamic pattern of dependencies between resources implies that various compromises are necessary when organizing a product development project. It is, therefore, equally relevant to ask what dependencies have *not* been considered and dealt with in a particular development project. Defining a product architecture based on physical component interfaces may imply that functional interfaces are not considered to any significant extent. This will also be reflected by various "imprints" in the existing resource structure, which need to be considered in future projects. It can therefore be questioned whether the same basic principles for organizing development should be used, time after time, in different development projects. By *altering* the principles for organizing development projects, different (and complementary) patterns of dependencies may be considered. This, however, may also imply that some benefits associated with utilizing "imprints" from previous projects, for example in terms of "carry-over," are lost.

Thus, as the development organization induces as well as it is exposed to dynamics in the existing resource structure, it may be necessary to change the organizing of development teams during and between projects. Thereby, the organizing of interactive product development is a dynamic process. Such changes need to be performed in a way that considers the possibilities to utilize "imprints" from previous projects, as well as influences from other actors on the existing resource structure need to be taken into account. By continuing important relationships, knowledge and experience regarding certain dependencies may be retained and utilized in future projects.

7.2.9. Summary

To summarize, interaction between business units is important for the possibilities to confront, adapt, and combine different business units' resources, something that is also important for innovation. This interaction can be achieved by organizing product development in teams including several different business units. A key implication of team development is that the team boundaries, which the development activities are grouped within, are *different* from the boundaries of the represented business units. The delimiting and the relating functions of the team boundary imply that team development may provide benefits associated with both differentiated and integrated organizational structures. The decomposition of the product (e.g. into modules) is important for the organizing of product development and vice versa. There is, however, no one-to-one relationship between (nearly) decoupled product elements and firms. Thereby, the study provides a view on the organizing of product development that is different from most existing research, which has mainly been focusing on the boundary of the firm. Thus, this study not only questions the established view on how development is differentiated between firms, but also on where the development takes place, i.e. not within firms but in interaction between firms. Further, depending on how the delimiting and relating functions of the development team are utilized, the team may achieve different characteristics. A team may even be regarded as an actor by business units and other teams. Then, the organizing of interactive product development was elaborated concerning projects that are dispersed in time. The adaptation and combination of resources implies that "imprints" are made in the existing resource structure. These "imprints" may be used in future projects. However, due to a continuously changing resource structure and a need for considering dependencies not dealt with in previous projects, the team organization may have to be modified between development projects.

7.3. Conclusions

With regard to the research issues identified in Section 2, and with the analyses in Sections 5 and 6 and the above discussion of implications as a basis, the following main conclusions are drawn:

- *Dependencies* between components, but also numerous dependencies related to other resources need to be considered when developing a product. In the present study, a complex *pattern* of dependencies related to the four resource categories products, production facilities, business units and business relationships has been identified. This pattern of dependencies stretches far beyond the boundaries of individual business units. Therefore, in order to enable adaptation and combination of resources across the boundaries of these business units, *interaction* between business units is needed. The dependencies between resources also imply that what can be achieved in the technical structure (products and production facilities) is closely related to the organizational structure (business units and relationships). This also implies that the *organizing* of product development needs to be subject to interaction between business units.
- The overall complexity of the pattern of dependencies implies that, regardless of how product development is organized, there will be dependencies that stretch across the organizational boundaries. Therefore, organizing product development is always a compromise with regard to what dependencies should be dealt with within and between organizational units respectively. In other words, there is no "best" way of organizing interactive product development. In addition, when organizing interactive product development, it is relevant to also consider what dependencies may not be dealt with. Further, not all dependencies can be foreseen. As resources are adapted and combined in the development process, new dependencies are created and the pattern of dependencies continuously

changes. This dynamics implies that neither the dependencies that need to be dealt with, nor the developed product, may be regarded as "given."

- Certain dependencies between resources may be dealt with within *relationships*. However, the complex pattern of dependencies also implies a need for dealing with dependencies across several relationships. By organizing product development in *teams*, simultaneous interaction among several different business units, and thus within and across relationships, can be achieved. An important feature of the team boundary is that it is *different* from and partly overlapping the boundaries of involved business units. This implies, with regard to the adaptation and combination of resources, that product development is performed jointly among several business units, rather than within individual business units. In turn, the business units that are represented in the team may function as "integrators" with regard to other business units not represented in the team.

- The team boundary has two principally important functions, a *delimiting* function and a *relating* function. By delimiting the development performed within the team from the larger resource structure, complexity is reduced and the team members can focus on the task at hand (cf. differentiation). This may be done by temporarily "freezing" interfaces to the existing resource structure (i.e. regarding them as "given"). However, the development within the team cannot be performed in isolation. By utilizing the relating function, not only individual resources but the whole *set* of resources represented in the team, can be related to the existing resource structure (i.e. integration). The two functions of the team boundary are not mutually exclusive, implying that the team may achieve benefits associated with *both* a high degree of differentiation and a high degree of integration. This, in turn, implies that a team may function and be regarded as an *actor* by business units as well as by other teams. Further, the relating function of the team boundary may be an alternative to the use of a static product architecture (i.e. product interfaces are regarded as "given") for the coordination of loosely coupled development tasks. The relating function of the team boundary enables *continuous* organizing of development activities with regard to the technical structure, within as well as beyond the scope of the team. This facilitates confrontation of resources and interaction and, thus, may improve innovation.

- The decomposition of a complete product (e.g. a car or a truck) into smaller building blocks (e.g. modules) may be important for the division of development activities among organizational units. However, due to the need for interaction, it may neither be possible, nor desirable, to internalize the development of specific modules within individual business units. Consequently, there may not be a one-to-one relationship between the modular product structure and the organizational structure of *business units*. Instead, development of different modules may be performed within different development *teams*. Thereby, modules are developed within an organizational structure that is complementary to the structure of business units, and that may be modular with regard to these teams. Further, the decomposition of the product into modules is always a compromise with regard to what (types of) dependencies can be dealt with within the teams. Therefore, there will always be a need for also dealing with dependencies across development teams. It is therefore relevant to question suggestions put forward in the current literature regarding the outsourcing of development of complete modules or "black box" components to "independent" suppliers.

• Every development project leaves certain *"imprints"* in the existing structure of products, production facilities, business units and business relationships. With regard to this existing resource structure, these "imprints" may be regarded as investments that can be utilized also in future development projects. However, requirements regarding the utilization of these investments also imply restrictions to what can be developed in the future. By maintaining important relationships in the organizational structure, knowledge regarding specific "imprints," as well as knowledge regarding "fruitless" resource combinations, can be revived and utilized in future development projects. It is therefore important to consider the strong connection between the technical structure and the organizing. This implies that policies regarding how to manage the technical structure (e.g. in terms of targets concerning "carry-over" and "commonality") cannot be separated from the management of the organizational structure (e.g. the supplier structure).

ACKNOWLEDGMENTS

I express my sincere thanks to Anna Dubois, Christer Karlsson and Sten-Olof Gustavsson. I express my gratitude to my other colleagues at Chalmers University of Technology and to researchers within the IMP Group. I thank the representatives from Volvo Car Corporation, Dayco, Autoliv, Delphi, Lear, and Scania.

REFERENCES

Alchian, A. A., & Demsetz, H. (1972). Production, information costs, and economic organization. *The American Economic Review, 62*, 777–795.

Allen, T. J. (1979). *Managing the flow of technology*. Boston, MA: MIT Press.

Allen, T. J. (1986). Organizational structure, information technology, and R&D productivity. *IEEE Transactions on Engineering Management, EM-33*(4).

Andersson, U., Jönsson, P.-A., Larsson, S., Lindgren, M., Magnusson L., & Strömberg, M. (1995). *Multiplexed vehicle electronics tutorial.* Gothenburg: Mecel AB.

Antonelli, C. (1997). The economics of path-dependence in industrial organization. *International Journal of Industrial Organization, 15,* 643–675.

Araujo, L., & Harrison, D. (2002). Path dependence, agency and technological evolution. *Technology Analysis and Strategic Management, 14*(1), 5–19.

Asanuma, B. (1989). Manufacturer-supplier relationships in Japan and the concept of relation-specific skill. *Journal of Japanese and International Economies, 3*(1), 1–30.

Axelsson, B. (1987). Supplier management and technological development. In: H. Håkansson (Ed.), *Industrial Technological Development: A Network Approach* (pp. 128–176). London: Croom Helm.

Axelsson, B., & Easton, G. (Eds) (1992). *Industrial networks: A new view of reality.* London: Routledge.

Baldwin, C. Y., & Clark, K. B. (1997). Managing in an age of modularity. *Harvard Business Review* (September–October), 84–93.

Baldwin, C. Y., & Clark, K. B. (2000). *Design rules – the power of modularity.* Massachusetts: MIT Press.

Barney, J. B. (1991). Firm resources and sustained competitive advantage. *Journal of Management, 17,* 99–120.

Bauer, H. (Ed.) (2000). *Automotive handbook* (5th ed.). Stuttgart: Robert Bosch GmbH.

Bensaou, M., & Venkatraman, N. (1995). Configurations of interorganizational relationships: A comparison between U.S. and Japanese automakers. *Management Science, 41*(9).

Bergman, B., & Klefsjö, B. (1994). *Quality from customer needs to customer satisfaction.* Lund: Studentlitteratur.

Bidault, F., & Cummings, T. (1994). Innovating through alliances: Expectations and limitations. *R&D Management, 24*(1), 33–45.

Bidault, F., Despres, C., & Butler, C. (1998). *Leveraged innovation: Unlocking the innovation potential of strategic supply.* London: Macmillan.

Blau, P. M. (1964). *Exchange and power in social life.* New York: Wiley.

Blois, K. (1971). Vertical quasi-integration. *Journal of Industrial Economics, 20*(3), 253–272.

Bonaccorsi, A., & Lipparini, A. (1994). Strategic partnerships in new product development: An Italian case study. *Journal of Product Innovation Management, 11,* 134–145.

Browning, T. R. (2001). Applying the design structure matrix to system decomposition and integration problems: A review and new directions. *IEEE Transactions on Engineering Management, 48*(3), 292–306.

Brusoni, S., & Prencipe, A. (2001). Unpacking the black box of modularity: Technologies, products and organizations. *Industrial and Corporate Change, 10*(1), 179–205.

Brusoni, S., Prencipe, A., & Pavitt, K. (2001). Knowledge, specialization, organizational coupling, and the boundaries of the firm: Why do firms know more than they make? *Administrative Science Quarterly, 46,* 597–621.

Burt, D. N. (1989). Managing suppliers up to speed. *Harvard Business Review* (July–August), 127–135.

Chandler, A. D., Jr. (1962). *Strategy and structure: Chapters in the history of the American industrial enterprise.* Cambridge, MA: MIT Press.

Chesbrough, H. W., & Teece, D. J. (1996). When is virtual virtuous? Organizing for innovation. *Harvard Business Review* (January–February), 65–73.

Clark, K. B. (1989). Project scope and project performance: The effect of parts strategy and supplier involvement on product development. *Management Science, 35*(10), 1247–1263.

Clark, K., & Fujimoto, T. (1991). *Product development performance: Strategy, organization, and management in the world auto industry.* Boston: Harvard Business School Press.

Coase, R. (1937). The nature of the firm. *Economica* (4), 386–405.

Cook, K. S., & Emerson, R. M. (1978). Power, equity and commitment in exchange networks. *American Sociological Review, 43*(October), 721–739.

Cooper, M. C., Ellram, L. M., Gardner, J. T., & Hanks, A. M. (1997). Meshing multiple alliances. *Journal of Business Logistics, 18*(1), 67–89.

Cyert, R. M., & March, J. G. (1963). *A behavioral theory of the firm.* Englewood Cliffs, NJ: Prentice-Hall.

Dacin, M. T., Ventresca, M. J., & Beal, B. D. (1999). The embeddedness of organizations: Dialogue & directions. *Journal of Management, 25*(3), 317–356.

David, P. A. (1985). Clio and the economics of QWERTY. *American Economic Review, 75*(2), 332–337.

Denzin, N. K., & Lincoln, Y. S. (Eds) (1994). *Handbook of qualitative research.* Thousand Oaks, CA: Sage.

Dessler, G. (1980). *Organization theory: Integrating structure and behavior.* Englewood Cliffs, NJ: Prentice-Hall.

Dowlatshahi, S. (1998). Implementing early supplier involvement: A conceptual framework. *International Journal of Operations and Production Management, 18*(2), 143–167.

Doz, Y. L. (1996). The evolution of cooperation in strategic alliances: Initial conditions or learning processes? *Strategic Management Journal, 17*, 55–83.

Doz, Y., & Hamel, G. (1997). The use of strategic alliances in implementing technology strategies. In: M. L. Tushman & P. Anderson (Eds), *Managing Strategic Innovation and Change: A Collection of Readings.* Oxford: Oxford University Press.

Doz, Y. L., & Prahalad, C. K. (1991). Managing DMNCs: A search for a new paradigm. *Strategic Management Journal, 12*, 145–164.

Dubois, A. (1994). *Organising industrial activities – An analytical framework.* Ph.D. thesis, Chalmers University of Technology, Gothenburg.

Dubois, A., & Gadde, L.-E. (2002). Systematic combining: An abductive approach to case research. *Journal of Business Research, 55*, 553–560.

Dyer, J. H. (1994). Dedicated assets: Japan's manufacturing edge. *Harvard Business Review* (November–December), 174–178.

Dyer, J. H. (1996). How Chrysler created an American Keiretsu. *Harvard Business Review* (July–August), 42–56.

Dyer, J. H., & Ouchi, W. G. (1993). Japanese-style partnerships: Giving companies a competitive edge. *Sloan Management Review* (Fall), 51–63.

Easton, G. (1992). Industrial networks: A review. In: B. Axelsson & G. Easton (Eds), *Industrial Networks: A New View of Reality.* London: Routledge.

Eccles, R. G. (1981). The quasifirm in the construction industry. *Journal of Economic Behavior and Organization, 2*, 335–357.

Eisenhardt, K. (1989). Building theories from case study research. *Academy of Management Review, 14*(4), 532–550.

Ellram, L. M. (1991). Supply chain management: The industrial organisation perspective. *International Journal of Physical Distribution and Logistics Management, 21*(1), 13–22.

Emerson, R. M. (1962). Power-dependence relations. *American Sociological Review, 27*, 31–40.

Eppinger, S. D., Whitney, D. E., Smith, R. P., & Gebala, D. A. (1994). A model-based method for organizing tasks in product development. *Research in Engineering Design, 6*, 1–13.

Evans, S., & Jukes, S. (2000). Improving co-development through process alignment. *International Journal of Operations and Production Management, 20*(8), 979–988.

Fine, C. H. (1998). *Clock speed*. Reading, MA: Perseus Books.

Ford, D., Gadde, L.-E., Håkansson, H., Lundgren, A., Snehota, I., Turnbull, P., & Wilson, D. (1998). *Managing business relationships*. Chichester: Wiley.

Forsgren, M., Hägg, I., Håkansson, H., Johanson, J., & Mattsson, L.-G. (1995). *Firms in networks: A new perspective on competitive power*. Studia Oeconomiae Negotiorum 38, Uppsala University, Uppsala.

Foss, N. J. (1998). The resource-based perspective: An assessment and diagnosis of problems. *Scandinavian Journal of Management, 14*(3), 133–149.

Fredriksson, P. (2002). *A framework for analyzing the operative performance of sequential module flows*. Ph.D. thesis, Chalmers University of Technology, Gothenburg.

Freeman, C. (1995). The 'national system of innovation' in historical perspective. *Cambridge Journal of Economics, 19*, 5–24.

Gadde, L.-E., & Håkansson, H. (2001). *Supply network strategies*. Chichester: Wiley.

Gadde, L.-E., & Jellbo, O. (2002). System sourcing – opportunities and problems. *European Journal of Purchasing and Supply Management* (March), 43–51.

Gadde, L.-E., & Snehota, I. (2000). Making the most of supplier relationships. *Industrial Marketing Management, 29*, 305–316.

Galbraith, J. K. (1967). *The new industrial state*. Boston: Houghton Mifflin.

Galbraith, J. R. (1977). *Organization design*. Reading, MA: Addison-Wesley.

Glaser, B. G., & Strauss, A. L. (1967). *The discovery of grounded theory*. Chicago: Aldine.

Granovetter, M. (1985). Economic action and social structure: The problem of embeddedness. *American Journal of Sociology, 91*(3), 481–510.

Granovetter, M. (1992). Problems of explanation in economic sociology. In: N. Nohria & R. G. Eccles (Eds), *Networks and Organizations: Structure, Form, and Action*. Boston, MA: Harvard Business School Press.

Hägg, I., & Johanson, J. (Eds) (1982). *Enterprise in networks: New perspective on competitiveness*. Stockholm: SNS.

Håkansson, H. (Ed.) (1982). *International marketing and purchasing of industrial goods*. London: Wiley.

Håkansson, H. (Ed.) (1987). *Industrial technological development: A network approach*. London: Croom Helm.

Håkansson, H., & Johanson, J. (1984). A model of industrial networks. Working Paper, Department of Business Administration, University of Uppsala.

Håkansson, H., & Johanson, J. (1992). A model of industrial networks. In: B. Axelsson & G. Easton (Eds), *Industrial Networks: A New View of Reality*. London: Routledge.

Håkansson, H., & Lundgren, A. (1997). Path in time and space – path dependence in industrial networks. In: L. Magnusson & J. Ottosson (Eds), *Evolutionary Economics and Path Dependence*. Cheltenham: Edward Elgar.

Håkansson, H., & Snehota, I. (1995). *Developing relationships in business networks*. London: Routledge.

Håkansson, H., & Waluszewski, A. (2001). Co-evolution in technological development: The role of friction. Paper presented at The 17th Annual IMP Conference (September 9–11).

Håkansson, H., & Waluszewski, A. (2002). *Managing technological development*. London: Routledge.

Halinen, A., & Törnroos, J.- r i n g A . (1998). The role of embeddedness in the evolution of business networks. *Scandinavian Journal of Management, 14*(3), 187–205.

Hamel, G. (1991). Competition for competence and inter-partner learning within international strategic alliances. *Strategic Management Journal, 12*, 83–103.

Hammarkvist, K. O., Håkansson, H., & Mattsson, L.-G. (1982). *Marknadsföring för konkurrenskraft* (Marketing for competitive power) (in Swedish). Malmö: Liber.

Harland, C. M. (1996). Supply chain management: Relationships, chains and networks. *British Journal of Management, 7*(Special Issue), S63–S80.

Harland, C., Lamming, R. C., & Cousins, P. D. (1999). Developing the concept of supply strategy. *International Journal of Operations and Production Management, 19*(7), 650–673.

Hayes, R. H., & Wheelwright, S. C. (1984). *Restoring our competitive edge: Competing through manufacturing*. New York: Wiley.

Helper, S. R., & Sako, M. (1995). Supplier relations in Japan and the United States: Are they converging? *Sloan Management Review* (Spring), 77–84.

Hines, P., Lamming, R., Jones, D., Cousins, P., & Rich, N. (2000). *Value stream management: Strategy and excellence in the supply chain*. Harlow: Prentice-Hall.

Hobday, M. (1998). Product complexity, innovation and industrial organization. *Research Policy, 26*, 689–710.

Hochfelder, D., & Helper, S. (1996). Suppliers and product development in the early American automobile industry. *Business and Economic History, 25*(2), 39–51.

Holmen, E. (2001). *Notes on a conceptualisation on resource-related embeddedness of inter-organisational product development*. Unpublished Ph.D. thesis, University of Southern Denmark, Sønderborg.

Holmen, E., & Pedersen, A.-C. (1999). The resource-related embeddedness of product development. In: D. McLoughlin & C. Horan (Eds), *Proceedings of the 15th Annual IMP Conference*. Dublin: University College.

Holmqvist, T. K. P. (2001). Visualization of product structure and product architecture for a complex product in a mass customization company. Paper presented at International Conference on Engineering Design, Glasgow (August 21–23).

Hubka, V., & Eder, W. E. (1988). *Theory of technical systems: A total concept theory for engineering design*. Berlin: Springer-Verlag.

Hughes, T. P. (1983). *Networks of power: Electrification in western society 1880–1930*. Baltimore: John Hopkins University Press.

Imai, M. (1986). *Kaizen: The key to Japan's competitive success*. New York: McGraw-Hill.

Inkpen, A. C. (1996). Creating knowledge through collaboration. *California Management Review, 39*(1), 123–140.

Jellbo, O. (1998). *Systemköp: En definitionsfråga* (in Swedish). Licentiate thesis, Gothenburg: Chalmers University of Technology.

Johanson, J. (1966). *Svenskt kvalitetsstål på utländska marknader* (in Swedish). Licentiate thesis, Uppsala University, Uppsala.

Johanson, J., & Mattsson, L.-G. (1987). Interorganizational relations in industrial systems: A network approach compared with the transaction-cost approach. *International Studies of Management and Organization, XVII*(1), 34–48.

Johnson, H. T., & Bröms, A. (2000). *Profit beyond measure*. New York: Free Press.

Kamath, R. R., & Liker, J. K. (1994). A second look at Japanese product development. *Harvard Business Review* (November–December), 154–170.

Karlsson, C., Nellore, R., & Söderquist, K. (1998). Black box engineering: Redefining the role of product specifications. *Journal of Product Innovation Management, 15*, 534–549.

Kraljic, P. (1983). Purchasing must become supply management. *Harvard Business Review* (September–October), 109–117.

Lakemond, N. (2001). *Managing across organizations: Intra- and interorganisational aspects of supplier involvement in product development projects.* Ph.D. thesis, Linköping Studies in Management and Economics, No. 52, Linköping.

Lambe, C. J., & Spekman, R. E. (1997). Alliances, external technology acquisition, and discontinuous technological change. *Journal of Product Innovation Management, 14*, 102–116.

Lambert, D. M., & Cooper, M. C. (2000). Issues in supply chain management. *Industrial Marketing Management, 29*, 65–83.

Lamming, R. (1990). Strategic options for automotive suppliers in the global market. *International Journal of Technology Management, 5*(6), 649–684.

Lamming, R. (1993). *Beyond partnership – Strategies for innovation and lean supply.* London: Prentice-Hall.

Langlois, P. R., & Robertson, P. L. (1992). Networks and innovation in a modular system: Lessons from the microcomputer and stereo component industries. *Research Policy, 21*, 297–313.

Langlois, R. N. (2002). Modularity in technology an organization. *Journal of Economic Behavior and Organization, 49*, 19–37.

Lawrence, P. R., & Lorsch, J. W. (1967a). New management job: The integrator. *Harvard Business Review* (November–December), 142–151.

Lawrence, P. R., & Lorsch, J. W. (1967b). Differentiation and integration in complex organizations. *Administrative Science Quarterly, 12*, 1–47.

Leonard-Barton, D. (1990). A dual methodology for case studies: Synergistic use of a longitudinal single site with replicated multiple sites. *Organisation Science, 1*(1), 248–266.

Lincoln, Y. S., & Guba, E. G. (1985). *Naturalistic inquiry.* Beverly Hills, CA: Sage.

Littler, D., Leverick, F., & Bruce, M. (1995). Factors affecting the process of collaborative product development: A study of UK manufacturers of information and communications technology products. *Journal of Product Innovation Management, 12*, 16–32.

Loasby, B. J. (1998). The concept of capabilities. In: N. J. Foss & B. J. Loasby (Eds), *Economic Organization, Capabilities and Co-ordination: Essays in honour of G. B. Richardson* (pp. 163–182). London: Routledge.

Loasby, B. J. (1999). *Knowledge, institutions and evolution in economics.* London: Routledge.

Lorsch, J. W., & Lawrence, P. R. (1965). Organizing for product innovation. *Harvard Business Review* (January–February), 109–122.

March, J. G., & Simon, H. A. (1958). *Organizations.* New York: Wiley.

Mattsson, L.-G. (1985). An application of a network approach to marketing. Defining and changing market positions. In: Dholakia & J. Arndt (Eds), *Alternative Paradigms for Widening Market Theory.* Greenwich, CT: JAI Press.

McCutcheon, D. M., & Meredith, J. R. (1993). Conducting case study research in operations management. *Journal of Operations Management, 11*, 239–256.

Melnyk, S. A., & Handfield, R. B. (1998). May you live in interesting times ... the emergence of theory-driven empirical research. *Journal of Operations Management, 16*(4), 311–319.

Meredith, J. (1998). Building operations management theory through case and field research. *Journal of Operations Management, 16*, 441–454.

Meyer, M. H., & Lehnerd, A. P. (1997). *The power of product platforms.* New York: Free Press.

Millson, M. R., Raj, S. P., & Wilemon, D. (1992). A survey of major approaches for accelerating new product development. *Journal of Product Innovation Management, 9*(1), 53–69.

Mintzberg, H. (1983). *Structure in fives: Designing effective organizations.* Englewood Cliffs, NJ: Prentice-Hall.

Mizruchi, M. S., & Schwartz, M. (Eds) (1987). *Intercorporate relations: The structural analysis of business.* Cambridge: Cambridge University Press.

Mohr, J., & Spekman, R. (1994). Characteristics of partnership success: Partnership attributes, communication behaviour and conflict resolution techniques. *Strategic Management Journal, 15,* 135–152.

Nelson, R. R., & Winter, S. G. (1982). *An evolutionary theory of economic change.* Boston, MA: Harvard University Press.

Nishiguchi, T. (1994). *Strategic industrial sourcing: The Japanese advantage.* Oxford: Oxford University Press.

Norén, L., Norrgren, F., & Trygg, L. (1995). Product development in inter-organizational networks, *International Journal of Technology Management* (Special Publication).

Olson, E. M., Walker, O. C., Jr., & Ruekert, R. W. (1995). Organizing for effective new product development: The moderating role of product innovativeness. *Journal of Marketing, 59*(January), 48–62.

O'Neal, C. (1993). Concurrent engineering with early supplier involvement: A cross-functional challenge. *International Journal of Purchasing and Materials Management* (Spring), 3–9.

Orton, J. D., & Weick, K. E. (1990). Loosely coupled systems: A reconceptualization. *Academy of Management Review, 15*(2), 203–223.

Pahl, G., & Beitz, W. (1996). *Engineering design: A systematic approach.* Berlin: Springer-Verlag.

Palmer, A. (2000). Cultural influences on relationship marketing. In: T. Hennig-Thurau & U. Hansen (Eds), *Relationship marketing: Gaining competitive advantage through customer satisfaction and customer retention.* Berlin: Springer.

Penrose, E. T. (1959). *The theory of the growth of the firm* (3rd ed., published in 1995). Oxford: Basil Blackwell.

Persson, M. (2003). The impact of organizational functions on modular structure – experiences from Volvo car corporation. *International Journal of Automotive Technology and Management* (forthcoming).

Pettigrew, A. M. (1990). Longitudinal field research on change: Theory and practice. *Organization Science, 1*(3), 267–292.

Polanyi, K. (1944). *The great transformation: The political and economic origins of our time.* Boston: Beacon Press.

Powell, W. W. (1990). Neither market nor hierarchy: Network forms of organization. *Research in Organizational Behavior, 12,* 295–336.

Powell, W. W. (1998, Spring). Learning from collaboration: Knowledge and networks in the biotechnology and pharmaceutical industries. *California Management Review, 40*(3), 228–240.

Prahalad, C. K., & Hamel, G. (1990). The core competence of the corporation. *Harvard Business Review* (May–June), 79–90.

Ragatz, G. L., Handfield, R. B., & Scannell, T. V. (1997). Success factors for integrating suppliers into new product development. *Journal of Product Innovation Management, 14,* 190–202.

Ragin, C. C. (1992). "Casing" and the process of social inquiry. In: C. C. Ragin & H. S. Becker (Eds), *What is a Case?* Cambridge: Cambridge University Press.

Ramsay, J. (1996). The case against purchasing partnerships. *International Journal of Purchasing and Materials Management* (Fall), 13–19.

Richardson, G. B. (1972). The organization of industry. *The Economic Journal* (September), 883–896.

Ring, P. S. (1996). *Networked organization: A resource-based perspective*. Studia Oeconomiae Negotiorum 39, Uppsala University, Uppsala.

Ring, P. S., & Van de Ven, A. (1994). Developmental processes in cooperative inter-organizational relationships. *Academy of Management Review, 19*, 90–118.

Robertson, P. L., & Langlois, R. N. (1995). Innovation, networks, and vertical integration. *Research Policy, 24*, 543–562.

Rosenberg, N. (1982). *Inside the black box: Technology and economics*. Cambridge: Cambridge University Press.

Rothwell, R., & Whiston, T. G. (1990). Design, innovation and corporate integration. *R&D Management, 20*(3), 193–201.

Rubenstein, A. H. (1957). Liaison relations in research and development. *IRE Transactions on Engineering Management* (June), 72–78.

Sanchez, R. (2000). Product and process architectures in the management of knowledge resources. In: N. J. Foss & P. L. Robertson (Eds), *Resources, Technology and Strategy: Explorations in the Resource-based Perspective*. London: Routledge.

Sanchez, R., & Mahoney, J. T. (1996). Modularity, flexibility, and knowledge management in product and organization design. *Strategic Management Journal, 17*(Winter), 63–76.

Scott, W. R. (1998). *Organizations: Rational, natural, and open systems*. New Jersey: Prentice-Hall.

Silverman, D. (2001). *Interpreting qualitative data: Methods for analysing talk, text and interaction*. London: Sage.

Simon, H. A. (1962). The architecture of complexity. *Proceedings of the American Philosophical Society, 106*(6), 467–482.

Smith, A. (1776). *An inquiry into the nature and causes of the wealth of nations*. E. Cannan (Ed.). New York: Modern Library.

Smith, P. G., & Reinertsen, D. G. (1992). Shortening the product development cycle. *Research Technology Management, 35*(3), 44–49.

Snehota, I. (1990). *Notes on a theory of business enterprise*. Ph.D. thesis, Uppsala University, Uppsala.

Spekman, R. E., John, W., Jr., & Myhr, N. (1996). An empirical investigation into supply chain management: A perspective on partnerships. *International Journal of Physical Distribution and Logistics, 28*(8), 630–650.

Tashakkori, A., & Teddlie, C. (1998). *Mixed methodology: Combining qualitative and quantitative approaches*. London: Sage.

Taylor, F. W. (1911). *Scientific management*. New York: Harper Bros.

Teece, D. J. (1989). Inter-organizational requirements of the innovation process. *Managerial and Decision Economics* (Special Issue), 35–42.

Thompson, J. D. (1967). *Organizations in action*. New York: McGraw-Hill.

Tilly, C. (1994). The time of states. *Social Research, 61*(2), 269–296.

Tunälv, C. (1996). *Profit impact from change strategy-1996 års benchmarking av svensk fordonsindustri* (in Swedish). Center for Organizational Renewal, Chalmers University of Technology.

Tushman, M. L., & O'Reilly, C. A. (1997). *Winning through innovation: A practical guide to leading organizational change and renewal*. Boston, MA: Harvard Business School Press.

Twigg, D. (1997). *Defining the concept of 'guest engineering'*. Warwick Business School Research Papers, No. 268, Warwick Business School Research Bureau.

Twigg, D., & Slack, N (1998). Lessons from using supplier guest engineers in the automotive industry. *International Journal of Logistics, Research and Applications, 1*(2).

Ulrich, K. (1995). The role of product architecture in the manufacturing firm. *Research Policy, 24*, 419–440.

Ulrich, K., & Tung, K. (1991). Fundamentals of product modularity. *Issues in Design Manufacture/ Integration, 39*, 73–79.

Ulrich, K. T., & Eppinger, S. D. (1995). *Product design and development*. New York: McGraw-Hill.

Utterback, J. (1994). *Mastering the dynamics of innovation*. Boston, MA: Harvard Business School Press.

Uzzi, B. (1997). Social structure and competition in interfirm networks: The paradox of embeddedness. *Administrative Science Quarterly, 42*, 35–67.

Venkatesan, R. (1992). Sourcing: To make or not to make. *Harvard Business Review* (November–December), 98–107.

von Corswant, F. (2000a). Product development and the supply chain. Paper presented at the Third International Conference on Operations and Quantitative Management in Sydney (December 17–20).

von Corswant, F. (2000b). *PICS 1999: Benchmarking av företag inom svensk fordonsindustri* (in Swedish). Research Report, Chalmers University of Technology.

von Corswant, F., Dubois, A., & Fredriksson, P. (2001). Organisering av aktiviteter i industriella nätverk – Fallet Volvo S80 (in Swedish). *Nordiske Organisasjonsstudier, 3*(4), 39–60.

von Corswant, F., & Fredriksson, P. (2002). Sourcing trends in the car industry: A survey of car manufacturers' and suppliers' strategies and relations. *International Journal of Operations and Production Management, 22*(7), 741–758.

von Corswant, F., & Tunälv, C. (2002). Coordinating customers and proactive suppliers: A case study of supplier collaboration in product development. *Journal of Engineering and Technology Management, 19*(3–4), 249–261.

von Hippel, E. (1990). Task partitioning: An innovation process variable. *Research Policy, 19*, 407–418.

von Hippel, E. (1994). "Sticky information" and the locus of problem solving: implications for innovation. *Management Science, 40*(4), 429–439.

Voss, C., Tsikriktsis, N., & Frohlich, M. (2002). Case research in operations management. *International Journal of Operations and Production Management, 22*(2), 195–219.

Wasti, S. N., & Liker, J. K. (1997). Risky business or competitive power? Supplier involvement in Japanese product design. *Journal of Product Innovation Management, 14*, 337–355.

Weber, M. (1946 trans.). *From Max Weber: Essays in sociology*. First published in 1906–1924. H. H. Gerth & C. W. Mills (Eds). New York: Oxford University Press.

Wedin, T. (2001). *Networks and demand: The use of electricity in an industrial process*. Ph.D. thesis No. 83, Uppsala University, Uppsala.

Wheelwright, S. C., & Clark, K. B. (1992). *Revolutionizing product development: Quantum leaps in speed, efficiency, and quality*. New York: Free Press.

Williamson, O. (1979). Transaction cost economics: The governance of contractual relations. *Journal of Law and Economics, 22*, 233–261.

Williamson, O. E. (1975). *Markets and hierarchies: Analysis and antitrust implications*. New York: Free Press.

Williamson, O. E. (1985). *The economic institutions of capitalism*. New York: Free Press.

Womack, J. P., & Jones, D. T. (1996). *Lean thinking*. New York: Simon & Schuster.

Womack, J. P., Jones, D. T., & Roos, D. (1990). *The machine that changed the world*. New York: Rawson Associates.

Wynstra, F., & ten Pierick, E. (2000). Managing supplier involvement in new product development: A portfolio approach. *European Journal of Purchasing and Supply Management, 6*, 49–57.

Yin, R. (1994). *Case study research*. California: Sage.

CO-CREATING SUCCESSFUL
NEW INDUSTRIAL NETWORKS
AND PRODUCTS

Magnar Forbord

ABSTRACT

In every industry there are resources. Some are moving, others more fixed; some are technical, others social. People working with the resources, for example, as buyers or sellers, or users or producers, may not make much notice of them. A product sells. A facility functions. The business relationship in which we make our money has "always" been there. However, some times this picture of order is disturbed. A user having purchased a product for decades may "suddenly" say to the producer that s/he does not appreciate the product. And a producer having received an order of a product that s/he thought was well known, may find it impossible to sell it. Such disturbances may be ignored. Or they can be used as a platform for development. In this study we investigate the latter option, theoretically and through real world data. Concerning theory we draw on the industrial network approach. We see industrial actors as part of (industrial) networks. In their activities actors use and produce resources. Moreover, the actors interact — bilaterally and multilaterally. This leads to development of resources and networks. Through "thick" descriptions of two cases we illustrate and try to understand the interactive character of resource development and how actors do business on features of resources. The cases are about a certain type of resource, a

Managing Product Innovation
Advances in Business Marketing and Purchasing, Volume 13, 211–335
Copyright © 2005 by Elsevier Ltd.
All rights of reproduction in any form reserved
ISSN: 1069-0964/doi:10.1016/S1069-0964(04)13002-0

product — goat milk. The main message to industrial actors is that they should pay attention to that products can be co-created. Successful co-creation of products, moreover, may require development also of business relationships and their connections ("networking").

1. A THEORETICAL FRAMEWORK FOR STUDYING AND UNDERSTANDING RESOURCE DEVELOPMENT

The theme we will be dealing with in this study is resource development in industrial (business) networks. More precisely we are interested in how products are developed in such a context, particularly how actors develop new uses of physical products. In this section and in the last part of Section 2, we will develop a theoretical basis for addressing this problem.

1.1. The Industrial Network Approach

The subject matter of the industrial network approach is firms operating in business markets. One claim made (within this approach) is that business markets differ from consumer markets in that not only sellers but also buyers are *active* (Håkansson, 1982). Hence, interaction between business sellers and buyers tends to be "thick"; more varied and complex as regards contents and function and more lasting (Håkansson, 1982; Håkansson & Snehota, 1995). One consequence of this is that firms can manage and do business in only few relationships with other firms. This makes the business relationships a firm has all the more important.

Moreover, relationships are *connected* forming networks (Cook & Emerson, 1978; Pedersen, 1996). Hence, business markets are better viewed as networks. In the words of Johanson and Mattsson (1987):

> The network approach bases its analyses on characteristics of systems of interdependent dyadic relations. Thus, if A first buys from B, but then merges with B, not only is the relationship between A and B changed . . . but also A's reaction to B's other customers, suppliers, competitors, etc. What might be gained in the A-B relationships might very well be lost through the changes in the other relationships that B had before the merger (p. 180).

In other words, if we analyse single relationships in isolation we might lose sight of the effect indirect relationships (third parties) have on a certain actor or relationship, and vice versa. Thus:

A business enterprise looks more like a linking unit where its strategic attributes lie in how it connects other market participants to each other (Håkansson & Snehota, 1995, p. 21).

The "network way" of viewing markets leads to that the division between market and firm, which is sharp (and an important assumption) within neo-classical economics and new institutional economics, becomes less sharp. That is, interaction is not necessarily much "thicker" within firms than between firms (Granovetter, 1985, 1992; Johanson & Mattsson, 1987). Piore (1992) even claims that "economic landscapes" basically consist of networks of which markets and firms represent two extremes:

> If one understands the process of technological change in terms of the priorities of specialization and integration, it may be that what we think of as networks are a natural form of organization and that markets and hierarchies are two extremes. The market extreme involves no integration at all. The hierarchical organization involves completely rigid integration (p. 443).

A third aspect is that business networks are not static but *dynamic*. This view has been established and reinforced by many studies of technological development in business networks (cf. Håkansson, 1989; Håkansson & Waluszewski, 2002; Lundgren, 1995; Waluszewski, 1989; Wedin, 2001). These studies have also demonstrated that technology (products, processes) does not "live a life of its own" in business networks. Technological development is linked to use and takes place in interplay with social beings in firms and organizations. This finding is formulated in a theoretical model, which contains and describes the relationship between three "basic" elements in business networks; activities, resources and actors (the "ARA-model"). Activities represent the economic dimension, resources point to the technological dimension and actors constitute the social "factor" (Håkansson, 1989). In other words, business networks operate on three interdependent levels; an activity (or economic) level, a resource (or technological) level and an actor (or social) level (Håkansson & Snehota, 1995).

The question now is to what extent the industrial network approach in general and the ARA-model in particular can help us understand our empirical problem (see next section), which concerns how a "poorly" used resource can be used better. Since use has to do with activities having a closer look at this concept seems logical. In addition pursuing the issue of resources appears mandatory. But we also "feel" that the actor dimension cannot be completely "ruled out."

1.1.1. Activities
In general activities are necessary to create an output. In the business world a huge number of various activities are carried out (Håkansson & Snehota, 1995, p. 28). Alderson (1965) makes a distinction between sorting activities and transformation activities; before every transformation there has to be a sorting

in order to provide the appropriate collection of different resources which are to be transformed into new resources. Transformation activities can change the form of resources (production) or their location in time and space (storing, transportation, display). More compound activities like product development, purchasing and marketing can involve both sorting and different transformation activities.

The critical point is that all these various activities have to be co-ordinated (or organized) in order to make desired outputs. Such co-ordination can come about in three principal ways; by firms, by the market or through relationships (Dubois, 1998; Richardson, 1972). If, in general, the *scale* of an activity does not affect its efficiency and no special *capabilities* are required for performing that activity, one firm could co-ordinate and do all activities; buy inputs, produce, and sell directly to consumers (Richardson, 1972, p. 890). When this is not the case – that is, when there are economies of scale and special capabilities – there will exist more than one firm in the "economic landscape." Hence, activities have to be co-ordinated *between* firms also.

Activities that result in standard products can be expected to be co-ordinated impersonally through "market forces" (Richardson, 1972). However, if the input is of a *special-purpose* kind where the quantity and the quality of it has to be known in advance, a firm cannot rely on impersonal market forces. Insofar as the firm does not possess the appropriate capability itself the solution is to *co-operate* with a firm that has it. This demands that the firms match their respective enterprise plans beforehand the physical transformation is carried out (Richardson, 1972, p. 892). This creates activity interdependencies.

Research within the industrial network approach has confirmed that activity interdependencies are common in business markets. Håkansson and Snehota (1995, pp. 52–54) relate activity interdependencies to economics and find two principal ways such interdependencies can be exploited. One is the *cost* dimension, leading to an emphasis on standardization and economies of scale and scope (Chandler, 1990); in other words efficiency (Torvatn, 1996). Building on a "behavioural" view of the firm and seeing activities as reciprocally enacted (Weick, 1979) the other dimension regards effectiveness. This dimension highlights the possibilities for customization and thereby *value* creation and corresponds to the third co-ordination mechanism (co-operation) described by Richardson (1972).

Dubois (1994, 1998) applies this theory of activity interdependencies to analyse "make-or-buy" problems in a business network. According to her, since an activity analysis concerns efficiency and effectiveness, it reveals "status quo" (stability) in a business network. In other words, an activity pattern (structure of interdependent activities in a business network) can say something about efficient and effective use of a *given*, known resource. That is, a certain activity pattern requires given resources. For example, the activity "use of goat milk for making brown cheese," which will be described in Section 2, exists and is as it is because actors involved regard it as efficient and effective within the *particular activity pattern* in which this (single) activity is embedded.

We could have gone much deeper into this activity pattern. Then, we might have been able to say something more about the efficiency and effectiveness of this activity compared to, for example, the activity of using the resource as e.g. feed. However, in order to understand why Namdalsmeieriet changes from using goat milk for making a (certain) food product to selling it as feed, pointing to activity patterns only is not sufficient. According to Dubois (1998) we then should take the resource dimension of industrial networks into consideration. Change in one or more resources impacts on what activities and activity patterns are efficient and effective and thus what is "economic." The question that we will be posing in Section 2 is how the use of a physical resource can be improved through new products and new markets. We realize that this resource is used in, and hence is part of, a business network. Thus, enhanced understanding of resources in this network may help us answer this question.

1.1.2. Resources

A resource need not *necessarily* be used as it is. Actors can develop pictures of changed uses or become convinced that other uses can be found. The resource then turns from something given to something "open." What is a resource then? Any element that some actor regards as valuable "counts" as a resource. Thus, Emerson (1981) proposes that:

> [Possessions and capabilities] we shall call [...] resources if they are valued by specific other actors (p. 41).

This means that elements, like possessions and capabilities, which are not valued by specific other actors are not resources. Håkansson and Snehota (1995) state that with knowledge of use any element changes status from "element-that-is-not-a-resource" to "element-that-is-a-resource." A resource can be a physical product (like goat milk) or something that facilitates production or use of a product. An organization, like a firm, can also be a resource. Also a relationship can be a resource. If we refer to the resources combined within the boundaries of a firm as a resource collection, a relationship ties two resource collections and forms a (supra-firm) resource constellation (Håkansson & Snehota, 1995). Such a constellation can embrace more than two firms and represent constraints as well as opportunities for new uses. Hence, a relationship can be regarded as a "space" where resources can be developed, but also as a hindrance for development.

Furthermore, any resource has features. In general the term feature refers to a distinctive trait of an individual or a class; *an outstanding or marked property which attracts attention* (Webster's, 1989). The important message for us, considering possibilities of better uses of a poorly used resource, is that features can give resources value if actors are able to tie them to certain other resources with *their* specific features. This presupposes actors with some knowledge of features of different resources.

The resource dimension thus incorporates dynamics, reminding us that the "status quo" in a business network can change. An important "driving force" here can be said to be the reciprocal influence between different resources (cf. Penrose, 1995); more precisely the reciprocal influence between actors' knowledge and physical resources. Technology, for example, can be seen as a resource resulting from such reciprocal influence. Håkansson and Snehota (2000) identify three ways in which resource ties become manifest in business networks; through technicians, products and projects. Technicians solve technical problems appearing over time and by this means gain knowledge about how products and production processes are mutually adjusted. Products of the seller have to fit the technical system of the buyer; on a continuing basis this fit can only be found via mutual learning in interaction. Special projects aiming at solving technical problems or developing technical solutions can involve two or more parties in a network. If this is the case business relationships and networks can be infused with technical content, thereby creating resource ties across firm boundaries.

1.1.3. Actors

Although the resource dimension seems most relevant for approaching our problem, the picture is not complete without the actor dimension. The discussion above revealed that resources do not develop by themselves; development is dependent on actors. In the industrial network approach the actor dimension enters our conceptual scheme indirectly via the term interaction. Nevertheless, explicating the "network actor" to some extent can be helpful. Companies are represented by interested actors pursuing not only economic purposes but also non-economic ones like prestige and status (Granovetter, 1985, 1992). Because of humans there are *will, intention* and *purpose* in business networks, "life" if you wish (Håkansson & Snehota, 1995).

The understanding of the "network actor" has undergone development since it was introduced as part of the ARA-model. Håkansson (1989, p. 16) defines actors by their performance of activities and their control over resources and specifies various sub-entities within the actor concept; people, groups of people, departments in a company, whole companies and groups of companies. However (on p. 21) he recognizes that actors are *more than* performers of activities and controllers of resources. Actors also possess particular *identities*. The legitimacy of referring to companies, firms and other individuals and collectives that carry out economic activities as actors, rests on the assumption that these:

> have an identity and thus [can be] ascribed purposeful action (Håkansson & Snehota, 1995, p. 193).

Since actors interact, identity is developed *in response to* other actors' actions and reactions. Thus, identity is not something that a single actor "has" and "controls" alone, but something that it shares — more or less — with other actors in the network. An actor's identity is thus as much a result of how other actors perceive this actor. An important consequence of seeing businesses as actors with identity is that their uniqueness comes to the forefront. To be ascribed identity points to what makes an actor *different* from other actors and its *specific* role in a business network. This role does not so much stem from some common goal, but rather the identity the actor is ascribed by the actors it interact with. The term *actor bond* refers to this shared, interacted identity (Håkansson & Snehota, 1995).

Applied to our problem this implies that we should not view resource development purely as a question of knowledge. We should also pay attention to how the use of resources relates to the identity of actors. For example, one thing is that an actor *knows* that a resource has these and these features. Another thing is whether the actor would *appreciate* it if these features were put to use. In our opinion appreciation has to do with feelings and thus identity. Hence we should at least have a picture of the actor dimension in mind when we set out to study our problem further. The actor dimension reminds us that new or improved uses of a resource are not only a question of *our* (the researchers') view. The view of the *actors* in the actual network also matters. Then there is the possibility that actors in a network view the same resources and resource ties differently.

1.2. Understanding Development in Business Networks

If we accept that actors in business networks need not treat resources as given, then development of resources becomes an opportunity. This means that *processes* can take place in business networks. Johanson and Mattsson (1987) argue that a "market-as-network" approach provides opportunities to describe and analyse problems related to dynamics in industrial systems:

> For us, industrial markets are characterised by lasting relationships among firms because such relationships can . . . promote knowledge development and change (p. 180).

Continuous change characterizes industrial networks. Thus, changes in networks are by and large evolutionary, consisting for the most part of many, small changes rather than few, large ones. Actors have to relate to change both in single relationships and on a network level. Sometimes change can be absorbed, sometimes actively promoted (Håkansson & Snehota, 1995, p. 22).

Continuous change stems from interaction between actors in the network. Håkansson and Snehota (2000, pp. 80–82) identify two *economic effects* of such interaction. One is using it to exploit *complementarities* between activities performed by different actors and their resources. The other is *knowledge* creation.

1.2.1. Technological Change

The type of change that has been mostly studied within the industrial network approach is technological change. Broadly speaking technological change concerns development of products and processes (Gressetvold, 2003; Håkansson & Snehota, 1995). Many of the mutual adaptations that firms do vis-à-vis one another stem from the technical side of products or processes:

> as a relationship develops, possible technical misfits have to be avoided (Håkansson & Snehota, 1995, p. 13).

Within the network products and processes are part of a larger technical system. In our case we can reckon goat milk, the focal resource, as a product. Technological change in one part of the network can influence, as well as be influenced by, rather distant technological changes in other parts of the network:

> ... The technical connections make relationships at a certain stage of transformation subject to, or the origin of, changes in other sometimes rather distant areas of the technological system (Håkansson & Snehota, 1995, p. 13).

Technological changes can also affect other functions of business, in the firm, relationship or network:

> The technology employed by the parties to a business relationship tends to influence not only the characteristics of the products and services exchanged but also the ways to do business in general, such as logistics, routines, planning and so on (p. 14).

Hence, we can look at the way Norwegian goat milk was used in the 1980s (see next section) partly as a result of previous technological development in the network in which this resource was embedded. But development in "business in general," like logistics, routines and planning, must also have had an impact. This recognition evokes the multi-content view of business relationships that we stressed earlier. The multi-content understanding of business relationships makes industrial network theory different from other approaches to technological change where the relationship is perceived to have a single content only, namely technical content (Håkansson & Snehota, 1995, p. 357). In other words, since goat milk can be regarded as a product, developing it must be reckoned as technological development. However, we must look for more than "pure" technical influences "behind" this technological development. Let us theorize in more detail how resources develop in business networks.

1.3. Resource Heterogeneity and Potential Uses of Resources

> If there are circumstances in which a businessman acquainted with the properties of the resources at his disposal (including his own abilities) says to himself regarding a particular resource, 'there ought to be some way in which I can use that', and subsequently proceeds to explore the possibilities of using it, then we can fairly conclude that he believes there are productive services inherent in that resource about which as yet he knows little or nothing (Penrose, 1995, p. 77).

This quotation reminds us that there in any resource, beyond the actual uses, are *potential* uses. We touched upon this earlier when we stated that actors can treat resources as given or "open." The two case stories that will be presented in Section 3 will demonstrate that resource development is a question of actors believing "strongly enough" in potential uses of a resource and interesting in seeking knowledge about potential uses.

In fact, actors will never reach a "state of balance" where there are no more "unused uses" of a resource. There will be *a continuing availability* of unused productive services (Penrose, 1995, p. 68). (However, instead of service we prefer the term use, which we perceive as denoting the same.) Resources may be *indivisible*; in which case there can be idle capacity to exploit. Or a potential of *specializing* in using the properties of the resource appearing most valuable may exist.

But there is also a third type of potential uses; *new uses*. Penrose (1995, p. 74) points to this as the *heterogeneity* of resources. Of course, the situation may be that a resource "already" has different actual uses. Thus, the heterogeneity concept refers to more than potential (new) uses. For example, we will in Section 2 learn that Norske Meierier in the 1980s used goat milk to produce more than one product. Hence, Norwegian goat milk is a resource that exhibits *heterogeneity in use* (Håkansson & Snehota, 1995). Since use of a resource requires that it be combined with some other resources, heterogeneity points to the diverse combinations that one and the same resource may enter. As mentioned this means that the value of a resource is highly affected by how it is combined with other resources. And to the extent that these combinations differ, the value of the resource may also differ. Hence, searching for potential uses of a resource also means trying to increase or, alternatively, secure its value.

Actual heterogeneity seems to have much in common with the term *variety* of resources (Håkansson & Waluszewski, 1999), which is regarded as a precondition for learning (Håkansson et al., 1999):

> A large number of interfaces [between resources] increase the variation, which is one basic condition for learning (p. 445).

As we identified learning as a precondition for resource development, actual heterogeneity (or variety), then, should facilitate development. (This is not to say that actors *always* treat resources as heterogeneous. Often actors reduce or ignore variability in order to carry out e.g. production efficiently (Alderson, 1965)). Penrose (1995, p. 76) finds that development of resources can occur if the people who work with them get different ideas about how they can be used:

> ... there is an interaction between the two kinds of resources of a firm – its personnel and material resources – which affects the productive services available from each.

In other words, actors may have little or no knowledge of potential uses of a resource, but can *gain* such knowledge; through research into the features of the resource, or via research into ways of combining its known features with those of other resources (Penrose, 1995, p. 77). Research is here understood in broad sense (cf. March, 1991, p. 71). Håkansson and Snehota (1995, pp. 133, 134) argue along the same lines:

> There always seems to be potential both to change and develop the resource itself and/or to change the way in which it is used.

Hence, searching for new potential uses of a resource can focus on the constitution of the resource itself or new combinations in which it can be of use. Since there is value tied to resources in combinations, actors carry out such searches with at least some economic interest. For example, when Ola and Kari in case 1 (see Section 3) search for new use combinations of goat milk they do so with an eye to new combinations paying off better than the existing (actual) combination (see Section 2).

1.4. The Double-faced Nature of Resources

Penrose (1995) discusses resource development with the purpose of explaining why firms grow. Hence, her perspective on ways of finding new uses of resources is the perspective of the firm; that is, from one side. Håkansson and Snehota (1995, p. 132) suggest that we should view resources from two sides, the use side and the provision side. Thus, they argue that resources have a "double face":

> . . . resources are a result of activities as much as a condition that makes certain activities possible (p. 132).

On these grounds they claim that research into the resource itself – its features – is typically carried out from the provision side, while research regarding new combinations typically is done from the use side. In a business network this means that:

> The provision and use, and thus the value, of resources hinge on the knowledge of resource use and on how it is spread and coordinated among the providers and users in the existing business network. Relationships activate and develop specific resource elements and different resource constellations (p. 133).

The provision and use of a resource may be spread and co-ordinated in different ways. In the 1980s, Skånaliseter was a provider of goat milk, and the only user was Namdalsmeieriet (see Section 2). In Section 3 we will learn that in the 1990s the "spread" of knowledge regarding provision and use of this resource changed. Moreover, this development seemed to have little to do with changed distribution of *existing* knowledge in the network and more to do with *new* knowledge being developed, of which some was distributed in the network and "put to good use."

What Håkansson and Snehota (1995, p. 136) stress is that *relation of provision and use* is critical in resource development. However, the weight put on each may vary. For example, case story 1 in Section 3 will illustrate that a provider can develop new uses (combinations) of a resource. Case 2 also centres around the provision side, but focuses on research into features of the resource. Nevertheless, in none of the cases do the actors involved ignore actors "on the other side;" there is *interaction* between them. This interaction varies in scope and depth, but takes place in a network. Many actors on the provision and/or the use side interact in developing the resource. Sometimes several providers and one user interact, at others one provider and many users. Moreover, the actors on the provision side or the use side respectively may be quite diverse or relatively homogeneous. Also actors on the same side may interact, in different ways or not at all. And one and the same actor may be involved in development both on the provision side and the use side, more or less in interaction with other actors. Hence, we are getting close to a picture of a dynamic network where interaction seems to be at the heart of the dynamism. Let us therefore discuss the concept of interaction more explicitly.

1.5. From Unknown to Known: The Role of Interaction

> Develop[ment of] resources and resource combinations . . . often originate in relationships with
> other companies because it is in a relationship that the use of a resource is confronted with how
> it is produced (Håkansson & Snehota, 1995, p. 132).

Hence, looking for the origin of development solely on the side of the provider *or* the user may be futile. For example, in case 1 (Section 3) judging whether it was Ola's (the provider's) complaints *or* complaints made by Namdalsmeieriet (the user) that triggered the development of the resource, is difficult. A small act from a user can lead to a small counter-act from a provider leading to several rounds of "interacts" (Weick, 1979). This can make the origin of the interaction (and hence the development) obscure. Also in case 2, we will see, saying that the development of the focal resource started as a confrontation within a business relationship is reasonable. The difference from case 1, however, is that the confrontation did not occur in the relationship between the provider and user of the *focal* resource, but between the provider of a *product made from the focal resource* and the user of this product. After some "initial" interaction between these two actors the rest of the development process moves to other business relationships involving other actors. Then technical scientists become central in the interaction. This interaction results in new knowledge about the *feature* that the "end user" does not appreciate. Moreover, this knowledge is *codified* in the form of written texts, like research reports and scientific articles. This knowledge seems to contrast with that of case 1, which appears to be more tacit and implicit, based on experience. Moreover, Ola and Kari seem to be more engaged in searching for new use combinations of the resource, while the scientists in case 2 are more occupied in investigating the resource "itself" and (some of) its features.

Claiming that interaction about the features of a resource is carried out from the provision side is tempting. Such interaction results in codified, explicit knowledge. Interaction concerning new combinations (of existing features) is done from the user side, and such interaction results in tacit, implicit knowledge. However, Ola and Kari are also providers of the resource and seem to apply some of their knowledge about provision when developing products. Moreover, they also explicate some of their experiences; e.g. they keep a diary about their cheese making and provide a description of their products on their web-site. And the researchers in case 2 co-operate with users of the resource when developing their knowledge. In fact, Anne and Clara together represent science on each side of the resource; Anne (as food scientist) holds knowledge about the use of the resource, while Clara (as animal scientist) has knowledge about the provision of the resource. Since they interact they both learn about the other side of the resource also. Thus, it may be that the *combined knowledge* that they are able to create in this way is more valuable for the users of this knowledge than the "sum of knowledge pieces" that they created had they been doing research separately on each "side" of the resource.

Hence, seemingly interaction can develop a physical resource by actors in the network creating and applying knowledge "to" it. But remembering that interaction about the resource occurs at many places in the network — between shifting and partly connected dyads, simultaneously as well as subsequently — also seems important. Thus, actors can easily get the impression of a chaotic network. This faces actors with a dilemma; they could try to reduce this chaos by decreasing the variety of resources and stronger structuring of relationships within the network. But then the innovativity in the network would be put at stake. According to Quinn (1988) chaos is necessary for resource development. Too much structuring can kill a network. Hence, to think of development as a stepwise, linear process is unfruitful since it is incompatible with how resources are developed in reality (Van de Ven, 1988). On the other side "chaos only" would also destroy the network and paralyse the actors in it; they would have no common point to refer to. Interaction can be seen as a "practical" way to respond to this dilemma as, on the one hand, it contributes to chaos and non-linearity and, on the other hand, dissolves chaos through clarification of actors' appreciations, interests and knowledge vis-à-vis one another.

1.5.1. The Concept of Interaction

While all living creatures are active in one way or another, only human beings can *act* (Østerberg, 1986, p. 11). Following this statement we have action when a human being acts. In that case we can call a human being an actor. Also a group of human beings is an actor if the participants are organized such that they can be mobilized for a common purpose (Brox, 1991, p. 63). This is a kind of "rational actor" definition. Another more "social constructivist" definition is the one described earlier in this section emphasizing identity. The two case stories in Section 3 reveal actors in the form of e.g. individuals, companies, associations of firms, departments within companies, public agencies and research institutions. Thus, actors are concrete; abstract and faceless categories like "agriculture," "information technology," "science" and "Norway" are not actors (Brox, 1991).

What is interaction then? The prefix "inter-" denotes among other things "between" and "among" (Webster's, 1989). Thus, interaction signifies "action between" or "action among." More precisely Webster's (1989) defines interaction as "reciprocal action or influence." As we have stated that actors act, interaction can denote "reciprocal action between or among actors." Thus, social interaction is defined as *interstimulation and response* taking place between individuals and between groups (Webster's, 1989).

Interaction "between or among" actors in the form of human individuals is one of the building blocks of the sociological tradition called agency (social constructivism) (Waters, 1994). One of the founders of this tradition, Georg Simmel (1858–1918), answers the question "How is society possible?" by pointing to the minds of individuals. More precisely he claims that society is built up by the actions of individuals. These actions comprise two inseparable elements: *content* (an interest, a purpose or a motive) and a form or mode of *interaction* (among individuals) through which, or in the shape of which, that content attains social reality (Simmel, 1950). Or in the words of Waters (1994):

> The motivations which propel life (e.g. hunger, love, religiosity, technology, intelligence) are not strictly social until they operate to transform isolated individuals into interactive relationships (p. 22).

Thus, according to Simmel, social interaction is not only important for the actors taking part, but is *one of the building blocks of the structure called society*. For us, studying use of a resource within a business network, we could rewrite this formulation and state that *business interaction is one important building block of the structure called business network*. In the quotation we also meet the word relationship and we realize that social interaction is something that often goes on within relationships between actors. We also realize that social interaction can take on different forms. Waters (1994) mentions imitation and differentiation.

Giddens (1993, p. 90) shows that theory of social interaction is characterized by direct, face-to-face communication, and via such communication meaning experiences are exchanged. Symbolic interactionists (e.g. Mead, cf. Waters, 1994) emphasize the prominent role of language in this communication. Only through interaction involving language is it possible for an individual to understand the meaning of others and not merely react to the other's act, goes the claim (Waters, 1994, p. 24). Other theorists influenced by Simmel and Mead – like Goffman – in addition point to non-verbal communication like facial expressions and movements of the body as important means in social interaction (Giddens, 1993, p. 91). Interacting individuals then not only *exchange* meaning experiences; they also *develop* meaning experiences as they use parts of existing experiences in order to make sense of new situations (Goffman, 1974). With reference to the same theoretical foundation Weick (1979) argues that interaction is the basic element in organizing. He describes interaction as a *contingent response pattern*. On the other hand, interaction does not presuppose equality or equal abilities among the participants (Aschehoug & Gyldendal, 1995–1998).

Co-operation is a term that is often used in parallel with interaction. To be sure the two terms have much in common, but they are not identical. While "co-" means: with-, together-, common-; "inter-" denotes: among, between, (a)cross. Hence, co-operation may be thought of as one side of interaction, where two or more actors jointly strive for a goal or object controlled by an actor other than those who co-operate (Stern, 1996, p. 4). The actors act *together, with* each other, for some *common* purpose. A picture of harmony arises.

But harmony is not a suitable description of what is going on between Ola and Namdalsmeieriet (see beginning of Section 2). The two actors disagree, yet they "act, respond and act back," something that also evokes the impression of a contingent response pattern. Hence, conflict seems to be "the other side" of interaction. This accords with findings from research on industrial networks; coexistence of co-operation and conflict is one of the process characteristics of business relationships (Håkansson, 1982). This coexistence is interesting from a development point of view. A "portion" of conflict is necessary in order to develop; and confrontation is an expression of conflict that can contribute to development. On the other hand, mere confrontation would not be constructive either. (Note, moreover, that competition between actors in a market is not regarded as interactive as these actors are not assumed to be "visible" and known to each other (Stern, 1996, p. 7)).

Another aspect of interaction is that it is *situated* – in a particular place and in a specific period of time (Giddens, 1993, p. 105). Moreover, the span in time and space can vary. For example, in a fencing match an interaction can take less than a second and occur within a few square meters, while occurring over thousands of kilometres and many months when a person sends out a message enclosed in a bottle and another person responds to this message. On the other hand any interaction can be separated in time and space from the one before and from others "beside." A relationship constitutes the context of an interaction in two ways. One is by linking the interaction to the participants' experiences of the past and expectations about the future. Another is, because of relationships being connected, through transmitting the results of the interaction to other relationships in the network. Hence, to understand any single interaction we must pay attention to the business network in which it is situated.

Interaction, then, can produce new meaning and develop the persons that interact. They may gain a new interpretation of a situation, or their existing interpretation may be confirmed. In comparison in a situation where there are two parties, but not any interaction, only isolated acts, the parties have very limited opportunities to develop their interpretations, and no social relationship is created. But interaction can also develop elements of a more physical nature. To avoid misconceptions on this point in this study, we have chosen to use the term interaction *only* in relation to actors. This is the dominant way in which the concept of interaction has been used within the industrial network approach (Håkansson, 1982, 1989; Håkansson & Snehota, 1995). For "interaction" between resources or between resources and actors we will use the term *reciprocal influence*.

1.5.2. Interaction Concerning Resources

Business actors may or may not be individuals. This need not necessarily imply that theory of social interaction is inapplicable for understanding business interaction. Firstly, collective business actors consist of individuals and can be perceived as the result of interacting individuals. The difference, of course, is that these individuals, when interacting with individuals of another collective business actor, do not represent only themselves. They also represent – more or less – the collective actor. Gadde and Håkansson (2001, p. 100) suggest that we study interaction between specific functions within or between companies. A function is impersonal and usually more stable and lasting than the individuals who "happen" to occupy that function at a certain time. In some situations investigating interaction even on a corporate level may be relevant. But we will argue that interaction between individuals is an important component in the "total" interaction between companies (Halinen & Salmi, 2001). For example, individuals may continue to interact after having changed function or moved to another company.

On a more abstract level, the theory of social interaction shows us that interaction can be interesting partly in *itself* and partly through its *results*. We have seen that social interaction develops "meaning" – a non-material product. But what about interaction in relation to products with physical features like goat milk? "Even" Goffman, a social constructivist, accepts that at the most microscopic level, behind all interpretations, there are *realities which cannot be contradicted and interpreted any further, especially the material constraints of the physical world* (Waters, 1994). We will use this formulation to state that both "the material constraints of the physical world" and meaning (ideas) are important entities for business actors and for resource development. Moreover, the physical world is not only a constraint; it is also an *enabling entity* (Giddens, 1993). The same can be said about ideas. In "real" business life actors work with many different types of resources. Some of them are physical, others non-physical. Consequently we need a clarification of physical and non-physical resources in relation to interaction.

1.6. Interaction and Four Types of Resources

Over time mutual development of a number of different resources across firm boundaries may create "heavy" resource combinations (Håkansson &

Waluszewski, 1999). We can experience this in the form of "worked in" solutions – dominant designs (Utterback, 1994) – like the Windows Operating System with all its resources developed specifically in relation to it over the years. The heaviness of different resource combinations is not only due to intricate technical *interfaces* between resources, but also heavy investments in economic and social interfaces. The resource constellation involving Norske Meierier (described in Section 2 and in more detail in Section 3) includes e.g. technical and social resources between which there are necessarily technical and social interfaces. But we can also observe variety in this resource constellation. In fact, the tension between heaviness and variety might be a source of development. The confrontation between Ola and Namdalsmeieriet (Section 2) can in many ways be said to reveal a tension between a heavy resource constellation and variety. In other words, there may be reason to focus on the *interface* between resources when understanding development.

1.6.1. The Concept of Interface
The term interface is logically consistent with the relational view of resources. Like Gadde and Håkansson (2001, p. 82) we will let the concept interface refer to "what is between resources." We stress "is" because interface is a noun and thus static not grasping what *happens* between resources. In the encyclopaedia interface is recognized as:

> a common boundary or interconnection between systems, equipment, concepts, or human beings (Webster's, 1989).

The term has been applied within computer technology to denote the interconnection between units that shall work together. Thus, like the concept relationship, interface denotes something *relational*. In other words, an interface has a paradoxical feature; it both separates and connects. And as we have pointed to interfaces can be of different types. The interface can for example be physical (like the interface between goat milk, milk pails and the physical location of a dairy described in Section 2). Or it can be conceptual (e.g. "mass production" vs. "customization"), or human (e.g. the way the food researcher and the animal researcher relate to each other in the research project described in case 2 in Section 3) (Webster's 1989). Earlier we pointed to how crucial combinations are for resources. The term interface is compatible with the term combination but points more specifically to the *border area* between resources. Figure 1 illustrates this.

1.6.2. Activating Resource Features by Systematic Relating
Like reciprocal influence between human resources reciprocal influence between human resources and physical resources can result in new ideas about use of

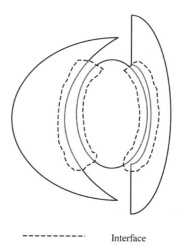

-----------· Interface

Fig. 1.   A Resource Combination Consisting of Three Resources with Two Interfaces.

physical resources as well as human resources (Penrose, 1995). Furthermore, if a series of reciprocal influences is taking place, a relation in the form of an interface between the human and physical resource can be developed. In order to be useful – or "potent" (Alderson, 1965) – a resource combination often must include several resources. As a consequence actors working with developing resources face multiple interfaces. In the interfaces certain features of each involved resource are activated. *Resource development can thus be seen as a question of finding new interfaces*; either through new features of resources that already are part of the combination or by altering the combination itself, through adding or removing resources to/from the combination. Actual activation (resource interfaces at a specific point in time) somewhere in the business network is the result of interaction processes over time, where:

> resources have been systematically related and where a solution of how to combine them has been gradually chiselled out (Håkansson & Waluszewski, 2001, p. 4).

This can explain why we often find heavy resource constellations; thousands of small changes in interfaces have been implemented over a long time. It can also explain why actors, like Ola in Section 2, are met by so much resistance when they try to identify "deviant" interfaces for resources.

As already noted, development is contingent upon new knowledge being created. Or as expressed by Håkansson and Waluszewski (2000, Chap. 2) in relation to technical development:

...to deal with technological development is to deal with the unknown. Per definition, what will be found in the search process can never be known in beforehand. Further, even when a new solution is found...it is only possible to capture fragments of its constitution and function.

In interaction between actors new knowledge can be created. Insofar as the new knowledge relates to a specific resource, unknown parts of the resource become known. This, we may say, is one ingredient in the development of the resource. Because of existing combinations development of the resource (by new combinations and/or new features) will affect other resources. Development must necessarily always begin with some existing resource combination (Håkansson & Waluszewski, 1999). Moreover, the existing combination can be very complex. Thus, when we see an opportunity to develop a certain resource, restricting (focusing) the analysis of resource interfaces may be necessary (Gadde & Håkansson, 2001, p. 84). Distinguishing to some extent between different types of resources can also be helpful.

1.6.3. Four Aspects of Interaction and Resources

Various schemes can be used for distinguishing between resources. Thus, we can distinguish between resources that are *internal* to a firm and resources that are *external* to it. Resources that the firm controls – via ownership, beneficial right or otherwise – are internal. External resources are resources the firm has been involved in creating in relationship with other firms – suppliers, customers (Gadde & Håkansson, 2001, p. 80) or other partners.

Another way is to classify resources as *physical* and *non-physical*, a distinction that we already have made. Håkansson and Snehota (1995) point to buildings, machines, manpower, materials and commodities as tangible resources as opposed to intangible resources. All these tangibles can also be referred to as material resources, but – as we have seen – the term physical also includes the elements of *time* and *space*. In order to use and create physical resources actors also need resources of another kind. Penrose (1995) points to the crucial role of knowledge, which is created when human and physical resources influence each other reciprocally. In the same way Itami (1991, p. 12) emphasizes the role of information, which he terms an invisible asset, to be distinguished from visible assets (people, goods and capital, including money). He finds that skill, artistic sense, morale, brand image and consumer trust, loyalty and reputation are examples of invisible assets. He regards people as especially important assets because they embody much of the invisible assets (p. 14). In other words, non-physical resources have emotional and symbolic components that physical resources lack. Emotional components are manifest in resources like brand

(Kotler et al., 1999; Thomson, 1998). Language is an example of a symbolic component.

We find the conceptual "pairs" "tangible-intangible," "material-non-material," "visible-invisible" and "physical-human" to denote aspects of the same fundamental distinction about resources. Since the term physical incorporates the terms tangible, material and visible, but in addition time and space, we prefer to use the term physical. The term non-physical then refers to resources and features that are not physical. We could also have used the term idea, and the subsequent discussion will show that this is an important type of resource when it comes to development. However, we can also find non-physical resources that are difficult to call ideas; emotions and morale are two. Our empirical material however has not much to say about emotional and morale resources, but much to tell about ideas. So when we talk about non-physical resources in the following we could just as well have used the word idea.

A key question is how certain features of single resources are developed and embedded into combinations of resources when business actors interact. Håkansson and Waluszewski (2000, Chap. 2) identify four types of resources, each influenced by a certain aspect of interaction:

> Interaction that deals with co-operation influences *business units*.
> Interaction regarding selling and buying influences *products*.
> Interaction regarding producing and using influences *facilities*.
> Interaction concerning networking influences *business relationships*.

Figure 2 illustrates a situation where resources of the four types are related in a certain way. The illustration resembles a routine "production – use" situation in a business network and is probably much more "ordered" than what actors experience in development situations. Business unit C has in interaction with the business units A and B developed the resources X and Y respectively. A sells X to C, B sells Y to C and C buys X and Y. Hence X and Y are *products* in our terminology. A uses the resources 1 and 2 to transform X and Y into another product Z. Hence 1 and 2 are means and thus *facilities* in our terminology. Viewed from the *production* side 1 and 2 are used in the production of product Z. Viewed from the *use* side 1 and 2 are used in the *use* of products X and Y. C sells Z to business unit D and D buys Z. Moreover, Z has been developed in interaction between C and D. The interaction between the four business units has been repeated over time, resulting in three business relationships, A:C, B:C and C:D. These three business relationships are connected, forming a business network (Fig. 2).

Let us now make (a first) visit to business realities before we give a more thourough account of interaction and the four resource types.

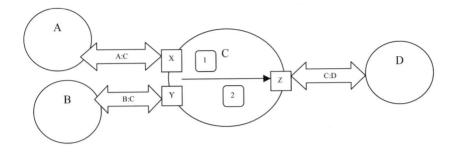

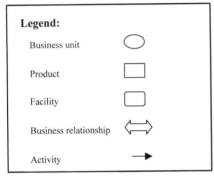

Fig. 2. Four Types of Resources Related in a Specific Way.

2. USE OF A RESOURCE – FORMULATING THE PROBLEM

A Norwegian goat farmer, Ola, described his customer's view of the resource he was selling:

> But then it was, that we heard a little bit, that the goat milk was not so very popular in the Tine system. We felt it was regarded somehow as a bit of rubbish in the machinery.

Ola's view concerned experiences he had in the early 1980s.

In 1998, at another location, a food researcher writes in an article published in a popular Norwegian dairy periodical:

> Knowledge about the composition and features of goat milk as a raw material for different products is far more limited than for cow milk. Some research has, however, been done . . . One may . . . ask if we in Norway have been clever enough to capitalize on the knowledge that nevertheless exists about goat milk in the manufacture of different goat milk products. The reason for this may of course be that goat milk in Norway so far for the most part has been

used in the making of brown cheese. There is ... reason to believe ... that one not has to the same extent demanded knowledge about the character of the raw material when making brown cheese compared to when making white cheese (Author's translation from Skeie, 1998).

Both these statements point to a problem: poor exploitation – or poorer exploitation than could have been the case – regarding a specific resource, goat milk. Each of the utterances also points to one specific aspect of resources and their use. Ola's utterance shows that a resource that is sold is not something that is determined solely by the seller or solely by the buyer. There are two parties, and both have interests and opinions regarding the resource. Hence, a resource seems to be a *relational* question. Ola refers to "a limited" and more specific goat milk, that which he is producing himself on his farm. He is worried about his customer's (at the time his only customer's) lack of interest regarding continuing use of the resource. Ola's worry is understandable, since he has recently bought the farm he is running and has planned to make a living from producing goat milk. Moreover, we notice that Ola terms the customer a system – "the Tine system," which suggests that the customer is more complex than a "simple" firm.

The researcher – whom we will name Anne – refers to a "broader" concept of goat milk; Norwegian goat milk. We will simply term this goat milk Norwegian goat milk. The most important element in Anne's utterance is, in our view, that the use of the resource is related to knowledge. More specifically, she claims that knowledge about the resource exists and that the reason for poor exploitation is not lack of knowledge, but lack of use of knowledge.

2.1. Goat Milk: Problem — or Possibility?

The two statements above thus seem to raise the following basic question:

Is the problem that the resource *is* poor or is the problem that the resource is poorly *used*?

The view that we take in this study is that the problem is poor use and not that the resource is poor per se. Standard textbooks in marketing distinguishes rather sharply between two ways in which the resource, then, could be used better:

Selling more of existing products made from it; that is, find new *markets*, or:
Developing (goat milk based) *products;* new or improved ones.

In this study we will look at both these options, but we shall not make a very sharp division between them. This has to do with that we see markets as networks. Our main assumption will be that resources and their value are dependent upon relations that are connected and thus forming networks. For actors in a network, we shall see, cultivating "new market" and "new product" as separate, "grand" directions for strategy is difficult and maybe not desirable. In fact the two options are intertwined and reinforce each other. Moreover, both strategies require some physical (real) resources and knowledge about them. This knowledge must be seen as part of the network and not outside of it. Put simply, better use of goat milk, thus, can be accomplished through development and application of knowledge of "real products" and "real markets" within a network.

Let us now return to the empirical "scene." Goat milk, together with other resources, is part of this scene. First we describe further the "local picture" – the use of the milk Ola was producing. Thereafter we present a "national picture" – use of the milk Anne referred to (Norwegian goat milk). In both cases we are dealing with the 1980s, the immediate antecedents regarding development of the focal resource. Then we will combine our theoretical concepts into a research model and formulate a couple of more precise research questions. In Section 3 we will describe and in Section 4 analyse how some new uses of the resource were developed in the 1990s. In Section 5 we discuss resources in relation to economics in business networks, before we draw some conclusions in Section 6. In the last section (7) we describe and reflect upon the research process in the study.

2.2. A Local Picture: Use of Goat Milk Produced at Skånaliseter Farm in the 1980s

Ola had taken over the goat milk farm Skånaliseter in the municipality of Røyrvik from his uncle in 1981. Then Skånaliseter delivered its goat milk to Namdalsmeieriet (literally "The Namdal Dairy"), which at that time was a regional dairy company. Together with other regional dairy companies it would merge into a new company (Tine Midt-Norge) 1.1.1996 (Erland, 1996). Ola married Kari in 1985. (These as well as other persons' names in the empirical parts of this study are fictitious.) Kari was qualified as nursery nurse.

In Trøndelag – a region in the middle of Norway – goat milk has never been the basis for more than a very limited dairy activity (Pettersen, 1984). This contrasts with the situation in some other Norwegian regions, such as Troms and the mountainous areas of Southern/Western Norway, where the production of goat milk always has been much larger and therefore better "adapted" to modern industrial dairying. Around 1980, Røyrvik was one of very few places in Trøndelag with a continuous tradition of goat milk production and processing.

Ola and Kari's farm – Skånaliseter – was located in the municipality of Røyrvik, about 500 meters above sea level at the entrance of Børgefjell National Park. Goat milk had for long been the main production on this farm. Skånaliseter's goat milk, together with the other goat milk produced in Indre Namdal, was delivered to Namdalsmeieriet's dairy in Namsos, about 150 km south-west of Røyrvik.

2.2.1. Little Volume in a "Mass Production Setting"

Some time after Ola had taken over the farm he received comments from persons handling the goat milk at the dairy in Namsos, which indicated that the goat milk he delivered was not so popular in Namdalsmeieriet. As Ola explains it:

> But then it was, that we heard a little bit, that the goat milk was not so very popular in the Tine [Norske Meierier] system. It was regarded somehow as a bit of rubbish in the machinery. A dairyman in Namsos, he said something like: 'This is some junk.' And we were struggling with milk pails. While the cow farmers got their milk collected from the farm by the dairy's tank lorries, we had to fill milk pails and transport them ourselves to the main road a little distance from here and take them back again . . . and with trouble in some ways. . . . I felt that we were in a way 'a ball and chain' for the Tine system.

According to the director of Namdalsmeieriet from 1981 to 1992, advising the goat milk suppliers to terminate their production was never official policy in the company. He is confident that officials in the company never gave such advice to any of the goat milk suppliers. In addition to Skånaliseter there were around ten other farmers that delivered goat milk to Namdalsmeieriet. In 1980 they supplied 109,565 litres of goat milk. This was very little compared to 47 million litres of cow milk supplied from around 800 cow farmers (Erland, 1996, p. 262). In hindsight (in 2002) the director of Namdalsmeieriet from 1981 to 1992 regards *small volume* as a main source of the problem:

> I must say that we did not exhibit the most outstanding creativity in finding a solution to the problem of using the goat milk that we purchased. The company had severe problems in finding an economical utilization of this small amount of goat milk given the company's industrial – as opposed to craftsmanlike – operations, although the company within the context of Norske Meierier was not totally hindered from developing, producing and marketing its own products (Director 1981–1992 Namdalsmeieriet).

Whey (the carbohydrate fraction of milk) was the only component of the goat milk that Namdalsmeieriet used to produce food products at the actual time. There were two products, pure brown goat cheese and mixed brown goat cheese. (The latter consists of about 90% cow milk whey and 10% goat milk.) Nevertheless, Namdalsmeieriet had some years before – in the 1970s – made an effort to make a special casein based product from the goat milk; goat milk gum. It was developed, produced and marketed by the company. However, the sales of the product never became sufficient to make it profitable and it was terminated after a few years. After that Namdalsmeieriet made no more efforts to find uses for goat milk "beyond" brown cheese.

2.2.2. Satisfactory Quality Given a Less Demanding Product
The *quality* of the goat milk was not a problem:

> My overall impression is that the quality of the goat milk that we purchased was more than good enough. To the degree that the goat milk was not satisfactory it was due to our handling subsequent to the farmer's handling of it . . . Nevertheless, I will say that the quality of the goat milk was not a problem. But then you have to remember that the product that we made of this goat milk [brown cheese] did not demand as high a milk quality as the making of real (white) cheese would demand. So you can say that there was some logic in the use of this resource from our side. We had a resource in small amounts; hence transportation on cooling tank lorries would be too expensive. We knew that transportation in non-cooled milk cans would lower the quality of the goat milk and hence we did not use it to produce demanding products, but instead less demanding products. Brown cheese demands less of the milk than white cheese does (Director 1981–1992 Namdalsmeieriet).

2.2.3. "Quasi"-Organizing and Price Compensation
But there is an additional factor that helps to make sense of Namdalsmeieriet's use of Skånaliseter's goat milk in this period. As already said, Namdalsmeieriet was not an independent company. A main part of this independence was Namdalsmeieriet's membership in Norske Meierier. One of the effects of this membership stemmed from an "instrument" called *price compensation*. The idea behind this instrument was economic equality among the member companies.

The member companies made dozens of products. However, the profitability of the different products varied, and the distribution of profitable products was not even across the companies. Hence some companies produced less profitable products, while others made highly profitable ones. This situation was regarded as unfair by the members of Norske Meierier (and also by state authorities and the two national farmers' organizations) and hence the practice of price compensation. Each company's income from sales of products was therefore transferred to and decided upon by a milk board ("Riksoppgjøret"), which was administered by Norske Meierier. Based on *standardized calculations* of cost and revenue for each product Norske Meierier compensated each company economically every year. For companies making profitable products this meant "giving away" income, while for companies producing less profitable products this meant "extra" money.

Seen in isolation the price compensation probably favoured goat milk at the expense of cow milk since goat milk products on average were less profitable than cow milk products within the quasi-organizational system of Norske Meierier. Nevertheless, the instrument may also have *hindered* use of the goat milk since:

> to the extent that a dairy company like Namdalsmeieriet used some of their resources to develop a goat milk product, eventual profit from this product had in any case to be 'paid back' to the

fellowship [Norske Meierier]... All in all, in my opinion in those days most development efforts within Norske Meierier and its member companies were centred on technology and little on products (Director 1981–1992 Namdalsmeieriet).

The product part of the price compensation system was implemented via production quotas. Each product within Norske Meierier had its specific quota. This quota was distributed among the member-companies' dairies. Regarding goat milk Namdalsmeieriet had production quotas for pure goat brown cheese and mixed brown cheese and nothing else (Erland, 1996, p. 265). In 1984 the dairy produced around 25,000 kg of pure goat brown cheese and around 75,000 kg of mixed brown cheese. In addition was produced nearly 80,000 kg of pure cow milk brown cheese. However, altogether brown cheese represented a small amount (ca. 5%) of the other products in the company: (white) cheese, butter and drinking milk. All these products were made from cow milk only.

Seen from the point of view of the goat milk the "problem" was that pure goat brown cheese as well as mixed brown cheese were produced in many other member-companies in Norske Meierier also and for the most part on a significantly larger scale than in Namdalsmeieriet. This meant that the cost efficiency of the brown cheese production in Namdalsmeieriet was low relative to the production in most of the other member-companies. Low cost efficiency was *not* compensated for by the price compensation instrument, but was something that the members of Namdalsmeieriet had to "pay" for.

2.2.4. Goat Milk Becoming Feed

However, as members of a co-operative company the goat farmers had a right to deliver goat milk to Namdalsmeieriet at a certain price regardless of what Namdalsmeieriet used this milk for. In fact, all members of Tine Norske Meierier were (and still are) paid full price for the milk that they delivered within their quota, even if selling the milk as feed to a lower price. The difference in price was compensated for via a national, semi-public fund financed from a fee paid by every milk producer (Omsetningsrådet, 1999). By 1985 the brown cheese boiler at the dairy in Namsos, where all the goat milk from Indre Namdal was processed, had become "worn out" and had to be renewed. Given the small amount of brown cheese, Namdalsmeieriet hesitated to renew it.

In 1986, Namdalsmeieriet, in co-operation with Norske Meierier, decided not to renew the boiler. Yet, all the goat farmers continued to deliver goat milk to Namdalsmeieriet. From now on the company mixed the goat milk with "cow buttermilk" – a by-product from butter-making – and eventually superfluous cow milk. This mixed product was sold to animal farmers that used it to feed pigs and calves. At this moment this was the most profitable use of goat milk produced in Indre Namdal.

2.3. A National Picture: Use of Goat Milk in the "Norwegian Dairy System" in the 1980s

2.3.1. Dairies in Norske Meierier – Main User of "Norwegian Goat Milk"

Around 1980 only small amounts of goat milk produced in Norway were processed on farms. Several specialized plants – dairies – took hold of the goat milk that was not processed on the farms. Most of these dairies also processed cow milk, and cow milk represented much more volume than goat milk in these dairies. In 1990 dairies within Norske Meierier processed 26.5 million litres of goat milk (Kvam, 1999, p. 14) and around 1,700 million litres of cow milk. Hence, goat milk represented in volume around 1.5% of all milk handled. Individual dairies were owned by one of the various dairy companies that again were owned co-operatively by cow milk and goat milk producing farmers in a specific geographical area.

Now, all these dairy companies, each covering "their" part of Norway, had for many years had a common organization, Norske Meierier. This organization carried out different tasks that the dairies regarded as common, among other things; product development, allocation of tasks between different dairies, logistics, quality control and marketing. Each dairy company purchased milk from its farmer members and only from them. Dairies within these companies processed the milk into various products defined and marketed on a national – and, for some products, international – level by Norske Meierier. Each dairy and dairy company must therefore be regarded semi-independent, as they could decide on some topics, while Norske Meierier decided upon other topics on the behalf of all the dairy companies. In Norway there existed at this time no dairy or dairy company beyond the companies that formed Norske Meierier.

2.3.2. Brown Cheese – The Main Use of Norwegian Goat Milk

Dairies within Norske Meierier had for long used the goat milk to produce brown cheese. For example, in 1990, 68% of the goat milk was used for brown cheese (Kvam, 1999). This use of goat milk differed from the use in other countries, e.g. France, where white cheese unquestionably was the main product (Alme, 1999; Masui & Yamada, 2000). In Norway cow milk was also used for making brown cheese, but this special application was clearly minor compared to other uses; liquid products, "real" cheese and butter.

Brown cheese is not a "real" cheese. According to World Health Organization (WHO) and Food and Agriculture Organization (FAO) only cheese made of casein, from which whey (the carbohydrate fraction of milk) is separated, can be termed cheese (Aschehoug & Gyldendal, 1995–1998; FAO, 1999). Curd is the usual English word for casein separated from whey and from which "real" (white) cheese can be made (Webster's, 1989). As a consequence brown cheese can be seen as a secondary product to cheese.

The dairies in Norske Meierier that processed goat milk used it in the production of two types of brown cheese: pure goat brown cheese (FG33) and mixed brown cheese (G35). The first was made of whey from goat milk, where goat milk and cream from goat milk was added (Kielland, 1976, pp. 120, 121). The latter was produced of whey from cow milk, where cow milk, cream from cow milk and around 10% goat milk was added. This cheese goes under the popular name Gudbrandsdalsost ("Cheese from the Gudbrandsdal Valley"), since adding milk and cream to the whey when making brown cheese first started in this valley. In addition a pure cow milk brown cheese (F33 – "Fløtemysost") was produced.

In the late 1980s around two-thirds of all brown cheese produced in Norway was mixed brown cheese. Thirty percent of all goat milk handled by Norske Meierier was used in the manufacture of this cheese (Kvam, 1999). Around 40% of the goat milk was used to make pure goat brown cheese. One difference between these two brown cheeses is that production of pure goat brown cheese results in casein as by-product, while in mixed brown cheese all the components in goat milk are used. Gudbrandsdalsost therefore represented the "easiest" way of utilizing goat milk in the dairies of Norske Meierier. Or as a development consultant in Tine Norske Meierier expressed to us in 2001:

> Gudbrandsdalsost represents a very good utilization of goat milk.

Involving one input product only and less equipment, making brown cheese was regarded as less complicated than making real cheese. No microbes and no ripening store were for example necessary. Moreover lactose in cow milk and goat milk was similar; hence equipment and skills developed for making brown cheese from cow milk could easily be used in the making of brown cheese from goat milk. In addition, there were stable customers that seemingly demanded few changes regarding the brown cheeses produced under the umbrella of Norske Meierier. For example they seemed to regard the relatively strong taste of pure goat brown cheese as a special – and positive – quality of this cheese. The market for brown cheese was stable; in a way brown cheese "sold itself." On the other hand, this meant that Norske Meierier did not foresee any increase in the market for brown cheese either, hence they were very restrictive in giving dairies larger quotas for brown cheese of any kind. Rather Norske Meierier was more interested in withdrawing quotas from dairies that had small quotas and giving them to dairies with larger quotas.

2.3.3. Brown Cheese: Less Demanding – Less Knowledge Required?

One consequence of the major part of goat milk being used to make "uncomplicated," standard brown cheese was that little effort was made to influence the quality of goat milk (Skeie, 1998). In comparison, for cow milk other and more complicated and vulnerable products represented the major application. Products like cheese and drinking milk demanded a higher quality of cow milk as raw material. Thus the dairy companies and Norske Meierier used considerable resources in developing and securing the quality of cow milk as raw material compared to goat milk. For instance, taste became an element in setting the price of cow milk in the early 1970s, while for goat milk this practice was not introduced until 2001. Norske Meierier also used many resources communicating information to cow milk farmers about milking routines and environment in the barn. In addition Norske Meierier used few resources to explore new features and other uses of lactose, for either cow milk or goat milk.

The consequence of the long reliance on brown cheese then that the knowledge about goat milk was limited compared to the knowledge about cow milk.

2.3.4. Exploitation of "Surplus" Goat Milk

Still, brown cheese could not "absorb" all goat milk that Norske Meierier handled in the 1980s. From the 40% or so of the goat milk that was used to make pure goat brown cheese, most of the casein was left over. The rest of the goat milk, around 30% when the quantity used in mixed brown cheese (30%) is subtracted, found entirely other applications, which we describe below.

2.3.5. Two White Goat Cheeses: Rosendal and Balsfjord

Around 1970 Norske Meierier's department of Product Engineering developed a semi-hard goat cheese called Rosendal. Rosendal was sold in Norway and exported to Germany and Australia among other countries, but the sales never took off. According to one consultant in Tine, the cheese was too loose. The cause of this is probably, according to Anne, an assistant professor at Department of Food Science at the Norwegian University of Agriculture, that goat milk casein has a different composition from cow milk casein. This easily results in a looser curd.

However, according to the consultant, making a satisfactory hard goat cheese is not impossible provided that one has special skills and knowledge, particularly regarding control of temperature and pH during the cheese making process. The dairy in Storsteinnes in Troms produced a mixed white cheese of 75% cow milk and 25% goat milk. This cheese was for the most part sold locally. In the years 1986–1992 the same dairy also made another cheese called Balsfjord. This was a fat cheese with weak goat taste made of 50% cow milk and 50% goat milk. At most (in 1988) the dairy made 135 tons of Balsfjord annually. This cheese was also for the most part sold locally and regionally. In other words, neither of these white cheeses was launched as "national" products like brown goat cheese. The sales never "took off." Thus, in the late 1980s real cheeses "absorbed" only 5% of Norwegian goat milk.

2.3.6. Mixing Goat Milk with Cow Milk: Dried Casein

The rest of the goat milk, 25%, was used to produce products with rather low value. Altogether around 65% of the goat milk casein was left over. And of the rest, 30% was not used to produce real, fermented cheese, but to make (mixed) brown cheese. The solution was to mix the goat milk casein left over with cow milk casein left over and dry it. One of the reasons for drying a mix of cow milk casein and goat milk casein is that drying pure goat milk casein was – and still is – technologically very difficult. Norske Meierier sold dry casein at rather low prices to Norwegian and foreign food companies, which used it as water-binding agent in, among other things, meat stuffing and fish stuffing.

2.3.7. Dried Goat Milk and Goat Milk as Feed

Surplus of "whole" goat milk in Norske Meierier came into being in areas of the country where there was no dairy company with equipment to process goat milk (Kvam, 1999). In addition all goat milk that lacked sufficient quality to be used in the production of food products, ended up as surplus. Both these types of surplus goat milk were sold to animal farmers as feed. Surplus goat milk also emerged at times of the year when the production of goat milk was higher than could be handled by the dairies. This goat milk again was dried and sold as goat milk powder. As with dried casein goat milk fodder and goat milk powder were products on which Norske Meierier obtained low prices.

In addition to describing the use of a certain resource in a particular network at a specific time, the text above also gave examples of interaction and the four types of resources introduced in Section 1; business units, products, facilities and business relationships. Let us now discuss in more detail what we mean by these four concepts.

2.4. A Discussion of Interaction and the Four Resource Types

2.4.1. Interaction Influencing Business Units: Co-Operation

The farm dairy firm Skånaliseter, which we have been introduced to in this section, can serve as an example of a business unit. Ola and Kari are the persons responsible of running this business unit. They also own it as real (as opposed to legal) persons. Moreover, in Section 3 we will be told how they use different resources (cheese making vat, knowledge, manpower etc.) in order to make certain cheese products. By using other facilities again the products are related to the resource collections of different customers; firms as well as households. Each customer can also be regarded as a business unit. By relating their products to these business units, Skånaliseter get access to resources they control; e.g. monetary resources and information of different kinds. The rationale behind business units is to co-ordinate the production and use of the different resources, because on their own resources cannot produce any meaningful outcome. The facilities, for example, have to be systematically related to (adapted to) the product in a certain way. More precisely the facilities have to carry out certain activities (pouring milk into the vat, regulating temperature and pH of the milk, handling customer orders, checking cheese on store etc.). Thus, organizing is necessary, or in the words of Weick (1979):

> To organize is to assemble ongoing interdependent actions into sensible sequences that generate sensible outcomes (p. 3).

The main purpose of a business unit is thus to organize activities to generate *sensible outcomes*. Organizing involves co-ordination of use of different facilities for transforming certain products into other products. A departure from the example above is of course that many firms command several different physical and non-physical facilities (although they may employ only one human individual) in its transformation of various products into other products. Thus simply to aggregate certain products and facilities does not generate any sensible outcome (Håkansson & Waluszewski, 2000, Chap. 2, p. 17). All activities necessary to generate sensible outcomes must be co-ordinated in sequence (complementarity) and parallel (similarity) (Dubois, 1998). A firm can thus be viewed primarily as an administrative resource (Penrose, 1995, p. 24).

It thus seems reasonable to regard business units as a *specific resource category*. However, referring to a legal entity (e.g. a unit registered in public business records) the word firm can restrict our imagination. In many firms different internal sub units may be so responsible for the economic result that studying them as firms makes sense. To avoid any misapprehension we choose, like Håkansson and Waluszewski (2000), to use the more abstract term *business unit*. Hence firms represent one example of business units.

What are the basic elements of a business unit? The answer is not straightforward, but let us make a suggestion. While products and facilities can be thought of as *technical* and *individual* resources, we perceive a business unit (and also a business relationship) primarily as a *social* entity (Håkansson

& Waluszewski, 2000, Chap. 2, p. 17). This entity is a resource to the extent that it has a use potential; more precisely, if it can serve to organize the use of technical and individual resources so that sensible products can be made. Implicit in "organizing" and "sensible product" is some sense of "economy"; the business unit must organize the activities in some economical way.

A comment regarding the physical/non-physical dimension is in order here. Since they are organizational and social thinking of business units (and also business relationships, see later) as purely non-physical resources and of products and facilities as physical resources can be tempting. However, on the pages to follow we hope it will become clear that there are also non-physical products and facilities. For example knowledge – a non-physical resource – can be transformed into a product or used as a facility. The same applies for business units and business relationships; also these contain physical and non-physical elements; they have a physical structure and an image (non-physical) structure (Waluszewski & Håkansson, 2001). For example, in the case of Skånaliseter (next section) we are told how a certain product, goat milk, undergoes specific handling (activities) in sequence and parallel, is mixed with different other products, until a customer has a meaningful product (cheese) in her hands. These activities are "physical" or real since we can observe them as they unfold. We may term the pattern we observe a physical (real) activity structure (Dubois, 1998; Håkansson & Snehota, 1995) to be distinguished from an imaged, non-physical activity structure. But a business unit does not only consist of organizational resources, it also contains social resources in terms of relationships between human individuals in the business unit.

The humans within the business unit have images (Morgan, 1997) of the organization they are part of and images of other organizations they deal with. We can extend this argument by invoking the term organizational knowledge (Nonaka & Takeuchi, 1995). We have already stated that knowledge can be found as or in the form of products and facilities. Saying that knowledge can be a business unit is probably to stretch the point too far. But knowledge can be a *part* of a business unit as is suggested by the concept organizational knowledge. Nonaka and Takeuchi (1995) describe and explain the process in which knowledge of individuals is transformed to common knowledge in an organization. In the same way Nelson and Winter (1982) argue that the routines of an organization parallel the skills of individuals. The term routine has much in common with the term activity structure mentioned above. In other words, the facility skill has its parallel in the business unit in the form of routines and organizational knowledge. Loasby (1998), for example, argues that the reason for the existence of economic organizations is that they develop and use knowledge. Skill (capabilities) is seen as crucial, as it is tacit, emergent and manifested in action and therefore difficult to copy.

> The organisation of capabilities is the organisation of systems for generating and testing new and improved skills (p. 157).

This view contrasts with the assumption within economics and transaction cost theory (cf. Williamson, 1975) that organizations exist because they allocate resources more *cost-efficiently* than the market. However, there is reason to believe that business units exist, both because they develop skills and knowledge and because they allocate resources efficiently (Håkansson & Snehota, 1995). Moreover a business unit may also develop physical resources and not only non-physical resources. But, as we have found, unless new knowledge is created, physical resources cannot be developed either.

Business units do not exist in isolation from each other. They are affected by actors' interaction. Håkansson and Waluszewski (2000, Chap. 2, p. 17) find that interaction in the form of co-operation influences business units in particular. Hence, co-operation can develop organizational features of a business unit; its activity structure, its image as seen by its members or by counterparts. Features of the routines may be changed and new, shared knowledge among the members may be created. The social interaction and social relationships *within* the business unit may likewise be influenced through co-operation with external counterparts. In this way various features of the business units involved may be mutually adjusted and developed over time as the co-operation continues.

Håkansson and Waluszewski (2000, Chap. 2, p. 17) put forward the suggestion that the *ability* to co-operate is crucial in interacting with other actors. We agree, but would like to qualify this observation in light of our discussion of resource types above. We identify a skill as a type of facility residing in individuals, while routine is a part of the business unit and can only be understood on a supra-individual level. Thus we can distinguish between individual's ability to co-operate with another actor, and the routines a business unit possess when it comes to co-operating with other actors. We think both are important for interaction. Not only the ability to co-operate, but also some knowledge of the business unit of the counterpart and how to work with it is critical for interaction (Håkansson & Waluszewski, 2000, Chap. 2, p. 17). Here the use of previous experience in co-operating with that counterpart *in new situations* is important as it influences the development of products and facilities.

Gadde and Håkansson (2001, p. 84) suggest that a buying firm perceives suppliers as resource elements. The important issue, and the highly strategic question, is then how a supplier – another business unit – fits in with the internal resources of the buyer. Here not only products and facilities of the two parties have to be considered in relation to each other, but also the business units of the two as such. In this consideration not only past events and the present situation have to be evaluated, but also expectations regarding the future. In an early contribution in the industrial network approach it was identified that interaction between industrial firms was not only marked by co-operation, but also by conflict (Håkansson, 1982). Thus in fitting resources two parties must also be aware of the need to confront resources, for example images of their own and the counterpart's different resources and resource combinations.

2.4.2. Interaction Affecting Products: "Selling – Buying"

A product can be viewed as the yield, result, or outcome of something (Penguin, 1992). In economics the term product refers to the result of a production process (Samuelson & Nordhaus, 1998). Products that are used to produce this product are not referred to as products, but factors of production. What is problematic in a theory of resource development is not that separate words are used for input and output, but the assumptions that are made regarding both factor and product within economics. They are both regarded as given. A factor for example is given since no distinction is made between a resource and the services the resource renders (Penrose, 1995, p. 25). A resource viewed as a factor, then, is identical to its actual (given) uses. Potential uses are ignored. Products are viewed in the same, given way within economics. Moreover, products are made in firms with no other contact with the external world than via price signals. The quality of the product is thus a result of development internal to firms.

Within logistics (Persson & Virum, 1989) and quality management (Aune, 1996) the product as output is also highlighted, but the perspective is wider. In logistics one is engaged in making the flow of materials through different transformation processes efficient and effective. Since this normally involves several firms, co-operation between firms is often called for. But we suggest that the conception of "flow" is not well suited for analysing development processes since, once the producer has made the product his or her job is over. The very separation between purchasing and marketing, in academia (Håkansson, 1982, p. 1) and to a significant extent in practice, seems to build on this conception of flow. This applies whether we support a market-oriented view of the firm or a product-oriented view (Van de Ven, 1988). In both cases we assume a unidirectional flow, in the first case from the seller to the buyer, in the latter case from the buyer to the seller.

The problem is that no *interaction* between seller and buyer is "allowed," and thus an important mechanism in the development of products is ruled out. But buyers must accept new products; products must match needs and needs must match products (Alderson, 1965). We regard matching as an interactive process. This accords with the relational view of resources taken in this study. In a relational view of resources, products become outputs *and* inputs. If a product cannot be used as input, it has no value and hence is no resource. And unless being an output it simply does not exist. In the empirical material (this section and Section 3) goat milk is the resource we have in focus; it is the focal resource that we follow. In this specific business network goat milk is a product. Like any other product it is both an output and input; it is sold and bought. But a resource need not be *either* a product *or* a facility. In one activity pattern the resource may be a product that is transformed by a facility. In another activity pattern the resource may be a facility that transforms another product. In our two cases, we will see, goat milk clearly is a product. But it would be a facility if it were used as a means to transform or sort (other) products. Thus, the basic distinction between facility and product resembles that between means and end.

Assuming interaction makes separate analysis of selling and buying rather meaningless; they are part of one and the same process (Håkansson, 1982). This (combined) "buying – selling" process can lead to development of products. Industrial products "changing" because of buyer and seller interacting during the "buying – selling" process are well documented (Håkansson & Snehota, 1995). In case 1 in the next section Skånaliseter sells cheese. Some of the buyers of this cheese have bought it for many years. One of the buyers sees a new opportunity for a more ripened cheese, interacts with Kari, who decides to make a new variant of an existing cheese (riper). Afterwards she can offer this special cheese also to other customers.

The rationale for a producing firm to sell a product that it produces – and vice versa for a user – may thus be that this gives better opportunities for interaction with the user about products than if the products were sold via one or more middlemen (Alderson, 1965). When the buyer is not a firm, but a private household finding middlemen between the user and the "ultimate" producer is more common. But we will see that Skånaliseter also interacts directly with private households. The cheese, which is not sold directly, is sold from manned cheese counters, and then the buyer has an opportunity to interact with the seller. The seller may be able to deal personally with some of the user's complaints about the product. He may give the user another product of the same or similar type, repair it or give him some extra information regarding the use of the product. Afterwards he or she can tell Kari in Skånaliseter how the customer has reacted to different products Skånaliseter is producing. This may make her change a certain product or develop a new product. Using abstract and indirect methods – instead of direct interaction – when they develop products seems to be more common for producers of mass-produced consumer products. Hence, products can be improved by collecting survey data from a sample of consumers and analysing these data statistically (Page & Rosenbaum, 1988).

Empirical research within the Industrial network approach has documented that industrial (business) sellers and buyers seldom regard the product as given (Håkansson & Snehota, 1995). This is of course important from a development point of view. The reason that the buyer "questions" the product may be that her or his production would be more *cost efficient* if certain features of the product were changed; for example it would better suit the producer's facilities. An even "more" interactive way would be co-operation where the product of the seller and the facility of the buyer were mutually developed. Or via a change in one of the features of the product or by adding another product the buyer can be able to make *better products*; products that suit her or his customers better or that attract new customers. In this case it is not only the *single* relationship that influences the development of the product, but also more, *connected* relationships (Håkansson & Snehota, 1995, p. 2). The seller may respond to these inquiries because he wants to secure further business with the buyer, or he may not. He may even find that during the efforts to alter the product he discovers some new features of it that will solve problems in relation to a second buyer.

Products can be of many different kinds. A common distinction is between goods and services (Håkansson & Waluszewski, 2000, Chap. 2, p. 13). With reference to the distinction we made earlier between physical and non-physical resources distinguishing between physical and non-physical products we find more logical. Goods then are surely physical products. They can be sold and bought, and formed, stored and transported as raw materials, processed materials, components and equipment (Håkansson, 1982) or in the shape of systems or art. The term service then we will only use in the Penrosian (1995) way; as something a resource does or potentially can do (that is, an activity) and not a resource in itself.

Products can range from exclusively physical ones to purely non-physical ones. Examples in the latter category are scientific concepts and theories (Latour, 1987) and metaphors, stories, beliefs and values (Morgan, 1997). An example in the first category is a resource in the natural state (Alderson, 1965), that is, an unprocessed raw material (Håkansson, 1982). In addition to "pure knowledge products," knowledge can also be embedded in physical products (Håkansson et al., 1999).

"Selling – buying interaction" can be used to help develop physical and non-physical products. Some products a firm may develop and produce internally for its own use, while other products the firm "just" has access to, either because of beneficial rights or due to the product being free (Penrose, 1995, p. 78). Air and sunlight are in this category. These products are free in the sense that no person, household or firm has to pay for them or make them. Thus one can discuss whether such natural, free resources are in fact resources. However, at least in an analysis of resource development it seems that free resources should be counted as resources. Like any other resource, free resources can render valuable services for firms that *acquire knowledge* of the resource and use of it (Penrose, 1995, p. 78).

To sum up this discussion of the resource type product and its relation to "buying – selling" interaction, we can say that within the discipline of economics (cf. e.g. Samuelson & Nordhaus, 1998) "buying – selling" interaction never occurs. If we take a relational view of resources we realize that a resource, which in the context of the selling firm is referred to as an output, is referred to as input in the context of the buying firm. This product can be developed through "buying – selling" interaction. Here features of the product "itself" can be questioned and eventually changed. Or existing features of the product can be related to existing features of resources the product has not been related to before. In the next section case 1 will provide good illustration on the former and case 2 on the latter of these possibilities.

2.4.3. Interaction Concerning Facilities: "Producing – Using"
The term facility has meanings like ease and aid, means, skill and ability (Penguin, 1992). Thus the concept of facility contrasts the concept of product as the latter refers to end, a result. In a business network, then, facility can be said to refer to any means or ability that aids or eases transformation and sorting (Alderson, 1965) of resources. As said earlier transformation can regard change in form and location in time and space. Another way to put it is to say that facility points to method (Loasby, 1998, p. 142) and not goal.

Facilities are necessary to produce a meaningful outcome, a result in the form of a product. But once production has started the actors involved may look for means that ease or speed up the production of the product. This may lead to a search for new features of the means, eventually giving them new features. Or a new means – facility – is developed. Moreover, the words ease and aid remind us that a facility does not replace an actor. A facility is something that so to speak "elongates" the actor; makes him or her more able.

Like products, facilities can have physical as well as non-physical dimensions. For example, the data-tomograph that Clara, the food researcher, uses to measure energy balance of goats in case 2 (next section) is a physical ("hard") facility. The skill to operate it is a non-physical ("soft") facility. Data programs, like that in the tomograph, are also usually regarded as non-physical (as associated with the term "software") since they consist of symbolic representations of the physical world. But knowledge is embedded both in the physical tomograph and in the software in it, thus any physical facility has a non-physical dimension tied to it. The concepts of skill (Nelson & Winter, 1982), capability (Loasby, 1998) and knowledge (Nonaka & Takeuchi, 1995) all highlight this non-physical dimension of facilities.

Moreover, Loasby (1998) refers to two types of knowledge, "knowledge-how" and "knowledge-that." "Knowledge-how" is knowledge that an individual has acquired by doing things. "Knowledge-that" is acquired by observing others doing things or by learning reference (codified, symbolic) knowledge. "Pure" scientific knowledge, then, is "knowledge-that." We regard skill and capability as synonyms for "knowledge-how." But like Nelson and Winter (1982) we prefer the term skill. In this scheme the word knowledge is quite wide, encompassing both codified knowledge and skill. Hence, to the extent that it has known use knowledge can be a facility. But knowledge can (as discussed on previous pages) be a product, too. Knowledge can also constitute a layer in a business unit or a business relationship, e.g. in the form of routines (Nelson & Winter, 1982) or organizational knowledge (cf. Nonaka & Takeuchi, 1995).

To discuss skill, then, seems to be the same as to discuss the knowledge dimension of facilities. Skill resides in human individuals. Both "knowledge-how" and "knowledge-that" indicate that knowledge is *a question of context*. It is only when a piece of information has been embedded in a specific human being that genuine knowledge has been created. And not before someone is able to do something has knowledge-how been created. A piece of knowledge taken out of its context is only information, not knowledge. It does not become knowledge in a new business network before it has been embedded in that network.

A skill is a specific combination of tacit knowledge (Nelson & Winter, 1982) and the ability to use physical or symbolic resources, including our own body. Manpower is thus a physical facility. The ability to judge what actions to take in a specific situation is a skill. Skill is related to technology and can be thought of as practical intelligence (Loasby, 1998, p. 146). Like physical facilities, skill aids and eases transformation and sorting of resources.

Sometimes distinguishing a product from a facility is easy. In other cases it might be more difficult. First of all the resource must be seen from the perspective of a specific firm, because what is a product for a selling (or producing) firm can be a facility for a using firm. Next, taking the side of the using firm, we must ask, does the resource only aid and ease transformation (eventually sorting) of resources? If the answer is yes, the resource is a facility. For example in making cheese, certain microbes are necessary, as they are means that transform certain chemical compounds in the cheese so that it gains a sought-after taste and texture. These microbes stay in the cheese and do their job as long as the cheese exists. The microbes, however, are not constituents of the product, but only means in the production of the product and its features. Hence in this case the microbes are a facility for the dairy. But if the dairy buys bacteria that enhance digestion and mixes them into the milk before making cheese, we can regard these bacteria as a product; both bacteria and milk *are transformed* by facilities that *transform*.

In Section 3 we will see that facilities change over time. Facilities used to transform goat milk in the early 1980s in e.g. Namdal are not the same as those used in the late 1990s. Physical facilities had developed in the meantime. From the cases (Section 3) we will also learn that the skills concerning manufacture of cheese were different in 2000 than in 1980. In fact, skills that actors in the network at a certain time had come to regard as obsolete would later become judged as having economic potential. Moreover, these developments concerning facilities were not entirely internal; business units outside e.g. Tine took part in many of the developments. The companies' interactions had an impact on various facilities, both "hard" and "soft" ones. During the interactions they discovered, for example, that the user firm's facility could be adjusted in a way that would make a firm's cheese making process more efficient or, in other cases, more effective, e.g. increasing the possibilities of differentiating existing products (Håkansson & Snehota, 1995, p. 54).

The aspect of interaction that first and foremost contributes to development of facilities, then, is "producing – using" interaction. For example, in case 2 we will learn that the milking goat – a facility – undergoes change. This change stems from interaction between production and use of this facility, but in a somewhat complex and indirect way. Tine and the breeding organization are two actors involved. In this case Tine is on the use side (not as a "direct" user of milking goats, but as user of a product that is dependent on milking goats' features). The breeding organization is on the production side as this actor is capable of affecting features of milking goats, more precisely their genetic "composition." The two actors effect a change in this composition, not because of (many separate) one-sided actions, but because of *inter*action.

However, it is not only interaction between a firm that produces a product and another firm that uses this product as a facility that is interesting for development of facilities. Facilities can also be developed due to interaction between two or more firms that sell and buy each other's products. Håkansson and Waluszewski (2000, Chap. 2, p. 16) point out that facilities in this case can be developed in order to mutually adapt production, production schedules, delivery or handling of products. Such mutual development can lead to certain features of the facility being "frozen" in order to make it possible (at all) to transform products with particular features. An example of this is the agitator in the milk-cooling tank, which will be described in case 2 (next section). The agitator was designed for using cow milk as input, while it was less suitable for goat milk, which had a different fat characteristic. In the process of adjusting the agitator so that it suited goat milk better, the actors involved learned more about both the facility and the product.

2.4.4. Interaction Impacting on Business Relationships: Networking
If interaction between two actors is repeated a relationship between the two may develop (Håkansson & Snehota, 1995, p. 273). We discussed the concept of business relationship earlier in this section. What interests us here is the recognition that a business relationship, once it has been developed, can be a valuable resource (Håkansson & Snehota, 1995, p. 31). Thus, a business relationship can be used for linking activities, tying resources and bonding actors. A business relationship can provide access to resources and therefore have economic consequences in terms of productivity. But a business relationship can also facilitate the confrontation of resources of different actors, which eventually can lead to development. Hence, business relationships have economic consequences in that they can influence productivity and innovativity in a business network.

This means that, like business units, business relationships bring economic logic into business networks. Moreover, like all types of resources we have discussed, business relationships have one real (objective) side and one imaged (subjective) side. Hence a business relationship can exist as an idea – knowledge – in the mind of people in the network. To the extent that such ideas are realized we can talk about business relationships as facts – as real (Berger & Luckmann, 1967, p. 30). And a business relationship is realized when two actors *really* start to interact repeatedly; *really* orient mutually towards each other and *really* commit themselves to each other. This "relationship reality" can be observed; in activities mutually co-ordinated between two actors (Dubois, 1998; Richardson, 1972), through resources reciprocally adapted and in social interaction over time between individuals of the two actors.

A business relationship, then, is a resource insofar as actors know to use it. In the cases that we shall visit in the next section there are several examples of relationships being used. Via its relationship with Åsbygdens Naturbruksgymnasium, Skånaliseter gains knowledge about cheese recipes and becomes aware of a company that supplies cheese making vats especially suited for small dairies. Through the relationship with a food consultant Skånaliseter becomes related – as a supplier – to a tourist firm. Via this business relationship Skånaliseter is able to sell some of its produce. Via its relationship with the goat breeding association, Tine influences the goat breeding goals. Thus, in relationships actors can get access to products and facilities that are more suitable than those that can be bought in the market or made internally. Moreover, it is in a business relationship that a product that an actor produces attains value. Or as Emerson (1981, p. 41) states:

> Notice that a resource is not an attribute or a "possession" of an actor in the abstract, but is rather an attribute of his relation to another or set of other actors whose values define resources.

Therefore, for example:

> A mother's capacity to offer approval is a resource in her relation with her child but may not be in her relation with someone else's child (Molm & Cook, 1995, p. 216).

In other words, the value of a resource is something specific; it depends on there being a relationship between actors, and any relationship is unique (Håkansson & Snehota, 1995). An actor can obtain resources from others that *match* its other resources better. This can lead to a more *potent* resource collection (Alderson, 1965), than if the resources were obtained in the "faceless" market (Richardson, 1972). This is also an advantage for the selling firm as it can expect to get a higher price when it sells its products through relationships with specific other firms than by competing for atomized customers in a market. This *relationship benefit* stems from the firm being able to produce a product that matches the buyer's collection of resources better (Alderson, 1965), or in our terminology more adapted with "better" interfaces.

Through interaction in the relationship the selling firm can also expect to *learn* more about the products it is producing – how they are used, for what purpose, how they could be used better or differently and discover new features in them. A nice example of this, we will see, occurred when Skånaliseter, because of incidentally having a surplus of goat milk, was urged to make brown cheese with double content of goat milk. Because some customers, among them shops, responded their positive taste experiences with this cheese "back to" Skånaliseter, Skånaliseter learned more about its brown cheese products and how they attained value. Since the relationship to the customers in this case also contained trust and commitment (Håkansson & Snehota, 1995) Skånaliseter was reasonably sure that if they "converted" the "occasional cheese" into a standard product, this product could be sold and hence that resources spent on its development would pay off. This, again, illustrates that economic logic underlies business relationships.

Recalling the dual face of resources – that any resource has a provision side and a use side – we realize that purchasing and selling are two sides of the same coin (Håkansson, 1982). There is no difference in principle between a customer searching for a seller and a seller searching for customers (Alderson, 1965). In both cases the crucial thing is *matching*; there can be no purchasing without sale and no sale without purchasing. Interaction between provider and buyer may be thought of as one way in which matching takes place. The unique "feature" of interaction is that it "allows" not only static matching of given and pre-existing products and needs. As we realized in the discussion of social interaction, interaction has a dynamic component as it may lead to *reinterpretation* of products and needs. We may say that interaction stimulates a kind of double loop learning, where not only means, but also ends are questioned and – eventually – changed (Argyris & Schön, 1996). Much of the "power" of interaction rests on information handling; it gives the parties "rich" and specific knowledge. This may recontextualize the situation relating to a product, a facility or a business unit, opening up new possibilities for development. The rationale for letting the interaction unfold in the context of a relationship, then, may be to increase the efficiency (output – input ratio) of the development process and to reduce the uncertainty about the effectiveness of it (will its output be valued by some buyer?).

However, business relationships develop not only via interaction in dyads. Most firms have more than one business relationship – be it with suppliers, customers, public agencies or R&D institutions. To the extent that actors regard their business relationships as resources *systematically relating two or more relationships* can be fruitful (Gadde & Håkansson, 2001, p. 84). Hence, we can imagine a more complex pattern of "multilateral" interaction. (When discussing the other three resource types we assumed "bilateral" interaction and not "multilateral" interaction.) We will refer to such multilateral interaction as *networking*. An important point is that networking can affect the business relationships involved.

As with combination of other types of resources, there may be two types of economic rationale "behind" networking; increased productivity or better innovativity. Networking for improved productivity will typically be to relate business relationships that are similar (homogeneous) to each other by terminating "deviant" relationships, establishing similar relationships with new actors and/or making "deviant" relationships more similar. This can create opportunity for an actor to relate in the same, and therefore efficient, way towards many counterparts. Networking for innovativity requires the opposite; establishing a portfolio of different (heterogeneous) relationships in order to introduce variation, which is a prerequisite for learning (Håkansson et al., 1999).

An example of the first situation is when Namdalsmeieriet (this section) in co-operation with Norske Meierier decides to stop using goat milk for making cheese and starts selling it as fodder. However, Norske Meierier continues to relate to these goat farmers in the same way as it does towards goat farmers who deliver goat milk that *is* used for producing cheese. The project for solving the taste problems of Frozen Curd (case 2 next section) illustrates networking affecting innovativity. Here Tine "assembles" different relationships. For example, one is with an actor competent within animal science. Another is with an actor with competence in food science. Tine's business relationship with the dairy producing the product (Tine Haukelid) and this dairy's relationships with its suppliers of goat milk are also part of the "ensemble" of relationships within the project. And ultimately Tine adapts all of these relationships to its relationship with its customer Laura Chenel.

Consequently networking is a highly *strategic* task as it affects the firm's position in the business network it is part of. Networking can be carried out in order to create *functional* improvements or be used for *political* purposes (Håkansson & Waluszewski, 2000, Chap. 2, p. 18). Functional improvements may be made when a firm tries to adjust its own facilities to a product supplied by one of its suppliers and a product sold to a certain customer. Once the possibility of improvement is identified, this may be a simple task to accomplish. But relationships may also be characterized by conflict, for example due to different images of what constitutes an ideal solution and how to share costs and benefits among network partners. In such a situation *trust*, which is built up through previous interaction between the parties, may be a critical feature, likewise *social competence* – the ability to manage social relations. Trust and social competence may improve when individuals from different firms strive for functional improvements or new political solutions.

Håkansson (1982) claims that power and dependence are also common features of many business relationships. Therefore we are likely to find enemies as well as friends in business networks. Hostility and friendship may be linked to social relations; sympathies and antipathies on the personal level across firm boundaries. One interesting situation is when former enemies become friends. This can be due to changes external to their relationship, for example because of specific technological or political changes in connected relationships (Håkansson & Waluszewski, 2000, Chap. 2, p. 18). Another situation is when two customers start to co-operate in order to gain more attention from their common supplier. There is also the situation when a business unit wants to terminate the relationship with one or more business units. The reason may be that the company wants to prioritize other relationships that for different reasons seem more promising or important. The termination can also be part of a strategy to reduce the firm's total number of relationships, thereby simplifying its handling of relationships. A firm can also decide to terminate a relationship because it wants to improve the way it is seen by other actors in the network. This is the case for a retailer who is severely criticized by environmental organizations for purchasing and selling furniture from a supplier who uses wood from a rain forest and therefore terminates the relationship with this supplier.

To sum up, actors can utilize business relationships. A business relationship can therefore be seen as a resource. Moreover, it can be developed by systematically relating many relationships. This, again, can facilitate development of other types of resources, for example a product.

2.5. Web of Actors Constraining and Enabling Interaction

In the second half of this section we have discussed interaction and the four types of resources. Even though the concept of interaction is general, referring to "reciprocal action" (between humans) as well as "reciprocal influence" (between other types of entities), we have in this study chosen to restrict the concept to the former notion. This does not mean that "interaction" between resources and between actors and resources are non-existent or irrelevant in relation to development. For example, a crucial element in the development problem in case 2 (next section) is "bad" interaction between two resources – milking goat and fodder. As the goats grazed late in summer the remaining grass at the nearest pastures became poorer, leading the goats to make longer trips, which "tapped" their energy, leading them to eat at nearer locations with poorer grass etc. In other words, the pasture influenced the goats, but the goats also influenced the pasture. But instead of talking about interaction between these two resources we use the expression reciprocal influence.

Interaction between actors, then, can involve two parties. But interaction can also include many parties; if not networks would not come into being. The discussion of interaction in the form of "networking" above showed this. As actors develop and use resources, bonds are created between actors. These bonds build on mutual identity and a certain character in terms of activity links and resource ties. Like business relationships bonds are connected and form a web of actors (Håkansson & Snehota, 1995). What is important from our point of view is not the web of actors per se, but the recognition that *the web of actors constrains and enables interaction regarding development of resources*. In other words, we think that the web of actors affects resources, as it constitutes part of the context in which interactive, systematic relating takes place. Thus, if we ignore the actor dimension we miss an important influence on resource use and resource development.

The actor dimension concerns organizing:

> Management issues involved in handling the actor dimension of relationships revolve . . . about organizing (Håkansson & Snehota, 1995, p. 261).

The term "web of actors" points to the organizing of several actor bonds; how the relationships between purposeful and interested actors are structured and combined to form a "meaningful whole." Identity, we think, is perhaps the concept that best captures the meaning of the concept of actor. Identity points to what makes an actor specific in a business network. Thus, we can apply the same logic to actors in business networks as we already have done regarding resources; because actors are different, combinations matter. In actor terms we refer to such a combination as a web of actors. This web can be regarded as a "quasi organization" (Håkansson & Snehota, 1995, p. 40). Like activity patterns and resource constellations a web has no natural boundaries, nor any clear centre, although actors' positions in a web may vary with respect to strength.

From this view of actors a web contrasts with a "conventional, rational" organization, as it has no common goal that unifies its members and directs their action by fiat. It can only be held together by some shared identity, for example regarding resources and their use in the network. Thus, one actor in a web may appreciate a certain use of a resource, while another actor in the same web may find another use of this resource more interesting. Put in another way, in a web more than one actor can have purposes and interpretations concerning a resource.

So interaction regarding a specific resource does not occur in vacuum, but is shaped by the web the involved actors are part of. In other words, we can assume that there exist inter-organizational effects on resource development. Or as Van de Ven (1988, p. 115) puts it:

> Innovation is not the enterprise of a single entrepreneur. Instead, it is a network-building effort that centers on the creation, adoption, and sustained implementation of a set of ideas among people who, through transactions, become sufficiently committed to these ideas to transform them into "good currency."... this network-building activity must occur both within the organization and in the larger community of which it is a part.

The author refers to the "larger community network" as the extra-organizational infrastructure or context "in which innovation can flourish." This formulation seizes what we think of when we use the concept "web of actors," with the exception that we would prefer the term interaction to transaction.

As we have emphasized many times in this section, development of resources hinges on knowledge. Actors hold this knowledge individually and collectively. But no single actor has full knowledge of any resource. Thus, the actors' knowledge does not exist in concentrated or integrated form but rather as dispersed bits of incomplete and often contradictory knowledge:

> The problem ... is how the spontaneous interaction of a number of people, each possessing only bits of knowledge, brings about a state of affairs in which prices correspond to costs, etc. (Hayek, 1949, referred in Kirzner, 1992, p. 163).

Fragmented knowledge means, on the other hand, that different actors have *specific* knowledge to offer. Via interaction such knowledge can be combined in new meaningful ways:

> [Actors] relate their intentions and understanding to those of others making it thus possible to transcend their limits (Håkansson & Snehota, 1995, p. 194).

And further:

> No actor can embrace all the complexities of the environment of which it is part. The web of bonds of an actor to others . . . provides a frame for knowledge development with respect to what exists and is happening beyond the horizon (provided that a common language exists) (p. 200).

Thus, the term web of actors is not empty (Alderson, 1965). It is meaningful as it refers to "realities" out there. Managers know that being part of a web of actors is important if new knowledge of a resource shall be created. Hence:

> The important thing is to ensure that the set of counterparts forms a meaningful totality (Håkansson & Snehota, 1995, p. 267).

From such a meaningful totality an actor can, through interaction, gain access to resources of others, including their specific knowledge. This access hinges on the actor receiving a minimum of commitment from the other actors, which again presupposes that the others ascribe some identity to the actor and trust him or her.

2.6. A Research Model

We will now make an effort to integrate some of the concepts accounted for in Sections 1 and 2 into a research model. Development takes place when purposeful (interested) actors in a business network confront and combine resources of different categories. According to Håkansson and Waluszewski (2000, Chap. 11, p. 8) this:

> can be expressed as efforts undertaken in order to utilize several different but related resources. This systematic relating appears as important both for the utilisation of individual resources and of larger constellations of resources. During this relating, features of some of the resource elements become successively embedded into each other [heaviness], while others are left out [variety].

Thus, resource development in a business network can be seen as purposeful, systematic relating of resources. This means that development is about creating and managing many and diverse interfaces between resources. This also makes it clear that development never starts from "nothing," hence having some picture of the prevailing resource constellation is important. But since this constellation in principle is infinite, any actor trying to understand and act in relation to the "total" combination would be paralysed at the outset. However, actors can approach *parts* of constellations and interfaces. In this way their approach to resources can be characterized as sub-optimal, local and limited (Cyert & March, 1963; Håkansson, 1989, p. 5). But in a network actors' searches are limited not necessarily in a geometrical sense. Hence, searches can reach far beyond the focal company and way beyond a local plant or community, but nevertheless encompass only a small portion of the "total" network.

The exploitation side and development side are both necessary in a model to explain development of physical resources. Moreover, the physical dimension is not sufficient; no resource can be a resource without the non-physical dimension. And regarding the non-physical dimension we have especially been interested in knowledge, which is of two kinds. One is knowledge that already *exists* and hence can be exploited more or less directly. The other is knowledge that does not exist, but can be *developed*. In relation to resource development in a network interaction takes the form of systematic relating. The relating is supposed to be systematic because the actors doing it are supposed to be purposeful. Hence, without purpose there can be no systematic relating.

As we define it, purposeful actors carry out interactive systematic relating. As a consequence we have found digging deeper into the actor dimension – the "driver" of resource development – "purposeful." The actor dimension can be studied at many levels. Håkansson and Snehota (1995, p. 45) identify three: organizational structure on company level, actor bond on relationship level and web of actors on network level. We found the last level – the web – especially fruitful given our interest in the inter-organizational context in which our resource was sold and bought and produced and used. A web of actors constitutes an important part of the industrial network in which development of a resource can take place. Hence, we incorporate the concept "web of purposeful actors" in our research model (Fig. 3).

The model can be interpreted in this way: On the right side we have the resources in the network, e.g. a physical resource to which actors interactively and systematically have related non-physical resources. Knowledge is an important non-physical resource because, as we found, an element is no resource if no actor has knowledge of it. On the right side in the model we also distinguish between resources that are used and resources that have been developed, but that, of various reasons, are not used in the network at the actual time. This applies both to physical and non-physical resources. Moreover, resources that are used have a role to play also in development of resources because, as we stated, development never starts from "nothing." Hence, resources in use as

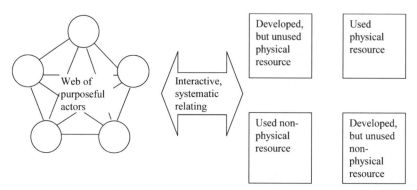

Fig. 3. Development as Interactive, Systematic Relating of Used and Unused Physical and Non-Physical Resources by Purposeful Actors in a Web.

well as "developed, but unused" resources are part of a process of systematic relating.

On the left side in Fig. 3 we find the "drivers" of resource development in an industrial network – purposeful actors. The actors have bonds to each other because they interact over time, and they are part of a web. (Note that the bonds and the actors may be more varied than is suggested in Fig. 3.) Moreover, interactive, systematic relating is an *on-going process*. Therefore, the model does not refer to "something" static, but to "something" *dynamic*, it is one possible depiction of the process of resource development in a network. However, we can "freeze" the process at a certain point in time and analyse outcomes of the process in terms of resources — activated features and combinations — as well as the actors involved and their bonds.

We can take the focal resource in this study as an example. In this section (2) Ola tells us about goat milk being poorly used, hence this goat milk is an example of the box labelled "used physical resource" in the figure. We regard Ola and Kari at Skånaliseter as purposeful actors, and we will learn in the next section that the poor exploitation of the resource in question leads these two actors, but not others, to interact with certain other actors. This leads to development of new knowledge ("developed, but unused non-physical resource"). Some of this knowledge is used and hence becomes an example of a "used non-physical resource." A result of this use of a non-physical resource is development of a physical resource ("developed, but unused physical resource"). An example of this is the "space" for a future dairy that Ola and Kari reserved when they built a new outbuilding in 1985. Ola and Kari started to use this space only ten years later when they built a dairy there. Then this space became a "used physical resource." However, this space might have remained an "unused physical resource."

The model (Fig. 3) does not distinguish between search for new features and search for new combinations of a certain resource; we regard both these options as included (implicitly) in the term "developed, unused resource." Combination is implicitly also part of the entity "used resource" since we have found that resources can be used only *if they are part of a combination with other resources.* In other words, the term "used resource" *presupposes* that the resource is part of a combination. Nor are the four types of resources discussed in this section explicitly "pictured" in the model. But each of them can be found in each of the four resource "states." For example, instead of the rather general "developed, but unused physical resource" we could refer to the more specific entity "developed, but unused physical *product.*"

2.7. Research Questions

In this section we have "met" a certain resource – goat milk – and become acquainted with three actors' (one producer's, one user's and one researcher's) view of the actual use of this resource. A joint concern was that the resource was poorly used, implying that it could have been used "better." On the background of the theoretical perspective developed in this section we may say that the problem is that the resource is dominated by the structure in which it is embedded. We view this structure as a business network made up of a specific connection of activity links, resource ties and actor bonds. The problem, then, seen from the perspective of our focal resource is that "its" business network is structured around another, almost similar, but much "larger" resource, cow milk. The actual business network (the "Norwegian milk network") at the time was efficient for cow milk, but less efficient for goat milk – the "smaller" resource. In other words, the milk network made cow milk a rather valuable resource, while it turned goat milk into a less valuable resource. This had something to do with that cow milk "existed" in far larger volumes than goat milk and is the reason why we use the adjectives "large" and "small" respectively in relation to these two resources. Thus, economies of scale and scope could within this network to a much higher degree be applied in relation to cow milk than in relation to goat milk. As long as the activity pattern in the network was dominated by efficiency logic goat milk would be the subordinate resource. As a consequence we may say that the network was a structure that confined goat milk as a resource.

From this two problems arise. The first is of an abstract, *theoretical* nature and can be put this way; what can actors do to develop new uses of a product that is subordinate in a business network? Håkansson and Ford (2002, pp. 138, 139) point to the paradox that if an actor in a business network "succeeds" in acquiring "final" control over the surrounding network, the network will die; thus, the development "vigour" may vanish through one-sided planning and too much structuring. Thus, we should be looking for the existence of a dynamic element in business networks. How can value of a resource, e.g. a product, be created? And what is the role of actors then? As the reader might have understood these are questions that we have been dealing with in Section 1 and in (the last part of) this section.

The other problem is *empirical* and concerns what the concrete actors in the Norwegian milk network introduced and described in this section can do to improve the use of the actual product. For example, should Ola and Kari at Skånaliseter let their goat milk remain marginal, or should they break out of the prevailing milk network? Or should this structure be broken? And can Ola and Kari do all this on their own? This (empirical) problem will be addressed in the next section (3). After a general introduction concerning actors in the milk network and features of the focal resource, we present two case stories. The first story begins around 1987 and departures in the "local picture" of the network presented in this section (2). The other story begins some years later − in 1995 − and is a continuation of the "national picture" of the milk network given in this section. Moreover, the first story centres around a business unit (Skånaliseter) and its role in relation to development of the focal resource, while the second story revolves around a product (Frozen Curd) and its impact on development of the resource.

3. DEVELOPING NEW USES: TWO CASE STORIES

3.1. Organizational Features and Use of Names in Tine/Norske Meierier

As we mentioned in Section 2, dairy companies that together have covered the whole of Norway have, under different names and since 1928 had a common organization. In 1984 its name was changed to Norske Meierier. When Tine was introduced in 1992 as common brand for all products produced by the dairy companies that owned Norske Meierier, the name of the common organization became Tine Norske Meierier (Tine. [http://www.tine.no/kunder/tine/TineStruktur.nsf]). In this section we will use the term Tine when being specific about what part of Tine we refer to is not so important. We will also in this section use the term Tine when the actual time is before 1992. When being more specific is necessary we will add the organizational name. Hence, individual dairies we will term Tine followed by the name of the place where the dairy is located, for example Tine Verdal. Companies are called

Tine followed by the name of the region that the company covers, for example Tine Midt-Norge. These companies' common organization will be called Tine Norske Meierier, which is also the official name.

All the regional dairy companies that own Tine are co-operatives owned by milk producing farmers in that region. In fact Tine is owned "double" as all the milk farmers in the different regions also have their share in Tine. In 2000 there were approximately 21,500 milk farmers. Of these nearly 700 produced goat milk. The others produced cow milk. Numbers of cow milk and goat milk producers have steadily decreased over the years. Around 1990, when the case stories "begin," the number was around 30% higher. In 2000 there were 10 regional companies running altogether 62 dairies (Tine Årsmelding, 2000). Both numbers of companies and dairies within Tine have steadily decreased during the years. The conditions for milk production, transportation distances and distance to customers vary between the different regions. Thus, nearly 90% of the goat farmers are found in five of the ten regions. This situation has not changed very much during the period we mainly deal with in this study, 1980–2001.

Tine makes various types of milk products; liquid products like milk for drinking, yoghurt and sour cream and solid products like butter and cheese. Tine widened their range of dairy products in the 1980s and 1990s (Stræte, 2001, pp. 23, 24). In 1999 retailers marketed in Norway 50 liquid products from Tine representing 205 product variants. The same year 1,630 different variants of cheeses were marketed. However, variants of two cheeses – Tine Gudbrandsdalsost (made of cow milk and goat milk mixed) and gouda (in the form of TINE Norvegia and the competitor Synnøve Finden's Gulost) represented 49% of sales value. From 1997 Tine Norske Meierier also allows "its" regional companies to develop their own products as supplement to the range of products that are marketed under the Tine brand (Stræte et al., 2000, p. 23). These regional products are not marketed centrally by Tine Norske Meierier, but can "instead" add the name of the producing dairy and the dairy company on the product. By contrast "ordinary" Tine products cannot – and shall not – be identified with the dairy and the dairy company producing the product, only Tine as such. The overall impression, then, is that Tine produces a considerable range of dairy products and that, regarding cheeses, only two represent the bulk of sales.

Tine Norske Meierier has defined different functions. These have mainly been constant in the period we are dealing with. Various departments take care of the different functions. In 2000 there were departments for:

(1) Information and Organization
(2) International

(3) Economy, Logistics, Information Technology, Controller and Purchasing
(4) Market
(5) Research and Development

The Department for Research and Development (R&D) is, moreover, subdivided into two R&D Centres. Tine R&D Voll in Rogaland deals mainly with product development. Tine R&D Kalbakken is purposely located next to the dairy Tine Fellesmeieriet in Oslo and deals mostly with technology and process development (Tine Årsmelding, 2000).

The regional companies are thus semi-independent in the sense that Tine is responsible for some types of decisions and tasks, while the regional companies are responsible primarily for production. Within the "Tine system" some companies, departments, dairies, employees and members have been more engaged in the development of goat milk than others.

3.2. Identification and Description of Some
"Accepted" Features of Goat Milk

As for other resources, the features of goat milk are important for the use and development of it. For the actors involved in the development work knowing at least some of the features of the resource is important. Having some idea of how one goes about discovering or developing new features is also important. Furthermore, knowing features of some other resources is mandatory. The aim of the cases is to describe how actors discover and use features related to the actual resource and how they combine it with other resources. The purpose of the list below, however, is to list some features of goat milk that have been described in the literature independent of the case stories. Actors in the cases are aware of and use some of these features, while they are not aware of and do not use others.

Let us first suppose that we are novices regarding milk in general. Somebody has given us the task to identify features of something called goat milk. How would we go about it? One strategy is to seek to get hold of "an exemplar" of the resource in order to wrest the mysteries from it with our own senses. One solution could be to search for a retailer that sells goat milk and buy some cartons. Then we probably would do something to the resource; look at it, smell it, pour it, shake it, and maybe warm it up and see what happened. But could we be sure that this "white liquid stuff" would not be dangerous for us? Could we take the chance of feeling it with our hands, or drink it to feel its taste? Maybe we should test it on a few rats first and observe their reactions. But probably, since we already from the start knew that the stuff was a sort of milk, and we already knew that stuff called milk in general is not dangerous for humans, we would be convinced that the actual stuff was not dangerous. We would also be reassured by the fact that the stuff was placed in a refrigerating counter together with other types of milk and dairy products and not together with detergents, insecticides or shampoo for example. It even had the word "milk" written on the packaging. Then we could give it to our kittens, and maybe members of our family, and notice the effects. The milk could also be purchased from a Norwegian goat farmer, or a dairy. A more exciting method would be to hijack a tank lorry with goat milk and demand some litres of the elixir from the driver.

No doubt by these actions we could gain some knowledge of features of goat milk. If we had some previous knowledge of a more common milk, cow milk, and its features, we could to a certain extent test if goat milk had some of the same features. Then we would have further increased our knowledge of Norwegian goat milk. But we could still not be sure if there were not additional features to be discovered. The time we could spend on further investigation would be limited, since we had other tasks to do. If a friend of ours asked if we could make a creamy cheese for him from the goat milk, we probably would realize that we lacked some ingredients and equipment, in addition to some basic knowledge. And if we managed to make such a cheese, what should we answer if our friend asked about the health effects of eating the cheese, or in which types of food this cheese could fit as an ingredient? And did it matter for making the cheese whether we used milk bought in the retail store, purchased from the farm, obtained in the dairy or stolen from the tank lorry? It is clear that what initially seemed to be a relatively easy task, had gradually grown above our heads.

Fortunately there exist scientists and science about goat milk. Thus we have approached the Department of Food Science at the Norwegian Agricultural University. Here we found two scientists whom we interviewed. Moreover, we read two articles, one written by one of these scientists (Skeie, 1998) dealing with goat milk as raw material and another written by the other scientist together with some colleagues at the Department (Vegarud et al., 1999) about the relation between genetics and features of goat milk. In addition we studied abstracts of two other publications from the Department; two postgraduate theses, one on "Laktoferrin in Norwegian goat milk" (Grøtte, 2001) and one on "Goat milk – genetic variants of $\alpha s1$-casein and effects on milk properties" (Nordbø, 2001). We also interviewed a scientist at the Department of Animal Science at the same university and examined some publications from this department (Eknæs et al., 1998; Eknæs & Hove, 2002). In addition we have interviewed two consultants in Tine, one working with processes related to goat milk, the other with product development. We have also used a foreign article (Haenlein

& Caccese, 1984). This article is part of a larger work – Extension Goat Handbook – published by the Extension Service, United States Department of Agriculture.

Defined chemically milk is a mixture (emulsion) of fat in water, where sugar and salts are dissolved, and where the proteins exist in colloidal solution (Aschehoug & Gyldendal, 1995–1998).

(1) Milk in general is the food article that has the most versatile composition of all food articles (Eeg-Larsen, 1976, p. 148). All nutrients in milk can be easily digested and absorbed. The nutrients are resolved in water in a special proportion, ca. 90% water and 10% nutrients. Like any milk, then, goat milk is *nutritious*. It contains proteins, carbohydrates, fat, minerals, trace elements and vitamins in proportions and amounts well suited for the new-born kid to develop and move during the first period of its life. The protein fraction (casein, albumin and globulin) contains most of the vital amino acids and has thus a very high biological value (Eeg-Larsen, 1976, p. 148). Protein in goat milk consists of more whey proteins (albumin and globulin) and less casein than the protein of cow milk (Skeie, 1998). There are also relatively more short and medium sized saturated fatty acids in goat milk, fewer carbohydrates and more potassium.

(2) Thus goat milk has a certain consistency; it is *liquid* and consequently "pourable," "pumpable," "suckable" and drinkable.

(3) In addition it is *tasty*. Human taste referees can tell that goat milk has a distinct taste different from cow milk (Skeie, 1998).

(4) Goat milk appears in a certain *colour*: white. But it is whiter than cow milk (Skeie, 1998, p. 308). This is because the fat in goat milk contains much smaller amounts of red β-carotene, since it already is converted to colourless vitamin A. The white colour in general is due to the amount of calcium in the casein-micells particles.

(5) Because they are smaller and lack a fat globule clustering agent (Agglutinin) *fat globules are more evenly dispersed* in goat milk than in cow milk (Maree, 1978). Thus goat milk creams much more slowly and less completely than cow milk. It is hypothesized that the *membrane* around the fat globules is more fragile in goat milk than in cow milk. All this makes goat milk fat easier to digest than cow milk fat, but also more susceptible for developing off-flavours (Haenlein & Caccese, 1984).

(6) When it is exposed to a certain digestive enzyme – rennet – one fraction of the protein in milk – casein – *coagulates* to solid matter as a gel. The gel of goat milk casein is softer and more brittle because milk from most goats

lacks the Alfa S-1 type of casein (Skeie, 1998; Vegarud et al., 1999). This gives a lower curd tension. It is argued that goat milk protein is easier to digest than cow milk protein (Haenlein & Caccese, 1984).

(7) As in all milk the whey proteins (albumin and globulin) coagulate when goat milk is warmed above their denaturation temperature.

(8) In certain states dried goat milk casein, like any casein, has the ability to bind water.

(9) A certain component in goat milk – *lactose* (the type of carbohydrate that one finds in milk in general) – can be isolated, for example by membrane filtering or by heating whey left over from the making of white cheese.

These are features that both our scientific informants and the scientific literature that we have studied regard as scientifically proven at the time being. Regarding:

(10) If goat milk has specific *health features* (in addition to its nutritious qualities).

Our two scientists have different opinions. One of them regards the health issue in relation to goat milk as highly controversial and argues that specific health effects of goat milk is a claim put forward by "fanatics." The other scientist disagrees and points to a recent study at the department (Grøtte, 2001) which shows that the content of lactoferrin (a glycoprotein) is higher in goat milk than in cow milk. Since lactoferrin has antibacterial properties and increases the body's absorption of iron, the study concludes that goat milk has specific health benefits (at least compared to cow milk).

Moreover, on the Internet, one producer of goat milk soap claim that:

(11) Soap made of goat milk is closer to the pH of the human skin and thus has better *softening, moisturizing and cleansing properties* than conventional soap because goat milk contains alpha-hydroxy acids and has a low pH (Home Soap Works, Millington, New Jersey. [http://www.cidigital.net/homesoapworks]).

One of "our" scientists strongly rejects this claim. And we have found no verification of this claim in the scientific literature that we have read.

Finally, we have ourselves found that:

(12) When putting cubes of (white) cheese made of goat milk into hot water the cubes remained cohesive and relatively solid, while cubes of (white) cheese made of cow milk put into equally as hot water melted and dissolved.

This is an observation that our scientific informants have no opinion about.

3.3. Case 1: Producer Becoming User — Skånaliseter Farm Dairy

3.3.1. Negotiations About Joint Production of "Niche Cheese"

Ola and Kari had ever since they discovered that the goat milk they produced was unpopular in Tine, speculated about doing the processing themselves on the farm. The reason for this was threefold: (1) They regarded their goat milk as an excellent raw material; (2) they were convinced that there were customers "out there" who wanted special goat cheese; and (3) they were convinced that they themselves could serve these customers better than Tine could. Their view gained support when, on a study trip to Jämtland in Sweden in 1985, they talked to goat farmers that had successfully started farm dairies. They had done this because the co-operative dairy company in the region (NNP) by 1980 had found using the small amount of goat milk produced in Jämtland in a meaningful way impossible. Ola says that:

> After this trip I saw somehow 'the Writing on the Wall' and how things would turn out. So therefore we started a process to take responsibility for the goat milk ourselves. But it has taken time, because it is not that easy. Those within the dairy co-operative system 'sat down on their hind legs' and did not find it quite acceptable that I steered the process.

When the outbuilding on Skånaliseter burned down in 1985 and a new building had to be set up, Ola and Kari secured sufficient space for a possible cheese factory in the future.

The couple had to solve some problems before they could realize their dairy. Most of the problems were related to public regulations regarding production and processing of milk and Tine Norske Meierier' own rules. In 1983 the agricultural authorities introduced *quotas* on all milk production in Norway including goat milk production. Skånaliseter got their quota. Similarly all milk producers had, according to national regulation, not only right to, but also the duty to deliver to the co-operative Tine dairy in their region. Also significant state subsidies were given to dairy farmers only if they delivered milk to Tine. Consequently the rules had to be adjusted on these points if farm processing should be legally allowed and economically possible. Skånaliseter was the first farm in Norway to confront the prevailing rules at this point and met resistance. But the problems were solved, although it took more years. In 1988 all goat farmers in Indre Namdal assembled for a meeting to discuss what to do with the goat milk. A working group was established and was assisted by consultants from the agricultural authorities and politicians in the county of Nord-Trøndelag. A new trip was arranged to study goat milk processing in Jämtland and Undredal in the county of Sogn & Fjordane. Undredal is a small, hilly community that was not connected to the public road system until 1987 (Gardsosten nr. 1 1998, p. 12). The goat farmers there had for long been doing craft-based processing of their goat milk. Their products were cheese and brown cheese. The group wrote a report that concluded positively about farm processing of goat milk in Indre Namdal. The group also sent an inquiry to the Ministry of Agriculture in 1988. This lead to certain regulations being changed so that processing their own milk without losing subsidies became possible for farmers under specific conditions.

A project was then (1992–1994) carried out in co-operation between Namdalsmeieriet and the goat farmers in Indre Namdal and agricultural consultants in the county of North-Trøndelag. The objective was to establish a new Tine cheese factory aimed at producing "niche" cheese in Namdal. Ola was the person among the goat farmers who most clearly engaged in this effort to obtain a more satisfactory use of the goat milk from *all* goat farms in Indre Namdal and not only Skånaliseter. One element in the plan was to locate the factory next to the newly established Namsskogan Familiepark, a Deer Park in the region, near the highway E6 and Nordlandsbanen railway. The park had around 50,000 visitors per year. Ola knew of such "symbiotic" solutions in Finland and Ireland, where the businesses involved experienced more sales through such a co-localization. Another detail in the plan was to design the factory such that customers could observe the cheese making process. A consulting firm was hired and carried out a study among the goat farmers and a market study. Landteknikk – a company that supplies Tine with dairy equipment [http://www.landteknikk.no] – analysed the technical aspects of such a "niche dairy." The group also urged changes in certain regulations in "Jordbruksavtalen" – an agreement between the Ministry of Agriculture and the two Farmers Unions in Norway that among other things set the terms of prices and subsidies in Norwegian agriculture. The request resulted in local, small-scale processing of goat milk being allowed in 1993.

The plan regarding a "niche dairy" became stranded. Even though the idea at the outset seemed to be to produce special cheese, the representatives of Tine could not imagine other products than:

standard white and brown cheese. Period (Ola).

And the price for these was, according to Tine's calculations, 60 Norwegian kroner per kg. Given such assumptions the prospect of the planned dairy would never become profitable, and Tine stopped their involvement in the project. This was in 1994. With Tine out of the plan, the goat farmers also withdrew. Moreover, the study showed that Ola and Kari were the only ones among the goat farmers that wanted to process milk on the farm.

For Ola and Kari this represented a clarification. For eight years they had worked to find a solution so that cheese could again be made out of the goat milk from Indre

Namdal. Now, when it was clear that a joint solution could not be reached, they returned to their original plan: farm-based processing. Another "breakthrough" was that Tine now stated that they would not hinder Ola and Kari in establishing a farm-based dairy provided that their products did not collide with Tine's products. Earlier Tine did not allow members to process milk themselves. Now Tine, firstly, admitted that there existed a "niche market" for dairy products, and secondly, that serving such a market was not Tine's responsibility. Moreover, Tine declared that they wanted to facilitate conditions for members who wanted to serve such markets.

As mentioned, the other goat farmers did not want to process milk themselves. But since many of them had invested relatively recently, around 1980, in plants for goat milk production, and these plants had very limited alternative uses, continuing goat milk production was clearly most economical for them. And the only buyer of this goat milk was Namdalsmeieriet that, as already mentioned, sold it to other animal farmers as feed. But the certainty that the goat milk that they produced ended up unprocessed as feed made the production less meaningful to the goat farmers. In addition they felt a bit insecure, being uncertain how long Tine and the dairy regulation system would continue to support this use of goat milk.

3.3.2. Ola and Kari Establish a Farm Dairy

Ola and Kari realized their plan regarding a farm dairy and started to produce cheese in 1995. The same year Kari ended her work as a nursery nurse at the local day-care centre, because she felt that work in the farm dairy would be more appealing. She could then escape early morning travelling to work with small children, often in snowy and windy weather. In the beginning Tine allowed Ola and Kari to use 15% of their total goat milk quota for farm processing. The rest had to be delivered to Tine. In the shed they had around 100 goats producing 40,000 litres of milk annually. This meant that they could dispose of 6,000 litres for cheese production. Normally this gives 600 kg cheese. There were some advantages from starting with this quite small volume when learning to master a new business. If something went wrong with the cheese making equipment for example they could deliver the goat milk to Tine and get paid for it. And bad batches of cheese production did not represent large losses, and experimenting with different products and processes in the dairy was less risky. In 1997 Tine increased Skånaliseter's processing quota to 50%, and in 1999 Tine allowed them to use the whole quota for cheese making. Skånaliseter has remained a member of Tine all the time, and Ola and Kari want to continue the membership:

> We have nothing against the established co-operatives within agriculture like Tine, and would gladly go along with these organizations if they could take activities like the cheese-making we are doing here on the farm under their umbrella. We have not given up the idea that creative

people can establish subsidiaries under co-operative organizations. To the extent that one can open up new markets and establish niche products in existing markets by this means, this will be a more efficient way of organizing than the way it can be organized within a large enterprise that 'thinks' bulk and big production.

Ola and Kari's basic idea behind farm-based processing was to supply a niche market that they were convinced existed. They also argued that goat milk was an excellent raw material that deserved a better fate than being used as feed. This fitted well in with Tines condition for letting Ola and Kari take care of the goat milk themselves: that their products should differ from Tine's products.

3.3.3. Developing Goat Milk Cheeses in Skånaliseter

In earlier times coffee cheese was an obvious part of the food supply when people in Indre Namdal and northward – both on the Norwegian and Swedish side of the border – made trips in the mountains. Not least Lapps frequently used this special dairy product. Putting cubes of unsalted and dried white goat cheese into hot coffee was customary. The special taste of the cheese appears more distinctive then (Bondebladet Julenummer, 1999, p. 18). Unlike cheese made of cow milk, goat milk cheese does not melt when it is heated, it only softens a little. The coffee cheese was easy to carry and provided a versatile meal with much energy. The tradition of making and using coffee cheese was about to disappear. Recognizing this made Ola and Kari start to think of a farm dairy at Skånaliseter; the couple wanted to "rescue" the coffee cheese. In an interview given to Landbrukstidende (nr. 4, 2001, p. 8) Ola tells that:

> The idea to start our own dairy on the farm started with the coffee cheese. The old tradition was about to vanish.

Ola's mother, who lived on the farm, had made coffee cheese and provided the couple with the first information regarding the making of it. Ola and Kari also learned to produce brown goat cheese from Ola's mother. They later developed a decoratively formed version of this cheese and "baptized" it Heidrun.

The couple found that they relatively soon mastered making brown cheese. The reason was that this "craft" primarily depends on technical competence; for example avoiding material burning on the boiler walls and controlling the consecutive cooling so that the lactose crystallizes is critical. Making cheese, however, involves living organisms "from start to finish," and Ola and Kari had more trouble with this part of the production. In 1997 they therefore decided that Kari should attend a course in cheese making at Åsbygdens Naturbruksgymnasium outside Östersund. This is a Folk High School that in the 1980s and 1990s developed a centre that offers courses in craft-like cheese making. They both knew the centre from earlier study trips. At the course Kari learned basic cheese making processes like adding of acid, control of pH and temperature, cutting and packing. She also got to know recipes of some "basic" cheeses. All in all, the course led to more stable production and product quality and a broader range of products at Skånaliseter. In 2000 Skånaliseter made the following cheeses:

- Coffee cheese (solid, without salt)
- Balder (solid and ripened, with or without caraway)
- Snøkvit (semi-solid, ripened with white mould on the surface)
- Blåmann (ripened, white, with blue mould on the surface)
- Real Feta (pickled or oil marinated on jar)
- Gomme (gum – made of goat milk, rennet, cinnamon, egg and wheat flour)
- Soft cheeses (to order)

The brown cheeses are:

- Brown goat cheese (solid)
- Heidrun (formed solid brown cheese)
- Prim (soft brown cheese)

They have written down the recipes for all of these cheeses.

The couple also tried to make a Camembert, but have found that goat milk based Camembert easily becomes too soft and thus too perishable. Moreover, Ola and Kari are considering producing a special cheese – ricotta – from albumin and globulin that precipitates as a by-product when whey is heated. Ricotta is Italian for "re-cooked" (Webster's, 1989), denoting re-cooked whey. Ricotta is a soft and sometimes smoked cheese. In its "homeland" Italy it is often used in salads and in pasta dishes like lasagne and ravioli ([http://countrylife.net/yoghurt/postings/2383.html]; Aschehoug & Gyldendal, 1995–1998). So far Ola and Kari use this by-product as feed for their goats.

In the beginning the couple felt that developing a quite broad range of products relatively quickly was important in order to "test the market." After five years – in 2000 – they feel that the range of products is satisfactory. Quality is doubtless the most important sales promoting factor. In the couple's opinion lack of quality due to inferior goat milk may have given goat cheese a bad reputation among many people. The couple thus put much effort into persuading potential customers to try tasting their products. This they do in the farm shop they have established next-door to the dairy and at exhibitions. Ola says:

> Some people are very sceptical, but we 'fool' them to try [tasting], and then they become customers at once.

Ola and Kari have frequent contact with a food consultant in Namsos in order to learn new "secrets" of goat milk and how their goat milk products can be used together with other products in new ways and new settings.

3.3.4. Finding and Getting a Price

Ola and Kari looked askance at the price that their colleagues in Jämtland received for their products when they decided the price of their own products. It meant about double of the price of an "average" Tine cheese, which was about 60 Norwegian kroner per kg. Ola and Kari soon found that their customers willingly accepted a price of 120 kroner per kg for their standard cheese. With more treatment – for example special packaging and extra long ripening – they get up to double the price. For example Feta on jar or in special packaging "makes good money." Ola puts it this way:

> We are gaining experience now . . . what pays best. The more you process the cheese; the better
> is the pay. Either in particular packaging or on jar like Feta. It gives a completely different price.

They sell Feta cheese pickled in jars for up to 170 kroner per kg. This is quite a high price, but Kari says that this is a very popular cheese, and they could have sold much more of it.

3.3.5. Developing Production Facilities

Ola and Kari needed various facilities to be able to transform their goat milk into special cheeses for sale. Barn, milk tank, dairy, cheese store and farm shop exist in separate rooms in the same outbuilding. The dairy lies next to the room where the milk tank is, and goat milk can be pumped automatically from the milk tank into the cheese-making tank.

Finding an appropriate cheese-making tank was one of the first tasks. The couple first inquired of Landteknikk A/L, a firm owned jointly by all the farmers' co-operatives in Norway. Among other things Landteknikk plans and delivers installations in food processing plants, has made and delivered milk cooling tanks to most dairy farms in Norway and tanks for transportation of milk. They also sell various special products like detergents, packing and packing equipment. Landteknikk has been involved in planning and delivering equipment to most dairies within Tine over the years. But Skånaliseter needed equipment that was quite different from the equipment in Tine dairies. The equipment in a cheese dairy in Tine is developed for handling up to about hundred times the volume of milk to be processed in Skånaliseter's farm dairy. And the equipment in Tine was designed for a continuous process, while in Skånaliseter they had to make cheese in a batch-wise process and with much cheaper equipment. A vat of around 500 litres would suit. Landteknikk could make such a vat, but had to calculate some special development costs, which would make the vat quite expensive. The couple then chose a very simple solution; they bought a much cheaper 400 litres milk cooling tank and made cheese in this. This tank had double walls and could be warmed and cooled by pumping warm and cold water in between the walls. However, obtaining a temperature sufficient for pasteurizing in this tank proved difficult. Another solution had to be found.

During a visit to Åsbygdens Naturbruksgymnasium in 1995 they discovered that the training centre there used a tank made by a Dutch firm – Rademaker – that supplied food processors and large-scale households [http://www.exportant.nl/gmv/expcat98/rademakers.html]. They were told that many farm dairies in Jämtland also used this kind of tank and experienced very few problems with it. Rademaker could deliver a tank specially made for small-scale batch-wise cheese making at a price far below that of Landteknikk. The couple decided to buy such a tank after Kari attended the course in Åsbygden in 1997. The boiler for making brown cheese however Ola and Kari bought from Landteknikk.

Precipitated curd in the vat must be transformed into cheeses of appropriate shape, size and hardness. Kari uses special cheese moulds for this. None of the Tine dairies form cheese manually, and there is no Norwegian producer of manual moulds. The couple found that Rademaker could also deliver cheese moulds, and they bought moulds of 0.5 kg, 1 kg, 2.5 kg and 5 kg. Moreover the cheese in the moulds has to be pressed in order to get the right compactness. Ola and Kari ordered a special cheese press from Tine, but nothing happened. The couple then approached the Department of Food Science at the Norwegian University of Agriculture. The workshop at this department then made a simple cheese press for them.

Most of the cheese in Skånaliseter is packed in plastic film. This film has to be of a certain kind because the cheese must be able to "breathe" during the whole ripening period. Again Kari and Ola approached Landteknikk, which supplies Tine with this special plastic film. Landteknikk could also supply Skånaliseter with the same film. A German firm, Süd Pack, produces the film. From a supplier of equipment to large-scale households in Trondheim they bought a vacuum packing machine.

However, Kari came to that packing the cheese in a stiffer paper would be better. She asked again Landteknikk, who informed her about a French firm who produced such a paper. On behalf of Kari Landteknikk ordered a sample of the paper. Kari received the sample after five months. She then asked Landteknikk about the price, but never got any answer. She still packs cheese in plastic film, but has in later years progressively started to use coating, that is, putting wax around the cheese. She learned this method when she attended the course in Åsbygden in 1997.

Coating makes the cheese special and suits the basic philosophy of Skånaliseter farm dairy, which is to produce cheese products that "stand out from the multitude." The couple has realized that all types of packaging and design can make a cheese product special. Hence they have developed gift versions of certain cheeses. One version is cheese in chip boxes. They searched in Norway for a supplier of appropriate chip boxes, but found none, where upon they approached Tine. Tine referred them to a French supplier. This supplier did not normally take orders less than 10,000 boxes, but could this first time accept an order of 6,000 boxes. This was far too much for Skånaliseter, but they knew of other firms that also had expressed interest in chip boxes as packaging. Together with these firms they managed to make an order of 6,000 chip boxes.

To be able to make Heidrun the couple came to an agreement with a mechanical firm, which made a specially designed, manual mould press for them.

3.3.6. Developing Distribution and Sales

Ola and Kari had to find and reach customers for Balder, Gjeta, Heidrun and the other cheese products that they made. As members of Tine they could have aimed at Tine's customers and used Tine's resources for distribution, including the resources of retailers that sell Tine's products. But Ola thought that Tine's delivery times were too long and made customers dissatisfied:

> Some have found that the Tine system has worked somewhat poorly and that deliveries have taken a long time. I know somebody in the restaurant branch, . . . among other things foreign cheeses going through that system took a very long time. This is not acceptable.

Thus Ola and Kari sought other ways to reach customers. Hard cheese can stand two days of travel at room temperature. If packed in expanded polyester and supplied with cooler bricks soft cheese and brown cheese can also endure two days of travel. Hence distribution with refrigeration would not be necessary if the cheese could reach the customer within two days. And there turned out to be more possibilities of reaching customers within two days.

Making the delivery time to each of its customers as short as possible is important, thinks the couple. Kari says:

> It is so that people have wishes about when . . . In one case a private customer planned a special event, and had to have the cheese the same day. And then, one has to do it. The same with those that run shops and say: Now it's empty, now we must have cheese . . . Of course you execute that order as fast as possible. Because . . . then the shop also sells more . . . because then they avoid being out of stock for a week or two.

The couple therefore handles each order individually, unless more orders that can use the same means of transportation have arrived in the meantime. Normally Ola and Kari get along with post, train or bus. However, customers are not always in a big hurry. In such cases Ola and Kari wait until they have to do another errand by car in the same direction. Then co-handling orders from several customers along the same route is possible also.

3.3.6.1. Mail service. Ola and Kari found that individual, private customers that ordered directly could get their cheese via mail. An order is then packed as parcel post and the postal services take it to the customer. In the beginning Ola or Kari had to take the parcel to the post office in the nearest small town, Røyrvik, 10 km away. When their sales grew bigger, Skånaliseter was able to become a business customer of the postal services. A parcel sent by a business customer has first priority and the invoicing is easier. A rural postman collects parcels from the farm. In recent years in certain localities postal services have been out-sourced. This is the case in Røyrvik, and the firm that handles the postal services is happy the more parcels that are sent, because this contributes to the persistence of postal services in the area. Skånaliseter has very good experience with sending parcels by mail. The list of customers has gradually increased and consists late in 2000 of 175 names. About half of them order quite regularly, the rest more occasionally. They order either by telephone or via e-mail.

3.3.6.2. Railway. For their part Ola and Kari preferred to ship orders by post, because this meant least work for them. But postal shipment did not suit most of the customers who were not private individuals. On the other hand these also made larger orders. Two types of collective transportation existed in the area. The railway from Trondheim to Bodø has a station in Namsskogan about 40 km west of Skånaliseter along the road. From Trondheim there are two railway lines to Oslo, one through the valley of Østerdalen and one through the valley of Gudbrandsdalen. From Oslo there are several railway lines to the east, south and west. Hence Ola and Kari could reach customers in Trondheim and the region of Østlandet by transporting orders first by their own car to Namsskogan and then by train. They reached agreements with the three specialized food shops Fenaknoken in Oslo, Byhaven Delikatesse in Trondheim and Ost & Bakst in Stjørdal. They send orders to all these customers by train. Later Byhaven Delikatesse went bankrupt, but was soon succeeded by another specialized food shop in Trondheim, Torvdelikatessen. Skånaliseter became a supplier of Torvdelikatessen. Later Skånaliseter got two more customers "along the railway," a farm shop in Siljan in Telemark and a farm shop in Verdal in Nord-Trøndelag.

3.3.6.3. Bus. But not all customers were located near railway. Hence Ola and Kari had to consider other means of transportation for these. There was a bus route from

Røyrvik to Grong and from there to Overhalla and Namsos and other localities in western Namdal. Skånaliseter could send orders by bus to their customers Grong Vertshus (an inn in Grong), Overhalla Hotell, Røthe (a specialized food shop) in Namsos, and Mo Gård in Salsnes. Packages by post, train or bus are not dispatched on Thursdays and Fridays in order to avoid them lying unattended over the weekend.

3.3.6.4. Farm shop. Ola and Kari have also established their own farm shop. In this shop they sell cheeses produced in the farm dairy. Skånaliseter is located 50 meters from the road that leads to Store Namsvatn ("Great Nams Lake"). In the summer season many tourists use this road in order to visit their private cottages, fish for trout in the lake or make excursions to Børgefjell National Park near by. Skånaliseter is an approved member of Norsk Gardsmat, an organization of nearly 200 farm-based specialized food producers in Norway [http://www.norskgardsmat.org]. Thus Skånaliseter can use Norsk Gardsmat's name and logo – a weathercock – on its signboards, leaflets and packaging. Near the "gateway" to the farm Ola and Kari have put up the weathercock with the name Norsk Gardsmat. Both people travelling by car and bus tourists make a stop at Skånaliseter, some on their way to or from Store Namsvatn, others having Skånaliseter as their only destination in the area.

In some cases people have driven 300 km in order to visit Skånaliseter and buy cheese "on the spot." These customers want to see the farm, the cheese making and the surroundings of the farm. Many of them and other private customers that order directly have come to know the farm dairy via coverage in newspapers and weekly papers or Skånaliseter's home page on the web. These customers are searching for food that is new and exciting. Skånaliseter has been featured many times in Hjemmet, and also in Dagbladet, Universitetsavisa in Trondheim, Adresseavisen and SAS Magasinet nr. 7/8, 2001. Out of curiosity Tine Midt-Norge visited Skånaliseter farm dairy as part of a course for employees. In order to accommodate visitors better, Ola and Kari want to build a separate reception and serving room next to the dairy and the shop.

Ola and Kari also take part in exhibitions. They do this primarily to promote their cheeses. They do not regard it as an important way of distributing the cheeses. At an exhibition they can inform the general public that Skånaliseter farm dairy exists. Furthermore visitors that stop at their stand can have a look at the cheeses and obtain information about them, where and how to buy them and how to use them. Visitors also have a chance to try a sample of the cheeses and eventually buy some of them "on the spot." And lastly visitors get to know the people in Skånaliseter farm dairy. However, a stand at an exhibition demands resources, and since Ola and Kari are a bit unsure about how much it generates beyond the immediate sales, they only take part in a few exhibitions.

Ola and Kari wanted to sell their cheese products together with rich information about them. They put information about the content of the product and advice regarding handling and what food to use with the product, on the label. The same information is given on the product list. The product list is part of the web page Ola and Kari have made about Skånaliseter and its farm dairy. There is of course not room to put all the information on a label or a web page, hence much information must be disseminated and much promotion done using other means, for example by word of mouth. This is the reason why Skånaliseter up to now has chosen not to let some of the four large retail chains in Norway sell its products. To be sure the chains have cheese counters in the shops that they run, but most of them are not staffed and thus cannot give oral information. Thus information on the package is the only information a customer can obtain. Both in their own farm shop, the other farm shops where their products are sold and in the specialized food shops there are assistants who can inform customers about each different cheese from Skånaliseter and cut it individually. Moreover the whole range of products that these shops have fits in well with the products of Skånaliseter farm dairy. Also if customers order directly by telephone Kari or Ola can provide specific information about the actual cheeses.

3.3.6.5. Co-operation between Skånaliseter and other farm shops. About 20% of the cheese is sold in Skånaliseter's own Farm Shop, for the most part in the period July to October. Skånaliseter has also developed co-operation with four other farm shops, all located in Norway; Gangstad Farm Dairy in Inderøy, Mikvold Farm in Verdal, Løpstikka in Brønnøysund and Auen Herb Farm in Siljan (Telemark). None of the five farms produces exactly the same products. By operating together each farm shop is able to offer a broader assortment, at the same time as none of the shops has a totally identical range of products.

Gangstad farm dairy was established in 1998. As in Skånaliseter a farm shop is located next-door to the farm's dairy, which again uses fresh cow milk produced in the barn next-door to produce, as it is put on their home page on the Internet, "*delicacy cheeses.*" (Information about Gangstad, Løpstikka and Auen farm shops is taken from the web page of Norsk Gardsmat [http://www.norskgardsmat.org]). For example, Ost & Bakst in Stjørdal and Fenaknoken in Oslo sell the products. These shops also sell cheeses from Skånaliseter. Thus Gangstad has resources in common with Skånaliseter. But there are differences too. Gangstad also sells cheeses via a retail chain – Coop's Mega's shops in Namsos, Steinkjer, Verdal and Levanger. Furthermore cows, and not goats, produce the milk from which the various cheeses are made. The cheeses are: Feta pickled in rape oil with herbs and garlic or leek and paprika, two types of white mould cheeses and a soft, spreadable cheese with garlic and herbs, and a special confectionary brown cheese where coffee, sugar and dog rose vinegar are added. Nannas Kjøkken ("Nannas Kitchen") has developed the recipe of this brown cheese and also sells cheeses made in Gangstad Farm Dairy. Nannas Kjøkken is a small firm, located on a farm in Hønefoss and develops new dishes from traditional recipes and local raw material (Landbruksdepartementet, 1996).

The married couple Hans and Grete established a farm shop on their farm Mikvold Gård in 1994. In the shop they sell *cured ham* produced from pigs that they breed themselves, five kinds of potatoes grown on the farm and products from other farm food producers. They run the farm shop on a round-the-year basis. In 1997 and 1998 Grete attended meetings arranged by the agricultural authorities in the county of Nord-Trøndelag. The meetings were part of a nation-wide project, initiated by the Ministry of Agriculture, where the purpose was to recruit producers of "farm food." At one meeting, in 1997, Grete became acquainted with Ola who told her about Skånaliseter farm dairy. This led them to start co-operating and to sell and promote each other's products. Mikvold offers all the cheeses that Ola and Kari produce. When Mikvold established the farm food production and the farm shop they made a special agreement with the butchery to which they had delivered animals for many years. The butchery slaughters Mikvold's pigs and cut up the meat. Mikvold, then, "buys back" some of the hams and makes cured ham of it. If the product is to be allowed to bear the name "farm food" the raw material has to be produced on the farm. The pigs at Mikvold are fed with remnants from potato production, which results in a special quality of the fat. Cured meat from Mikvold is then sold in Mikvold's own farm shop and in Skånaliseter, among other farm shops. Most customers of Mikvold live in Verdal, but some also come all the way from Trondheim to buy products. Many of them come because they want to buy white goat cheese. Most of the customers are "returners."

Løpstikka farm shop on the Tilrem farm was established in 1997 and has specialized in *herbs*. In the garden are grown culinary and medical herbs. From the herbs are produced four different blends of tea and seven different blends of spice. Herbs from the garden are also used in the manufacture of three types of red wine that the farm couple has developed. Vinmonopolet also sells these three wines. In addition the couple have developed raw syrup from crowberries, which they make and sell. They have also invested in a small restaurant on the farm where visitors can have among other things herb soup, herb bread, herb tea, wine and coffee. In addition they have established a picture-gallery where visitors can see and buy original paintings. Visitors can also have a guided tour of the herb garden.

Also in Auen farm shop near the river Siljan in Telemark, *herb* is the main product. The couple running the shop sells different products made on the farm from raw material produced on the farm. All products are organically grown and approved by Debio, the institution in Norway that approves organic farms and organic food products. Herb products are fresh herbs, blends of herb (specially made for among other things fish, game, pizza, lamb, potatoes, casseroles, marination of meat and meddling in brandy — "snaps") and different blends of tea. The couple also sells strawberries produced on the farm and meat cut according to the customer's wish, from lambs bred on the farm. Some products are also sold via mail order. From other producers Auen herb farm sells Debio approved vegetables like tomato, cucumber, salad, cabbage, onion and potato, and – as we have seen – goat cheese from Skånaliseter. A small restaurant is built on the farm, and the couple runs herb courses.

3.3.6.6. Co-operation between Skånaliseter and specialized food shops. Ost & Bakst ("Cheese & Baking") in Stjørdal is one of the four specialized food shops that sell cheeses made in Skånaliseter. Gitte ran Ost & Bakst until 2001. The contact between the shop and Skånaliseter came about because Gitte's husband as co-worker in Landteknikk several times helped Skånaliseter with solving technical problems. In August 1998 the couple made a trip to Northern Norway. They then made a little detour via Røyrvik to visit Skånaliseter and have a look at the farm dairy. During the visit Kari asked Gitte if she could imagine selling cheese made in Skånaliseter. Gitte found the production and the products exciting and accepted the inquiry. Since then, and also after Gitte left the shop, Ost & Bakst has sold cheeses from Skånaliseter.

Gitte thinks the cheeses from Skånaliseter fit in well with the rest of the products that the shop sells. These consist of various dairy products, bakery products and fruit wine. Most of the cheese that Ost & Bakst sells comes from Tine. This is because Tine produces standard cheeses that are relatively cheap. But Gitte found that Tine did not produce special cheeses. And they had problems with white goat cheese. For a while she purchased a white goat cheese that Tine made. But she never felt comfortable with it; it was too unripe and thus too soft and hence difficult to cut with a cheese slicer. The white, hard goat cheese from Skånaliseter does not have these problems, she says:

> There is a huge difference between the goat cheese that I got from Tine and the goat cheese that I get now from Skånaliseter. I think this has something to do with 'body' and ripening. Tine never managed to ripen the cheese completely. The cheese from Skånaliseter has a rich taste – it is not insipid, it is sufficiently firm so that the cheese slicer can cut all the way through, and it has taste.

And she also put forward other reasons:

> [The cheese from Skånaliseter] is not mixed with something, and you do not find E-substances in it. I have one example of an elderly customer who came in and bought goat cheese for several hundred kroner. I asked if he did not think this was expensive. He answered: 'I consider this as a health food, you see. I have arthritis'. To be sure, I know that goat milk can be used in connection with health. Earlier Ost & Bakst in many cases sold small cartons of goat milk to people who needed it for health reasons. And I also know that the goats [in Skånaliseter] are not fed with silage, but hay. They get better digestion then. I have seen cows myself that have been fed with silage and how lax dropping they have.

Ost & Bakst purchase special cheese from three firms. Oluf Lorentzen, a specialized food retailer located in Oslo, supplies French and some German cheeses. From Gangstad farm dairy in Inderøy Ost & Bakst purchases different craft-made cheeses made of cow milk. These then differ from the cheeses the shop buys from Skånaliseter. Gitte says that:

> it is funny to have two so different farm dairies as suppliers.

Gitte takes care that the customers who buy cheese from Skånaliseter and Gangstad are informed that the cheeses are made in the region on specific locations. She also emphasizes that the cheeses therefore differ from Tine's cheeses and thus must be more expensive. She has found that Ost & Bakst has sold more of a certain Tine cheese after she has begun to tell customers that the cheese is made in Tine's dairy in the neighbouring municipality.

From Skånaliseter Ost & Bakst deal in Balder, Blåmann and Snøkvit plus brown cheese and Heidrun, totalling 200–300 kg altogether. So far they are not selling the coffee cheese and the Feta cheese Gjeta. Gitte thinks Gjeta could fit in salads, but fears that it is too strong and prefers to deal in the cow milk based Feta produced in Gangstad farm dairy instead. This Feta is moreover served as snack in a pub near Ost & Bakst.

Gitte and the other co-worker in Ost & Bakst make a point of talking with the customers about the products. Gitte says that:

> the products do not sell themselves. The most important thing is that after the sale the customer shall have reason to say that: 'here we got help'.

Hence the background of the two co-workers is essential; both have worked within the dairy business for years and know the products and how they are made very well. They serve the customers by answering their questions and tell them things about the products that they have not thought of. In addition they can hand out leaflets and offer samples. Gitte asserts that cutting the cheese "on the spot" is important:

People want cheese that is newly cut. In a nearby shop of one of the retail chains they cut the cheese beforehand. Then the cheese deteriorates.

Regarding goat cheese samples are especially important, thinks Gitte:

Norwegians seem to associate goat cheese with very strong taste. When they taste the Skånaliseter cheese many customers are surprized; it is milder than they had expected. Often elderly customers say that the Skånaliseter cheese reminds them of cheese they ate at the mountain pasture when they were young.

Most of the customers of Ost & Bakst are "regulars;" they have been customers for years and both Gitte and her co-worker know them well. They also make cheese dishes from the cheeses that they deal in. In some cases, then, a friend of the customer enters the shop and asks for a specific cheese that was in the cheese dish. In summer many tourists enter the shop. Many of them did not know of the existence of farm dairies and because of that are curious about the cheeses that Ost & Bakst sells. In some cases Gitte has had to show a picture of Gangstad farm dairy in order to convince customers that it exists. The shop has private customers only and does not have the capacity to serve business customers.

Gitte orders cheese from Skånaliseter about one week before she is out of stock, by fax if it is a "straight" order, by telephone if special explanations are necessary. An order lasts normally 2–3 weeks. Gitte knows that Ola or Kari have a long way to drive, even when they send the order by railway from Namsskogan to Stjørdal, as is normal. Hence Gitte does not want to bother them by ordering more frequently than is strictly necessary.

3.3.6.7. Co-operation between Skånaliseter and tourist firms. Concerning the products of Skånaliseter Ola and Kari have found firms within the tourist industry business in their own region, Namdal, interesting. They sell products to three such businesses, Mo Gård in Salsnes, Grong Vertshus and Overhalla Hotell. One reason that these firms have cheese from Skånaliseter on their menu is that their customers asked for cheese from the region they visited. This was the case for Mo Gård. Mo Gård is part of the company Firma Albert Collett, which operates businesses within power production, agriculture, forestry and tourism in Namdal [http://www.collett.no]. Besides producing cow milk, since 1988 Mo Gård has offered full board and lodging, elk and roe-deer hunting and salmon fishing in the 570 square km of forest and outfield areas that Firma Albert Collett owns. The season lasts from June to October. Most customers are Norwegian, mainly from Oslo. Many of them have been customers of Mo Gård for years.

Frida is a Namsos-based food consultant with training from the Department of Food Science at the Norwegian University of Agriculture. She works partly as an independent consultant and partly as a co-worker in Firma Albert Collett. Frida gives advice regarding food and dishes at Mo Gård. Around 1998 she was responsible in Nord-Trøndelag for a nation-wide project run by MATFORSK, a research foundation doing research and development regarding food. The project aimed at assisting small-scale food-processing firms. Skånaliseter took part in the project and hence got to know Frida. Frida knew that Mo Gård wanted to give their guests varied taste experiences as part of their offering. Regarding cheese they had until then served Norvegia (a gouda cheese) and other traditional cheeses from Tine together with more special cow milk and goat milk based French cheeses supplied by Røthe in Namsos. But many customers had commented that they missed special cheeses from the region, cheeses with a history and origin in Namdal. Thus, when Frida got to know about the cheeses that Skånaliseter made, she realized that these cheeses could satisfy the demand for cheeses with "a regional anchoring" at Mo Gård. Skånaliseter was invited to deliver cheese to Mo Gård in 1998 and has since then been a supplier. However, because the French cheeses are somewhat different from the cheeses from Skånaliseter, the latter have not replaced the French cheeses; they have supplemented them and made Mo Gård's total offering more varied. In addition some of the customers have individual preferences and bring with them their own cheeses, which the personnel at Mo Gård prepare for them.

Cheese is served at all meals – breakfast, lunch and dinner. It is used as cold cuts and as ingredients in different dishes. Regarding cheese Frida thinks the challenge at Mo Gård is to learn to exploit cheese in new ways, for example in grilled dishes and warm dishes. She emphasizes that telling customers about the specific history behind each cheese is important. Hence, she has trained the cooks at Mo Gård in telling the histories. For the same reason she appreciates the fact that Ola and Kari have written information about the origin, contents and making of their cheeses. So far Mo Gård does not buy products from any other farm food producer, because none except Skånaliseter produces food with a sufficiently strong "Namdal anchoring."

3.3.7. New Ways of Standardizing and Customizing Manufacture and Sales of Goat Cheese

The milking season in Skånaliseter starts in the middle of February, when the goats bring forth, and lasts until early November, about 8.5 months altogether. In winter the goats eat dry feed. Earlier, when they delivered goat milk to Namdalsmeieriet, they used silage. But after they started to make cheese on the farm, Ola and Kari found that silage sometimes transferred bad microbes to the goat milk, resulting in wrong fermentation of cheese. From 1999 they have only used hay. In summer the goats graze in the mountain pastureland surrounding the farm.

Until 1999 Skånaliseter used only its own goat milk for cheese making. They make both cheese and brown cheese. Kari is responsible for cheese, while Ola takes care of brown cheese and goat milk production.

The cheese making is done batch-wise. Four batches are done every week: two of white cheese and two of brown cheese. Of white cheese each batch – on average from about 550 litres of goat milk – gives 55 kg of cheese. From whey, the by-product, a batch of brown cheese is done, resulting in about 40 kg of cheese. The process is craft-like and builds on quite simple technology and manual work. No part of the process is automated. Cheese is made on Mondays and Thursdays from goat milk produced the 3–4 previous days. Because the whey must not become sour, the making of brown cheese must follow immediately after the cheese making. Brown cheese is therefore made later every Tuesday and Friday. On the other days there are no cheese making.

Kari starts the manufacturing of white cheese around 8.30 a.m. by letting the goat milk in the cooling tank in the neighbouring room be pumped into a metal vat. The vat – delivered by Rademaker – is specially made for cheese making and can handle up to 700 litres per batch. One batch lasts around eight hours. In the vat the goat milk is pasteurized. Ola and Kari have, like Tine, for health safety considerations, decided to make no unpasteurized cheese. In order to regulate the temperature, the vat has double walls where warm and cold water can flow in and out. Kari uses a method of pasteurizing where milk is held at 63 °C for half an hour. This gives a result equivalent to the much quicker continual pasteurizing process in Tine Verdal where the milk is held at 72 °C for 15 seconds. Kari controls time and temperature manually by using watch and a thermometer standing in the milk. Landteknikk can offer Ola and Kari equipment for automatic pasteurizing, but the couple finds this equipment too expensive in relation to the amount of milk they are processing.

After pasteurizing she lowers the temperature to 28–32 °C, depending on the type of cheese to be made. Kari thinks bactofugation – a centrifugation process where microbes are "thrown out" of the milk at high speed – is not necessary. This is because their milk is produced on dry feed. This gives little risk of heat resistant bacteria, like clostridia, which survive pasteurizing, in the milk. In addition bactofugation also removes bacteria that can have a beneficial effect on the ripening of cheese, she thinks. The fat content in the milk is not standardized because Skånaliseter, unlike Tine, does not have to adjust to public regulations regarding fat content in food. Skånaliseter's goat milk contains around 3.5% fat.

Then Kari puts a blend of bacteria into the milk. All cheese making – in Tine too – is based on the use of blends of bacteria and not pure cultures. Blends are specific compositions of certain pure cultures. Kari prefers to use freeze-dried bacteria, which she buys from the Danish firm Chr. Hansen's retailer in Oslo. Freeze-dried bacteria are less perishable than "natural" bacteria and hence more suitable for sending by post. Tine also buys some of their blends of bacteria from this firm. The blend is an essential determinant for the type of cheese to come out of the cheese making process. Kari sees to it that she always has a minimum of all cheeses in store and chooses what cheese to produce accordingly. Feta, as a typical ingredient in salads, is a popular cheese in summer and consequently she produces more Feta then. "Within" each cheese she can, against a 50–100% increase in price, make variations regarding shape, size, salting, ripening and packaging, all depending on customer orders or what she has noted specific customers want.

For example one customer wanted an especially well ripened cheese, which Kari made against a doubling in price. In another case, late in the season of 2000, she received unexpectedly a big order of 1000 cheeses of the type Blåmann from the shop Fenaknoken, an important customer in Oslo. Skånaliseter could not produce enough goat milk this season to meet the whole order, but Kari immediately made several batches of Blåmann in a row to meet as much of the order as possible. In another case, she got an order for the cheese Balder from the shop Torvdelikatessen. She knew that this shop had a cheese counter with service. Therefore she thought that Balder in 5 kg sizes would be suitable, because then the staff could cut cheese according to individual customers' preferences. But soon Torvdelikatessen made contact and told Kari that the customers rather preferred uncut Balder of the size 0.5 kg. This was a practical size for an average household and the customers did not have to "exert themselves" to give the staff information about the appropriate size and then wait for the cheese to be cut and packed.

However, Kari emphasizes that she has to set limits to customization. For example, she said no to a customer who wanted to by unripe coffee cheese that he wanted to ripen himself. Cheese ripening is not for "amateurs," she believes. If the customer had failed, he could have put the blame on Kari's part of the process, giving Skånaliseter a bad reputation.

When the bacteria have worked in the milk for $\frac{1}{2}$ – 1 hour, Kari puts rennet (an enzyme) into the milk. Each type of cheese requires specific amounts of rennet. Rennet causes the casein in the milk to precipitate as one lump of jelly in the vat. In order to form cheese out of it, the lump has to be cut in small pieces of around 1 cm3. Kari observes how the consistence of the lump changes and assess when cutting it is appropriate. For this, she puts horizontal and vertical harp strings (cutting strings) on the rotator in the vat and the lump gradually converts into grains. There are different sizes of harp strings. Smaller grains give more compact cheese; thus Kari selects strings according to the type of cheese she is going to make. The time needed for conversion varies during the lactation. In each individual batch Kari evaluates the compactness of the mass by squeezing some of it in the hand. She checks acidity in the mass with a pH-meter. Acidity has to be adjusted to each specific type of cheese; if not, the cheese will not ripe in the right way. When Kari finds the mass appropriate, she bails it into cheese forms.

Kari has cheese forms of different form and size. Rademaker also delivers these. Mostly she uses 0.5 kg, 1 kg, 2.5 kg and 5 kg forms. What type of form Kari uses depends on orders received and what sizes of the actual cheese are lacking in store. The whey is tapped into a boiler where Ola makes brown cheese from it. To give the cheeses appropriate compactness Kari puts the moulds into the press. The couple bought the pressing equipment, which is quite simple, from the workshop at the Department of Food Science at the Norwegian University of Agriculture. After about four hours Kari takes the forms out of the press and each cheese out of its form.

She then salts the cheeses, either by putting dry salt on the surface or laying them in a salt bath. One type of cheese is unsalted. The duration of the salting affects the bacteria and with that the speed of ripening. The cheese has no taste and character before it has undergone fermentation in store. The more compact the cheese is, the longer time in store is needed. Each type of cheese requires therefore distinct salting, temperature and storing time. Some customers have their "favourites" regarding salting and ripening. Some types of cheese demand mould on the surface. She then packs each cheese manually in plastic film with special pore size before the cheese is put in store. Kari also experiments with coating, which is melting wax on the surface instead of film. She learned about waxing on a course at Åsbygdens Naturbruksgymnasium. On request Kari puts some types of cheese in special gift packaging. The transportation to store is done manually with a trolley table. There is one store, lying next door in the same building as the vat.

The whey that is poured into the brown cheese boiler is warmed up as fast as possible in order that it shall not become sour, first to 70 °C. At this temperature the heat labile proteins albumin and globulin – which do not react with rennet – precipitate. After albumin and globulin are removed, goat milk is mixed into the whey. In the beginning Ola used 25% goat milk, but changed it later to 50%. Once when they had surplus of goat milk as an emergency solution they mixed goat milk and whey in the proportion 50–50%. The shops that sold the brown cheese, however, reported that their customers found the "new" brown cheese much better. Since then Ola has continued to make brown cheese of 50% goat milk and 50% goat milk whey. In the process this mixture is "steamed in" and cooked under low pressure. This results in a solid mass with a brown colour. The colour is due to caramelized lactose. Depending on how much water that is removed the mass becomes soft brown cheese or hard brown cheese. The latter type Ola and Kari produces in a "plain" and a formed version.

Ola and Kari write a diary during each batch of cheese making.

3.3.8. A Visit to Farmers that Continued Delivering Goat Milk to Tine

Hans and Inge are two of the goat milk producers in Indre Namdal that have not established farm processing of goat milk. They have continued to deliver the goat milk to Namdalsmeieriet and, after 1.1.96, to Tine Verdal. Hans and Inge are neighbouring farmers in Namsskogan around 60 km south-west of Skånaliseter. Both farms have access to huge outfield and mountain pastures.

Originally sheep farming was the basic activity on both farms. Around 1980 the farmers – Hans and Inge's fathers – felt that expanding their farms was necessary. They considered investing in milking cows, but found that milking goats were easier to purchase and relatively cheaper. Goats start to milk when they are one year old, while cows have to be two years. In addition goats normally get two offspring per birth and year, while cows get one. Hence, building up a herd of milking goats would take shorter time than building up a herd of milking cows. Goats were also better suited for outfield pastures than cows. An additional factor was that the outlook for sales and price of goat milk seemed good at the time and one could count on abundant state subsidies. Agricultural consultants at the public county administration encouraged farmers in Indre Namdal to start up goat milk production at the time. Hans and Inge's fathers decided to start up. Around 1980 they invested in female kids and new buildings suited for goat milk production. The herds on both farms reached 100–110 milking goats. Both farmers continued their sheep breeding. Hans in addition had 15 nurse cows.

Like the other goat milk farmers in Indre Namdal both farmers from the start delivered their goat milk to Namdalsmeieriet. They continued goat milk production and delivery of goat milk to Namdalsmeieriet also after the shutting down of the brown cheese production there in 1986. As long as they obtained the same price for their goat milk as other goat farmers in Norway, from an economical standpoint, goat milk production represented the best use of the new buildings that they had built for goat milk production in 1980. Nevertheless, Hans and Inge started to feel somewhat insecure after Namdalsmeieriet shut down the production of brown cheese. They started to wonder if Tine would continue to purchase goat milk from Indre Namdal in the future. And if not, would they get quotas for producing cow milk instead? The certainty that they were producing a product that was good enough for human consumption, but all the same ended up as "pig feed for farmers in Verdal," meant that putting all their heart into goat milk production was hard for them. Hans' wife also had the same feeling about the goat milk production on their farm, although her main income was obtained from work off the farm. The fact that Tine tested the quality of their goat milk at every collection by the tank lorry did not change this feeling of meaninglessness. Hans and Inge (who took over after his father in the late 1990s) asked themselves:

For how long does Tine intend to continue operating like this?

Against this background Hans and Inge thought it was a good thing when Ola and Kari early in 2000 presented plans for expanding Skånaliseter farm dairy and purchasing all goat milk produced in Indre Namdal. All the goat farmers were informed about the plans. For their part Hans and Inge make it a condition that they still can be members of Tine. Hans and Inge look upon Skånaliseter as a small firm and they wonder if Skånaliseter has enough customers for output that will be four times as large. Are their products good enough? Do they have sufficient competence? They want Tine as a guarantor in case Skånaliseter fails with their expanded production.

Both Hans and Inge have sometimes had ideas about starting processing goat milk on the farm combined with some form of tourist business. They have, however, not found it probable that these ideas will be realized. As for the rest there has never been any tradition of goat milk processing on their farms and neither in Namsskogan at large. In addition the production on each farm is so large already that they have no idle labour within the family to handle a new enterprise.

3.3.9. Increased Sales – Need for More Raw Material in Skånaliseter

Ever since they established their farm dairy in 1995 Ola and Kari have received inquiries that exceed their capacity. Inquiries come from existing customers and new customers. For the time being they give priority to their existing customers. Their annual sales of cheese in 2000 were about 500,000 kroner. Their goal is 1 million. The limit is therefore not lack of customers; rather it is lack of raw material, goat milk. Ola and Kari have been working for a while to get more goat milk. Indeed they worked implicitly with this problem in 1992–1994 when they, together with the other goat farmers, tried to establish a special Tine dairy in Namsskogan, a project which we have seen, failed.

Ola took up the idea again after the establishing of the farm dairy. As last time Tine and the other goat farmers have been negotiating. An agreement was made in the spring of 2000. The other goat farmers do not want to resign from Tine, because Tine in any case is obliged to pay full price for the goat milk that they produce. On the other hand these farmers are more motivated to produce raw material for a more meaningful use. Ola and Kari, for their part, want additional supplies, but only from sources that can guarantee the quality of the raw material and also can transport it satisfactorily. Tine offered a solution. The solution is briefly that the other eight goat farmers as before sell their entire goat milk to Tine. Tine buys the goat milk, checks the milk quality and transports it to Skånaliseter, which buys it from Tine.

In June 2000 Tine made five test deliveries. Kari made cheese from the "new" raw material. In one of the batches all the cheese fermented wrongly and had to be scrapped. Personnel from Tine tested the cheese and found Clostridia bacteria in it. Pasteurizing does not kill clostridia. The source of the bacteria was traced to silage bales on one of the farms. Until further notice the delivery of the "new" goat milk was stopped until Tine together with the goat farmers had solved the problem. Ola and Kari are prepared to insist that the farmers shift from silage to hay, because unwanted bacteria like Clostridia thrive in moist feed. Kari points to a farm dairy in the neighbouring region Jämtland where the farmer says he has obtained a significantly higher price for cheese after guaranteeing that the cheese is manufactured only from milk produced from hay. Kari also is aware that hay is a critical element in the concept of the highly priced Italian Parmesan cheese.

In the autumn of 2000 Ola and Kari enlarged the goatshed from 100 to 115 milking goats. The reason is that Kari then will be able to use the whole capacity of the cheese-making vat. The couple is convinced that the Clostridia problem will be solved, and that Tine can start regular deliveries of goat milk from the other farms in 2001. As a consequence Ola and Kari have already planned to enlarge the cheese factory and the store on Skånaliseter in 2001.

3.4. Case 2: Inquiry from a Foreign User of Goat Milk – Frozen Curd

In 1994 the packing machine in Tine Haukelid broke down. 15 employees were granted leave and the production of real goat brown cheese was stopped (Gardsosten nr. 1, 1999, p. 26). Almost at the same time Tine Norske Meierier received, via its subsidiary in USA – Norseland Inc. – a request from Laura Chenel's Chèvre Inc. in California. This company needed extended deliveries of frozen goat milk curd to be used in the production of various products (Tine Meieriet Sør, 2001).

Laura Chenel's Chèvre Inc. in California has produced "French style" fresh and aged goat's milk cheeses since 1979 (Farm World, 1998). The firm is located in the county of Sonoma, a wine district around 100 km north of San Francisco. Laura Chenel runs a dairy and has its own goatherd. Unlike in Norway, goats in California are held within fences and fed with hay, straw and concentrated fodder all the year round. The firm also purchases goat milk from around ten other farms in the district. The number of speciality cheese makers in USA increased significantly in the 1990s, from a handful in the 1980s to about 200 in 1998 (Werlin, n.d.). Many of them, like Laura Chenel, process goat milk that is produced on the farm. From most of the goat milk Chenel makes fresh, unripened frozen curd. Under the name Frozen Curd, Chenel has marketed this product as a health product in USA since 1979. Frozen Curd is sold mainly to industrial customers, e.g. "gourmet" restaurants. It is produced in a pure version (Naturell) and a spiced version (Tine Meieriet Sør, 2001) and is used among other things in pizza as flavouring. In addition the company makes ripened goat cheese.

Norseland is a company that markets speciality cheeses in USA and Canada. The company's main task is to market selected Tine cheeses. The cow milk based Jarlsberg has been marketed since 1965, and is the most important. The brand Jarlsberg is regarded uppermost among cheeses imported to USA (Bondebladet 5; juli 2001, p. 18). Norseland also sells Tine's Norvegia, Ridder and Nøkkelost, mixed brown cheese, and Snøfrisk (Bondebladet 16. august 2001: 18). In order to broaden the range of products Norseland has in recent years also started to market cheeses from other companies, Unilever, Tholstrup and – as we will see below – Laura Chenel (Tine's nyhetsarkiv, 22.06.2000).

In 1995 Tine decided to start production of Frozen Curd. There were several dairies to choose among (Tine Meieriet Sør, 2001). In the end the board of Tine chose to locate the new production to Tine Haukelid. The farmers supplying goat milk to this dairy were enthusiastic about the plans for a new production there.

Tine Haukelid started the production early in 1995. In the beginning, Chenel was very satisfied with the quality of the product. But in April the same year, she complained that the taste of the curd had become too strong. Tine's Frozen Curd continued to have a strong taste the whole summer. She made it clear that she could not purchase more of the product until the taste had become milder. This time, as opposed to the earlier case of Feta production at Haukelid, Tine put much effort in solving the problem. Because she produced Frozen Curd herself, Chenel knew the product and the production of it very well. She sent one of her dairymen to assist Tine Haukelid in improving the process in the dairy.

However, it was discovered that the main problem was not connected to processes in the dairy. It seemed more likely that the problem had to do with the raw material – goat milk that was supplied to the dairy. Since Frozen Curd was a 100% goat milk based product adding or subtracting components in the goat milk was not an actual solution. Hence, the problem had to be localized and solved in the production, transportation and storing of the goat milk before it reached the dairy. Tine now asked the Departments of Food Science and Animal Science at the Norwegian Agricultural University for help. In addition, personnel at Tine's own departments for Organization and Research & Development took part in the effort to find the causes of the problem and solve it. Tine's Department of Organization deals with questions related to animal health, breeding, feeding and milking operations, while the R&D department deals with product development and new and improved technological solutions. A project group with participants from the organizations mentioned above was set up. The project went on from 1995 to 1999. The group identified three problem areas related to strong taste in the goat milk: feeding, breeding and transportation and storage.

3.4.1. Taste Problems – Change of Feeding

Personnel at the Department of Food Science and the Department of Animal Science co-operated to research the connection between taste and feeding. Anne – today (2002) associate professor – was one of the main participants from Department of Food Science. Clara – a doctoral student – was one of the leading persons from Department of Animal Science. Anne had already become involved in the problems regarding goat milk quality in 1994, at Haukelid, in other words before the problems related to Frozen Curd happened. Anne is especially interested in fermentation and ripening processes in cheese.

Chenel had complained about strong taste. Since Tine and the various panels of taste referees set up to evaluate taste traditionally had perceived strong taste as a positive quality of goat milk, the very notion of taste had to be re-evaluated. For example, Anne found in an experiment at The Department of Food Science that a sensory panel of older "taste referees" gave a sample of goat milk that was fresh (about four hours old) the description "normal," whereas a younger taste panel classified the same sample as tart and rancid. This convinced Anne that the "right taste" of goat milk might vary from generation to generation. Earlier a scale from 1 to 5 had been used when characterizing taste in goat milk. 1 represented 'weak taste' while 5 meant "strong taste." Instead, Anne and Clara proposed to divide the taste into three components, goat taste, rancid taste and tart taste (Skeie, 1998). Goat milk with goat taste has a distinct taste that is easy to distinguish from the taste of cow milk, but is neither rancid nor tart, they claimed. In this scheme strong taste is entirely tied to the two latter elements and is a negative feature of goat milk, they claimed. Consequently, the causes of rancid and tart taste in the goat milk that Tine Haukelid purchased had to be found and fought.

Anne and Clara now carried out some experiments at a small number of goat farms. From the experiments they learned that goat milk produced on mountain pastures, especially late in summer, tended to have a stronger taste than goat milk produced during other seasons. The main finding from their research was that strong taste was mostly related to the *amount of free fatty acids* in the goat milk. At the outset, the fat in milk is contained in globules enclosed by a membrane. Free fatty acids are produced when the membrane is broken. Then an enzyme – lipase – attacks the fat molecules and splits them into free fatty acids. This is a process called *lipolysis* and which subsequently gives rancid and tart taste.

What Anne and Clara were able to show, was that *lipolysis was related to feeding*. In an article (Eknæs et al., 1998) they and two colleagues write that rancid and tart flavour is negatively correlated ($r = -0.2$ to -0.5) to the dry matter content in the milk. They found that reduced dry matter content of milk was related to a negative energy balance resulting from low energy intake, high milk yield or both. From this connection, Clara and her colleagues stated a hypothesis; *energy deficit is the main cause of lipolysis and thus strong taste in goat milk*. An energy deficit means that the goats mobilize energy resources from their own bodies in addition to exploiting the fodder they eat. Energy deficit occurs especially late in the grazing season when the weather is colder and more humid and there is less and poorer grazing, which urges the milking goats to make more and longer grazing trips.

Clara now advises farmers who find that their milking goats produce "strong milk" in the out-door period to avoid the top of the lactation curve falling in the late mountain grazing period. This can to some extent be regulated through the timing of the goats' kidding. However, more important in Clara's view is avoiding the lactation curve becoming steep. A moderate lactation curve is better; very high yields are often connected to low content of dry matter in the milk and thus tart and rancid taste. The lactation curve can be evened out if the goats gradually get more feed before and around kidding.

But type and quality of feed were found to matter maybe the most. First of all it is a question of versatile feed with a quality that suits goats that produce milk. To investigate the significance of high quality fodder, Clara and her colleagues carried out an experiment. Twenty-four milking goats in-door were given as much hay as they could eat (appetite feeding) in 48 hours and 24 other goats grazed outdoors for 48 hours on a mountain pasture. Only 10% of the goats in the first group produced milk with off-flavour, while 90% of the goats in the last group produced milk with unacceptable flavour. Clara concluded that to allot additional feed in the late grazing season could prevent energy imbalance.

In direct co-operation with the project, Felleskjøpet – a farmers' supply co-operative – therefore developed and started to produce a special feed concentrate for milking goats (FORMEL) (Felleskjøpet Øst Vest, 2001). This feed could complement grass fodder, prevent energy deficit and thus contribute to reducing the occurrence of off-flavour in goat milk.

In the beginning Clara had to measure the status of the goats regarding their energy balance by feeling with her hands and looking at the "firmness" of their bodies. Judging firmness from the outside could only give a very rough estimation of energy balance at a certain time and change from time to time. Because of this measurement problem, Clara looked for an interior method that did not destroy the subject of measurement – the goat. An instrument called x-ray tomograph, which the Department of Animal Science had purchased in the 1980s, caught her eye.

The x-ray tomograph was developed in the 1970s and by 1980 it had become a rather well known and common instrument by which to screen internal structures of human patients. The Department bought such an instrument in order to measure, among other things, fat marbling in pigs. In 2000, Clara gained access to the Department's tomograph and could measure the energy status of "her" goats much more precisely. She measured energy status of 12 of her experimental milking goats at 6 different points in time; before, during and after mountain pasture. At the same times she also measured milk yield, milk composition, evaluated its taste and measured certain blood parameters of the goats. Until the time of our interview, she had been able only to do provisional evaluation of the data. But as far as she could assess, they confirmed Anne's and her earlier findings that milking goats mobilize energy resources from their own bodies during the first months of lactation. This mobilization results in higher frequency of lipolysis in the milk, especially in the last part of the grazing season. According to Clara, to prevent off-flavour in goat milk, the goats should be fed towards their energy balance point.

3.4.2. Taste Problems – Altering the Breeding Goals
Contrary to feeding, breeding is a much more long term undertaking. In 1997 Anne and Clara investigated 50 milking goats from the herd at the Agricultural University and found that five animals (10%) produced milk with a strong (rancid and tart) taste. In 1998 they investigated 60 milking goats of the same herd and got a similar result. Since Anne and Clara obtained data from animals representing several generations in these investigations, they were also able to conclude that the characteristics of producing strong milk was due to heredity. Consequently systematic work to identify and remove individual animals producing strong milk in individual herds is one way to obtain a more mild-tasting goat milk.

However, breeding organized above the farm level is also important. Norsk Sau- og Geitalslag – NSG (literally "Norwegian Association for Sheep- and Goat Breeding") have worked to develop what they term "the Norwegian goat race" for many years ([http://www.nsg.no]). NSG is a member organization for sheep farmers and goat farmers in Norway and is responsible for the goat breeding in Norway. Landsrådet for geiteavl (literally "The National Goat Breeding Board") gives advice to NSG when it comes to goat breeding. This board consists of different competencies and represents different organizations. Two goat farmers, of whom one heads the board, represent NSG. There is one member from Tine and one from Department of Animal Science on the board. The Ministry of Agriculture is represented by the animal consultant (Fylkesagronom i husdyrbruk) at one of the County Governor Offices. NSG alone has not sufficient expertise to carry out the organized system of goat breeding. In addition breeding scientists at the Department of Animal Science and regional consultants in Tine contribute in specific ways.

One main task of the board is to shape the goat breeding goals. In general, animals that produce good milk have efficient exploitation of natural resources, and good health and fertility are chosen for further breeding. Regarding the feature "milk," high yield was the primary goal until 1996. Then the board changed the goal and introduced a new formulation: "Develop a goat that produces milk with good and distinct taste." High yield was not a goal in itself any more. However, obtaining a reliable and valid measure of the taste of the milk from every milking goat in the country is a too complicated undertaking. But it is known that goat milk with a high relative portion of dry matter has a more mild taste. Therefore the breeding board doubled the weight that was put on the parameter "relative portion of dry matter in the milk" when crossing within the population of Norwegian goats. In addition genes from the Swiss race Saanen has been used. Saanen goats are recognized as the best milking goats in the world (Haenlein & Ace, 1984), and they produce milk with a mild taste.

That this change in the breeding goals occurred in 1996 was not a coincidence. It was a direct result of the problems of strong taste in Frozen Curd that Tine experienced in 1995 combined with the fact that Tine had a representative in the breeding board. And as a participant in the breeding board, Tine could directly influence the actors who were responsible for and carried out goat breeding.

3.4.3. Taste Problems – Changing Storage and Transportation

Feed and genetics are two – of many influences – affecting goat milk. Transportation and storage facilities are a third group. Since, in the case of Frozen Curd, the processing of the goat milk was organized in such a way as to take care of milk produced at many farms, the milk had to be transported from (all) these farms to the dairy. This demanded specific transport facilities and storage facilities. That is, one could not take it for granted that fresh goat milk on the farm had the same taste as the goat milk that arrived at the gate of the dairy.

Tine's department of research and development work to improve the transport and storage facilities so that the taste of the goat milk remains mild along the way from the farms to the dairy. In the case of Tine Haukelid, goat milk is transported to the dairy from farms that are situated up to 350 km away. Tine has chosen to collect milk every third day, which of course has the consequence that milk has to be stored on the farms for up to so long. On the farm the normal practice is, immediately after milking with milking machine, to pump the milk into a pipe leading to a cooling tank. In the cooling tank there is an agitator. Agitation implies that all the milk is mixed, that the fat does not rise to the top, and that all the milk at no time gets warmer than +4 °C. Until around 2000 the tank solution with the agitator has been the same for cow milk and goat milk in the Tine system. Since cow milk is produced in far larger volumes than goat milk, the design of the agitator has been made on the basis of requirements for cow milk:

> Goat milk does not have the same need to be agitated as the distribution of fat is easier to maintain in goat milk [than in cow milk] (David, a consultant in Tine R&D).

This has to do with the fact that goat milk, in contrast to cow milk, lacks agglutinin (Skeie, 1998, p. 308). The supplier, Landteknikk, started to deliver milk tanks in which programming the intensity of agitation was possible. David and his colleagues believed that the fat in goat milk had been too intensely treated in the former type of tank and started to experiment with lower intensity. However, their analysis showed that there was no less splitting of fat (into fatty acids) when the intensity of the agitation was reduced.

David and his colleagues have also been working to find other improvements regarding transportation and storing of goat milk. One is based on the observation that *lipases are inactivated at temperatures above 60–70°C*. Some farmers are taking part in this work by letting David use their milk handling facilities in his experiments. David envisages two technical solutions. One is to plug in a *heater* on the milk pipe between the milking machine and the cooling tank. In addition a small water cooler has to be plugged in after the heater to bring the temperature in the milk down to the level it had before it entered the heater. This solution will be quite expensive and is considered only for livestock where so-called spontaneous lipolysis is a serious problem. Spontaneous lipolysis is lipolysis that starts immediately after milking. David carried out a small-scale experiment in the summer of 2000 in a setting where the goats grazed on a mountain pasture. He experienced what he terms "dramatic effects." Goat milk that was heated was almost without exception classified as having "mild taste," "1. class" and "low content of free fatty acids." Contrary to this, untreated goat milk generally obtained the classification "tart and rancid taste," "2. or 3. class" and "high content of free fatty acids." In 2001 David plans to carry out the "inactivation experiment" on a larger scale.

A cheaper solution is to heat up the goat milk after it has been pumped from the tank on the farm to the tank lorry that transports the goat milk to the dairy. In this case, the lorry must be equipped with two tanks. Untreated goat milk (from the tank on the farm) is pumped into a small buffer tank. During the trip to the next farm this milk is pumped into the heater and then the cooler before it enters the largest tank on the lorry. In the autumn of 2002 Tine will decide whether a prototype of such a "rolling dairy" shall be installed. If so, Tine will start to use the prototype in 2003.

Half versus full tank during transportation to the dairy also makes a difference. One of David's colleagues carried out an experiment and found that if the tank was full, the goat milk had fewer free fatty acids after the transportation than when the tank was half full. The explanation is that in the former case the goat milk does not "splash" so much. Splashing may destroy the membrane around the fat globules so that fat is released and can be attacked by the lipase enzyme.

On her side Anne has made experiments and found that goat milk that was 72 hours old had a significantly stronger taste than goat milk that was 4 hours old. Clara points to France where making cheese the same day as the milk is milked is common because the quality of it is regarded better then.

3.4.4. Epilogue 2002: Satisfactory Goat Milk – Tine Norseland Starts to Sell Chenel Products

In March 2001 the director at Tine Haukelid was able to report that the situation regarding taste of the goat milk had improved considerably. He now considers that the production of Frozen Curd is "on track." Already in 1995, when they first experienced taste problems, Tine Haukelid started a new routine with weekly evaluations of the taste of each producer's goat milk. The practice until then had been to measure taste in samples from each carload arriving in the dairy. Carloads consist of a mix of goat milk from many farms and thus do not tell anything about the quality of goat milk from single farms. Since then Tine Haukelid have, for the production of Frozen Curd, only used goat milk with no taste defects from the farms. Goat milk with taste defects is, however, collected, but is priced less (Bondebladet, 7 September 2000, p. 15) and sold as feed (Gardsosten nr. 1, 1999, p. 26).

In August and September 1997 the whole production of Frozen Curd at Tine Haukelid was stopped (Tine Årsmelding, 1998). In 1998 – the first year with full round-the-year production of Frozen Curd – 65% of the goat milk had to be rejected because of too strong a taste. In 2000, the figure had declined to 15%. Since then the figure has changed very little, which means that the dairy still has to sort all the incoming goat milk. But all in all the director boasts of the suppliers:

> They have been very motivated and have made a redoubtable contribution in changing the quality of the goat milk that they deliver. Without this effort our dairy would have had no chance ... Now, with the new quality of the goat milk we can even go further and develop new products that we can produce and market.

In the director's opinion (interview June 2002) the reason for the improvement in quality of the goat milk is not solely a question of new fodder and improved feeding routines among the suppliers. Neither is it solely a question of outdoor conditions. It is a compound problem, which includes climate *and* feeding, indoors *as well as* outdoors. For example, he finds that farmers who manage to establish good ventilation in their barns deliver better milk. This is because milking goats staying in stalls with bad ventilation lose their appetite and eat less. Moreover, most of the bulk fodder used in the indoor season is silage, and this loses quality during the season. Hence it is "worst" late in the indoor season, which in this case means April. Thus, providing extra concentrated fodder then is as important as in the outdoor season.

4. ANALYSIS OF SOME CHANGES IN RESOURCE INTERFACES

In this analysis we will separate out important single resources in the resource constellations the focal resource was part of, examine how some of these resources are related (interfaces) and how this has affected the use of the focal resource. In particular, since the problem that interests us is development, we will analyse some changes in interfaces. We will do this simply by looking at interfaces at two points in time. First, based on Section 2, we analyse some interfaces involving the focal resource at "the beginning" (1980s) before new uses of it were developed. Then we analyse some new and changed interfaces after the development − at "the end" (2001) − described in our two cases (Section 3).

4.1. Important Resource Interfaces at "The Beginning" (1980s)

The focal resource was combined with certain other and various types of resources at "the beginning." Hence there are interfaces to consider; to other products, to facilities, business units and business relationships. Moreover, there are physical and non-physical resources. Through these interfaces the focal resource was locked in a specific resource constellation making certain uses of it possible. In Fig. 4 we have mapped some of this resource constellation and some interfaces that we consider was important for Norwegian goat milk in the 1980s. We notice goat milk products like goat brown cheese, goat white cheese, mixed brown cheese and mixed goat milk and rinsing milk. Also we notice a product idea, "coffee cheese." We also recognize certain facilities necessary to make these products and different business units, e.g. Norske Meierier, a goat milk farmer and a cow milk farmer. The fourth category of resources in the constellation is business relationships. Three of them, all including Norske Meierier, are depicted in the figure (Fig. 4).

What are the important interfaces at "the beginning?" A resource that we did not pay so much attention to in Section 2 appears in the map as rather central − *cow*

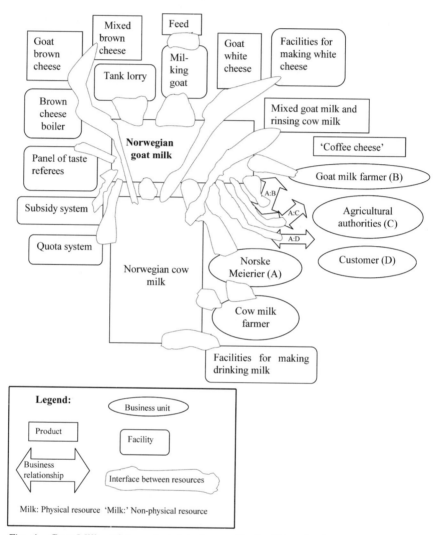

Fig. 4. Goat Milk and Important Interfaces with Facilities, Business Units, Business Relationships and Other Products in the Norwegian Milk Network at "The Beginning" (1980s).

milk. Regarding volume and income this product was much larger than goat milk in the network. Let us analyse some of the ways in which goat milk had interfaces with cow milk at "the beginning."

A major impression is that the *facilities*, which Norske Meierier and their dairy companies and dairies use in relation to goat milk seem to have been developed mainly for cow milk. No facility is used *solely* and *specifically* for goat milk in the network in the 1980s. All goat milk products are produced with facilities that are also used for producing cow milk products. However, the extent to which the various goat milk products fit business relationships between Norske Meierier and their customers vary. Goat brown cheese, for example, sells rather well, while white goat cheese sells poorly and is regarded almost as a failure by one of the customers (Ost & Bakst). In other words goat brown cheese fits rather well in to the business relationships between Norske Meierier and its customers (A:D) while goat white cheese fits poorly.

There may be a *technical* explanation for this difference. Any type of milk, we learn from the empirical material, consists of *components*. Lactose and casein are two milk components that actors in the cases use; hence these components are resources. Lactose in goat milk and cow milk are similar from a physical point of view. Norske Meierier handles these two resources with similar facilities, and both outputs, be it goat brown cheese or cow brown cheese are reasonably well valued by customers of Norske Meierier. Goat milk casein and cow milk casein on the other hand differ with respect to physical features. Nevertheless they also are related to similar facilities. However, Norske Meierier's customers value the products that come out of these two interfaces *differently*. In other words, relating two physically different products to the same facilities may result in products that have very different value in the same business relationship.

One reason contributing to similarity in valuation in the first case (lactose) and difference in the latter (casein), thus, seems to be *technical* interfaces which Norwegian goat milk has to other resources at "the beginning." For nearly 30 years (1970–1999) Tine/Norske Meierier continuously keeps up the technically rather inappropriate interface between goat milk casein and facilities designed for producing products from cow milk casein. However, *why* this technical interface is kept up is more difficult to understand given our case material. But, given our theory we should also look for *social/economic* interfaces; for example the one between goat milk and the milk *quota* system and the one between goat milk and the *subsidy* system. We have regarded these two systems as facilities here and both have also interfaces with goat milk's "big brother" in the network (cow milk). Moreover, at "the beginning" both these economic facilities have the same interface (are similar in relation to) goat milk and cow milk. In addition some of the goat milk has also direct, physical interfaces with cow milk at "the beginning." For example, goat milk is mixed with cow milk in various ways in order to produce products like mixed brown cheese and "mixed goat milk and rinsing cow milk."

Regarding business units goat milk has only one interface on the user side at "the beginning." It is with Norske Meierier. Even if this business unit is a rather "quasi" one – constituted of many, partly independent business units it has nevertheless the final word when it comes to the *use* of the goat milk that these business units buy from their member suppliers. On the supplier side, however, goat milk's interfaces with business units are different. Most of them are specific producers and suppliers of this product, and there are many of them.

To sum up, goat milk had at "the beginning" interfaces with many different resources; technical ones as well as social and economic ones. Many of these interfaces included, directly and indirectly, goat milk's "big brother" cow milk. This heavy embeddedness in a resource constellation developed mainly for another, almost similar but much "larger" product, directed goat milk into some few, rather undemanding, but not unprofitable uses. Nevertheless, some uses (products) were failures in relation to customers in the network. Common to all these products was that they used a certain component in goat milk – casein. However, during the next 15–20 years the situation changed, not at least concerning use of goat milk casein.

4.2. Change in Interfaces Affecting the Focal Resource: Case 1

Figure 5 visualizes some of the effects of interactive, systematic relating in case 1 (Skånaliseter) until 2001. We see that goat milk has got many new interfaces, although some are the same, e.g. the goat farm is still there. But cow milk is not a central resource in this goat milk's constellation at the actual moment in time (Fig. 5).

In the case we learn that Ola – the farmer – believes that the goat milk he produces is "an excellent raw material" and that there are "special cheese customers out there." His knowledge of the coffee cheese is important, too. Hence, physical resources as well as non-physical resources in the form of ideas and beliefs are part of goat milk's constellation in this case. Moreover, the constellation develops. For example "special cheese customer" is an idea Ola has before 1995. This idea develops as Ola interacts with certain other actors over time, for example goat farm dairymen in Jämtland. Moreover, Ola has will to realize this idea by systematically relate goat milk to resources it has not been related to before in the Norwegian milk network. But changes had to be and were made also in goat

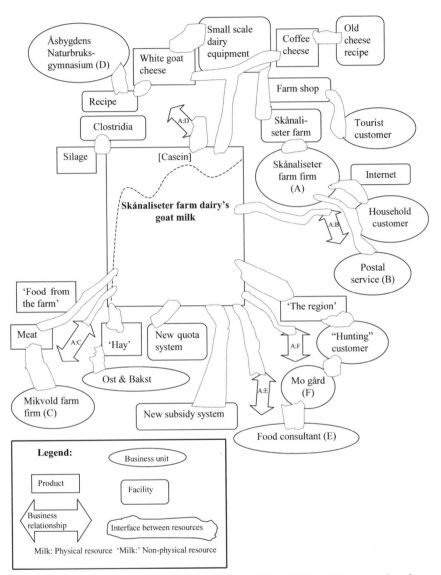

Fig. 5. Goat Milk Used by Skånaliseter at "The End" (Year 2001) and Important Interfaces with Facilities, Business Units, Business Relationships and Other Products.

milk's existing interfaces, e.g. in relation to two economic facilities previously analysed, the quota system and the subsidy system. Note that removing these interfaces would be economic hazard for Skånaliseter. Therefore adaptation was the solution.

"Goat milk – hay" is another new interface at "the end." It is an interface between a product and a product. It replaces a former product – product interface; "goat milk – silage" at Skånaliseter. However, the new interface gives meaning first when other interfaces also are taken into account. When Namdalsmeieriet used goat milk it used it only for producing brown cheese. Brown cheese does not have interface with the whole goat milk, but only a part of it – lactose (the carbohydrate component). Goat milk does not have to be activated by microbes in order to result in the product brown cheese.

Moreover, eventual interfaces between goat milk and microbes have no consequences for the features of brown cheese whatsoever. For example, an interface "Clostridia – goat milk" has no consequences for the interface "goat milk – brown cheese." Furthermore we know that there is an interface between silage and Clostridia, but this interface does not influence the interface "goat milk – brown cheese" either. In other words, because the business unit Namdalsmeieriet related only to a part – a specific component – of goat milk (of which Skånaliseter produced some), it could ignore the interface between goat milk and the "facility" Clostridia.

However, for resource interfaces that include another component of goat milk – casein – the interface "Clostridia – goat milk" matters. Clostridia facilitate transformation of goat milk into certain products. But these products were not sought after neither by Tine's nor Skånaliseter's customers. Exchanging the interface "goat milk – silage" with "goat milk – hay" was Skånaliseter's way of avoiding the unwanted interface "goat milk – clostridia."

Moreover, there also is a new interface between Skånaliseter's hay and the *business unit* Ost & Bakst, as the shopkeeper there has a more positive image of the interface "milking goat – hay" than the interface "milking goat – silage." Hence she seems prepared, when interacting with customers, to argue more positively about cheeses from Skånaliseter. The shopkeeper's knowledge of a certain interface (she had herself visited Skånaliseter) has a bearing on the resource – Skånaliseter's goat milk.

All in all we will argue that the effects on this resource of about 15 years of development has much to do with new interfaces between existing resources. In other words, in the Skånaliseter case the *use* side of the resource is developed and not so much the provision side. And one component in the resource (casein) is particularly affected. Let us analyse the effects on the resource of some new interfaces between this component and other resources.

4.2.1. New "Product – Product" Interfaces

In 2001 Skånaliseter uses the goat milk that it produces to make seven different products in which casein is the major ingredient. When Namdalsmeieriet used the goat milk, only lactose-based products were made. Skånaliseter on their part sorts this component out and makes specific products from it. In addition Skånaliseter continues to use the lactose component in its goat milk.

4.2.2. A New "Product – Facility" and "Product – Business Unit" Interface

The specific goat milk of Skånaliseter has in 2001 a very weak interface with cow milk, but a strong interface with meat, that is, a specific meat; meat produced and used by Mikvold farm firm (see Fig. 5). These two products (Skånaliseter's goat milk and Mikvold's meat) have an interface, we believe, because the actors "behind" them have managed to connect the products to a common *idea*, "food from the farm." This idea can be understood in terms of resource interfaces. In relation to Skånaliseter there is a facility in the form of a farm (Skånaliseter farm), a business unit (Skånaliseter farm firm) controlling this – and mainly this – facility and a farm product (goat milk) made with the help of this facility. In addition there are products made from the farm product (food products, for example white goat cheese 7), facilities for producing this food product and a facility (shop) for selling the product to a certain kind of customers (tourist customers).

The peculiarity of the "food-from-the-farm" concept seems primarily related to two interfaces. The first is *technical* and is between the facility for *producing* a (farm) product – farm – and the facility for *using* this product in the manufacture of another (food) product. In the Skånaliseter case this latter facility is a farm dairy. The other interface concerns *economy* and is between the business unit holding these facilities (the farm firm) and another business unit (the customer). In the Skånaliseter case there are various economic interfaces. One is between Skånaliseter farm firm and a household customer; others are with the tourist firm Mo Gård and with Ost & Bakst. However, food products really become "food from the farm" when a third – technical – interface is established, that between the facility "farm" and the facility "shop." Then Skånaliseter *really* can refer to their food products as "food from the farm." This third interface again leads to still new economic interfaces, between Skånaliseter firm and customers transported physically to the farm, in Fig. 5 called "tourist customer." In addition to obtaining specific products in exchange for money, these customers also *experience* the products' interfaces; e.g. with the specific facilities and capabilities that have produced them.

4.2.3. Novel "Product – Business Relationship" Interfaces

After 1987 Skånaliseter establishes many new business relationships with other actors. These relationships are used – for different purposes – and are hence resources. Five of them are depicted in Fig. 5. Each business relationship has a certain interface with the focal resource. Some of the relationships give Skånaliseter *access* to various facilities and capabilities. Others facilitate confrontation of resources and thus affect development. An example of the first is the relationship between Skånaliseter and the Postal Service (A:B). Here Skånaliseter gets access on a long-term basis to certain resources; transportation facilities and capabilities that suit its food products and some of its customers. In fact this relationship not only gives access to "stationary" resources, but resources *in use* – a certain activity pattern – that *physically* moves goat milk products from Skånaliseter to particular customers.

The business relationship between Skånaliseter and Mikvold (A:C) provides access to other resources; the retail facility and capability at Mikvold and food products produced there. The business relationship with Åsbygdens Naturbruksgymnasium (A:D) not only gives access to resources but also facilitates confrontation of resources and hence development. For example, Skånaliseter obtains a recipe for white cheese through this relationship. However, Skånaliseter does not use this recipe as it is but develops it in specific relation to other of its resources. In A:D Skånaliseter also develops capabilities in white cheese making and obtains knowledge about appropriate dairy facilities and business units that supply such specific facilities.

The A:E relationship (Skånaliseter – Food Consultant) also has many uses. In this relationship Skånaliseter develops its knowledge about the uses of the resource. It also connects them to a third party, Mo Gård, with which it develops a business relationship (A:F). The most innovative element in this relationship is maybe that here the specific (physical) *location* of Skånaliseter *farm* is valued.

4.3. Change in Interfaces Affecting the Focal Resource: Case 2

While establishment of new combinations of *existing* resource features marks the development in the Skånaliseter case, *change* of a feature is central in the development in the Frozen Curd case — taste. Nevertheless, both the origin to the change — the realization *that* a change has to be made — and *how* the change is attained involves several interfaces. There are new ones as well as (modification of) old ones. Technical interfaces are surely important, especially concerning how the feature is *physically* altered. Here many technical researchers are engaged over several years. But the case also illustrates how *views* — non-physical resources — play a role in development. During the development process the Norwegian actors (of whom Tine is the most prominent) changes the view of what constitutes "proper" goat milk taste. Hence, "new view of goat milk taste" is one of the many resources that affect the development in the case. Some of these resources and some interfaces that seem important are pictured in Fig. 6.

Like in case 1, the development can be linked to a specific component in the focal resource — casein. But unlike in case 1, a third component turns out as central — goat milk fat. The technical researchers identify this component as "responsible" for the unwanted feature in the, for the Norwegian actors, new product Frozen Curd. This is the only product that is traded in the new business relationship between Laura Chenel and Tine (A:C in Fig. 6). The start of the specific development of the focal resource described in the case originates in the establishment of this business relationship. But to fully understand what happens later we have to include the customers of the (new) customer, e.g. restaurants. And we have to distinguish between the Frozen Curd made by Tine and that made by Laura Chenel. Then we see that what triggers the development is confrontation of a product made of the focal resource (Frozen Curd made by Tine) and customers of the customer, e.g. restaurants. These can here be regarded as business units.

The confrontation of these two resources – a product and a business unit – is a real "crash." What is it that crashes? The actual business unit ("Restaurant") already has an interface with Frozen Curd (made by Laura Chenel). Hence it has a clear picture of what a proper Frozen Curd should be, e.g. regarding taste. It experiences a clear misfit between this and the same product made by Tine; there is a "bad" interface.

In principal this "friction" between a customer's customers and Tine's Frozen Curd can be removed by changing the features of these customers, or by changing the features of Tine's Frozen Curd, or by changing both. In the case the second solution is chosen; the features of Tine's Frozen Curd has to be changed. If not Tine's business relationship with Laura Chenel will terminate. Tine then uses some of its established relationships with certain research institutions in order to change the feature of the product. In this way the "bad" interface is repaired. Altering a specific feature in a certain product that has *interface* with Tine's Frozen Curd brings about this change. This product is our focal resource goat milk. More specifically in Fig. 6 we distinguish between goat milk as it is when newly produced on the farm (Farmer's goat milk) and goat milk as it is when arriving at the dairy (Tine Haukelid's goat milk). In this case, we learn, these two "goat milks" differ with respect to the problematic feature, and part of the development activities is to make the latter milk more similar to the former with respect to this feature. The agitator speed regulating device is a new resource (facility) introduced in the

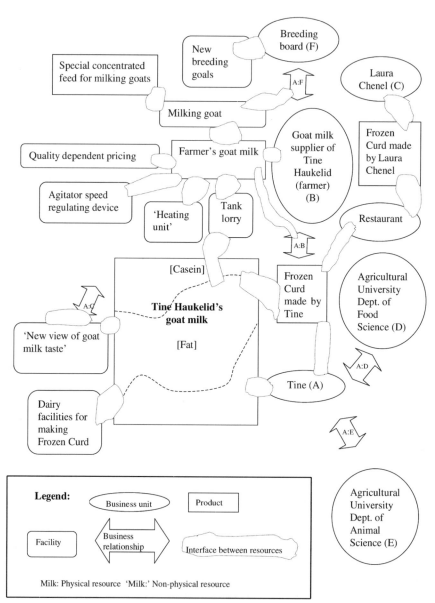

Fig. 6. Goat Milk Used by Tine Haukelid at "The End" (Year 2001) and Important Interfaces with Facilities, Business Units, Business Relationships and Other Products.

constellation to do this. An idea about another facility for accomplishing the same ("heating unit") also comes out of the development process.

There are crucial changes also with respect to other interfaces in the story. Several of them are depicted in Fig. 6. One is a "product – facility" interface:

(1) Special concentrated feed for milking goats – Milking goat

Two others has to do with the relation between a facility and a business relationship:

(2) Milking goat – Business relationship between Tine and the Breeding board (A:F)
(3) "New view of goat milk taste" – Business relationship between Tine and Laura Chenel (A:C)

A fourth one is a "product – business relationship" interface:

(4) Farmer's goat milk – Business relationship between Tine and Goat milk supplier (A:B)

There is no room here for analysing all these interfaces, but let us analyse two of them, number 1 and 3.

4.3.1. A New "Product – Facility" Interface

One of the physical results of the research described in case 2 is a new product, a concentrated feed specially designed for milking goats. Milking goats fed with this fodder produce a "farmer's goat milk" with a different feature; a better ability to maintain mild taste. Thus this is a new interface between a product and a facility that affects one of the focal resource's features. Note that this interface has little value for example for the Californian goats that produce milk purchased by Laura Chenel. These are fed in barns and live in a different climate during the summer season. Hence, the interface has a function only given certain other interfaces, e.g. between milking goat and climate and milking goat and feeding facilities (for example grazing vs. feeding in barn).

4.3.2. A Novel "Facility – Business Relationship" Interface

Tine was not unaware of the taste feature of the focal resource before it established the business relationship with Laura Chenel (A:C). Tine/Norske Meierier and other actors in the Norwegian milk network had rather precise views regarding what constituted "proper taste" of goat milk. This view was formally explicated in a scheme for evaluating taste. Both the view and the scheme can be seen as facilities – non-physical such. Hence, "New view of goat milk taste" is mapped as a facility in Fig. 6. This facility is different at "the end" than at "the beginning." One crucial difference is that during the development process this facility has been affected by the new relationship between Tine and Laura Chenel. In other words, a new interface between a facility and a business relationship has emerged. This interface has contributed to changing physically the taste feature of the focal resource.

The change in view of goat milk taste had also to do with other resources, e.g. the taste panel and the technical researchers. At least on one occasion different panels had different views concerning the taste of the same goat milk. And as a result of research the taste scheme was changed. But the scheme per se is not changed, but rather the *view* underlying it. The new view is explicated in form of changes in a pair of concepts for characterizing taste; from "weak – strong" to "mild – strong." The new scheme builds on *mild* being the sought-after taste of Norwegian goat milk, while strong was the proper taste according to the old view. We say this because we believe that the word "strong" has negative connotations in *relation* to the word "mild," while positive connotations in relation to the word "weak."

To sum up, the change of the taste feature in case 2 was not solely a technical matter. It also had to do with certain actors changing their view – idea – regarding this feature in relation to the focal resource. Combined with technical facilities for *physically* sorting goat milk with one feature (strong taste) from goat milk with another (mild taste), together with economic facilities (a new pricing system for goat milk) the new scheme had a positive effect on the new business relationship between Tine and Laura Chenel. Hence, saying that there is an interface between this relationship and the facility "New view of goat milk taste" gives meaning. From the many goat milk supplier's point of view, then, the product they were producing in this way increased in value.

5. DISCUSSION: RESOURCES AND ECONOMICS

What can actors do to improve the use of a resource? This was the research problem that we formulated early in Section 2. Later in that section, after having developed a more thourough theoretical framework, we refined the problem. We stated that resources are always used within the context of a business network. Furthermore we came to see the arriving at better uses as a development problem. Hence, at the end of Section 2, we could formulate a more precise research question; what can actors do to develop new uses of a product that is subordinate in a business network? Moreover, we proposed that development of a product (as well as other resources) is something driven by interaction between actors. Since we found the use, and hence value, of a resource as depending on the match (combination) between its features and the features of other resources, "better" use turned into a question of arriving at a "better" combination. In a network various actors can arrive at "better" combinations through interaction where different resources are systematically related. In Section 4 we analysed some of the focal product's improved combinations and their interfaces. The analysis showed that the focal resource was part of a specific resource constellation at "the beginning." At "the end," however, it entered the two resource constellations in another way, and the actors considered it differently. The difference between the "start constellation" and the "end constellations" turned partly on new combinations of existing features of the resource, partly on new features.

Certain actors have been instrumental in creating these specific constellations of resources. This means that the constellations are not "natural" or "accidental." Moreover, the constellations represent *investments* for the actors. In this way the actors have economic interests tied to the various constellations (Håkansson & Waluszewski, 2002). Thus, improved use of our focal resource is also a question of economics, that is any aspect that is economically significant (Webster's, 1989). Or to put it in more everyday terms; how to make "new" money on features of a resource, in this case a product? The purpose of this section is to assess – reason in terms of – economics on the background of the preceding descriptions and analysis.

5.1. Economics of Combinations

One of the terms most frequently used by companies in their annual reports is "synergy" – the combined action of two or more elements in order to produce an effect or enhance the effect of each element (Webster's, 1989). Possibly they use this term as a catchword without it reflecting company realities. Nevertheless it demonstrates that actors are aware that there are economic effects tied to the very combination of resources. Thus, the word synergy points exactly to the limitations of assessing economics only in terms of quantity and suggests that an important aspect of economics is "hidden" in resource combinations. And a resource combination is a question of different resources that match or are made to match. Resource heterogeneity, a term we introduced in Section 1, is a key concept here. The same resource can enter into more than one resource combination and have different values in different combinations. This fact is helpful when trying to develop a way of assessing how actors in a business network assess economics of resources.

5.2. Viewing the Resource as a Cost

Namdalsmeieriet in the 1980s has problems with the goat milk that it purchases. More precisely it views the resource "by itself" as satisfactory; the technical features of it represent no problems. What is problematic is getting the resource to fit economically into the *specific* combination of other resources that Namdalsmeieriet use and produce. The calculation for the dairy (which can be regarded as a facility) overrides the calculation for goat milk. In this calculation goat milk is first and foremost *a cost*. Why it is regarded as a cost has to do with the other resources that this actor enters in the calculation, that is the "large" technical resource cow milk around which a certain constellation of facilities is developed, and from which practically all the company's revenues (value) is created.

The shift in use of the resource in 1986 – from brown cheese to fodder – confirms that Namdalsmeieriet regards it first and foremost as a cost. What prevents the company from ceasing to purchase goat milk entirely (which would totally have eliminated costs of goat milk) is probably that this would have affected the company's *relationships* with other business units, namely the cow milk farmers in the region. At first sight we might think that dropping goat milk would unequivocally be positive for the economics seen from the side of Namdalsmeieriet. On closer scrutiny the picture becomes more complex; there is more than one *resource tie* to consider when assessing the economic effect. "Dropping" goat milk would require a change in the bylaws, an important element in the business relationship between the company and its suppliers. Such a change would presuppose the company disclaiming, in one way or another, its formal duty to *purchase* milk from its supplying members. In addition this would conflict with one central principle for all co-operative enterprises; it could mean that some or all members for their part terminated their formal obligation to *deliver* milk exclusively to the company. To the extent that this occurred the dairy would experience negative economics; negative economic effects in other (technical as well as social) resource ties would exceed the positive economic effect of stopping purchasing goat milk. The crucial economic question concerning the focal resource seen from the resource perspective of Namdalsmeieriet then was: "How can we in the most economical way reduce the *costs* per litre of goat milk?"

5.3. Emphasizing the Value Side of the Resource

In 1995, after nearly ten years of being fed to livestock, the focal resource (more specifically a part of it) is again being used to produce human food. Now, in Skånaliseter, the focus is on goat milk as having a value, the most prominent question being: "How can we get the most out of 1 litre of goat milk?" This leads to a calculation where the revenue side is highlighted. But this calculation is not very explicit, and it is not especially precise as it contains few figures. Ola and Kari have learned that colleagues in a neighbouring region in another country obtain double the price per kg of goat milk product compared to the large, established dairy companies and "adopt" this level of price for the resource that they control. The costs were mere conjecture, but not totally disconnected from the costs of real resources. For example, before establishing the farm dairy Ola and Kari visited many farm dairies and saw the facilities used. Via these observations they gained some rough ideas about costs in the production and marketing also in an eventual dairy on their farm. In other words, calculations were present when Ola and Kari searched for ways to realize a dairy.

Actors consider economics in different ways; getting more out of a resource is truly something else than using a resource more efficiently. First and foremost such a job has qualitative aspects. Traditionally the identification of other resources to tie the resource with has been emphasized (cf. Håkansson & Snehota, 1995; Penrose, 1995). Thus we note that many of the resources, to which Skånaliseter later tied goat milk, existed long before the farm dairy was established. Most customers existed, some of the special food shops existed, the postal service existed, and expanded polyester existed. Even the special cheese-making vat existed. Børgefjell National Park existed. Namdal as a regional identity existed. Skånaliseter as a farm existed. On the other hand case 1 also demonstrates how important *untying* can be for getting more out of a resource and hence for economic effects. In this case goat milk was untied from e.g. the system of production quotas and product calculations within Tine Norske Meierier and the business relationships that Namdalsmeieriet had with cow milk suppliers. This untying seemed to be necessary for establishing new ties for the resource.

Namdalsmeieriet found none of these new resource ties relevant in relation to the focal resource. Ola and Kari did. *This discrepancy cannot be explained by one of these actors being uneconomical and the other economical.* Both actors acted economically and produced economic effects. But since the actors' resource ties differed, the resources that they considered relevant in relation to the focal resource came to differ. Hence one and the same resource (goat milk) came to enter differently in their respective calculations. Figure 7 is an attempt at visualizing this situation, a situation that we believe is not unique for this case but rather an example of a relatively common circumstance in business networks.

5.4. Confronting Different Calculations

However, the latter calculation was not developed in isolation from the former. One link between the two was the calculation about using goat milk in the 1992–1994 project. Here Namdalsmeieriet's cost-centred calculation was directly confronted – for the first time, as it seems – by a value-centred calculation. This latter built

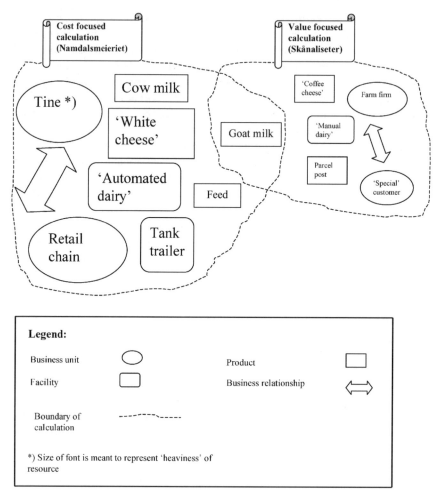

Fig. 7. An Illustration of How Two Actors Calculate the Same Resource Differently.

on an idea of a match between goat milk and a certain collection of resources. Some of these were absent from Namdalsmeieriet's calculation. They also differed from the combination exploited later by Skånaliseter farm dairy. New resources not considered by Namdalsmeieriet included two facilities (a Deer Park that was already in existence and the idea of a special ("niche") dairy located next to the Deer Park). In addition there was the idea of some new products made from the resource and the expectation that many customers of the Deer Park, because of the co-localization, would also become customers of the new dairy. An actor not taking directly part in the project calculated the costs of the new dairy facility. Seemingly neither Namdalsmeieriet nor Skånaliseter questioned this calculation regarding a *facility* (Fig. 7).

What they did not agree upon was the calculation of the *product* to be made with the facility — the new dairy. Skånaliseter emphasized the value of this product and found it to be considerably higher than the value of ordinary products of the same category made by Tine dairies. One basis for this assessment was differences in value for these types of products that Ola and Kari had observed in Sweden. Namdalsmeieriet on the other hand emphasized costs and assumed the value to be exactly the same as the value of ordinary products of the same category. With this value and estimated costs of other resources, Namdalsmeieriet made a calculation for the dairy facility and found the economics of the new dairy to be negative. This contrasted with the other calculation backed by Skånaliseter.

In other words, here one and the same resource entered into different calculations made by two different actors. The resource was assessed differently in economic terms in the various calculations. Firstly, Namdalsmeieriet lets its calculation centre on a facility (the "niche" dairy) while products (like goat milk and products made from it) are secondary. As a consequence the cost side of the focal resource is emphasized. Skånaliseter, on the other hand, focuses on products and customers while the facility is secondary; hence it emphasizes the value side of the focal resource. Moreover, in the project the two calculations are confronted. This seems to change both actors' view of the resource and hence impact how Skånaliseter calculates the focal resource in relation to using it itself.

Regarding the old calculation, Namdalsmeieriet as a business unit of a certain kind, has for a long time been tied to other business units of the same kind through membership in a common business unit (from 1992 called Tine). This common business unit develops and markets non-fluid products on behalf of all "its" business units. Moreover, this common business unit also makes standard calculations for each of these products. These calculations seem to be influenced by a policy that prices should not be too high. In other words, there exists within the business network of Tine a certain (national) portfolio of dairy products, each with its standard calculation. Thus, we imagine that Namdalsmeieriet in the project cannot move very far from these products and calculations when making the calculation for the "niche" dairy. If it does it will probably put its business relationship with the common business unit and thereby the other dairy companies at stake. These relationships are crucial for the economy of the business unit Namdalsmeieriet.

As a dairy farm Skånaliseter is also a member of the common business unit Tine. But its business relationship with Tine is different. First of all Skånaliseter is a producer of the focal resource and not a user. This means that it is not bound to the dairy products and calculations created by the common business unit in the same way as Namdalsmeieriet is. Furthermore, Skånaliseter has already secured an important part of its economy by having influenced changes in public regulations regarding milk subsidies and milk quotas. Thus, when Skånaliseter makes its calculation in the project and later for its farm dairy it can let goat milk enter in another way because it can ignore some resources that cannot be ignored by Namdalsmeieriet.

5.5. Calculations and Interaction

As producers, users or in other ways actors have economic interests related to resources. Actors make, more or less consciously, calculations in order to handle these interests. They may make calculations for, and enter into calculations, "whole" business units, products and facilities. They "even" calculate business relationships. Our focal resource entered in several calculations; for products like brown cheese; for facilities like dairy and transportation; for business units like a dairy and a farm; and for business relationships like that between Namdalsmeieriet and Tine. Goat milk entered differently in the calculations in 1980 compared to twenty years later. This is so not only in case 1 (which we have chosen to build most extensively on in this discussion) but also in case 2.

Moreover, not only does one and the same resource enter into different calculations; different actors might "stand behind" these different calculations. This can be due to differences in interests regarding the same resource. One actor may prioritize a certain resource and therefore put it in centre of its calculation. Another actor may judge the same resource only as "a necessary evil" and let it enter at the fringe in the calculation. Both actors, however, have *interests* in relation to the resource, but necessarily also in relation to other resources. At least some of these resources will not be common for the two actors. In other words, *the boundary that each actor sets in the resource constellation will "only" partly overlap*. Hence, there can be a chance of conflicting interests in relation to the "common" resource. Assuming a business world consisting of firms (hierarchies) in a (neo-classical) market, this conflict can be resolved in two ways. If the conflict is between firms (or between a firm and a consumer) the involved actors have either to accept or reject each other's calculations regarding the resource; that is, the price mechanism is at work. To the extent that the conflict is within a firm, it can be resolved through authority; that is, by use of power.

Within the world of a business network there is also the possibility that this conflict, when being between firms, can be approached through interaction. Then, the boundaries that each actor sets around the resource and how they "locate" the resource within this boundary (at the centre or at the fringe) can be directly confronted. This may lead the actors to change what resources are in focus respectively at the fringe. But it may also lead them to alter their view of their own calculations and the counterpart's calculation. This reasoning is in line with Torvatn's (1996: pp. 190, 191) argument about efficiency; actors in an industrial network should be able to vary the "network borders" in which they assess efficiency and not cling only to one border.

In other words, willingness and ability to understand and accept a counterpart's boundary setting as basis for calculation is crucial. For example, in case 1 (in the project 1992–1994) it was essential for the subsequent development of the focal resource that Namdalsmeieriet changed its view regarding the *counterpart's* (Skånaliseter's) calculation. This made Namdalsmeieriet loosen its ties to the resource. On the basis of this change Skånaliseter could create a new calculation in which the value side of the focal resource was emphasized, but *in another way* than planned at the outset of the project.

Hence, calculations – in explicit or implicit form – can be seen as instruments that influence actors' view of resources and how they are developed and used within a business network. Here, in the interaction, "having the 'right' calculation" seems more important than "having the calculation 'right.'" On the other hand, actors cannot construct any calculation they like. Calculations must reflect some resources that are seen as real by some other actor. Thus, creating a calculation and *make other actors appreciate it* is quite a "social" job. Case 1 in particular demonstrates this.

A reasonable inference, then, is that calculations are a consequence of resource constellations and actors' view of them; what resources they attach importance to and where they draw boundaries for their calculations. But the reverse is also true; calculations affect the way actors combine resources across firm boundaries and hence what resources are developed. The price of a product may be decided before it is developed, a researcher's level of pay settled before s/he starts working, and the budget of a development project determined prior to it. A customer may demand certain future reductions in price of a product provided by a supplier, something that necessarily must lead to some development on the side of the supplier in order for it to stay in business. This implies that calculations can be, and in fact are, used as instruments for change.

6. CONCLUSION

On an "exterior" (empirical) level the problem that we have been pursuing in this study concerns how concrete actors can improve the use of a particular resource;

an agricultural product that at a certain time is subordinate in the industrial network of which it is part. On these grounds one result of the study is – or, rather, can be found in – its documentation of concrete development processes in the actual network in subsequent years, leading to certain outcomes in the form of new or improved uses of the product in question. However, these new or improved uses did not concern Norwegian goat milk in its entirety, but certain *parts* of it.

In the Skånaliseter case (case 1) the goat milk produced on *one farm* was incrementally detached from certain resources in the network and attached to other resources. On these grounds use of one (small) portion of the product was improved. Moreover, this improved use had most to do with a certain component (casein) in the product. This component differed in some features from the corresponding component of cow milk. Because cow milk was economically most important in the prevailing network, facilities and capabilities for making casein-based products had been developed in relation to the features of cow milk and not in relation to the features of goat milk. In the new, smaller milk network which Skånaliseter was instrumental in creating, investments in and development of facilities and capabilities that were better suited to goat milk casein were made. This lead to new use of this component in a portion of Norwegian goat milk in the form of various white goat cheeses. Previously this component had been used as feed, a use that generated low incomes.

The Frozen Curd case (case 2) demonstrates how use of another portion of the product (all goat milk supplied to a certain dairy) is improved while *remaining* attached to most resources in the prevailing network. Starting from a product (Frozen Curd) that is already developed and manufactured, and taken as granted by the involved actors, the clue is not to combine existing features of the focal product in new ways with other resources. Rather, in order to suit the "new" product the focal product "itself" is changed, through alteration of a certain feature (taste). Moreover, while this "new" product mainly is based on the same component as the products in case 1, the *critical* feature in case 2 is tied to a second component in the focal product, fat. By altering a feature (taste) in this component new use of another specific portion of the focal product is established.

Hence, not only have we demonstrated that the use of the actual, "underestimated" product was improved; we have also shown how a *variety* of new uses was developed and implemented. This variety concerning new uses had to do with discovery of new combinations of different resources involving several firms and institutions in the network. But the variety in new uses and hence development had also to do with "opening" the resource "itself"; recognizing that it consisted of many and diverse components, each with certain features that could be exploited, together or in combination with other resources. In fact, we could alternatively have regarded goat milk casein as the focal product and let the study be about improved uses of *this* product.

And then we inevitably have turned to the "interior" side of our research problem; does the study have transferability on a theoretical level? In the next (last) section we will discuss the concept of transferability in more detail. There we will argue that the one who is to use the study, the reader, primarily must do eventual "transfer." The responsibility of the writer is "restricted" to provide thick descriptions so that the reader gets a chance to compare the context described in the study with the context in which the study shall be applied. On these grounds we should strictly speaking, as authors, desist from suggesting applications of the study. However, if we imagined ourselves as users of the study, what would we emphasize? Again, this would depend on e.g. in what industrial network we were located, the function we had in this network, the type of resources we were working with, and what other actors we could interact with. For example, it might be that this study is easily applicable to problems of poor use of other physical products, while less employable to problems of poor use of non-physical resources (like knowledge) or social resources (e.g. a business relationship).

Nevertheless, let us point at a couple of more general lessons from the study concerning developing better uses of resources. As we have seen, use of a resource requires it being combined with other resources, and by logic better use therefore becomes a question of better combinations. As shown, better combinations really were found for our focal product. But the word "better" here has no meaning unless we take two other "factors" or dimensions into consideration, economy and actors.

Firstly, better combinations will not be identified and implemented, in fact cannot be understood, in isolation from economic considerations (economics). Moreover, there is interplay between economics and development. In one way or another actors will have or make calculations in relation to any resource that they consider or handle. These calculations build on selected combinations of resources, where some resources are regarded as more "central" than others. Often actors will be economically "conservative" in the sense that they will try to get the most out of investments in combinations already made. Therefore, arriving at new combinations can be difficult. On the other hand, without development an industrial network will sooner or later die, hence there will always be a need of new combinations and features. This means that there at any time in a network exist possibilities for using a resource better. But this provides among other things that actors in the network confront, compare and discuss – that is, interact about – each other's calculations. In other words, interaction can be a way to clarify the resource combination "behind" different actors' calculations and hence making it easier identifying "better" combinations and therefore uses. In addition, economics also can provide a way to encourage development of better uses.

If all actors in a business network were similar, we could as researchers approach the problem of finding better uses of a resource with a few general assumptions prevailing to all actors. However, this study confirms other studies within the industrial network approach that actors, as well as resources, are heterogeneous. Hence, we leave out of the picture a crucial element if we ignore the actor dimension when searching for and studying new ways to use a resource. The actor dimension is important because actors interact to discover and implement new resource combinations and to calculate resources. Not only do actors *activate* resources, they also have *views* about resources. They seem to appreciate some resources more than others, and this appreciation concerns more than economy, technology and knowledge. Hence, we might say that the actor dimension concerns the *sociology of business networks*. This sociology also affects the use of a resource and the possibilities of developing it. Improvement in use may thus as much be about changing actors view of what constitutes "better use" as changing physical combinations and features. This makes interaction the more important.

The study, therefore, confirms other studies of resource development in the industrial network approach, for example Wedin (2001), that has shown that the economics of a resource is something "larger" than single organizations and relationships. Economics depends on a complex pattern of ongoing interaction by actors in a business network. In other words, no sole buyer or seller – user or producer – determines value. On the other hand, neither is economics of a resource a result of aggregated acts by a multitude of anonymous actors. Actors are concrete and unique in terms of identity and character and handle heterogeneous resources. This is why interaction is possible and can be worthwhile. And actors know this. On the other hand, this makes predicting changed use and value of a resource through intellectual exercise only highly difficult and rather uninteresting. Instead we can, as researchers, in relatively detailed ways, describe concrete, interactive processes in business networks through which certain resources are developed over time. By attempting to see these processes through conceptual lenses (like the one that we have been applying in this study) we can hope to learn from process descriptions and experiences and perhaps become better at understanding resources and seize ways in which they could be used better. Managerial implications of the study can be sought in this direction.

7. THE RESEARCH JOURNEY

We are convinced that learning in the research society as a whole would be improved if more of the processes of how we have learned were revealed to the reader (Dubois & Gadde, 2002, p. 560).

This last section is an attempt to follow up this request. We start with a presentation of the research process and discuss the impact of being in different research networks during the research process. Then we describe the intertwined relation between data and theory and how we developed cases. Thereafter sources and types of data are presented and discussed. We finish with assessing trustworthiness of the study.

7.1. The Research Process: Impact of Different Research Networks

We have not carried out this study in isolation. This might not be surprising. According to Kuhn (2002) scientific activity normally takes place within a community of researchers sharing some "received views" (p. 17). The special thing about the actual study is that it started in one research community and moved into another. In itself this suggests that the boundaries between different research communities need not be absolute. Hence the term research network may be as suitable as research community.

The study started through discussions in the research network at our place of employment, Centre for Rural Research in Trondheim. Later we became part of another network — the "industrial network approach." A "branch" of this network has since the early 1990s developed at the Department of Industrial Economics and Technology Management at the Norwegian University of Science and Technology, also in Trondheim (hereafter referred to as the Department). However, during most of the doctoral studies we were physically located at the Centre for Rural Research.

The idea of a case within the food "sector" originated in a program launched at the Centre in 1993 aimed at studying the food system from "earth" to "table." This theme also fitted with the purpose of a new regional development program (Interreg) from which we got our funding in 1998. Then our doctoral studies could begin. For the first three and a half years we had our place of work in our "old" research network at the Centre for Rural Research. From here we tried to enter the new research network in various ways. Our first step was an individual doctoral course in industrial network theory supervised by one of our two supervisors. We wrote an essay about what would later become case story 1 in this study and analysed the case by the ARA (Activities, Resources and Actors) model. We discussed the essay with the industrial networks group at the Department (hereafter called the Group) and discovered some confusion regarding e.g. the role of the research question in the research process and what would count as appropriate data.

In 1999 our second supervisor advised us to follow a doctoral course in industrial networks theory led by him at the Norwegian School of Management

BI. Here we got to know a larger group of persons, some – like us – trying to enter the industrial network approach and some already within and quite experienced in it. We wrote a new essay in interaction with the participants where we imitated the "tribal language" of our new research network. We wrote a new case story and were set to analyse it from the three main perspectives of the ARA-model. The essay was criticized but we were also encouraged to go on with our research.

From 1998 to 2002 we also had 28 meetings with one or both our supervisors at the Department. Often other persons from the group and visiting researchers participated. The meetings were all based on texts that we had been writing. In addition we presented and received comments on papers at several research conferences and workshops, among other things the annual IMP conference.

In retrospect we see that all these discussions and comments on texts were to a large extent about language; the use of concepts, the description of empirical material; the use of wrong concepts or not having appropriate concepts to "express the world" with. According to the philosopher Quine (cf. Aschehoug & Gyldendal, 1995–1998; Føllesdal et al., 1990) learning language *is* learning theory. The theory is in the language, not outside of it. Hence, learning the specific "industrial network approach" meant learning the particular "industrial networks language." In retrospect we see that the way in which we learnt the industrial networks theory was by studying other industrial network researcher's texts, commenting on these, writing our own texts, and presenting and getting comments on these.

In 2001, after three and a half years of doctoral studies, we were invited by one of our supervisors to stay at the Department of Industrial Economics and Technology Management. We "took office" there for one year and most of the study was written in this period. The study now obtained a much sharper perspective building on the industrial network approach. The language of rural sociology and other approaches (like economics and transaction cost theory) was "thrown out" of our texts. One important reason for this was that we then had weekly, often daily, dialogue with people practising research within the industrial network approach. This year was professionally very productive and personally very satisfying. At the end of the year we had produced an outline of the study which later was discussed at an end seminar. Such a seminar is usually held about half a year before one expects the final thesis to be delivered. At this seminar we obtained extensive comments from an experienced researcher within the industrial network approach. We incorporated most of her suggestions in the study.

Building on Kuhn (2002) we can say that effective research cannot come into being without the existence of a network of researchers sharing some set of views on questions like: What basic elements build up the universe that we are studying?

How do these elements interact with each other and with us as researchers? What questions are legitimate to ask about these elements, and what techniques should we use to find answers to the questions? The industrial network approach is such a set of received views. However, the set of views may not be "fully" explicit, but exist as tacit knowledge in the network. Hence, reading and writing texts are not sufficient; oral discussions and physical proximity to other researchers within the network are also crucial.

7.2. Developing Cases

We developed our empirical data (see later this section) into case stories. The literature that we studied in our first doctoral course in industrial network theory revealed that typical studies within this approach built on such empirical material. For example, Smith and Laage-Hellman (1992) start by presenting a short case study describing a supplier's relationships with other significant organizations during the years of the development of a new market. They remark that:

> The above case is a typical example of the 'raw material' used by interaction and network researchers (p. 39).

During the process neither our supervisors nor we ever questioned that "case" should constitute the empirical material of the study. The first attempt to make such a case was done when we wrote the essay (later published as Forbord, 1998) in our first course in industrial network theory. The empirical data for the case was rather simple; a couple of written documents and one short dialogue with one of the two persons running Skånaliseter farm dairy. At the time we wrote it we felt the case to be rather insignificant. In retrospect we see that writing this small text was the first step towards case story 1.

After three more years of research experience within the industrial network approach a couple of issues related to development of empirical material stands out. One is the theory relatedness of empirical data. The other is the process of developing cases ("casing").

7.2.1. Relation Between Empirical Material and Theory
The "collection" – or, maybe better, co-creation (Kvale, 1997) – and processing of empirical data were influenced by theory through the ARA-model and the 4R-model. But the empirical data also affected the theory during the research process. In other words, there was reciprocal influence between theory and empirical data during the research process. Dubois & Gadde (2002) have termed this process "systematic combining" and propose that:

> this approach creates fruitful cross-fertilization where new combinations are developed through
> a mixture of established theoretical models and new concepts derived from the confrontation
> with reality (p. 559).

They emphasize that systematic combining is about refining existing theories. The original (theoretical) framework is successively modified:

> partly as a result of unanticipated empirical findings, but also of theoretical insights gained
> during the process (p. 559).

How has this cross-fertilization been "spelled out" in our study?

We became interested in the first case (Skånaliseter) because we were interested in new business activities and value creation in agriculture, and this farm "firm" had newly extended its activities to include processing of their main product (goat milk). Moreover, this "way of doing business" broke with a more than century long pattern within the dairy industry in Norway. In our 1998 essay we made use of the ARA-model to understand this transition (from producing and using milk in two separate firms to carrying out these two activities within one firm). We used Dubois' (1994) model of activity patterns in industrial networks to gain understanding of the difference between the "before-the-new-activity-situation" and "in-the-new-activity-situation."

Thus, we see that our first case written within the perspective of the ARA-model aroused first an interest in the concepts of activity and activity pattern. From this derived an interest in resources. The interest in the network level, then, came from reading Håkansson and Snehota (1995) and discussing their ideas with "the Group" at the Department. By doing this case analysis we also obtained a "first warning" of how detailed and complex analysis on a network level can be. Hence, in dialogue with our supervisors, we decided to reduce our original plan of writing 10–12 cases to 2, 3 cases.

One year later, on the second course in industrial network theory, we were presented with a new theoretical model, the 4R(esources)-model. We regarded this as a specific model within the more general ARA-model; a specification of the resource dimension in this model. The plan was then to use interview data to develop a new case describing the transition from "production only" to "production and use" of goat milk within the same firm. However, the case turned into a story – the historical background of the transition, not the transition itself.

Our interest within the ARA-model had thus turned from activities to resources and our focus had changed from network structures to network processes. Our interest before the whole study started was also change and innovation, but the "encounter" with the 4R-model and the text surrounding it inspired us to dig much deeper into our empirical world regarding change. In other words, here had occurred cross-fertilizing between empirical material and theory. We realized that our study ought to deal with the resource dimension; more precisely development of a product within a business network.

In other words, development of the theoretical perspective now turned to "refinement" of one element in the ARA-model, resources; in fact one dimension of this element, development. As a consequence of this reciprocal influence between theory and "reality" the research problem became more specific – development of a (subordinate) product in a business network. This was late in 2000. One of our supervisors now advised us to drop our original plan for a second "farm dairy" case and instead obtain empirical material about technical research of the product that over time had become the central "object" of our study.

We obtained this material in 2001 and developed case story number 2. And as a consequence of the shift in theoretical perspective (from "static" activities to "dynamic" resources) we rewrote, based on much the same "raw" material, case 1 so that it primarily illustrated how the goat milk was developed across firm boundaries during the 1980s and 1990s.

The last cross-fertilizing between empirical material and theory was when we developed our theoretical argument about resources. During the process of writing, thinking and interaction with supervisors we realized for the first time the impact of the relational view of resources (provision – use) and its close connection to the concept interaction. Unfortunately rewriting the cases once more was too late. However, we realized that it was a serious lack in the original case 1 that we had no data about the use side in "the beginning." Hence we did a last interview and rewrote this part of the empirical material (cf. first half of Section 2).

7.2.2. Processing Cases

In a way Smith and Laage-Hellman (1992) are wrong when they state that a case is "raw material." Our experience in this study has been that a case is the result of *processing* of "raw" empirical material (like interview transcripts and documents) and not raw material in itself. A case "contains" – at least implicitly – theory. Thus, a written case represents *a first step* towards analysis. Both our case stories were the result of at least two rounds of writing. Explaining exactly why the case texts ended up as they did is difficult. To a large extent "casing" rests on tacit knowledge. But we believe a desire for some point and coherence "drove" the writing. The second round of writing was important not at least because it made the case more "pointed" and coherent. This again was undoubtedly facilitated by us obtaining new theoretical insights during the research process.

This illustrates two points. The first point is that the empirical material in the study is not "objective" data simply collected by us; it is highly influenced by us. On the other hand the material is not "pure poetry"; all the activities, resources and actors described actually exist. The material has been approved by the informants (cf. the last subsection in this section). Any other observer could in principle have observed the same entities. The other point is that the cases were not "given" at the outset, ready to be collected and entered into the text by us. For example, the cases had to be delimited, and in our case *we* set the final boundaries around the cases; there existed no "natural" boundaries around (and between) them. Moreover, these boundaries had to be meaningful and again we must point to the importance of "writing up" the cases more than once. Hence, the process of writing not only made the cases more "emphasized" and coherent; it also somehow resulted in meaningful boundaries of the cases. In this we follow the view put forward by Hammersley and Atkinson (1995, p. 239) that qualitative research to a large extent is produced through active writing and not only via simply and technically collecting and analysing "data."

7.3. Sources and Types of Empirical Material

The means by which we have obtained the empirical "raw" material for the study have been interviews, documents and, to some degree, observation. We think that interviews have been the most important. We have made personal interviews as well as telephone interviews. Various documents have also been a major source of data. Observation was done in connection with three personal interviews underlying case story 1.

7.3.1. Interviews

The interviews were carried out between October 1998 and June 2002. All in all we made 44 interviews. Of these 30 interviews have been used in this study. Table 1 provides an overview. 10 were personal and 20 were telephone interviews. The personal interviews lasted for about 60–120 minutes each. The telephone interviews took from 10 to 30 minutes; the shortest of them aimed at checking or completing information already obtained via other interviews or documents. All the telephone interviews were carried out without prior appointment with the informant. This was the case also for one personal interview (with a food shopkeeper). All the other interviews were arranged beforehand. Only in one case (a U.S. food firm) was our request for an interview turned down (Table 1).

At the start of the interview we stated the purpose of the study, our role in it, place of work and professional connection. We made it clear before the interview started that none of the informants would be recognized by name in any publication from the project and that all recordings and notes would be handled confidentially. As a consequence all interviewees were given fictitious names.

Table 1. Overview of Interviews.

Organization	Job Description of Informant	Number of Interviews			Time of Interview (Year)	Observation
		Personal Recorded		Telephone		
		Yes	No			
Case 1						
Skånaliseter Gårdsysteri	Farmer/dairyman	1		1	1999/2000	
	Farmer/dairymaid		1	2	2000/2000/2000	X
Goat farm in Stroplsjødalen, Namskogan	Farmer	1			2000	
Another goat farm in Stroplsjødalen, Namskogan	Farmer	1			2000	
Landteknikk AL	Consultant			1	2000	
MATFORSK	Project manager			1	2000	
Nord-Trøndelag Næringsservice	Marketing adviser			1	2000	
Mo Gård, Albert Collet	Food consultant			1	1999	
Mikvold Gård	Food-producer/shop-keeper			1	2000	
Ost & Bakst	Shop-keeper		1		2000	X
Fenaknoken	Shop-keeper		1		2001	X
Namdalsmeieriet	Managing Director (1981–1992)			1	2002	
Case 2						
Tine Nord-Norge, avd. Tromsø	Project Manager			1	2001	
Tine Meieriet Sør, avd. Haukelid	Dairy Manager			2	2001/2001	
Tine Norske Meierier, Senter for Forskning & Utvikling, Kalbakken	R&D Consultant	1			2001	
Tine Norske Meierier, Senter for Forskning & Utvikling, Voll	R&D Consultant			2	2001/2001	
	R&D Consultant			1	2001	

Table 1. (*Continued*)

Organization	Job Description of Informant	Number of Interviews			Time of Interview (Year)	Observation
		Personal Recorded		Telephone		
		Yes	No			
Tine Norske Meierier Ås (Husdyrkontrollen)	Consultant			1	2001	
Tine Norske Meierier, Internasjonal avdeling	Consultant			1	2001	
Tine Norske Meierier, Industriavdelingen	Consultant			1	2001	
Norges Landbrukshøgskole, Institutt for næringsmiddelfag	Assistant professor	1			2001	
Norges Landbrukshøgskole, Institutt for husdyrfag	Professor	1			2001/2001	
	Doctoral student	1		1	2001	
Norsk Sau- og Geitalslag	Breeding Consultant			1	2001	

An interview guide was made before each interview. As we found each informant to be very competent in his or her job we let him or her talk freely interrupted only by follow-up questions from our side. As soon as we felt that a topic was exhausted we introduced a new topic based on the guide or information revealed through the interview. Thus, the interviews had the character of dialogue. We experienced that the personal interviews provided considerably richer and "livelier" material than the telephone interviews. Telephone interviews were typically made after personal interviews had been carried out and often when an outline of a case story had been written. Thus, the main purpose of telephone interviews was to fill gaps in a story.

7.3.2. Documents

Documents of various types, printed as well as electronic, have been the other major data source (cf. Table 2). All in all 44 documents have been used. All these documents are referred in the reference list. We found 13 of these on the World Wide Web. The rest we accessed in printed form. Many of the documents were obtained after the first draft of the cases had been written in order to confirm, specify or extend information given in the interviews. In some cases we studied documents as preparation for interviews. This was especially the case before the interviews with technical researchers (case 2). Studying scientific articles and other written information beforehand combined with our professional training in agricultural science made us feel able to take part in a dialogue with these interviewees (Table 2).

Table 2. Overview of Documents Used as Sources of Empirical Data.

	Number of Documents	Used for Empirical "Background"	Used for Case 1	Used for Case 2
Web – home pages	11		x	x
Web – articles	2		x	x
Scientific articles and theses	8	x		x
Popular articles in newspapers and journals	7		x	x
Specialized books incl. Encyclopaedia	7	x		x
Research reports	4	x		
Annual reports	3	x		x
Company- and branch-histories	2	x	x	

As indicated in the table certain documents were used for case 1, while others were exploited in case 2. For example, web documents were our only source of information about the U.S. company Laura Chenel. In case 2 scientific articles, theses and specialized books were important, while we found company and branch histories fruitful in the making of case 1. Documents were the most critical source of data for the empirical introduction (first part of Section 2 and the two first subsections of Section 3). That we ended up using so many and rather diverse documents was not planned at the outset of the study. Rather, it was the result of theoretical 'moves' made at certain points during the research process. That we ended up with these 52 *particular* documents, was a consequence of e.g. systematic searches on the web and regular reading of certain newspapers and journals.

7.3.3. Observations

Observation influenced our writing of case 1 to some degree. To the extent that we observed we did it openly in connection with three particular personal interviews. In one case observation was primary. This was in relation to case 1 when we for one day observed, and to some extent participated, when "Kari" and "Ola" carried out one ordinary batch of cheese-making at Skånaliseter and during which we also conversed with them about the resource, products, facilities and suppliers. We also stayed in the farm shop and could see facilities and products "in use" there. Observations were made primarily in order to provide empirical material for illuminating activity patterns, our theoretical interest then. But the observations were also valuable for illustrating resources, our final theoretical interest. During the observations we came physically close to some concrete technical and social resources that informants and documents could only describe indirectly and sym-bolically. In this way the observations fertilized our understanding of concepts like "efficiency," "effectiveness" and "capability" and convinced us that there is sense in treating activities, resources and actors as separate entities in business networks.

7.4. Assessing Trustworthiness of the Study

After having described and reflected upon our research process and sources and types of empirical data we will in this last subsection assess the scientific "quality" of the study. Can it be defended as science? A question, then, is what should count as "good science" in our case, in other words what research standard or scientific canon (cf. Strauss & Corbin, 1990, p. 249) to use as "benchmark?" Our research standard has in important ways followed from the theoretical approach that we have used — the industrial network approach. In that way we did not make an independent choice of method, and the question of scientific canons could as well be discussed in relation to our basic theoretical model (the ARA-model). We have tried to "live up to" the standards of this approach, which among other things builds upon ideals reflected in qualitative method and case method (cf. Yin, 1994). Especially, we think, the "care" for the unique (as opposed to the general) in these methods are interesting (Maaløe, 1996). The unique is here regarded not only as a legitimate but also important object of research. Moreover, Andersen (1994, p. 21) finds that:

> any phenomenon consists of a unique combination of qualities, and that one therefore cannot count, measure or weigh (Andersen & Gamdrup, 1994, p. 60) (Our translation).

This is a description that seems valid for our research phenomenon too; a unique resource in reciprocal influence with a certain business network. Knowledge of such a unique phenomenon can only be obtained through holistic, comprehensive descriptions. Such descriptions can best be produced from interpretations based on two-way communication between researcher and respondent.

Lincoln and Guba (1985) have developed a scheme for assessing qualitative studies. A qualitative study, like ours, should meet four criteria. Firstly, while rigour is appropriate in the research process, the researcher must also allow flexibility; adjust to changes in the entity being studied and capitalize on growing insight as the study emerges – *dependability*. For the second, in qualitative research "neutrality" becomes a question of characteristics of the data and not the objectivity of the researcher – *confirmability*. Thirdly, a qualitative study can be "true" in the sense that it reflects multiple constructions of reality – *credibility*. Lastly, "applicability" of a qualitative study is a question of knowledge of both the sending and receiving context – *transferability*. If these four criteria are met our study should be *trustworthy*, which according to Lincoln and Guba (1985, p. 290) is the "ultimate" ideal of a qualitative study.

7.4.1. Dependability During the Research Process

In the first two subsections of this section we described how we considered methodological aspects of the study at the beginning and how some of these were changed during the research process. Basically these changes regarding method and data had two sources; interaction with other researchers and co-development of theoretical perspective and empirical data. This changed our view of the research "object" during the research journey, and we went for empirical data that we had not thought relevant at the beginning. On the other side we were faithful to the general scope formulated at the outset of the study. In this way we lived up to the dependability criterion; we were flexible in some respects and rigorous in others during the research process.

A question is if and how the dependability could have been improved. Not following every "whim" along the way was a good thing, we think. In other words, we believe that some steadfastness was fruitful for the study. On the other hand, the final product might have been better if we had revised the cases — especially case 1, which is much longer than case 2 — after the process of analysis.

7.4.2. Confirmability of the Study

Confirmability concerns the research product; more precisely if the different parts of the final text – data, conceptual framework and interpretations — hang together. In other words, confirmability has to do with internal coherence (Lincoln & Guba, 1985, p. 318). We think the "litmus test" here is not whether we have chosen an appropriate theoretical approach for the research problem. Rather, the point is whether the interpretation (analysis and discussion in this study) is based on the cases *and* applies the concepts and theory described. When developing the analysis we put much effort into using the conceptual apparatus of the "4 resources model" in order to understand change in the use of the focal resource. Our experience is that using a theoretical model helps in creating coherence both within a case and between it and the analysis of it. The challenge is rather to avoid becoming a *prisoner* of the model. The question is whether the dependability could have been improved. We might e.g. have reduced the amount of different resources illustrated in the analysis and concentrated on fewer, presumably more interesting interfaces for our resource.

7.4.3. Credibility of the Study

According to Lincoln and Guba (1985, p. 296) the credibility of our study depends on two factors. The first is whether we have carried out the inquiry in such a way that the *probability* that the findings will be found credible is enhanced. Here, the authors describe four different techniques. The other, and perhaps most obvious factor is letting informants *approve* our representations of their multiple realities. Let us take the last factor first.

7.4.3.1. Informants' approval of cases. In the empirical material (Sections 2 and 3) we represent different views of one and the same resource. For example, in Section 2 we represent a producer's, a user's and a researcher's view of goat milk respectively. A preliminary text was sent to these and other involved informants for verification before the text was all set. The same procedure was followed also for the two cases and the empirical background in Section 3. All informants accepted the text in broad outline. But most of them also suggested particular changes in the text, for the most part regarding facts and quotations. We found that almost all the suggestions could fruitfully be incorporated in the final text.

7.4.3.2. Enhancing the likelihood of credibility. Lincoln and Guba (1985, p. 328) suggest four ways to enhance the probability of credibility in a qualitative study.

Of these we regard two, "negative case analysis" and "referential adequacy," as less relevant to our study. The other two prescriptions, however, have been rather crucial in our case. These are "peer debriefing" and various "activities in the field."

Peer debriefing. Interaction with other researchers has in various ways been crucial in making this study. The number of meetings with supervisors and papers presented on conferences demonstrate this. Peer debriefing has helped keep us honest, led us into new theoretical directions and given concrete advice regarding next step in the research process. A case in point was when we had made the first outline of case 1. One of our supervisors then advised us to obtain data about technical research of our resource. At that moment we were not able to see ourselves that the study would benefit from including this kind of empirical material. On another occasion we had made the first draft of an analysis and received a clear message from one of our colleagues that certain parts in it did not build on data but rather on our hypothesis regarding data. Confirmability was at stake, and we rewrote the actual part of the analysis.

Activities in the field. Lincoln and Guba (1985, p. 301) identify three types of field activities for enhancing the probability of a credible study.

One of the main ways of reaching credibility in our case has been *prolonged engagement*. It has given us the chance to become familiar with a resource and its ties in a specific business network. We "met" what would become case 1 for the first time in 1996. We read and wrote about it in 1998, made several interviews from August 1999 to June 2002 in addition to studying many documents. Hence we were engaged for quite a time with this case. Our engagement in case 2 was shorter; from December 2000 to September 2002 (when we revised the case on the basis of informants' comments). However, the data collection and processing (into cases) took place in shorter and more concentrated periods of time; the winter of 2000 and the winter of 2001. In this way, by steadily building up the object with more detail, we have probably been able to come closer to some "truth" about the object (cf. Diesing, 1971, cited in Maaløe, 1996, p. 17).

Another field activity contributing to credibility was *triangulation*. This is use of e.g. multiple sources of data, and/or methods in relation to the same fact or phenomenon (Yin, 1994, p. 92). Especially if one is able to allow this variety in data, methods etc. produce a converging line of inquiry, the credibility of a study can be enhanced. In our case the phenomenon to be described and understood was changed use of a resource. As shown in the previous subsection we have used both multiple sources of data and methods to obtain information about this phenomenon. Moreover, different and partly independent persons in the network provided this information. We think that this variety in data sources and methodological "tools" to a great extent enhanced the credibility of the empirical parts of this study.

Regarding the third type of field activity, *persistent observation*, we are somewhat unsure regarding our study. Persistent observation is to "dig deep" into (some few) characteristics or elements that seem most relevant to the phenomenon (Lincoln & Guba, 1985, p. 305). For quite a time we worked to reveal the resource aspect of the problem. Thus, to the extent that we have been digging deep into something related to our problem, it is resource development. On the other hand, we chose a network perspective, which meant concentrating on the context – the breadth – surrounding the phenomenon. We may have felt too loyal towards this breadth perspective in the sense that we did not dare to narrow the number of elements to be analysed in relation to the resource.

7.4.4. Is the Study Transferable?

Transferability refers to the possibilities of applying a case study in another context. This requires first of all effort from the person seeking to make an application elsewhere (Lincoln & Guba, 1985, p. 298). The responsibility on our side is to provide sufficiently "thick" descriptions to make assessing similarities and differences regarding context of the actual research object possible for a user. In our opinion we have provided a fairly thick description of the context surrounding a resource. We have even described how this context has changed over some time. Both cases became thick as they drew upon many and versatile types and sources of data. Our experience is nevertheless that "proximate" methods, like personal interviews and direct observation, in particular provide basis for thick descriptions. Telephone interviews and documents may be necessary, but does not in the same way give life and "nerve" to a story insofar this is an aim. However, there is another aspect that may be as important for transferability – theory. Yin (1994) puts forward that case studies can be transferred on an analytical (that is theoretical, in contrast to empirical) level. In other words, an important reason for having a theoretical framework at all may be that it provides the necessary common language for discussing and comparing cases across contexts, for example use of goat milk in different business networks.

REFERENCES

Literature

Alderson, W. (1965). *Dynamic marketing behaviour. A functionalist theory of marketing.* Homewood, IL: Richard D. Irwing.

Andersen, H. (1994). Hvad er videnskabsteori og metodelære? (In Danish). In: H. Andersen (Ed.), *Videnskabsteori & Metodelære*. Samfundslitteratur. Fredriksberg C.

Andersen, V., & Gamdrup, P. (1994). Forskningsmetoder (In Danish). In: H. Andersen (Ed.), *Videnskabsteori & Metodelære*. Samfundslitteratur. Fredriksberg C.

Argyris, C., & Schön, D. A. (1996). *Organizational learning II. Theory, Method, and Practice*. Addison-Wesley.

Aschehoug & Gyldendal (1995–1998). *Store Norske Leksikon. 3. Utgave*. Oslo: Kunnskapsforlaget.

Aune, A. (1996). *Kvalitetsstyrte bedrifter* (In Norwegian). Oslo: Ad Notam Gyldendal.

Berger, P., & Luckmann, T. (1966, 1967). *The social construction of reality*. London: Penguin Books.

Brox, O. (1991). *Praktisk samfunnsvitenskap* (In Norwegian). Oslo: Universitetsforlaget.

Chandler, A. D., Jr. (1990). *Scale and scope. The dynamics of industrial capitalism*. Cambridge MA/London: Belknap Press of Harvard University Press.

Cook, K. S., & Emerson, R. M. (1978). Power, equity, and commitment in exchange networks. *American Sociological Review*, *43*(October), 721–739.

Cyert, R. M., & March, J. G. (1963). *A behavioral theory of the firm*. Englewood Cliffs, NJ: Prentice-Hall.

Diesing, P. (1971). *Patterns of discovery in the social sciences*. Illinois: Adine.

Dubois, A. (1994). *Organising industrial activities – An analytical framework*. Doctoral Thesis. Department of Industrial Marketing, Chalmers University of Technology. Göteborg.

Dubois, A. (1998). *Organising industrial activities across firm boundaries*. London, NY: Routledge.

Dubois, A., & Gadde, L.-E. (2002). Systematic combining: An abductive approach to case research. *Journal of Business Research*, *55*, 553–560.

Emerson, R. M. (1981). Social exchange theory. In: M. Rosenberg & R. H. Turner (Eds), *Social Psychology: Sociological Perspectives*. New York: Basic Books.

Føllesdal, D., Walløe, L., & og Elster, J. (1990). *Argumentasjonsteori, språk og vitenskapsfilosofi* (In Norwegian). Oslo: Universitetsforlaget.

Forbord, M. (1998). *Småforetak i matvaresektoren i lys av industriell nettverksteori: vurderinger av teori og metode* (In Norwegian). Unpublished essay. Senter for bygdeforskning, Trondheim.

Gadde, L.-E., & Håkansson, H. (2001). *Supply network strategies*. Wiley.

Giddens, A. (1993). *Sociology* (2nd ed.). Cambridge, UK: Polity Press.

Goffman, E. (1974). *Frame analysis. An essay on the organization of experience*. Boston: Northeastern University Press.

Granovetter, M. S. (1985). Economic action and social structure: The problem of embeddedness. *American Journal of Sociology*, *91*(3), 481–510.

Granovetter, M. S. (1992). Problems of Explanation in economic sociology. In: N. Nohria & R. G. Eccles (Eds), *Networks and Organizations. Structure, Form, and Action*. Boston, MA: Harvard Business School Press.

Gressetvold, E. (2003). *Developing relationships within industrial networks – effects of product development*. Doctoral thesis, draft. Department of Industrial Economics and Technology Management, Norwegian University of Science and Technology, Trondheim.

Håkansson, H. (Ed.) (1982). *International marketing and purchasing of industrial goods*. An Interaction Approach. Wiley.

Håkansson, H. (1989). *Corporate technological behaviour. Co-operation and networks*. London and New York: Routledge.

Håkansson, H., & Ford, D. (2002). How should companies interact in business networks? *Journal of Business Research*, *55*, 133–139.

Håkansson, H., Havila, V., & Pedersen, A.-C. (1999). Learning in networks. *Industrial Marketing Management*, *28*, 443–452.

Håkansson, H., & Snehota, I. (Eds) (1995). *Developing relationships in business networks*. London: International Thomson Business Press.

Håkansson, H., & Snehota, I. (2000). The IMP perspective. Assets and liabilities of business relationships. In: J. N. Sheth & A. Parvatiar (Eds), *Handbook of Relationship Marketing*. Sage.

Håkansson, H., & Waluszewski, A. (1999). Path-dependence: Restricting or facilitating technical development? Paper to the 15th IMP Conference, Dublin (2–4 September).

Håkansson, H., & Waluszewski, A. (2000). *Managing development in interaction or how white paper was made green* (Forthcoming).

Håkansson, H., & Waluszewski, A. (2001). Co-evolution in technological development. The role of friction. Paper to the 17th IMP Conference, Oslo (9–11 September).

Håkansson, H., & Waluszewski, A. (2002). *Technological development. IKEA, the environment and technology*. London and New York: Routledge.

Halinen, A., & Salmi, A. (2001). Managing the informal side of business interaction: Personal contacts in the critical phases of business relationships. Paper to the 17th Annual IMP Conference, Oslo (Sept. 9–11).

Hammersley, M., & Atkinson, P. (1995). *Ethnography. Principles in practice* (2nd ed.). Routledge.

Hayek, F. A. (1949). The use of knowledge in society. In: *Individualism and Economic Order*. London & Kegan Paul: Routledge (originally published in *American Economic Review*, *35*(4) (1945), 519–530).

Itami, H. (1991). *Mobilizing invisible assets*. Cambridge, MA: Harvard University Press.

Johanson, J., & Mattsson, L.-G. (1987). Interorganisational relations in Industrial Systems. A network approach compared with the transaction-cost approach. *International Studies of Management and Organisation*, *17*(1), 34–48.

Kirzner, I. M. (1992). *The meaning of market process. Essays in the development of modern Austrian economics*. London & New York: Routledge.

Kotler, P., Bowen, J., & Makens, J. (1999). *Marketing for hospitality and tourism*. Prentice-Hall.

Kuhn, T. S. (2002). *Vitenskapelige revolusjoners struktur* [The structure of scientific revolutions 1962/1970]. Oslo: Spartacus Forlag.

Kvale, S. (1997). *Det kvalitative forskningsintervju* (In Norwegian). ad Notam Gyldendal.

Latour, B. (1987). *Science in action. How to follow scientists and engineers through society*. Cambridge, MA: Harvard University Press.

Lincoln, Y. S., & Guba, E. G. (1985). *Naturalistic inquiry*. Sage.

Loasby, B. J. (1998). The organisation of capabilities. *Journal of Economic Behaviour and Organization*, *35*, 139–160.

Lundgren, A. (1995). *Technological innovation and network evolution*. London and New York: Routledge.

Maaløe, E. (1996). *Case-studier – af og om mennesker i organisationer* (In Danish). Akademisk Forlag.

March, J. G. (1991). Exploration and exploitation in organizational learning. *Organizational Science*, *2*(1), 71–87.

Molm, L. D., & Cook, K. S. (1995). Social exchange and exchange networks. In: K. S. Cook, G. A. Fine & J. S. House (Eds), *Sociological Perspectives on Social Psychology*. Allyn and Bacon.

Morgan, G. (1997). *Images of organization*. Sage.

Nelson, R. R., & Winter, S. G. (1982). *An evolutionary theory of economic change*. Belknap Press of Harvard University Press.

Nonaka, I., & Takeuchi, H. (1995). *The knowledge-creating company*. New York/Oxford: Oxford University Press.

Østerberg, D. (1986). *Fortolkende sosiologi* (In Norwegian). Oslo: Universitetsforlaget.

Page, A. L., & Rosenbaum, H. F. (1988). Redesigning product lines with conjoint analysis: How sunbeam does it. In: M. L. Tushman & W. L. Moore (Eds), *Readings in the Management of Innovation*. Harper Business.

Pedersen, A.-C. (1996). *Utvikling av leverandørrelasjoner i industrielle nettverk – en studie av koblinger mellom relasjoner* (In Norwegian). Doctoral thesis. Norwegian University of Science and Technology, Trondheim.

Penguin (1992). *Dictionary of English synonyms and antonyms* (Rev. ed.).

Penrose, E. ([1959] 1995). *The theory of the growth of the firm* (3rd ed.). Oxford University Press.

Persson, G., & Virum, H. (red.) (1989). *Materialadministrasjon for konkurransekraft* (In Norwegian). Oslo: Ad Notam forlag AS.

Piore, M. J. (1992). Fragments of a cognitive theory of technological change and organizational structure. In: N. Nohria & R. G. Eccles (Eds), *Networks and Organizations. Structure, Form, and Action*. Boston, MA: Harvard Business School Press.

Quinn, J. B. (1988). Innovation and corporate strategy: Managed chaos. In: M. L. Tushman & W. L. Moore (Eds), *Readings in the Management of Innovation*. Harper Business.

Richardson, G. B. (1972). The Organisation Of Industry. *The Economic Journal, 82*(September), 883–896.

Samuelson, P. A., & Nordhaus, W. D. (1998). *Economics* (16th ed.). McGraw-Hill.

Simmel, G. (1950). Sociability – An example of pure, or formal, sociology. In: K. H. Wolff (Ed.), *The Sociology of Georg Simmel*. New York: Free Press.

Smith, P. C., & Laage-Hellman, J. (1992). Small group analysis in industrial networks. In: Axelsson & Easton (Eds), *Industrial Networks – A New View of Reality*. Routledge.

Stern, L. W. (1996). Relationships, networks, and the three Cs. In: D. Iacobucci (Ed.), *Networks in Marketing*. Sage.

Strauss, A., & Corbin, J. (1990). *Basics of qualitative research. Grounded theory procedures and techniques*. Sage.

Thomson, K. M. (1998). *Emotional capital: Maximising the intangible assets at the heart of brand and business success*. Oxford: Capstone.

Torvatn, T. (1996). *Productivity in industrial networks – A case study of the purchasing function*. Doctoral Thesis. Norwegian University of Science and Technology, Trondheim.

Utterback, J. M. (1994). *Mastering the dynamics of innovation: How companies can seize opportunities in the face of technological change*. Boston, MA: Harvard Business School Press.

Van de Ven, A. H. (1988). Central problems in the management of innovation. In: M. L. Tushman & W. L. Moore (Eds), *Readings in the Management of Innovation*. Harper Business.

Waluszewski, A., & Håkansson, H. (2001). To investigate interaction between companies concerning use of heterogeneous resources – a methodological dogma. Paper to 11th Nordic Workshop on Interorganisational research (August). Chalmers University of Technology, Gothenburg.

Waters, M. (1994). *Modern sociological theory*. Sage.

Webster's (1989). *Encyclopedic Unabridged Dictionary of the English Language*. Random House.

Wedin, T. (2001). *Networks and demand. The use of electricity in an industrial process*. Doctoral Thesis. Department of Business Studies, Uppsala University.

Weick, K. E. (1979). *The social psychology of organizing*. McGraw-Hill.

Williamson, O. E. (1975). *Markets and hierarchies: Analyses and antitrust implications*. New York: Free Press.

Yin, R. K. (1994). *Case study research* (2nd ed.). Sage.

Written Sources of Empirical Data

Alme, E. (1999). Rapport om geithold, geitprodukter, og omsetning i Frankrike (In Norwegian). Vedlegg 2 in: G.-T. Kvam (Ed.), *Muligheter for Geithold i Norge.* Rapport 15/99. Senter for bygdeforskning, Trondheim.

Aschehoug & Gyldendal (1995–1998). *Store Norske Leksikon. 3. Utgave.* Oslo: Kunnskapsforlaget.

Bondebladet Julenummer 1999.

Bondebladet 7. September 2000.

Bondebladet 16. August 2001.

Bondebladet 5. Juli 2001.

Eeg-Larsen, N. (1976). *Ernæringslære* (In Norwegian). 4. Opplag. Oslo: Landsforeningen for kosthold og helse.

Eknæs, M., Eik, L. O., Skeie, S., & Havrevoll, Ø. (1998). Fôring og mjølkekvalitet hos geit (In Norwegian). *Meieriposten* Nr. 9.

Eknæs, M., & Hove, K. (2002). Endringer i geitas fettreserver gjennom laktasjonen sett i forhold til sensorisk kvalitet på mjølka (In Norwegian). *Husdyrforsøksmøtet* 2002, Norwegian Agricultural University.

Erland, S. (1996). *Meieribruket i Namdalen* (In Norwegian). Namsos: Tine Midt-Norge.

FAO (1999). *Codex general standard for the use of dairy terms.* Codex stan 206–1999.

Farm World (1998). [http://www.farmworld.com/trade/aa004961.html].

Felleskjøpet Øst Vest (2001). *Spesialfôr til melkegeit* (In Norwegian). [http://www2.felleskjopet.no/Fink/FKOV/index.cfm].

Gardsosten nr. 1 1998.

Gardsosten nr. 1 1999.

Grøtte, C. B. (2001). *Laktoferrin i norsk geitemelk* (In Norwegian). Post graduate thesis. Department of Food Science, Norwegian Agricultural University.

Haenlein, G. F. W., & Ace, D. L. (Eds) (1984). *Extension goat handbook.* Washington, DC: United States Department of Agriculture.

Haenlein, G. F. W., & Caccese, R. (1984). Goat milk versus cow milk. In: G. F. W. Haenlein & D. L. Ace (Eds), *Extension Goat Handbook.* Washington, DC: United States Department of Agriculture.

Home Soap Works, Millington, New Jersey [http://www.cidigital.net/homesoapworks].

http://countrylife.net/yoghurt/postings/2383.html.

http://www.collett.no.

http://www.exportant.nl/gmv/expcat98/rademakers/catrademaker.html.

http://www.landteknikk.no.

http://www.norskgardsmat.org

http://www.nsg.no

Kielland, R. M. (1976). *Takk for melken. Om utvikling og bruk av meieriprodukter* (In Norwegian). Oslo: Landbruksforlaget.

Kvam, G.-T. (1999). *Muligheter for geithold i Norge* (In Norwegian). Rapport 15/99. Trondheim: Senter for bygdeforskning.

Landbruksdepartementet (1996). [http://kimen.dep.no/ld/publ/lkontakt/96-6/Piff.htm].

Landbrukstidende nr. 4 (2001).

Maree, H. P. (1978). Goat milk and its use as a hypo-allergenic infant food. *Dairy Goat Journal* (May).

Masui, K., & Yamada, T. (2000). *French cheeses.* London: Dorling Kindersley.

Nordbø, R. (2001). Geitmjølk – genetiske variantar av αs1-kasein og effektar på eigenskapar i mjølka (In Norwegian). Post graduate thesis. Norwegian Agricultural University: Department of Food Science.

Omsetningsrådet (1999). *Årsmelding 1999* (In Norwegian).

Pettersen, R. (1984). *A/L Innherredsmeieriet 1973–1983* (In Norwegian). Innherredsmeieriet, Verdal.

Skeie, S. (1998). *Geitemjølk som råstoff* (In Norwegian). Meieriposten Nr. 10 and 11.

Stræte, E. P. (2001). *Produktmangfold i verdikjeden for melk* (In Norwegian). Rapport 5/01. Trondheim: Norsk Senter for Bygdeforskning.

Stræte, E. P., Stavrum, T., Kvam, G.-T., & Almås, R. (2000). *Omstilling i meierisamvirket* (In Norwegian). Rapport 12/00. Trondheim: Senter for Bygdeforskning.

Tine [http://www.tine.no/kunder/tine/TineStruktur.nsf].

Tine *Årsmelding* (Annual Report) 1998.

Tine *Årsmelding* (Annual Report) 2000 [http://www.tine.no].

Tine Meieriet Sør (2001) [http://tms.tine.no/drift/haukelid.htm].

Tine's nyhetsarkiv 22.06.2000 [http://www.tine.no].

Vegarud, G. E., Devold, T. G., Opheim, R., Loeding, E., Svenning, C., Abrahamsen, R. K., Lien, S., & Langsrud, T. (1999). Genetic variants of Norwegian goats milk composition, micellar size and renneting properties. *International Dairy Journal, 9,* 367–368.

Werlin, L. (n.d.). *The new American cheese*. Wisconsin: American Cheese Society.

THE ROLE OF PERSONAL CONTACTS OF FOREIGN SUBSIDIARY MANAGERS IN THE COORDINATION OF INDUSTRIAL MULTINATIONALS

Ricardo Madureira

ABSTRACT

This paper illuminates the distinction between individual and organizational actors in business-to-business markets as well as the coexistence of formal and informal mechanisms of coordination in multinational corporations. The main questions addressed include the following. (1) What factors influence the occurrence of personal contacts of foreign subsidiary managers in industrial multinational corporations? (2) How such personal contacts enable coordination in industrial markets and within multinational firms? The theoretical context of the paper is based on: (1) the interaction approach to industrial markets, (2) the network approach to industrial markets, and (3) the process approach to multinational management. The unit of analysis is the foreign subsidiary manager as the focal actor of a contact network. The paper is empirically focused on Portuguese sales subsidiaries of Finnish multinational corporations, which are managed by either a parent country national (Finnish), a host country national (Portuguese) or a third country national. The paper suggests eight scenarios of individual dependence and uncertainty, which are determined by individual, organizational, and/or

Managing Product Innovation
Advances in Business Marketing and Purchasing, Volume 13, 337–521
Copyright © 2005 by Elsevier Ltd.
All rights of reproduction in any form reserved
ISSN: 1069-0964/doi:10.1016/S1069-0964(04)13003-2

market factors. Such scenarios are, in turn, thought to require personal contacts with specific functions. The paper suggests eight interpersonal roles of foreign subsidiary managers, by which the functions of their personal contacts enable inter-firm coordination in industrial markets. In addition, the paper suggests eight propositions on how the functions of their personal contacts enable centralization, formalization, socialization and horizontal communication in multinational corporations.

1. INTRODUCTION

This section introduces, in separate sub-sections, the theoretical background, objectives, scope and key concepts of the paper. The remaining sub-section presents the overall structure of the paper.

1.1. Background

It is now more than twenty years since the so-called Industrial Marketing and Purchasing (IMP) group published the results of an empirical study (e.g. Cunningham, 1980), which demonstrates the existence of lasting relationships between customers and suppliers in industrial markets (Håkansson, 1982). Such buyer-seller relationships were characterized in the so-called interaction model (IMP group, 1982) as encompassing not only economic exchanges, but also social aspects. Personal contacts have, ever since, been regarded as a crucial factor in the development of lasting inter-firm relationships in industrial markets (Easton, 1992; Forsgren et al., 1995; Halinen & Salmi, 2001; IMP group, 1982). In particular, they are thought to reduce the perceived distance (Ford, 1980) or uncertainty (Ford et al., 1998; Forsgren et al., 1995) between the parties, especially in periods of problematic or temporarily inexistent transactions (IMP group, 1982).

In addition to such transactions or exchange episodes, business relationships are thought to encompass unilateral or reciprocal adaptations by the parties (IMP group, 1982). Such relationship-specific investments may concern product specifications, product design, manufacturing processes, planning, delivery procedures, stockholding, administrative procedures or financial procedures (Håkansson, 1982). A particular type of adaptation is the allocation of managerial time for inter-firm social exchange (Ford, 1980), once that personal contacts often constitute a scarce human resource in industrial markets (Cunningham & Homse, 1986). Taken together, exchange and adaptation episodes (Håkansson & Snehota, 1995; IMP group, 1982) constitute the two elements of short-term interaction and long-term relationships in industrial markets.

Based on the concept of inter-firm relationship (Håkansson & Snehota, 1995; IMP group, 1982) the notion of industrial network has been developed (Axelsson & Easton, 1992; Hägg & Johanson, 1983; Håkansson, 1987). The so-called "market-as-network" approach (Easton, 1992; Johanson & Mattsson, 1987; Mattsson, 1997) suggests that industrial markets can be described as networks of connected business relationships, in which actors, resources, and activities are interdependent (Håkansson & Johanson, 1984; Håkansson & Snehota, 1995). Such interdependence is justified with the assumption of heterogeneity in industrial markets (Easton, 1992; Forsgren et al., 1995; Hägg & Johanson, 1983), which leads to a certain division of labor among the firms (Thorelli, 1986). The coordination of such a division of labor is, in turn, thought to occur through inter-firm interaction rather than market prices (Easton, 1992; Håkansson & Johanson, 1993; Johanson & Mattsson, 1987). Inter-firm interaction is thus thought to support efficiency as well as the development and control of operations in industrial markets (Håkansson & Johanson, 1993).

In recent managerial studies of Multinational Corporations (MNCs), the concept of network (Araujo & Easton, 1996) has equally been adopted in order to capture internal relationships among sister units and the headquarters as well as external relationships to counterparts in the local market (Forsgren & Johanson, 1992; Ghoshal & Bartlett, 1990; Hedlund, 1986). The so-called "network paradigm of the MNC" (Birkinshaw, 2000) encompasses numerous accounts, which describe such an organization, among others, as heterarchy (Hedlund, 1986, 1993; Hedlund & Ridderstråle, 1998; Hedlund & Rolander, 1990), multifocal corporation (Doz, 1986; Prahalad & Doz, 1987), transnational corporation (Bartlett, 1986; Bartlett & Ghoshal, 1987a, b, 1989, 1995a, b), multi-centre firm (Forsgren, 1990b; Forsgren et al., 1992), horizontal organization (White & Poynter, 1990), metanational (Doz et al., 1996, 2001), differentiated network (Nohria & Ghoshal, 1997), and individualized enterprise (Ghoshal & Bartlett, 1998).

Such models are thought to share a view of the MNC as becoming "less-hierarchical" (Marschan, 1996, 1997), once that they challenge traditional views of both hierarchy (e.g. Hedlund, 1993) and formal structure (e.g. Bartlett & Ghoshal, 1990). In particular, the network paradigm of the MNC attempts to circumvent the inability of studies inspired by the so-called strategy-structure paradigm (Chandler, 1962) to generate a structural design, which could simultaneously support strategies for global efficiency, local responsiveness, and worldwide learning (Bartlett & Ghoshal, 1989). In other words, it is suggested that a single broad design provides the MNC with more flexibility to cope with environmental and strategic change than tightly specified designs under contingency theory (Egelhoff, 1999).

In general, less-hierarchical MNCs are thought to share five basic dimensions (Marschan, 1997), which include: (a) delegation of decision-making authority; (b) delayering of organization levels; (c) geographical dispersal of key functions; (d) de-bureaucratisation of formal procedures; and (e) differentiation of work, responsibility and authority among subsidiaries. Such a differentiation of subsidiaries (Ghoshal & Nohria, 1989) in geographically dispersed and heterogeneous settings (Prahalad & Doz, 1987) is thought to constitute a rather complex task for managers at the headquarters (Doz & Prahalad, 1991) and in subsidiaries (Gupta et al., 1999). Models of less-hierarchical MNC thus tend to suggest the adoption of informal mechanisms of coordination (Harzing, 1999; Martinez & Jarillo, 1989) at the level of individuals and groups (Bartlett & Ghoshal, 1990; Egelhoff, 1999), which are thought to supplement rather than replace formal mechanisms of coordination and control[1] (O'Donnell, 2000). In the present study coordination and control are used interchangeably under the assumption that the former leads to the latter (e.g. Harzing, 1999; Marschan, 1996; Martinez & Jarillo, 1989).

Informal mechanisms of coordination include inter-unit communication (e.g. Baliga & Jaeger, 1984; Edström & Galbraith, 1977) through personal contacts of individuals in general (Marschan, 1996) and of managers in particular (Ghoshal et al., 1994). Such personal contacts are thought to support the efficiency and innovativeness of the MNC by allowing the development of trust and shared values across the organization (Nohria & Ghoshal, 1997). In addition, personal contacts are regarded as a crucial mechanism, by which the MNC increases its information-processing capacity (Egelhoff, 1991, 1993) to cope with environmental and organizational complexity (Bartlett & Ghoshal, 1989, 1998; Hedlund, 1986, 1993). In this respect, subsidiary managers may be regarded as boundary spanning individuals (Tushman, 1977), given their wide range of contacts within and across the subsidiary's boundaries (Nohria & Ghoshal, 1997). In other words, they are expected to bridge otherwise disconnected entities within and across the MNC (Burt, 1992, 1997; Granovetter, 1973).

The point of departure for the present paper is, therefore, the assumption that industrial foreign subsidiaries are simultaneously part of a network of units belonging to the MNC and of a network of organizations in the host country (Birkinshaw, 2000; Forsgren & Johanson, 1992; Ghoshal & Bartlett, 1990). In addition, it is assumed that, through personal contacts, Foreign Subsidiary Managers (FSMs) contribute to inter-firm coordination both within the MNC (Harzing, 1999; Martinez & Jarillo, 1989) and in the local industrial market (Easton, 1992; Håkansson & Johanson, 1993; Johanson & Mattsson, 1987).

1.2. Research Gap

As mentioned in the previous section, studies inspired by the original findings of the IMP group (e.g. Håkansson, 1982; Turnbull & Valla, 1986) recurrently acknowledge that personal contacts are at the heart of inter-firm interaction in industrial markets (Brennan & Turnbull, 1999; Cunningham & Turnbull, 1982; Halinen & Salmi, 2001). On the one hand, it is claimed that exchange episodes include inter-firm social exchange (IMP group, 1982; Easton, 1992; Forsgren et al., 1995), which, in turn, may require personal contacts from general managers (Cunningham & Homse, 1986). On the other hand, adaptation episodes may include human adaptations such as the investment of managerial time in inter-firm personal contacts (Ford, 1980; Forsgren et al., 1995).

The definition of actor within the "market-as-networks" approach (Easton, 1992; Johanson & Mattsson, 1987; Mattsson, 1997) has remained, however, a rather elusive concept for theoretical and empirical reasons. On the one hand, IMP research tends to define actors as a theoretical construct (Håkansson & Johanson, 1993), which may refer to an individual, a department, a business unit, a firm, or even a group of firms (Håkansson & Johanson, 1984, 1992). On the other hand, in practice, several individuals may be involved in inter-firm interaction (Ford et al., 1986; Håkansson & Snehota, 1995), leading to multiperson interactions (Ford et al., 1998). Further research is needed on the extent to which managers think and behave as "networkers" in domestic (Axelsson, 1992) as well as in foreign industrial markets (Axelsson & Agndal, 2000).

In models of less-hierarchical MNC, efficiency (e.g. Nohria & Ghoshal, 1997) and innovativeness (e.g. Doz et al., 2001) is thought to require the adoption of not only formal, but also informal mechanisms of coordination (Harzing, 1999; Martinez & Jarillo, 1989; O'Donnell, 2000). Personal contacts are thus regarded as a key mechanism for the integration of dispersed, differentiated and interdependent subsidiaries (Ghoshal & Bartlett, 1990), but the extent to which they may be oriented in the interests of the MNC as a whole remains open to debate (Andersson & Holm, 2002; Marschan et al., 1996). In this respect, it has been suggested the need for further research on interpersonal relationships of individuals (Marschan, 1996) and subsidiary managers (Gupta et al., 1999; O'Donnell, 2000) both within and across the MNC's boundaries.

A research gap can, therefore, be identified: the need to examine the extent to which FSMs act: (a) as actors who contribute to inter-firm coordination in industrial markets; and (b) as boundary spanning individuals who contribute to inter-firm coordination within MNCs.

1.3. Purpose of the Paper

The general purpose of the paper is to describe and conceptualize the implications of FSMs' personal contacts for inter-firm coordination in industrial markets and within MNCs. The focus on FSMs rather than other individuals or managers is based on two basic assumptions about the nature of managerial work (Mintzberg, 1973). The first assumption is that managers may be distinguished from other individuals in terms of legal authority (Astley & Sachdeva, 1985), by which they retain a certain degree of control over organizational decision-making (Barnard, 1938). This implies that, due to higher decisional authority than other subsidiary employees, FSMs are expected to be involved in inter-firm exchange (Cunnningham & Homse, 1986; Forsgren et al., 1995) and adaptation (Brennan & Turnbull, 1999; Ford, 1980) in industrial markets.

The second assumption is that decision-making requires not only formal authority, but also personal contacts, by which information may be gathered to support such decisions (Mintzberg, 1973, 1975, 1990). This implies that, due to a broader range of intra-group contacts than other subsidiary employees (Nohria & Ghoshal, 1997) and of local contacts than other managers at the MNC (Bartlett & Ghoshal, 1992, 1997), FSMs are expected to be involved in the local implementation of multinational strategies (Gates, 1994; Ghoshal & Bartlett, 1998).

The purpose of the present paper may thus be synthesized in two basic research questions:

(i) What factors influence the occurrence of FSMs' personal contacts in industrial MNCs?
(ii) How FSMs' personal contacts enable coordination in industrial markets and within MNCs?

The first research question addresses the context of FSMs' personal contacts in terms of individual, organizational, and market factors. The second research question addresses the implications of FSMs' personal contacts for inter-firm coordination. The second research question may also be regarded as two separate questions, which address inter-firm coordination: (a) in industrial markets (Easton, 1992; Håkansson & Johanson, 1993; Johanson & Mattsson, 1987); and (b) within MNCs (Harzing, 1999; Martinez & Jarillo, 1989).

1.4. Scope and Limitations

As mentioned in the previous section, the present paper examines personal contacts of FSMs only, thus precluding those of other individuals in the local industrial market (e.g. Cunningham & Homse, 1986; Hallén, 1992) and within the MNC (e.g. Bartlett & Ghoshal, 1992, 1997; Marschan, 1996). Such delimitation in terms of individuals considered has been traded-off with the scope of personal contacts examined, which includes the subsidiary, other units and headquarters within the MNC as well as any entity in the local industrial market.

At the subsidiary level, the paper is focused on wholly owned subsidiaries with a sales function in the local industrial market. In addition, the paper is restricted to local implementer subsidiaries (Birkinshaw & Morrison, 1995) in the sense that they are net receivers of knowledge within the MNC (Gupta & Govindarajan, 1991, 1994) and small and medium-sized enterprises (SMEs) in a non-strategic market (Bartlett & Ghoshal, 1986). At the corporate level, the paper is focused on Finnish MNCs instead of other European MNCs (e.g. Harzing, 1999) or American and Japanese MNCs (e.g. Bartlett & Ghoshal, 1989, 1998).

By focusing on industrial markets, the present paper is also restricted to subsidiaries and MNCs, which make business with other firms rather than end users. In other words, the paper is focused on business-to-business markets rather than business-to-consumer markets. On the other hand, the paper is focused on small and open economies (Kirpalani & Luostarinen, 1999) in terms of both the country in which the MNC is based (e.g. Ghauri, 1992) and the market in which the subsidiary operates.

Theoretically, the present paper may be delimited not only for what it is (see Section 2.1), but also for what it is not. On the one hand, the paper is not about organizational communication (e.g. Stohl, 1995) in the sense that it examines individual rather than collective contact networks and for other purposes than information exchange. On the other hand, it is not a paper of social capital (e.g. Baker, 1990) in the sense that it examines the occurrence of personal contacts as the result of several individual, organizational and market factors rather than structural properties of social networks (e.g. Adler & Kwon, 2002).

1.5. Key Concepts

The multidisciplinary scope of the present paper requires a brief introduction to its key concepts. As it can be inferred from the basic research questions (see Section 3), the key concepts of the paper are personal contacts and coordination. Personal contact is here defined as "an instance of meeting or communicating with another person." Coordination is defined as "any means for achieving integration among different entities both within and outside an organization."

In addition to the key concepts, it is worth introducing related but secondary concepts, which include contact, dependence, uncertainty and buyer-seller relationship. In the present paper a contact is defined as "an individual with whom one takes personal contacts." Dependence is defined as "an individual's lack of authority to control and be obeyed to" (Astley & Sachdeva, 1985; Forsgren, 1990a). Uncertainty is defined as "an individual's inability to predict something accurately, including internal and external changes to the organization, their outcomes and possible responses" (Milliken, 1987). Finally, a buyer-seller relationship is defined as "a chronological sequence of interaction episodes" (Håkansson & Snehota, 1995).

In spite of constituting sub-sets of dependence, the concepts of informational- and decisional dependence also deserve a separate definition, given their relevance for the theoretical contribution of the present paper. Informational dependence is defined as "an individual's lack of authority to control a process of information exchange, in which (s)he participates," whereas decisional dependence is defined as "an individual's lack of authority to control a process of decision-making, in which (s)he participates."

1.6. Structure of the Paper

The first section introduces the phenomenon under study in terms of theoretical background, objectives, scope and key concepts. The second section reviews the theoretical context of the paper, which is based on three research traditions: the interaction and network approaches to industrial markets as well as the process approach to MNC management. The corollary of such a review of literature is an a priori theoretical framework for analysis, which positions the present paper within previous research.

The third section positions the paper in philosophical and methodological terms, which bridge its theoretical and empirical context. The philosophical stance of the paper is discussed in terms of key ontological, epistemological and axiological assumptions. In addition, the adopted research strategy is discussed as an instance of qualitative research and of multiple-case study approach. This is followed by a discussion of the research design in terms of data collection and analysis, which precedes an assessment of the general quality of the study on which the paper is based.

The fourth section discusses the evidence from the selected cases in terms of context, content and process of FSMs' personal contacts. The discussion of context includes some considerations on the distinctive features of FSMs' interpersonal context, which is then illustrated with quotations from interviews. In this section, the content and process of FSMs' personal contacts is equally discussed in the light of extant literature and illustrated with quotations from interviews.

The fifth and final section presents the conclusions of the paper. Its academic implications are discussed in terms of a refined theoretical framework, interpersonal roles of FSMs, and propositions on MNC coordination and control. Such academic implications are also discussed in terms of the overall theoretical and empirical contribution of the paper to the research traditions, which form its theoretical context. The paper's managerial implications are also addressed, namely at the individual-, organizational- and country-level. The final section provides some suggestions for further research.

2. LITERATURE REVIEW

This second section of the paper reviews previous research on the phenomenon under study. The theoretical context of the paper and respective research traditions are thus presented in the following sub-sections. The final sub-section presents the a priori theoretical framework for analysis based on such literature review.

2.1. Theoretical Context of the Paper

The theoretical context of the present paper consists of three research traditions: (1) the interaction approach to industrial markets (e.g. Håkansson, 1982); (2) the network approach to industrial markets (e.g. Axelsson & Easton, 1992); and (3) the process approach to MNC management (e.g. Doz & Prahalad, 1991; Forsgren & Johanson, 1992). Figure 1 depicts the relevance of such research traditions for the paper.

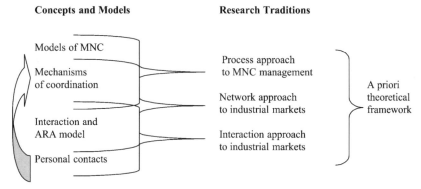

Fig. 1.   Rationale Behind the Selection of Research Traditions.

As it can be inferred from Fig. 1, the main goal of the present paper is to explore and understand the relationship between personal contacts and inter-firm coordination in industrial markets and within MNCs. For that purpose, the paper takes the interaction approach to industrial markets as its theoretical point of departure both in terms of conceptual elaboration and empirical focus. Such a research tradition conceptualizes personal contacts in industrial markets as part of inter-firm social exchange (Håkansson, 1982; Möller & Wilson, 1995) itself associated with buyer-seller relationships (Håkansson & Snehota, 1995) in the so-called interaction model (IMP group, 1982).

Inter-firm relationships are, in turn, the sine qua non for a network approach to industrial markets (Easton, 1992), which moves beyond the analysis of dyads to sets of connected buyer-seller relationships. Such networks are distinguished from mere social networks (Cook & Emerson, 1978) by the importance that activities and resources have for the overall network. Such simultaneous interdependence of actors, resources, and activities (Håkansson & Johanson, 1984) is conceptualized in the so-called A-R-A model (Håkansson & Snehota, 1995) in terms of actors bonds, resources ties, and activities links. In addition, it is suggested that a network of inter-firm relationships may be regarded as a mechanism of coordination (Easton, 1992) or governance structure (Håkansson & Johanson, 1993) by which goal-oriented actors coordinate interdependent activities and resources. The network approach conceptualizes personal contacts as social bonds (Easton, 1992) among actors, which may be firms or individuals (Håkansson & Johanson, 1984, 1992).

The process approach to MNC management equally adopts the concept of network (Araujo & Easton, 1996) as the basis for a single broad design (Egelhoff, 1999), which is expected to provide the MNC with sufficient flexibility for simultaneous global efficiency, local responsiveness and worldwide learning (e.g. Bartlett & Ghoshal, 1989). Several designs or models of MNC have been suggested, which depict the MNC as a network of inter-firm relationships within and across its legal boundaries (Birkinshaw, 2000; Ghoshal & Bartlett, 1990). Such models of MNC often suggest the adoption of informal mechanisms of coordination (Harzing, 1999; Martinez & Jarillo, 1989) in order to facilitate the management of differentiated subsidiaries (Ghoshal & Nohria, 1989) in geographically dispersed and heterogeneous settings (Prahalad & Doz, 1987). The process approach conceptualizes personal contacts as interpersonal networking (Nohria & Ghoshal, 1997), which is regarded as a key mechanism of coordination in MNCs (e.g. Bartlett & Ghoshal, 1990).

The three research traditions may be generally compared in network terms, once that they all assume the existence of inter-firm relationships. Such relationships are regarded as links within the network approach and the process approach. In spite of not adopting the concept of network as a tool for theoretical development,

Table 1. Comparison of the Three Research Traditions.

	Interaction Approach to Industrial Markets	Network Approach to Industrial Markets	Process Approach to MNC Management
Exemplary works	Håkansson (1982), Turnbull and Valla (1986)	Axelsson and Easton (1992), Håkansson and Snehota (1995), Ford et al. (1998)	Hedlund (1986), Bartlett and Ghoshal (1989), Forsgren (1990b), Nohria and Ghoshal (1997), Ghoshal and Bartlett (1998)
Research goals	Describe and explain industrial dyadic inter-organizational relationships	Describe and explain industrial/organizational market structures	Explain decentralized, less-hierarchical organizations
Nature of actors	Organizations, individuals	Organizations	Individuals, groups
Nature of links	Resources, information	Resources, information	Communication, power, information, resources
Focus	Process	Structure and process	Structure and process
Unit of analysis	Buyer-seller relationships	Networks of relationships	Individual manager
Methodology	Case studies	Case studies	Case studies
Disciplinary background	Organization theory, Economic theory	Marketing and Purchasing	Organization theory, International business
Cross references	Contract law	Social networks	Social networks

Source: Adapted from Araujo and Easton (1996).

the interaction approach takes such links as its unit of analysis (Easton, 1992; Ford, 1997). A systematic comparison of the three research traditions can thus be provided (see Table 1) in terms of: main goals, nature of actors and links analyzed, focus in terms of process and/or structure, unit of analysis, research strategy, disciplinary background, and cross references.

More generally, the three research traditions may be compared in terms of theories of the firm. On the one hand, the assumptions of the interaction and network approaches may be traced back to the theory of the growth of the firm (Penrose, 1959), the behavioral theory of the firm (Cyert & March, 1963) and the resource-dependence view of the firm (Pfeffer & Salancik, 1978). On the other hand, the process approach, in spite of constituting a rather fragmented body of knowledge, equally shares assumptions from the behavioral theory of the firm (Cyert & March, 1963) and the resource-dependence view of the firm (Pfeffer & Salancik, 1978), which often combines with contingency theory (Lawrence & Lorsch, 1967).

The integration of previous findings within the three research traditions thus seems appropriate, requiring, however, a critical evaluation of more specific assumptions such as bounded rationality (Cyert & March, 1963) and micro-politics (Pettigrew, 1973). The insights of previous studies within the interaction and network approaches to industrial markets as well as the process approach to MNC management are reviewed in the remainder of this section.

2.2. The Interaction Approach to Industrial Markets

The so-called interaction approach to industrial markets results from research conducted within the IMP group (e.g. Cunningham, 1980). Its theoretical context consists of two major theoretical models from outside the marketing literature: Inter-organizational Theory and New Institutional Economic Theory (IMP group, 1982). On the one hand, the interaction approach shares the view that organizations are part of a group of interacting entities dependent on their environment (Pfeffer & Salancik, 1978), which characterizes some studies within Inter-organizational Theory. On the other hand, the interaction approach shares with "New Institutionalists" (Williamson, 1975) in micro-economic theory, some assumptions concerning the functioning of industrial markets. The key assumptions and findings of the interaction approach are discussed in the following sub-sections.

2.2.1. The Interaction Model

The interaction approach has been developed in reaction to traditional marketing literature, which was thought to disregard specific features of industrial markets. In particular, marketing studies tended to: (a) analyze marketing and purchasing processes separately; (b) concentrate on the purchasing process for a single purchase, and (c) assume that buyers were individually insignificant, passive and part of a relatively homogeneous market (Ford, 1997). In contrast, the interaction approach suggests that in industrial markets: (a) both buyers and sellers are active; and (b) they often relate in a long-term basis; (c) by which their interdependence is institutionalized; (d) even in the absence of continuous purchases (IMP group, 1982).

The interaction approach identifies four groups of variables that describe and influence the interaction between buying and selling firms in industrial markets.

Such groups of variables are conceptualized as the four basic elements of the so-called interaction model (IMP group, 1982):

– The interaction process
– The participants in the interaction process
– The environment within which interaction takes place
– The atmosphere affecting and affected by the interaction

Such basic elements are, in turn, subdivided into other elements, reflecting the descriptive nature of the research tradition. The interaction process is subdivided into episodes and relationships. Episodes involve four types of exchange: product or service, information, financial, and social exchange. Such exchange episodes may, in turn, become institutionalized over time, leading to expectations of further exchanges. In addition to such types of exchange, the parties may make adaptations in the elements exchanged or in the process of exchange (IMP group, 1982). These may include adaptations of the product specification, product design, manufacturing processes, planning, delivery procedures, stockholding, administrative procedures or financial procedures (Håkansson, 1982).

In addition to the elements of the interaction – exchange and adaptation – the process of interaction is thought to depend on the characteristics of the participants. These may be organizations or the individuals who represent them. Organizations are characterized in terms of technology, size, structure and strategy as well as experience whereas individuals are characterized by their functional area, hierarchical level, personality, experience and motivation. On the other hand, the environment within which the interaction takes place is characterized in terms of market structure, dynamism, internationalization, position in the manufacturing channel, and social system. Finally, the atmosphere affecting and being affected by the interaction is described in terms of power-dependence relationships, conflict or cooperation, closeness or distance, and mutual expectations.

The four basic elements of the interaction model are interrelated in the sense that the interaction process, which involves short-term exchange episodes and long-term adaptations, is influenced by the characteristics of the participants and the environment in which it takes place. Over time, the interaction process may institutionalize into a relationship, which is characterized by a certain atmosphere between the parties (IMP group, 1982).

The interaction approach is the first research tradition on which the present paper is based, given its explicit recognition of individuals as participants in industrial transactions (e.g. Turnbull, 1979). In the terminology of contract law, such an approach emphasizes relational exchange instead of discrete transactions (Macneil, 1980), once that the latter implies very limited communication and narrow content. Relational exchange presupposes that each transaction is the result of a certain history and/or anticipated future based on implicit and explicit expectations, trust and planning. In Dwyer's et al. (1987, p. 12) words: "dependence is prolonged, performance is less obvious, uncertainty leads to deeper communication, the rudiments of cooperative planning and anticipation of conflict arise, and expectations of trustworthiness may be cued by personal characteristics."

Such a relational exchange view underlines the focus of the interaction model "on a two party relationship" (IMP group, 1982, p. 14), which is also reflected in the present paper's definition of personal contact (see Section 1.5). As mentioned above, the interacting parties include individuals representing buyer and seller organizations under the assumption that "though the transaction cost approach is highly relevant for the study of economic relationships, business relationships also include social aspects" (Hallén et al., 1991, p. 32). Exchange episodes between the parties thus include social exchange, which has been described as "a crucial element in the development of lasting business relationships" (Forsgren et al., 1995, p. 24). In particular, social exchange is thought to reduce uncertainty, especially in the case of geographical or cultural distance as well as short-term difficulties or lack of transactions. In other words, it is through a long-term social process that organizational trust is built, in addition to successful execution of product/service-, information- and financial types of exchange (IMP group, 1982).

In addition to exchange, the interaction approach notes the existence of inter-firm adaptations, which are primarily seen as the result of deliberate decisions. In the original words of the IMP group (1982, p. 18): "although adaptations by either party can occur in an unconscious manner as a relationship develops, it is important to emphasize the conscious strategy which is involved in many of these adaptations." Brennan and Turnbull (1999, pp. 481–482) add that: "it is at the individual level that interactions between buyers and suppliers take place, and it is at this level that the well-being of buyer-supplier relationships is affected. However, those individuals responsible for developing and managing buyer-seller relationships need to work within a strategic framework, so that the "right" relationships are developed in the "right" ways." Ford (1980, p. 40) acknowledges such an "allocation of managerial resources" as human adaptations, which generate familiarity and trust between the interacting parties.

The original interaction model (IMP group, 1982) has inspired subsequent research on its basic elements and respective interrelation. Ford et al. (1986) suggest four aspects, which concern both the implementation and the effects of interaction. The implementation of interaction implies a certain degree of particularity towards individual counterparts as well as of inconsistency or ambiguity given the coexistence of conflict and cooperation. In particular, the authors refer to interpersonal inconsistency once that "companies consist of individuals and subgroups, and it is these who are involved in the company's interactions" (Ford et al., 1986, p. 63). In other words, each individual involved in interaction between firms will have his or her own expectations and degree of commitment to inter-firm interaction. In similar fashion, Thorelli (1986, p. 453) considers that "power, expertise, perceived trustworthiness and social bonds are often person-specific rather than firm-specific."

More recently, Möller and Wilson (1995) reiterate the importance of social exchange, namely as a vehicle for communication and learning of meanings and values. The authors also note that episodes refer to actions of organizations and their representatives thus encompassing personal contacts in such episodes. In similar fashion, Håkansson and Snehota (1995, p. 204) consider that: "as individuals act within relationships between two companies they bring in their limits (the bounded rationality) but also their capabilities to learn and reflect. They develop bonds to overcome their limits." Such social bonds may thus be conceptualized as either social exchange between the firms or personal contacts between the individuals who represent them. In Easton's words (1992, p. 12) "social relations between firms are the resultant of the relations of the individuals involved."

2.2.2. Personal Contacts in Industrial Markets

As mentioned in the previous section, social exchange between firms in industrial markets takes place through personal contacts, which are also acknowledged in the following quotation (IMP group, 1982, p. 17):

> The communication or exchange of information in the episodes successfully builds up inter-organizational contact patterns and role relationships. These contact patterns can consist of individuals and groups of people filling different roles, operating in different functional departments and transmitting different messages of a technical, commercial, or reputational nature. These patterns can interlock the two parties to a greater or lesser extent and they are therefore an important variable to consider in analyzing buyer-seller relationships.

Cunningham and Turnbull (1982), discuss such inter-organizational contact patterns in terms of their importance, relation to other variables in the interaction model (see Section 2.2.1), roles, intensity and style. The importance of personal contacts results from their ability to reduce buyers' perceived risk, to improve the credibility of the supplier, and to provide market knowledge. The authors also claim that buyers perceive personal contacts with technical and general management personnel as important as with sales representatives.

Cunnigham and Turnbull (1982, p. 311) emphasize, however, that: "the intensity of personal contact patterns is not capable of explanation by a single phenomenon or variable." In this respect, the authors suggest that the occurrence of personal contacts in industrial markets reflects the resources allocated by the interacting parties as well as the complexity of the product being purchased. They also claim that factors such as the age of the relationship, the volume of business being transacted, language and cultural barriers as well as industry norms of behavior equally influence the occurrence of personal contacts. In addition, the authors consider that, at the individual level, the influence and power of the interacting parties will partly depend on their hierarchical level.

The same authors identify several roles, which personal contacts may simultaneously perform within industrial inter-organizational relationships. Such functions of personal contacts include an information exchange, assessment, negotiation and adaptation, crisis insurance, social, and ego-enhancement role (Cunningham & Turnbull, 1982). Personal contacts perform an information exchange role when carrying "soft" information, which is particularly useful in promoting mutual trust, respect, and personal friendships. In addition, personal contacts support buyers' assessment of suppliers' competencies based on subjective judgments, which supplement objective facts. The negotiation and adaptation role of personal contacts is more relevant in the case of high value, highly complex products, in which negotiations may involve a wide range of topics and several hierarchical levels over considerable periods of time. In addition, personal contacts may be activated to insure against crisis when existing channels of influence are insufficient to handle a major problem.

The four roles of personal contacts just mentioned – information exchange, assessment, negotiation and adaptation, and crisis insurance – are task-related in the sense that they serve organizational objectives. Conversely, the two other roles of personal contacts – social and ego-enhancement – are non-task related in the sense that they primarily serve individual interests. The social role implies that, in addition to their working relationship, some individuals may take personal contacts for private reasons. The ego-enhancement role refers to personal contacts established with senior people of a counterpart organization in order to enhance the individual's status in his or her own organization.

Cunningham and Turnbull (1982) also suggest that the intensity of inter-organizational personal contacts may be assessed in terms of the number and hierarchical level of people involved, the diversity of functional activities encompassed, and the frequency with which such personal contacts take place. In addition, the authors examine the style of personal contacts, namely in terms of closeness, formality and institutionalization. In terms of closeness, it is suggested that suppliers' representatives seek closer personal interaction with buyer's personnel than vice-versa. On the other hand, the degree of formality of buyer-seller personal contacts is thought to increase with the involvement of individuals of upper hierarchical levels, although it may be deliberately kept low.

Moreover, it is expected that the intensity of inter-firm personal contacts will institutionalize over time.

In a subsequent contribution, Cunningham and Homse (1986) further distinguish inter-organizational personal contacts between those which involve: (a) a salesman and a buyer; (b) functional staff; (c) functional managers; and (d) general managers. They recognize the importance of such contacts in reducing perceived distance (Ford, 1980) between the interacting parties, particularly in the case of "key accounts with major customers in concentrated and highly competitive international markets" (Cunningham & Homse, 1986, p. 272). Equally inspired by the interaction model (see Section 2.2.1), the authors suggest factors associated with suppliers' allocation of resources for personal contacts with customers in industrial markets. Such factors include the stage of inter-organizational relationships, market structure, customer importance, product complexity, and supplier strategy.

The same authors specify the purpose of personal contacts into commercial and technical information exchange, negotiation and problem solving, in addition to technical training and advice as well as delivery and technical progressing (Cunningham & Homse, 1986). Such purposes of personal contacts can be said to resemble the information exchange, negotiation and adaptation, as well as crisis insurance roles of personal contacts previously identified (Cunningham & Turnbull, 1982).

Cunningham and Homse (1986) also reiterate that the intensity of personal contacts may be evaluated in terms of frequency, breadth across different functions, and hierarchical level of the individuals involved. In this respect, they note that a matching hierarchical level in terms of inter-organizational personal contacts often occurs, although suppliers are more likely to commit their senior management. Finally, they speculatively suggest three types of coordination and control of inter-organizational personal contacts. These include: (a) marketing and purchasing controlled personal contacts if the latter are channeled through seller's marketing and buyer's purchasing department; (b) marketing and purchasing coordinated personal contacts if the latter are mediated by such departments; and (c) stratified personal contacts if the latter are taken directly by the functional staff involved. The stratified type of coordination and control of inter-organizational personal contacts is thought to require one of three conditions: (a) good internal communications; (b) an explicit strategy for handling the organizational counterpart; and (c) a trustable inter-organizational relationship.

Hallén (1992) refers to non-task personal contacts of top executives in industrial markets. The author is focused on infra-structural relations, which may emerge either around the firm's business activities or around specific individuals' professional and private activities. Such personal contacts are regarded as important to handle the firm's dependence on business and non-business parties for marketing purposes and/or long-term influence. The author associates several factors with non-task personal contacts, including the individual's career background, deliberate planning and tenure, in addition to "national culture, business habits and traditions" (Hallén, 1992, p. 88). Hallén also notes the information exchange role of personal contacts as well as the prestige with which they may be associated. Finally, the author argues that attempting to manage networks of infra-structural contacts may backfire in the sense that "they must not appear opportunistic" (Hallén, 1992, p. 91).

Based on insights from the interaction approach, personal contacts in industrial markets have also been investigated in specific geographical contexts such as China (Björkman & Kock, 1995) and California (Andersson et al., 1996). Björkman and Kock (1995) associate personal contacts with the cultural context, the age of relationships, individual background, and employee turnover among employers. Andersson et al. (1996) also focus on cultural differences associating personal contacts with language, individual background, and age of relationships. Both studies acknowledge the information exchange role of personal contacts, which Björkman and Kock (1995) specify into information about possible customers and upcoming purchases.

More recently, Axelsson and Agndal (2000) note the importance of individuals' network of contacts as opportunity networks in the context of industrial internationalization. The authors associate personal contacts with individual background and professional experience. Axelsson and Agndal (2000) also emphasize the multidimensional role of personal contacts as the latter provide: solutions to specific problems, access to other networks, and legitimacy. In addition, the authors conceptualize the intensity of personal contacts in terms of availability (on-going or dormant) and reach (e.g. geographical, industry). Moreover, Axelsson and Agndal (2000) discuss the extent to which managers may either coordinate – through human resource practices – or control – through systematic charting efforts – individuals' network of contacts.

Halinen and Salmi (2001, p. 7) regard "personal contacts as forces of stability and of change" which they associate with individual background, personality, and employee turnover among employers. In addition to the roles of personal contacts within business relationships in general (Cunningham & Turnbull, 1982) the authors suggest roles of personal contacts in the development of such relationships, including negative aspects. In particular, Halinen and Salmi (2001) identify positive and negative dynamic functions of personal contacts, which include: (a) door opener and gatekeeper in relationship initiation; (b) peace maker and trouble maker in relationship crisis; and (c) door closer and terminator in relationship ending. The authors also suggest that the dynamic feature of such roles allows increased managerial control of individuals' network of contacts.

2.2.3. Conclusion

The interaction approach contributes to our understanding of industrial markets with the concept of buyer-seller relationship, which is richly described in a four element analytical framework (IMP group, 1982). The concept of relationship remains, however, difficult to define. In this respect, Håkansson and Snehota (1995, p. 25) argue that "interaction between companies in industrial markets can be fruitfully described in terms of relationships essentially for two reasons: one is that actors themselves tend to see their interactions as relationships, another is that the interaction between companies over time creates the type of quasi-organization that can be labeled a relationship."

As mentioned in Section 1.5, a buyer-seller relationship in industrial markets is here defined as "a chronological sequence of interaction episodes." Such interaction episodes consist of exchange episodes including social exchange (IMP group, 1982) and adaptations usually decided by certain individuals (Brennan & Turnbull, 1999). It has been recognized, however, that "empirically it is difficult to distinguish between the social, information and business exchanges taking place when actors interact" (Björkman & Kock, 1995, p. 521). The present paper addresses such a distinction between the individual and the organizational level of analysis in buyer-seller relationships by focusing on personal contacts of general managers (Cunningham & Homse, 1986). Such managers – FSMs – are conceptualized as individuals representing upper hierarchical levels of an interacting firm who may participate in social exchange episodes as well as in adaptation-related decision-making processes.

Within the interaction approach, the study of personal contacts in inter-firm interaction has, in some cases, relied on a slightly narrower definition of personal contact than the one adopted in the present paper (see Section 1.5). Cunningham and Turnbull (1982), for instance, appear to equate personal contacts with face-to-face meetings thus precluding written communication from their definition. This and other idiosyncrasies have, however, been taken into account in the review of studies within the interaction approach, which provide insights on the importance, context, roles, intensity, and style of personal contacts. Such aspects of personal contacts in industrial markets constitute the first conceptual block of the a priori theoretical framework for analysis (see Section 2.5.1).

2.3. The Network Approach to Industrial Markets

The interaction approach took the relationship among business organizations as its unit of analysis, in order to study simultaneously the processes of selling and purchasing in industrial markets (IMP group, 1982). Such an approach came to realize, however, that understanding an industrial firm requires the examination of not only its relationships, but also of the network they form (Ford, 1997). This wider perspective inspired the emergence of the so-called "markets-as-networks" approach, which can be seen as a development of the interaction approach beyond the analysis of dyads to networks (Axelsson & Easton, 1992; Hägg & Johanson, 1983; Håkansson, 1987).

Such a network approach to industrial markets has been systematically compared with the "transaction-cost approach" (Williamson, 1975, 1979, 1981) by Johanson and Mattsson (1987) as well as with "relationship marketing" (Grönroos, 1994; Sheth & Parvatiyar, 1995) by Mattsson (1997). The "markets-as-networks" approach has also been briefly compared with the resource dependence view of the firm (Pfeffer & Salancik, 1978), social exchange theory (Cook & Emerson 1984), communication and social networks research (Rogers & Kincaid, 1981), as well as industrial organization theory (e.g. Porter, 1980) by Easton (1992). The key assumptions and findings of the network approach are discussed in the following sub-sections.

2.3.1. The A-R-A Model

Within the "market-as-networks" approach, industrial markets are described as networks of connected relationships between firms, in analogy to social networks, which have been defined as sets of connected exchange relationships between social actors (Cook & Emerson, 1978). These two types of networks are primarily distinguished by the importance that activities and resources have for the overall network. In social networks, activities and resources are basically attributes of actors, whereas in industrial networks they may be equally interdependent.

Håkansson and Johanson (1984) suggest a conceptual model of industrial networks, in which the basic classes of variables – actors, activities and resources – are described as interrelated networks. The interrelatedness of the variables results from their circular definitions. Actors are defined as entities (ranging from single individuals to groups of firms) that perform and control activities based on access (directly by ownership or indirectly through relationships) to resources. Actors develop relationships with other actors through exchange processes (Johanson & Mattsson, 1987) and are goal oriented in the sense that they attempt to increase their control over the network (Håkansson & Johanson, 1992). Activities consist of the combination, development, exchange, or creation of resources with other resources. They can be grouped into transformation activities, which are controlled by an actor, and transfer activities, which transfer direct control over a resource from an actor to another. Resources are heterogeneous and can be characterized by the actors controlling them and by their utilization in activities (Håkansson & Johanson, 1992).

Such a view of industrial markets emphasizes the interdependence of actors, activities and resources, as well as a power structure, once that relationships between actors are based on the control of resources. In addition to a structure of power, an industrial network is thought to encompass a knowledge structure, once that the design of activities and the use of resources equally reflect the knowledge and experience of present and earlier actors (Håkansson & Johanson, 1992).

More recently, Håkansson and Snehota (1995, p. 26) discuss the substance of business relationships in terms of the "existence, type and strength of the activity links, resource ties, and actor bonds." In particular, the authors distinguish between the role of a business relationship for: (a) the dyad or conjunction of two actors; (b) each of the two actors separately; and (c) other relationships and actors. In addition, Håkansson and Snehota (1995, p. 35) contend that: "the interplay of bonds, ties and links is at the origin of change and development in relationships," which reflects conscious and goal-seeking actors, organized patterns of activities as well as constellations of resources. The authors thus conceptualize an industrial network as a structure of dynamic actor bonds, resources ties, and activity links – the so-called A-R-A model – in a context of simultaneous stability and change (Gadde & Mattson, 1987).

The structural or stable aspect of industrial networks results from the assumption of firm interdependence. In Easton's (1992, p. 16) words: "interdependence introduces constraints on the actions of individual firms which create structure 'in the large'." Such an emphasis on firm interdependence reflects, in turn, the assumption within the "markets-as-networks" approach that industrial markets are essentially heterogeneous in nature (Hägg & Johanson, 1983). In particular, such markets are characterized by heterogeneous supply of multidimensional resources as well as by heterogeneous demand for goods and services (Alderson, 1965). One such a resource is human capital (Alchian & Demsetz, 1972), which combined with specialized equipment (Richardson, 1972) and environmental complexity and uncertainty (Williamson, 1975, 1979) gives rise to heterogeneous firms and relationships in industrial markets. In addition to human capital, heterogeneity has been associated with adopted techniques in firms due to different: (a) input goods; (b) timing of long-term investments; (c) and technical installations (Forsgren et al., 1995).

Industrial firms are thus seen as idiosyncratic in terms of their "structure, employee preferences, history, resources, investments, skills, etc" (Easton, 1992, p. 17) and involved in relationships, which further promote heterogeneity. In particular, by specializing in certain activities, firms are expected to coordinate complementary activities with other firms (Richardson, 1972). Such a coordination of activities is, in turn, likely to require transaction-specific investments (Williamson, 1981) such as inter-firm training and learning-by-doing, which lead to further specialization. In this respect, Forsgren et al. (1995) distinguish between naturally determined and acquired heterogeneity in industrial markets. Naturally determined heterogeneity includes, among others, physical location, qualities of raw materials, and human nature. Acquired heterogeneity is generated over time and based on naturally determined differences, thus reinforcing the idiosyncratic nature of both firms and their relationships.

2.3.2. Coordination in Industrial Markets

As mentioned in the previous section, heterogeneity in industrial markets implies that activities and resources of actors may be interdependent. In particular, "heterogeneity implies that the company will live in a world characterized by uncertainty" (Forsgren et al., 1995, p. 32) thus possessing a limited overview of the options available in input and sales markets. It follows that, due to such a lack of information, the firm's efficiency will largely depend on costs associated with transfer activities (Håkansson & Johanson, 1992), which Forsgren et al. (1995) refer to as exchange costs.

Exchange costs may be current or result from certain investments. One such an investment is the channel by which the firm seeks to obtain information about other firm's offers, requirements, possibilities and limitations. An information channel represents an investment of not only physical means, but more importantly of "time spent in building up the contact with the opposite party" (Forsgren et al., 1995, p. 33). In other words, it is the information channel that allows the interacting parties to engage in social exchange (IMP group, 1982), and to build up trust, which, in turn, renders costly defensive measures unnecessary.

In addition to costs, the firm's efficiency in industrial markets may be assessed in terms of benefits from transfer activities (Håkansson & Johanson, 1992). In this respect, Håkansson and Snehota (1995, p. 39) argue that: "costs and benefits of engaging in a relationship are related to the consequences that a relationship has on the innovativeness, productivity and competence that stem from the impact it has on the activity structure, the set of resources that can be accessed, but also for the perceived goal structure of the actor." The contribution of relationships to an industrial firm's efficiency may thus be synthesized as: (a) a more effective acquisition of resources and sales of products through learning by doing; (b) a higher degree of control over the environment through mutual relationship-specific investments; and (c) a more effective development and application of new knowledge based on buyer-seller cooperation (Forsgren et al., 1995).

At the network level, lasting relationships are thought to form the basis for a certain division of labor among the firms (Thorelli, 1986), which requires some sort of coordination (Richardson, 1972). In this respect, Easton (1992) distinguishes between three kinds of coordination mechanisms: the invisible hand, the visible hand, and network processes. The invisible hand (Smith, 1776) presupposes perfect markets in which the division of labor follows firms' reaction to price formation, whereas the visible hand emphasizes the discretion of firms as self-directing hierarchies (Williamson, 1975). Network processes are regarded as "a form of coordination which is neither market nor hierarchy or yet an intermediate form" (Easton, 1992, p. 22). In a "markets-as-networks" perspective firms are characterized as relatively independent from market prices and relatively dependent on supplementary activities and heterogeneous resources of other firms. It follows that an alternative form of coordination to the invisible hand and the visible hand is required in industrial markets. Johanson and Mattsson (1987, pp. 34–35) formulate such a view as follows:

> In industrial systems, firms are engaged in production, distribution, and use of goods and services. We describe such systems as networks of relationships among firms. There is a division of work in a network that means that firms are dependent on each other. Therefore, their activities need to be coordinated. Coordination is not achieved through a central plan or an organizational hierarchy, nor does it take place through the price mechanism, as in the traditional market model. Instead, coordination takes place through interaction among firms in the network, in which price is just one of several influencing conditions.

Håkansson and Johanson (1993, p. 218) discuss the coordinating aspect of industrial networks in terms of specific governance structures, which they define as "organizational forms and processes through which activities are directed in a field." The authors take into account external forces, which are subdivided into specific- and general relations among the actors as well as internal forces, which are subdivided into interests and norms by which the actors are guided (see Fig. 2). In other words, external forces are relational conditions in which actors perform or direct their activities, whereas internal forces are motives behind the actions of such actors. The combination of such external- and internal forces leads to four governance structures, which are labeled: network, hierarchy, market, and culture.

In an industrial network, interdependent activities are coordinated through specific relationships among goal-oriented actors (Håkansson & Johanson, 1992;

	Internal force based on:	
External force based on:	**Interests**	**Norms**
Specific relations	Network	Hierarchy
General relations	Market	Culture

Source: Adapted from Håkansson and Johanson 1993.

Fig. 2. Classification of Governance Structures.

Johanson & Mattsson, 1987). The relational conditions are thus specific inter-firm relationships rather than general market relations. On the other hand, the motives of the actors are based on individual interests rather than shared norms.

In a hierarchy, activities are also coordinated through specific relationships among actors, but their actions are driven by norms imposed by a central authority (Williamson, 1975). A hierarchy thus allows efficient coordination of activity interdependences, but precludes the dynamic confrontation of actors' interests, which is assumed by the network approach to industrial markets.

In a market, activities are coordinated through the total interplay of all actors, who pursue their own interests. A market thus implies goal-oriented actors, but, in contrast to the network approach, ignores the potential for efficiency gains through specific rather than general supply/demand relations.

Finally, in a culture or profession, activities are coordinated through general rather than specific relations between actors, whose behavior is determined by shared norms rather than individual interests. A culture or profession thus allows a stable and uniform coordination of actors, but not of specific interdependent activities as assumed by the network approach.

Håkansson and Johanson (1993, p. 45) recognize that such pure types of governance coexist in industrial markets, claiming, however, that an industrial network constitutes the most effective and viable governance structure in the context of "many, changing, strong specific activity interdependencies." Such a context has been characterized in the previous section, as the coexistence of stability and change in industrial markets (Gadde & Mattson, 1987), which requires a structure of dynamic actor bonds, resources ties, and activity links (Håkansson & Snehota, 1995). Concerning actor bonds, Håkansson and Johanson (1993, p. 38) note that: "actors in a network can be an individual, a department in a company, a business unit in a company, a whole company, or even a group of companies." In spite of such a broad definition, the authors assume that actors in industrial markets share: (a) purposeful actions towards general economic gain (Penrose, 1959); (b) bounded knowledge (Cyert & March, 1963); and (c) control of certain resources/activities (Richardson, 1972). In addition, Håkansson and Johanson (1993, p. 46) note the relevance of individual perceptions in industrial inter-firm coordination as follows:

> In the comparison between different governance structures we suggested that structural conditions affect the viability of the governance modes differentially. But, given the way we have characterized industrial networks, structural conditions shall not be viewed as external constraints but as enacted structures, in which the perceptions and experiences of actors are important. Hence, activity interdependencies are enacted and they are based on cognitive models of the interdependencies. Similarly, the network structure is enacted and the actors base their action on their network perceptions. Thus, the network viability in a certain industrial field

is largely dependent on the network perceptions of the actors involved and in their ability to mobilize other actors in realizing network structures rather than on any external structural conditions.

In other words, the emergence of an industrial network as a structure of knowledge and power (Håkansson & Johanson, 1992) and, ultimately, as a mechanism of coordination (Easton, 1992; Håkansson & Johanson, 1993) largely depends on the network theory (Johanson & Mattsson, 1992) or strategic framework (Brennan & Turnbull, 1999) of the individuals involved. In this respect, Axelsson (1992, p. 249) suggests that an "appealing task would be to examine empirically the extent to which managers think and behave like 'networkers'."

2.3.3. Conclusion

The network approach contributes to our understanding of industrial markets with the assumptions of heterogeneity (e.g. Forsgren et al., 1995) and inter-firm interdependence (e.g. Easton, 1992). The notion of interdependence is captured with the concept of industrial network as a set of connected buyer-seller relationships (Cook & Emerson, 1978), which encompasses not only actors, but also activities and resources (Håkansson & Johanson, 1984). Such a structure is characterized by simultaneous stability and change (Gadde & Mattsson, 1987) based on long-lasting actor bonds, resource ties, and activity links (Håkansson & Snehota, 1995), which do not preclude the confrontation of actors' interests.

Interdependence in industrial markets implies a certain division of labor among firms (Thorelli, 1986), which requires, in turn, some sort of coordination (Richardson, 1972). In this respect, it has been suggested that an industrial network constitutes an alternative governance structure to both markets and hierarchies (Williamson, 1975). In particular, it is considered a viable mechanism of coordination in the context of changing and specific activity interdependencies (Håkansson & Johanson, 1993) by allowing a stable yet dynamic distribution of power and knowledge among the actors (Håkansson & Johanson, 1992). In practice, it is argued that: "coordination takes place through interaction among firms" (Håkansson & Mattsson, 1987, p. 35).

In such a context, personal contacts are regarded as social bonds among actors, which may reduce their uncertainty in terms of options available in input and sales markets, and increase their control over the environment through relationship-specific investments (Forsgren et al., 1995). In other words, social bonds in the context of a network encompass both social exchange (Forsgren et al., 1995) and human adaptations (Ford, 1980) in the context of inter-firm relationships (see Section 2.2.1).

Personal contacts may thus be conceptualized as playing a crucial role in industrial coordination, by enabling actors' participation in inter-firm knowledge and power structures (Håkansson & Johanson, 1992). Because resource- and activity interdependencies (Håkansson & Snehota, 1995) are enacted rather than objectively defined (Håkansson & Johanson, 1993), personal contacts are relevant both at the individual- and organizational level. Such aspects of coordination in industrial markets constitute the second conceptual block of the a priori theoretical framework for analysis (see Section 2.5.1).

2.4. The Process Approach to Multinational Management

In the field of international business, MNCs have been extensively studied both in economic and managerial terms. The first economic studies of the Multinational Enterprise (MNE) were conducted in the 1950s and 1960s (e.g. Vernon, 1966) culminating in a widely accepted "theory of the MNE" in the 1980s (e.g. Dunning, 1980). More managerially oriented studies emerged in the 1970s focusing on strategy, structure and administrative processes of MNCs. Such managerial studies of MNCs may, in turn, be subdivided in two streams of research following Whittington's (1993) distinction between a classical and a processual approach to strategy. The classical approach is associated with profit-oriented rational analysis, whereas the processual approach takes bounded rationality (Cyert & March, 1963) and organizational micro-politics (Pettigrew, 1973) as the driving forces behind organizational strategic behavior.

Correspondingly, managerial studies of MNCs may be classified into studies inspired by: (a) the so-called strategy-structure paradigm (Chandler, 1962) and (b) the process perspective of strategy (Bower, 1970). The former studies (e.g. Daniels et al., 1984; Egelhoff, 1982, 1988; Franko, 1976; Hulbert & Brandt, 1980; Stopford & Wells, 1972) may be labeled the classical approach to MNC management by assuming that organizational structure reflects firms' strategy itself associated with a relatively stable environment (Egelhoff, 1999). The latter studies, including the so-called "process school" of the diversified MNC (Doz & Prahalad, 1991), may be labeled the process approach to MNC management as they assume a constant dilemma between integration and responsiveness needs (Doz & Prahalad, 1984), which is to be resolved by confronting managers' conflicting views (e.g. Prahalad & Doz, 1981a, b; Doz, 1986).

The process approach to MNC management does not emphasize, therefore, a causal chain between environment, strategy and structure (Chandler, 1962). It assumes, instead, that organizational structure may as well determine strategic change (e.g. Hall & Saias, 1980) without being necessarily triggered by the environment (Hedlund & Rolander, 1990). In recent years, research within the process approach has increasingly attempted to model the MNC as a network

(Forsgren & Johanson, 1992; Ghoshal & Bartlett, 1990; Hedlund, 1986). In this respect, Birkinshaw (2000, p. 108) even refers to a network theory of the MNC "in which each unit has both its internal network relationships (to sister units and to HQ) and its external network relationships (to the local marketplace and beyond)." The author notes, however, that: "in its current form it probably deserves to be called a paradigm or framework rather than a theory" (Birkinshaw, 2000, p. 98). The following sections review the key assumptions and findings of the process approach.

2.4.1. Models of Less-hierarchical MNC

Within the process approach to MNC management, the trade-off between global integration and local responsiveness (Prahalad & Doz, 1987) is thought to be permanent, implying a quest for balance between formal structure, communication systems and organizational culture (Bartlett & Ghoshal, 1990). Several models of MNC have been proposed, which share elements of formal and/or informal matrix management. Table 2 briefly describes five of such models, including the heterarchy (Hedlund, 1986, 1993; Hedlund & Ridderstråle, 1998; Hedlund & Rolander, 1990), the multifocal corporation (Doz, 1986; Prahalad & Doz, 1987), the transnational corporation (Bartlett, 1986; Bartlett & Ghoshal, 1987a, b, 1989, 1995a, b, 1998), the multi-centre firm (Forsgren, 1990b; Forsgren et al., 1992) and the horizontal organization (White & Poynter, 1990).

More recently, other models of MNC have been suggested including the metanational (Doz et al., 1996, 2001), the differentiated network (Nohria & Ghoshal, 1997), and the individualized enterprise (Ghoshal & Bartlett, 1998). Such models can be said to share a view of the MNC as becoming less-hierarchical (Marschan, 1996, 1997). The less-hierarchical MNC is expected to operate as a network of highly differentiated (Ghoshal & Nohria, 1989) and functionally interdependent subsidiaries (Hedlund, 1986), resulting in a complex flow of products, people and information (Bartlett & Ghoshal, 1989) beyond the constraints of formal, bureaucratic structures (Bartlett & Ghoshal, 1990). In particular, geographically dispersed subsidiaries are granted responsibility and decision-making authority to perform strategically important functions, being coordinated primarily through informal mechanisms such as organizational culture, interlocking board of directors and personal relationships (Bartlett & Ghoshal, 1990; Hedlund, 1986; Hedlund & Rolander, 1990).

Marschan (1997) justifies the term "less-hierarchical MNC" with the fact that the process approach to MNC management challenges traditional views of both hierarchy (e.g. Hedlund, 1993) and formal structure (e.g. Bartlett & Ghoshal, 1990). The author identifies five distinctive dimensions of less-hierarchical MNCs, which include: (a) delegation of decision-making authority;

Table 2. Comparison of Five Models of MNC.

	Heterarchy	Multifocal	Transnational	Multi-centre	Horizontal
Theoretical background	Cybernetics, Organization theory	Political influence, Diversified MNC	Strategy-structure paradigm, Contingency theory	Resource-dependence view	Decision-making processes
Focus	Innovation, change, flexibility	Balancing global/local challenges	Internal differentiation	External and internal networks	Horizontal exchange of information
Organizational structure	Multiple and shifting heterarchies through projects	Between conventional and matrix	Integrated network of HQ and subsidiaries	Multi-centered network of HQ and subsidiaries	Horizontal network of functions
Strategic implications	Matching knowledge, action and people	Balancing global integration, national responsiveness	Aiming global efficiency, local responsiveness, learning transfer	Considering network relationships	Achieving globally and locally based advantages
Driving force	Change in information technology, acquisitions	Industry characteristics	Industry characteristics	Power structures, politics	Competitive advantage
Relationship between units	Interdependent, circular, shifting	Interdependent	Interdependent	Interdependent	Interdependent, horizontal

Source: Adapted from Marschan (1996).

(b) delayering of organization levels; (c) geographical dispersal of key functions; (d) de-bureaucratisation of formal procedures; and (e) differentiation of work, responsibility and authority among subsidiaries.

In general, such models of MNC attempt to circumvent the inability of studies inspired by the strategy-structure paradigm (Chandler, 1962) to generate a structural design, which could simultaneously support strategies for global efficiency, local responsiveness, and worldwide learning (Bartlett & Ghoshal, 1989). In other words, the multidimensionality, complexity and heterogeneity of an MNC are thought to require a single broad design (Egelhoff, 1999), which takes into account the following aspects of their management (Doz & Prahalad, 1991, p. 147):

- structural indeterminacy (little usefulness of any stable uni-dimensional structural design or concept)
- internal differentiation (recognition in management processes of various countries, products, and functions)
- integrative optimization (recognition of decision-making trade-offs)
- information intensity (formal and informal information flows as a source of competitive advantage)
- latent linkages (facilitated rather than pre-specified interdependences)
- networked organization and "fuzzy" boundaries (recognition of business counterparts and network relationships)
- learning and continuity (tension between low cost interaction and innovation and change)

Based on such assumptions, Doz and Prahalad (1991, p. 153) recognize the relevance of both contingency theory (Lawrence & Lorsch, 1967) and "research on external power and dependence" (Pfeffer & Salancik, 1978) for studies of MNCs. Correspondingly, two perspectives appear to coexist within the process approach, which may be labeled the design and the organic approach to less-hierarchical MNC management (Andersson & Holm, 2002).

The design approach is inspired by contingency theory (Lawrence & Lorsch, 1967) and more normative in orientation whereas the organic approach is based on the resource dependence view of the firm (Pfeffer & Salancik, 1978) and more descriptive in nature. Most studies of less-hierarchical MNCs (e.g. Bartlett & Ghoshal, 1989, 1998; Ghoshal & Bartlett, 1998; Nohria & Ghoshal, 1997; Prahalad & Doz, 1987) appear to subscribe the design approach, by assuming that headquarters control subsidiaries and decide the overall strategy. Other studies (e.g. Forsgren, 1990b; Ghoshal & Bartlett, 1990) appear to subscribe the organic approach, by assuming that MNC coordination reflects both headquarters' authority (Forsgren, 1990a) and subsidiary influence based on the control of critical resources (Larsson, 1985).

Given its assumptions, the organic approach has been considered "consistent with empirical findings and theories about the function of business networks, as developed by researchers in Sweden, Great Britain and the USA" (Holm & Pedersen, 2000, p. 4). In other words, studies of MNCs within the organic approach may be informed by research within the IMP group (see Sections 2.2 and 2.3) which regards the control of resources as dependent on specific inter-firm relationships (e.g. Cunningham & Homse, 1986; Ford, 1997; Forsgren & Johanson, 1992; Forsgren et al., 1995; Håkansson, 1982; Håkansson & Snehota, 1989, 1995; Turnbull & Valla, 1986). Such inter-firm relationships have been conceptualized as internal and external networks to the MNC by Ghoshal and Bartlett (1990) requiring, in Melin's (1992, p. 113) words, further research on "the interplay regarding exchange processes and political processes between these two types of networks."

2.4.2. Roles of Foreign Subsidiaries

As mentioned in the previous section, one dimension of less-hierarchical MNCs is differentiation, by which "subsidiary units are granted highly specialized roles in terms of functional and geographical responsibilities" (Marschan, 1997, p. 440). Subsidiary roles have been addressed both within the design and the organic approaches to less-hierarchical MNC management. Within the design approach, the headquarters are thought to deliberately differentiate the formal structure as well as formal and informal management processes to match different national contexts (Lawrence & Lorsch, 1967). Within the organic approach, such organizational processes are supposedly differentiated based on internal power relationships, which, in turn, are dependent on the control of resources (Pfeffer & Salancik, 1978). In similar fashion, Birkinshaw and Morrison (1995) arguably contend that the term "role" suggests an imposed function on the subsidiary, whereas the term "strategy" implies a higher degree of freedom on the part of subsidiary management to decide its own destiny.

Bartlett and Ghoshal (1986, p. 87) appear to subscribe the design approach by stating that: "corporate management can benefit the company by dispersion of responsibilities and differentiating subsidiary's tasks." The authors identify four subsidiary roles based on the strategic importance of the local environment and on the level of local resources and capabilities of the subsidiary. The four roles are labeled: strategic leader with substantial resources in a strategic market, black hole with few resources in a strategic market, contributor with many resources in a non strategic market, and implementer with few resources in a non strategic market.

Inspired by the integration-responsiveness framework (Prahalad & Doz, 1987), Jarillo and Martinez (1990) also suggest three generic roles for subsidiaries, which are based on the degree of integration and localization of their activities. Such roles include: receptive subsidiary performing few highly integrated and little differentiated activities, active subsidiary performing many highly integrated and differentiated activities, and autonomous subsidiary performing many little integrated and highly differentiated activities. Such roles are also seen as typical subsidiary strategies of global, transnational, and multinational MNCs, respectively (Bartlett, 1986).

On the other hand, White and Poynter (1984) suggest five generic strategies of subsidiaries, based on the product-, market-, and value added scope of their activities. Such strategies include: miniature replica with a small-scale replica business of the parent company, marketing satellite with final product processing at the subsidiary, rationalized manufacturer with worldwide component part or product production, product specialist with limited world product line development, production and marketing, and strategic independent with autonomy and resources to develop any worldwide lines of business. Roth and Morrison (1992) examine the last strategy in further detail, distinguishing between integrated subsidiaries with worldwide responsibility for a narrow set of value added activities, and global subsidiary mandate subsidiaries with worldwide responsibility for the complete set of value added activities for a single product or product line.

Gupta and Govindarajan (1991, 1994) focus on inter-subsidiary knowledge flows such as technology and/or skill transfer, in order to distinguish between four generic subsidiary roles. Such roles include: global innovator with high outflow and low inflow of knowledge, integrated player with high outflow and inflow of knowledge, implementor with low outflow and high inflow of knowledge, and local innovator with low outflow and inflow of knowledge. The authors appear to subscribe the organic approach with the following statement (Gupta & Govindarajan, 1994, p. 455):

> In suggesting the presence and criticality of autonomous bottom-up processes within MNCs, this study also reinforces the notion that, if researchers' intent is to understand strategic processes within MNCs, then focusing only on corporate "induced" (i.e. centrally managed) processes would run the risk of overlooking important and directly relevant phenomenon.

Birkinshaw and Morrison (1995) synthesize previous studies of subsidiary roles into a three-fold typology (see Table 3), which includes: local implementer with limited geographic and value added scope, specialized contributor with extended geographic scope but narrow value added scope, and world mandate with worldwide or regional responsibility for a product line or entire business.

Table 3.   Typologies of Subsidiary Roles.

Authors	Local Implementer	Specialized Contributor	World Mandate
White and Poynter (1984)	Miniature Replica	Rationalized, Manufacturer, Product Specialist	Global Mandate
D'Cruz (1986)	Branch Plant	Globally Rationalized	World Product Mandate
Bartlett and Ghoshal (1986)	Implementer	Contributor	Strategic Leader
Jarillo and Martinez (1990)	Autonomous	Receptive	Active
Gupta and Govindarajan (1991)	Local Innovator, Implementor	Global Innovator	Integrated Player
Roth and Morrison (1992)		Integrated	Global Subsidiary Mandate

Source: Adapted from Birkinshaw and Morrison (1995).

More recently, Taggart (1997a) suggests four subsidiary roles based on decision-making autonomy and procedural justice (Kim & Mauborgne, 1991, 1993). Such roles include: collaborator subsidiary with high procedural justice and low autonomy, vassal subsidiary with low procedural justice and autonomy, militant subsidiary with low procedural justice and high autonomy, and partner subsidiary with high procedural justice and autonomy. The author generally associates militant and collaborator subsidiary roles with Birkinshaw and Morrison's (1995) local implementer and specialized contributor roles, respectively.

The same author (Taggart, 1997b) supplements Jarillo and Martinez's (1990) taxonomy of subsidiary roles with a low integration/low responsiveness role, which he labels quiescent subsidiary i.e. performing little integrated and differentiated activities. Such a role is seen as the typical subsidiary strategy of international MNCs (Bartlett & Ghoshal, 1989) and equivalent to Bartlett and Ghoshal's (1986) black hole, which is excluded from Birkinshaw and Morrison's (1995) typology. The author also renames Jarillo and Martinez's (1990) active subsidiary into constrained independent subsidiary, which he considers "much less bound to the parent's network" (Taggart, 1997b, p. 310). Taggart (1997b, p. 301) appears to subscribe the organic approach by stating that: "there seems no prima facie reason why an MNC subsidiary should not adopt a low integration-low responsiveness strategy, either pro-actively or due to negligence on the part of the parent corporation."

Finally, Andersson and Forsgren (2000) focus on inter-subsidiary product flows in terms of purchases and sales, in order to distinguish between four generic subsidiary roles. Such roles include: external subsidiary with low inflow and outflow of products, backward vertical subsidiary with high inflow and low outflow of products, forward vertical subsidiary with low inflow and high outflow of products, and mutually integrated subsidiary with high inflow and outflow of products. Such subsidiary roles may be interpreted as equivalent to quiescent, local implementer, specialized contributor, and world mandate roles, respectively (Birkinshaw and Morrison, 1995; Taggart, 1997b). Moreover, the authors appear to subscribe the organic approach by stating that: "literature to a large extent ignores that an MNC, as other firms, are organic entities rather than instruments. The headquarters intentions to orchestrate an integration within the MNC are always in conflict with every sub-units history, interest and business context" (Andersson & Forsgren, 2000, p. 162). In this respect, it is also worth noting the similarity between the latter part of such a statement and Easton's (1992, p. 17) characterization of firm heterogeneity in industrial markets (see Section 2.3.1).

2.4.3. MNC Coordination and Control

As mentioned in Section 2.4.1, less-hierarchical MNCs are characterized not only by differentiation of subsidiaries, but also by delayering of organization levels, geographical dispersal of key functions, delegation of decision-making authority, and de-bureaucratisation of formal procedures (Marschan, 1997). It follows that, similarly to subsidiary roles, the MNC's "internal coordination mechanisms might be differentiated to match the variety of subunit contexts" (Ghoshal & Bartlett, 1990, p. 620).

Martinez and Jarillo (1989) identify eight coordination mechanisms, which may be adopted in MNCs, subdividing them into: (a) structural and formal mechanisms; and (b) other mechanisms, more informal and subtle (Barnard, 1938). The former sub-set of coordination mechanisms includes: formal structure of organizational units, hierarchical locus of decisional authority, formalization and standardization, planning, and output and behavior control. The latter sub-set of coordination mechanisms includes: cross-departmental relations, informal communication, and socialization. Hennart (1993) refers to a ninth mechanism of coordination – price control – which the author conceptualizes as a form of output control, by which individuals in an MNC are informed, motivated and rewarded.

The mechanisms of coordination suggested by alternative models of MNC are briefly reviewed in the following paragraphs. In addition, Table 4 depicts the mechanisms of coordination, which are suggested by the five models of MNC described in Table 2 (see Section 2.4.1).

The authors of the model of MNC as a heterarchy suggest that coordination is achieved through a continuous flow of information across the MNC in a flexible and integrated manner, in addition to normative mechanisms such as shared culture and

Table 4.   Mechanisms of Coordination in Five Models of MNC.

	Heterarchy	Multifocal	Transnational	Multi-centre	Horizontal
Mechanisms of coordination	Shared culture, continuous information flow	Sub-processes of change, management tools	Structural configurations, administrative processes, management mentalities	Power structure, politics	Lateral decision-making, shared premises

ethics (Hedlund, 1986; Hedlund & Ridderstråle, 1998; Hedlund & Rolander, 1990). The authors of the model of MNC as a multifocal corporation recommend instead a matrix of sub-processes of change and a collection of management tools. The sub-processes of change involve three dimensions: cognitive perspective, strategic priorities, and power allocation, whereas the management tools are of three kinds: data management tools, managers' management tools and conflict resolution tools (Doz & Prahalad, 1981, 1984, 1987; Prahalad & Doz, 1981a, b, 1987).

In particular, Prahalad and Doz (1981a, b) suggest that in MNCs the need to balance national and global priorities flexibly from decision to decision requires the management of several orientations, which are expected to differ among individual managers. The authors identify a cognitive orientation i.e. the perception of the relevant environment; a strategic orientation i.e. the competitive posture and methods adopted; and a power orientation i.e. the locus of power to commit resources. MNCs' top managers can then use a variety of management mechanisms in order to influence and control these three orientations as well as a fourth, the administrative orientation i.e. the orientation of supporting systems. Management mechanisms include: data management mechanisms that generate and regulate the flow of information; manager management mechanisms, which determine the assignments, compensation, development, evaluation and socialization of managers; and conflict resolution mechanisms such as task forces, planning committees, integrators and coordinating groups (Prahalad & Doz, 1981a, b).

The authors of the model of MNC as a transnational corporation distinguish between different structural configurations, administrative processes and management mentalities in order to simultaneously achieve global efficiency, local responsiveness, and worldwide learning (Bartlett & Ghoshal, 1989, 1998). In particular, they suggest that coordination through centralization, formalization and socialization, correspond to the most common processes of Japanese, American and European MNCs, respectively.

Centralization allows rapid decision-making and minimizes headquarters-subsidiary arm wrestling, but can become expensive not only in terms of travel costs, but also for the strain it puts on managers at the centre. Formalization is largely based on formal systems, policies, and standards, thus decreasing the power of both headquarters and subsidiaries and increasing decision-making efficiency due to routines. Formalization implies, however, high fixed costs of establishment and may induce lack of flexibility toward complex or changing tasks. Socialization is based on careful recruitment, development and acculturation of key decision-makers, therefore overcoming both headquarters' overload and formalization's inflexibility. The major disadvantage of socialization is the cost of intensive indoctrination and training, in addition to the eventual ambiguity, slowness and complexity of decision-making and management processes.

The authors of the model of MNC as a multi-centre firm emphasize the subsidiary's point of view in its relationship with headquarters, namely in terms of strategic influence and control (Forsgren, 1990b; Forsgren et al., 1992). They are thus focused on power structures and politics as a means of coordination from a resource-dependence perspective. The authors of the model of MNC as a horizontal organization refer, instead, to lateral decision-making processes in a context of functional networking, which requires shared values as the basis for consensus among managers (White & Poynter, 1990).

More recently, the authors of the model of MNC as a differentiated network (Nohria & Ghoshal, 1997) suggest conditions of "fit" between the structure of each headquarters-subsidiary relation and the subsidiary context. They believe that such a contingency framework may enhance performance both at the subsidiary (Ghoshal & Nohria, 1989) and at the MNC level (Nohria & Ghoshal, 1994). The structure of the headquarters-subsidiary relation is differentiated in terms of a combination of centralization, formalization, and normative integration, whereas the subsidiary context is differentiated in terms of local resource levels and environmental complexity (Ghoshal & Nohria, 1989; Nohria & Ghoshal, 1997). In particular, the authors suggest four specific structures of a headquarters-subsidiary relation (see Fig. 3), which supposedly "fit" four different subsidiary contexts.

Such a contingency framework at the subsidiary level is based on particular assumptions concerning: (a) the degree of headquarters-subsidiary interdependence and (b) the cost efficiency of centralization, formalization, and normative integration in each context. In particular, interdependent headquarters-subsidiary interests are seen as positively associated with environmental complexity. In addition, both environmental complexity and local resource levels are seen as positively associated with formalization and normative integration, and negatively associated with centralization (Ghoshal & Nohria, 1989; Nohria & Ghoshal, 1997).

At the MNC level, the authors suggest that it is more difficult to differentiate the degree of normative integration among various subsidiaries than it is to differentiate centralization and formalization (Nohria & Ghoshal, 1994, 1997).

Local resources

	Low	High
Environmental complexity — High	Centralization: Moderate Formalization: Low Socialization: High	Centralization: Low Formalization: Moderate Socialization: High
Environmental complexity — Low	Centralization: High Formalization: Low Socialization: Low	Centralization: Low Formalization: High Socialization: Low

Fig. 3.   Fit Structures of a Headquarters-Subsidiary Relation. *Source:* Adapted from Nohria and Ghoshal (1997).

The authors thus distinguish between differentiated fit consisting of centralization and formalization, and shared values through normative integration, which are akin to Baliga and Jaeger's (1984) administrative control and normative-cultural control, respectively. Nohria and Ghoshal (1997, p. 115) contend, however, that: "differentiated fit and shared values are equally effective alternatives for managing headquarters-subsidiary relations." In addition, the authors claim that: "firms that can simultaneously create both a strong set of shared values and differentiated fit will outperform those that rely on one or the other of these administrative approaches" (Nohria & Ghoshal, 1997, p. 126). They justify such a prescriptive tone with the adoption of contingency theory (e.g. Donaldson, 1995) as their theoretical perspective, which, in turn, may be associated with the design approach to less-hierarchical MNC management (see Section 2.4.1).

In their model of MNC as a differentiated network, Nohria and Ghoshal (1997) also emphasize the importance of inter-unit communication for effective MNC management (Baliga & Jaeger, 1984; Edström & Galbraith, 1977; Ghoshal et al., 1994) as it increases information processing capacity (Egelhoff, 1991, 1993) to cope with environmental and organizational complexity (Bartlett & Ghoshal, 1989; Hedlund, 1986, 1993; Martinez & Jarillo, 1991; Prahalad & Doz, 1987). In this respect, the authors note that: "interpersonal networking has significant positive effects on the ongoing communication of subsidiary managers, both with their counterparts in the headquarters and with managers in other subsidiaries (Nohria & Ghoshal, 1997, p. 146) as well as that: "in MNCs, interpersonal networks are vital because they serve as the glue that holds these vast geographically dispersed and internally differentiated organizations together" (Nohria & Ghoshal, 1997, p. 151).

Nohria and Ghoshal (1997) recognize, however, that interpersonal networking can be constrained by human cognitive capacity as well as by different time zones, language, and culture. For the particular case of functional departmental heads and general managers in subsidiaries, the authors suggest, in addition to individual personality and motivation, key career-related factors, which influence the formation of a contact network. Such factors include: tenure, mobility, expatriate status, initial socialization, and mentoring relationships.

Finally, the authors of the model of MNC as an individualized enterprise (Ghoshal & Bartlett, 1998) emphasize coordination through three core organizational processes: the entrepreneurial process, the integration process, and the renewal process. The entrepreneurial process supports externally focused opportunity-seeking entrepreneurship; the integration process links dispersed resources and competencies; and the renewal process supports strategic revitalization. These processes are, in turn, associated with roles rather than tasks and responsibilities of front-line, middle, and top managers. Ghoshal and Bartlett (1998, p. 209) synthesize their view as follows:

> The Individualized Corporation can be examined in terms of its core processes and the new management roles embedded within these processes. Because these new roles are what lie at the heart of the new organizational model, the key challenge in transforming a company into an Individualized Corporation lies in transforming the frontline, middle, and top-level managers so that they are willing and able to play their respective roles of entrepreneurs, capability developers, and institutional leaders.

2.4.4. Roles of FSMs

The importance of managerial hierarchies for coordination and control of economic activities in general (Chandler, 1977; Williamson, 1975) and organizational decision-making in particular (Barnard, 1938; Fayol, 1916; Taylor, 1911) has long been recognized. Mintzberg (1973) distinguishes between eight major schools of thought on the manager's job: classical, great man, entrepreneurship, decision theory, leader effectiveness, leader power, leader behavior, and work activity. Mintzberg's own study belongs to the latter school, which the author describes as "the school of inductive research, in which the work activities of managers are analyzed systematically; conclusions are drawn only when they can be supported by the empirical evidence" (Mintzberg, 1973, p. 21).

Mintzberg (1973) also notes that a basic distinction can be made between the content and the characteristics of managerial work. Content consists of activities that managers carry out such as negotiating, whereas characteristics describe where, with whom, how long, and with what media managers work. Moreover, categorizations of content and purpose lead to statements of functions or roles of managerial work, which the author defines as "organized sets of behaviors identified with a position" (Mintzberg, 1990, p. 168).

Interpersonal roles are a particular type of managerial roles, being characterized by the establishment and maintenance of interactions with superiors and subordinates as well as individuals outside the formal chain of command. Such interpersonal roles, which result from managers' formal authority, are interrelated with informational roles, which provide access to information, and with decisional roles by which information supports decision-making (Mintzberg, 1973, 1975). Three main types of managerial roles are thus identified:

(i) Interpersonal roles: Figure head (ceremonial), leader (staff responsibility), and liaison (outside the vertical chain of command)
(ii) Informational roles: monitor (central access to information), disseminator (informing staff), and spokesperson (informing external people)
(iii) Decisional roles: entrepreneur (initiating and supervising projects), disturbance handler (reacting to change), resource allocator (time, approval), and negotiator (commitment)

Such interrelated roles constitute a challenge to the classical view of management, which associates managerial work with activities such as long-term planning, efficient organizing, goal-oriented directives, and systematic control (e.g. Carroll & Gillen, 1987; Hemphill, 1959). Mintzberg's (1973) findings dismiss such an image of managers as rational and plan-oriented decision-makers, by noting that a large part of their job consists of short, fragmented and verbal interactions of mainly a reactive kind. Kotter (1982a, b) and Stewart (1974, 1976, 1982) equally question the usefulness of the classical view of managerial work, based on their own conceptualizations of managers' job.

Mintzberg's study (1973) has, however, been criticized for: (a) its exclusive reliance on observable work activities; (b) particular conceptualization of managerial roles; (c) lack of relationship between such roles and organizational theory; (d) simplistic definition of management; and (e) lack of explanatory power (Carroll & Gillen, 1987; Hales, 1986, 1989, 1999; Martinko & Gardner, 1985; Stewart, 1998; Watson, 1994; Watson & Harris, 1999; Whitley, 1988, 1989; Willmott, 1984, 1987). Nevertheless, several other studies can be identified, which adopt role theory to conceptualize managerial work (e.g. Dalton, 1959; Fondas & Stewart, 1994; Kotter, 1982a, b; Martinko & Gardner, 1990) or provide support to the general validity of Mintzberg's roles (e.g. Carroll & Teo, 1996; Hannaway, 1989; Kurke & Aldrich, 1983; Lau et al., 1980; Snyder & Glueck, 1980; Stewart, 1982).

In the case of MNCs, Bartlett and Ghoshal (1997) suggest that rather than sharing identical behavior and responsibility, top-level, middle-level and front-line managers have their roles differentiated by organizational hierarchy.

In the authors' words: "top-level managers set direction by formulating strategy and controlling resources; middle-level managers mediate the vertical information processing and resource allocation processes by assuming the role of administrative controllers; and, swamped by direction and control from above, front-line managers find themselves in the role of operational implementers" (Bartlett & Ghoshal, 1997, p. 1). The authors further argue that MNCs' transition away from a traditional authority-based hierarchy implies that front-line managers are increasingly required to take the initiative to create and pursue new business opportunities. In particular, country managers may play three roles: "the sensor and interpreter of local opportunities and threats, the builder of local resources and capabilities, and the contributor to and active participant in global strategy" (Bartlett & Ghoshal, 1992, p. 128).

In his study of American, European and Asian FSMs, Gates (1994) reiterates that the work of such managers includes entrepreneurial challenges such as meeting local customer needs, satisfying local government requirements, and defending the company's position vis-à-vis local and foreign competitors. The author reports an increasing number of local nationals in that position (e.g. Harzing, 2001) due to their "knowledge of local customers and government" (Gates, 1994, p. 7) as well as an increasing concern of FSMs' with marketing and customer relations including deal making and approval. Conversely, traditional planning and budgeting procedures, manufacturing, and research and development are all expected to account less for FSMs' time in the future.

Such findings, although convergent with Mintzberg's roles for the particular case of FSMs, challenge the author's proposed sequence of roles, especially that "formal authority gives rise to the three interpersonal roles" (Mintzberg, 1990, p. 168). In other words, the need for knowledge of local market requirements combined with compliance to parent company's rules and programs requires FSMs whose contact network not only results from, but also adds to their formal authority. In retrospect, Mintzberg (1990, 1991) equally considers his list of roles as over-rational by emphasizing a one-way sequence of separate aspects of managerial work rather than their holistic and interdependent nature. The author thus recommends further research on the content of managerial work (Mintzberg, 1991), in addition to calls for further research on the context of managerial work (e.g. Fondas & Stewart, 1994). In this respect, opinions remain divided on whether recent models of network organization require different managerial roles (e.g. Harvey & Novicevic, 2002) or not (e.g. Hales, 2002).

2.4.5. Conclusion

The process approach to MNC management contributes to our understanding of MNCs with the assumptions of bounded rationality (Cyert & March, 1963) and micro-politics (Pettigrew, 1973) in such organizations. In addition, by assuming that subsidiaries are differentiated and interdependent (e.g. Hedlund, 1993) such a research tradition suggests that MNCs are increasingly complex and heterogeneous (Doz & Prahalad, 1991; Gupta et al., 1999). Such a view of MNCs as becoming less-hierarchical (Marschan, 1997) has been labeled the network paradigm of MNCs (Birkinshaw, 2000), which emphasizes non-structural and informal mechanisms of coordination (e.g. Bartlett & Ghoshal, 1990; Hedlund & Rolander, 1990).

Different views on the extent to which network linkages are facilitated rather than pre-specified (Doz & Prahalad, 1991) justify, however, a further distinction between an organic and a design approach to less-hierarchical MNC management (Andersson & Holm, 2002). The former approach is inspired by the resource dependence view of the firm (Pfeffer & Salancik, 1978) and is primarily descriptive, whereas the latter approach tends to adopt contingency theory (Lawrence & Lorsch, 1967) as the basis for normative implications (Donaldson, 1995).

The present paper shares the assumptions of the organic approach to less-hierarchical MNC management thus attempting to integrate findings within the process approach to MNC management with those of studies within the IMP group (see Sections 2.2 and 2.3). As mentioned in Section 2.1, the three research traditions are thought to share the assumption of bounded rationality (Cyert & March, 1963), resource dependency (Pfeffer & Salancik, 1978), and asymmetrical distribution of power (Forsgren & Johanson, 1992). In addition, the three streams of research address the implications of personal contacts for inter-firm coordination, in spite of distinct terminology such as social exchange (IMP group, 1982) and interpersonal networking (Nohria & Ghoshal, 1997).

Within the MNC, the coordination of interdependent subsidiaries is thought to require that their differentiated roles be taken into account. In this respect, and as mentioned in Section 1.4, the present paper is limited to subsidiaries generally labeled local implementers (Birkinshaw & Morrison, 1995). In particular, such subsidiaries are thought to operate with few resources in a non-strategic market (Bartlett & Ghoshal, 1986), being net receivers of knowledge flows (Gupta & Govindarajan, 1991).

In terms of specific mechanisms of coordination at the subsidiary level, network models of MNC refer to interpersonal networking (e.g. Nohria & Ghoshal, 1997), but also to centralization, formalization, and socialization (e.g. Ghoshal & Nohria, 1989). Bartlett and Ghoshal (1989, 1998) generally associate the latter three mechanisms of coordination with Japanese, American, and European MNCs, respectively. Nohria and Ghoshal (1997) associate them with specific subsidiary contexts in terms of environmental complexity and local resources levels (Ghoshal & Nohria, 1989). Such studies (Bartlett & Ghoshal, 1989, 1998; Nohria & Ghoshal, 1997) subscribe the design approach to less-hierarchical MNC management (see

Section 2.4.1) in the sense that they prescribe contingency-frameworks that headquarters are supposedly able to design and implement.

On the other hand, the model of the MNC as an individualized enterprise (Ghoshal & Bartlett, 1998) explicitly associates MNC coordination with specific managerial roles. In particular, the role of FSMs is distinguished from that of middle and top-level managers (Bartlett & Ghoshal, 1997) as entrepreneurs (Ghoshal & Barlett, 1998) who sense the local environment, build local resources, and contribute to MNC strategy (Bartlett & Ghoshal, 1992). In the present paper and due to its focus on interpersonal roles (Mintzberg, 1973) and local implementer subsidiaries (Birkinshaw & Morrison, 1995) only sensing and building roles of FSMs (Bartlett & Ghoshal, 1992) are considered.

In sum, coordination in less-hierarchical MNCs may be discussed in terms of differentiated subsidiary roles (e.g. Birkinshaw & Morrison, 1995), specific mechanisms of coordination (e.g. Ghoshal & Nohria, 1989), and managerial roles (e.g. Bartlett & Ghoshal, 1997). Such aspects of coordination in MNCs constitute the third and final conceptual block of the a priori theoretical framework for analysis, which is discussed in the following section.

2.5. Theoretical Framework for Analysis

The present paper adopts two conceptual frameworks, which represent "the current version of the researcher's map of the territory being investigated" (Miles & Huberman, 1994, p. 20) before and after data collection and analysis. They are labeled the a priori theoretical framework for analysis (see Section 2.5.1) and the final theoretical framework (see Section 5.1), respectively.

An a priori theoretical framework for analysis may be characterized by its degree of elaboration as well as by the extent to which it is deductive (Miles & Huberman, 1994). In the present paper, the a priori theoretical framework for analysis is deductive to the extent that it is based on literature review (see Fig. 1 in Section 2.1), but little elaborated once that the research questions are rather exploratory (see Section 1.3). On the other hand, the a priori theoretical framework for analysis is meant to guide subsequent data collection and analysis. In Yin's (1994, p. 46) words, it specifies "the conditions under which a particular phenomenon is likely to be found (a literal replication) as well as the conditions when it is not likely to be found (a theoretical replication)," thus supporting case selection and analysis (Eisenhardt, 1991).

Miles and Huberman (1994, p. 18) acknowledge the usefulness of conceptual frameworks in qualitative research by stating that "a conceptual framework explains, either graphically or in narrative form, the main things to be studied

– the key factors, constructs or variables – and the presumed relationships among them." In the present paper the a priori theoretical framework for analysis is presented graphically in the following sub-section and refined into a final theoretical framework in Section 5.1.

2.5.1. A Priori Theoretical Framework for Analysis

As mentioned in Section 2.2, studies within the interaction approach to industrial markets demonstrate that in such markets, transactions are unlikely to occur without the establishment of personal contacts. The importance of the latter is, however, supposedly contingent on the levels of uncertainty and risk perceived by the interacting parties (e.g. Cunningham & Turnbull, 1982; Forsgren et al., 1995). In this respect, social exchange has been emphasized and associated with the exchange of information, product and/or services as well as money in transactions (Håkansson, 1982; IMP group, 1982).

The network approach to industrial markets (see Section 2.3) assumes that inter-organizational relationships are connected to the extent that a stable structure of relationships may be observed (Easton, 1992). In such a context, coordination of actors, activities and resources (Håkansson & Johanson, 1984) is expected to occur by means of inter-organizational interaction (Johanson & Mattsson, 1987), which consists, in turn, of both exchange and adaptation processes (IMP group, 1982; Håkansson & Snehota, 1995). Although interaction is primarily discussed as occurring among firms, the role of individuals in such a process is equally acknowledged (e.g. Brennan & Turnbull, 1999).

The occurrence of personal contacts in industrial markets is thought to be contingent on individual, organizational and market factors. In particular, on the perceptions, attitudes and behavior of individuals (IMP group, 1982), which are, in turn, affected by their personality (Halinen & Salmi, 2001) as well as cultural- (Andersson et al., 1996; Björkman & Kock, 1995; Cunningham & Turnbull, 1982; Hallén, 1992), language- (Andersson et al., 1996; Cunningham & Turnbull, 1982), and professional background. The latter has also been specified into the individual's career (Andersson et al., 1996; Axelsson & Agndal, 2000; Björkman & Kock, 1995; Halinen & Salmi, 2001; Hallén, 1992) and tenure (Hallén, 1992).

At the organizational level, factors such as the age of the inter-firm relationship (Andersson et al., 1996; Björkman & Kock, 1995; Cunningham & Homse, 1986; Cunningham & Turnbull, 1982), the business volume exchanged (Cunningham & Homse, 1986; Cunningham & Turnbull, 1982), supplier strategy (Cunningham & Homse, 1986), and employee turnover among employers (Björkman & Kock, 1995; Halinen & Salmi, 2001) are also expected to influence the occurrence of personal contacts in industrial markets. At the market level, such factors include the complexity of technology involved (Cunningham & Homse, 1986;

Cunningham & Turnbull, 1982), industry norms of behavior (Cunningham & Turnbull, 1982), and market structure (Cunningham & Homse, 1986).

In terms of the role or function of personal contacts, information exchange (Cunningham & Turnbull, 1982) has been specified into commercial information exchange as well as technical information exchange and advice, in addition to delivery and technical progressing (Cunningham & Homse, 1986). Such an information exchange role of personal contacts may also be associated with non-task socializing for friendship and ego-enhancement (Cunningham & Turnbull, 1982) or prestige (Hallén, 1992). In addition, the assessment role of personal contacts (Cunningham & Turnbull, 1982) has been associated with information about possible customers and upcoming purchases (Björkman & Kock, 1995), legitimacy (Axelsson & Agndal, 2000) and door opening (Halinen & Salmi, 2001).

On the other hand, the negotiation and adaptation role of personal contacts (Cunningham & Homse, 1986; Cunningham & Turnbull, 1982) may be subdivided, once that the adaptation role implies deliberate decision-making (Brennan & Turnbull, 1999; IMP group, 1982). Such a decision-making function of personal contacts is expected to enable problem solving (Axelsson & Agndal, 2000; Cunningham & Homse, 1986; Cunningham & Turnbull, 1982; Halinen & Salmi, 2001) as well as allocation of resources namely in terms of training (Cunningham & Homse, 1986).

Personal contacts can thus be regarded as contributing to inter-firm coordination in industrial markets by influencing the quality of inter-organizational exchange as well as the intensity of adaptations (see Fig. 4). The quality of exchange is perceived not only in terms of information and communication concerning products/services, but also in terms of social exchange in times of business inactivity or even crisis (IMP group, 1982). Adaptations are closely related to the negotiations between the parties, which reflect, in turn, their differences in terms of interests and power (Easton, 1992). In this respect, control over resources and knowledge may be determinant for the distribution of power among the actors (Håkansson & Johanson, 1992).

In other words, inter-firm coordination in industrial markets may be described in terms of the function or role of personal contacts. On the one hand, personal contacts may increase the trust between the parties by reducing the uncertainty, which eventually prevents them from engaging in an exchange process. On the other hand, personal contacts may enable the parties to persuade each other into integrating their resources and/or activities in spite of conflicting interests, which eventually prevent them from engaging in an adaptation process. The lower question mark in Fig. 4 represents, therefore, the second research question of the present paper. The upper question mark represents the first research question of the paper, and concerns not the function or role of personal

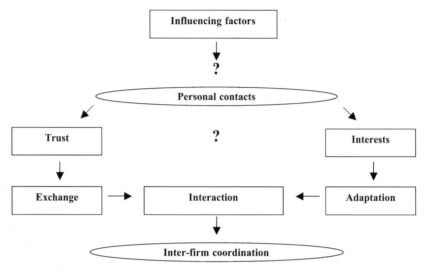

Fig. 4. Research Questions and Industrial Inter-Firm Coordination.

contacts, but the factors which influence their occurrence in the first place (see Section 1.3).

Within the MNC, similar processes of exchange and adaptation are expected to occur, as large and diversified companies move away from a classical authority-based hierarchy of vertically oriented relationships towards higher decentralization of responsibility (Marschan, 1997) and individual accountability (Bartlett & Ghoshal, 1997). As mentioned in Section 2.4, subsidiaries of less-hierarchical MNCs are increasingly coordinated through informal mechanisms such as organizational culture, interlocking board of directors and personal relationships (Bartlett & Ghoshal, 1990; Hedlund, 1986; Hedlund & Rolander, 1990). Network models of MNC thus suggest that individuals establish personal contacts by joining different teams as well as by taking direct contact with other individuals (e.g. Ghoshal et al., 1994). It has been suggested, however, that such a degree of interpersonal networking depends on individual factors such as personality, motivation, tenure, mobility, expatriate status, initial socialization, and mentoring relationships (Nohria & Ghoshal, 1997).

On the other hand, network models of MNC appear to agree on three basic roles or functions of personal contacts of FSMs, which enable coordination at the MNC level: (a) information exchange; (b) decision-making; and (c) resource allocation (e.g. Bartlett & Ghoshal, 1992, 1997). In particular, the models of MNC as a heterarchy (Hedlund, 1986), transnational corporation (Bartlett, 1986;

Bartlett & Ghoshal, 1989, 1998), horizontal organization (White & Poynter, 1990), differentiated network (Nohria & Ghoshal, 1997), and individualized enterprise (Ghoshal & Bartlett, 1998) emphasize the importance of a continuous flow of information within the MNC, in order to support transfer of knowledge and decision-making.

The influence of FSMs on decision-making is also addressed in the models of MNC as a multifocal corporation (Prahalad & Doz, 1981a, b), multi-centre firm (Forsgren, 1990b), transnational corporation (Bartlett, 1986; Bartlett & Ghoshal, 1989, 1998), horizontal organization (White & Poynter, 1990), differentiated network (Nohria & Ghoshal, 1997), and individualized enterprise (Ghoshal & Bartlett, 1998), especially to achieve decisional consensus. Finally, FSMs' influence and control over resource allocation is discussed in the models of MNC as a multi-centre firm (Forsgren, 1990b), transnational corporation (Bartlett, 1986; Bartlett & Ghoshal, 1989, 1998), multifocal corporation (Prahalad & Doz, 1981a, b) and individualized enterprise (Ghoshal & Bartlett, 1998).

The extent to which the reviewed literature (see Section 2.1) answers the basic questions of the present paper (see Section 1.3) is graphically synthesized into an a priori theoretical framework for analysis (see Fig. 5). On the one hand, research within the interaction and the network approaches to industrial markets (see Sections 2.2 and 2.3) suggests several contextual factors which influence the occurrence of personal contacts as well as possible functions of such personal contacts. Such research traditions rarely specify, however, the individuals who take personal contacts (for an exception see Cunningham & Homse, 1986; Hallén, 1992). On the other hand, research within the process approach to MNC management does make a distinction between the roles of FSMs and other managers (Bartlett & Ghoshal, 1992, 1997), but rarely specifies factors and functions of their personal contacts (for an exception see Ghoshal et al., 1994; Nohria & Ghoshal, 1997).

The a priori theoretical framework thus lists all individual, organizational, and market factors, which have been identified through literature review as associated with the occurrence of personal contacts. In this respect, motivation, expatriate status and mobility (Nohria & Ghoshal, 1997) were integrated with attitude, nationality and employee turnover (Andersson et al., 1996; Björkman & Kock, 1995; Halinen & Salmi, 2001; IMP group, 1982), respectively. On the other hand, initial socialization and mentoring relationships (Nohria & Ghoshal, 1997) were integrated with career (Andersson et al., 1996; Axelsson & Agndal, 2000; Björkman & Kock, 1995; Halinen & Salmi, 2001; Hallén, 1992).

In addition, the a priori theoretical framework lists all functions of personal contacts, which have been identified through literature review as enabling coordination within the MNC and in the local industrial market. In this respect,

Individual	Personality, Attitude, Nationality, Career, Tenure, Language
Organizational	Age of relationships, Business volume, Supplier strategy, Employee turnover
Market	Technical complexity, Industry norms, Market structure

Information exchange	Commercial info Technical info Technical advice Delivery progress Technical progress Friendship
Assessment	Customers
Negotiation	Negotiations
Decision-making	Problem solving
Resource allocation	Training

Fig. 5.   A Priori Theoretical Framework for Analysis.

the negotiation and adaptation role of personal contacts (Cunningham & Turnbull, 1982) has been subdivided into negotiation On the one hand, and decision-making and resource allocation in the other. Such a subdivision of functions of personal contacts is meant to acknowledge the distinctive features of managerial work in general (e.g. Mintzberg, 1973) and of subsidiary management in particular (Bartlett & Ghoshal, 1992, 1997).

On the other hand, the specification of such functions of personal contacts into certain contents was mostly based on previous findings within the IMP group (Axelsson & Agndal, 2000; Björkman & Kock, 1995; Cunningham & Homse, 1986; Cunningham & Turnbull, 1982; Halinen & Salmi, 2001). In this respect, ego-enhancement (Cunningham & Turnbull, 1982) or prestige (Hallén, 1992) has been excluded from the a priori theoretical framework under the assumption that

FSMs may be regarded as part of an elite (Welch et al., 2002), which does not take personal contacts exclusively for such purposes.

The a priori theoretical framework for analysis also emphasizes the lack of an explicit relationship between the factors and functions of personal contacts in previous research. In other words, the relationship between the context and content of social exchange (IMP group, 1982) in industrial markets and of interpersonal networking (Nohria & Ghoshal, 1997) in MNCs has remained unspecified. Such a relationship could be illuminated with the dynamic aspects of personal contacts, following Pettigrew's (1987, p. 6) claim that sounding theorizing on managerial phenomena requires "the continuous interplay of ideas about the context, the process and the content of change, together with skill in regulating the relations among the three."

The dynamic aspects of personal contacts in industrial markets have been examined by IMP researchers, namely in terms of frequency and institutionalization (Cunningham & Homse, 1986; Cunningham & Turnbull, 1982) as well as deliberate planning and control (Axelsson & Agndal, 2000; Halinen & Salmi, 2001; Hallén, 1992). Such findings are, however, excluded from the a priori theoretical framework for analysis for two main reasons. On the one hand, they are too general in order to specify the relationship between certain factors and functions of personal contacts. On the other hand, they were less influential in the study's collection and analysis of data, following the adoption of a cross-sectional rather than longitudinal research strategy (see Section 3.3). The following section discusses the research strategy and other methodological aspects of the study on which the present paper is based.

3. METHODOLOGY

This section examines the philosophical and methodological stance of the present paper in relation to other possible approaches to social science in general and management studies in particular. Key ontological, epistemological, and axiological assumptions are thus made explicit in order to justify the research strategy and design of the study. In sum, the present paper is based on a cross-sectional multiple-case strategy primarily based on semi-structured interviews, which are interpreted from a realist perspective.

3.1. Philosophical Stance of the Study

It is almost twenty-five years since Burrell and Morgan (1979, p. 23), in reaction to the hegemony of functionalist orthodoxy in social science, suggested four paradigms as "meta-theoretical assumptions, which underwrite the frame of reference, mode of theorizing and *modus operandi* of the social theorists who operate within them." The authors claimed that such paradigms are mutually exclusive as they are based on at least one set of opposing meta-theoretical assumptions. Jackson and Carter (1991, p. 110) reiterate the impossibility for a synthesis between such paradigms, implying "that each paradigm must, logically, develop separately, pursuing its own problematic and ignoring those of other paradigms as paradigmatically invalid, and that different claims about organizations would, in an ideal world, be resolved in the light of their implications for social praxis."

Such an assumption of paradigm incommensurability as a necessary condition for pluralism in organization studies (Jackson & Carter, 1993) has been challenged based on the argument that "it locks analysis into a series of parallel narratives that disqualifies them from engaging with each other" (Willmott, 1993, p. 727). Although I recognize the slippery nature of such arguments, namely due to the lack of agreement on paradigmatic boundaries, my view is that a separatist paradigm mentality may compromise scientific progress rather than promote its pluralism (Weick, 1999). In similar fashion, Lincoln and Guba (2000, p. 164) maintain that: "to argue that it is paradigms that are in contention is probably less useful than to probe where and how paradigms exhibit confluence and where and how they exhibit differences, controversies, and contradictions."

Furthermore, I agree that "one *can* operate in different paradigms sequentially over time" (Burrell & Morgan, 1979, p. 25) but not necessarily that "for a theorist to switch paradigms calls for a change in meta-theoretical assumptions, something which, although manifestly possible, is not often achieved in practice" (Burrell & Morgan, 1979, pp. 24–25). In other words, I believe in the distinction between fanatically-, firmly-, and weakly held assumptions (Zaltman et al., 1982), which suggests that only some meta-theoretical assumptions may indeed be inseparable from the researcher. I thus prefer referring to the philosophical stance of a study rather than that of a researcher.

In an article which reviews the methods generally employed by the interaction and the network approaches to industrial markets, Easton (1995, p. 421) defines orientation as a "fixed profile of positions" in terms of axiology, ontology, and epistemology, which, in turn, is thought to determine methodological choice. The author emphasizes the idea of consistency as "the necessary metacriterion required to create an orientation" (Easton, 1995, p. 422), which he illustrates with Burrell and Morgan's (1979) subjectivist and objectivist approaches to social science (see Table 5).

Such a dichotomy between qualitative and quantitative methodology has been further elaborated by Morgan and Smircich (1980), who subdivide the subjectivist-

Table 5. Assumptions About the Nature of Social Science.

Objective-Subjective Dimensions	Subjectivist Approach to Social Science	Objectivist Approach to Social Science
Ontology	Nominalism	Realism
Epistemology	Anti-positivism	Positivism
Human nature	Voluntarism	Determinism
Methodology	Ideographic	Nomothetic

Source: Adapted from Burrell and Morgan (1979).

objectivist continuum into six distinct positions (see Table 6). The authors acknowledge, however, that it "is often the case that the advocates of any given position may attempt to incorporate insights from others" (Morgan & Smircich, 1980, p. 42).

In terms of ontological assumptions, the present paper shares the view of the social world as a contextual field of information, which consists of activities based on the transmission of information. Human beings are thought to participate in such activities by receiving, interpreting, and acting upon information (Arbnor & Bjerke, 1997; Morgan & Smircich, 1980). Such an ontological position implies that some forms of activity are more stable than others reflecting relative rather than fixed and real relationships (Morgan & Smircich, 1980). The way such relationships are viewed in the present paper eventually comes closer to the next ontological position towards the objectivist end of the continuum. In particular, because this paper shares the realist view that relationships may be necessary or contingent depending, respectively, on whether the identity of social entities is mutually dependent or not (Sayer, 1992). In other words, I do not regard inter-firm or inter-personal relationships as constantly modified as a result of patterns of learning and mutual adjustment (Morgan & Smircich, 1980) but rather as relationships, which, in some cases, may be fixed and real.

According to Morgan and Smircich (1980) viewing reality as a contextual field of information implies the adoption of epistemologies based on cybernetic metaphors. One such a metaphor, which is central to the theoretical context of the present paper (see Section 2.1), is the concept of "network" namely for the network approach to industrial markets and the process approach to MNC management. A key feature of such an epistemological stance is the concern with contexts rather than boundaries (Morgan & Smircich, 1980).

In other words, social entities such as organizations and their environment are conceptualized in terms of a reciprocal rather than a one-sided relationship. Such an emphasis on the interactive rather than causal nature of relationships is reflected

Table 6. The Subjective-Objective Debate Within Social Science.

	Reality as a projection of human imagination	Reality as a social construction	Reality as a realm of social discourse	Reality as a contextual field of information	Reality as a concrete process	Reality as a concrete structure
Core ontological assumptions	Reality as a projection of human imagination	Reality as a social construction	Reality as a realm of social discourse	Reality as a contextual field of information	Reality as a concrete process	Reality as a concrete structure
Assumptions about human nature	Man as pure spirit, consciousness, being	Man as a social constructor, the symbol creator	Man as an actor, the symbol user	Man as an information processor	Man as an adaptor	Man as a responder
Basic epistemological stance	To obtain phenomenological insight, revelation	To understand how social reality is created	To understand patterns of symbolic discourse	To map contexts	To study systems, process, change	To construct a positivist science
Favored metaphors	Transcendental	Language game, accomplishment, text	Theatre, culture	Cybernetic	Organism	Machine
Research methods	Exploration of pure subjectivity	Hermeneutics	Symbolic analysis	Contextual analysis of Gestalten	Historical analysis	Lab experiments, surveys

Source: Adapted from Morgan and Smircich (1980).

on the research goals of the interaction and network approaches to industrial markets, which are mainly descriptive in nature (Easton, 2000). Also primarily descriptive, the process approach to MNC management questions the assumptions of studies inspired by the so-called strategy-structure paradigm (Chandler, 1962), which emphasizes a one-sided relationship between organizational strategy and environment (Whittington, 1993). The focus of the present paper on managerial work (Mintzberg, 1973) also justifies such an epistemological stance once that studies of management roles have been considered the most contextual type of management studies (Tsoukas, 2000).

A recent taxonomy of social research paradigms is provided by Guba and Lincoln (1998), who distinguish between positivism, postpositivism, critical theory et al., and constructivism, namely in terms of ontology, epistemology, and methodology. In brief, critical theory and constructivism assume the co-existence of multiple social realities, which cannot be dissociated from particular belief systems, whereas positivism assumes a single apprehensible reality. Correspondingly, critical theory and constructivism assume knowledge to be value-dependent, whereas positivism assumes value-free researchers (Guba & Lincoln, 1998) and independent non-reflective respondents (Numagami, 1998).

Realism – postpositivism in Lincoln and Guba's (2000) terminology – constitutes a somewhat intermediate stance by assuming simultaneously that: (a) the world exists independently of our knowledge of it (Sayer, 1992); but (b) knowledge can only be produced in terms of available descriptions or discourses (Sayer, 2000). In other words, scientific theories and discourse change over time, but the world they address largely remains the same. It follows that social science goals are neither nomothetic i.e. the postulation of invariant laws, nor idiographic i.e. the documentation of idiosyncrasies (Sayer, 2000).

The present paper shares the view that although social phenomena are concept-dependent, they exist regardless of researchers' interpretation of them. Furthermore, although our knowledge of the world is fallible and theory-laden it is not immune to empirical check and critical evaluation (Sayer, 1992). The following sub-sections enable such an evaluation by justifying the methodological choices of the study on which the present paper is based.

3.2. Qualitative Research

The study represents an instance of qualitative research within the realist paradigm (Healy & Perry, 2000). A general distinctive feature of qualitative research is its reliance on a few cases and many variables in contrast to quantitative research's concern with a few variables and many cases (Ragin, 1987). There is, however, a general lack of consensus on what constitutes a "case" (Ragin & Becker, 1992) and "qualitative research" (e.g. Creswell, 1998). The present paper shares the view that a "case" is "a phenomenon of some sort occurring in a bounded context" (Miles & Huberman, 1994, p. 25). From such a perspective, the "case" is the unit of analysis of the study. A study may, in turn, consist of one or several cases, constituting a single- or multiple-case study, respectively.[2]

The present paper also shares the view that rather than a specific research design (Hakim, 2000), qualitative research is "an umbrella term covering an array of interpretative techniques that seek to describe, decode, translate and otherwise come to terms with the meaning, not the frequency, of certain more or less naturally occurring phenomena in the social world" (Van Maanen, 1983, p. 9). In the present paper such an emphasis on meaning rather than frequency does not necessarily reflect conventionalist or constructivist epistemology (Easton, 1995) once that realism also takes into account "the meanings and purposes that people ascribe to their actions" (Guba & Lincoln, 1998, p. 205). In other words, the present paper takes the perceptions of FSMs and their meaning not as multiples realities, but as alternative perspectives of a single but not perfectly apprehensible reality (Healy & Perry, 2000).

The present paper is, therefore, qualitative in the sense that it builds a complex and holistic picture of a phenomenon in its natural setting, based on the analysis of words and on the report of detailed views of informants (Creswell, 1998). The informants are FSMs in industrial markets, who constitute the cases of the study (Miles & Huberman, 1994). The following section discusses the reasons behind the adoption of a multiple-case study approach in the study on which the present paper is based.

3.3. Case Study Approach

According to McGrath (1982, p. 70) "*all research strategies and methods are seriously flawed*, often with their very strengths in regard to one desideratum functioning as serious weaknesses in regard to other, equally important, goals. Indeed, *it is not possible, in principle, to do 'good'* (that is, methodologically sound) *research*." Such a methodological dilemma has to do with the inability of any research strategy to simultaneously minimize threats to data integrity i.e. absence of error and bias, and to currency i.e. generalizability of research results (Campbell & Stanley, 1963). In Bonoma's (1985, p. 200) words: "high degree of data integrity requires a precise operationalization of the research variables, a relatively large sample size and quantitative data for statistical power, and the ability to exercise control over persons, settings, and other factors to prevent causal contamination." In the same author's words: "high currency typically demands situationally unconstrained operationalizations of variables to allow cross-setting generalization, and observations within natural, ecologically valid settings – "noisy" settings – where large samples, quantitative measures, and control are more difficult to achieve" (Bonoma, 1985, pp. 200–201).

The study adopts a cross-sectional multiple-case study approach, which is primarily justified with three interrelated factors: (1) the research questions; (2) the nature of the phenomenon under study; and (3) practical constraints. Each of these issues is addressed in the following paragraphs.

As mentioned in Section 1.3, the purpose of the present paper is to describe and conceptualize the implications of FSMs' personal contacts for inter-firm coordination in industrial markets and within MNCs. In particular, the paper attempts to answer two basic research questions:

(i) What factors influence the occurrence of FSMs' personal contacts in industrial MNCs?
(ii) How FSMs' personal contacts enable coordination in industrial markets and within MNCs?

On the one hand, the exploratory and descriptive nature of such questions requires a methodological approach, which supports the development of in-depth information on contextual factors and their association with the phenomenon under study (Bonoma, 1985). One such approach is case study research, which Yin (1994) considers appropriate to answer both exploratory types of "what" questions and "how" questions. In Easton's (1995, p. 476) words: "case research allows the researcher the opportunity to tease out and disentangle a complex set of factors and relationships."

On the other hand, the research questions help narrowing down the scope of the study into "*some* actors in *some* contexts dealing with *some* issues" (Miles & Huberman, 1994, p. 22). In other words, they influence both the theoretical context of the study (see Section 2.1) and the a priori theoretical framework for analysis (see Section 2.5.1). Such a theoretical framework supports, in turn, the adoption of a multiple- rather than single-case design by stating "the conditions under which a particular phenomenon is likely to be found (a literal replication) as well as the conditions when it is not likely to be found (a theoretical replication)" (Yin, 1994, p. 46). In Miles and Huberman's (1994, p. 22) words: "we begin with some orienting constructs, extract the questions, and then start to line up questions with an appropriate sampling frame and methodology."

The second factor behind the adoption of a case study approach is the nature of the phenomenon under study. In particular, whether the phenomenon can be studied outside its natural setting, and whether it may be meaningfully quantified

(Bonoma, 1985). In the present paper, personal contacts of FSMs are regarded as highly contextual requiring a methodological approach, which does not interfere with their natural setting. On the other hand, the complex and interdisciplinary nature of such a phenomenon makes it less amenable to meaningful quantification. The adoption of a case study approach in the study thus seems appropriate as it is "an empirical inquiry that investigates a contemporary phenomenon within its real-life context, especially when the boundaries between phenomenon and context are not clearly evident" (Yin, 1994, p. 13).

The discussion of factors influencing methodological choice in the study would not be complete without referring practical constraints, which "could be overcome in principle, but are not necessarily easy to overcome in practice" (Easton, 1995, p. 420). In the study, the main constraint has been what Bonoma (1985, p. 206) defines as executional problem, that is, "access to corporations *appropriate for the research objectives*." Such a barrier is, in turn, primarily justified with a second constraint, which is time. On the one hand, FSMs had limited availability to support collection of data for the study and to comment its findings. On the other hand, the research project itself has been financed from September 1999 to September 2003 thus restricting the time available for literature review, data collection and analysis as well as reporting. Such practical constraints partly justify the implementation of a cross-sectional research design, as longitudinal research would have required more access and time by involving "the collection of data that refer to different points in time" (Easton, 1995, p. 480).

In terms of sample, a case study approach usually relies on one or a few cases. As mentioned above, the study adopted a multiple-case approach, which Stake (2000) labels collective case study as distinct from intrinsic- and instrumental case studies. In an intrinsic case study "the purpose is not to come to understand some abstract construct or generic phenomenon," but the particular features of the case, whereas in an instrumental case study the case is of secondary interest, but it facilitates our understanding of something else (Stake, 2000, p. 437). In an instrumental case study "the case still is looked at in depth, its contexts scrutinized, its ordinary activities detailed, but all because this helps the researcher pursue the external interest" (Stake, 2000, p. 437). From this perspective, a collective case study is a collection of instrumental cases, which are selected under the assumption that understanding them will lead to better theorizing about a phenomenon (Stake, 2000).

In similar fashion, Eisenhardt (1991, p. 620) argues that: "multiple cases are a powerful means to create theory because they permit replication and extension among individual cases." Replication supports the identification of patterns through independent corroboration of specific propositions across individual cases, whereas extension supports a more complete theoretical picture based on the complementary nature of the cases (Eisenhardt, 1991). Such a replication logic reflects the concern of the present paper with conceptual instead of statistical representativeness (Strauss & Corbin, 1990), which analyses the frequency of a particular phenomenon with inferential statistics (Yin, 1994). The sampling procedures of the study are discussed in the following section.

3.4. Case Selection

As mentioned in Section 3.2, a "case" in the present paper is a FSM as the focal actor of a contact network in the context of an industrial MNC. Such delimitation follows Miles and Huberman's (1994, p. 26) assertion that a case "may be an *individual* in a defined context." Bonoma (1985, p. 204), on the other hand, defines a case as "a description, directly obtained, of a management situation based on interview, archival, naturalistic observation, and other data, constructed to be sensitive to the context in which management behavior takes place and to its temporal restraints." It may be concluded, therefore, that a case study "is both a process of inquiry about the case and the product of that inquiry" (Stake, 2000, p. 436).

In the study, the selection of cases has been primarily based on the research questions, following the deductive reasoning of Miles and Huberman (1994) and Yin (1994) to whom "the cases are opportunities to study the phenomena" (Stake, 2000, p. 446). The selection of cases was thus aimed at replication and extension (Eisenhardt, 1991) and preceded by literature review (see Section 2.5.1) under the assumption that "an important step in all of these replication procedures is the development of a rich, theoretical framework" (Yin, 1994, p. 46). In other words, the study adopted a logic of theoretical sampling based on the potential for replication and extension instead of a logic of random sampling for statistical purposes (Glaser & Strauss, 1967).

The final sample of cases was determined by the characteristics of the phenomenon under study and its context – personal contacts of FSMs in the coordination of industrial MNCs – but also by some practical constraints (see Section 3.3). The characterization of the phenomenon and its context was based on literature review (see Section 2) leading to a criterion for the selection of cases (see Table 7). Such a criterion was designed to ensure uniformity across cases, while preserving some degree of variety (Stake, 2000) in order to facilitate both replication and extension (Eisenhardt, 1991).

At the individual level, the cases were selected in order to share a position of FSM, which has been associated with interpersonal roles (Mintzberg, 1973, 1975) in general and with a sensor-, builder-, and contributor role in particular (Bartlett & Ghoshal, 1992). In addition, the sample was designed to include managers of

Table 7.   Criterion for the Selection of Cases.

Level of Analysis	Insights from Literature	Attributes of Sample
Country	Socialization in European MNCs (Bartlett & Ghoshal, 1989); European roots of IMP group (Cunningham, 1980)	11 Portuguese subsidiaries of Finnish MNCs
Industry	Social exchange and bonds in industrial markets (Håkansson, 1982; Easton, 1992); Industry norms (Cunningham & Turnbull, 1982)	11 business-to-business subsidiaries; 6 product industries
MNC	Less-hierarchical models of MNC (Marschan, 1996)	11 divisions of 9 MNCs coordinated through formal and informal mechanisms
Subsidiary	Marketing orientation (Gates, 1994); Subsidiary roles (Gupta & Govindarajan, 1991)	10 sales subsidiaries and 1 service subsidiary; 11 SMEs as net knowledge receivers
Individual	Roles of managers (Mintzberg, 1973); Roles of front-line managers (Bartlett & Ghoshal, 1997)	11 FSMs including 3 PCNs, 4 HCNs, and 4 TCNs

various nationalities, in order to assess the extent to which such a background influences their interpersonal roles.

At the subsidiary level, the selection of firms with sales or service function reflects the assumption that FSMs responsible for such functions are more likely to engage in personal contacts within and external to the MNC (Gates, 1994). Still at the subsidiary level, the selection of SMEs, which are net receivers of knowledge within the MNC, reflects the assumption that firm size and resourcefulness equally influences the engagement of FSMs in inter-firm communication.

At the corporate level, the multinational divisions selected resemble less-hierarchical MNCs (Marschan, 1996) given their adoption of both formal and informal mechanisms of coordination such as matrix structures and inter-unit communication. Together with the subsidiary level, the corporate level of analysis constitutes the organizational context of the cases i.e. the FSMs and their contact network within the MNC.

At the industrial level, the selected firms operate in business-to-business instead of business-to-consumer markets reflecting the assumption of intensive social interaction in such markets (Håkansson, 1982). In addition, the selected firms may be grouped into five pairs of product industries[3] in order to assess the extent to which personal contacts in business-to-business markets are contingent on industry norms of behavior (Cunningham & Turnbull, 1982).

Finally, at the country level, the selected firms share the nationality of the parent company – Finnish – as well as the local market in which they operate – Portugal. Such a selection is justified with the assumption that coordination of European MNCs tends to rely on socialization rather than formalization or centralization, which are more typical of American and Japanese MNCs, respectively (Bartlett & Ghoshal, 1989, 1998). Together with the industrial level, the country level of analysis constitutes the market context of the cases i.e. the FSMs and their contact network in the local industrial market.

In addition to the characteristics of the phenomenon under study and its context, the final sample was molded by practical constraints, namely the degree of access to corporations (Bonoma, 1985). At the outset of the research no personal contact had ever been established with any representative of a Finnish MNC in Portugal. A first personal contact was made with Mr. Tapani Lankinen at the office of FinPro in Lisbon, who kindly provided a list of 18 Finnish firms with direct investments in Portugal. Initial personal contacts with such firms were aimed at characterizing them in terms of offered products and services, business functions, year and type of entry mode, as well as nationality of the manager. One firm has shown no interest to participate in the study whereas six others were excluded from the final sample based on the criterion for case selection (see Table 7).

In particular, two subsidiaries had no sales function in Portugal, a third subsidiary had spin-off following the merger of its parent company with a competitor, a fourth subsidiary represented a Finnish SME rather than an MNC, a fifth subsidiary was not managed by a FSM but by several functional managers, and a sixth subsidiary was operating in a business-to-consumer instead of business-to-business market. Taken together with the only firm, which refused to participate in the study, the final sample of eleven (11) firms thus constitutes the total population of firms, which suits the selection criterion (see Table 7).

3.5. Data Collection

A case study approach typically involves the collection of multiple sources of evidence in order to allow in depth and holistic understanding of a small number of social entities or situations (Creswell, 1998; Eisenhardt, 1989; Yin, 1994). In Yin's (1994, p. 92) words: "any finding or conclusion in a case study is likely to be much more convincing and accurate if it is based on several different sources of information, following a corroboratory mode." In similar fashion, Jick (1979, p. 602) contends that: "organizational researchers can improve the accuracy of their judgments by collecting different kinds of data bearing on the same phenomenon." For case studies aimed at theory generation it is equally claimed that: "triangulation made possible by multiple data collection methods provides stronger substantiation of constructs and hypotheses" (Eisenhardt, 1989, p. 538).

Such claims that through data triangulation (Patton, 1987) the strengths of one source of evidence may compensate the weaknesses of another (e.g. Yin, 1994) implicitly assume a single and apprehensible reality and measurable convergence of findings (Easton, 1995). Although the present paper shares such an ontological realism (see Section 3.1), comparability of data is seen here as contingent on the data collection methods employed (Easton, 1995), which, in turn, should reflect the nature of the phenomenon studied. In this respect, personal contacts of FSMs in the coordination of industrial MNCs constitute a simultaneously social, economic and technical phenomenon (Easton, 1995), requiring collection methods, which suit restricted access to and measurement of data (Bonoma, 1985). In the study on which the present paper is based, the main sources of evidence[4] were, therefore, interviews, documents, audio-visual materials, and observations (Creswell, 1998; Yin, 1994).

According to Alvesson (2003, p. 15), the study adopts a neopositivist position on research interviewing aimed at establishing "a context-free truth about reality 'out there' through following a research protocol and getting responses relevant to it, minimizing researcher influence and other sources of bias." In particular, the study adopts a standardized open-ended interview approach, which, according to Patton (1990, p. 280), "consists of a set of questions carefully worded and arranged with the intention of taking each respondent through the same sequence and asking each respondent the same questions with essentially the same words." A standardized open-ended interview is an intermediate option between a general interview guide by which the order and actual wording of questions is not determined in advance, and a closed, fixed response interview by which respondents must fit their knowledge, experience and feelings into the researcher's categories (Patton, 1990).

The relatively low degree of flexibility and spontaneity associated with such a type of structured interviewing (Fontana & Frey, 2000) has been compensated with the use of probes and follow-up questions (Patton, 1990). Such probes were not written out in the standardized open-ended interview guide,[5] but proved crucial in enhancing the degree of comfort, accuracy, and honesty with which the interview questions were answered. In this respect, the respondents may be regarded as elite interviewees (Welch et al., 2002), which constitutes both an opportunity and a challenge in terms of access, power, openness, and feedback.

In the study interviewees were selected on the basis of their knowledge rather than convenience, which is recommended, particularly "if only one informant per organization is to be questioned" (Huber & Power, 1985, p. 174). In terms of access, the general lack of time from managers (cf. Mintzberg, 1973) has been compensated with support from gatekeepers and the adoption of a formal approach (Welch et al., 2002). In particular, the study has benefited from contact information provided by the representative office of FinPro in Lisbon (see Section 3.3.3) and from a cooperative attitude of FSMs' secretaries. The actual interview was preceded by a first personal contact well in advance in order to characterize the firms (see Section 3.3.3) as well as personal contacts in order to agree the date and place of the interview. The approach was formal in the sense that the standardized open-ended interview guide (see Appendix C) and a consent form[6] were sent to the interviewees beforehand.

The issue of power imbalance between the researcher and the interviewee was not detected in the study. Although a few interviewees did express lack of time even during the interview, most of them did praise the relevance of the topic in general and of some of the questions in particular. The physical setting of the interviews – a meeting room with the exception of two instances in which the FSM's own office was used – did not constitute a source of power imbalance either. In general, the formal approach mentioned above appears to have stimulated a respectful and even proactive response from interviewees, who in some cases gathered unsolicited documents before the interview. The use of English as the working language during the interview also appears to have leveled any power imbalance, which could have persisted in favor of the interviewee.

The openness of interviewees was stimulated with an explicit mention in the consent form (see Appendix D) to the implications of the study in general and to the anonymity and confidentiality of responses in particular (Huber & Power, 1985). On the other hand, as expatriates and/or frequent travelers, the interviewed managers appeared to have appreciated my own international experience. The fact that I am a resident in the home country of the MNC they represent as well as a national of the host country they serve appears to have contributed to a certain degree of identification while preserving my status of a neutral outsider. In this respect, the extent to which some interviewees have elaborated on some issues indicates that they may have appreciated "the presence of an attentive and neutral listener" (Welch et al., 2002, p. 623).

In terms of feedback, interviewing FSMs appears to have constituted an opportunity rather than a challenge "as elites are comfortable with written correspondence and they may be willing to engage directly in the process of factual verification of the findings" (Welch et al., 2002, p. 618). In the study, interviewees were required to provide feedback in two stages. In the first stage, the interview transcripts were sent to interviewees for factual verification, whereas in the second stage the preliminary conclusions of the study were sent for their evaluation and approval. Interview transcripts were sent by email, whereas the preliminary conclusions were sent and received by post in order to facilitate handwriting notes in a ready-made printout. The preliminary conclusions were illustrated with quotations from the interviewee to whom they were sent and adapted in terms of form in order to include an executive summary. No interviewee has objected the facts of the interview transcript or the contents of the preliminary conclusions.

As mentioned in Section 3.3.3, at the firm level, the final sample of 11 cases can be said to represent the total population of firms, which suit the selection criterion (see Table 7). Correspondingly, the "cases" in the study – the managing directors of such firms – may be said to constitute an instance of population sampling (Breakwell, 1990), once that all the people who share the characteristics of interest for the study were interviewed. In this respect, it may be argued that other individuals than FSMs themselves could have been interviewed in order to analyze their personal contacts in the coordination of industrial MNCs. Such a possibility was ruled out in the study based on the assumption that "when the knowledge of the informants varies, and the most knowledgeable people are likely to be queried first, responses from additional but less knowledgeable informants can actually decrease the accuracy of responses" (Huber & Power, 1985, p. 175). The same reasoning is put forward by Golden (1992, p. 885) concerning retrospective accounts to whom "the benefits of using multiple respondents has to be balanced against the possibility of introducing greater systematic error into the measurement of certain phenomena." In other words, it was assumed in the study that a contact network is a social phenomenon, which is difficult to perceive for other individuals than the focal actor of such a network. Moreover, interviewing other individuals than the FSM could have been interpreted as lack of confidence in the manager (Welch et al., 2002).

The study is thus based on a total of 11 semi-structured interviews, that is, an interview to each of the FSMs included in the final sample of cases. Such interviews were preceded by a pilot interview to the managing director of the Portuguese subsidiary of a German business-to-business MNC, in order to evaluate the standardized open-ended interview guide. Such a pilot interview was conducted on the 3rd of May 2001 whereas the interviews to the FSMs were conducted between the 10th of May 2001 and the 7th of January 2002. Excluding the pilot interview, the average length of interviews was two hours. All interviews were tape recorded with permission from the interviewees (Patton, 1990) and transcribed. The resulting data amounted to nearly 350 pages or 160 thousand words of transcribed text.

As mentioned above, in addition to interviews, the study relies on documents, audio-visual materials, and observations (Creswell, 1998; Yin, 1994) as sources of evidence. Documents included annual reports, other corporate publications, internal documents, and research reports. Annual reports were a major source of contextual data. On the one hand, they have supported the selection of cases by providing information with which the corporation could be characterized as a less-hierarchical MNC (Marschan, 1996). On the other hand, they have supported the preparation of the interview, by providing information on the formal structure of the MNC and the characteristics of its business. In particular, all interviews were preceded by a brief discussion of the subsidiary activities, based on a printout of the organizational structure of the MNC, valid at the beginning of year 2001.

In addition to annual reports, the study relies on other corporate publications such as Press and stock exchange releases, promotional brochures, and group magazines. Internal documents, whenever possible, included organizational charts at the divisional and subsidiary level, which were not available in the annual report, reports on subsidiary performance, and job descriptions of the interviewed FSMs. Research reports included doctoral reports concerning the MNCs which provide the context for the cases in the study.

On the other hand, interviews and documents were supplemented with audio-visual materials and observations. Audio-visual materials were as crucial as documents in terms of contextual data, once that the studied MNCs provide extensive information in their web sites. Useful data for the study available in the World Wide Web included corporate key figures, divisions, organization, history, and contact information, among others. In addition to data collected from web sites, the study relies on electronic mail messages exchanged with the FSMs and respective secretaries. Although primarily concerned with practical arrangements such as the date for an interview, such messages provided sometimes information on the MNC and/or the subsidiary, which was not available in annual reports or in web sites.

To some extent, observations were also a source of evidence in the study, particularly on the day of the interviews. Before the interview, some notes were made concerning the subsidiary physical setting, which could provide some clues on the relationship of FSMs with subordinates and on the degree of subsidiary integration in the MNC. During the interview, notes were also made whenever the FSM displayed emotional involvement (Huber & Power, 1985) concerning an issue or was interrupted by either a knock on the door or a phone call, thus communicating "live" with a counterpart. In sum, the study relies on data collected through semi-structured interviews, which were supplemented, ex-ante and ex-post, with data from published and internal documents, audio-visual materials such as web sites and emails, and non participant observations (Creswell, 1998). The findings of the study are thus mainly based on primary rather than secondary data.

3.6. Data Analysis

There is no consensual definition of qualitative data analysis (Coffey & Atkinson, 1996; Creswell, 1998), which in case studies largely "depends on an investigator's own style of rigorous thinking, along with the sufficient presentation of evidence and careful consideration of alternative interpretations" (Yin, 1994, pp. 102–103). Stake (1995) distinguishes between direct interpretation and categorical aggregation as two strategies of making sense of case study evidence. The former refers to meaning, which emerges from a single instance, whereas the latter refers to meaning from the repetition of phenomena. The author adds that: "with instrumental case studies, where the case serves to help us understand phenomena or relationships within it, the need for categorical data and measurements is greater" (Stake, 1995, p. 77). In similar fashion, Silverman (2000) distinguishes between a narrative and a realist approach to interview data. The former attempts to access various stories or narratives through which people describe their worlds, whereas the latter equally searches for the "subjective" meanings of people, but relates them to "objective" social structures (Silverman, 2000).

As mentioned in Section 3.3, the study is a collection of instrumental cases primarily based on evidence from interviews (see Section 3.5), which are analyzed from a realist perspective (see Section 3.1). Data analysis was therefore based on categorical aggregation (Stake, 1995) in general and a realist approach to interview data (Silverman, 2000) in particular.

Miles and Huberman (1994) define data analysis as three linked sub-processes of data reduction, data display, and conclusion drawing and verification. Data reduction begins even before data collection with the specification of the research questions, the theoretical framework for analysis, the case selection criterion, and the data collection methods, by which the scope of data collection is set. During and after data collection, data reduction proceeds with summaries, coding, and identification of themes. Data display implies the organization and display of reduced data for further examination. Conclusion drawing and verification involves the interpretation of displayed data. Creswell (1998, p. 141) provides a synthesis of Miles and Huberman's (1994) and two other general data analysis strategies (Bogdan & Biklen, 1992; Wolcott, 1994), which was adopted in the study as follows:

(i)   Sketching ideas
(ii) Displaying data
(iii) Identifying codes
(iv) Reducing information

(v)   Counting frequency of codes
(vi) Relating categories
(vii) Relating to analytic framework in literature

In the study sketching ideas consisted of reading through all collected information in order to obtain a sense of the overall data (Tesch, 1990). Interview transcripts – the main source of evidence – were read several times during the process of transcription, increasing the familiarity with the 11 cases selected (Eisenhardt, 1989). Once the transcription was concluded, the interview text was read again and margin notes were written down. Such notes referred to initial impressions about the data such as eventual categories or conceptual relationships.

The second step in the analysis was the creation of a matrix, which displays the data collected by case. In addition to such a data matrix (see Appendix B), a table was created in order to visualize variables by theme. The themes were based on the research questions thus encompassing variables (1) triggering or (2) inhibiting the (3) establishment or (4) maintenance of FSMs' personal contacts, supposedly (5) enabling, in turn, certain coordination tasks to be performed. Some of the variables with which such five themes were associated have been identified in extant literature and included in the a priori theoretical framework for analysis (see Section 2.5.1).

Such themes and variables can be regarded as the a priori hierarchical coding frame (Richards & Richards, 1995) of the study, following the view that "coding must start with a frame that is well grounded in a theory or conceptual scheme" (Araujo, 1995, p. 97). In other words, the themes constitute single categories at the top of a coding hierarchy, which define the scope of the data through general-to-specific links to other categories immediately below (Richards & Richards, 1995). In the present paper, such categories are codes, which are empirically grounded by relating to chunks of text as well as theoretically relevant by only acquiring meaning in relation to other categories (Dey, 1993). The final hierarchical coding frame[7] results, therefore, from a bottom-up or data-driven method of building coding trees (Richards & Richards, 1995), which is also informed by the a priori theoretical framework for analysis (Araujo, 1995).

The actual process by which the hierarchical coding frame was developed implied, in turn, a reduction of information in terms of the number of categories considered. The first list of codes consisted of 128 categories including the five a priori themes referred above, whereas the final list of codes (see Appendix E) encompasses 82 categories, including 17 themes: inf.dependence-/uncertainty+, inf.dependence−/uncertainty−, inf.dependence+/uncertainty+, inf.dependence +/uncertainty−, dec.dependence−/uncertainty+, dec.dependence−/uncertainty−, dec.dependence+/uncertainty+, dec.dependence+/ uncertainty−, channels, direction, frequency, paths, information exchange, assessment, negotiation, decision-making and resource allocation. The first eight themes in the final list of codes correspond to the a priori triggering and inhibiting contextual factors, once that FSMs' personal contacts may be triggered and inhibited by the very same factor. The four following themes in the final list of codes correspond not to the context, but to the process or dynamic aspects of FSMs' personal contacts, once that both their establishment and maintenance may be characterized in terms of channels, direction, frequency and paths. The last five themes in the final list of codes correspond to a sub-categorization of the a priori enabling theme into five types of content or function of FSMs' personal contacts.

The several updates of the hierarchical coding frame also implied a reduction of information in terms of the amount of text to which codes were attached. Although the codes have been attached to lines of text instead of sentences or paragraphs, substantial chunks of text were coded for each category in the first coding phase in order to avoid atheoretical decontextualization (Araujo, 1995). Subsequent retrieval of coded data allowed, however, the refinement of categories (Eisenhardt, 1989) reducing the amount of text to which codes were attached. The overall amount of coded text was also reduced whenever such a process of refining categories involved the merger of two different codes and respective text.

The retrieval of coded data also allowed "counts" of data in order to determine how frequently codes appeared in the database (Miles & Huberman, 1994). Counting the frequency of codes across cases (Eisenhardt, 1989) helped confirming or disconfirming patterns, which were initially noted through data reduction. In particular, it was possible to identify 29 categories from the final list of 82 codes (see Appendix E), which were not attached to the text of at least one case. On average, each of such 29 categories was not attached to the text of 1.75 cases out of the 11 selected. On the other hand, the text of a case was not coded, on average, with 4.6 categories out of the final list of 82 codes. As mentioned in Section 3.3, the counting of such frequencies has followed a logic of replication across individual cases (Eisenhardt, 1991) aiming at conceptual rather than statistical representativeness (Strauss & Corbin, 1990; Yin, 1994).

The process of counting frequencies of codes preceded the development of a final theoretical framework (see Section 5.1), which underlines the overall relation between the categories. In Miles and Huberman's (1994, p. 261) words: "when you're trying to determine what someone's behavior 'means', the mental exercise involves connecting a discrete fact with other discrete facts, and then grouping these into lawful, comprehensible, and more abstract patterns." In this respect, an effort was made in the study to preserve the holistic nature of the phenomena by considering simultaneously its content, context and process (Pettigrew, 1987).

The analysis of data was concluded with the discussion of findings in the light of previous research (see Sections 5.1 to 5.3). Eisenhardt (1989) refers to such a step as enfolding literature by which emerging concepts or propositions are compared with a broad range of extant literature. In this respect, the present paper considers the three research traditions, which constitute its theoretical context (see Section 2.1), the body of knowledge to which it contributes (see Section 5.4).

The seven steps just described were all supported with computer software including MS Word, MS Excel and NUD × IST N5, the latter as an acronym for Non-numerical Unstructured Data Indexing Searching and Theorizing. The development and use of computer software programs for qualitative data analysis has become widespread over the last decade (Weitzman, 2000; Wolfe et al., 1993). Correspondingly, literature on the topic has been proliferating, reviewing different software packages (e.g. Fielding & Lee, 1991; Tesch, 1990; Weitzman & Miles, 1995) as well as their methodological capabilities and limitations (e.g. Dey, 1993; Kelle, 1995; Weitzman, 1999). NUD × IST is specifically developed to support text interpretation and theory building (Wolfe et al., 1993) having been categorized as a text analysis program by Tesch (1990) and as a code-based theory builder by Weitzman and Miles (1995). The program has basically three tools: the coders, text search, and node search. Such tools operate on two complementary sets of data: the document system, which holds documents, notes and memos, and the node system, which represents themes and categories. The two systems are related through hierarchical coding (Richards, 2000).

In the study, the use of computer software supported the following data analysis tasks: transcribing, storage, data display, coding, memoing, search and retrieval, data "linking," content analysis, conclusion-drawing and verification, and theory-building (Weitzman, 1999). The interviews were transcribed with MS Word and subsequently stored as separate documents in the document system of NUD × IST. Such interview transcripts and other sources of evidence were displayed in a data matrix (see Appendix B) which was created with MS Excel. The same program was used to create a table in order to display the total number of categories emerging over time. Such categories corresponded to the codes displayed in the node system of NUD × IST thus including themes and variables (see Appendix E). Coding itself was performed with the coders of NUD × IST which allow memoing of both documents and nodes. Search and retrieval of coded text was performed with the text- and node-search tools of NUD × IST. By allowing the simultaneous update of documents and nodes, NUD × IST has also allowed data "linking" by which segments of text were connected to each other in order to form categories.

Content analysis was supported with NUD × IST's browser menu for nodes, which allows the researcher to review all codes which have been attached to a particular quotation (coded text), and to "jump" to the respective interview transcript (document) in order to review the context of such a quotation. In addition, NUD × IST's node explorer automatically counts the number of both lines and interview transcripts coded by a certain node or category, thus having supported the counting of codes within and across cases. Understandably, such tasks also supported the drawing and verification of conclusions, based on the on-going refinement of the hierarchical coding frame in NUD × IST's tree node. Theory building, by which the study findings are justified and confronted with extant literature, was performed with MS Word.

3.7. Validity and Reliability

The quality of the study may be assessed in terms of tests commonly adopted in the social sciences such as construct validity, external validity, and reliability (Yin, 1994). Construct validity refers to the adoption of appropriate operational measures for the concepts being studied, whereas external validity concerns the extent to which findings may be generalized beyond the scope of the study. Reliability implies that the repetition of the study's procedures would ensure identical findings (Yin, 1994).

In the study on which the present paper is based, the tactics adopted in order to increase construct validity included: (1) a pilot interview; (2) clarifications in interviews; (3) feedback from interviewees; and (4) interviewees' verbatim responses. As mentioned in Section 3.5, the study included a pilot interview in order to evaluate the standardized open-ended interview guide (Patton, 1990), namely in terms of sequence and wording of questions. In addition, some concepts such as "personal contact" were clarified at the beginning of the interviews as well as during the interviews when necessary. In this respect, the adoption of a single working language – English – in addition to my own background and international experience (see Section 3.5) appears to have reduced the likelihood of misunderstandings with the interviewees.

A third tactic to improve construct validity in the study was the request for feedback concerning the interview transcript and its interpretation (see Section 3.5). Such a factual verification, evaluation and approval from interviewees is thought to have further reduced eventual misunderstandings. A fourth and final tactic to improve construct validity was the extensive use of quotations from the interviews in preliminary and final reports in order to illustrate the studied concepts and their relationships. Such quotations relate conceptual variables based on the a priori theoretical framework for analysis (see Section 2.5.1) with empirical accounts from the interviewees (see Sections 4.2. to 4.4) thus contributing to a logical chain of evidence (Yin, 1994), which allows readers to make their own interpretation (Patton, 1990).

Concerning external validity, the present paper aims at analytical rather than statistical generalization (Yin, 1994), based on replication logic (see Section 3.3). Such a conceptual representativeness (Strauss & Corbin, 1990) requires, in turn, a careful selection of cases based on theoretical rather than random sampling (Glaser & Strauss, 1967). In this respect, it is the criterion for the selection of cases adopted in the study (see Table 7 in Section 3.3.3), which defines the domain to which its findings may be generalized (Yin, 1994). However, even within such a domain, the study's findings should be cautiously generalized. In particular, because the study's sample does not necessarily represents the population of individuals, subsidiaries, MNCs, industries, and countries, which constitute the referred domain.

On the one hand, the sample may not be representative of other European countries (e.g. Bartlett & Ghoshal, 1989) or industries (e.g. Håkansson, 1982), especially in terms of contextual factors of FSMs' personal contacts such as market idiosyncrasy and business culture (see Section 4.2.3). On the other hand, the sample may not be representative of other MNCs, given the eventual influence of MNCs' nationality in the adoption of formal and informal mechanisms of coordination (e.g. Harzing, 1999) and the general difficulty of operationalizing the distinctive features of less-hierarchical MNCs (e.g. Marschan, 1996). Moreover, the fact that the sample includes subsidiaries with more than one function (see Appendix A) may restrict the extent to which the findings can be generalized to a larger population of sales subsidiaries (e.g. Gates, 1994). Finally, the specificity of the sample in terms of nationality, educational background, gender, prior international assignments, and tenure of the FSMs (see Section 4.1) must also be taken into account when generalizing the findings to a larger population of front-line managers (e.g. Bartlett & Ghoshal, 1997). In addition to such sampling issues the limited amount of interviews and the difficulties encountered in terms of data- and respondent triangulation (see Section 3.5) further justify a cautious generalization of the paper's findings.

In terms of reliability, the study has been enhanced with the adoption of explicit procedures for data collection and analysis including: (1) a data matrix; (2) a consent form; (3) a standardized open-ended interview guide; and (4) computer software for qualitative data analysis. The data matrix (see Appendix B) specifies the types of data collected per case following Yin's (1994, p. 36) reminder that reliability implies "doing the *same* case over again, not on "replicating" the results of one case by doing *another* case study." In other words, such a data matrix identifies the sources of evidence, which were collected for each of the cases selected, contributing to the reliability of data collection. The access to such sources of evidence was facilitated by the adoption of a consent form (see Appendix D), which explicitly states the requirements of the study in terms of sources of evidence as well as the implications for those who may provide such types of data. Such a consent form can therefore be regarded as a further factor of reliability in terms of data collection in the study.

For the particular case of interviews – the main source of evidence – the standardized open-ended interview guide (see Appendix C) is also thought to

Chronology	Theory and methodology	Empirical data
September 1999	- first doctoral course - first term paper - initial literature review	- list of 18 Finnish firms with FDI in Portugal
November 2000	- change of topic from "foreign market entry" to "MNC coordination" - first a priori theoretical framework	- selection of 11 cases
May 2001	- data matrix - interview guide - consent form - first transcriptions	- access negotiations - secondary data - pilot interview - first interviews
January 2002	- initial data analysis	- final interview
May 2002	- first conference paper (IMP)	- initial feedback on transcripts
September 2002	- second conference paper (EIBA)	
January 2003	- final data analysis	- initial feedback on conclusions
May 2003	- third conference paper (IMP)	
June 2003		- closing negotiations
July 2003	- doctoral study (submitted version)	
August 2003	- fourth conference paper (VCIB)	
October 2003	- fifth conference paper (EIBA)	
December 2003	- doctoral study (revised version)	

Fig. 6. The Research Process.

have reduced research error and bias (Fontana & Frey, 2000). The contribution of such an interview guide to the reliability of the study may, however, be questioned in two ways. On the one hand, the standardized open-ended interview guide was supplemented with probes and follow-up questions (see Section 3.5), which trades-off reliability for construct validity due to an increased but less transparent control over the interview (Patton, 1990). On the other hand, collecting data in different moments in time (Yin, 1994, p. 36) even with the same interview guide may involve bias and error due to respondents' inability to recall past events accurately (Huber & Power, 1985).

A final procedure to enhance the reliability of the study was the adoption of computer software for qualitative data analysis (see Section 3.6). In particular, the adoption of NUD $\times$ IST contributed to the reliability of the study by allowing its document and node systems to be saved as a separate version of the study in different moments in time. Such an electronic database of interview transcripts and respective coding has been saved in four different dates, over a period of one year. Such versions thus allow a subsequent audit trail of notes, memos, and more importantly, themes and categories (Richards, 2000). In similar but paper-based fashion, the overall study has been chronologically documented over a period of four years. Figure 6 briefly depicts such a process, providing general guidance on the aspects of the research project which may be scrutinized.

4. DISCUSSION OF CASE EVIDENCE

This fourth section presents and discusses the evidence from the cases. The following sub-section introduces the cases and the remaining sub-sections examine the context, content, and process of FSMs' personal contacts, respectively.

4.1. Introduction to the Cases

As mentioned in Section 3.3.3, although the "cases" in the present paper are FSMs as the focal actors of a contact network, the criterion for their selection also took into account their context at the subsidiary-, corporate-, industrial- and national level.

At the subsidiary level, and as mentioned in Section 1.4, the context of the eleven cases is a local implementer subsidiary (Birkinshaw & Morrison, 1995), in the sense that it operates with few resources in a non-strategic market (Bartlett & Ghoshal, 1986) and that it is a net receiver of knowledge within the MNC (Gupta & Govindarajan, 1991, 1994). In the present paper, the size of the subsidiary, measured in terms of absolute and relative amount of sales and employees, is adopted as a proxy for both the level of local resources (Ghoshal & Nohria, 1989) and strategic importance of the local market (Bartlett & Ghoshal, 1986). In this respect, the studied subsidiaries are typically SMEs with an average of EUR 28.8 million in sales and of 51 employees in 2001. The relative weight of the subsidiary's sales and employees on the MNC as a whole was, on average, 1.4% and 1.8%, respectively. In terms of knowledge flows (Gupta & Govindarajan, 1991), all subsidiaries were classified as net knowledge receivers by their respective FSM.

At the corporate level, the context of the cases is an MNC with an average of EUR 7,598 million in sales and of 22,562 employees in 2001. The smallest MNC had sales of EUR 131 million and a total of 1,360 employees in 2001, whereas the largest MNC had sales of EUR 31191 million and a total of 53,849 employees. At the industrial level, and as mentioned in Section 1.4, the context of the 11 cases are six general product industries, which include telecommunications, pulp and paper, technical textiles, minerals, mechanical engineering and plastic pipes (see Appendix A). Finally, at the country level, and as equally mentioned in Section 1.4, the context of the eleven cases is a small and open economy for both the MNCs – Finland – and their subsidiaries – Portugal.

The cases themselves – FSMs – can be characterized in terms of their nationality, educational background, gender and prior international assignments as well as tenure in the host country, in the industry, in the MNC, in the subsidiary, and in their current position. In terms of nationality, the final sample of cases includes three Finnish nationals or PCNs (Parent Country Nationals), four Portuguese nationals or HCNs (Host Country Nationals) as well as a Belgian, a Dutch, a French and a Spanish national as four TCNs (Third Country Nationals). In terms of educational background, the final sample of cases includes seven degrees in engineering and four degrees in economics or business administration. The final sample only included male managers.

On average the eleven cases had had three international assignments prior to their current position. However, five out of 11 had had none. The FSM with most international experience had had 10 international assignments.

In terms of tenure in the host country, and excluding HCNs, the cases had been, on average, 11 years in Portugal. In this respect, the most experienced FSM had been 31 years in the country, whereas the least experienced one had been two years.

On the other hand, the cases had, on average, worked for 21 years in the industry. In this respect, the most experienced FSM had been working for 35 years, whereas the least experienced one had been working for six years.

Within the MNC, the cases had, on average, worked for 15 years. The most experienced FSM had been working for 30 years, whereas the least experienced one had been working for six years.

Table 8. Key Figures of the Cases and Their Context.

Key Figures 2001	Average	Minimum	Maximum
Subsidiary[a] sales (EUR million)	28.8		
Subsidiary employees	51		
Subsidiary weight on MNC sales	1.4%		
Subsidiary weight on MNC employees	1.8%		
MNC[b] sales (EUR million)	7598	131	31191
MNC employees (thousand)	22.562	1.360	53.849
FSM's international assignments	3	0	10
FSM's tenure in host country	11	2	31
FSM's tenure in industry	21	6	35
FSM's tenure at the MNC	15	6	30
FSM's tenure at the subsidiary	12	2	29
FSM's tenure at the position	8	2	12

[a] The minimum and maximum figures concerning the subsidiary are undisclosed as requested by some FSMs.
[b] The average figures concerning the MNC are calculated for 9 rather than 11 MNCs (see Table 7 in Section 3.4).

In addition, the cases had, on average, worked for 12 years in the subsidiary. In this respect, the most experienced FSM had been working for 29 years, whereas the least experienced one had been working for two years.

Finally, the cases had, on average, worked for eight years in their current position at the subsidiary. The most experienced FSM had been working for 12 years, whereas the least experienced one had been working for two years. Table 8 depicts the key figures concerning the cases and their context.

As mentioned in Section 3.3.3, such characteristics of the final sample of cases and their context were defined in order to ensure some degree of both uniformity and variety, thus facilitating replication and extension in the analysis of case evidence (Eisenhardt, 1991). Such case evidence is discussed in the following sections in terms of context, content and process of FSMs' personal contacts. As mentioned in Section 2.5.1, the adoption of such a specific structure for the discussion of case evidence is based on Pettigrew's (1987) call for a simultaneous account of context, content and process in theories of dynamic managerial phenomena.

4.2. Context of Personal Contacts

In order to examine the context of personal contacts of FSMs this sub-section is subdivided into one section on the general interpersonal context of FSMs and another section on the different contact networks of such managers. The remaining eight sub-sections examine alternative scenarios of individual dependence and uncertainty.

4.2.1. Interpersonal Context of FSMs

As mentioned in Section 2.5.1, previous studies within the IMP group (see Sections 2.2 and 2.3) and the process approach to MNC management (see Section 2.4) do not explicitly account for the distinctive features of FSMs' personal contacts. Research within the IMP group tends to examine personal contacts in industrial markets without specifying the individuals who are involved in social exchange (IMP group, 1982) or the actors who are involved in industrial coordination (Håkansson & Johanson, 1993). The process approach to MNC management increasingly suggests the relevance of personal contacts for coordination at the subsidiary and MNC level, without specifying the individuals who are involved in interpersonal networking (Nohria & Ghoshal, 1997). The present paper attempts, therefore, to clarify the distinctive features of FSMs' interpersonal context following the suggestion that social networks of "managers and nonmanagers do differ" (Carroll & Teo, 1996, p. 437). For that purpose, two main constructs are adopted: dependence and uncertainty.

According to social exchange theory, the dependence of one party in an exchange relationship corresponds to the power of the other. In this respect, Emerson (1962, p. 32) argues that: "the dependence of actor A upon actor B is (1) directly proportional to A's motivational investment in goals mediated by B, and (2) inversely proportional to the availability of those goals to A outside the A-B relation." Earlier, Weber (1947) equally asserted that bureaucratic authority is based on formal decree, but also on the superior's ability to control resources upon which the subordinate depends. Astley and Sachdeva (1985) label such two sources of authority the legal and the rational components of authority, respectively.

In the context of MNCs, Forsgren (1990a, p. 74) equates authority with "power based on a right to control and a concomitant obligation to obey" and influence with "power based on the control of critical resources" (Larsson, 1985). Authority is thought to affect organizational decisions directly and to flow unilaterally downward, whereas influence is seen as more informal and multidirectional in nature. Forsgren (1990a) thus seems to restrict authority to its legal component by equating its rational component with influence (Astley & Sachdeva, 1985). More recently, Hewett and Bearden (2001, p. 53) define dependence of one party on another "as the extent to which the first party relies on the relationship for the fulfillment of important needs" such the case of FSMs on the headquarters. The authors do not specify, however, whether such a dependence and concomitant authority is legal or rational (Astley & Sachdeva, 1985).

In the context of industrial markets, dependence is primarily discussed in terms of mutual control of activities (Håkansson & Johanson, 1984) through inter-firm relationships, which provide access to external resources (Pfeffer & Salancik, 1978). Such an emphasis on mutuality (Ford et al., 1986) thus seems to equate dependence with Forsgren's (1990a) notion of influence, given the assumption of interdependent actors, resources, and activities (Håkansson & Johanson, 1992) in those markets.

Uncertainty, on the other hand, has been generally defined as the difference between the amount of information required to perform a task and the amount of information already possessed by the organization (Galbraith, 1973, 1977). Tushman (1979, p. 483) refers to both internal and external sources of work related uncertainty, which require organizations "to gather information from the environment, process information within the organization, and then export information back to the environment." Earlier, Thompson (1967) had identified technologies and environments as major sources of uncertainty for organizations.

In his review of literature employing the concept of uncertainty, Milliken (1987, p. 134) notes that environmental uncertainty may be used "both as a descriptor of the state of the organizational environment and as a descriptor of the state of a person who perceives himself/herself to be lacking critical information about the environment." The former implies that uncertainty can be objectively measured (e.g. Starbuck, 1976), whereas the latter takes such measurements as incompatible with contrasting perceptions due to contextual factors and individual attributes (e.g. Downey et al., 1975). Milliken (1987, p. 136) appears to subscribe the latter view by defining uncertainty "as an individual's perceived inability to predict something accurately." The author suggests three types of environmental uncertainty, which can be experienced by the organization's administrators: state, effect and response uncertainty. State uncertainty refers to perceived unpredictability of changes in the general environment or of actions by key organizational counterparts. Effect uncertainty refers to the inability to predict what impact a change or action will have on the organization. Response uncertainty refers to the lack of knowledge of own response options and/or the inability to predict their consequences.

In the context of industrial markets, uncertainty has been associated with heterogeneity (Hägg & Johanson, 1983) and equated with lack of information on the options available in input and sales markets (Forsgren et al., 1995). Ford (1980) refers to uncertainty in terms of potential costs and benefits associated with the adaptation to a specific counterpart, including opportunity costs of not doing it with other potential partners. More recently, Ford et al. (1998) refer to need-, market- and transaction uncertainty of buyers as well as capacity-, application- and transaction uncertainty of suppliers in industrial markets. Such views of uncertainty in industrial markets seem to generally correspond to Millikon's (1987, p. 138) notion of response uncertainty, which is usually experienced "in the course of choosing from a number of possible strategies."

In the context of less-hierarchical MNCs, Gupta et al. (1999) discuss heterogeneity in terms of country differences, strategic roles assigned to subsidiaries, and clarity of roles assigned to FSMs. The authors suggest that FSMs may experience uncertainty "about the manner in which goals should be prioritized, and the appropriate behaviors needed to achieve results" (Gupta et al., 1999, p. 208). Such a view of uncertainty equally seems to correspond to Millikon's (1987) notion of response uncertainty.

As mentioned in section 1.5, the present paper equates dependence with FSMs' lack of authority (Weber, 1947), which, in turn, may be legal or rational (Astley & Sachdeva, 1985). Legal authority is based on the formal right to control and be obeyed to, whereas rational authority is based on the control of resources upon which others depend. As also mentioned in Section 1.5, uncertainty is here equated with FSMs' inability to predict something accurately, including internal and external changes to the organization, their outcomes and possible responses (Milliken, 1987). In the present paper, both dependence and uncertainty are thus viewed as perceptions of FSMs rather than objectively measurable characteristics of their context. Such a view is based on the assumption of FSMs' bounded rationality (see Section 2.1) in a single but not perfectly apprehensible reality (see Section 3.1).

In terms of FSMs' interpersonal context, a distinction can be made between an owner system and a business network to which "any unit in an international firm, be it a subsidiary or a business unit, belongs at the same time" (Forsgren & Johanson, 1992, p. 24). The owner system or MNC is primarily based on formal relationships established by a central authority (Williamson, 1975), whereas the business network or the local industrial market is primarily based on long-term business relationships among goal-oriented actors (Johanson & Mattsson, 1987). Figure 7 depicts such a distinction with a vertical dotted line, which separates FSMs' counterparts within the MNC from those in the local industrial market. This follows the assumption that FSMs have boundary spanning roles (Tushman, 977), that is, "act as link pins between subunits and external information areas" (Tushman, 1979, p. 498).

In terms of dependence it is assumed (see Fig. 7) that FSMs generally perceive an obligation to obey to hierarchical superiors, the right to control subsidiary subordinates, and an even legal authority (Astley & Sachdeva, 1985) vis-à-vis other subsidiary managers and corporate staff. In addition, it is assumed that, in general, FSMs have more influence (Forsgren, 1990a) over suppliers than over customers following evidence that suppliers' managing directors participate more often than their customers' counterparts in buyer-seller social exchange (Cunningham &

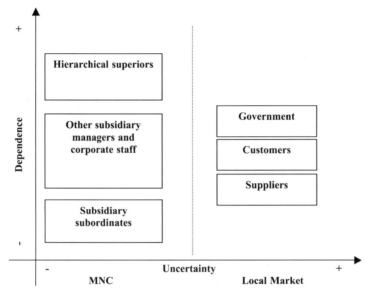

Fig. 7.   Interpersonal Context of FSMs in Industrial MNCs.

Homse, 1986). In terms of uncertainty, it is assumed (see Fig. 7) that FSMs generally perceive more uncertainty in the local industrial market than within the MNC due to a higher degree of heterogeneity in the former (Forsgren et al., 1995; Hägg & Johanson, 1983) than in the latter context (Doz & Prahalad, 1991; Gupta et al., 1999).

The degree of dependence and uncertainty perceived by FSMs, may, in turn, be associated with contextual factors of personal contacts (see Section 2.5.1). In this respect, the present paper suggests individual, organizational, and market factors,[8] which were identified in the analysis of case evidence (see Section 3.6). The discussion of such contextual factors in the following sections is, however, restricted to FSMs' degree of dependence or lack of legal authority within the MNC and to FSMs' degree of uncertainty or inability to predict something accurately in the local industrial market. In other words, the case evidence (see Section 3.5) did not allow the analysis of FSMs' degree of dependence based on the control of resources within the MNC (e.g. Larsson, 1985) or in the local industrial market (e.g. Håkansson & Johanson, 1984), nor the analysis of FSMs' degree of uncertainty within the MNC (e.g. Gupta et al., 1999).

The following sections thus discuss case evidence only in terms of FSMs' perceived lack of legal authority within the MNC (left section of Fig. 7) and perceived inability to predict something accurately in the local industrial market (right section of Fig. 7). In addition, FSMs may perceive lack of legal authority within the MNC for different purposes. Two such purposes, which have been previously associated with the interpersonal role of managers, are information exchange and decision-making (e.g. Mintzberg, 1990). Such purposes may be regarded as goals (Emerson, 1962) or needs (Hewett & Bearden, 2001), which form the basis for a manager's dependence on other actors. FSMs' lack of legal authority within the MNC may, therefore, be sub-divided into informational- and decisional dependence. Such types of dependence are defined in the present paper (see Section 1.5) as "an individual's lack of authority to control a process of information exchange, in which (s)he participates" and "an individual's lack of authority to control a process of decision-making, in which (s)he participates," respectively.

Such definitions of dependence reflect the focus of the present paper on legal rather than rational authority (Astley & Sachdeva, 1985). Informational dependence does not refer to dependence on information as a resource controlled by others (Pfeffer & Salancik, 1978), but to the participation of an individual in a process of information exchange, which (s)he does not control. An example of a process of information exchange within the MNC, in which a FSM participates but does not control, is a bureaucratic reporting system (e.g. Child, 1973, 1972). An example of a process of information exchange within the MNC, in which a FSM participates and controls, is benchmarking other subsidiaries by own initiative.

Likewise, decisional dependence does not refer to lack of control over the outcome of decision-making – decisions – but to lack of control over the process of decision-making, in which an individual participates. An example of a process of decision-making within the MNC, in which a FSM participates but does not control, is bureaucratic goal setting (e.g. Galbraith, 1973). An example of a process of decision-making within the MNC, in which a FSM participates and controls, is coaching a subordinate by own initiative.

The notions of informational dependence and decisional dependence may, therefore, be combined with the notion of uncertainty in order to analyze the interpersonal context of FSMs. On the one hand, the combination of informational dependence with uncertainty results in four scenarios (see Fig. 8). On the other hand, the combination of decisional dependence with uncertainty equally results in four scenarios (see Fig. 9).

As mentioned above, FSMs' degree of dependence and uncertainty may be associated with individual, organizational, and/or market factors of personal contacts (see Appendix F). Such contextual factors were identified in the analysis of case evidence (see Section 3.6) and subsequently associated with a particular scenario of informational- or decisional dependence. In other words, each contextual factor has been associated with only one of the eight possible scenarios

	High informational dependence Low uncertainty (section 4.2.6)	High informational dependence High uncertainty (section 4.2.5)
	Low informational dependence Low uncertainty (section 4.2.4)	Low informational dependence High uncertainty (section 4.2.3)

+ Informational dependence −

−   Uncertainty   +

Fig. 8. Case Evidence on FSMs' Informational Dependence.

depicted above. Arguably, the association of certain contextual factors with more than one scenario would have been equally plausible. It has been assumed, however, that associating each contextual factor only with the scenario that it appears to be primarily related to, would enhance the clarity of the analysis.

On the other hand, the focus of the present paper on dependence within the MNC (left section of Fig. 7) and uncertainty in the local industrial market (right section of Fig. 7) made the association between contextual factors and scenarios relatively straightforward. Market factors of personal contacts were associated with FSMs' degree of uncertainty, whereas organizational factors were associated with their degree of dependence. Individual factors of personal contacts were associated with uncertainty in the local industrial market and/or dependence within the MNC.

As mentioned in Figs. 8 and 9, the eight scenarios are discussed in separate sections. Each section starts by listing the contextual factors associated with the respective scenario and proceeds with their separate analysis. Each contextual factor is thus: (a) briefly described in terms of insights from the eleven cases; (b) illustrated with quotations from the interviews; and (c) reviewed in the light of extant literature. Such a procedure is intended to increase the construct validity of the study on which the present paper is based (see Section 3.7) by allowing readers to follow the chain of evidence and make their own interpretation.

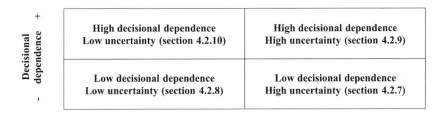

	High decisional dependence Low uncertainty (section 4.2.10)	High decisional dependence High uncertainty (section 4.2.9)
	Low decisional dependence Low uncertainty (section 4.2.8)	Low decisional dependence High uncertainty (section 4.2.7)

+ Decisional dependence −

−   Uncertainty   +

Fig. 9. Case Evidence on FSMs' Decisional Dependence.

4.2.2. Contact Networks of FSMs

Before addressing the contextual factors of FSMs' personal contacts a distinction can be made between different types of FSMs' contact networks. In particular, it is assumed in the present paper that FSMs' overall contact network may be sub-divided into private-, business-, formal-, and informal contact network. The private contact network includes FSMs' relatives, friends, acquaintances and ex-colleagues external to the MNC. The business contact network consists of individuals equally external to the MNC, but who represent governmental, customer, supplier and other organizations in the local industrial market. The formal contact network consists of FSMs' colleagues at the MNC. Finally, the informal contact network also includes FSMs' relatives, friends, acquaintances and ex-colleagues, but who are employed at the MNC.

Such contact networks of FSMs are illustrated with quotations from the interviews in the following paragraphs, ahead of the discussion of contextual factors in Sections 4.2.3 to 4.2.10. In terms of private contact network, most of the interviewed FSMs mention personal contacts with friends and acquaintances. A few of the interviewed FSMs mention personal contacts with relatives.

> Sometimes you have a private guy who knows more than these legal guys . . . (. . .) that's a bit what type of circles you are moving yourself and what are the basic contacts for you . . . in this case how Finland is established in Portugal, can you use your Finnish colleagues or some other companies you know and this is quite . . . I mean, in some cases I have an English friend whose company is extremely active in Portugal and I ask him: "Can you introduce me to this man in Portugal?" . . .
>
> PCN manager

> I call to the embassy, I call to the chambers, I call my friend . . .
>
> TCN manager

> Outside the group I have a lot, but basically on the Portuguese and the Spanish market. This is where I have my contacts. (. . .) [In local firms] production and marketing I know. (. . .) But, apart from those contacts, all what I consider the company references in Portugal, I have regular contacts with them. (. . .) I am also the president of ISO certified companies in Portugal, so I know . . . now there are almost one thousand companies . . . (. . .) Politically, because of this position of president of the ISO certified companies, I am member of a national quality counsel as well. So, politically, I have some good contacts on the government level. You know, all the ministries are part of the national quality counsel . . . (. . .) Then, perhaps one of the most important, because is also a hobby I have, is the schools. (. . .) And in our neighborhood all those important people which can influence in society. I know all those local authorities quite well. (. . .) actually, I have a lot of friends from other activities I had before coming here. I still use them . . . (. . .) And I have still a lot of contacts with my family. (. . .) I am quite close with more eleven companies to found a benchmarking club saying in our country what are the best practices in the several areas of management.
>
> HCN manager

Because some of FSMs' acquaintances represent trade centers, chambers of commerce and associations, their private contact network may be regarded as including their business contact network i.e. individuals who are primarily business-related contacts (see Section 1.5 for the definition of contact). In other words, the distinction between private- and business contact may become blurred due to the multiplexity or variety of contents comprised in FSMs' personal contacts (Mitchell, 1969). In this respect, Rangan (2000, p. 814) argues that the relevance of social networks is "greatest in those spheres of economic activity where search and deliberation pertaining to potential exchange partners are important but problematic." The author equates search with the identification of potential partners, and deliberation with the assessment of their quality and intentions.

In addition to their private- and business contact network, FSMs may take personal contacts with relatives, friends, acquaintances and ex-colleagues within the MNC, who are defined in the present paper as their informal contact network. Most of the interviewed FSMs mention personal contacts with acquaintances. A few of the interviewed FSMs mention personal contacts with ex-colleagues.

> Depends on your personal network within the company. (. . .) of course there is a formal structure, which you find out one way or another, which helps you, but usually is much easier just to call where you know the people and they know you, so you just pick up the phone and call them. (. . .) I have some contacts, which I have been [having] all my working time in this specific company . . .

PCN manager

> I know quite a number of people in Switzerland, in France, in Holland, and in Trieste, but this is because I am working in this group since ten years, so I have contacts, of course. (. . .) I know a very good friend, who moved from [. . .] to [. . .] and he is head of [. . .] division, so I call him . . .

TCN manager

> In some units I only know the managing director or perhaps also the marketing manager, but if its one organization on which I used to go through to understand their processes and how they developed their processes, I know not only the managing director. I know all the managers and even the operators. (. . .) at least five persons you use to call them even if you have no points. Just to see how life is going. And that at least five contacts I have. (. . .) With the group reorganization some of them went out to other divisions, but of course friendship is very transversal, so you can keep it wherever they are.

HCN manager

The informal contact network of FSMs is thus seen in the present paper as a subset of the MNC's informal organization (Barnard, 1938), with which FSMs take personal contacts. In this respect, Krackhardt (1990, p. 344) distinguishes between an advice network, which "represents the instrumental, workflow-based network in the organization" and a friendship network, which "is not necessarily linked to the routine work done in the organization, but it does capture important affective and social bonds." In a latter contribution the same author further distinguishes between an advice network related with technical information, a trust network related with political information, and a communication network related with work-related matters (Krackhardt & Hanson, 1993).

Finally, some personal contacts of FSMs may involve hierarchical superiors, subsidiary subordinates, corporate staff and other subsidiary managers within the MNC. Such a scope of contacts is defined in the present paper as the FSM's formal contact network. Most of the interviewed FSMs mention formally assigned contacts for reporting, planning and approval purposes. A few of the interviewed FSMs mention formally assigned contacts for technical or marketing support.

> I have a very thin link to the actual organization formally. So the formal restrictions in my job are almost non-existent. I have my boss, but that's the president of the Iberian company and is purely administrative, looking formally. All the functional contacts I create myself through the necessities of my work ... (. . .) As a negotiator you follow very clearly the organigram.

> PCN manager

> We don't have direct access to [. . .], for example, people of technology and research and development. If we have problems of this kind it will always go through an expert in [. . .] and expert will go to [. . .] and we will get the answer the same way. (. . .) Everything goes through [. . .], because if you start to accept that kind of organization then the group starts to be totally unmanageable.

> TCN manager

> These people are assisting all the sales offices in the world so I have my contact in each location. I have one contact for quotations and also I have my order handling people, which is different matters. (. . .) We have specialists for everything, so I can use my contact, it takes a little bit longer, but ok it's the channel or I can use directly the specialists ... (. . .) In a daily basis is very good to have that person, [or] when he is on holidays ... he is sending a message that: "from this day to that day, please contact our colleague," because otherwise it would be a mess, everybody calling everybody.

> HCN manager

The formal contact network of FSMs is thus seen in the present paper as a subset of the MNC's formal structure, with which FSMs take personal contacts. Bartlett and Ghoshal (1990) regard formal structure and interpersonal relationships as complementary mechanisms of coordination (Martinez & Jarillo 1989), which they label the MNCs' anatomy and physiology, respectively. In this respect, Egelhoff (1993, p. 204) argues that: "a key function of formal MNC structure is that managers across the company know where specific sources of knowledge and capability lie, the locations tend to be fairly stable, and managers are generally familiar with how to access them."

The four contact networks of FSMs – private, business, formal, informal – are not addressed in the discussion of contextual factors (see Sections 4.2.3 to 4.2.10), which only refers to general personal contacts of FSMs. Such contact networks will form the basis, however, for some of the managerial implications and suggestions for further research of the present paper (see Sections 5.5 and 5.6).

4.2.3. Low Informational Dependence/High Uncertainty

A scenario of low informational dependence and high uncertainty as perceived by FSMs in industrial MNCs may be associated with the following contextual factors: market idiosyncrasy, market dynamism, supplier closeness, customer closeness, business culture, corporate culture, background, career, language skills, initiative, sales orientation, social skills, personality, attitude, and availability. Such market, organizational, and individual factors of FSMs' personal contacts in industrial markets (see Appendix F) are illustrated with three quotations from the interviews (see Section 3.5) and discussed in the light of extant literature in the following paragraphs.

As mentioned in Section 4.2.1, the discussion of contextual factors in the present paper is restricted to FSMs' degree of uncertainty in the local industrial market and to FSMs' degree of dependence within the MNC. Therefore, high uncertainty for FSMs is associated with the market factors listed above, whereas their low informational dependence is associated with the organizational factor. The individual factors are associated with high uncertainty in the local industrial market and/or low informational dependence within the MNC.

Market idiosyncrasy is the first market factor listed, being assumed to increase FSMs' degree of uncertainty. In this respect, most of the interviewed FSMs mention local specificity in terms of market size and educational level. A few of the interviewed FSMs mention local specificity in terms of legislation and market concentration.

> When they plan the strategy so we participate in the planning of those strategies, is very difficult to consider all the details of various countries and various companies. (. . .) Portugal is still fairly person or family oriented in all the businesses, so you talk about influential families and persons. (. . .) Portugal, especially, is in that sense in a quite rapid process of establishing some of the European Union laws and manners and that you need to know it, not to make a mistake that will cost you financially.

> PCN manager

> Social organization of Portugal is such that you have a very close world, only 5% makes 95% of the business in Portugal, this is a close club with very famous families in Portugal. (. . .) We

are interested to have consultant who can see where you are good and bad to compare with the other. But this is not really [the case] in Portugal.

TCN manager

When I started with this business, in our customers you never met any engineer. Ten years ago or twelve ago and now all customers have an engineer, who have the responsibility for the plant. (. . .) In this type of mining engineers, I think that there are five or six per year, not more.

HCN manager

In the context of industrial markets, Cunningham and Homse (1986, p. 262) also speculate that: "market structure will have a major impact upon the amount of interaction and, therefore, on the human resources committed to develop or defend special relationships."

Market dynamism is related with, but distinct from *market idiosyncrasy*, being equally assumed to increase FSMs' degree of uncertainty. In this respect, most of the interviewed FSMs mention uncertain demand in the local industrial market.

There are also changes in the market place, mergers between our customers and takeovers. (. . .) The business environment changes continuously, that means that we have to be on a continuous search for new opportunities, and also it's a continuous follow-up of threats, new competition or due to changes at the customers, maybe a financial crisis of a customer or even a certain business segment.

PCN manager

If the competitors reduce 20% the level of prices, what do you do? You stop your work? No. You need to convince to the marketing director that the competitors have another level in the market. And you need to convince that is necessary to maintain the customer and the product and everything.

TCN manager

Nowadays it has become more and more difficult because we are surviving in a world with lots of speed as you know, but I am used to have one meeting every fifteen days with the local management, where we analyze the evolution of the company, the most important problems, the most interesting opportunities . . .

HCN manager

In the context of industrial markets, Cunningham and Turnbull (1982, p. 305) similarly contend that: "there are several groups of variables, identified in the theoretical model of interaction, which affect or are affected by, personal contacts." One such variable is dynamism once that: "in a dynamic environment the opportunity cost of reliance on a single or small number of relationships can be very high when expressed in terms of the developments of other market members" (IMP group, 1982, p. 20).

In addition to market dynamism, a high degree of uncertainty perceived by FSMs may be associated with supplier closeness. Most of the interviewed FSMs mention personal contacts to understand customers' hierarchy and decision-making process. A few of the interviewed FSMs mention suppliers' initiative to take personal contacts with customer counterparts.

> Our suppliers it's quite usual, and it goes quite straightforward: they have a little bit the responsibility to create the relationship with us . . . (. . .) Also we are consciously dividing the hierarchies of the organization into responsibility areas of certain people. (. . .) Is of course that people are doing the decisions, is not the company making the decisions, is a group of people within the company who make the decisions. Your personal influence on those people is crucial value. . .

> PCN manager

> You go over the head of the purchasing manager and he may get a little annoyed when you do that, so usually it's better to do it straight to the purchasing manager. (. . .) He is the decision-maker after all. And he should be your friend, if he is not your friend, he doesn't buy from you . . .

> TCN manager

> Normally my contacts they go through the people with top-level positions, with power for decision process as much as we can. However, we and I also develop some contacts on lower levels, medium and high level, as soon as I think that they are going to take decisions. (. . .) So decision-makers for me they are very important on every company, on every department.

> HCN manager

In the context of industrial markets, Cunningham and Turnbull (1982, p. 312) acknowledge supplier closeness as a dimension of the style of personal contacts, arguing that: "marketers seek a much closer personal interaction with customer's personnel than the buyers do with suppliers."

The reverse of supplier closeness is customer closeness, which is also associated with a high degree of uncertainty for FSMs. Most of the interviewed FSMs mention personal contacts by customers' initiative as well as close relationships with suppliers.

> We may get an impulse from a customer saying that: "I would like to have that and that change in your product to suit better to my needs, can you make it?" . . . (. . .) a managing director of a customer, who called me and said that he knew that we had an investment project which would affect them in a positive sense, [to ask if] there were any news, was it going according to the plan, what would happen to the prices . . .

> PCN manager

> All customers that call me to ask or write to ask or send information or inquiries to ask, I try to know, I try to visit.

TCN manager

Each time I sell machines we are obliged to sell a structure to support the machines and this structure we make in Portugal with our plans. That means that we have a good relationship with these two enterprises...(...) The idea is to have some local suppliers and maintain these suppliers. Is very important for this type of business. (...) during one exhibition we decided to contact one of these suppliers in France, the best in France, and I propose to work together...(...) we had a lot of demands of customers for this type of the plants and we decided to work and to sell this kind of plants.

HCN manager

In the context of industrial markets, Cunningham and Turnbull (1982, p. 304) contend that: "buyers are by no means passive and personal contacts can be initiated by either the buying or the selling company."

The last market factor listed in this section is business culture, being equally assumed to increase FSMs' degree of uncertainty. Most of the interviewed FSMs mention personal contacts, which are initially difficult to take due to a high degree of ceremony in local counterparts, but subsequently frequent due to a high degree of centralization in such counterparts.

Portugal is a country which has a lot of very specific cultural issues, when it comes to the business behavior and we need to implement the strategies of ours knowing all that. (...) In the Portuguese culture there is quite often that before you close the deal, actually is formally closed, the president of the company, the owner of this kind of whatever, [...] or [...] company, he wants to close it and he doesn't close it with the salesman, he wants to close it with this part. Is structured so. (...) In Finland you can call almost everyone, you just pick the phone and call and introduce yourself and say: "I want to talk to you about this subject." Unless he is a government official you can invite him even for a lunch and talk. It's no problem at all. In United States you can do almost the same. In Portugal you cannot. Somebody needs to present you and if you can't find, then you at least need to write a letter and say: "I have this and this," you ask his permission too: "could I call, could our secretaries find some common time for us?" and then he says: "yeah, that's alright. Let's put for lunch or whatever." But this is quite...it's different, you need to do it in a civilized way.

PCN manager

The owner of a big company in Portugal will not accept to discuss with our vice-president. (...) People who I am meeting and certainly at the end of the day most of the industry, the boss does not delegate. (...) And this is very special in Portugal, which is not the case here. Here we have clear share of responsibility and [a subordinate] knows to which point he can negotiate in our company. Other partner, most of the time, everything is going to the top, which makes some of the problems very difficult.

TCN manager

Mill managers and the project managers usually they want to discuss and to talk to the other managers. (...) A certain person that it was a decision maker, that it was replaced by another person that we never met, it's not easy, in almost one 100% of the cases is not easy. We must be introduced . . .

HCN manager

In the context of industrial markets, Cunningham and Turnbull (1982, p. 311) similarly refer to industry norms of behavior as a factor of the intensity of personal contacts.

As mentioned in Section 4.2.1, the association of the market factors just described with other scenarios of high uncertainty (see Sections 4.2.5, 4.2.7 and 4.2.9) would have been eventually plausible. The analysis of case evidence suggests, however, that market idiosyncrasy, market dynamism, supplier closeness, customer closeness, and business culture are primarily related with a scenario of low informational dependence as defined in Section 1.5.

On the other hand, corporate culture is the only organizational factor listed in this section, being assumed to decrease FSMs' degree of informational dependence. In this respect, most of the interviewed FSMs mention relatively common interests as well as open communication within the MNC. A few of the interviewed FSMs mention, however, heterogeneous interests within the MNC due to mergers and acquisitions.

Instead of having a very formal structure we have this kind of informal structure where you basically do your work by contacting people. (. . .) In theory we all try to do the best for the shareholders, so in that sense there should not be a conflict of interest, [but] there might be a difference of opinion of what would be the best benefit for the shareholders.

PCN manager

There is no limitation and I don't need to contact first the director, because I am in contact with another people, salesman directly or something like this. (. . .) of course there is inside the group cooperation about the way each profit centre reaches the targets . . . (. . .) I think that one thing very positive in the group is exactly the fluency in the contacts. They are very simple, they are normally very constructive in general and very easy to maintain.

TCN manager

There is a sub-culture in France and there is a sub-culture in Finland. (. . .) I can see very good and very complicated also with this fusion with [. . .]. We decided to work with some guys with a different culture of enterprise and I think that it is a challenge . . .

HCN manager

The MNC's corporate culture is thus seen in the present paper as a common set of values that minimizes divergent interests, emphasizes mutual interdependence, and leads to domain consensus (Van Maanen & Schein, 1979). In similar fashion, Bartlett and Ghoshal (1990, p. 140) refer to MNC's psychology or "shared norms, values and beliefs that shape the way individual managers think and act."

As mentioned in Section 4.2.1, the association of this organizational factor with other scenarios of low informational dependence (see Section 4.2.4) and even of low decisional dependence (see Sections 4.2.7 and 4.2.8) would have been eventually plausible. The analysis of case evidence suggests, however, that corporate culture is primarily related with a scenario of low informational dependence and high uncertainty as defined in Section 1.5.

Background is the first individual factor listed in this section, being associated with both FSMs' high degree of uncertainty and/or low degree of informational dependence. In this respect, most of the interviewed FSMs mention personal contacts within the MNC or in the local industrial market, which are either enhanced or inhibited by their nationality and/or profession.

> Not being engineer as such, really, I delegate the engineering discussions, and anyway that's not really my specialty . . . (. . .) I think that here actually being a foreign is easier to establish contacts, than if you would be a local. It's a question actually in many countries/cultures because then you are free of any other background issues, which might affect the relationship otherwise.

> PCN manager

> [Within the MNC] I am a foreigner so I have a different background than the background from Portugal, so I have to defend the house and Portugal and with my Northern European background and that makes it easier for the Finns to understand what the situation is . . . (. . .) [In the local market] I feel that I have more opportunities and more possibilities to maintain or start those contacts because I am a foreigner.

> TCN manager

> [Within the MNC] [. . .] was an economist and this guy is the same formation that I have, it means mechanical engineer. He's not a French, is a Swedish guy, it means that with [. . .] I spoke in French, with this guy I am obliged to speak in English, is a challenge.

> HCN manager

In this respect, Mishler (1965, p. 560) considers nationality as especially "important in affecting the kind of contacts made and their potential for becoming long-term relationships" in the case of students and scholars who become sojourners abroad. In the context of less-hierarchical MNCs, Nohria and Ghoshal (1997, p. 158) argue that expatriates or "individuals whose home country is the MNC's corporate headquarters" typically have a larger range of inter-subsidiary contacts. In the context of industrial markets, an individual's national and professional background has also been referred, albeit implicitly, as a factor of personal contacts (Andersson et al., 1996; Axelsson & Agndal, 2000; Björkman & Kock, 1995; Halinen & Salmi, 2001; Hallén, 1992).

Related to, but distinct from background, the career of FSMs is also associated with their high degree of uncertainty and/or low degree of informational dependence. Most of the interviewed FSMs mention personal contacts within the

MNC or in the local industrial market with contacts that they first met in another job.

> There is lot of my ex-colleagues from [...], for example, joining the same multinational, so yes I had a lot of contacts already before. (...) same people who might have been working within our customers in Italy, Poland, here, so usually I knew the people sometimes quite intimately before even coming here.

PCN manager

> Sometimes I know the companies, I have a relationship with the companies because I was selling other products in these companies, in another markets...

TCN manager

> Two of my colleagues I already knew before I joined this company, because I used to be a customer.

HCN manager

In the context of less-hierarchical MNCs, Nohria and Ghoshal (1997) distinguish between initial socialization by which a newcomer is formally introduced to key individuals in the organization, and mentoring relationships by which individuals are informally advised by a more senior member of the organization. The authors claim that "ties formed early in our careers are the most important and durable contacts we form" (Nohria & Ghoshal, 1997, p. 169). In the context of industrial markets, an individual's career has also been referred as a factor of personal contacts (Andersson et al., 1996; Axelsson & Agndal, 2000; Björkman & Kock, 1995; Halinen & Salmi, 2001; Hallén, 1992).

In addition to FSMs' career, their language skills are also associated with their high degree of uncertainty and/or low degree of informational dependence. Most of the interviewed FSMs mention personal contacts within the MNC or in the local industrial market, which are either inhibited or enhanced by their language skills.

> [In the local market] language is an enormous barrier. You feel always difficulties to get close to the people if you are talking a foreign language. (...) basically to be part of the social life there you should be speaking fluently Portuguese.

PCN manager

> [Within the MNC] the language barrier, so if we are together with the Finns and they start talking in Finnish then you feel an outcast, and then you must have the confidence and the trust that they are not discussing something different, but sometimes is difficult to accept this...

TCN manager

> I think the big handicap is the language, but I can speak in English not very fast, not very well, but I understand the people, it's very easy for me to speak French, Spanish... (...) The

relationship is different if you speak the same language. (. . .) I am convinced that I have a good relationship with my boss, because I can speak with him in French.

HCN manager

In the context of less-hierarchical MNCs, language constraints on individuals' ability to maintain an extensive number of ties, has been acknowledged by Nohria and Ghoshal (1997) and examined in further detail by Marschan et al. (1997, 1999). More recently, Charles and Marschan-Piekkari (2002) further distinguish language constraints in less-hierarchical MNCs into: (a) problems caused by absence of a common language; and (b) comprehension problems caused by inadequate knowledge of a shared language. In the context of industrial markets, individuals' language skills have also been referred as a factor of personal contacts (Andersson et al., 1996; Cunningham & Turnbull, 1982).

In addition to language skills, a high degree of uncertainty and/or low degree of informational dependence may be associated with FSMs' initiative to take personal contacts. Most of the interviewed FSMs mention personal contacts within the MNC and in the local industrial market by their own initiative.

One thing is to be personally active in the company, so go around and meet people and get to know them . . . (. . .) [In the local market] in most cases you need to seek the opportunity to meet the people, just as simple. You call as many times as required to get the meeting, to get to know the people.

PCN manager

Always there are opportunities for maintaining the contact. Always. If you want you can talk everyday. If somebody doesn't want to attend your call, there are another people that you can have a possibility to talk with also. Depends of you, you are the manager. You need to decide if it is good for your company these people or another people, this contact or another contact.

TCN manager

From my initiative I also have more contacts to the big customers . . . (. . .) if I want to make an advertisement or send a technical article to the magazine, in that case, it's my initiative.

HCN manager

In the context of less-hierarchical MNCs, Barlett and Ghoshal (1997, p. 95) equally emphasize "the initiative to create and pursue new business opportunities" of front-line managers. In similar fashion, Cunningham and Turnbull (1982, p. 306) argue that personal contacts in industrial buyer-seller relationships "provide both companies with the dynamic necessary to respond to new opportunities and threats."

FSMs' initiative may, in turn, be associated with their sales orientation. Most of the interviewed FSMs mention personal contacts with customer representatives. A few of the interviewed FSMs admit giving priority to sales.

If I would restrict something I would restrict to sales and marketing. So, the administration is the part which I have to do, the marketing and sales is the one I want to do.

PCN manager

If you are one hour by phone with the marketing director of the factory or the manager of the business line, you cannot develop your work. (. . .) I am worried calling to the customers, not calling to my colleagues. If they want to talk with me, they can call. My work is with the customer.

TCN manager

The price it's one thing that is very important, but for me not the most important. The most important is the quality of relationship with the customers . . . (. . .) I work with some customers, not all the customers, but I know all customers personally. (. . .) The idea is the market share. It means that you are obliged to contact new customers.

HCN manager

In similar fashion, Gates (1994, p. 12) suggests that: "FSMs devote over a third of their time, the largest share, to marketing and customer relations." Quelch and Bloom (1998, p. 376) also refer to traders as country managers who "focus primarily on sales and distribution," but in consumer- rather than industrial markets.

In addition to sales orientation, FSMs' initiative may be contingent on their social skills. Most of the interviewed FSMs mention the importance of being able to engage in personal contacts within the MNC or in the local industrial market.

[Within the MNC] is a question of your personal networking skills, basically, so you learn to know people. (. . .) I have personally been always able to establish very close relationships with the local people and one thing I believe is affecting is that usually if your social skills are good, you are able to establish personal relationships in general . . .

PCN manager

Well, I think that the contact with the person is for me something easy to get, so I don't see any problem related with this. On the contrary I see pleasure and benefits.

TCN manager

For me is very easy to do the contacts [within the MNC] . . . (. . .) It means that for me is not a problem to speak with anybody. The same with customers, with subcontractors, I have no problems to do the relationship.

HCN manager

In practice, however, it may be difficult to dissociate FSMs' social skills from their personality. Most of the interviewed FSMs mention the importance of matching personalities within the MNC or in the local industrial market.

[Within the MNC] of course, the chemistry between people affects . . .

PCN manager

[Within the MNC] it depends on the character of the people. (. . .) they don't like you or you don't like them . . . (. . .) [In the local market] depends on the personality of the customer. It is necessary to study the people that it is in front of you. (. . .) You need to put your best, but always is impossible. Sometimes your character is different . . .

TCN manager

[Within the MNC] depends on the persons. Sometimes there are shy [persons], it's very difficult, but for me it is not a problem. (. . .) The first contact it's very important and the chemistry.

HCN manager

In similar fashion, Nohria and Ghoshal (1997, p. 155) acknowledge that, in principle, "individual factors such as personality and motivation, can influence an individual's social capital." In the context of industrial markets, Halinen and Salmi (2001, p. 12) refer to personal chemistry, which "may have various negatives consequences for business relationships."

The personality of FSMs may, in turn, be difficult to dissociate from their attitude. Most of the interviewed FSMs mention attitudes within the MNC or in the local industrial market, which either enhance or inhibit the intensity of their personal contacts.

[Within the MNC] there are sometimes conflicts, but I would say that conflict mainly arises if you are not willing to accept that maybe your view of the things is more narrow than should be. (. . .) [In the local market] you need to be persistent to create them as well as you need to be able to provide some value added to the relationships . . .

PCN manager

[Within the MNC] there is conflict, he is optimistic, he is realistic and there is many in between.

TCN manager

I am curious about what others are doing, I am always asking and I try to be polite with them, so I would say that nowadays I think I have a quite big list of potential and good friends. (. . .) You know, I am an optimistic. (. . .) [In the local market] if somebody decided to call me, I can't be impolite and say: "no, I don't want to talk." (. . .) my persistence is strong enough to keep insisting.

HCN manager

As mentioned above, Nohria and Ghoshal (1997) also acknowledge motivation as an individual factor of personal contacts. In the context of industrial markets, Halinen and Salmi (2001, p. 12) implicitly acknowledge the negative side of individual attitude, by stating that: "people necessarily get involved with inter-firm conflicts and, in the worst case, even aggravate them by their own behavior."

Finally, the attitude of FSMs may, in turn, be contingent on their availability. Most of the interviewed FSMs mention limited time for personal contacts within the MNC and in the local industrial market.

> [Within the MNC] you would need to have time to have the relationships and I don't think there is any kind of barriers, except this kind of natural barrier, lack of time or availability... (...) [In the local market] a personal relationship doesn't happen over night, you need time to create it... (...) getting time to meet them also because usually the people I meet are very busy people.

PCN manager

> [Within the MNC] I don't have many free time or everyday to talk with the people. (...) if you go with the customer, you have no time practically for the day.

TCN manager

> The difficulty is time. I think that you are involved in lot of things and sometimes you don't have time to do the things correctly... (...) [In the local market] the customer can see the difference of availability...

HCN manager

In the context of less-hierarchical MNCs, Nohria and Ghoshal (1997, p. 152) argue that: "individuals simply do not have enough time or cognitive capacity to maintain such an extensive number of ties, especially since many of these ties have to span the globe." In the context of industrial markets, Cunningham and Turnbull (1982, p. 305, italics added) implicitly acknowledge the relevance of FSMs' availability by stating that: "personal contacts between buyers and the technical and *general management personnel* were rated as highly as sales representatives as necessary channels of communication."

As mentioned in Section 4.2.1, the association of the individual factors just described with another scenario of low informational dependence (see Section 4.2.4) would have been eventually plausible. The analysis of case evidence suggests, however, that background, career, language skills, initiative, sales orientation, social skills, personality, attitude, and availability are primarily related with a scenario of high uncertainty as defined in Section 1.5.

4.2.4. Low Informational Dependence/Low Uncertainty

A scenario of low informational dependence and low uncertainty as perceived by FSMs in industrial MNCs may be associated with the following contextual factors: geographical proximity, age of relationships, tenure and delegation. Such organizational and individual factors of FSMs' personal contacts in industrial markets (see Appendix F) are illustrated with three quotations from the interviews (see Section 3.5) and discussed in the light of extant literature in the following paragraphs.

As mentioned in Section 4.2.1, the discussion of contextual factors in the present paper is restricted to FSMs' degree of uncertainty in the local industrial market and to FSMs' degree of dependence within the MNC. Therefore, low informational dependence for FSMs is associated with the organizational factors listed above. The individual factors are associated with low uncertainty in the local industrial market and/or low informational dependence within the MNC.

Geographical proximity is the first organizational factor listed in this section, being associated with a low degree of informational dependence for FSMs. In this respect, most of the interviewed FSMs mention physical location as either enhancing or inhibiting the intensity of their personal contacts within the MNC.

[Within the MNC] maybe the most frequent contacts, as far as exchange of market information is concerned, is with Spain.

PCN manager

On the business side we have a close relationship with Spain, and this is easy to understand... (...) if I was closer from Helsinki I would probably have a meeting one, two, three times per week and to see how the things are progressing, but I am too far. (...) We are very far, we are not in Europe... in Portugal, but the central activities in Helsinki means at least five hours trip or all day trip and is significant. I mean, within the product company and in Europe, really France, Italy and all these countries they are meeting often and actually sharing quite a lot of things, but Portugal is too far, even Spain is too far. We are not involved...

TCN manager

It doesn't mean that abroad we don't talk together. But because also we are too far away from those countries, we are really in the Iberia, so we cannot receive lots of support from them. (...) It has been very difficult for me, for instance with Finland, it's difficult because Finland it's too far away...

HCN manager

In the context of less-hierarchical MNCs, Marschan (1996, p. 157) found that: "geographical distance and differences in time zones caused problems in running inter-unit communication and the daily business."

Age of relationships is the last organizational factor listed in this section, being equally associated with a low degree of informational dependence for FSMs. In this respect, most of the interviewed FSMs mention personal contacts within the MNC, which are enhanced by long-lasting relationships.

[Within the MNC] it's easy to approach the people whom you already met and had contact and business with... (...) After a certain time working together you get an image of the other person... (...) [In the local market] when we reorganized our sales responsibilities we took very much into account that was there a longer existing relationship and a good working relationship with certain customers... (...) Completely new customers maybe less... of course it's easier to expand the cooperation with customers that you already have relationships with.

PCN manager

[In the local market] very close relationship between customer and company. Of course that this work is during years. (...) We started with one company and we worked with them ten years more or less ... (...) New customers, is difficult ... if you have opened of course the door is easy for you. If you are a new salesman perhaps you have a problem because the purchasing man has a habit of receiving another salesman and you need to change. ...

TCN manager

[Within the MNC] if you want to negotiate with a person you know, if this person knows me it's very easy to negotiate because he knows me, he knows my work, my reputation, he knows a lot of things. (...) [In the local market] all local suppliers started to work with us ten years ago, twelve years ago, at the beginning or creation of this local sales unit. (...) when we arrive to a relationship with a customer is necessary a lot of years of relationship ...

HCN manager

In the context of less-hierarchical MNCs, Marschan (1996, p. 153) suggests that: "building personal relationships within a large MNC takes time." In the local industrial market, Cunningham and Turnbull (1982, p. 311) refer to inter-firm age of relationships due to "the progressive institutionalization of contact patterns" over time. Cunningham and Homse (1986, p. 257) suggest as well that perceived distance between two firms "is reduced in stages as the personal contacts change from a simple salesman-buyer relationship to a multi-functional network of contacts."

As mentioned in Section 4.2.1, the association of the organizational factors just described with other scenarios of low informational dependence (see Section 4.2.3) and even of low decisional dependence (see Sections 4.2.7 and 4.2.8) would have been eventually plausible. The analysis of case evidence suggests, however, that geographical proximity and age of relationships are primarily related with a scenario of low informational dependence and low uncertainty as defined in Section 1.5.

Tenure is the first individual factor listed in this section, being assumed to decrease FSMs' degree of uncertainty and/or informational dependence. In this respect, most of the interviewed FSMs mention larger scope of personal contacts over time within the MNC and in the local industrial market. A few of the interviewed FSMs mention less frequent personal contacts over time within the MNC.

In most of these types of operations, my colleagues were fairly senior guys. And the reason for that selection is obviously that due to our personal career we have been able to establish quite numerous contacts in various developments during the recent years. So for us is very easy to call, ask, introduce ideas without always need to introduce who you are, why you are calling. So you make more right questions and your approach in that sense is more effective. The younger guys are actually the operative guys. There we have a different structure. And in my case, as you saw, being working that long, for me personally is extremely easy. I am one of those who probably know best all the organization by person.

PCN manager

I know what is the situation in Portugal, I am living here for many, many years, so, I know exactly what the situation is, and that means that I can easily work with these two worlds.

TCN manager

A lot of trainings when I joined the company, so much more than now, because I needed in the beginning, now not so many. (. . .) In terms of customers (. . .) In the beginning I didn't know almost anybody, but ok after these eleven years . . .

HCN manager

In the context of less-hierarchical MNCs, Nohria and Ghoshal (1997, p. 156) consider intuitively obvious that: "the longer an individual has worked in any organization, the more opportunities he or she has to meet and form contacts through the organization." In the context of industrial markets, Hallén (1992, p. 90) similarly states that: "the number of contacts is also likely to multiply over time."

Delegation is the last individual factor listed in this section, being assumed to decrease FSMs' degree of uncertainty and/or informational dependence. In this respect, most of the interviewed FSMs mention having delegated the operative side of relationships, namely with customers and suppliers as well as with accountants, auditors, lawyers, banks and forwarding agents. A few of the interviewed FSMs mention having delegated the operative side of relationships with local authorities.

With some of them like with the accountants and auditors and lawyers, banks, it's not only myself. In many cases it is in parallel with our controller or with our sales director . . .

PCN manager

Also the local authorities, the municipalities, local government is very important that you know exactly where you can find your information or get your information. (. . .) Sometimes I do it myself, and most of it I delegate. (. . .) I have contacts with Portuguese customers as well, but on the daily basis is better to leave it to the local people than to do it yourself.

TCN manager

I don't like to operate just by myself on the majority of the cases, because I cannot go to maintain a certain kind of regularity . . . (. . .) I delegate as much as I can in terms of business, but I like to participate when I decide that the business in terms of supplier or in terms of customer is important, is relevant for the company.

HCN manager

Delegation is thus seen in the present paper as the transfer of assigned tasks and responsibilities to lower levels in the organizational hierarchy. In the context of

MNCs, delegation has been identified as one of five dimensions of less-hierarchical structures (Marschan, 1997), which is expected to translate into a broader rather than narrower set of tasks and responsibilities for FSMs. Such a view of delegation at the MNC rather than subsidiary level is captured in the present paper's notion of extra duties (see Section 4.2.7) rather than delegation.

As mentioned in Section 4.2.1, the association of the individual factors just described with other scenarios of low informational dependence (see Section 4.2.3) and even of low decisional dependence (see Sections 4.2.7 and 4.2.8) would have been eventually plausible. The analysis of case evidence suggests, however, that tenure and delegation are primarily related with a scenario of low uncertainty and low informational dependence as defined in Section 1.5.

4.2.5. High Informational Dependence/High Uncertainty

A scenario of high informational dependence and high uncertainty as perceived by FSMs in industrial MNCs may be associated with the following contextual factors: technical complexity, market internationalization, start-up, organizational change and employee turnover. Such market and organizational factors of FSMs' personal contacts in industrial markets (see Appendix F) are illustrated with three quotations from the interviews (see Section 3.5) and discussed in the light of extant literature in the following paragraphs.

As mentioned in Section 4.2.1, the discussion of contextual factors in the present paper is restricted to FSMs' degree of uncertainty in the local industrial market and to FSMs' degree of dependence within the MNC. Therefore, FSMs' high degree of uncertainty is associated with the market factors listed above, whereas their high degree of informational dependence is associated with the organizational factors.

Technical complexity is the first market factor listed in this section, being assumed to increase FSMs' degree of uncertainty. In this respect, most of the interviewed FSMs mention personal contacts within the MNC and in the local industrial market concerning technical issues.

> If you don't know it, you find someone who knows. This is very complex business that we have, which means that even simple questions like what is the price is not easily defined. (. . .) Most likely I don't even understand the question what I am doing myself properly, but I am just transferring the question and I am trying to apply the answer. (. . .) [In the local market] usually our customers demand that there has to be a certain amount of expatriates in the organization otherwise they cannot trust that our competence is on the right level.

> PCN manager

> I never try, and this is my philosophy, I never try to solve a problem myself when I can find somebody more competent in the group to solve it. (. . .) [In the local market] [. . .] knows more about our engine than [. . .], because when you have fifty engines to deal with in a day-to-day business, I mean, you know much more on the engine than any service engineer . . .

TCN manager

[Within the MNC] if we have on the sales area a technical problem, and we need to clarify this technical problem on the business level to have some explanation about some specifics then I will talk with the technical director for international operations . . . (. . .) basically related with technical information on some equipments, assistance for training sessions, for supporting technical information to our sales people, drawings, designs, recommendations, doubts about certain kinds of utilizations of products that should be taken in consideration, this kind of things. (. . .) In one business, just like this one, it's quite difficult. Very often many things are brand new. The situations are brand new. It's a question of assuming risks . . .

HCN manager

In the context of local industrial markets, Cunningham and Turnbull (1982, p. 305) contend that: "the type and level of technology of the customer's organization and the complexity of the product being purchased, have profound effects on the amount of information exchange which is required." Such a view is reiterated by Cunningham and Homse (1986), who refer to product- and transaction complexity.

Market internationalization is the second market factor listed in this section, being equally assumed to increase FSMs' degree of uncertainty. In this respect, a few of the interviewed FSMs mention personal contacts concerning information on competitors and legislation.

It may be that a certain competitor has increased or decreased prices, which affects us on a number of markets, so it's a clear policy decision from the competition and then we have to react in whatever way . . .

PCN manager

Portugal is part of the European Union and that's very important because laws are more or less the same in all countries, so what we have here, if we have a problem here is more or less the same solution it will need in Portugal as in another country and everybody is aware of that. (. . .) More and more companies will come to Portugal, foreign companies, and I see this as an opportunity.

TCN manager

For me it's important to know the price of the competitors but for him [the product manager] is very important also, because he can influence the transfer price or he can influence the cost price. (. . .) From the multinational and the other multinationals, the other competitors.

HCN manager

Market internationalization may be regarded as negatively associated with psychic distance, which Johanson and Vahlne (1977, p. 24) define as "the sum of factors preventing the flow of information from and to the market." Such a negative relationship is, however, not clear-cut when sub-dividing the concept of psychic distance into cultural affinity at the national level, trust at the organizational level, and experience at the individual level (Hallén & Wiedersheim-Paul (1984). In this respect, Johanson and Mattsson (1986, p. 258) argue that when the local industrial market is highly internationalized the MNC may coordinate positions in different national nets, requiring, in turn, "that the lateral relations within the firm are rather strong."

As mentioned in Section 4.2.1, the association of the market factors just described with other scenarios of high uncertainty (see Sections 4.2.3, 4.2.7 and 4.2.9) would have been eventually plausible. The analysis of case evidence suggests, however, that technical complexity and market internationalization are primarily related with a scenario of high informational dependence as defined in Section 1.5.

The start-up of subsidiary operations is the first organizational factor listed in this section, being associated with a high degree of informational dependence for FSMs. A few of the interviewed FSMs mention having participated in the establishment of the subsidiary in the local industrial market as well as difficulties of delegation at that period.

> In the beginning of usually any activities, those escalations are more frequent and before people start learning things and those processes and decision-making criteria are well defined.

PCN manager

> In the beginning when I visited [...] I have been presented to the different directors and also the people that I should possibly contact later...

TCN manager

> [...] at that time was interested to invest in Portugal (...) after many talks and many meetings we have been all together making the studies for the investments in Portugal, we have been selecting the area to put the plant, what kind of strategy for Portugal (...) So at that time I have been establishing good contacts with some fellows in the company, so after one year and half of defining the majority of items, the details... (...) they decided to come and invited me (...) in a way that I should come to take care of the company in Portugal.

HCN manager

In the context of MNCs, it has been argued that young or recently established subsidiaries tend to be dependent on the headquarters for both resources and decision-making (Ghoshal & Nohria, 1989). In the context of industrial markets, Ford (1980, p. 40) argues that the early stage of buyer-seller relationships in industrial markets is characterized by considerable uncertainty, requiring human resource investments such as the "allocation of managerial resources."

Organizational change is the second organizational factor listed in this section, being equally associated with a high degree of informational dependence for FSMs.

In this respect, most of the interviewed FSMs mention changes within the MNC due to mergers and acquisitions.

> [Within the MNC] changes the people you are in terms of normal processes involved with. (. . .) In one way it expands you personal network, because you can know new people. The other one is of course that you might not keep contacts with those people you knew before so much, then is very much a question of your personal activities . . .
>
> PCN manager

> [Within the MNC] if there are some special changes in management, they notify the changes, the structure of the company . . . (. . .) Last year was a very special year, many changes inside the company. (. . .) I think that always there are opportunities. Inside the company because year by year changes the structure and you need to know new people or you know the people in the new positions.
>
> TCN manager

> [Within the MNC] if the situation is changing all the time, in my opinion, is not very good, because we have certain contacts and we have certain persons and then . . . (. . .) If they are changing all the time I am changing my contacts all the time . . . (. . .) Sometimes these changes make some confusion in the customer: "But, now what's the name of your company?", "But you are still selling the same?; so we have to talk to the customers or visiting them or by phone, because sometimes, this is true, it happened in the past, they are a little bit confused with several changes, but we explain of course and they understand.
>
> HCN manager

The present paper regards organizational change as the disruption of a status quo between opposing entities, which may be internal or external to the organization (Van de Ven & Poole, 1995). From such a dialectical perspective, change is explained by reference to the balance of power between opposing entities. In similar fashion, Prahalad and Doz (1981a, b) argue that in less-hierarchical MNCs national and global priorities are balanced by the confrontation of managers' differing cognitive-, strategic-, power- and administrative orientations. In the case of organizational change towards a less-hierarchical structure, it has also been suggested that personal relationships particularly at middle management and operating levels may be disrupted by such a process (Marschan, 1996).

Employee turnover is the last organizational factor listed in this section, being associated with a high degree of informational dependence for FSMs. Most of the interviewed FSMs mention employee turnover within the MNC as either increasing or decreasing the intensity of their personal contacts.

> Our organization develops continuously and new appointments are an everyday thing. If a person who knows the Portuguese market well for his or for her present or past job description, for instance, that the person has been responsible for this market as a marketing manager or area export manager, or sales director, if he has good experiences of this market, including [. . .]

Portugal or if he has bad experiences, that most probably will affect us in a negative or positive sense.

PCN manager

[Within the MNC] the managing directors change and they go for another business line or they go to another company, but there are another people in these positions. If you have the same person, you talk about the same business, but with a different person, of course. The problem is that you need to explain [the] whole market, all things, all problems, all questions and you need to convince . . .

TCN manager

[Within the MNC] is necessary to convince that my ideas for Iberia are good ideas. That means that all work that I made with [. . .] I need to start with the new [boss] . . .

HCN manager

In the context of MNCs, Nohria and Ghoshal (1997, p. 156) refer to horizontal mobility or "the number of different functions and subsidiaries in which an individual has worked during his or her tenure" as key mechanism for building social capital. Marschan (1996, p. 141) also suggests a "positive influence of staff transfers on inter-unit communication." In the context of industrial markets, Björkman and Kock (1995, p. 527) claim that: "the retirement or transfer of one key person can be enough to destroy the social relationships that existed." In similar fashion, Halinen and Salmi (2001, p. 11) argue that "people change jobs, get ill and retire, which always creates a risk for an on-going business relationship."

As mentioned in Section 4.2.1, the association of the organizational factors just described with a scenario of high decisional dependence (see Section 4.2.9) would have been eventually plausible. The analysis of case evidence suggests, however, that start-up, organizational change and employee turnover are primarily related with a scenario of high informational dependence as defined in Section 1.5.

4.2.6. High Informational Dependence/Low Uncertainty

A scenario of high informational dependence and low uncertainty as perceived by FSMs in industrial MNCs may be associated with the following contextual factor: reporting process. Such a factor of FSMs' personal contacts in industrial markets (see Appendix F) is illustrated with three quotations from the interviews (see Section 3.5) and discussed in the light of extant literature in the following paragraphs.

Reporting process is the only organizational factor listed in this section, being assumed to increase FSMs' degree of informational dependence. In this respect, most of the interviewed FSMs mention recurrent personal contacts concerning financial and marketing information. A few of the interviewed FSMs mention recurrent personal contacts concerning internal and external audits to the subsidiary.

> There is an organizational link. I report to my superior and to the board and then also to controllers and personnel management. So that is all established . . . (. . .) The same goes for the auditor.

PCN manager

> Usually, we maintain the structure of the company. We transmit to our chief, we transmit to the chief of the factory, to the marketing chief of the factory or the business guy . . . (. . .) if you forget to notify these persons and you notify the chief or the boss of these persons, tomorrow you have a problem with these . . . (. . .) We have also auditors every year . . . (. . .) From the multinational twice by year.

TCN manager

> I need also to report to my boss abroad on a monthly basis and to maintain a regular contact, at least once per week with my boss, in a way to cover more or less the most important issues in the Iberian area. (. . .) financial, because we need just to evaluate and just to cover the reports and so on, once or twice per month. (. . .) We have auditing and these kind of things internal and external.

HCN manager

The reporting process is thus seen in the present paper as a monitoring process (Baliga & Jaeger, 1984) of output (Ouchi, 1977) through bureaucratic control systems (Child, 1973, 1972). Ouchi (1978) argues that implementing output control presupposes organizational processes of selection, socialization, and peer pressure. In similar fashion, Martinez and Jarillo (1989, p. 491) equate output control in MNCs with "the evaluation of files, records, and reports submitted by organizational units to corporate management." According to Harzing (1999, p. 22) the distinctive feature of output control is that "certain goals/results/outputs are specified and monitored by reporting systems."

As mentioned in Section 4.2.1, the association of the organizational factor just described with another scenario of high informational dependence (see Section 4.2.5) would have been eventually plausible. The analysis of case evidence suggests, however, that the reporting process is primarily related with a scenario of low uncertainty as defined in Section 1.5.

4.2.7. Low Decisional Dependence/High Uncertainty

A scenario of low decisional dependence and high uncertainty as perceived by FSMs in industrial MNCs may be associated with the following contextual factors: job description and extra duties. Such individual factors of FSMs' personal contacts in industrial markets (see Appendix F) are illustrated with three quotations from the interviews (see Section 3.5) and discussed in the light of extant literature in the following paragraphs.

Job description is the first individual factor listed in this section, being assumed to increase FSMs' degree of uncertainty and/or decrease their degree of decisional dependence. In this respect, most of the interviewed FSMs mention total responsibility for the subsidiary, namely in administrative/legal, strategic/planning, marketing and sales, financial, and human resources issues. A few of the interviewed FSMs also mention responsibility for logistics, production, purchasing and public relations issues. A few of the interviewed FSMs mention that marketing and sales responsibility includes direct customer accountability.

> My responsibilities cover a number of different functions. I have the global responsibility for managing and representing the interests of the [. . .] group on the Portuguese market (. . .) And then of course there are legal aspects I have to administer. (. . .) A very important part of my work is an annual business plan (. . .) And then of course I have the responsibility of reaching the strategic targets in terms of market shares and of course the profitability targets of our sales and the cost-effectiveness of our company (. . .) I am responsible for securing adequate human resources at the sales office to meet the objectives of the group (. . .) and apart from my managing director function I also have a number of sales director functions for a certain number of customers active in different business areas. (. . .) I am responsible for all the communication with the [. . .] trade press . . .

PCN manager

> My responsibility is a total responsibility for the subsidiary in Portugal. It means that I am responsible for the financial results, and of course for the industrial results, and on top of that, which has not been foreseen in the beginning, I am also responsible for the sales and the marketing results. So it's an overall responsibility.

TCN manager

> I became the managing director of Portugal in June '93 and in that time managing director meant, as it means today, the total responsibility for managing the Portuguese site (. . .) the important areas of my main concern are how to define the strategy, how to deploy the goals and, most of all, how to commit all the people and organization to meet the goals.

HCN manager

The job description of the FSMs is thus seen in the present paper as tasks or demands, which Stewart (1982, p. 9) defines as "what anyone in the job *has* do." A decade later, the same author argues that "job descriptions no longer rigidly define a manager's domain: managers are expected to contribute more broadly, in areas that will enhance their unit's and organization's effectiveness" (Stewart & Fondas, 1992, p. 11). In the context of less-hierarchical MNCs, Ghoshal and Bartlett (1998) similarly argue that organizational processes require general managerial roles rather than specific tasks and responsibilities.

Extra duties are the second individual factor listed in this section, being equally assumed to increase FSMs' degree of uncertainty and/or decrease their degree of decisional dependence. In this respect, most of the interviewed FSMs mention marketing in other geographic region. A few of the interviewed FSMs mention an extension of the range of products and services offered by the subsidiary.

> I am responsible just like all the other sales office directors on other markets for projects in the group. The most important of them today is TQM (Total Quality Management). (...) the business unit has changed, they may discontinue with a product or they may introduce or want to introduce a new product. So you have this kind of projects, which happen with a variable frequency...

PCN manager

> On top of that, which has not been foreseen in the beginning, I am also responsible for the sales and the marketing results. (...) for Spain and for Portugal...

TCN manager

> The other point I am using [time] really is to take care of the quality and participate in the process of quality control, nowadays with the total quality systems... (...) we may have possibilities to present our proposals in doing business with other countries out of Iberian Peninsula. (...) I have been closing a business in Brazil, but this Brazilian business came after a talk with the mother company that we should be the ones to pick the business from Brazil...

HCN manager

Extra duties of FSMs are thus seen in the present paper as supplementary tasks and responsibilities, which extend FSMs' domain (Ghoshal & Bartlett, 1998; Stewart & Fondas, 1992).

As mentioned in Section 4.2.1, the association of the individual factors just described with another scenario of high uncertainty (see Section 4.2.9) would have been eventually plausible. The analysis of case evidence suggests, however, that job description and extra duties are primarily related with a scenario of low decisional dependence as defined in Section 1.5.

4.2.8. Low Decisional Dependence/Low Uncertainty

A scenario of low decisional dependence and low uncertainty as perceived by FSMs in industrial MNCs may be associated with the following contextual factors: size and experience. Such organizational and individual factors of FSMs' personal contacts in industrial markets (see Appendix F) are illustrated with three quotations from the interviews (see Section 3.5) and discussed in the light of extant literature in the following paragraphs.

As mentioned in Section 4.2.1, the discussion of contextual factors in the present paper is restricted to FSMs' degree of uncertainty in the local industrial market and to FSMs' degree of dependence within the MNC. Therefore, FSMs' low degree of decisional dependence is associated with the organizational factor listed above, whereas the individual factor is associated with low uncertainty in the local industrial market and/or low decisional dependence within the MNC.

The size of the subsidiary is the only organizational factor listed in this section, being assumed to decrease FSMs' degree of decisional dependence. In this respect, most of the interviewed FSMs mention personal contacts within the MNC due to the lack of subsidiary resources.

> Getting actual support, which means resources usually, not usually money, but is the resources, so you need a person, somebody to work ... (...) We don't have too much of the resources, so what happens is that there has to be some priorities, obviously my duty is to put the priority as high as possible for these our cases and then basically other people who have more responsibility or wider responsibility they try to look it from the wider perspective ...

PCN manager

> We have no legal department here in [. . .] Portugal, so if I have a problem of a legal matter, if I have a financial matter, a tax problem, there is always people available by this group to advise me.

TCN manager

> Because we are, first of all, small company in terms of human resources, the point is that our daily activities are a bit spread on the field and also in the company, so I take care of the main issues and the main subjects in the company trying to coordinate the main activities connected with the various departments ...

HCN manager

Hedlund (1981, p. 52) argues that: "increased size means that the subsidiary can build up its own resources and become less dependent on management." Harzing (1999) implicitly suggests personal contacts among managers (Martinez & Jarillo, 1989) as a mechanism of coordination in small subsidiaries of Finnish MNCs, by claiming a positive relationship between subsidiary size and output control in such MNCs.

As mentioned in Section 4.2.1, the association of the organizational factor just described with other scenarios of low decisional dependence (see Section 4.2.7) and even of low informational dependence (see Sections 4.2.3 and 4.2.4) would have been eventually plausible. The analysis of case evidence suggests, however, that *size* is primarily related with a scenario of low decisional dependence and low uncertainty as defined in Section 1.5.

Experience is the only individual factor listed in this section, being assumed to decrease FSMs' degree of uncertainty and/or decisional dependence. In this respect, most of the interviewed FSMs mention their participation in negotiations within the MNC and in the local industrial market, which are affected by their working experience.

[Within the MNC] is as any sales, because we are talking internal sales (...) also depends on the credibility of the people doing the proposal ... (...) [In the local market] this business is complex and you cannot learn it from the books and if you are a local person who has not been in the business before obviously you cannot have real experience of the business unless you have been working abroad so usually our customers demand that there has to be a certain amount of expatriates in the organization ...

PCN manager

[In the local market] we are not talking about the contents, technical contents, which is always the same, but it's is the conditions, responsibilities, payments, liability ... and in this respect, they don't have any experience, they could have, I mean, probably they agree, but this part of work I have some decades of experience in negotiating the contract, which is not the case of our operational people, which are more practitioners ...

TCN manager

But if you are becoming a guy with, after a couple of years in the company, and you have been showing a certain kind of sense and good sense making the company control and so on, probably if you are presenting some investments it's much easier to get the approval if they know you comparing with other people that don't know ...

HCN manager

In the context of industrial markets, it has been argued that "the varied personalities, experience and motivation of each company's representatives will mean that they will take part in the social exchange differently" (IMP group, 1982, p. 19). In the context of less-hierarchical MNCs, Nohria and Ghoshal (1997, p. 156) argue that: "an experienced individual is often seen as a credible and valuable source of information and may thus be sought out by other individuals trying to build their own contact network."

As mentioned in Section 4.2.1, the association of the individual factor just described with another scenario of low uncertainty (see Section 4.2.4) would have been eventually plausible. The analysis of case evidence suggests, however, that experience is primarily related with a scenario of low decisional dependence as defined in Section 1.5.

4.2.9. High Decisional Dependence/High Uncertainty

A scenario of high decisional dependence and high uncertainty as perceived by FSMs in industrial MNCs may be associated with the following contextual factors: customer internationalization, planning process, approval process, business volume and intra-group transactions. Such market and organizational factors of FSMs' personal contacts in industrial markets (see Appendix F) are illustrated with three quotations from the interviews (see Section 3.5) and discussed in the light of extant literature in the following paragraphs.

As mentioned in Section 4.2.1, the discussion of contextual factors in the present paper is restricted to FSMs' degree of uncertainty in the local industrial market and to FSMs' degree of dependence within the MNC. Therefore, FSMs' high degree of uncertainty is associated with the market factor listed above, whereas their high degree of decisional dependence is associated with the organizational factors.

Customer internationalization is the only market factor listed in this section, being assumed to increase FSMs' degree of uncertainty. In this respect, most of the interviewed FSMs mention having negotiated the terms offered to multinational customers.

> I have a lot of contacts with my colleagues, because we want to share some of the resources, some of the key things and timings and also because, it's even more important, the customers are usually linked very much between themselves. (. . .) if we are making a tender for one of the international operators here which are operating in Portugal, with one subsidiary in Portugal, we are ensuring that we are in line with the pricing that we have been providing as a multinational company in other locations . . .

PCN manager

> If I have some problem with marketing or then always there is some customer, which is also operating, let's say, in the Benelux, then I call marketing, Mr. [. . .], and discuss it with him and what should we do, what we can do with this customer and that customer and what we can offer on prices, so that is joint strategy, we always discuss . . .

TCN manager

> Some customers with very close frontier with another country, the idea is to ask the price in our country and the neighbor country, and it is necessary to pass this information to prevent some problems with price, with different price. (. . .) I spoke a lot of times with the general manager of France, because we have common customers. It means French customers or French enterprises which work in Portugal and it means [that] sometimes is necessary to speak with my colleague in France for these matters.

HCN manager

Customer internationalization is thus regarded in the present paper as positively associated with international integration, which Johanson and Mattsson (1986, p. 249) define as "increasing coordination between positions in different national nets." The same authors argue that an MNC facing internationally active counterparts in a local industrial market is expected to use its network of positions across countries for strategic decision-making rather than for mere knowledge development (Johanson & Mattsson, 1988).

As mentioned in Section 4.2.1, the association of the market factor just described with other scenarios of high uncertainty (see Sections 4.2.7, 4.2.5 and 4.2.3) would have been eventually plausible. The analysis of case evidence suggests, however, that customer internationalization is primarily related with a scenario of high decisional dependence as defined in Section 1.5.

Planning process is the first organizational factor listed in this section, being assumed to increase FSMs' degree of decisional dependence. In this respect, most of the interviewed FSMs mention a budget, which is supplemented with more qualitative long-term planning.

> The basic thing is the budgeting for the next six months in time and we have this kind of rolling planning for the one year ahead, and then we have this kind of long range planning for the three years. And the planning itself for Portugal is defined by our team here. (. . .) I would say that final approval is done somewhere else, the planning itself is done here. (. . .) Having this kind of common planning and reporting, budgeting meetings, it's one way of meeting those people . . .

PCN manager

> We make meetings during the year usually in October and the budgets we establish during this meeting together. Production, quality, marketing and accounting also, sometimes . . . We make a discussion of these budgets, we agree usually. Or, if we don't have together the meeting we make a proposal to the company that are in this position to sell at this price, with this level of costs to the company and they approve or not. (. . .) The final approval always is the top of the division, is the manager of division who establishes . . . (. . .) In October usually we make the strategic budget forecasts for the next year and we make a report of the nine or the ten months in that year. During the month, in March, we make a revision of the first quarter of the year [and] we establish the objectives for the rest of the year . . .

TCN manager

> When I am preparing the budget I have many talks with my staff . . . (. . .) Then I have to send the budget to several people because there are lots of entities involved . . . (. . .) As far as I know, my boss and all the other bosses with more or less his duties in Europe and Asia Pacific and North America and Latin America, have certain targets and then they try to reach these targets asking to the country managers what they need. Then you reply if it's possible or not and reasons if is not possible, which are the reasons behind. (. . .) Usually we have only one meeting in September/October, where we discuss the budget for the next year. (. . .) With my boss, with the controller of Europe, with some guys from key accounts from marketing . . .

HCN manager

The planning process is thus seen in the present paper as goal setting (Galbraith, 1973), which requires FSMs' personal contacts within the MNC. In similar fashion, Cray (1984, p. 88) argues that: "to agree upon a budget generally necessitates a great deal of communication." In the context of MNCs, planning is indeed thought to "guide and channel the activities and actions of independent units" (Martinez & Jarillo, 1989, p. 491) especially through vertical communication (e.g. Hulbert & Brandt, 1980; Marschan, 1996).

The planning process within the MNC may also include the submission of investment proposals for evaluation and approval, which is the second organizational factor listed in this section – approval process – and thus assumed to increase FSMs' degree of decisional dependence. In this respect, most of the interviewed FSMs mention their participation in a process by which subsidiary investments over a certain limit are evaluated concerning human resources and infrastructure. A few of the interviewed FSMs mention that such a process results in slower and/or less transparent decision-making.

> If there is a certain investment or thing that [. . .] has to do of course, as in any company, there is a certain process to accept the investments. (. . .) So you have a pre-defined process for the approval, sometimes you have also pre-defined process in terms of who are participating in terms of creating the proposal . . . (. . .) Sometimes I don't know the objective criteria, I just know the result. I am trying to influence the result obviously, but I don't know exactly always what are the criteria used to decide.

PCN manager

> Investments it always depend on what [. . .] tells us to do and that's always a yearly fight to get investments, money for investments. And that's mostly decided by the president, Mr. [. . .], and together with Mr. [. . .]. And that sometimes is not easy to understand . . . (. . .) You have really to fight and try to convince people to give you the money. Is very personal, if you don't do anything, they don't do anything at all. (. . .) it takes a long time for the Finns to take a decision, and if you are not used to it, you get nervous . . .

TCN manager

> Some investments you can proceed locally without any kind of approval, but there are some limitations over which you need to present the program payback for those investments in a way that you can prove that the investment is a need. (. . .) Next year, if you still have some previous ones without approval and if you think that they are still important and with the kind of priority, then you continue the process and you put more. So this is a dynamic process, you talk, you justify. (. . .) It's a question of confidence and also according with the confidence it's a question of sense . . . (. . .) I would say that normally we are not used to have a too fast decision in the company internationally wise . . .

HCN manager

The approval process is thus seen in the present paper as hierarchical referral (Galbraith, 1973). In the context of MNCs, Egelhoff (1993, p. 185) has similarly argued that: "when uncertainty increases, exceptions must be referred up the hierarchical authority structure for decision-making."

In addition to investments, the approval process may also concern the business volume of the subsidiary, which is the third organizational factor listed in this section and equally associated with a high degree of decisional dependence for FSMs. Most of the interviewed FSMs mention having negotiated their sales targets with hierarchical superiors as well as restricting their participation in customer negotiations to large deals. A few of the interviewed FSMs mention restricting their participation in supplier negotiations to large deals.

If there is a major subcontractor in Portugal I might take the responsibility of taking personal relations with the president . . . (. . .) The bigger the deal, the more important is and because of the nature of the business, is more and more difficult to measure things. As I said if we are talking about some kind of delivery or whatever the business relationship is usually something between five and ten years after decision-making.

PCN manager

The final approval always is the top of the division, is the manager of division who establishes . . . sometimes they make a proposal to sell more quantities than we have the possibilities, but we discuss that it is too high that level for our sales (. . .) and we refuse to sell, but sometimes is an imposition . . . (. . .) For the most important customers sometimes, well I make special invitations . . .

TCN manager

As far as I know, my boss and all the other bosses with more or less his duties in Europe and Asia Pacific and North America and Latin America, have certain targets and then they try to reach these targets asking to the country managers what they need. Then you reply if it's possible or not and reasons if is not possible, which are the reasons behind. (. . .) In big customers, my [contacts] are everybody, are the mill manager, are the project manager, are the maintenance manager, are the purchasing department manager, are also people that are not manager, but reporting to all these people. In terms of very small mills, in those cases I just know two or three key people . . .

HCN manager

The subsidiary's business volume is thus seen in the present paper as either a budget item, which is negotiated through the planning process, or the volume of business, which is exchanged with other firms. In the context of industrial markets, the volume of business transacted has indeed been associated with the allocation of suppliers' resources for personal contacts with customers (Cunningham & Homse, 1986; Cunningham & Turnbull, 1982).

The business volume of the subsidiary may, in turn, include intra-group transactions, which is the last organizational factor listed in this section and equally associated with a high degree of decisional dependence for FSMs. In this respect, all the interviewed FSMs mention their participation in the negotiation of transactions with supplier firms within the MNC. A few of the interviewed FSMs mention their participation in the negotiation of transactions with customer firms within the MNC.

It covers also all the supply chain. So looking for solutions, how to get the [. . .] best to the customers, what the most economical or responsive to the customers requirements, all that stuff, and that's quite . . . logistics, is fairly complicated part, because as you understand this kind of multinational company has [. . .] mills who supply to Portugal from almost all over the world. How to orchestrate it in a way that we get the best economical results is an important part. (. . .) As a negotiator you follow very clearly the organigram.

PCN manager

We make a proposal to the business lines according to the total consumption of the market and according to our share of the market. (. . .) they have the final decision because sometimes they have more attractive markets in another countries with better margins . . . (. . .) The problem is that you need to explain all market, all things, all problems, all questions and you need to convince . . .

TCN manager

I work with these products, I sell a lot of machines of these two product managers and I pass the information that I consider very important for him. (. . .) because he can influence the transfer price . . . (. . .) If I try to sell some kind of machines and I have a problem with the price or with the delay, it's necessary to negotiate these things with the product managers.

HCN manager

Intra-group transactions are thus seen in the present paper as negotiated through the planning process or the approval process. In similar fashion, Harzing (1999) distinguishes between interdependence between the subsidiary, the headquarters, and other subsidiaries, and dependence of the subsidiary on headquarters. According to the author, subsidiary-dependent subsidiaries "experience a higher level of control by socialization and networks than headquarters-dependent subsidiaries" (Harzing, 1999, p. 292).

As mentioned in Section 4.2.1, the association of the organizational factors just described with another scenario of high decisional dependence (see Section 4.2.10) would have been eventually plausible. The analysis of case evidence suggests, however, that planning process, approval process, business volume and intra-group transactions are primarily related with a scenario of high uncertainty as defined in Section 1.5.

4.2.10. High Decisional Dependence/Low Uncertainty

Finally, a scenario of high decisional dependence and low uncertainty as perceived by FSMs in industrial MNCs may be associated with the following contextual factors: rules and programs and performance. Such organizational and individual factors of FSMs' personal contacts in industrial markets (see Appendix F) are illustrated with three quotations from the interviews (see Section 3.5) and discussed in the light of extant literature in the following paragraphs.

As mentioned in Section 4.2.1, the discussion of contextual factors in the present paper is restricted to FSMs' degree of uncertainty in the local industrial market and to FSMs' degree of dependence within the MNC. Therefore, FSMs' high degree of decisional dependence is associated with the organizational factor listed above, whereas the individual factor is associated with their low degree of uncertainty in the local industrial market and/or high degree of decisional dependence within the MNC.

Rules and programs are the only organizational factor listed in this section, being assumed to increase FSMs' degree of decisional dependence. In this respect, most of the interviewed FSMs mention group wide policies concerning marketing and procurement. A few of the interviewed FSMs mention group wide policies concerning human resources.

> If you are a low-cost provider then you show the product and the price and that's it, you don't put a lot of value on this. If you look for more service type of approach like as you see that we have even segmented the customers, we think that the customers behave differently and if your strategy is that, then you put a lot of emphasis to these relationship issues . . .
>
> PCN manager
>
> Internally too I am responsible that everything is done according to our guidelines. (. . .) [. . .] Portugal has to follow those guidelines in terms of administration and technical and material . . .
>
> TCN manager
>
> We have an international agreement with suppliers duly coordinated by our vice-president and after that each company is more or less independent to negotiate with each one, according to the local means. (. . .) the board is defining a kind of global strategies for different kind of subsidiaries. We need as much as we can, at least on those specific areas which can be adapted to the local markets, to try to implement also those strategies on the local markets in a way to follow an image, something related with the overall idea of the board . . .
>
> HCN manager

Rules and programs are thus seen in the present paper as written policies and rules (Galbraith, 1973; Pugh et al., 1968) including corporate strategies. In particular, it has been argued that such sets of rules, regulations, and procedures "clearly limit subsidiary management's role and authority" (Baliga & Jaeger, 1984, p. 26) by "pre-specifying, mostly in a written form, the behavior that is expected from employees" (Harzing, 1999, p. 21).

As mentioned in Section 4.2.1, the association of the organizational factor just described with another scenario of high decisional dependence (see Section 4.2.9) would have been eventually plausible. The analysis of case evidence suggests, however, that rules and programs are primarily related with a scenario of low uncertainty as defined in Section 1.5.

Performance is the only individual factor listed in this section, being associated with FSMs' low degree of uncertainty and/or high degree of decisional dependence. In this respect, most of the interviewed FSMs mention the intensity of their personal contacts in the local industrial market as contingent on their degree of professionalism.

During the time you have been working with the other people you have created a certain image of your company and you have been transferring not only your personal relationship but more a part of, let's say, the company you are working for, its values, its way of operating, and giving an image of that. (. . .) when you have had this kind of operational problems, then part of the decision process of solving those problems is of course easily related to the fact that you need to have the relationship to communicate with other parties and to be able to solve the problems, so of course personal relations play a big role in terms of solving those issues, but between two companies I would say that typically is the question of the actual real life performance issues . . .

PCN manager

When we have a problem with our products in most cases the customer continues to buy from us, so that's an indication that we solve it in the right way . . . (. . .) in most of those cases I negotiate a solution. I don't let it go for years, and for weeks or for months.

TCN manager

[Within the MNC] it's the figures that make the trust. If the product managers see that all years you sell the machines, you make the budget and you win the money, it's very easy after. (. . .) if people see in my person a competent person, it's easier to establish the contacts. (. . .) I have a reputation. . . [In the local market] the idea, if the customer has a problem, is to solve the problems immediately . . . (. . .) Time is very important and the quality of support. If the customers see that we are interested to solve their problems is easier after to sell something to these customers.

HCN manager

In the context of less-hierarchical MNCs, Nohria and Ghoshal (1997, p. 156) argue that: "more experienced individuals may maintain key contacts in other areas whom they have found over time to be helpful in their performance." In the context of industrial markets, social exchange has been associated with trust, which, in turn, is supposedly based on the successful execution of product-, information-, and financial exchange (IMP group, 1982, p. 17).

As mentioned in Section 4.2.1, the association of the individual factor just described with other scenarios of high decisional dependence (see Section 4.2.9) and even of low decisional dependence (see Sections 4.2.7 and 4.2.8) would have been eventually plausible. The analysis of case evidence suggests, however, that performance is primarily related with a scenario of low uncertainty and high decisional dependence as defined in Section 1.5.

4.3. Content of Personal Contacts

In Section 4.2, the context of FSMs' personal contacts has been discussed in terms of individual, organizational, and market factors which are thought to influence the occurrence of such personal contacts. In addition, the referred contextual factors have been associated with the degree of dependence and uncertainty perceived by FSMs. Such a discussion was illustrated with three selected quotations from the interviews (see Section 3.5) for the reader to assess the extent to which case evidence allows the present paper to answer the first research question (see Section 1.3).

The following sections discuss, in the light of extant literature, the content of FSMs' personal contacts in terms of five basic functions: information exchange, assessment, negotiation, decision-making, and resource allocation (see Section 2.5.1). Such a discussion is also illustrated with three selected quotations from the interviews (see Section 3.5) for the reader to assess the extent to which case evidence allows the present paper to answer the second research question (see Section 1.3).

4.3.1. Information Exchange

In terms of information exchange, FSMs' personal contacts may enable contact transfer, socializing, friendship, advice, follow-up, knowledge transfer, and benchmarking. In particular, FSMs may take personal contacts to receive and transfer third party's contact information. Most of the interviewed FSMs mention having received third party's contact information within the MNC and in the local industrial market. A few of the interviewed FSMs mention having transferred third party's contact information within the MNC and in the local industrial market.

> Expatriates are bringing their own personal networks also to the company. (...) [In the local market] if you know somebody who knows somebody else then that's a way of getting to know third persons. (...) lots of requirements in terms of what kind of entity we need to work with come from our teams, who are defining their needs and then it's my job to create the relationship. (...) some part of them are transferred naturally in the sense that we are doing this intentionally, so we are introducing people: "so, this is the one, who is going to do this work from now on" and things like that...
>
> PCN manager

> Normally if I have some doubt about the people or a person to contact I can get this information through the director of the division or through the Corporate Planning manager. (...) [In the local market] if I need a contact in financial, public institutions or something I can call a friend...
>
> TCN manager

> Usually the customers contact us if we know somebody in some organization and if I know I say: "yes I know one person you can call and you can speak in my name." (...) Sometimes when I visit a customer he makes a contact with also other persons.
>
> HCN manager

Contact transfer is thus seen in the present paper as a specific content of FSMs' personal contacts within the MNC and in the local industrial market. In the context of less-hierarchical MNCs, Marschan (1996, p. 140) similarly suggests that: "some of the expatriate's contacts may also be transferred to local personnel." In the context of industrial markets, Hallén (1992, p. 79) argues that, in contrast to person-centered infrastructural networks of contacts, organization-centered infrastructural networks "can mostly be transferable to other individuals." By infrastructural, the author refers to non-task relationships i.e. little oriented towards actual business deals. The analysis of case evidence suggests that contact transfer is primarily related with a scenario of low informational dependence and high uncertainty (see Section 4.2.3) influenced by factors such as the FSM's career and background in addition to corporate culture (see Appendix F).

FSMs may also take personal contacts for mere socializing. Most of the interviewed FSMs mention personal contacts at gatherings within the MNC. A few of the interviewed FSMs mention personal contacts at gatherings in the local industrial market.

[Within the MNC] in structured meetings, whether it's sales organization meeting or sales meetings of the divisions, we always exchange information with the colleagues.

PCN manager

[In the local market] for the most important customers sometimes, I make special invitations to my house, parties, or I try to go to lunch during the weekend or to visit, travels to the factory or to pass the holidays during the Summer or during the Christmas . . . because I have the confidence of the manager or the owner, his wife, his sons, my sons, my family, his family, everything . . . in this form I obtain information that is very important for me, you know, sometimes about competitors, about strategic plans for the future of the companies, for example.

TCN manager

I have been part of some training courses the group has promoted. (. . .) And living five weeks together, naturally, by the end, we are committed. We can't say that we don't know the others, because we know, we lived together. And with some of them, perhaps the only thing we have had is that we lived together for that period, but with most of them we have used then all the possible, all the potential help they could give us.

HCN manager

Socializing is thus seen in the present paper as a specific content of FSMs' personal contacts within the MNC and in the local industrial market. In the context of MNCs, Edström and Galbraith (1977) equate socialization with the process of selecting, training and transferring managers across units, by which they are able to create a verbal communication network. The authors thus largely equate socialization with the present paper's notion of employee turnover (see Section 4.2.5) rather than socializing. In the context of industrial markets, Andersson et al. (1996,

p. 150) implicitly refer to socializing by suggesting that: "it is easier to deal with business colleagues from a land with a culture close to that in their home country." The analysis of case evidence suggests that socializing is primarily related with a scenario of low informational dependence and high uncertainty (see Section 4.2.3) influenced by factors such as the FSM's language and social skills (see Appendix F).

FSMs' personal contacts may also promote friendship. Most of the interviewed FSMs mention personal contacts for friendship in the local industrial market. A few of the interviewed FSMs mention personal contacts for friendship within the MNC.

Also I made friends, I mean, personal friends, which I will keep.

PCN manager

[Within the MNC] I know a very good friend, who moved from [. . .] to [. . .] and he is head of [. . .] division . . .

TCN manager

Some of them are old friends, which for any reason I noted in our division. With the group reorganization some of them went out to other divisions, but of course friendship is very transversal, so you can keep it wherever they are. (. . .) [In the local market] I have a lot of friends as well.

HCN manager

Friendship is thus seen in the present paper as a specific content of FSMs' personal contacts within the MNC and in the local industrial market. In the context of less-hierarchical MNCs, Marschan et al. (1996, p. 142) argue that: "both company-based and individual-based personal networks can be used for either company or individual purposes." In the context of industrial markets, Cunningham and Turnbull (1982, p. 308) similarly suggest that it may happen "that personal liking develops as a consequence of instrumental action and the two people then tend to interact more frequently for the social reasons." The analysis of case evidence suggests that friendship is primarily related with a scenario of low informational dependence and low uncertainty (see Section 4.2.4) influenced by factors such as the FSM's tenure and geographical proximity (see Appendix F).

FSMs may also exchange information in terms of marketing-, technical-, financial-, and legal advice. Most of the interviewed FSMs mention personal contacts within the MNC for advice on marketing and technical issues. A few of the interviewed FSMs mention personal contacts within the MNC and in the local industrial market for advice on financial and legal issues.

In this kind of business decision things, then you involve people like finance and trade finance, for example, you might even employ people from legal department . . . (. . .) is very complicated thing to define what is the price, it's not simple like "the price is this," because there is a lot of variables and it can mean a lot of different things, so actually that's one part of it, so you need to seek for those basic answers, which can be very complicated. The same is about technical issues, for example, what are our capabilities in certain technical things. Most likely I don't even understand the question what I am doing myself properly, but I am just transferring the question and I am trying to apply the answer.

PCN manager

If I have some problem with marketing or then always there is some customer, which is also operating, let's say, in the Benelux, then I call marketing . . . (. . .) [In the local market] we have a contact with a lawyer's office in Lisbon and we have our accounting company, that's [. . .] in Porto, and they give us advice on legal issues.

TCN manager

[Within the MNC] contact people in all the factories mainly for support and marketing activity. (. . .) pricing that is not in our system yet, this kind of things, also in some cases is technical support . . . (. . .) I have contacts for instance with Legal Affairs, to Human Resources, to Strategy and Marketing . . . because sometimes I have other tasks different from sales and management. (. . .) in certain cases, certain applications, you always need to be supported by someone.

HCN manager

Advice is thus seen in the present paper as a specific content of FSMs' personal contacts within the MNC and in the local industrial market. The need for advice in less-hierarchical MNCs, is implicit in Marschan's (1996) discussion of limited "know who" information especially among middle managers and operating staff. In the context of industrial markets, Cunningham and Homse (1986, p. 261) suggest technical advice and general commercial information exchange as "topics dealt with through these personal contacts." The analysis of case evidence suggests that advice is primarily related with a scenario of high informational dependence and high uncertainty (see Section 4.2.5) influenced by factors such as the start-up of subsidiary operations, organizational change, technical complexity and market internationalization (see Appendix F).

A related purpose of personal contacts is the follow-up of transactions. Most of the interviewed FSMs mention personal contacts within the MNC and in the local industrial market concerning delivery times. A few of the interviewed FSMs mention personal contacts within the MNC and in the local industrial market for the settlement of receivables.

With our logistics partner I am in contact with the managing director. Our sales assistants are in contact mostly with the person responsible for the stock management and the deliveries. If the customer calls us and says that he has a problem with a delivery then we have to resolve it. (. . .) If a customer has a payment problem, the sales director may contact our lawyers or we do it together and then we proceed, but as the overall responsibility towards the parent company is mine, it also implies that I have to be informed and I want to be informed . . .

PCN manager

I am just in between, so I say to the customer: "sorry, sir, but I am not a bank and you have to settle your bill and if you don't, I stop to deliver any spare parts and services: (. . .) within the group, if for example we should receive a commission for sets of spare parts in the Portuguese territory and we haven't received any commissions and we haven't been kept informed that sales have been done directly from the production company to the ship owner for example, it's my duty to claim. I will do it and I have done it. (. . .) if we are missing one or two spare parts they can come from [. . .], it is day-to-day business.

TCN manager

[Within the MNC] these people are assisting all the sales offices in the world so I have my contact, in each location I have one contact for quotations and also I have my order handling people, which is different matters. (. . .) [In the local market] the equipment is not always delivered exactly according the requirements . . . (. . .) if it's involving costs of any type, transportation costs, they know that I am the only person that can decide this . . .

HCN manager

Follow-up is thus seen in the present paper as a specific content of FSMs' personal contacts within the MNC and in the local industrial market. The need for follow-up in less-hierarchical MNCs, is also implicit in Marschan's (1996) discussion of limited "know who" information. In the context of industrial markets, Cunningham and Homse (1986) suggest progressing (delivery and technical) as a topic dealt with through personal contacts. The analysis of case evidence suggests that follow-up is primarily related with a scenario of low informational dependence and low uncertainty (see Section 4.2.4) influenced by factors such as the FSM's delegation and age of relationships (see Appendix F).

FSMs may also engage in the transfer of knowledge originated within the MNC. Most of the interviewed FSMs mention personal contacts within the MNC and in the local industrial market for knowledge transfer.

Part of the responsibility, yes, is the knowledge transfer. We are a knowledge-based company, of course, so ensuring that the knowledge is transferred and that we are keeping ourselves competent in part with the technological development as well with the market development, yes, that's part of my job description, ensure knowledge transfer actively. (. . .) Being in my case a friend of the mother company or anyway an expatriate . . . the assumption is that I should bring some kind of knowledge, which doesn't exist here.

PCN manager

[In the local market] we inform in technology, in quality the requirements of the products to the customers . . . (. . .) We try to teach, to supply one more thing for another machine because is better in productivity, we try to teach new system of production, we try to teach new methodology, we try to teach our systems of production, visiting our factories . . . (. . .) visits to the factory in technical production to look the machines, to look mechanical characteristics of chemical compositions . . .

TCN manager

[Within the MNC] I receive a lot of information, of types of information, technical information, marketing information . . . (. . .) when I speak of marketing information is marketing information as new products. (. . .) [In the local market] we give all information.

HCN manager

Knowledge transfer is thus seen in the present paper as a specific content of FSMs' personal contacts within the MNC and in the local industrial market. In the context of less-hierarchical MNCs, Marschan (1996, p. 140) suggests that: "generally, the role of the expatriate was seen as a teacher who was sent over to share technical knowledge and expertise with local personnel." In the context of industrial markets, Cunningham and Homse (1986) suggest general technical information exchange as a topic dealt with through personal contacts. The analysis of case evidence suggests that knowledge transfer is primarily related with a scenario of high informational dependence and high uncertainty (see Section 4.2.5) influenced by factors such as the start-up of subsidiary operations and technical complexity (see Appendix F).

A related issue is FSMs' benchmarking of best practices. Most of the interviewed FSMs mention personal contacts within the MNC concerning organizational and technical issues. At least one of the interviewed FSMs mentions personal contacts in the local industrial market concerning organizational issues.

I work with my colleagues as well, to understand things better, number one, to benchmark cases, the bigger sales units than Portugal have more resources, so I call them: "hey, how have you clever guys thought about this?"

PCN manager

If we have a problem that is known by Helsinki and if they have the same problem in Philippines so they know how to serve it . . . (. . .) We have a problem in one plant in Portugal and I want to know technically if this problem was known by this group . . .

TCN manager

I am in a position, which allows me to know most of the good achievements in the several areas of the different units, so I access to that information, which means that I can define who are more interesting to me. (. . .) Those, which I could call benchmarking relationships they are occasional, but they are so many. (. . .) [In the local market] all what I consider the company references in Portugal, I have regular contacts with them. (. . .) to develop my leadership skills or my research management skills or whatever (. . .) I am quite close with more eleven companies to found a benchmarking club saying in our country what are the best practices in the several areas of management.

HCN manager

Benchmarking is thus seen in the present paper as a specific content of FSMs' personal contacts within the MNC and in the local industrial market. In the context of less-hierarchical MNCs, Nohria and Ghoshal (1997, p. 152) implicitly acknowledge benchmarking by arguing that: "information obtained through interpersonal contacts can greatly enhance innovation." In the context of industrial markets, Cunningham and Turnbull (1982, p. 307) implicitly refer to benchmarking by mentioning confidential information exchange "which provides market and technological feedback to the customer and supplier alike." The analysis of case evidence suggests that benchmarking is primarily related with a scenario of low informational dependence and high uncertainty (see Section 4.2.3) influenced by factors such as the FSM's background and initiative (see Appendix F).

4.3.2. Assessment

In terms of assessment, FSMs' personal contacts may enable trust enhancement, reporting, corporate reputation as well as MNC-, market-, customer-, and supplier assessment. In particular, FSMs may take personal contacts, which enhance individual counterparts' trust. Most of the interviewed FSMs mention the importance of face-to-face personal contacts in the local industrial market. A few of the interviewed FSMs mention negative perceptions of bypassing decision-makers within the MNC and in the local industrial market.

> Without personal contacts is very difficult to do any business. You need to be able to trust people you are dealing with so you need to be able to establish mutual trust and mutual respect. (. . .) The decision is based on the evaluation of things, but then the last thing is the trust. You trust that this company is able to provide what they are promising? And the trust you need to create in personal relationships and there is no other way of creating it. (. . .) you as person are functioning as some kind of guarantee of this thing . . .

> PCN manager

> [Within the MNC] if you forget to notify these persons and you notify the chief or the boss of these persons, tomorrow you have a problem with these . . . (. . .) [In the local market] I visit and I try to find the confidence with the customers. It is very important when you visit one customer to talk with the top of the customer. Top in management or with the owner, because you need to go where is the decision.

> TCN manager

> [In the local market] all the big opportunities I would lose, because the mill managers and the project managers just want, usually they want to discuss and to talk to the other managers.

> HCN manager

Trust enhancement is thus seen in the present paper as a specific content of FSMs' personal contacts within the MNC and in the local industrial market. In the context of less-hierarchical MNCs, Nohria and Ghoshal (1997, p. 152) argue that: "interpersonal ties are also mechanisms for building trust." In the context of industrial markets, it has also been acknowledged that a buyer-seller relationship is based on mutual trust and that "building up this trust is a social process" (IMP group, 1982, p. 17). The analysis of case evidence suggests that trust enhancement is primarily related with a scenario of low informational dependence and high uncertainty (see Section 4.2.3) influenced by factors such as the FSM's availability, attitude and personality in addition to supplier closeness (see Appendix F).

FSMs may also take personal contacts within the MNC for vertical reporting. Most of the interviewed FSMs mention top-down and bottom-up requests for information.

> Our business environment is in constant change so if I see or our sales directors see that a new opportunity arises, say for instance, a new [. . .] or a new [. . .], if this happens in January we certainly don't wait until September or October, but we approach the respective business unit or all of them potentially involved in different ways.

PCN manager

> If it's technical then it is more our initiative, and if it's financial then it's mostly from the group.

TCN manager

> An estimate sometimes is requested. One or several estimates concerning mainly net sales, order intake, gross profit, and sometimes the expenses . . . (. . .) Mainly by their initiative, mainly in what concerns these Legal Affairs and this Strategy and Marketing . . . (. . .) I receive requests and "please reply up to fifteen days later" . . .

HCN manager

Reporting is thus seen in the present paper as a specific content of FSMs' personal contacts within the MNC. In similar fashion, Egelhoff (1993, p. 185) refers to "vertical information-processing systems that increase the organization's information-processing capacity" and "frequently include computer-based information systems and staff groups." The analysis of case evidence suggests that reporting is primarily related with a scenario of high informational dependence and low uncertainty (see Section 4.2.6) influenced by factors such as the reporting process (see Appendix F).

On the other hand, FSMs may take personal contacts in order to promote the reputation of their subsidiary in the local industrial market. Most of the interviewed FSMs mention personal contacts in order to become a reference for customers. A few of the interviewed FSMs mention personal contacts in order to publish MNC-related information.

> Sometimes we are approached by these associations sometimes we approach them and the same goes for the trade Press. (. . .) in a way the managing director of any multinational

company on any market is seen by customers and by associations as the counterpart if they want information...

PCN manager

As a managing director is what I am doing very often, I am an ambassador of the group. I mean, I will certainly participate to seminars, to professional meetings to show up ... (. . .) you meet a lot people in the same time, in the same day, so there is some message you can send through ...

TCN manager

I know all those local authorities quite well. Actually one of our values is to be a good neighbor and being a good neighbor is not only a declaration is to be a good neighbor. (. . .) On the customers, when we pass concepts, one of the aims is to be a reference for them ... (. . .) the people/company image was a key question to me. (. . .) a social reference for the business and outside the business as well.

HCN manager

Corporate reputation is thus seen in the present paper as a specific content of FSMs' personal contacts in the local industrial market. In this respect, Hallén (1992, p. 82) argues that: "a basic difference exists between influence through mass communication (e.g. public relations) on the one hand and individual contacts on the other," by which managers may get involved in political or social activities in order to influence opinions. The analysis of case evidence suggests that corporate reputation is primarily related with a scenario of high informational dependence and high uncertainty (see Section 4.2.5) influenced by factors such as technical complexity and market internationalization (see Appendix F).

FSMs may also take personal contacts to assess their own *MNC*. Most of the interviewed FSMs mention personal contacts within the MNC in search of support. A few of the interviewed FSMs mention personal contacts within the MNC in order to assess organizational change.

It takes you a lot of time to understand how various functions are led because the styles are never the same. Although we try to establish [. . .]'s style it depends a lot of the managers themselves. When you go to the function and you need the help of that function you need to ask around a bit and how it's really working and who's really the decision-maker, is it the team or is it a "one man show" or what...

PCN manager

Of course through my contacts I see what's going on. (. . .) Maybe sometimes you are aware the situation a little bit before the other, because, ok, you know that this will happen ... (. . .) so I knew also two years before that they would be re-organized and they would be moved to [. . .] or we know that one engine will be phased out ...

TCN manager

> We have a lot of people, you know, in the exhibitions, that I have no idea what kind of work they [do] in the multinational, in our group. (. . .) The big problem is the change of organization, because a lot of times we don't know these changes. (. . .) I know very well two or three persons key in this group. If I have a problem I speak with these persons.

HCN manager

MNC assessment is thus seen in the present paper as a specific content of FSMs' personal contacts within the MNC. In this respect, Marschan (1996, p. 155) suggests that: "while the lack of 'know who' information was perceived as a constraint among middle manager and operating staff, this was not the case in the interviews at top management level." The analysis of case evidence suggests that MNC assessment is primarily related with a scenario of high informational dependence and high uncertainty (see Section 4.2.5) influenced by factors such as organizational change and employee turnover (see Appendix F).

FSMs may also take personal contacts to assess the market. Most of the interviewed FSMs mention personal contacts within the MNC and in the local industrial market for assessment of local and eventually regional market trends.

> I could not be a good managing director unless I had direct sales responsibilities on the market, because that gives me the knowledge and the ideas of how to direct my sales directors. (. . .) If I find myself in a certain situation on the Portuguese market where the market is changing, the prices are going down or the prices are going up, or I get certain market information from my customers, I very frequently talk to my colleagues, very informally and I explain what I hear here and then I ask them: "well, how is it on your market, is the customer just bluffing that the prices are going down or how is it on your market, how did the competitors or that particular competitor behave?" and then I get a wider picture.

PCN manager

> There are innovations in the market and you need to be in this market. How it is possible if you don't attend faxes, calls, or inquiries, you listen to information . . . if you don't go? (. . .) I visited the associations in the country, industrial associations, because it was necessary to find information, for example, the directory of the companies. Or I visited the chambers of commerce, local chambers of commerce also to obtain information or asking to other customers about his competitors . . .

TCN manager

> By meaning knowing the business I am including the whole parts of the business. Not only customers but also the view point of investors, suppliers and competitors. (. . .) [Within the MNC] on the operative meetings the first agenda point is the business situation. So in that sense is not only the financial figures, is how is the market, how we are positioning, what are the trends, what are the expectations, what are the actions we are preparing to the several projects we are making . . .

HCN manager

Market assessment is thus seen in the present paper as a specific content of FSMs' personal contacts within the MNC and in the local industrial market. In the context MNCs, Keegan (1974, p. 414) suggests that: "when a headquarters executive in an international corporation with operations abroad acquires external information, the most likely single source of information is the corporation's own staff abroad." In the context of industrial markets, Björkman and Kock (1995, p. 524) refer to social relations in order "to obtain information about possible customers." The analysis of case evidence suggests that market assessment is primarily related with a scenario of low informational dependence and high uncertainty (see Section 4.2.3) influenced by factors such as market idiosyncrasy and market dynamism (see Appendix F).

In addition to market trends, FSMs may take personal contacts in order to assess customers. Most of the interviewed FSMs mention personal contacts in order to assess customers' needs and decision-making process. A few of the interviewed FSMs mention personal contacts in order to assess change in customer organizations.

> I have the role of contacting the people, having the contact with people corresponding to my level. (. . .) to understand the customer requirements correctly you need to have several different views from customer's side, because it's not homogeneous requirement, because it's a sum of several people. It's not a company. A company consists of decision-makers who are people. (. . .) the needs are so different. (. . .) how do they want we deliver the product, what are the personal contacts, how do they physically want, what are the time limits, and how do we follow-up, what's the technical service level, what's the whole package, is totally dependent of some individuals' own thinking. There are some companies where the organizational power is enormous, they have created standards, they do this and that, but those companies are an exception.
>
> PCN manager

> We transmit the necessities of the customer to the company . . . (. . .) who are the people responsible in the customer for purchases, the top in this direction, the manager for this function . . . (. . .) you need to go where is the decision. (. . .) When you visit the customer you know if they have twenty salesman, if they have trucks, if they have stocks in consignation, if they have money, many things . . .
>
> TCN manager

> On the exhibitions, at least twice a year, we use to make what we called a "tournée" on the most important customers. So, I know them, the top management and the second level, and their facilities. (. . .) When you are facing an external organization, depending on what is your aim, you have to find who is the key person for the decisions. (. . .) The purpose with private customers is basically to understand their business, what are the opportunities to help them to grow or, saying differently, to develop our common growth. With public [customers] is a little different because you know, changes are happening more times, so, we have to be very much updated with the status of the organization . . .
>
> HCN manager

Customer assessment is thus seen in the present paper as a specific content of FSMs' personal contacts in the local industrial market. In similar fashion, Björkman and Kock (1995, p. 520) argue that: "for companies marketing industrial products and large-scale projects a key question is how to obtain information about up-coming purchasing decisions, and how to establish and nurture relationships to potential buyers." The analysis of case evidence suggests that customer assessment is primarily related with a scenario of low informational dependence and high uncertainty (see Section 4.2.3) influenced by factors such as the FSM's sales orientation in addition to supplier closeness (see Appendix F).

Similarly to customers, FSMs may take personal contacts in order to assess suppliers. Most of the interviewed FSMs mention personal contacts in order to assess local service providers as well as subcontractors.

> The banks, insurance companies, operative logistic companies, and things like that, which are related to our business, whose services we need...(...) What comes to operative support like bankers and logistics varies... I don't need the managing director of any Portuguese bank, but I know some of the managers who run the businesses of ours, and their bosses.

PCN manager

> I have the normal contact that you can expect with public organizations, with financial organizations, with consulting organizations...(...) suppliers they don't know the structure of the company, so when I contact them this is in the role of managing director or president of the company, but inside a certain purpose of sales, of purchase or something else.

TCN manager

> And then to select the main suppliers on each moment according to pricing, conditions, technical facilities, needs in terms of production...(...) for sure I am assuming that banks and the insurance companies they are part of the suppliers. (...) I like to assist, because it might be many things around and then normally the contracts they are going to be signed by me representing the company and I would like to know some specifics on some specific businesses according with the size of the business and so on.

HCN manager

Supplier assessment is thus seen in the present paper as a specific content of FSMs' personal contacts in the local industrial market. In similar fashion, Cunningham and Turnbull (1982, p. 307) contend that: "the assessment of a supplier's competence, is a process frequently involving personal judgments as well as objectives facts; these judgments are improved through interacting with the other party in both formal and informal situations." The analysis of case evidence suggests that supplier assessment is primarily related with a scenario of low informational dependence and high uncertainty (see Section 4.2.3) influenced by factors such as customer closeness and business culture (see Appendix F).

4.3.3. Negotiation

In terms of negotiation, FSMs' personal contacts may enable negotiations and staff empowerment. In particular, FSMs may participate in negotiations both within the MNC and in the local industrial market. Most of the interviewed FSMs mention personal contacts in order to negotiate with customers and with suppliers. A few of the interviewed FSMs mention easier negotiations within the MNC than in the local industrial market.

> The computer neither written reports can ever replace the personal contact where you exchange information and you read between the lines and you develop a certain idea together and then at the end of the day you define your policy, make a price policy, all the targets and so forth. (...) we try to get first feedback from the customers and then we give that information probably by phone or by e-mail to the mill, we get their comments, the customer says one hundred, the mill may say one hundred-and-ten and then we start to develop it from that...

PCN manager

> [In the local market] I have negotiated the last maintenance contract. (...) We are not talking about the contents, technical contents, which is always the same, but it is the conditions, responsibilities, payments, liability... and in this respect, they don't have any experience, they could have, I mean, probably they agree, but this part of work I have some decades of experience in negotiating the contract, which is not the case of our operational people, which are more practitioners...

TCN manager

> Is easier to negotiate intra-group than to negotiate with the customers. (...) With one or two product managers, these guys gave me the cost price and we decided together if I have a problem in front of the customer "you can go until that price"... (...) [In the local market] if I do a business and my gross margin is much better than I think I can give something plus to the subcontractors... (...) our key success of this local sales unit is the negotiation with these subcontractors. (...) I know the boss of the enterprise and I negotiate always with the boss.

HCN manager

Negotiations are thus seen in the present paper as a specific content of FSMs' personal contacts within the MNC and in the local industrial market. In the context of less-hierarchical MNCs, Marschan (1996, p. 131) suggests that: "personal relationships were used for gaining influence in inter-unit communication." In the context of industrial markets, Cunningham and Turnbull (1982, p. 308) argue that: "personal contacts in buying and selling are the normal means of persuasion and negotiation both at the time of, and subsequent to the original order." The analysis of case evidence suggests that negotiations are primarily related with a scenario of low decisional dependence and low uncertainty (see Section 4.2.8) influenced by factors such as the FSM's experience in addition to subsidiary size (see Appendix F).

FSMs may also take personal contacts for staff empowerment. Most of the interviewed FSMs mention personal contacts in the local industrial market in order to mediate subsidiary-customer relationships as well as within the MNC in order to intervene in subsidiary-headquarters relationships.

> Sometimes the sales director may come and say: "I would need your support because it would be important that the customer understands that the terms of payment or the price policy or this and that does not depend on me personally and it's a group policy" (...) the sales director is involved, otherwise he would loose face, because in this kind of situations, sometimes it happens that the customer thinks that if he goes to a higher level or sends a fax or whatever directly to the parent company that then he gets what he wants. (...) What I never do is that I would go to meet or contact customers of my sales directors behind their backs. It has got to be always open, say, completely transparent and always with the idea of supporting my team.

> PCN manager

> What is important for [...] is to keep a good relationship with the rest of the group because he has to deal with those people everyday. I have to deal once a year so is totally different approach. And not the same level actually, so each time is necessary ... technically he doesn't need my contact, but as soon as we are talking about relationship, then I will take over, I will be in charge. [In the local market] I have received a copy of this claim. So there is two ways. Who is going to answer? We are taking about price, overall. It should be [...] because he made the proposal. I did it, because I don't see the point why he would fight against this customer when he has to deal with him everyday, when as the president of the company I can give all the explanations he wants...

> TCN manager

> Sometimes it happens that you have a subordinate, it might be a manager, trying to solve some problem and he has been trying once, twice, and three times and nothing was happening. So, maybe you can go directly or you can go first to the boss just to say: "well, I have a problem with this, do you like that you treat this on your way, or may I go straight?" (...) [In the local market] when I am trying to be in touch with these decision-makers, normally I would like to have one of my managers in this case, sales and marketing managers with me ... (...) you can say in the majority of the times, 95% of the cases I never establish any kind of contact with our customers without any previous contact with our people.

> HCN manager

Staff empowerment is thus seen in the present paper as a specific content of FSMs' personal contacts within the MNC and in the local industrial market. In the context of less-hierarchical MNCs, Marschan (1996, p. 139) suggests that: "in some situations local personnel or third country nationals use, for example, Finnish expatriates as stepping stones in inter-unit communication to overcome language barriers or gain more influence." In the context of industrial markets, Cunningham and Homse (1982, p. 269) refer to marketing and purchasing co-ordinated contact patterns by which, for example, "the sales representative 'brings along' a member of the engineering department." The analysis of case evidence suggests that staff empowerment is primarily related with a scenario of low decisional dependence and high uncertainty (see section 4.2.7) influenced by factors such as the FSM's job description and extra duties (see Appendix F).

4.3.4. Decision-making

In terms of decision-making, FSMs' personal contacts may enable approval, planning and problem solving. In particular, FSMs may take personal contacts for approval of their decisions. Most of the interviewed FSMs mention personal contacts within the MNC for marketing issues. A few of the interviewed FSMs also mention personal contacts within the MNC for human resources issues. A few of the interviewed FSMs mention personal contacts in the local industrial market concerning permits from local authorities.

> HR issues, basically. So simple things, salary increases, whatever. Those are usually done within the line organization. (...) is permission, basically, "shall we do this way, or that way" and get permission or approval for that our approach. (...) you need to get this kind of approval that "yes, you can offer this kind of offering to your customer" and typically that involves my line management ... (...) typically it involves usually two or three people, as a minimum ... (...) usually the proposal is related to extraordinary things like a tender or whatever.
>
> PCN manager

> If special decisions have to be made I have to get permission or discuss it with my colleagues from the other units. (...) strategic decisions that we say: – "ok, we do it with this price," if we produce it with a lower price because strategically it is better to do it now, and then make profit next year, but I cannot from here, from Portugal, I cannot oversee the situation, so that has to come from Finland ... (...) [In the local market] most is for special authorizations, if we need to construct something or if we need another permit authorization then we need to go to local authorities.
>
> TCN manager

> [My boss] if I decide to increase my team I need to discuss with him. (...) If I try to sell some kind of machines and I have a problem with the price or with the delay, it's necessary to negotiate these things with the product managers.
>
> HCN manager

Approval is thus seen in the present paper as a specific content of FSMs' personal contacts within the MNC and in the local industrial market. In the context of MNCs, Egelhoff (1993, p. 185) refers to hierarchical referrals by which "exceptions must be referred up the hierarchical authority structure for decision-making." In the context of industrial markets, Hallén (1992, p. 79) argues that: "the relationships with non-business actors such as government and local authorities, trade unions, industrial federations, and private-interest associations may be as important as the business relationships." The analysis of case evidence suggests that approval is primarily related with a scenario of high decisional dependence and high uncertainty (see Section 4.2.9) influenced by factors such as approval process and customer internationalization (see Appendix F).

FSMs may also take personal contacts for planning. Most of the interviewed FSMs mention personal contacts within the MNC to review marketing plans.

> I am a natural part of the process in the sense that if you are planning something to Iberian Peninsula then I am involved . . .

PCN manager

> You decide objectives, but it is not definitive objectives, you change because the markets change during the year, and the first tertiary for example is a very good level of the market, but the second tertiary reduce consumption and we don't sell nothing and is necessary a revision of forecasts. (. . .) you don't need to make ten or twelve persons together, you can establish information or strategy by phone, e-mail or private meetings, two, three persons, in factory, in market, in customers, it depends . . .

TCN manager

> I am preparing the budget right now, end of August/beginning of September, preparing the budget for 2002. In June, for instance in June 2002, my opinion will be completely different from now so what I am thinking now that will happen next year can change or not, but can change a lot, so an estimate sometimes is requested.

HCN manager

Planning is thus seen in the present paper as a specific content of FSMs' personal contacts within the MNC. In this respect, Nohria and Eccles (1992, p. 292) argue that: "the social dimension of organization is especially crucial in the network organization because the type of coordination action that is required is rarely routine." The analysis of case evidence suggests that planning is primarily related with a scenario of high decisional dependence and high uncertainty (see Section 4.2.9) influenced by factors such as the planning process, business volume, and intra-group transactions (see Appendix F).

Finally, FSMs may take personal contacts to solve problems. Most of the interviewed FSMs mention personal contacts in the local industrial market due to customer claims. A few of the interviewed FSMs mention personal contacts within the MNC concerning decisions on technical-, logistic-, financial- and legal problems.

> The customer calls us and says that he has a problem with a delivery then we have to resolve it. (. . .) if a problematic situation arises, then of course the ultimate responsibility is mine (. . .) Sometimes a customer may get in touch with me directly. (. . .) I have a certain control function, because the overall responsibility is mine regarding especially the payments and the legal aspects, because the legal responsibility of the company I cannot delegate, it's mine. So when it comes to problem solving of an impasse then it's my duty.

PCN manager

That's important that you know exactly whom to contact when you have a problem. (. . .) when there is a big problem, so then I have to solve the problem or take the decision to do something. (. . .) it's decision-making. (. . .) is my task and my position to say: "ok, let's do it then like this, and we accept this, and that's it." (. . .) most of it is technical. (. . .) it has to do with sometimes logistics, sometimes with the quality of the raw material, sometimes with the specifications, and sometimes with the product . . .

TCN manager

I may have additional contacts on the level of some directors in the mother company related with different kinds of eventual problems we face on the daily operations. (. . .) I am a kind of fireman. (. . .) [In the local market] If they are claiming, normally the bosses, I send immediately these claims to our people, asking them if they can give me the feedback. And before establishing contacts I would like to know details about these. (. . .) Sometimes because they have been facing some conflict or because they thought that the people didn't transfer the message in the company . . .

HCN manager

Problem solving is thus seen in the present paper as a specific content of FSMs' personal contacts within the MNC and in the local industrial market. In the context of less-hierarchical MNCs, problem solving is implicit in Marschan's (1996, p. 139) discussion of expatriates' conduit role by which "local personnel of third country nationals use, for example, Finnish expatriates as stepping stones in inter-unit communication." In industrial markets, Cunningham and Turnbull (1982, p. 308) refer to the crisis insurance role of personal contacts by which contacts are established for later use "when a major problem or crisis occurs." The analysis of case evidence suggests that problem solving is primarily related with a scenario of high decisional dependence and low uncertainty (see Section 4.2.10) influenced by factors such as the FSM's performance in addition to rules and programs (see Appendix F).

4.3.5. Resource Allocation

In terms of resource allocation, FSMs' personal contacts may enable coaching, buffer relations and resource leverage. In particular, FSMs may be required to allocate part of their time to coach subordinates. A few of the interviewed FSMs mention personal contacts in order to coach subordinates on marketing and management issues.

I am more a coach than a managing director, because the operations are done by [. . .] segments and by things like that. (. . .) I work more with the people, so that the people are motivated, people understand things correctly . . . (. . .) In some cases, I act as a trainer myself . . .

PCN manager

This is also part of my tasks. That's training . . .

TCN manager

Many proposals I don't make them or I just give the guidelines to my colleagues. In this case is not sales activities, is also management . . .

HCN manager

Coaching is thus seen in the present paper as a specific content of FSMs' personal contacts within the MNC. In similar fashion, Marschan (1996, p. 140) suggests that: "generally, the role of the expatriate was seen as a teacher" by local personnel. The analysis of case evidence suggests that coaching is primarily related with a scenario of low decisional dependence and low uncertainty (see Section 4.2.8) influenced by factors such as the FSM's experience in addition to subsidiary size (see Appendix F).

FSMs may also invest their time in buffer relations i.e. potential contacts. Most of the interviewed FSMs mention personal contacts in the local industrial market based on subsidiary business prospects. A few of the interviewed FSMs mention personal contacts within the MNC based on subsidiary business prospects. At least one of the interviewed FSMs mentions personal contacts within the MNC based on individual career prospects.

[In the local market] you also create a friendship with people, who do you think it will be useful . . . (. . .) you need to have the relationship before you get into difficulties.

PCN manager

[Within the MNC] take a guy of forty now in my shoes, he will have a tremendous connection in the group, he wants to be known from everywhere. He will make papers, he will show up because he has another twenty years in front of him, and is always useful to be known. (. . .) [In the local market] since we are not in charge [of the other Division's products], it would be a waste of money and a waste of time to try to build-up relationships . . .

TCN manager

[Within the MNC] the idea is to have some contacts per year, which mean that people don't forget you. (. . .) [In the local market] if you help these students, after you have some good experiences with these people. (. . .) These students in the future can come to work with our machines and it's easier for us to speak with a person who knows our machines, our equipment, than with a person that doesn't know anything about our machines.

HCN manager

Buffer relations are thus seen in the present paper as a specific content of FSMs' personal contacts within the MNC and in the local industrial market. In similar fashion, Marschan (1996, p. 145) suggests that the development of personal relationships depends on "the value perceived in personal communication networks." In industrial markets, buffer relations are implicit in Cunningham and Turnbull's (1982, p. 308) discussion of "personal contacts taking place between individuals in organizations for no immediately obvious reason." The analysis of case evidence suggests that buffer relations are primarily related with a scenario of low decisional dependence and high uncertainty (see Section 4.2.7) influenced by factors such as job description and extra duties (see Appendix F).

Finally, FSMs may take personal contacts in order to leverage the MNC's resources. Most of the interviewed FSMs mention personal contacts within the MNC concerning technical and logistic issues. A few of the interviewed FSMs mention personal contacts within the MNC and in the local industrial market concerning marketing issues.

[Within the MNC] I have a lot of contacts with my colleagues, because we want to share some of the resources...(...) in a lot of cases there might be some specific competence (...) the strength of each employee individually and in this networking organization is that you involve other people who are not part of the process to give their contribution.

PCN manager

[Within the MNC] if we need someone who is a specialist for a special operation, we ask the product company to send the guy with the tools or whatever. (...) It worked very well last time because I have this guy as the boss and, I would say, five days later they came to Portugal to solve the problem. And the problem has been solved. Not with me, with those people and the customer. But without me would not work, of course.

TCN manager

If you need, for example, small machines in Europe we decide to discuss with everybody and decide if the president of the region talks with the [...] divisions to influence to do another machines...(...) [In the local market] we have contacts with institutes of [...] and this type of institutes can help to solve not our problems, but the problems of the customers.

HCN manager

Resource leverage is thus seen in the present paper as a specific content of FSMs' personal contacts within the MNC and in the local industrial market. In the context of less-hierarchical MNCs, Nohria and Ghoshal (1997, p. 151) similarly argue that: "exchange of information allows the various subunits of the multinational to take advantage of opportunities for arbitrage" such as ad hoc allocation of stocks among subsidiaries. In the context of industrial markets, Cunningham and Turnbull (1982, p. 308) contend that: "adaptations to the product, manufacturing processes and delivery systems are discussed and agreements reached through personal discussions," which may include the "allocation of managerial resources" (Ford, 1980, p. 40). The analysis of case evidence suggests that resource leverage is primarily related with a scenario of low decisional dependence and high uncertainty (see Section 4.2.7) influenced by factors such as job description and extra duties (see Appendix F).

4.4. Process of Personal Contacts

In addition to the context (see Section 4.2) and content (see Section 4.3) of FSMs' personal contacts, the present paper discusses, in the light of extant literature, the process by which such personal contacts take place, namely in terms of channels, direction, frequency and paths. Such a discussion is also illustrated with three selected quotations from the interviews (see Section 3.5) for the reader to assess the extent to which case evidence allows the present paper to explore the dynamics of FSMs' personal contacts.

4.4.1. Channels
The channels, by which FSMs take personal contacts, include: telecommunications and information systems, meetings, visits, training, events, memberships, and leisure.

Telecommunications and information systems are the most frequent channel, by which FSMs take personal contacts within the MNC and in the local industrial market. Most of the interviewed FSMs mention personal contacts within the MNC through fixed and mobile phone, email and fax. A few of the interviewed FSMs mention that verbal personal contacts are more appropriate than written personal contacts for negotiation purposes.

> An e-mail, or a fax, or earlier it was a telex...(...) you give the basic information and as the first contact is good (...) And then normally whatever is then talked over the phone, then the next step is mutually to confirm it, just to take an order summarizing our telephone conversation and previous e-mail exchange...(...) The computer neither written reports can ever replace the personal contact where you exchange information and you read between the lines and you develop a certain idea together and then at the end of the day you define your policy, made a price policy, all the targets and so forth. (...) we try to get first feedback from the customers and then we give that information probably by phone or by e-mail to the mill (...) it's always a combination of written and personal information.

> PCN manager

> You have the opportunity to communicate with many people, now you have a new technology, e-mails...(...) You can establish information or strategy by phone, e-mail or private meetings...

> TCN manager

> I spend a lot of time at the mobile phone...(...) [Within the MNC] you can do the things together, you can put the mail or make the email and after call the persons, if the matter is very urgent or is very complicated or is a big problem. It's easier to write the problem and after call this person. (...) [In the local market] if you help the customer in this situation...if he has a problem later he will call you.

> HCN manager

In the context of MNCs, it has been suggested that vertical information systems "frequently include computer-based information systems" (Egelhoff, 1993, p. 185), but also that: "the viability and effectiveness of this electronic network will depend critically on an underlying network of social relationships based on face-to-face interaction" (Nohria & Eccles, 1992, p. 290). In the context of industrial markets, it is also claimed that: "information technology improves the ability of organizations to communicate with one another through interorganizational systems and other forms of electronic data interchange" (Nohria & Eccles, 1992, p. 291).

In addition to telecommunications and information systems, FSMs may take personal contacts through meetings within the MNC and in the local industrial market. Most of the interviewed FSMs mention meetings with subordinates and hierarchical superiors for planning purposes as well as with customers and suppliers for negotiation purposes. A few of the interviewed FSMs mention meetings with corporate staff, other subsidiary managers and hierarchical superiors for approval and problem solving purposes.

> The overall strategy not only for Portugal but also for the other markets is more or less set in what is called "sales meetings" that take place in the Autumn, September/October. (. . .) Two annual board meetings in the Autumn and then in the Spring a kind of a follow-up meeting. (. . .) Apart from that, the corporate marketing and sales organizes normally once or twice a year a meeting with the sales offices . . . (. . .) There you meet your colleagues, your superior, the key people from the divisions, from the support functions . . . So that is a very common way of establishing contacts . . . (. . .) [In the local market] the customer wants to have a meeting. We talk about a future contract or if he has a problem . . .

> PCN manager

> This is my business I am the only one who knows that we need a meeting to solve one issue . . . (. . .) so I am in contact with one people I have never met before, but we have a problem and I need his help, so, we have discussed . . . If I was closer from Helsinki I would probably have a meeting one, two, three times per week and to see how the things are progressing, but I am too far.

> TCN manager

> This can come from these personal conversations, these can come from the normal meetings or annual meetings, in the particular case of the divisional meetings, they are twice a year. So, you have more than thirty people with whom you are talking or you can talk. (. . .) [In the local market] when we are talking about suppliers or customers, all the needed represented operationals are present, always present. And sometimes they lead the meeting.

> HCN manager

In the context of less-hierarchical MNCs, Marschan (1996, p. 132) argues that: "personal relationships are most effectively created through participation in international meetings." In industrial markets, Cunningham and Turnbull (1982, p. 304) note that: "face to face meetings are desirable and that negotiations between the parties are best conducted on a person-to-person basis."

FSMs may also take personal contacts through visits within the MNC and in the local industrial market. Most of the interviewed FSMs mention visits to customers for assessment purposes. A few of the interviewed FSMs mention visits to/from corporate staff and other subsidiary managers for benchmarking purposes.

> We receive visits from the business units and divisions on the sales and marketing side and also on the technical side. (. . .) I visited the customers, two potential customers . . .
>
> PCN manager
>
> I visit and I try to find the confidence with the customers. (. . .) [Within the MNC] we visit, for example [. . .] in Spain and there factories are the same, the system of production, the factory has the same resources, technical and everything.
>
> TCN manager
>
> [Within the MNC] I decided at that time to visit as maximum as I could other group companies. I remember that I used very much the Danish company to see what they were doing and what they were not doing. So trying to understand their success and their failures as well. (. . .) Because we have got this silver trophy of EFQM methodologies, my contacts with the group have increased very much, especially on the last part of last year and early this year, because I have got a lot of visitors from the group.
>
> HCN manager

In the context of less-hierarchical MNCs, Marschan (1996, p. 134) reports a "positive effect on relationship building" among middle managers and operatives who visit other units. In the context of industrial markets, Cunningham and Turnbull (1982, p. 313) acknowledge "periodic visits of salesman from supplier" which the authors apparently distinguish from "higher level meetings of senior management from the two companies."

Some meetings or visits within the MNC are arranged specifically for training purposes. Most of the interviewed FSMs mention personal contacts with other subsidiary managers through training at the MNC, which also allows socializing.

> I am one of those who, in spite of the age, is training himself all the time.
>
> PCN manager
>
> We have in this group a permanent development of the personnel . . . and this is probably an opportunity to build-up a relationship and to meet physically people . . .
>
> TCN manager
>
> I have been part of some training courses the group has promoted. (. . .) And with some of them, perhaps the only thing we have had is that we lived together for that period, but with most

of them we have used then all the possible, all the potential help they could give us. (. . .) It happened many times that I never had a direct connection with those guys. They are in different divisions, in different tasks. But sometimes I use them to understand something . . .

HCN manager

Training is thus seen in the present paper as a channel by which FSMs take personal contacts within the MNC. In similar fashion, Marschan (1996, p. 135) suggests that: "participants in the same training course or meeting build contacts among themselves."

In addition to training within the MNC, FSMs may take personal contacts through events in the local industrial market. Most of the interviewed FSMs mention personal contacts with corporate staff, customers and suppliers through seminars or exhibitions for knowledge transfer and trust enhancement purposes.

I believe that all relationships are based on informal creation of the relationships, but it might be done in a formal environment or formal occasions.

PCN manager

When the customers organize events and they invite you, my system is to go to all events, because if they invite you, they recognize that you are something in his organization. It is necessary to be present. (. . .) If you make the event in Finland or in Spain . . . some customers like to go . . .

TCN manager

Last month I was closing the three days conference of the innovation educational institute (. . .) and there I can find a lot of teachers, which are also managers in other companies. (. . .) On the exhibitions, at least twice a year, we use to make what we called a "tournée" on the most important customers. (. . .) By being invited to seminars, by being member of certain institutions, you have no other chance than to meet people. (. . .) Most of them are managerial seminars. (. . .) the best way to access to the political or public companies . .. (. . .) By being invited as well for technical seminars related with our industry, we make ourselves somehow a reference for the technicians . . .

HCN manager

Events are thus seen in the present paper as a channel by which FSMs take personal contacts in the local industrial market. Andersson et al. (1996, p. 150) implicitly discuss events in their discussion of "a business lunch" as an "important means of meeting people."

In addition to events, FSMs may take personal contacts in the local industrial market through memberships. Most of the interviewed FSMs mention personal contacts through industrial or national associations and clubs for market assessment purposes.

Some of our customers belong to an association, which has the objective of promoting the interests of that whole business branch or business area in Portugal. And sometimes we are approached by these associations sometimes we approach them . . .

PCN manager

I am a member of the Finnish business . . . (. . .) We have an international organization, is called [. . .], but we are not member at the moment, but we will be a member again in a very few period of time and there you meet all your colleagues, your friends, your enemies, everybody. So, is just an informal way of meeting those people.

TCN manager

I am also the president of ISO certified companies in Portugal, so I know now there almost a thousand companies . . . (. . .) Because of this position of president of the ISO certified companies, I am member of a national quality counsel as well. So, politically, I have some good contacts on the government level. (. . .) by being member of certain institutions, you have no other chance than to meet people. (. . .) I am quite close with more eleven companies to found a benchmarking club saying in our country what are the best practices in several areas of management. (. . .) Not only to establish further contacts, but to develop much more the ones we have.

HCN manager

Memberships are thus seen in the present paper as a channel by which FSMs take personal contacts in the local industrial market. In similar fashion, Axelsson and Agndal (2000, p. 12) acknowledge "membership in clubs" as an origin of contacts.

Finally, FSMs may take personal contacts within the MNC and in the local industrial market in leisure time. A few of the interviewed FSMs mention personal contacts with customers in leisure activities such as golf, tennis, hunting, kart driving, and holidays for customer assessment purposes.

[In the local market] you establish the contact purely business related and if in the conversation it comes up that you share same hobbies you may develop that kind of relationship that you invite them . . .

PCN manager

We sometimes go hunting with one of our customers and things like that or we have dinner with them . . .

TCN manager

Some of the people they are using the golf tournaments and tennis . . .

HCN manager

Leisure is thus seen in the present paper as a channel by which FSMs' take personal contacts in the local industrial market. In this respect, Andersson et al. (1996,

Table 9. Content of FSMs' Personal Contacts per Channel.

	Information Exchange	Assessment	Negotiation	Decision-Making	Resource Allocation
T&IS	Contact transfer, Advice, Follow-up	Reporting, MNC assessment	Staff empowerment	Problem solving	Buffer relations, Resource leverage
Meetings		assessment	Negotiations	Approval, Planning, Problem solving	Coaching
Visits	Benchmarking	Customer assessment, Supplier assessment			
Training Events	Socializing Knowledge transfer	MNC assessment Trust enhancement, Corporate reputation			
Memberships Leisure	Socializing Friendship	Market assessment Customer assessment			

p. 150) equally acknowledge "a tennis match or a golf match" as an "important means of meeting people."

In general (see Table 9), the case evidence suggests that telecommunications and information systems are the only channel by which FSMs take personal contacts with all functions: information exchange, assessment, negotiation, decision-making, and resource allocation (see Section 4.3). In particular, telecommunications and information systems may be used for contact transfer, advice and follow-up (see Section 4.3.1), reporting and MNC assessment (see Section 4.3.2), staff empowerment (see Section 4.3.3), problem solving (see Section 4.3.4) as well as buffer relations and resource leverage (see Section 4.3.5).

In addition, the case evidence suggests that meetings are primarily arranged for negotiation, decision-making, and resource allocation purposes. In particular, meetings may be used for negotiations (see Section 4.3.3), approval, planning, and problem solving (see section 4.3.4) as well as coaching (see Section 4.3.5).

On the other hand, the case evidence suggests that visits, training, events, memberships and leisure are channels by which FSMs take personal contacts primarily for information exchange and assessment purposes. In particular, visits may be used for benchmarking (see Section 4.3.1) as well as customer- and supplier assessment (see Section 4.3.2); trainings may be used for socializing (see Section 4.3.1) and MNC assessment (see Section 4.3.2); events may be used for knowledge transfer (see Section 4.3.1) as well as trust enhancement and corporate reputation (see Section 4.3.2); memberships may be used for socializing (see Section 4.3.1) and market assessment (see Section 4.3.2); and leisure may be used for friendship (see Section 4.3.1) and customer assessment (see Section 4.3.2).

In spite of suggesting a direct relationship between the contents of FSMs' personal contacts and the type of channel by which they take place, the present paper equally acknowledges that such a relationship is not necessarily exclusive. In particular, FSMs' personal contacts for problem solving, MNC- and customer assessment as well as socializing may take place by more than one channel (see Table 9).

4.4.2. Direction

The process of FSMs' personal contacts may also be discussed in terms of direction. In this respect, most of the interviewed FSMs mention personal contacts from their own initiative with hierarchical superiors and corporate staff for marketing and technical support. A few of the interviewed FSMs mention personal contacts from the initiative of hierarchical superiors and corporate staff for reporting and of customers for problem solving purposes.

> In terms of reporting the initiative always comes from up. In terms of getting help or getting some contribution to our specific issues, then the initiative is ours.

PCN manager

> If its technical then it is more our initiative, and if it's financial then it's mostly from the group.

TCN manager

> Many they are related with business requests from the field, in a way to make proposals for different kinds of countries, sending some kind of additional information, asking for some questions about some reports, some things like that. From our side the initiative, they are basically related with technical information . . . (. . .) [In the local market] if they are claiming, normally the bosses, I receive here claims directly . . .

HCN manager

The present paper thus suggests FSMs' personal contacts within the MNC due to top-down initiative for reporting and bottom-up initiative for advice. In addition, the present paper suggests FSMs' personal contacts in the local industrial market due to customer initiative for problem solving purposes. In the context of MNCs, Marschan (1996, p. 28) argues that: "inter-unit communication aimed at control (such as financial reports) tends to be more vertical by nature than the communication endeavoring to enhance coordination and socialization (such as cross-unit projects and training)." In the context of industrial markets, Cunningham and Turnbull (1982, p. 308) suggest that: "when a major problem or crisis occurs, which cannot be resolved through existing channels of influence" it may happen that "the supplier attempts to establish some links at a very high level."

As mentioned in the previous section, the case evidence suggests that the main channel by which FSMs take personal contacts for reporting, advice and problem solving is telecommunications and information systems.

4.4.3. Frequency
In addition to channels (see Section 4.4.1) and direction (see Section 4.4.2), the process of FSMs' personal contacts may be discussed in terms of frequency. In this respect, most of the interviewed FSMs mention yearly and monthly personal contacts with hierarchical superiors and corporate staff for planning and reporting purposes, respectively. A few of the interviewed FSMs also mention frequent personal contacts with customers as well as yearly personal contacts with suppliers and auditors.

> Part of my work is an annual business plan (. . .) Corporate Marketing and Sales organizes normally once or twice a year a meeting with the sales offices . . . (. . .) We report to the divisions, the business units. In most cases is monthly. (. . .) Most frequent contacts are of course with the customers . . .

PCN manager

Year by year we establish the objectives. (. . .) We have also auditors every year . . . (. . .) Every month, I visit the customers.

TCN manager

Usually we have only one meeting in September/October, where we discuss the budget for the next year. (. . .) I have one monthly report that I have to send . . . (. . .) I would say customers, everyday. (. . .) Audits, usually is once per year . . .

HCN manager

The present paper thus suggests recurrent FSMs' personal contacts for planning and reporting as well as customer- and supplier assessment purposes. In the context of MNCs, Egelhoff (1993, p. 194) refers to formal single-cycle planning systems as well as post-action control systems as routine information processing mechanisms, which deal with "inputs that are frequent and homogenous." In the context of industrial markets, Cunningham and Turnbull (1982, p. 313) suggest frequency as an indicator of the intensity of inter-organizational personal contacts, which is expected to increase over time, namely among lower hierarchical levels, which "are then supported by infrequent, more formal top level meetings."

As mentioned in Section 4.4.1, the case evidence suggests that the main channel by which FSMs take personal contacts for reporting is telecommunications and information systems, for planning is a meeting, and for customer- and supplier assessment is a visit.

4.4.4. Paths

Finally, the process of FSMs' personal contacts may be characterized in terms of paths. In particular, FSMs may extend the scope of their business- and informal contact network (see Section 4.2.2) through a snowballing path. Most of the interviewed FSMs mention personal contacts in the local industrial market by which their private contact network has been extended. A few of the interviewed FSMs mention personal contacts within the MNC by which their informal contact network has been extended.

Over the years you meet people by just working . . .

PCN manager

What we are doing now is quite good and I don't think that will be less. Not at all, I think that this will increase it will be better in the future, the contacts. I don't think it will be reversed now.

TCN manager

If you need you have to find the best way to meet them. (. . .) But then is like a snowball, since you know one, that one allows you to know somebody more and those somebody more, somebody more and it's a never ending ball.

HCN manager

On the other hand, FSMs may reduce the intensity of their personal contacts through a selecting path. Most of the interviewed FSMs mention personal contacts within their formal contact network (see Section 4.2.2), by which the intensity of personal contacts within their business- and informal contact network may be reduced.

> Because we have then delegated people to take care of our purchasing processes. Of course I am involved to certain extent and usually it's a question of hierarchy . . . (. . .) In the beginning of usually any activities, those escalations are more frequent and before people start learning things and those processes and decision-making criteria are well defined. Before that, of course they are more frequent.

> PCN manager

> Basically I try to delegate the most possible the contacts with external partners, unless in some sensitive case that I keep for myself or when I feel that the purpose is so important that I have to act by myself. In general this is the rule.

> TCN manager

> I think that you have steps. I would say that nowadays there are a few contacts that I know more or less that some of my people sales and marketing manager, is going to face some more difficulties . . . (. . .) So the delegation is a little bit in accordance with the positioning of the people [in customer organizations], knowing that these people they rather prefer to have some personal contacts instead of going with a different contacts.

> HCN manager

The present paper thus suggests a snowballing- and a selecting path of FSMs' personal contacts within the MNC and in the local industrial market. In the context of less-hierarchical MNCs, Nohria and Ghoshal (1997, p. 156) similarly argue that "the longer an individual has worked in any organization, the more opportunities he or she has to meet and form contacts throughout the organization" although "no individual could possibly maintain the thousands of contacts that a fully connected network would require" (1997, p. 152). In the context of industrial markets, Hallén (1992, p. 90) argues that: "the number of contacts is also likely to multiply over time."

This section concludes the discussion of case evidence, which includes insights not only on the process (see Section 4.4), but also on the context (see Section 4.2) and content (see Section 4.3) of FSMs' personal contacts. The extent to which such insights answer the research questions of the present paper (see Section 1.3) is discussed in the following section.

5. CONCLUSIONS

This final section discusses the conclusions of the paper. The following three sub-sections suggest a final theoretical framework as well as eight interpersonal roles of FSMs and eight propositions on MNC coordination and control. The remaining three sub-sections provide a summary of the theoretical and empirical contribution of the paper as well as its managerial implications and suggestions for further research.

5.1. Final Theoretical Framework

Based on the analysis of evidence from the cases, a refined version of the a priori theoretical framework for analysis (see Section 2.5.1) has been developed. Such a final theoretical framework (see Fig. 10) lists 36 factors and 22 contents of FSMs' personal contacts in industrial markets, which form the basis for the answer to the first and second questions of the paper, respectively (see Section 1.3). Thirteen factors and 10 contents had already been identified through literature review (see Fig. 5 in Section 2.5.1), being depicted in italic for better assessment of the present paper's contribution to such a listing.

In terms of contextual factors of FSMs' personal contacts, the present paper adds: nine individual factors to the six previously identified; nine organizational factors to the four previously identified; and five market factors to the three previously identified (see Section 2.5.1). In terms of specific contents of FSMs' personal contacts, the present paper adds: three information exchange contents to the six previously identified;[9] six assessment contents to the one previously identified; one negotiation content to the one previously identified; two decision-making contents to the one previously identified; and two resource allocation contents the one previously identified.

However, some of the factors and contents of FSMs' personal contacts, which are added in the present paper, may have been implicit in previous findings within the IMP group and/or the process approach to MNC management. In spite of being absent in the a priori theoretical framework for analysis (see Section 2.5.1) such findings are acknowledged in Sections 4.2 and 4.3, respectively.

The final theoretical framework also supplements the initial theoretical framework for analysis by making explicit the relationship between factors and functions of FSMs' personal contacts. Such a relationship is established through the notions of individual uncertainty and dependence (see Section 1.5) and the scenarios, which result from their combination (see Section 4.2.1). On the one hand, it is suggested that the four scenarios of informational dependence

	Inf. dep. (-) Uncertainty (+)	Inf. dep. (-) Uncertainty (-)	Inf. dep. (+) Uncertainty (+)	Inf. dep. (+) Uncertainty (-)	Dec. dep. (-) Uncertainty (+)	Dec. dep. (-) Uncertainty (-)	Dec. dep. (+) Uncertainty (+)	Dec. dep. (+) Uncertainty (-)
Individual	Background (inc. *Nationality*), *Career*, *Language skills*, Initiative, Sales orientation, Social skills, *Personality*, *Attitude*, Availability	*Tenure*, Delegation			Job description, Extra duties	Experience		Performance
Organizational	Corporate culture	Geographical proximity, *Age of relationships*	Start-up, Organizational change, *Employee turnover*	Reporting process		Size	Planning process, Approval process, Business volume, Intra-group transactions	Rules and programs (inc. *Supplier strategy*)
Market	Market idiosyncrasy (inc. *Market structure*), Market dynamism, Supplier closeness, Customer closeness, Business culture (inc. *Industry norms*)		Technical complexity, Market internationalization				Customer internationalization	
Information exchange	Contact transfer, Socializing, Benchmarking	Friendship, Follow-up (inc. *Delivery and Technical progress*)	Advice (inc. *Technical advice and Commercial info*), Knowledge transfer (inc. *Technical info*)					
Assessment	Trust enhancement, Market, *Customers*, Suppliers		Corporate reputation, MNC assessment	Reporting				
Negotiation					Staff empowerment	*Negotiations*		
Decision-making								*Problem solving*
Resource allocation					Buffer relations, Resource leverage	Coaching (inc. *Training*)	Approval, Planning	

Fig. 10. Final Theoretical Framework.

(see Sections 4.2.3 to 4.2.6) are associated with FSMs' personal contacts for information exchange and assessment. On the other hand, the four scenarios of decisional dependence (see Sections 4.2.7 to 4.2.10) are associated with FSMs' personal contacts for negotiation, decision-making and resource allocation. More specifically, it is suggested that each scenario results from particular contextual factors, which are associated, in turn, with specific contents of FSMs' personal contacts (see Sections 4.3.1 to 4.3.5).

Moreover, and in order to facilitate its comparison with the a priori theoretical framework for analysis, the final theoretical framework does not include dynamic aspects of FSMs' personal contacts. Such aspects were, however, equally discussed in the light of extant literature, namely in terms of channels (see Section 4.4.1), direction (see Section 4.4.2), frequency (see Section 4.4.3), and paths (see Section 4.4.4). In particular, the present paper identifies seven channels by which FSMs' personal contacts take place. The paper also suggests that the direction of FSMs' personal contacts is usually top-down concerning reporting, bottom-up concerning advice, and buyer-supplier concerning problem solving. In addition, it is suggested that reporting and customer assessment are the most frequent contents of FSMs' personal contacts. In terms of paths, the paper suggests a snowballing path mainly in the local industrial market and a selecting path within the MNC and in the local industrial market.

In sum, the present paper identifies factors and functions of FSMs' personal contacts (see Sections 4.2 and 4.3), which are listed in the final theoretical framework for analysis. In addition, the paper identifies channels, patterns of direction and frequency as well as long-term paths of such personal contacts (see Section 4.4). The identification of individual, organizational, and market factors influencing the occurrence of FSMs' personal contacts in industrial MNCs constitutes the answer to the first research question (see Section 1.3). The identification of functions and dynamic aspects of FSMs' personal contacts constitutes a preliminary, but still incipient answer to the second research question, which calls for a more integrated conceptualization of the phenomenon under study. Such a conceptualization of the interplay between context and content of FSMs' personal contacts is here captured by the notion of interpersonal role (Mintzberg, 1973). The following section thus discusses the extent to which the formulation of FSMs' interpersonal roles answers the second research question of the present paper.

5.2. *Interpersonal Roles of FSMs in Industrial Markets*

In his original conceptualization of managerial working roles, Mintzberg (1973, p. 54) defines role "as an organized set of behaviors belonging to an identified office or position." The author argues that roles are predetermined even if individuals may interpret them differently. An apparently less deterministic view is provided by Pettigrew (1973, p. 31) who argues that an individual's behavior is governed "not only by the structure of the situation in which he participates but also by his ability to shape and mould the structure to fit his interests." As mentioned in Section 4.2.5, the present paper shares such a dialectical perspective (Van de Ven & Poole, 1995), according to which members of an organization are able to retain some discretion in spite of situational constraints.

In order to emphasize FSMs' discretion in terms of personal contacts, the present paper refers to autonomous interpersonal roles. These roles are expected to co-exist with integrated interpersonal roles, which encompass FSMs' personal contacts primarily determined by situational constraints. FSMs' autonomous and integrated interpersonal roles are thus associated, respectively, with low and high degrees of dependence within the MNC. Such a dependence may, in turn, be informational or decisional (see Section 1.5), leading to four scenarios of dependence within the MNC. In order to distinguish between informational and decisional dependence, the present paper refers to sensor and allocator interpersonal roles of FSMs, respectively. Moreover, each of the four scenarios of dependence within the MNC may be associated with two scenarios of uncertainty in the local industrial market, leading to eight scenarios of uncertainty and dependence (see Section 4.2.1). In order to differentiate between the two scenarios of uncertainty, the present paper refers to certain and uncertain interpersonal roles of FSMs.

The explicit association between the eight scenarios of uncertainty and dependence (see Sections 4.2.3–4.2.10) and specific contents of FSMs' personal contacts (see Sections 4.3.1–4.3.5) may be interpreted as interpersonal roles of FSMs. In other words, each scenario may be regarded a structured situation molded by market, organizational and individual factors, which leads to an organized set of personal contacts with particular contents. The implications of FSMs' interpersonal roles for inter-firm coordination in industrial markets (see Sections 2.3.2 and 2.3.3) are discussed in the following paragraphs.

As uncertain autonomous sensors, FSMs are expected to perceive a high degree of uncertainty and a low degree of informational dependence (see Section 4.2.3). Such an interpersonal role implies that FSMs take personal contacts specifically for contact transfer, socializing, benchmarking, trust enhancement as well as market-, customer-, and supplier assessment (see Fig. 10 in the previous section).

As certain autonomous sensors, FSMs are expected to perceive a low degree of both uncertainty and informational dependence (see Section 4.2.4). Such an interpersonal role implies that FSMs take personal contacts specifically for friendship and follow-up (see Fig. 10).

As uncertain integrated sensors, FSMs are expected to perceive a high degree of both uncertainty and informational dependence (see Section 4.2.5). Such an interpersonal role implies that FSMs take personal contacts specifically for advice, knowledge transfer, corporate reputation and MNC assessment (see Fig. 10).

Finally, as certain integrated sensors, FSMs are expected to perceive a low degree of uncertainty and a high degree of informational dependence (see Section 4.2.6). Such an interpersonal role implies that FSMs take personal contacts specifically for reporting (see Fig. 10).

The four interpersonal roles of FSMs just mentioned correspond to the four scenarios of informational dependence discussed earlier (see Sections 4.2.3–4.2.6), being exclusively concerned with personal contacts for information exchange and assessment (see Sections 4.3.1 and 4.3.2). Conversely, the four interpersonal roles of FSMs mentioned below correspond to the four scenarios of decisional dependence discussed earlier (see Sections 4.2.7–4.2.10), being exclusively concerned with personal contacts for negotiation, decision-making and resource allocation (see Sections 4.3.3–4.3.5).

As uncertain autonomous allocators, FSMs are expected to perceive a high degree of uncertainty and a low degree of decisional dependence (see Section 4.2.7). Such an interpersonal role implies that FSMs take personal contacts specifically for staff empowerment, buffer relations and resource leverage (see Fig. 10).

As certain autonomous allocators, FSMs are expected to perceive a low degree of both uncertainty and decisional dependence (see Section 4.2.8). Such an interpersonal role implies that FSMs take personal contacts specifically for negotiations and coaching (see Fig. 10).

As uncertain integrated allocators, FSMs are expected to perceive a high degree of both uncertainty and decisional dependence (see Section 4.2.9). Such an interpersonal role implies that FSMs take personal contacts specifically for approval and planning (see Fig. 10).

Finally, as certain integrated allocators, FSMs are expected to perceive a low degree of uncertainty and a high degree of decisional dependence (see Section 4.2.10). Such an interpersonal role implies that FSMs take personal contacts specifically for problem solving (see Fig. 10).

Table 10 depicts the overall association between FSMs' interpersonal roles and the content of their personal contacts, corresponding to the lower section of Fig. 10. Given the characteristics of coordination in industrial markets (see Sections 2.3.2 and 2.3.3), it may be concluded that FSMs participate as sensors in processes of inter-firm exchange (Cunningham & Homse, 1986; Forsgren et al., 1995; IMP group, 1982) and as allocators in processes of inter-firm adaptation (Brennan & Turnbull, 1999; Ford, 1980; Håkansson, 1982). In other words, the present paper

Table 10. Content of FSMs' Personal Contacts per Interpersonal Role.

	Information Exchange	Assessment	Negotiation	Decision-Making	Resource Allocation
Uncertain Autonomous Sensors	Contact transfer, Socializing, Benchmarking	Trust enhancement, Market assessment, Customer assessment, Supplier assessment			
Certain Autonomous Sensors	Friendship, Follow-up				
Uncertain Integrated Sensors	Advice, Knowledge transfer	Corporate reputation, MNC assessment, Reporting			
Certain Integrated Sensors					
Uncertain Autonomous Allocators			Staff empowerment Negotiations		Buffer relations, Resource leverage Coaching
Certain Autonomous Allocators					
Uncertain Integrated Allocators				Approval, Planning Problem solving	
Certain Integrated Allocators					

suggests that although both sub-processes of inter-firm interaction – exchange and adaptation – presuppose FSMs' personal contacts, the contents of personal contacts they require are rather different.

In sum, personal contacts of FSMs enable inter-firm coordination in industrial markets (Easton, 1992; Håkansson & Johanson, 1993; Johanson & Mattsson, 1987) in the sense that such managers participate as sensors in social exchange (Forsgren et al., 1995; IMP group, 1982) and as allocators in human adaptations (Brennan & Turnbull, 1999; Ford, 1980) within inter-firm relationships (Håkansson & Snehota, 1995). The identification of FSMs' interpersonal roles thus constitutes the answer to the second research question (see Section 1.3) in the context of industrial markets. The extent to which such interpersonal roles answer the very same question in the context of less-hierarchical MNCs is discussed in the following section.

5.3. Propositions on MNC Coordination and Control

As mentioned in Section 2.4.1, the process approach to MNC management may be said to encompass a design and an organic approach to less-hierarchical MNC management (Andersson & Holm, 2002). The design approach (e.g. Bartlett & Ghoshal, 1989; Ghoshal & Bartlett, 1998; Nohria & Ghoshal, 1997; Prahalad & Doz, 1987) assumes that headquarters deliberately control subsidiaries, whereas the organic approach (e.g. Ghoshal & Bartlett, 1990; Forsgren, 1990a, b) assumes that headquarters' authority (Forsgren, 1990a) is contingent on subsidiaries' control of critical resources (Larsson, 1985). It has also been argued that the organic approach is generally consistent with findings within the interaction and network approaches to industrial markets (Holm & Pedersen, 2000), which further justifies the theoretical context of the present paper (see Section 2.1).

Nevertheless, in the present paper coordination of differentiated subsidiaries in less-hierarchical MNCs (see Section 2.4.3) is not equated with coordination of interdependent firms in industrial markets (Easton, 1992; Håkansson & Johanson, 1993; Johanson & Mattsson, 1987). In spite of downplaying hierarchy (e.g. Hedlund, 1993) and formal structure (e.g. Bartlett & Ghoshal, 1990) in favor of differentiation and heterogeneity (Doz & Prahalad, 1991; Gupta et al., 1999), headquarters of less-hierarchical MNCs are not expected to relinquish the very authority (Forsgren, 1990a), which prevents the MNC from breaking down into anarchy (Hedlund & Rolander, 1990). What is expected, instead, is that headquarters' authority may not translate into control over subsidiaries due to negligence of the former and/or pro-activeness of the latter (Taggart, 1997b).

Marschan et al. (1996) equally appear to subscribe the organic approach by questioning the extent to which headquarters are able to control informal communication and corporate culture. As mentioned in Section 2.4.3, informal communication and corporate culture are regarded in the present paper as two informal mechanisms of MNC coordination (Martinez & Jarillo, 1989). Based on the identification of FSMs' interpersonal roles (see previous section), the present paper may equally discuss the extent to which headquarters of less-hierarchical MNCs control informal communication and corporate culture. Such two informal mechanisms of coordination are here labeled horizontal communication and socialization, respectively. In addition, the present paper may discuss the adoption of centralization and formalization in less-hierarchical MNCs, which are here seen as two formal mechanisms of MNC coordination (Martinez & Jarillo, 1989).

In particular, eight propositions can be suggested, which relate the adoption of such mechanisms of coordination with specific contents of FSMs' personal contacts. In this respect, three remarks must be made. First, as mentioned in Section 4.2.1, the case evidence of the present paper (see Section 3.5) does not allow the analysis of dependence based on the control of resources within the MNC (e.g. Larsson, 1985) or in the local industrial market (e.g. Håkansson & Johanson, 1984). That means that, in spite of sharing the assumptions of the organic approach, the present paper can only discuss the adoption of mechanisms of coordination in terms of FSMs' legal dependence (see Section 4.2.1). Second, in contrast to previous research which has attempted to objectively measure environmental uncertainty (e.g. Harzing, 1999; Nohria & Ghoshal, 1997), the present paper only discusses the adoption of mechanisms of coordination in terms uncertainty as perceived by FSMs (see Section 4.2.1). Finally, and as mentioned in Section 2.4.5, coordination of interdependent subsidiaries requires that their differentiating roles be taken into account. That means that the suggested propositions only concern the type of subsidiaries analyzed in the present paper, that is, local implementers (Birkinshaw & Morrison, 1995).

Given the definition of decisional dependence adopted in the present paper (see Section 1.5), centralization and socialization may be equated with high and low decisional dependence of FSMs, respectively. On the other hand, the definition of informational dependence adopted in the present paper (see Section 1.5) implies that formalization and horizontal communication may be equated with high and low informational dependence of FSMs, respectively. It follows that the association between such mechanisms of coordination with specific contents of FSMs' personal contacts is here discussed as primarily contingent on FSMs' degree of uncertainty.[10]

Correspondingly, two scenarios of uncertainty may be considered per each mechanism of coordination, based on the distinction between certain and uncertain interpersonal roles of FSMs (see previous section). In particular, two propositions are suggested per each mechanism of coordination, which relate its adoption at the subsidiary level with specific contents of FSMs' personal contacts. Such propositions are discussed in the following paragraphs.

Centralization is a mechanism of coordination by which decision-making authority is concentrated at the higher levels of the organizational chain of command (e.g. Pugh et al., 1968; Simon, 1976). Centralization is relatively inexpensive once it allows administration by fiat (Ghoshal & Nohria, 1989; Williamson, 1975) requiring, however, administrative resources for continuous decision-making (Bartlett & Ghoshal, 1989). In addition, centralization is thought to allow fast decision-making (Bartlett & Ghoshal, 1989) and to enable headquarters' support to non-resourceful subsidiaries (Ghoshal & Nohria, 1989).

The present paper suggests that the adoption of centralization as a mechanism of coordination at the studied subsidiaries may occur in a scenario of both high and low uncertainty as perceived by FSMs. In a scenario of high uncertainty, centralization would be justified by the need to coordinate the terms offered to multinational customers, being contingent on the degree of customer internationalization. By definition, centralization would also presuppose a high degree of decisional dependence for FSMs, itself contingent on planning- and approval processes, business volume and intra-group transactions. In other words, the adoption of centralization as a mechanism of coordination in a scenario of high uncertainty may be associated with FSMs' personal contacts as uncertain integrated allocators. The following proposition is thus suggested:

Proposition 1a. FSMs' personal contacts for approval and planning are positively associated with centralization in a scenario of high uncertainty.

In a scenario of low uncertainty, centralization would still be justified by the need to ensure fast and resourceful response to local customers, that is, appropriate performance. By definition, centralization would also presuppose a high degree of decisional dependence for FSMs, itself contingent on rules and programs.[11] In other words, the adoption of centralization as a mechanism of coordination in a scenario of low uncertainty may be associated with FSMs' personal contacts as certain integrated allocators. The following proposition is thus suggested:

Proposition 1b. FSMs' personal contacts for problem solving are positively associated with centralization in a scenario of low uncertainty.

Formalization is a mechanism of coordination by which an organization's policies, rules and procedures are written down and established through routines (e.g. Galbraith, 1973; Pugh et al., 1968). Although it requires administrative resources for its establishment (Bartlett & Ghoshal, 1989), formalization is relatively inexpensive to maintain (Ghoshal & Nohria, 1989). In addition, formalization is thought to reduce the potential for conflict in headquarters-subsidiary relations

(Ghoshal & Nohria, 1989) and to induce lack of flexibility in complex or changing environments (Bartlett & Ghoshal, 1989).

The present paper suggests that the adoption of formalization as a mechanism of coordination at the studied subsidiaries may occur in a scenario of both high and low uncertainty as perceived by FSMs. In a scenario of high uncertainty, formalization would be justified by the need to recurrently exchange information on technical issues – contingent on technical complexity – as well as on competitors and legislation – contingent on market internationalization. By definition, formalization would also presuppose a high degree of informational dependence for FSMs, itself contingent on the start-up of subsidiary operations, organizational change and employee turnover. In other words, the adoption of formalization as a mechanism of coordination in a scenario of high uncertainty may be associated with FSMs' personal contacts as uncertain integrated sensors. The following proposition is thus suggested:

Proposition 2a. FSMs' personal contacts for advice, knowledge transfer, corporate reputation, and MNC assessment are positively associated with formalization in a scenario of high uncertainty.

In a scenario of low uncertainty, formalization would still be justified by the need to recurrently exchange information on financial issues. By definition, formalization would also presuppose a high degree of informational dependence for FSMs, itself contingent on the reporting process. In other words, the adoption of formalization as a mechanism of coordination in a scenario of low uncertainty may be associated with FSMs' personal contacts as certain integrated sensors. The following proposition is thus suggested:

Proposition 2b. FSMs' personal contacts for reporting are positively associated with formalization in a scenario of low uncertainty.

Socialization is a mechanism of coordination by which an organization's norms, values and beliefs are communicated to its members (e.g. Pfeffer, 1982; Van Maanen & Schein, 1979). Although it overcomes both the workload of headquarters and the inflexibility of formalized routines (Bartlett & Ghoshal, 1989), socialization is relatively expensive in terms of administrative resources required for continuous indoctrination and training (Ouchi, 1980). In addition, socialization is thought to reduce the potential for headquarters-subsidiary conflict (Ghoshal & Nohria, 1989) but also to induce ambiguity in decision-making (Bartlett & Ghoshal, 1989).

The present paper suggests that the adoption of socialization as a mechanism of coordination at the studied subsidiaries may occur in a scenario of both high and low uncertainty as perceived by FSMs. In a scenario of high uncertainty, socialization would be justified by the impossibility to specify the tasks and responsibilities of managers, being contingent on their job description and extra duties. By definition, socialization would also presuppose a low degree of decisional dependence for FSMs. In other words, the adoption of socialization as a mechanism of coordination in a scenario of high uncertainty may be associated with FSMs' personal contacts as uncertain autonomous allocators. The following proposition is thus suggested:

Proposition 3a. FSMs' personal contacts for staff empowerment, buffer relations and resource leverage are positively associated with socialization in a scenario of high uncertainty.

In a scenario of low uncertainty, socialization would still be justified by the need to ensure reliable interaction with local customers, contingent on FSMs' experience. By definition, socialization would also presuppose a low degree of decisional dependence for FSMs, itself contingent on the *size* of the subsidiary. In other words, the adoption of socialization as a mechanism of coordination in a scenario of low uncertainty may be associated with FSMs' personal contacts as certain autonomous allocators. The following proposition is thus suggested:

Proposition 3b. FSMs' personal contacts for negotiations and coaching are positively associated with socialization in a scenario of low uncertainty.

Finally, horizontal communication is a mechanism of coordination by which an organization's informal networks of personal relationships are promoted (e.g. Galbraith, 1973; Martinez & Jarillo, 1989). Horizontal communication is relatively expensive to establish, namely through lateral or cross-departmental relations, but relatively inexpensive to maintain depending on the channel of communication which is used (Marschan, 1996). In addition, horizontal communication is thought to develop beyond the control of headquarters (Marschan et al., 1996) and to promote information flows through the organization (Bartlett & Ghoshal, 1990).

The present paper suggests that the adoption of horizontal communication as a mechanism of coordination at the studied subsidiaries may occur in a scenario of both high and low uncertainty as perceived by FSMs. In a scenario of high uncertainty, horizontal communication would be justified by the need to understand the local environment and counterparts, itself contingent on local market idiosyncrasy and dynamism as well as supplier- and customer closeness, in addition to business culture. By definition, horizontal communication would also presuppose a low degree of informational dependence for FSMs, itself contingent on corporate culture.[12] In other words, the adoption of horizontal communication as a mechanism of coordination in a scenario of high uncertainty may be associated with FSMs' personal contacts as uncertain autonomous sensors. The following proposition is thus suggested:

Proposition 4a. FSMs' personal contacts for contact transfer, socializing, benchmarking, trust enhancement as well as market-, customer- and supplier assessment are positively associated with horizontal communication in a scenario of high uncertainty.

In a scenario of low uncertainty, horizontal communication would still be justified by the snowballing and selecting paths of FSMs' contact network (see Section 4.4.4), which are contingent on their tenure and use of delegation, respectively. By definition, horizontal communication would also presuppose a low degree of informational dependence for FSMs, itself contingent on geographical proximity and age of relationships. In other words, the adoption of horizontal communication as a mechanism of coordination in a scenario of low uncertainty may be associated with FSMs' personal contacts as certain autonomous sensors. The following proposition is thus suggested:

Proposition 4b. FSMs' personal contacts for friendship and follow-up are positively associated with horizontal communication in a scenario of low uncertainty.

Table 11 depicts the overall association between the content of FSMs' personal contacts and mechanisms of coordination in MNCs (e.g. Martinez & Jarillo, 1989).

Such a table is equally based on the lower section of Fig. 10 (see Section 5.1), but merges the two degrees of uncertainty per each scenario of dependence. In other words, the present paper suggests that each of the four mechanisms of coordination – centralization, formalization, socialization, horizontal communication – may be adopted regardless of FSMs' perceived degree of uncertainty. In addition, the present paper suggests that the simultaneous adoption of such mechanisms of coordination is possible in terms of FSMs' personal contacts.

In sum, personal contacts of FSMs enable inter-firm coordination in less-hierarchical MNCs (Martinez & Jarillo, 1989) in the sense that such individuals participate in interpersonal networking (Nohria & Ghoshal, 1997) in the MNC as an inter-organizational network (Ghoshal & Bartlett, 1990). In particular, it is suggested that, in local implementer subsidiaries (Birkinshaw & Morrison, 1995), FSMs participate in centralization as integrated allocators, in formalization as integrated sensors, in socialization as autonomous allocators, and in horizontal communication as autonomous sensors. The eight propositions, which associate such mechanisms of coordination at the subsidiary level with specific functions of FSMs' personal contacts, constitute the answer to the second research question (see Section 1.3) in the context of less-hierarchical MNCs. The overall findings of the paper are discussed in the light of extant literature in the following section.

Table 11. Content of FSMs' Personal Contacts per Coordination Mechanism.

	Information Exchange	Assessment	Negotiation	Decision-Making	Resource Allocation
Centralization				Approval, Planning, Problem solving	
Formalization	Advice, Knowledge transfer	Corporate reputation, MNC assessment, Reporting			
Socialization			Staff empowerment, Negotiations		Buffer relations, Resource Leverage, Coaching
Horizontal communication	Contact transfer, Socializing, Benchmarking, Friendship, Follow-up	Trust enhancement, Market assessment, Customer assessment, Supplier assessment			

5.4. Theoretical and Empirical Contribution

The present paper contributes theoretically to the research traditions, which form its theoretical context (see Section 2.1) by describing and conceptualizing the implications of FSMs' personal contacts for inter-firm coordination in industrial markets and within MNCs. On the one hand, FSMs' personal contacts are conceptualized in terms of interpersonal context, factors, functions and dynamics. On the other hand, inter-firm coordination is conceptualized in terms of individual interpersonal roles, inter-firm interaction as well as MNC centralization, formalization, socialization and horizontal communication. Such aspects of the role of FSMs' personal contacts in the coordination of industrial MNCs are discussed in the light of extant literature in the following paragraphs.

Following calls for a better understanding of the content (e.g. Mintzberg, 1991) and context (e.g. Fondas & Stewart, 1994) of managerial work, the present paper starts by addressing the distinctive features of FSMs' personal contacts compared to other individuals in general and other managers in particular. The paper thus conceptualizes the interpersonal context of FSMs in industrial MNCs (see Fig. 7 in Section 4.2.1) in terms of perceived dependence (Astley & Sachdeva, 1985; Forsgren, 1990a) and uncertainty (Milliken, 1987) at the individual level. In addition, such an interpersonal context is conceptualized in terms of counterparts with whom FSMs are expected to take personal contacts. Such counterparts are both external and internal to the MNC, once that FSMs are regarded as boundary spanning individuals (Tushman, 1977). By conceptualizing FSMs' interpersonal context, the present paper supplements previous findings, which do not specify the individuals who take personal contacts (see Cunningham & Homse, 1986; Hallén, 1992; Nohria & Ghoshal, 1997 for exceptions) nor their perceptions or counterparts.

Previous studies have identified, however, individual, organizational and market factors, which supposedly influence the occurrence of personal contacts in industrial markets (Andersson et al., 1996; Axelsson & Agndal, 2000; Björkman & Kock, 1995; Cunningham & Homse, 1986; Cunningham & Turnbull, 1982; Halinen & Salmi, 2001; Hallén, 1992) and in MNCs (Ghoshal et al., 1994; Marschan, 1996; Nohria & Ghoshal, 1997). Such contributions follow previous claims that: "a major problem of studying the process of personal interaction and communication between buying and selling companies is the large number of variables impinging on the nature and extent of the process" (Turnbull, 1979, p. 83). In this respect, the present paper identifies nine individual factors, nine organizational factors, and five market factors, which were either implicit or absent in such studies (see Fig. 10 in Section 5.1). In addition, the present paper suggests that contextual factors influence not only the occurrence of personal contacts, but also perceptions of dependence and uncertainty at the individual level (see Sections 4.2.3–4.2.10).

On the other hand, previous studies have identified functions of personal contacts and their specific contents in industrial markets (Axelsson & Agndal, 2000; Björkman & Kock, 1995; Cunningham & Homse, 1986; Cunningham & Turnbull, 1982; Halinen & Salmi, 2001) and in MNCs (Bartlett & Ghoshal, 1992, 1997). In this respect, the present paper identifies three information exchange contents, six assessment contents, one negotiation content, two decision-making contents, and tworesource allocation contents, which were either implicit or absent in previous findings (see Fig. 10 in Section 5.1). In addition, the present paper associates one information exchange content, three assessment contents, and two decision-making contents with the general direction and/or frequency of FSMs' personal contacts (see Sections 4.4.2 and 4.4.3).

Other dynamics aspects of FSMs' personal contacts than direction and frequency are the channels by which they take place and their general paths over time. In this respect, the present paper suggests seven channels (see Section 4.4.1), which have also been identified in previous studies of either industrial markets (Andersson et al., 1996; Axelsson & Agndal, 2000; Cunningham & Turnbull, 1982) or MNCs (Egelhoff, 1993; Marschan, 1996). In addition, the present paper suggests two general paths of FSMs' contact network (see Section 4.4.4), which have been implicitly identified in previous studies of industrial markets (Cunningham & Turnbull, 1982; Hallén, 1992) and of MNCs (Nohria & Ghoshal, 1997).

Before continuing with the review of the present paper's theoretical contribution to the three research traditions on which it builds upon (see Section 2.1), it may be worth noting its assumptions on what constitutes such a contribution. It is assumed here that a theoretical contribution should go beyond the mere listing of variables from data or literature review (Sutton & Staw, 1995) and specify the relationships among them, which, based on a certain set of assumptions (Whetten, 1989), are made explicit through diagrams and propositions (Weick, 1995). Correspondingly, the present paper moves beyond the mere identification of factors, functions and dynamics of FSMs' personal contacts by specifying relationships among them based on assumptions of FSMs' perceived dependence and uncertainty. Such relationships are made explicit with the conceptualization of four interpersonal roles (Mintzberg, 1973), which are discussed in Section 5.2.

Previous studies within the process approach to MNC management have suggested managerial working roles of FSMs (Bartlett & Ghoshal, 1992, 1997; Ghoshal & Bartlett, 1998) without acknowledging, however, a sub-set of interpersonal roles. In particular, Bartlett and Ghoshal (1992, 1997) distinguish FSMs from other managers in the MNC, by suggesting three roles of front-line managers: sensor and interpreter of local opportunities and threats; builder of local resources and capabilities; and contributor to and active participant in global strategy. The latter role is not addressed in the present paper due to its focus on local implementer subsidiaries (Birkinshaw & Morrison, 1995), which according to Taggart (1997a) tend to be militant subsidiaries, that is, with low procedural justice (Kim & Mauborgne, 1991, 1993). The two remaining roles – sensor and builder – are addressed in the present paper, but as specific interpersonal roles rather than general working roles. This follows the assumption that informational and decisional roles presuppose interpersonal roles (Mintzberg, 1973, 1975) rather than vice-versa.

The interpersonal roles of FSMs suggested in the present paper – sensor and allocator – may be said to supplement those proposed by Bartlett and Ghoshal (1992, 1997) by distinguishing the degree of individual dependence and uncertainty involved in their notion of sensing and building. In particular, FSMs are thought to interpret local opportunities and threats both as integrated- and autonomous sensors, and to build local resources and capabilities both as integrated- and autonomous allocators. An important assumption behind this distinction is that managerial roles are not exclusively determined by situational constraints such as the organization's formal structure, but also by individual agency (Pettigrew, 1973). On the other hand, FSMs are expected to perceive a varying degree of uncertainty in the local market, which leads to the present paper's distinction between certain and uncertain interpersonal roles.

The eight interpersonal roles of FSMs here suggested constitute the basis for a theoretical argument, which explicitly relates FSMs' personal contacts with coordination in industrial markets. On the one hand, it is suggested that FSMs' personal contacts as integrated- and autonomous sensors allow information exchange and assessment at the individual level, which supports processes of exchange at the organizational level. Such a relationship between personal contacts and inter-firm exchange in industrial markets has been acknowledged in previous studies as social exchange (Forsgren et al., 1995; IMP group, 1982) at the firm level, which may include personal contacts between general managers (Cunningham & Homse, 1986). The present paper supplements such studies by explicitly identifying specific contents of FSMs' personal contacts, which enable the firm's perception of other actors in industrial networks (see Section 5.2.). This follows Håkansson and Johanson's (1993) claim that the viability of an industrial network as a governance structure in industrial markets is largely dependent on the perceptions of the actors involved.

On the other hand, the present paper suggests that FSMs' personal contacts as integrated- and autonomous allocators allow negotiation, decision-making, and resource allocation at the individual level, which supports processes of adaptation at the organizational level. Such a relationship between personal contacts and inter-firm adaptation in industrial markets has been acknowledged in previous studies as human adaptations (Ford, 1980) at the firm level, which require a proper strategic framework (Brennan & Turnbull, 1999) at the individual level. The present paper supplements such studies by explicitly identifying specific contents of FSMs' personal contacts, which enable the firm's allocation of resources in industrial networks (see Section 5.2.). This follows Håkansson and Johanson's (1993) claim that the viability of an industrial network as a governance structure in industrial markets is dependent on the ability of actors to mobilize other actors.

As mentioned in Section 2.2.1, processes of exchange and adaptation constitute the two elements of inter-firm interaction in industrial markets (Håkansson & Snehota, 1995; IMP group, 1982). Interaction among firms in an industrial network (see Fig. 4 in Section 2.5.1) is, in turn, thought to enable inter-firm coordination in such markets (Easton, 1992; Håkansson & Johanson, 1993; Johanson & Mattsson, 1987). FSMs' personal contacts are thus conceptualized in the present paper as playing a crucial role in the coordination of industrial markets in the sense that they enable processes of exchange and adaptation at the firm level.

The present paper also suggests that FSMs' personal contacts may be explicitly associated with coordination in less-hierarchical MNCs. It is claimed, in particular, that in local implementer subsidiaries (Birkinshaw & Morrison, 1995) centralization is associated with FSMs' personal contacts for approval and planning in a scenario of high uncertainty. Such a proposition illuminates the inconclusive notion of moderate centralization in subsidiaries that have scarce local resources in highly complex environments (Nohria & Ghoshal, 1997). In addition, the present paper suggests that centralization is associated with FSMs' personal contacts for problem solving in a scenario of low uncertainty. Such a proposition gives little support to the notion of high centralization in subsidiaries that have scarce local resources in little complex environments (Nohria & Ghoshal, 1997). The authors equate, however, environmental complexity with local competition and technological dynamism, thus appearing to subscribe the view that perceived environmental uncertainty may be objectively measured (see Section 4.2.1) rather than constituting a subjective perception at the individual level (Milliken, 1987). In addition, the authors appear to subscribe the design approach to less-hierarchical MNC management (see Section 2.4.1) by prescribing rather than describing centralization at the subsidiary level based on the assumption that "there is a fit structure of the headquarters-subsidiary relation that leads to improved performance" (Nohria & Ghoshal, 1997, p. 111).

The present paper also suggests that in local implementer subsidiaries (Birkinshaw & Morrison, 1995) formalization is associated with FSMs' personal contacts for advice, knowledge transfer, corporate reputation, and MNC assessment in a scenario of high uncertainty and for reporting in a scenario of low uncertainty. Such a proposition contrasts with Nohria and Ghoshal's (1997) suggestion that subsidiaries with low levels of local resources are expected to adopt a low degree of formalization in both highly and little complex environments.

Moreover, the present paper suggests that in local implementer subsidiaries (Birkinshaw & Morrison, 1995) socialization is associated with FSMs' personal contacts for staff empowerment, buffer relations, and resource leverage in a scenario of high uncertainty. Such a proposition supplements the notion of high socialization, which has been put forward by Nohria and Ghoshal (1997) for subsidiaries with low levels of local resources in highly complex environments. In addition, the present paper suggests that socialization is associated with FSMs' personal contacts for negotiations and coaching in a scenario of low uncertainty. Such a proposition contrasts with Nohria and Ghoshal's (1997) suggestion that subsidiaries with low levels of local resources are expected to adopt a low degree of socialization in little complex environments.

Finally, the present paper suggests that in local implementer subsidiaries (Birkinshaw & Morrison, 1995) horizontal communication is associated with FSMs' personal contacts for contact transfer, socializing, benchmarking, trust enhancement as well as market-, customer- and supplier assessment in a scenario of high uncertainty. Such a proposition supplements Harzing's (1999) suggestion that networks[13] are positively related with environmental uncertainty. In addition, the present paper suggests that horizontal communication is associated with FSMs' personal contacts for friendship and follow-up in a scenario of low uncertainty. Such a proposition thus contrasts with Harzing's (1999) very same suggestion that networks are positively related with environmental uncertainty. Harzing (1999) attempts, however, to measure environmental uncertainty with questions concerning consumers, competition, technological change, and necessity for continuous adaptation, appearing to subscribe the view that perceived environmental uncertainty may be objectively measured (see Section 4.2.1) rather than constituting a subjective perception at the individual level (Milliken, 1987).

As mentioned in Section 4.2.1, the present paper subscribes the view that perceived environmental uncertainty is a subjective perception at the individual level rather than an objectively measurable phenomenon (Milliken, 1987). In addition, the present paper subscribes the organic approach to less-hierarchical MNC management (see Section 2.4.1) by describing the adoption of mechanisms of coordination in local implementer subsidiaries (Birkinshaw & Morrison, 1995) as the result of co-existing headquarters' authority (Forsgren, 1990a) and FSMs' discretion (Pettigrew, 1973). By contrast, other authors appear to subscribe the design approach to less-hierarchical MNC management (see Section 2.4.1) by prescribing an optimal "mix" of centralization, formalization and socialization, which headquarters are supposedly able to design and implement. In Nohria and Ghoshal's (1997) words: "managers must adjust the control mechanisms of centralization, formalization, and normative integration in the proper manner to achieve the administrative form that matches the structure appropriate for a particular subsidiary" (Nohria & Ghoshal, 1997, p. 111).

According to the present paper, Nohria and Ghoshal's (1997) view of coordination in their model of MNC as a differentiated network may be questioned in at least two ways. First, even if headquarters would deliberate a particular degree of centralization, formalization, and socialization at the subsidiary level their implementation would still be contingent on FSMs' opportunity, motivation and ability (Adler & Kwon, 2002) to take the personal contacts that such mechanisms require. This point can ironically be illustrated with Ghoshal's own words, when proposing another model of less-hierarchical MNC: "the key challenge in transforming a company into an Individualized Corporation lies in transforming the frontline, middle, and top-level managers so that they are willing and able to play their respective roles" (Ghoshal & Bartlett, 1998, p. 209).

Second, centralization, formalization and socialization are not necessarily mutually exclusive and should be discussed in combination with a fourth mechanism of coordination – horizontal communication. Nohria and Ghoshal (1997) appear to regard such mechanisms as mutually exclusive by proposing a "mix" of mechanisms for subsidiaries with few resources, which is primarily composed of either centralization or socialization (see Fig. 3 in Section 2.4.3). The authors acknowledge a fourth mechanism of coordination – interpersonal networking – but its adoption is not discussed in combination with the three former mechanisms (Nohria & Ghoshal, 1997). By contrast, the present paper suggests that the simultaneous adoption of the four mechanisms of coordination is possible in terms of FSMs' personal contacts (see previous section). In addition, it is here suggested that formalization (e.g.rules and programs) may reinforce centralization, whereas socialization (e.g.corporate culture) may reinforce horizontal communication. In this respect, Ouchi (1978) also suggests that socialization reinforces formalization (e.g.output control).

In sum, the present paper contributes to the interaction approach to industrial markets (see Section 2.2) with the conceptualization of FSMs' interpersonal context, which has not been distinguished from that of other individuals in previous research. In addition, the paper contributes to such a research tradition with the identification of factors, functions and dynamics of personal contacts, which have been only partially addressed in previous research. On the other hand, the paper contributes to the network approach to industrial markets (see Section 2.3) with the conceptualization of interpersonal roles, which enable FSMs' participation in inter-firm interaction in industrial networks. Finally, the paper contributes to the process approach to MNC management (see Section 2.4) with eight propositions, which associate specific contents of FSMs' personal contacts with the adoption of centralization, formalization, socialization, and horizontal communication in local implementer subsidiaries (Birkinshaw & Morrison, 1995).

The present paper also contributes empirically to the research traditions, which form its theoretical context (see Section 2.1) by confirming factors and functions of personal contacts, which have been identified in previous research (see Fig. 5 in Section 2.5.1). On the one hand, the paper illustrates, with quotations from the interviews (see Section 4.2), six individual factors, four organizational factors, and three market factors, which have been identified in previous studies of industrial markets (Andersson et al., 1996; Axelsson & Agndal, 2000; Björkman & Kock, 1995; Cunningham & Homse, 1986; Cunningham & Turnbull, 1982; Halinen & Salmi, 2001; Hallén, 1992) and of MNCs (Nohria & Ghoshal, 1997). On the other hand, the paper illustrates, with quotations from the interviews (see Section 4.3), six information exchange contents as well as one assessment, negotiation, decision-making, and resource allocation content of personal contacts. Such contents of personal contacts have been identified in previous studies of industrial markets (Axelsson & Agndal, 2000; Björkman & Kock, 1995; Cunningham & Homse, 1982, 1986; Halinen & Salmi, 2001; Hallén, 1992) and, more implicitly, of MNCs (Bartlett & Ghoshal, 1992, 1997).

Finally, the present paper confirms some dynamics of personal contacts, which have been previously identified within the three research traditions (see Section 2.1). In particular, the paper illustrates, with quotations from the interviews (see Section 4.4.1), seven channels, by which personal contacts take place. Such channels have also been identified in previous studies of industrial markets (Andersson et al., 1996; Axelsson & Agndal, 2000; Cunningham & Turnbull, 1982) and of MNCs (Marschan, 1996).

5.5. Managerial Implications

The findings of the present paper are expected to support the specification of FSMs' job as well as the selection, development and appraisal of such managers. The discussion of the paper's practical implications in the following paragraphs only concerns, however, FSMs in charge of local implementer subsidiaries in industrial markets.

In general, the present paper supports the specification of FSMs' job by identifying factors and functions of their personal contacts (see Fig. 10 in Section 5.1), which highlight the context and content of their work. Such a holistic yet structured framework is expected to provide a realistic picture of the complex interplay between individual agency and situational constraints, which characterizes FSMs' personal contacts. On the one hand, the framework lists individual factors of FSMs' personal contacts, which define the scope of managerial discretion as well as organizational and market factors of FSMs' personal contacts, which characterize their structural contingencies. On the other hand, the framework identifies functions of FSMs' personal contacts related with a low degree of dependence, which further characterizes their discretion, as well as a high degree of dependence, which further characterizes their situational constraints. Such interplay between individual agency and situational constraints is especially relevant for FSMs given their boundary spanning interaction with multiple, but often unconnected counterparts (see Fig. 7 in Section 4.2.1).

By specifying the factors and functions of FSMs' personal contacts, the present paper also supports the selection, development and appraisal of such managers. On the one hand, it is expected to help MBA students and candidate managers anticipate the specific job requirements of a FSM's position. On the other hand, it is expected to support current FSMs in terms of training, self-assessment and benchmarking of best practices. This is especially important in MNCs where the very adoption of a less-hierarchical design requires new managerial roles across the hierarchy (Ghoshal & Bartlett, 1998) in a context of increasingly differentiated subsidiary roles (Gupta et al., 1999).

By addressing the dynamics of FSMs' personal contacts, the paper is also expected to support the long-term planning of their contact network as well as the short-term handling of their hectic agenda. On the one hand, the paper lists channels, by which FSMs take personal contacts, and emphasizes two paths that their contact network is expected to follow over time. On the other hand, the paper specifies FSMs' counterparts as well as certain contents, which are expected to characterize the direction and frequency of their personal contacts (see Section 4.4).

Concerning the mechanisms of coordination discussed in Sections 2.4.3 and 5.3 – centralization, formalization, socialization, horizontal communication – several managerial implications may be outlined. First, through the various contents of their personal contacts, FSMs may participate in the simultaneous implementation of such mechanisms of coordination. It follows that, in spite of having different implications in terms of administrative and opportunity costs, such mechanisms of coordination should not be regarded as mutually exclusive in terms of FSMs' personal contacts. Second, subjecting the adoption of each mechanism of coordination to the degree of local complexity or uncertainty may be problematic, given the difficulties of monitoring, let alone measuring, environmental uncertainty. Third, several other variables than uncertainty should be taken into account when considering the adoption of each mechanism of coordination, including mimetic behavior, local market practices, MNC's administrative heritage, subsidiary history, and headquarters preferences.[14] To such a list, the present paper adds individual variables such as the background, career, language skills, initiative and availability of FSMs, which characterize their opportunity, motivation and ability to participate in the adoption of mechanisms of coordination at the subsidiary level. In other words, the choice of mechanisms of coordination should not be dissociated from the selection, development and appraisal of FSMs. Fourth, a more detailed way of taking FSMs into account in the choice of mechanisms of coordination is by considering the type of channels (see Section 4.4.1) and contact networks (see Section 4.2.2) required by such mechanisms. In this respect, the present paper provides some insights which are synthesized in the following paragraph.

FSMs' personal contacts enabling centralization usually take place through meetings as well as telecommunications and information systems, involving primarily their formal- and business contact network. FSMs' personal contacts enabling formalization tend to take place through telecommunications and information systems as well as events, and also involve mainly their formal- and business contact network. FSMs' personal contacts enabling socialization usually take place through telecommunications and information systems as well as meetings, involving their four contact networks. Finally, FSMs' personal contacts enabling horizontal communication tend to take place through visits, telecommunications and information systems, memberships, events, trainings, and leisure, also involving their four contact networks.

The remaining implications of the present paper concern the design of industrial and national programs of both FDI (Foreign Direct Investment) and export promotion. On the one hand, organizations in charge of attracting FDI should regard the selection of FSMs as a key factor in the promotion of their country as a potential recipient of FDI. On the other hand, organizations in charge of export promotion may contribute to intra-group exports of domestic MNCs, by equally supporting their recruitment needs in terms of FSMs. In other words, the availability of qualified FSMs at the corporate level may be regarded as a crucial requirement for the attraction of FDI and/or promotion of exports at the industrial- and, ultimately, national level.

5.6. Suggestions for Further Research

The findings of the present paper suggest several avenues for further research. On the one hand, the conceptualization of the distinctive features of FSMs' personal contacts here suggested could be compared with other individuals' interpersonal context. In this respect, the notion of elite (e.g. Welch et al., 2002) may prove useful in order to assess contrasting perceptions, namely between managers and non-managers (Carroll & Teo, 1996), of the role personal contacts play in inter-firm coordination. A related issue is the extent to which the roles of managers in MNCs differ. The findings of the present paper could thus be supplemented with the analysis of middle- and top managers (e.g. Ghoshal & Bartlett, 1998) as well as functional subsidiary managers (e.g. Nohria & Ghoshal, 1997). In this respect, the notions of role (e.g. Mintzberg, 1973) and network organization (e.g. Hales, 2002) would need to be considered, once that: (a) the distinction between interpersonal-, informational- and decisional roles is primarily conceptual (e.g. Mintzberg, 1990) and (b) the critical features of "less-hierarchical" MNCs tend to be difficult to operationalise (Marschan, 1996).

In terms of individuals appointed to such managerial positions, further research would be required on issues of gender and national background. In particular, it would be interesting to compare the findings of the present paper with a similar study of female managers. In addition, future studies could examine the extent to which national background combines with other variables such as tenure and experience to explain the increasing assignment of HCNs as FSMs (e.g. Harzing, 2001).

The present paper also provides an exploratory assessment of individual, organizational, and market factors of FSMs' personal contacts, which could be examined in further detail. In particular, the extensive list of factors here provided may constitute the basis for more explanatory and quantitative type of studies, in which key variables are measured. Two such variables are dependence and uncertainty, which are here analyzed only in terms of legal authority (e.g. Astley & Sachdeva, 1985) and inability to predict something accurately (e.g. Milliken, 1987), respectively. Further studies are thus recommended to collect data, which also allows the analysis of dependence based on the control of critical resources (e.g. Larsson, 1985) as well as other measures of perceived environmental uncertainty (e.g. Miller, 1993).

Further research needs to examine the findings of the present paper in other subsidiary-, corporate-, industrial-, and national settings. In particular, it would be interesting to assess the extent to which the analysis of other types of subsidiaries, namely in terms of knowledge flows (e.g. Gupta & Govindarajan, 1991) and level of resources (e.g. Bartlett & Ghoshal, 1986), would lead to contrasting findings. In addition, the scope of MNCs here analyzed could be extended through comparative studies, based on their national (e.g. Harzing, 1999) and regional (e.g. Bartlett & Ghoshal, 1989) background. The fact that the present paper only considers six product industries in a small and open economy, would also justify further research in other industrial and national settings.

Finally, longitudinal studies may shed light on the dynamic aspects of FSMs' personal contacts here suggested. Such studies could examine the channels, direction, frequency, and paths of personal contacts as well as the extent to which FSMs' interpersonal roles co-exist over time. In this respect, examining the relationship between the channels by which FSMs take personal contacts and the type of contact network involved may constitute a fruitful approach.

NOTES

1. In the present study coordination and control are used interchangeably under the assumption that the former leads to the latter (e.g. Harzing, 1999; Marschan, 1996; Martinez & Jarillo, 1989).

2. In addition, "the same case study may involve more than one unit of analysis" (Yin, 1994, p. 41), constituting a single- or multiple-case embedded design in which one or several subunits are also analyzed.

3. See Appendix A for further information on the selected firms and respective product industries.

4. See Appendix B for further information on the types of data collected in the present study.

5. See Appendix C for further information on the standardized open-ended interview guide.

6. See Appendix D for further information on the consent form.

7. See Appendix E for further details on the final hierarchical coding frame.

8. See Appendix F for an alphabetic list of variables and respective definition, which are identified in the present study as contextual factors of FSMs' personal contacts.

9. The six information exchange contents previously identified have been regrouped into four: friendship, progress, advice, and technical information.

10. As mentioned in Section 4.2.1, FSMs' degree of uncertainty is, in turn, contingent on individual and market factors.

11. Rules and programs thus constitute both an instance of formalization and a contextual factor of centralization. In other words, the two mechanisms of coordination may be mutually reinforcing.

12. Corporate culture thus constitutes both an instance of socialization and a contextual factor of horizontal communication. In other words, the two mechanisms of coordination may be mutually reinforcing.

13. The author refers to networks as comprising informal, lateral or horizontal exchange of information as well as formalized lateral or cross-departmental relations. Together with socialization such mechanisms of coordination are labeled by the author control by socialization and networks (Harzing, 1999, pp. 22–23).

14. I am grateful to an anonymous reviewer of my fifth conference paper (see Figure 6 in Section 3.7) for this point.

ACKNOWLEDGMENTS

Financial support from the Finnish Center for Service and Relationship Management, the Finnish Graduate School of International Business, and the Center for International Mobility is gratefully acknowledged.

REFERENCES

Adler, P., & Kwon, S.-W. (2002). Social capital: Prospects for a new concept. *Academy of Management Review, 27*(1), 17–40.

Alchian, A., & Demsetz, H. (1972). Production, information costs and economic organization. *American Economic Review, 5*, 705–777.

Alderson, W. (1965). *Dynamic marketing behavior. A functionalist theory of marketing.* Homewood, IL: Richard D. Irwin.

Alvesson, M. (2003). Beyond neopositivists, romantics, and localists: A reflexive approach to interviews in organizational research. *Academy of Management Review, 28*(1), 13–33.

Andersson, U., & Forsgren, M. (2000). Integration in global MNCs: The Swedish case. *Proceedings of the University of Vaasa. Reports, 58*, 150–163.

Andersson, U., & Holm, U. (2002). Managing integration of subsidiary knowledge in the multinational corporation: A note on the role of headquarters. In: V. Havila, M. Forsgren & H. Håkansson (Eds), *Critical Perspectives on Internationalization* (pp. 359–385). Oxford: Pergamon.

Andersson, U., Kock, S., & Thilenius, P. (1996). Moving from domestic to a foreign social network: The case of Finnish business professionals in California. *Finnish Journal of Business Economics, 2*, 141–153.

Araujo, L. (1995). Designing and refining hierarchical coding frames. In: U. Kelle (Ed.), *Computer-Aided Qualitative Data Analysis: Theory, Methods and Practice* (pp. 96–104). London: Sage.

Araujo, L., & Easton, G. (1996). Networks in socioeconomic systems: A critical review. In: D. Iacobucci (Ed.), *Networks in Marketing* (pp. 64–107). London: Sage.

Arbnor, I., & Bjerke, B. (1997). *Methodology for creating business knowledge* (2nd ed.). Thousand Oaks, CA: Sage.

Astley, W., & Sachdeva, P. (1985). Structural sources of intraorganizational power: A theoretical synthesis. *Academy of Management Review, 9*(1), 104–113.

Axelsson, B. (1992). Network research – future issues. In: B. Axelsson & G. Easton (Eds), *Industrial Networks: A New View of Reality* (pp. 237–251). London: Routledge.

Axelsson, B., & Agndal, H. (2000). Internationalization of the firm: A note on the crucial role of the individual's contact network. *Proceedings of the 16th IMP Annual Conference.* Bath, UK.

Axelsson, B., & Easton, G. (Eds) (1992). *Industrial networks: A new view of reality.* London: Routledge.

Baker, W. (1990). Market networks and corporate behavior. *American Journal of Sociology, 96*, 589–625.

Baliga, B., & Jaeger, A. (1984). Multinational corporations: Control systems and delegation issues. *Journal of International Business Studies, 15*(2), 25–40.

Barnard, C. (1938) [1968]. *Functions of the executive.* Cambridge, MA: Harvard University Press.

Bartlett, C. (1986). Building and managing the transnational: The new organizational challenge. In: M. E. Porter (Ed.), *Competition in Global Industries* (pp. 367–401). Boston, MA: Harvard Business School Press.

Bartlett, C., & Ghoshal, S. (1986). Tap your subsidiaries for global reach. *Harvard Business Review, 64*(6), 87–94.

Bartlett, C., & Ghoshal, S. (1987a). Managing across borders: New strategic requirements. *Sloan Management Review, 28*(4), 7–17.

Bartlett, C., & Ghoshal, S. (1987b). Managing across borders: New organizational responses. *Sloan Management Review, 19*(1), 43–53.

Bartlett, C., & Ghoshal, S. (1989). *Managing across borders: The transnational solution.* Boston, MA: Harvard Business School Press.

Bartlett, C., & Ghoshal, S. (1990). Matrix management: Not a structure, a frame of mind. *Harvard Business Review*, *68*(4), 138–145.

Bartlett, C., & Ghoshal, S. (1992). What is a global manager? *Harvard Business Review*, *70*(5), 124–132.

Bartlett, C., & Ghoshal, S. (1995a). Changing the role of top management: Beyond structure to processes. *Harvard Business Review* (January–February), 86–96.

Bartlett, C., & Ghoshal, S. (1995b). Rebuilding behavioral context: Turning process re-engineering into people rejuvenation. *Sloan Management Review* (Fall), 11–23.

Bartlett, C., & Ghoshal, S. (1997). The myth of the generic manager: New personal competencies for new management roles. *California Management Review*, *40*(1), 92–116.

Bartlett, C., & Ghoshal, S. (1998). *Managing across borders: The transnational solution*. London: Random House Business Books.

Birkinshaw, J. (2000). *Entrepreneurship in the global firm*. London: Sage.

Birkinshaw, J., & Morrison, A. (1995). Configurations of strategy and structure in subsidiaries of multinational corporations. *Journal of International Business Studies*, *26*(4), 729–753.

Björkman, I., & Kock, S. (1995). Social relationships and business networks: The case of Western companies in China. *International Business Review*, *4*(4), 419–535.

Bogdan, R., & Biklen, S. (1992). *Qualitative research for education: An introduction to theory and methods*. Boston, MA: Allyn & Bacon.

Bonoma, T. (1985). Case research in marketing: Opportunities, problems, and a process. *Journal of Marketing Research*, *22*(May), 199–208.

Bower, J. (1970). *Managing the resource allocation process: A study of corporate planning and investment*. Boston, MA: Harvard University Press.

Breakwell, G. (1990). *Interviewing*. London: BPS Books.

Brennan, R., & Turnbull, P. (1999). Adaptative behavior in buyer-seller relationships. *Industrial Marketing Management*, *28*(5), 481–495.

Burrell, G., & Morgan, G. (1979). *Sociological paradigms and organizational analysis. Elements of the sociology of corporate life*. London: Heinemann.

Burt, R. (1992). *Structural holes: The social structure of competition*. Cambridge: Harvard University Press.

Burt, R. (1997). The contingent value of social capital. *Administrative Science Quarterly*, *42*(2), 339–365.

Campbell, D., & Stanley, J. (1963). *Experimental and quasi-experimental designs for research*. Chicago: Rand McNally.

Carroll, G., & Teo, A. (1996). On the social networks of managers. *Academy of Management Journal*, *39*(2), 421–440.

Carroll, S., & Gillen, D. (1987). Are the classical management functions useful in describing managerial work? *Academy of Management Review*, *12*(1), 38–51.

Chandler, A. (1962). *Strategy and structure: Sections in the history of the American industrial enterprise*. Cambridge, MA: MIT Press.

Chandler, A. (1977). *The visible hand: The managerial resolution in American business*. Cambridge, MA: Harvard University Press.

Charles, M., & Marschan-Piekkari, R. (2002). Language training for enhanced horizontal communication: A challenge for MNCs. *Business Communication Quarterly*, *65*(2), 9–29.

Child, J. (1972). Organization structure and strategies of control: A replication of the Aston study. *Administrative Science Quarterly*, *17*, 163–177.

Child, J. (1973). Strategies of control and organizational behavior. *Administrative Science Quarterly,* *18,* 1–17.

Coffey, A., & Atkinson, P. (1996). *Making sense of qualitative data: Complementary research strategies.* Thousands Oaks, CA: Sage.

Cook, K., & Emerson, R. (1978). Power, equity and commitment in exchange networks. *American Sociological Review, 43*(5), 721–739.

Cook, K., & Emerson, R. (1984). Exchange networks and analysis of complex organizations. *Research in the Sociology in Organizations, 3,* 1–30.

Cray, D. (1984). Control and coordination in multinational corporations. *Journal of International Business Studies, 15*(2), 85–98.

Creswell, J. (1998). *Qualitative inquiry and research design: Choosing among five traditions.* Thousand Oaks, CA: Sage.

Cunningham, M. (1980). International marketing and purchasing of industrial goods: Features of a European research project. *European Journal of Marketing, 14*(5/6), 322–338.

Cunningham, M., & Homse, E. (1986). Controlling the marketing-purchasing interface: Resource development and organizational implications. *Industrial Marketing and Purchasing, 1*(2), 3–27.

Cunningham, M., & Turnbull, P. (1982). Inter-organizational personal contact patterns. In: H. Håkansson (Ed.), *International Marketing and Purchasing of Industrial Goods: An Interaction Approach* (pp. 304–316). Chichester: Wiley.

Cyert, R., & March, J. (1963). *A behavioral theory of the firm.* Englewood Cliffs, NJ: Prentice-Hall.

Dalton, M. (1959). *Men who manage.* New York: Wiley.

Daniels, J., Pitts, R., & Tretter, M. (1984). Strategy and structure of U.S. multinationals: An exploratory study. *Academy of Management Journal, 27*(2), 292–307.

Dey, I. (1993). *Qualitative data analysis: A user-friendly guide for social scientists.* London: Routledge.

Donaldson, L. (1995). *American anti-management theories of organization: A critique of paradigm proliferation.* Cambridge, UK: Cambridge University Press.

Downey, H., Hellriegel, D., & Slocum, J. (1975). Environmental uncertainty: The construct and its applications. *Administrative Science Quarterly, 20*(December), 613–629.

Doz, Y. (1986). *Strategic management in multinational companies.* Oxford: Pergamon Press.

Doz, Y., Asakawa, K., Santos, J., & Williamson, P. (1996). The metanational corporation. *Proceedings of the Academy of International Business Annual Meeting,* Banff, Canada, 26–29.

Doz, Y., & Prahalad, C. (1981). Headquarters influence and strategic control in MNCs. *Sloan Management Review, 1*(23), 15–29.

Doz, Y., & Prahalad, C. (1984). Patterns of strategic control within multinational corporations. *Journal of International Business Studies, 15*(June), 55–72.

Doz, Y., & Prahalad, C. (1987). A process model of strategic redirection in large complex firms: The case of multinational Corporations. In: A. Pettigrew (Ed.), *The Management of Strategic Change* (pp. 63–83). Oxford: Basil Blackwell.

Doz, Y., & Prahalad, C. (1991). Managing DMNCs: A search for a new paradigm. *Strategic Management Journal, 12*(Summer), 145–164.

Doz, Y., Santos, J., & Williamson, P. (2001). *From global to metanational: How companies win in the knowledge economy.* Boston, MA: Harvard Business School Press.

Dunning, J. (1980). Toward an eclectic theory of international production: Some empirical tests. *Journal of International Business Studies, 11*(Spring/Summer), 9–31.

Dwyer, R., Schurr, P., & Oh, S. (1987). Developing buyer-seller relationships. *Journal of Marketing, 51*(1), 11–27.

Easton, G. (1992). Industrial networks: A review. In: B. Axelsson & G. Easton (Eds), *Industrial Networks: A New View of Reality* (pp. 3–27). London: Routledge.

Easton, G. (1995). Methodology and industrial networks. In: K. Möller & D. Wilson (Eds), *Business Marketing: An Interaction and Network Perspective* (pp. 411–491). Boston, MA: Kluwer.

Easton, G. (2000). Is relevance relevant? *Proceedings of the 16th IMP Annual Conference.* Bath, UK.

Edström, A., & Galbraith, J. (1977). Transfer of managers as a coordination and control strategy in multinational organizations. *Administrative Science Quarterly, 22*(2), 248–263.

Egelhoff, W. (1982). Strategy and structure in multinational corporations: An information processing approach. *Administrative Science Quarterly, 27*(3), 435–458.

Egelhoff, W. (1988). *Organizing the multinational enterprise: An information-processing perspective.* Cambridge, MA: Ballinger.

Egelhoff, W. (1991). Information-processing theory and the multinational enterprise. *Journal of International Business Studies, 22*(3), 341–368.

Egelhoff, W. (1993). Information-processing theory and the multinational corporation. In: S. Ghoshal & E. Westney (Eds), *Organization Theory and the Multinational Corporation* (pp. 182–210). London: MacMillan.

Egelhoff, W. (1999). Organizational equilibrium and organizational change: Two different perspectives of the multinational enterprise. *Journal of International Management, 5*, 15–33.

Eisenhardt, K. (1989). Building theories from case study research. *Academy of Management Review, 14*(4), 532–550.

Eisenhardt, K. (1991). Better stories and better constructs: The case for rigor and comparative logic. *Academy of Management Review, 16*(3), 620–627.

Emerson, R. (1962). Power-dependence relations. *American Sociological Review, 27*(1), 31–41.

Fayol, H. (1916) [1950]. *Administration industrielle et générale.* Paris: Dunod.

Fielding, N. & Lee, R. (Eds) (1991). *Using computers in qualitative research.* London: Sage.

Fondas, N., & Stewart, R. (1994). Enactment in managerial jobs: A role analysis. *Journal of Management Studies, 31*(1), 83–103.

Fontana, A., & Frey, J. (2000). The interview. In: N. Denzin & Y. Lincoln (Eds), *The Handbook of Qualitative Research* (2nd ed., pp. 645–672). Thousand Oaks: Sage.

Ford, D. (1980). The development of buyer seller relationships in industrial markets. *European Journal of Marketing, 14*(5), 339–354.

Ford, D. (Ed.) (1997). *Understanding business markets* (2nd ed.). London: Dryden Press.

Ford, D., Gadde, L.-E., Håkansson, H., Lundgren, A., Snehota, I., Turnbull, P., & Wilson, D. (1998). *Managing business relationships.* West Sussex: Willey.

Ford, D., Håkansson, H., & Johanson, J. (1986). How do companies interact? *Industrial Marketing and Purchasing, 1*(1), 26–41.

Forsgren, M. (1990a). *Managing the internationalization process: The Swedish case* (2nd ed.). London: Routledge.

Forsgren, M. (1990b). Managing the international multi-center firm: Case studies from Sweden. *European Management Journal, 8*(2), 261–267.

Forsgren, M., Hägg, I., Håkansson, H., & Mattsson, L.-G. (1995). *Firms in networks: A new perspective on competitive power.* Uppsala: Acta Universitatis Upsaliensis.

Forsgren, M., Holm, U., & Johanson, J. (1992). Internationalization of the second degree: The emergence of European-based centers in Swedish firms. In: S. Young & J. Hamill (Eds), *Europe and the Multinationals* (pp. 235–253). Worcester: Edward Elgar Publishing.

Forsgren, M., & Johanson, J. (Eds) (1992). *Managing networks in international business.* Philadelphia: Gordon and Breach Science Publishers.

Franko, L. (1976). *The European multinationals: A renewed challenge to American and British big business*. Stanford, CT: Greylock Press.

Gadde, L.-E., & Mattsson, L.-G. (1987). Stability and change in network relationships. *International Journal of Research in Marketing, 4*, 29–41.

Galbraith, J. (1973). *Designing complex organizations*. Reading, MA: Addison-Wesley.

Galbraith, J. (1977). *Organization design*. Reading, MA: Addison-Wesley.

Gates, S. (1994). *The changing global role of the foreign subsidiary manager*. New York: Conference Board.

Ghauri, P. (1992). New structures in MNCs based in small countries: A network approach. *European Management Journal, 10*(3), 357–363.

Ghoshal, S., & Bartlett, C. (1990). The multinational corporation as an interorganizational network. *Academy of Management Review, 15*(4), 603–625.

Ghoshal, S., & Bartlett, C. (1998). *The individualized corporation: A fundamentally new approach to management*. New York: Harper Perennial.

Ghoshal, S., Korine, H., & Szulanski, G. (1994). Inter-unit communication in multinational corporations. *Management Science, 40*(1), 96–110.

Ghoshal, S., & Nohria, N. (1989). Internal differentiation within multinational corporations. *Strategic Management Journal, 10*(4), 323–338.

Glaser, B., & Strauss, A. (1967). *The discovery of grounded theory*. New York: Aldine Publishing.

Golden, B. (1992). The past is the past – or is it? The use of retrospective accounts as indicators of past strategy. *Academy of Management Journal, 35*(4), 848–860.

Granovetter, M. (1973). The strength of weak ties. *American Journal of Sociology, 78*(6), 1360–1380.

Grönroos, C. (1994). Quo vadis, marketing? Toward a Relationship Marketing paradigm. *Journal of Marketing Management, 10*, 347–360.

Guba, E., & Lincoln, Y. (1998). Competing paradigms in qualitative research. In: N. Denzin & Y. Lincoln (Eds), *The Landscape of Qualitative Research. Theories and Issues* (pp. 195–220). Thousand Oaks: Sage.

Gupta, A., & Govindarajan, V. (1991). Knowledge flows and the structure of control within multinational corporations. *Academy of Management Review, 16*(4), 768–792.

Gupta, A., & Govindarajan, V. (1994). Organizing for knowledge flows within MNCs. *International Business Review, 3*(4), 443–457.

Gupta, A., Govindarajan, V., & Malhotra, A. (1999). Feedback-seeking behavior within multinational corporations. *Strategic Management Journal, 20*, 205–222.

Hägg, I., & Johanson, J. (1983). *Firms in networks*. Stockholm: Business and Social Research Institute.

Håkansson, H. (Ed.) (1982). *International marketing and purchasing of industrial goods*. Chichester: Wiley.

Håkansson, H. (1987). *Industrial technological development: A network approach*. London: Croom Helm.

Håkansson, H., & Johanson, J. (1984). A model of industrial networks. Working Papers, Department of Business Administration, Uppsala: University of Uppsala.

Håkansson, H., & Johanson, J. (1992). A model of industrial networks. In: B. Axelsson & G. Easton (Eds), *Industrial Networks: A New View of Reality* (pp. 28–34). London: Routledge.

Håkansson, H., & Johanson, J. (1993). The network as governance structure: Interfirm cooperation beyond markets and hierarchies. In: G. Grabber (Ed.), *The Embbeded Firm. The Socio-Economics of Industrial Networks* (pp. 35–51). London: Routledge.

Håkansson, H., & Snehota, I. (1989). No business is an island: The network concept of business strategy. *Strategic Management Journal, 5*(3), 187–200.

Håkansson, H., & Snehota, I. (1995). *Developing relationships in business networks*. London: Routledge.

Hakim, C. (2000). *Research design: Strategies and choices in the design of social research*. London: Allen & Unwin.

Hales, C. (1986). What do managers do? A critical review of the evidence. *Journal of Management Studies, 23*(1), 88–115.

Hales, C. (1989). Management processes, management divisions of labor and managerial work: Towards a synthesis. *International Journal of Sociology and Social Policy, 9*(5/6), 9–38.

Hales, C. (1999). Why do managers do what they do? Reconciling evidence and theory in accounts of managerial work. *British Journal of Management, 10*, 335–350.

Hales, C. (2002). "Bureaucracy-lite" and continuities in managerial work. *British Journal of Management, 13*(1), 51–66.

Halinen, A., & Salmi, A. (2001). Managing the informal side of business interaction: Personal contacts in the critical phases of business relationships. *Proceedings of the 17th IMP Annual Conference*. Oslo, Norway.

Hall, D., & Saias, M. (1980). Strategy follows structure! *Strategic Management Journal, 1*, 149–163.

Hallén, L. (1992). Infrastructural networks in international business. In: M. Forsgren & J. Johanson (Eds), *Managing Networks in International Business* (pp. 77–92). Philadelphia: Gordon & Breach.

Hallén, L., Johanson, J., & Seyed-Mohamed, N. (1991). Interfirm adaptation in business relationships. *Journal of Marketing, 55*(April), 29–37.

Hallén, L., & Wiedersheim-Paul, F. (1984). The evolution of psychic distance in international business relationships. In: I. Hägg & F. Paul-Wiedersheim (Eds), *Between Market and Hierarchy* (pp. 15–27). Uppsala: University of Uppsala.

Hannaway, J. (1989). *Managers managing: The workings of an administrative system*. New York: Oxford University Press.

Harvey, M., & Novicevic, M. (2002). The hypercompetitive global marketplace: The importance of intuition and creativity in expatriate managers. *Journal of World Business, 37*(2), 127–138.

Harzing, A.-W. (1999). *Managing the multinationals: An international study of control mechanisms*. Cheltenham: Edward Elgar.

Harzing, A.-W. (2001). Of bears, bumble-bees, and spiders: The role of expatriates in controlling foreign subsidiaries. *Journal of World Business, 36*(4), 366–379.

Healy, M., & Perry, C. (2000). Comprehensive criteria to judge validity and reliability of qualitative research within the realism paradigm. *Qualitative Market Research, 3*(3), 118–126.

Hedlund, G. (1981). Autonomy of subsidiaries and formalization of headquarters-subsidiary relationships in Swedish MNCs. In: L. Otterbeck (Ed.), *The Management of Headquarters-Subsidiary Relationships in Multinational Corporations* (pp. 25–78). New York: St. Martin's Press.

Hedlund, G. (1986). The hypermodern MNC: A heterarchy? *Human Resource Management, 25*(1), 9–35.

Hedlund, G. (1993). Assumptions of hierarchy and heterarchy with applications to the management of the multinational corporation. In: S. Ghoshal & E. Westney (Eds), *Organization Theory and the Multinational Corporation* (pp. 211–236). London: Macmillan and St. Martin Press.

Hedlund, G., & Ridderstråle, J. (1998). Toward a theory of the self-renewing MNC. In: W. Egelhoff (Ed.), *Transforming International Organizations* (pp. 168–193). Cheltenham: Edward Elgar.

Hedlund, G., & Rolander, D. (1990). Action in heterarchies: New approaches to managing the MNC. In: C. Bartlett, Y. Doz & G. Hedlund (Eds), *Managing the Global Firm* (pp. 15–46). London: Routledge.

Hemphill, J. (1959). Job descriptions for executives. *Harvard Business Review, 37*(5), 55–67.

Hennart, J.-F. (1993). Control in multinational firms: The role of price and hierarchy. In: S. Ghoshal & E. Westney (Eds), *Organization Theory and the Multinational Corporation* (pp. 157–181). London: Macmillan and St. Martin Press.

Hewett, K., & Bearden, W. (2001). Dependence, trust, and relational behavior on the part of foreign subsidiary marketing operations: Implications for managing global marketing operations. *Journal of Marketing, 65*(October), 51–66.

Holm, U., & Pedersen, T. (2000). *The emergence and impact of MNC centers of excellence: A subsidiary perspective*. Great Britain: Macmillan.

Huber, G., & Power, D. (1985). Retrospective reports of strategic-level managers: Guidelines for increasing their accuracy. *Strategic Management Journal, 6*(2), 171–180.

Hulbert, J., & Brandt, W. (1980). *Managing the multinational subsidiary*. New York: Holt, Rinehart & Winston.

IMP group (1982). An interaction approach. In: H. Håkansson (Ed.), *International Marketing and Purchasing of Industrial Goods: An Interaction Approach* (pp. 10–27). Chichester: Wiley.

Jackson, N., & Carter, P. (1991). In defence of paradigm incommensurability. *Organization Studies, 12*(1), 109–127.

Jackson, N., & Carter, P. (1993). Paradigm wars: A response to Hugh Willmott. *Organization Studies, 10*(5), 721–725.

Jarillo, J., & Martinez, J. (1990). Different roles for subsidiaries: The case of multinational corporations in Spain. *Strategic Management Journal, 11*, 501–512.

Jick, T. (1979). Mixing qualitative and quantitative methods: Triangulation in action. *Administrative Science Quarterly, 24*(4), 602–611.

Johanson, J., & Mattsson, L.-G. (1986). International marketing and internationalization processes: A network approach. In: P. Turnbill & S. Paliwoda (Eds), *Research in International Marketing* (pp. 234–265). Kent: Croom Helm.

Johanson, J., & Mattsson, L.-G. (1987). Interorganizational relations in industrial systems: A network approach compared with the transaction cost approach. *International Studies of Management and Organization, 17*(1), 34–48.

Johanson, J., & Mattsson, L.-G. (1988). Internationalization in industrial systems: A network approach. In: N. Hood & J. Vahlne (Eds), *Strategies in Global Competition* (pp. 287–314). New York: Crooom Helm.

Johanson, J., & Mattsson, L.-G. (1992). Network positions and strategic action: An analytical framework. In: B. Axelsson & G. Easton (Eds), *Industrial Networks: A New View of Reality* (pp. 205–217). London: Routledge.

Johanson, J., & Vahlne, J.-E. (1977). The internationalization process of the firm: A model of knowledge development and increasing foreign market commitments. *Journal of International Business Studies, 8*(1), 23–32.

Keegan, W. (1974). Multinational scanning: A study of the information sources utilized by headquarters executives in multinational companies. *Administrative Science Quarterly, 19*, 411–421.

Kelle, U. (1995). *Computer-aided qualitative data analysis: Theory, practice and methods*. London: Sage.

Kim, W., & Mauborgne, R. (1991). Implementing global strategies: The role of procedural justice. *Strategic Management Journal, 12*(Summer), 125–143.

Kim, W., & Mauborgne, R. (1993). Effectively conceiving and executing multinationals' worldwide strategies. *Journal of International Business Studies, 24*(3), 419–448.

Kirpalani, M., & Luostarinen, R. (1999). Dynamics of success of smopec firms in global markets. *Proceedings of the 25th EIBA Annual Conference*. Manchester, UK.

Kotter, J. (1982a). *The general managers*. New York: Free Press.

Kotter, J. (1982b). What effective general managers really do. *Harvard Business Review, 60*(6), 156–167.

Krackhardt, D. (1990). Assessing the political landscape: Structure, cognition and power in organizations. *Administrative Science Quarterly, 35*(2), 342–369.

Krackhardt, D., & Hanson, J. (1993). Informal networks: The company behind the chart. *Harvard Business Review* (July), 104–111.

Kurke, L., & Aldrich, H. (1983). Mintzberg was right! A replication and extension of the nature of managerial work. *Management Science, 29*(8), 975–984.

Larsson, A. (1985). *Structure and change: Power in transnational corporations*. Doctoral Report. Acta Universitatis Upsaliensis, Stockholm: GOTAB.

Lau, A., Newman, A., & Broedling, L. (1980). The nature of managerial work in the public sector. *Public Management Forum, 19*, 513–521.

Lawrence, P., & Lorsch, J. (1967). Differentiation and integration in complex organizations. *Administrative Science Quarterly* (June), 1–47.

Lincoln, Y., & Guba, E. (2000). Paradigmatic controversies, contradictions, and emerging confluences. In: N. Denzin & Y. Lincoln (Eds), *The Handbook of Qualitative Research* (2nd ed., pp. 163–188). Thousand Oaks: Sage.

Macneil, I. (1980). *The new social contract. An inquiry into modern contractual relations*. New Heaven, CT: Yale University Press.

Marschan, R. (1996). *New structural forms and inter-unit communication in multinationals: The case of kone elevators*. Doctoral Report, Heslinki, Finland: Helsinki School of Economics and Business Administration.

Marschan, R. (1997). Dimensions of less-hierarchical structures in multinationals. In: I. Björkman & M. Forsgren (Eds), *The Nature of the International Firm: Nordic Contributions to International Business Research* (pp. 433–450). Copenhagen, Denmark: Munksgaard International Publishers.

Marschan, R., Welch, D., & Welch, L. (1996). Control in less-hierarchical multinationals: The role of personal networks and informal communication. *International Business Review, 5*(2), 137–150.

Marschan, R., Welch, D., & Welch, L. (1997). Language: The forgotten factor in multinational management? *European Management Journal, 15*(5), 591–598.

Marschan, R., Welch, D., & Welch, L. (1999). Adopting a common corporate language: IHRM implications. *International Journal of Human Resource Management, 10*(3), 377–390.

Martinez, J., & Jarillo, J. (1989). The evolution of research on coordination mechanisms in multinational corporations. *Journal of International Business Studies, 20*(3), 489–514.

Martinez, J., & Jarillo, J. (1991). Coordination demands of international strategies. *Journal of International Business Studies (Third quarter), 22*(3), 429.

Martinko, M., & Gardner, W. (1985). Beyond structured observation: Methodological issues and new directions. *Academy of Management Review, 10*(4), 676–695.

Martinko, M., & Gardner, W. (1990). Structured observation of managerial work: A replication and synthesis. *Journal of Management Studies, 27*(3), 329–357.

Mattsson, L.-G. (1997). Relationship marketing and the markets as networks approach: A comparative analysis of two evolving streams of research. *Journal of Marketing Management, 13*(5), 447–461.

McGrath, J. (1982). Dilemmatics: The study of research choices and dilemmas. In: J. McGrath, J. Martin & R. Kulka (Eds), *Judgement Calls for Research* (pp. 69–102). Beverly Hills: Sage.

Melin, L. (1992). Internationalization as a strategy process. *Strategic Management Journal, 13*, 99–118.

Miles, M., & Huberman, A. (1994). *Qualitative data analysis: An expanded sourcebook* (2nd ed.). Thousand Oaks: Sage.

Miller, K. (1993). Industry and country effects on managers' perceptions of environmental uncertainties. *Journal of International Business Studies, 24*(4), 693–714.

Milliken, F. (1987). Three types of perceived uncertainty about the environment: State, effect, and response uncertainty. *Academy of Management Review, 12*(1), 133–143.

Mintzberg, H. (1973). *The nature of managerial work*. New York: Harper & Row.

Mintzberg, H. (1975). The manager's job: Folklore and fact. *Harvard Business Review, 53*(4), 49–61.

Mintzberg, H. (1990). The manager's Job: Folklore and fact. *Harvard Business Review* (March–April), 163–176.

Mintzberg, H. (1991). Managerial work: Forty years later. In: S. Carlson (Ed.), *Executive Behavior: Reprinted with Contributions by Henry Mintzberg and Rosemary Stewart* (pp. 97–120). Uppsala: Acta Universitatis Upsaliensis.

Mishler, A. (1965). Personal contact in international exchanges. In: H. Kelman (Ed.), *International Behavior: A Social-Psychological Analysis* (pp. 550–561). New York: Holt, Rinehart & Winston.

Mitchell, J. (1969). *Social networks in urban situations*. Manchester: University of Manchester Press.

Möller, K., & Wilson, D. (Eds) (1995). *Business marketing: An interaction and network perspective*. Boston MA: Kluwer.

Morgan, G., & Smircich, L. (1980). The case for qualitative research. *Academy of Management Review, 5*(4), 491–500.

Nohria, N. & Eccles, R. (1992). Face-to-face: Making network organizations work. In: N. Nohria & R. Eccles (Eds), *Networks and Organizations: Structure, Form, and Action* (pp. 288–308). Boston, MA: Harvard Business School Press.

Nohria, N., & Ghoshal, S. (1994). Differentiated fit and shared values: Alternatives for managing headquarters-subsidiary relations. *Strategic Management Journal, 15*(6), 491–502.

Nohria, N., & Ghoshal, S. (1997). *The differentiated network: Organizing multinational corporations for value creation*. San Francisco: Jossey-Bass Publishers.

Numagami, T. (1998). The infeasibility of invariant laws in management studies: A reflective dialogue in defense of case studies. *Organization Science, 9*, 2–15.

O'Donnell, S. (2000). Managing foreign subsidiaries: Agents of headquarters, or an independent network? *Strategic Management Journal, 21*, 525–548.

Ouchi, W. (1977). The relationship between organizational structure and organizational control. *Administrative Science Quarterly, 22*(1), 95–113.

Ouchi, W. (1978). The transmission of control through organizational hierarchy. *Academy of Management Journal, 21*(2), 173–192.

Ouchi, W. (1980). Markets, bureaucracies and clans. *Administrative Science Quarterly, 25*(1), 129–141.

Patton, M. (1987). *How to use qualitative methods in evaluation*. Beverly Hills, CA: Sage.

Patton, M. (1990). *Qualitative evaluation and research methods*. Newbury Park, CA: Sage.

Penrose, E. (1959). *The theory of the growth of the firm* (3rd ed.). New York: Oxford University.

Pettigrew, A. (1973). *The politics of organizational decision-making*. London: Tavistock.

Pettigrew, A. (1987). *The management of strategic change*. Oxford: Basil Blackwell.

Pfeffer, J. (1982). *Organizations and organization theory*. Marshfield, MA: Pitman Publishing.

Pfeffer, J., & Salancik, G. (1978). *The external control of organizations: A resource-dependence perspective*. New York: Harper & Row.

Porter, M. (1980). *Competitive strategy: Techniques for analyzing industries and competitors*. New York: Free Press.

Prahalad, C., & Doz, Y. (1981a). Strategic control: The dilemma in the headquarters-subsidiary relationship. In: L. Otterbeck (Ed.), *The Management of Headquarters – Subsidiary Relationships in MNCs* (pp. 187–203). London: Gower.

Prahalad, C., & Doz, Y. (1981b). An approach to strategic control in MNCs. *Sloan Management Review, 22*(4), 5–13.

Prahalad, C., & Doz, Y. (1987). *The multinational mission: Balancing local demands and global vision*. New York: Free Press.

Pugh, D., Hickson, D., Hinings, C., & Turner, C. (1968). Dimensions of organization structure. *Administrative Science Quarterly, 13*(June), 65–105.

Quelch, J., & Bloom, H. (1998). The return of the country manager. In: W. Egelhoff (Ed.), *Transforming International Organizations* (pp. 370–380). Cheltenham: Edward Elgar.

Ragin, C. (1987). *The comparative method: Moving beyond qualitative and quantitative strategies*. Berkeley: University of California Press.

Ragin, C., & Becker, H. (1992). *What is a case? Exploring the foundations of social inquiry*. Cambridge: Cambridge University Press.

Rangan, S. (2000). The problem of search and deliberation in economic action: When social networks really matter. *Academy of Management Review, 25*(4), 813–828.

Richards, L. (2000). *Using N5 in qualitative research*. Melbourne: QSR International Pty.

Richards, T., & Richards, L. (1995). Using hierarchical categories in qualitative data analysis. In: U. Kelle (Ed.), *Computer-Aided Qualitative Data Analysis: Theory, Methods and Practice* (pp. 80–95). London: Sage.

Richardson, G. (1972). The organisation of industry. *The Economic Journal, 82*(September), 883–896.

Rogers, E., & Kincaid, D. (1981). *Communication networks: Toward a new paradigm for research*. New York: Free Press.

Roth, K., & Morrison, A. (1992). Implementing global strategy: Characteristics of global subsidiary mandates. *Journal of International Business Studies, 23*(4), 715–735.

Sayer, A. (1992). *Method in social science: A realist approach*. London: Routledge.

Sayer, A. (2000). *Realism and social science*. Thousand Oaks: Sage.

Sheth, J., & Parvatiyar, A. (1995). The evolution of relationship marketing. *International Business Review, 4*(4), 397–418.

Silverman, D. (2000). Analyzing talk and text. In: N. Denzin & Y. Lincoln (Eds), *Handbook of Qualitative Research* (2nd ed., pp. 821–834). Thousand Oaks: Sage.

Simon, H. (1976). *Administrative behavior* (3rd ed.). New York: Free Press.

Smith, A. (1776) [1937]. *An inquiry into the nature and causes of the wealth of nations*. New York: Modern Library.

Snyder, N., & Glueck, W. (1980). How managers plan: The analysis of managers' activities. *Long Range Planning, 13*(1), 70–76.

Stake, R. (1995). *The art of case study research*. London: Sage.

Stake, R. (2000). Case studies. In: N. Denzin & Y. Lincoln (Eds), *Handbook of Qualitative Research* (2nd ed., pp. 435–454). Thousand Oaks: Sage.

Starbuck, W. (1976). Organizations and their environment. In: M. Dunnette (Ed.), *Handbook of Industrial and Organizational Psychology* (pp. 1069–1124). Chicago: Rand McNally.

Stewart, R. (1974). The manager's job: Discretion vs. demand. *Organizational Dynamics, 2*(3), 67–80.

Stewart, R. (1976). To understand the manager's job: Consider demands, constraints, and choices. *Organizational Dynamics, 4*(4), 22–32.

Stewart, R. (1982). A model for understanding managerial jobs and behavior. *Academy of Management Review, 7*(1), 7–13.

Stewart, R. (Ed.) (1998). *Managerial work.* Aldershot: Ashgate.

Stewart, R., & Fondas, N. (1992). How managers can think strategically about their jobs. *Journal of Management Development, 11*(7), 10–17.

Stohl, C. (1995). *Organizational communication: Connectedness in action.* Beverly Hills: Sage.

Stopford, J., & Wells, L., Jr. (1972). *Managing the multinational enterprise. Organization of the firm and ownership of the subsidiaries.* New York: Basic Books.

Strauss, A., & Corbin, J. (1990). *Basics of qualitative research techniques and procedures for developing grounded theory.* London: Sage.

Sutton, R., & Staw, B. (1995). What theory is not. *Administrative Science Quarterly, 40*(3), 371–384.

Taggart, J. (1997a). Autonomy and procedural justice: A framework for evaluating subsidiary strategy. *Journal of International Business Studies,* 51–76.

Taggart, J. (1997b). An evaluation of the integration-responsiveness framework: MNC manufacturing subsidiaries in the UK. *Management International Review, 37*(4), 295–318.

Taylor, F. (1911) [1947]. *Scientific management.* New York: Harper & Row.

Tesch, R. (1990). *Qualitative research: Analysis types and software tools.* New York: Falmer Press.

Thompson, J. (1967). *Organizations in action.* New York: McGraw-Hill.

Thorelli, H. (1986). Networks: Between markets and hierarchies. *Strategic Management Journal, 7*(1), 37–51.

Tsoukas, H. (2000). What is management? An outline of a metatheory. In: S. Ackroyd & S. Fleetwood (Eds), *Realist Perspectives on Management and Organisations* (pp. 26–43). London: Routledge.

Turnbull, P. (1979). Roles of personal contacts in industrial export marketing. *Scandinavian Journal of Management, 16*(5), 325–337.

Turnbull, P., & Valla, J. (1986). *Strategies for international industrial marketing. The management of customer relationships in European industrial markets.* London: Croom Helm.

Tushman, M. (1977). Communication across organizational boundaries: Special boundary roles in the innovation process. *Administrative Science Quarterly, 22,* 587–605.

Tushman, M. (1979). Impact of perceived environmental variability on patterns of communication. *Academy of Management Journal, 22*(3), 482–500.

Van de Ven, A., & Poole, M. (1995). Explaining development and change in organizations. *Academy of Management Review, 20*(3), 510–540.

Van Maanen, J. (Ed.) (1983). *Qualitative methodology.* Beverly Hills, CA: Sage.

Van Maanen, J., & Schein, E. (1979). Toward a theory of organizational socialization. In: B. M. Staw (Ed.), *Research in Organizational Behavior* (Vol. 1, pp. 209–264). Greenwich, Connecticut: JAI Press.

Vernon, R. (1966). International investment and international trade in the product cycle. *Quarterly Journal of Economics, 80*(2), 190–207.

Watson, T. (1994). *In search of management: Culture, chaos, and control in managerial work.* London: Routledge.

Watson, T., & Harris, P. (1999). *The emergent manager.* London: Sage.

Weber, M. (1947). *The theory of social and economic organization.* New York: Free Press.

Weick, K. (1995). What theory is not, theorizing is. *Administrative Science Quarterly, 40*(3), 385–390.

Weick, K. (1999). Theory construction as disciplined reflexivity: Tradeoffs in the 90s. *Academy of Management Review, 24*(4), 797–806.

Weitzman, E. (1999). Analyzing qualitative data with computer software. *Health Services Research, 34*(5), Part II December, 1241–1263.

Weitzman, E. (2000). Software and qualitative research. In: N. Denzin & Y. Lincoln (Eds), *Handbook of Qualitative Research* (2nd ed., pp. 803–820). Thousand Oaks: Sage.

Weitzman, E., & Miles, R. (1995). *Computer programs for qualitative data analysis: A software sourcebook.* London: Sage.

Welch, C., Marschan-Piekkari, R., Penttinen, H., & Tahvanainen, M. (2002). Interviewing elites in international organizations: A balancing act for the researcher. *International Business Review, 11*(5), 611–628.

Whetten, D. (1989). What constitutes a theoretical contribution? *Academy of Management Review, 14*(4), 490–495.

White, R., & Poynter, T. (1984). Strategies for foreign-owned subsidiaries in Canada. *Business Quarterly, 49*(2), 59–69.

White, R., & Poynter T. (1990). Organizing for world-wide advantage. In: C. Bartlett, Y. Doz & G. Hedlund (Eds), *Managing the Global Firm* (pp. 95–113). London: Routledge.

Whitley, R. (1988). The management sciences and managerial skills. *Organization Studies, 9*(1), 47–68.

Whitley, R. (1989). On the nature of managerial tasks and skills: Their distinguishing characteristics and organization. *Journal of Management Studies, 26*(3), 209–224.

Whittington, R. (1993). *What is strategy and does it matter?* London: Routledge.

Williamson, O. (1975). *Markets and hierarchies: Analysis and antitrust implications.* New York: Free Press.

Williamson, O. (1979). Transaction cost economics: The governance of contractual relations. *Journal of Law and Economics, 22,* 233–261.

Williamson, O. (1981). The economics of organizations: The transaction cost approach. *American Journal of Sociology, 87*(3), 548–577.

Willmott, H. (1984). Images and ideals of managerial work: A critical examination of conceptual and empirical accounts. *Journal of Management Studies, 21*(3), 349–368.

Willmott, H. (1987). Studying managerial work: A critique and a proposal. *Journal of Management Studies, 24*(3), 170–249.

Willmott, H. (1993). Breaking the paradigm mentality. *Organization Studies, 10*(5), 681–719.

Wolcott, H. (1994). *Transforming qualitative data: Description, analysis, and interpretation.* Thousand Oaks, CA: Sage.

Wolfe, R., Gephart, R., & Johnson, T. (1993). Computer-facilitated qualitative data analysis: Potential contributions to management research. *Journal of Management, 19*(3), 637–660.

Yin, R. (1994). *Case study research: Design and methods* (2nd ed.). Thousand Oaks: Sage.

Zaltman, G., LeMasters, K., & Heffring, M. (1982). *Theory construction in marketing. Some thoughts on thinking.* New York: Wiley.

APPENDIX A: SELECTED FINNISH MNCS IN PORTUGAL

MNC/Division	Product Industry	Subsidiary Function
Nokia Networks	Telecommunications	Sales
Anonymous1	Pulp and Paper	Sales
UPM-Kymmene	Pulp and Paper	Sales
Anonymous2	Technical textiles	Production and sales
Rosenlew	Technical textiles	Production and sales
Outokumpu Cooper	Minerals	Sales
Metso Minerals	Minerals	Sales
Metso Automation	Mechanical engineering	Sales
Wärtsila Service	Mechanical engineering	Service
KWH Pipe	Plastic pipes	Production and sales
Uponor	Plastic pipes	Production and sales

Note: Two MNCs are kept anonymous as requested by their respective FSM in Portugal. The information reports to year 2001.

APPENDIX B: DATA MATRIX

Data/Cases	Case 1	Case 2	Case 3	Case 4	Case 5	Case 6
Annual reports	2000/2001	2000/2001	2000/2001	2000/2001	2000/2001	2000/2001
Other publications	P. release (28.700)	I. review (1.03.01)	Brochure (20001)	Brochure (1999)	Brochure (1999)	P. release (4.02.02)
Internal materials	Chart (28.3.01)	Job desc. (07.01)		Chart (1999)		
Personal correspondence	Consent (5.9.01)	Consent (30.08.01)	Consent (15.11.01)	Consent (30.07.0)	Consent (7.01.02)	Consent (10.05.01)
Research reports	Kulkki, S. 1994					Stenberg, E. 1992
Electronic messages	Received: Sent:	Received: Sent:	Received: Sent:	Received: Sent:	Received: Sent:	Received: Sent:
Internet text	13.09.00; 6.04.01	13.09.00; 31.07.01	4.10.01	13.09.00; 4.10.01	26.08.01	13.09.00; 10.05.01
Tapes	2 HF90 (5.9.01)	2 HF90 (30.08.01)	2 HF90 (4.10.01)	2 HF90 (30.07.0)	1 HF90 (7.01.02)	2 HF90 (10.05.01)
Transcripts	Interview	Interview	Interview	Interview	Interview	Interview
Notes	Meeting; I. Protocol	Meeting; I. Protocol	Meeting; I. Protocol	Meeting; I. Protocol	Meeting; I. Protocol	Meeting; I. Protocol
Verification comments	24.9.01; 04.03	04.03	21.11.01; 03.03	03.03	03.03	21.05.01; 03.03
Observation notes	29.5.01; 5.09.01	31.07.01; 30.08.01	15.11.01	30.07.01	7.01.02	12.07.99; 10.05.01

Data/Cases	Case 7	Case 8	Case 9	Case 10	Case 11
Annual reports	2000/2001	2000/2001	2000/2001	2000/2001	2000/2001
Other publications			Brochure (1999)	Brochure (2/2001)	Brochure (2000)
Internal materials	Chart (2000)			Manual (10.98)	Subsidiary (1999)
Personal correspondence	Consent (28.08.01)	Consent (3.09.01)	Consent (21.05.01)	Consent (18.07.01)	Consent (4.09.01)
Research reports			Stenberg, E. 1992		
Electronic messages	Received: Sent:	Received: Sent:	Received: Sent:	Received: Sent:	Received: Sent:
Internet text	13.09.00; 26.08.01	13.09.00; 26.08.01	13.09.01; 15.02.01	13.09.00; 18.07.01	13.09.00; 26.08.01
Tapes	2 HF90 (28.08.01)	2 HF90 (3.09.01)	2 HF90 (21.05.01)	2 HF90 (18.07.01)	2 HF90 (4.09.01)
Transcripts	Interview	Interview	Interview	Interview	Interview
Notes	Meeting; I. Protocol	Meeting; I. Protocol	Meeting; I. Protocol	Meeting; I. Protocol	Meeting; I. Protocol
Verification comments	1.10.01; 03.03	03.03	8.06.01; 04.03	29.08.01; 05.03	04.03
Observation notes	28.08.01	3.09.01	22.07.99; 21.05.01	5.07.99; 18.07.01	4.09.01

APPENDIX C: STANDARDIZED OPEN-ENDED
INTERVIEW GUIDE

Project: "Social networks of foreign subsidiary managers as a mechanism of coordination in industrial MNCs: the case of Finnish subsidiaries in Portugal."

(1) Could you please describe your work activities and personal responsibilities?

(2) Could you please draw a diagram of your personal contacts with other subsidiaries and with corporate headquarters?

(3) How did you establish these personal contacts?

(4) Could you please describe these personal contacts in terms of frequency and purpose?

(5) What opportunities and barriers, if any, do you perceive/experience to maintain these personal contacts?

(6) Could you please draw a diagram of your personal contacts with organizations not belonging to the multinational corporation you represent?

(7) How did you establish these personal contacts?

(8) Could you please describe these personal contacts in terms of frequency and purpose?

(9) What opportunities and barriers, if any, do you perceive/experience to maintain these personal contacts?

(10) What opportunities and barriers, if any, do you perceive to establish further personal contacts, both internal and external to the multinational corporation you represent?

Signature of Researcher: _____   Date: __/__/____

Ricardo Madureira, Researcher, Corporate Strategy, University of Jyväskylä, Finland

APPENDIX D: CONSENT FORM

The following information is provided for you to decide whether you wish to participate in the present study:

(1) You should be aware that you are free to decide not to participate or withdraw at any time without affecting your relationship with this department, the researcher, or the University of Jyväskylä.

(2) The purpose of this study is to describe and analyze the role of social networks of foreign subsidiary managers as a mechanism of coordination in industrial multinational corporations. The procedure will be a multiple case study design and the findings will be reported in the form of a Ph. D. report.

(3) Data collection will involve documents (annual reports, research reports, internal newsletters and other company material), audio-visual material (electronic messages and texts), interviews (transcripts of interviews and verification comments), and observation field notes.

(4) The expected benefits associated with your participation are the information about the role of social networks of foreign subsidiary managers in the coordination of industrial multinational corporations, and the opportunity to participate in a qualitative research study.

(5) There are no known risks and/or discomforts associated with this study.

(6) Your name will not be associated with the research findings in any way, and your identity will be known only to the researcher.

Signature of Researcher: _____   Date: ___/___/_____

Ricardo Madureira, Researcher, Corporate Strategy, University of Jyväskylä, Finland

APPENDIX E: HIERARCHICAL CODING FRAME

(1) Context
(11) Inf.
  dep.−/Uncertainty+
(111) Individual
(1111) Background
(1112) Career
(1113) Language skills
(1114) Initiative
(1115) Sales orientation
(1116) Social skills
(1117) Personality
(1118) Attitude
(1119) Availability
(112) Organization
(1121) Corporate culture
(113) Market
(1131) Market
  idiosyncrasy
(1132) Market dynamism
(1133) Supplier closeness
(1134) Customer closeness
(1135) Business culture
(12) Inf.
  dep.−/Uncertainty−
(121) Individual
(1211) Tenure
(1212) Delegation
(122) Organization
(1221) Geographical
  proximity
(1222) Age of
  relationships
(13) Inf.
  dep.+/Uncertainty+
(132) Organization
(1321) Start-up
(1322) Organizational
  change

(2) Content
(21) Information exchange

(211) Contact transfer
(212) Socializing
(213) Friendship
(214) Advice
(215) Follow-up
(216) Knowledge transfer
(217) Benchmarking
(22) Assessment
(221) Trust enhancement
(222) Reporting
(223) Corporate reputation
(224) MNC assessment
(225) Market assessment
(226) Customer assessment

(227) Supplier assessment
(23) Negotiation
(231) Negotiations
(232) Staff empowerment
(24) Decision-making

(241) Approval
(242) Planning
(243) Problem solving
(25) Resource allocation
(251) Coaching

(252) Buffer relations

(253) Resource leverage

(3) Process
(31) Channels

(311) T&IS
(312) Meetings
(313) Visits
(314) Training
(315) Events
(316) Memberships
(317) Leisure
(32) Direction
(33) Frequency
(34) Paths

(1323) Employee turnover
(133) Market
(1331) Technical
  complexity
(1332) Market
  internationalization
(14) Inf.
  dep.+/Uncertainty−
(142) Organization
(1421) Reporting process
(15) Dec.
  dep.−/Uncertainty+
(151) Individual
(1511) Job description
(1512) Extra duties
(16) Dec.
  dep.−/Uncertainty−
(161) Individual
(1611) Experience
(162) Organization
(1621) Size
(17) Dec.
  dep.+/Uncertainty+
(172) Organization
(1721) Planning process
(1722) Approval process
(1723) Business volume
(1724) Intra-group
  transactions
(173) Market
(1731) Customer
  internationalization
(18) Dec.
  dep.+/Uncertainty−
(181) Individual
(1811) Performance
(182) Organization
(1821) Rules and programs

APPENDIX F: GLOSSARY OF FACTORS OF FSMS' PERSONAL CONTACTS

Age of relationships is the time the subsidiary has been doing business with other firms within the MNC and in the local industrial market.

Approval process is the formal process within the MNC, by which the subsidiary's investments are decided.

Attitude is the way of thinking and behaving of the FSM towards his or her contacts.

Availability is the time available to the FSM for personal contacts.

Background is the nationality and educational background of the FSM.

Business culture is shared and informal norms of behavior in the local industrial market.

Business volume is the amount of transactions between the subsidiary and firms within the MNC and in the local industrial market.

Career is the positions, which the FSM has previously held in firms within and external to the MNC.

Corporate culture is shared and informal norms of behavior within the MNC.

Customer closeness is the initiative from customers to communicate with suppliers in the local industrial market.

Customer internationalization is the degree of internationalization of subsidiary's customers.

Delegation is the assignment of FSMs' tasks to subordinates.

Employee turnover is the change of position held by employees within the MNC.

Experience is the knowledge or skills previously acquired by the FSM.

Extra duties are responsibilities assigned to the FSM in addition to his or her initial job description.

Geographical proximity is the proximity between the subsidiary and other firms within the MNC and in the local industrial market.

Initiative is the active rather than reactive engagement of the FSM in personal contacts.

Intra-group transactions are transactions between the subsidiary and firms within the MNC.

Job description is the formal description of the FSM's duties.

Language skills are the ability of the FSM to communicate in a foreign language.

Market dynamism is the degree of change in the local industrial market.

Market idiosyncrasy is unique features of the local industrial market.

Market internationalization is the degree of internationalization of the local industrial market.

Organizational change is the formal establishment of a different status quo within the MNC.

Performance is the degree of competence of the FSM in performing his or her duties.

Personality is the ensemble of personal characteristics of the FSM.

Planning process is the formal process within the MNC, by which the subsidiary's plans are decided.

Reporting process is the formal exchange of information along the chain of command within the MNC.

Rules and programmes are formal policies and procedures within the MNC.

Sales orientation is the FSM's preference for personal contacts with customers.

Size is the subsidiary's amount of sales and employees.

Social skills are the ability of the FSM to engage in personal contacts.

Start-up is the establishment of subsidiary operations in the local industrial market.

Supplier closeness is the initiative from suppliers to communicate with customers in the local industrial market.

Technical complexity is the complexity of technology sold by the subsidiary.

Tenure is the time the FSM has been holding his or her current position.

LIFE CYCLE PERSPECTIVE IN THE MEASUREMENT OF NEW PRODUCT DEVELOPMENT PERFORMANCE

Petri Suomala

1. SYNOPSIS

The essential investments in new product development (NPD) made by industrial companies entail effective management of NPD activities. In this context, performance measurement is one of the means that can be employed in the pursuit of effectiveness.

The primary aim of the study is to structure and analyze the concept of product life cycle in the context of new product development. This objective includes answering the question of what elements comprise product life cycle and identifying the different types of life cycles relevant to NPD performance measurement.

The study is founded on two main elements. First, an extensive literature study on performance measurement and product life cycle has been made for conducting a conceptual analysis covering and synthesizing these two issues. On the basis of this, a conceptual framework comprising the idea of "life cycle conscious" NPD performance measurement is constructed. Second, the empirical base of the study relies on a case study of six industrial companies. This case study was carried out to provide empirical evidence on the product life cycles and their distinct phases in different industrial settings.

Managing Product Innovation
Advances in Business Marketing and Purchasing, Volume 13, 523–700
Copyright © 2005 by Elsevier Ltd.
All rights of reproduction in any form reserved
ISSN: 1069-0964/doi:10.1016/S1069-0964(04)13004-4

The primary contribution of the study is the constructed conceptual framework for the comprehensive performance measurement of product development. Especially its particular emphasis on life cycle requirements has some novelty value – both in practical and theoretical sense. Life cycle oriented performance measurement of NPD reported in the literature has been something of immature, and the novel approach presented in this study provides the doctrine with at least incremental improvement to this.

On the basis of the discussion of this study, a couple of potential research questions can be formulated for future studies. First, proper testing of the constructed framework entails real life cases that would employ the ideas presented in this study for the performance measurement of their product development activities. Second, quantitative evidence on the product life cycles in metal industry should be collected. This can be done either by survey research or by in-depth case studies.

Not everything that counts can be counted, and not everything that can be counted counts (Albert Einstein).

2. INTRODUCTION

New product development (NPD) is a complex and challenging activity. The challenge of managing NPD can be illustrated by addressing a number of difficult – and yet most essential – questions: How to anticipate future events in markets? How to foresee competitors' strategies and actions? How to understand the logic of potential customers in evaluating competing products and services? How to deal with the uncertainties of all the factors affecting the success of the new products being developed?

Edward De Bono (1991) states that our traditional way of thinking has proven its capacity in producing various technical innovations and developments, but he criticizes the effectiveness of our logic in social situations, in human interaction. He provides an example that describes well one of the strengths of ours, the utilization of routine model (De Bono, 1991, p. 54):

Consider a normal routine such as dressing up in the morning. If a person intended to wear 11 pieces of clothing he or she would have – theoretically – ca. 39 million different order options to put the cloths on. Of course, not all the options are feasible, like shoes before the socks etc. However, if the person judged each option even for one second it would take years to get the cloths on. Fortunately, it is not necessary for us to consciously do that kind of judging. We are able to utilize the models our brains have once created.

In the light of De Bono's example, it is a relief to notice that the human mind is capable of constructing different kinds of applications helping us to resolve many practical challenges that we face on a daily basis. However, there are many complex problems that necessitate tools and equipment also other than the human mind. The context of this study, industrial new product development, is argued to be among them. The dressing up – problem addressed the notion that in order to be properly conducted, even the simplest tasks require certain tools.

2.1. Pursuit of Successful Product Development

Industrial research and development (R&D) utilizes science and technology to construct new or improved products or processes for profit-seeking companies (IRI, 2000). New product development, which is an essential part of R&D, can be seen as an activity that is expected to improve a company's competitive advantage and future success in terms, for example, of profitability and market share (see for example Morbey & Reithner, 1990; Osawa & Murakami, 2002; Poh et al., 2001; Zif & McCarthy, 1997). Based on the hope and trust that tangible returns will be greater than expenditure, considerable sums of money are invested in R&D (Batty, 1988). According to IRI, in U.S. companies alone, representing over one-third of the entire world's allocation in R&D, 185.9 billion USD was invested in industrial research and development in 1999 (IRI, 2000). For comparison, U.S. R&D expenditure in 1950 was 2.5 billion USD (Jackson & Spurlock, 1966).

Industrial R&D can be seen as a continuum that starts from basic or applied research and ends with the development and design of a commercial product. It is unlikely that a project will straightforwardly pass all the phases of the continuum; rather, a company is typically able to maintain a certain amount of applied research, concept development,[1] and product development activities/projects. Each type of R&D can be seen as a pool of knowledge; only the most potential ideas of each pool can be further developed – often through many syntheses or even co-incidences – into commercial products.

When striving for effective new product development, R&D management faces several challenges, including project selection,[2] communication, team/individual performance evaluation, benchmarking, etc. In this context, performance measurement can be seen simply as a tool that is supposed to help in grasping "the big picture" and in making good decisions. It is noted that performance measurements drive behavior and they are needed and useful for fostering the prioritization of effort (Schumann et al., 1995). Thus, whatever the purpose (for example project selection, communication, etc.), measurement nevertheless may contribute to the way R&D efforts are managed.

Measurement can be seen as a systematic means for obtaining information and understanding concerning a phenomenon or issue that is rather complicated or broad in its nature, thereby hindering the possibility to manage it only by "gut feeling." The question then is what should be measured in the R&D and NPD context. The challenge of product development management and measurement has received both academic and practical attention. In the practical – industrial – sense, it is highly relevant for companies striving for effective and efficient R&D investments to seek operational tools for better management. Academia, on the other hand, has identified several potential research topics around the subject. Some writers (Chiesa & Masella, 1996; Kerssens-van Drongelen & Bilderbeek, 1999; McGrath & Romeri, 1994; Szakonyi, 1994a, b) have established holistic approaches for the assessment of R&D effectiveness, while others have concentrated on the project level (Ormala, 1986; Rouhiainen, 1997). There are advocates for continuous or in-process monitoring of development as well as for end-of-process evaluation (Schumann et al., 1995). There is a variety of methods available for R&D project selection (Cooper, 1985; Hollander, 2000), performance evaluation for managerial purposes, customer perspective (Hirons et al., 1998; Nixon, 1998), and benchmarking. Many creditable reports that describe the state of the art of R&D measurement have been published (Brown & Svenson, 1998; EIRMA, 1985, 1995; Griffin, 1997; Werner & Souder, 1997a, b).

Success in product development can be considered a general aim for any R&D activity. Unfortunately, success is very multidimensional. It is not only the viewpoint of a stakeholder but also the temporal orientation for product development that affects the definition of success. Despite this difficulty, the question of which dimensions of success one should include and how one can measure these dimensions is an essential question that must be resolved within R&D management (Hultink & Robben, 1995). However, relatively little discussion has focused on the resolution of this question. Yet, as Hart (1993) puts it:

> Clearly, the way in which NPD success is defined influences the findings which describe the factors contributing to NPD success.

Griffin and Page recognize that success is elusive, multifaceted and difficult to measure. Still, companies and academics use over 75 measures of success in product development (Griffin & Page, 1996). Basically, hand in hand with determining and selecting R&D performance measures for a company, one should also consider the concept of success. What is the form of success that is primarily pursued? Are there any other success dimensions that would be important for us? Knowing the type of success pursued would likely be helpful in choosing the appropriate set of R&D metrics. Further, the elusive nature of NPD success is not only due to the fact that the term *success* is multifaceted. It is evident that the term *new product* is also a challenging one to define succinctly and soundly. Depending on the degree of newness related to the product being developed, the nature of NPD might vary a lot.

As a general requirement, at least two kinds of objectives should be set for the utilization of performance measurement (PM) in new product development. First, the measures should convey essential information on the present state of activities. On the other hand, the measures should provide some guidance for long-term improvements. In contrast with this, it has been pointed out that the measures of NPD in many companies suffer from short-termism and an overemphasis on single projects (Meyer et al., 1997). Indeed, considering the importance of effective new product development, it seems that NPD performance measurement is not as developed as one might expect (see for example Hertenstein & Platt, 2000; Hyland et al., 2002).

At a general level, this study addresses the issue of the long-term focus of performance measurement in new product development. By reviewing the body of literature on product life cycle (PLC) theory and on NPD performance measurement, a conceptual analysis focusing on the synergy of these two broad themes is conducted. Further, empirical evidence on product life cycles gathered from six case companies is reflected against this conceptual framework.

From the performance measurement point of view, the concept of life cycle is multifaceted. The traditional marketing view that implies life cycle phases such as development, growth, maturity, and decline, focusing mainly on the sales volume, is only a narrow one. Life cycle can be generally defined as the period of time that begins when a system is conceived and ends when the system is no longer available for use. Analogously, the life cycle of an individual product begins with the acquisition of raw materials and includes processing of bulk materials, production of engineering materials, manufacture, use, retirement, disassembly, and disposal of residuals that might have resulted in each stage of the life cycle. Furthermore, from the business point of view, the management of product life cycle should not be restricted to the life cycle of an individual product, but rather should also include issues such as after sales impacts, product upgrades, and an assessment of their perceived potential, or life cycle assessment of production systems all of which are – either directly or indirectly – associated with the life cycle of the actual product.

Hence, life cycle analysis has the potential to provide the companies with a framework that depicts virtually all the circumstances and the stakeholders that are relevant for a product. Also, it could be employed as a basis that helps to evaluate the cumulative impacts of new products. As noted by Bauer and Fischer (2000), product life cycle theory is an enduring framework in business. Among many other things, it can be beneficial in analyzing the long-term economic and non-economic effects of NPD activities.

2.2. Research Questions

This study is founded on two broad research questions. Together, the questions cover the idea of life cycle consciousness in NPD and the organization of performance measurement on the basis of the concept of product life cycle. These questions are:

(a) Multifaceted performance measurement and the concept of product life cycle-conscious new product development: What would be the potential role of product life cycle in new product development performance measurement and management?
(b) How would it be possible and expedient to organize the measurement of (new) product development performance while taking into account the challenges and requirements that arise from the product life cycle and its discrete phases?

Question A is founded on the issue pointed out by the literature that there has been a very limited amount of discussion concerning the possible solutions for NPD performance measurement that is both multifaceted and has a long-term orientation. The question addresses the possibility that the concept of product life cycle could be engaged in new product development performance measurement.

On the basis of this, the second question – question B – is interested in the specific nature of the measurement framework that is founded on the combination of product life cycle and NPD performance measurement. The literature includes some examples of the life cycle-oriented NPD performance measurement, but overall, the utilization of the concept of PLC in NPD measurement seems to be far from mature. Importantly, the concept of product life cycle has to be fully analyzed in order to be able to use it as a foundation for NPD performance measurement. Also for establishing a foundation for the framework, the requirements and challenges of NPD performance measurement in general have to be discussed.

2.3. Objectives

To be able to respond to the challenges posed by the research questions, a number of more specific research objectives have been formulated. The aim of the study is:

(1) To structure and analyze the concept of product life cycle in the context of new product development. This objective includes answering the question of

what elements comprise product life cycle and identifying the different types of life cycles relevant to NPD performance measurement.

(2) To analyze the concept of life cycle-conscious NPD performance measurement. This includes identifying the various requirements for performance measurement that are founded on the characteristics of life cycle.

(3) To build a conceptual model that connects the product life cycle to new product development performance measurement. The construct should take into account the different stakeholders of the product and the interpretations regarding the product life cycle. As a result, the conceptual model should provide a multifaceted framework for measuring NPD performance.

Answering question A entails reaching objectives I and II, while objective III aims to produce answers mainly for question B. When pursuing these objectives and answers for the questions, the study relies on two main sources of data: a case study and an extensive literature study. The research design will be more fully discussed in the succeeding sections.

2.4. Scope

The overall intent of the study can be described as to produce an overall blueprint for multifacetedly measuring the performance of product development. The main focus is not on the individual measures or on the detailed description of a measurement system; rather, the study aims to produce fresh and well-founded ideas regarding the overall scheme of NPD performance measurement. In other words, the scope is on the analysis of the relationship between the performance measurement and the environment within which it is applied (Neely et al., 1995, p. 81). Long-term orientation and the consideration of various NPD stakeholders comprise the core idea of this scheme.

The definition of the concept of product affects the scope of this study to some extent. Although the definition of product is not intended to be strictly understood, all the products explicitly discussed within this study represent examples of industrial investment goods. The products referred to are either stand-alone industrial products or physical components or materials associated with investment goods. In other words, no consumer products are included in the study. Due to this restriction, the applicability of the study and its findings with respect to consumer products and markets cannot be discussed on the basis of this study. Above all, it is not the characteristics of the life cycle of a specific product but the overall applicability of the concept of product life cycle regarding a specific product that largely determines the applicability of the discussion and the findings in various market settings. If the PLC concept is feasible, the concept of the life cycle – conscious NPD performance measurement will be reasonably feasible as well.

The scope of the study is not very sensitive with respect to a specific industrial sector. Most of the studied cases represent the metal industry and machine manufacturing but there is also a representation of companies operating in the electronics industry. Again, the characteristics of a specific market – no matter how special they are – are not considered to be an obstacle for the applicability of the concept as such if the concept of life cycle seems feasible.

The primary scope of the study is the class of middle-sized or large companies that are active in product development. This statement is founded on the fact that the case companies are middle-sized if not large. In spite of this limitation, the discussion presented in this study might also be relevant for smaller companies if they practice active and systematic product development.

The temporal nature of business is one of the key issues regarding the scope of the study. The proposed framework is founded on the idea that products have various impacts (operational or directly monetary) on the operation of the company, on society, and on the customer over a period of time. The responsibility of the company pertaining to the product – either implicitly or explicitly – very often extends from development, manufacturing, and delivery to the end of life and, for instance, to the possible recycling. In addition, the issue of after sales service comprises a temporal aspect of its own for the manufacturing company. Especially in the case of an industrial product, the customer utilizes the product for several years and during this period, the product is expected to maintain its ability to produce value for the customer. Furthermore, society often has concerns regarding the life cycle impacts of products including, for instance, environmental hazards and pollution. As a result, if no temporal aspects seem to be feasible in a particular environment, the applicability of the proposed framework would be compromised in those settings.

Finally, the phase of the R&D cycle of interest is an important issue. This study, when discussing performance measurement, concentrates on new product development, which is interpreted as the development of commercial products. Talking about the R&D continuum, product development – contrary to basic or applied research – is seen as an activity that takes place near the market and that is focused on a specific product. Thus, the restrictions, requirements, and objectives of product development differ essentially from those of research (see for example Brown & Svenson, 1998). Considering these vast differences between the R(esearch) and D(evelopment) in R&D, this would be an important distinction to make.

3. CONCEPTUAL ANALYSIS

Rose by any other name would smell just as sweet (William Shakespeare).

Despite the apt remark by Shakespeare that a thing is what it is rather than what it is called, it can be argued that a piece of conceptual research without a proper concept definition would be a paradox. Hence, it is necessary to briefly discuss and define the key concepts of this study.

The primary locus of this study is performance measurement and thus also, in a wider sense, management accounting (Neilimo & Uusi-Rauva, 1999; Riistama & Jyrkkiö, 1991). Further, the particular context in which the performance measurement is discussed in this study is new product development and – as the boundary between new and old products is sometimes rather ambiguous – product development more generally. Importantly, the study introduces the inclusion of the concept of life cycle in this context for multifacetedly measuring the performance of product development.

Respectively, the key concepts of this study include performance and its measurement. Also the concepts of product and product development are important. In addition, understanding the concept of life cycle is essential in order to be able to address the research interests. On this account, these key concepts are briefly discussed in the following section prior to actual literature review and analysis. This section ends with a brief synthesis of the core concepts employed in this study.

3.1. Performance

Grönfors reminds that there are many definitions of performance that are founded on different paradigms and assumptions: The mechanistic view implies that performance is the difference between input and output (a measure of efficiency or productivity[3]). On the other hand, performance could also be seen as a function of effort, ability, and conditions (Grönfors, 1996, pp. 42–44).

Otley (1999) argues that performance is an ambiguous term. For instance, it does not inherently specify to whom the organization is delivering its performance. This notion leads Otley to recognize and to define that an organization is performing well if it is attaining its objectives or effectively implementing its appropriate strategy. Also Coccia (2001) argues that performance is the *result* of the organization in carrying out activities over a period of time. Further, Otley recognizes the importance of organizational stakeholders for defining the content of the term "performance" (Otley, 1999).

Laitinen gives a definition according to which performance can be defined as the ability of the company to gain output in the preferred dimensions (see for example Kaplan & Norton, 1992; Lynch & Cross, 1995) in relation to objectives and targets set. (Laitinen, 1998) This definition seems very compact and yet rather generic: performance is mainly related to the outputs and it can be assessed within various dimensions. That is, there is not only one dimension of performance. In addition, it is an important remark that performance is closely connected to the objectives set. It is only the existence of objectives and targets – they can be either explicit or implicit – that actually define the performance in any given situation.

Flapper et al. (1996) suggest that performance is something that is very important for an organization: the success and continuity of an organization depend on its performance. According to Flapper, performance may be defined as the way the organization carries its objectives into effect. Good performance is also about consistency: "it requires that all noses are pointing in the same direction." However, despite its practical appeal, the requirement of consistency seems to some extent questionable. Rather than coherence and consistency, good performance may also require versatile views and even differences in opinions. Furthermore, the fact that performance has a number of dimensions and that it is a relative concept to some extent implies that good performance is not solely founded on consistency.

If there are a number of dimensions that define the comprehensive performance, there also seems to be hierarchical levels of performance. According to Rummler and Brache (1995), the three levels of performance include:

- organization,
- process, and
- job/performer (see also Eloranta & Räisänen, 1986, pp. 45–46).

Organization-level performance emphasizes the relationship between the organization and the market and the variables that affect performance at this level are strategies, organization-wide goals and measures, and organization structure. If the organization structure represents a skeleton of an organization, the cross-functional processes comprise the musculature. To manage the performance at the process level, one must make sure that the processes are designed to meet customer needs and that the process goals are founded on the customers' and organization's requirements. Finally, processes are managed and performed by individuals. Thus, the overall performance of an organization is the result of the performance achieved at three interdependent levels. (Rummler & Brache, 1995) Importantly, when emphasizing the role of measurement in management, Rummler and Brache equate the concept of performance with the concept of output. That is, performance measurement should be focused on the output at three levels: organization, process, and job/performer (Rummler & Brache, 1995, pp. 134–137).

In the product development context, a more specific interpretation of the concept of performance has been presented by Ulrich and Eppinger (1995). Five dimensions that relate to profit achieved by (new products) can be used to assess the *performance* of a product development effort (adapted from Ulrich & Eppinger, 1995, pp. 2–3):

(1) Product quality: goodness of the product as interpreted by different stakeholders, the ability to satisfy customers' needs, robustness, and reliability.
(2) Product cost: manufacturing cost including spending on capital equipment, indirect cost caused by the product.
(3) Development time: the time frame of the product development effort (determines how quickly the organization receives the economic returns from the efforts).
(4) Development cost: the amount of money invested in product development.
(5) Development capability: have the product development effort and experiences associated with it enhanced the abilities of the development team to develop future products (development capability is an important asset the organization can use)?

It is noteworthy that the first, the second, and the fifth point in this list clearly relate to the outputs or outcomes of product development. In that sense, the performance of product development is to a large extent based on the achievements and results of product development activities. However, the third and the fourth point suggest that the performance of product development is not only determined by the outcomes but also by the process itself. Within certain settings, development time and cost may be very critical elements to product development success. Therefore, it seems feasible to regard them as components of product development performance.

3.2. Performance Measurement

Performance measurement is a topic that is often discussed but rarely defined (Neely et al., 1995). Of course, Neely's argument was made in 1995 and since then, the situation seems to have changed to a certain degree. Perhaps it can be said that performance measurement is both discussed and defined often but proper definitions are still hard to find. Neely (1995) suggests that performance measurement should be defined as:

the process of quantifying the efficiency and effectiveness of action.

In this context, measurement represents the process of quantification and action is something that leads to performance. In addition, being well in line with the definition by Neely, Hyland specifies that performance measurement is considered to be a process of data collection and analysis that provides information about the efficiency and effectiveness of ongoing activities (Hyland et al., 2002). On the other hand, quantification is not the only way to define measurement. Grönfors (1996) argues that if one wants to measure performance from a holistic point of view, instead of a mechanistic one, it is not possible to quantify all the variables. Rather, one has to rely on at least some subjective assessments (Grönfors, 1996, p. 47).

Andersin et al. (1994) argue that the concept of performance measurement emerged in the literature at the end of the 1980s. A major driver for this had been the critics – for example (Johnson & Kaplan, 1987) among the others – targeted at traditional financial control and management of organizations based on short-term historical data. Indeed, 1990s witnessed a trend of performance measurement literature. However, it was already some 20 years earlier when (Ijiri, 1975) stated that:

> Performance measurement is an evaluation of the performance of an organizational unit or corporate unit: hence not only the emotional but also the economic interest of the unit is tied to the measurement. As a result, there is likely to be more pressure to bias performance measures than other more neutral measures. For this reason, we cannot look at performance measures as merely additional information useful for some decisions. The measurement has to be more carefully constructed in order to protect it from such pressures.

Management control systems, according to Otley, are systems or "packages" that are intended to provide managers with information that is perceived as important in developing and maintaining viable patterns of behavior (Otley, 1999). If performance measures are defined and implemented properly, they will facilitate the implementation of change (Laakso, 1997, p. 77): measures are facilitators. The facilitating role of performance measurement underscores the importance of a well-defined focus of measurement. In addition, measures can be regarded as motivators. The purpose of performance measurement is to *motivate* behavior leading to continuous improvement in customer satisfaction, flexibility, and productivity (Lynch & Cross, 1995). Hence, it is crucially important to clarify what sort of changes or status quo is being facilitated by the measures. It has been said that the purpose of measurement has to be defined before designing a PM system and identifying the measures (Ojanen et al., 1998).

Performance measurement can also be placed into a larger context: Performance measurement can be interpreted as a part of a performance control process (Kerssens-van Drongelen & Cook, 1997), or measurement can be seen as a foundation for process management and for managing organizations as systems

(Rummler & Brache, 1995, pp. 134–137). It comprises at least information gathering, recording and processing. Hence, acquisition and analysis of information regarding the actual attainment of organizational objectives and plans are included in performance measurement. Further, according to Kerssens-van Drongelen and Cook (1997), performance measurement should also gather and analyze information that relates to factors that may contribute to goal attainment. A performance measurement system is interpreted as a set of tools and procedures that can be utilized to support the information gathering (Kerssens-van Drongelen & Cook, 1997, p. 347).

Bourne et al. (2000) proposed that the development of performance measurement systems consists of three main phases. These are similar to the three phases presented by IMA (1998a, b) for implementing an integrated performance measurement system:

(1) The design of the performance measures: this is principally a cognitive exercise, translating customer views and other stakeholder needs into business objectives and appropriate performance measures. A growing literature base is considering this domain of performance measurement.
(2) The implementation of the performance measures: this is basically a mechanistic exercise and should be susceptible to being managed by classic project management tools. An early involvement of IT specialists is encouraged to increase the speed of progress.
(3) The use of performance measures. This domain is lightly researched and few tools and techniques are available. The solutions in this area require more than simple application of project management techniques.

This scope of this study is on the first point. Due to the novelty of the idea of connecting product life cycle with NPD performance measurement, discussion on the implementation or the use of measures would not be feasible at this point.

According to Hyland (2002), performance measurement can be further divided into active and passive performance measurement. Passive PM is perceived as, for instance, evaluating performance or determining suitable rewards. In contrast, active measurement is characterized by motivating and encouraging desirable behavior or action. (Hyland et al., 2002) As regards the distinction between active and passive performance measurement, it remains somewhat unclear. Performance measurement seems to be a concept that is quite difficult to separate from the context of decision-making – it always has some kind of a connection to active behavior. For instance, it is noted that PM is intended to be a helpful tool in making good decisions and also, it is widely acknowledged that performance measurement affects the people that are in its realm. Therefore, a notion that there could be such an aspect as passive measurement seems arbitrary. In fact,

Kerssens-van Drongelen and Bilderbeek (1999) have provided a more appropriate internal typology of performance measurement: As a part of performance control, performance measurement relates to two different aspects of control, namely feed forward and feedback control. In the research and development context, feed forward control is intended to ensure that the right resources and organizational conditions are employed at the right time to promote good performance. Auditing or benchmarking, for instance, can be utilized to improve the alignment of the resources and conditions to increase the probability of success or good performance. On the other hand, the role of feedback control is to consider the actual attainment of goals in respect to the objectives set for the activities – such as new product development – in the first place. Also, the feedback control should comprise the comparison of expected and actual internal and external conditions affecting the performance.

It has been reminded that the terms "objectives" and "measures" are sometimes used as synonyms for each other. However, an objective is actually an abstract representation of quantity while a measure can be considered as a gauge that produces results or measurement values on that quantity (Fogelholm & Karjalainen, 2001). Consistently, a performance measure can be defined as the metric used to quantify the efficiency and/or effectiveness of an action (Neely et al., 1995). This study discussed performance measurement primarily on the level of objectives and performance measurement systems. Individual measures are very context-specific issues, which means that the selection of measures cannot be accurately and thoroughly discussed at a general level.

Performance measures are indicators of the work performed and the results achieved in an activity, process, or organizational unit. The measures may be both financial and nonfinancial (Player & Lacerda, 1999, p. 258). More generally, according to Ijiri (1975, p. 40), the primary purpose of measures is to communicate the state of something else. This purpose is similar to that of, for instance, a language. Figures that are produced as an output of measurement are of no interest as such. Thus, performance measures can be perceived as surrogates – things or phenomena that are used to convey information about the state of something else – and the subjects of performance measurement can be perceived as principals – things that are primarily concerned and represented by surrogates.

The inherent surrogate character of performance measures is also founded on the difficulty to directly measure the actual phenomenon or variable that is of interest. Consider, for example, the ability of an organization to measure a very typical performance dimension such as customer satisfaction (see Ellis & Curtis, 1995; Thomson, 1995, for more information regarding measuring customer satisfaction[4]). First, individual customer satisfaction cannot really be known without explicitly inquiring it. However, for an organization that serves thousands of customers, it would likely be too resource intensive to carry out such an inquiry in the first place (Thomson, 1995). Second, if the inquiry could and would be done, the act of inquiry itself would likely affect the result. Third, despite the previously mentioned problems, imagine that the opinion of each customer had been asked successfully without any bias. What do the results depict? They do not actually represent customer satisfaction but they illustrate the explicit comments of the customers when their satisfaction was inquired. Fourth, if the problems with direct evaluation of customer satisfaction lead to an adoption of clearly indirect measures, such as the number of reclamations, the surrogate nature of measurement is even more evident. Therefore, the notion by Sharman (1995) on the fundamental goal of performance measurement is a very important one. According to him, performance measurement frameworks are to provide an information infrastructure to *motivate and encourage* the organization and its members to attain its goals. Although it may be very difficult to accurately measure all the variables that affect the goal attainment, a well-structured performance measurement framework can nevertheless effectively communicate the assumptions on the causes and on the inter-relations of factors affecting the organizational goals.

It seems undisputable as such that performance measures are merely surrogates of real life phenomena that lack an independent utility. However, to fully understand the surrogate nature of measurement one has to distinguish the *process of developing the measures* from the process of *using the performance measures*. Clearly, using (calculating and communicating) the measures can be perceived as a surrogate activity that has no meaning unless it contributes to some meaningful purposes. In contrast, the process of developing the measures should not be seen merely as a surrogate of something else. This process includes elements that are essential in terms of the purpose and the essence of an organization. For instance, the priorization of objectives or discussion concerning the adopted strategies and methods that are all included in the process of developing the performance measures cannot be regarded as surrogate activities.

Considering the above, many requirements can be identified for performance measures. To some extent generic requirements for measures include (Kaplan & Norton, 1996a, b; Malmi et al., 2002; Olve et al., 1999):

- When taken together, the measures should cover all the relevant aspects of business.
- The measures that represent different viewpoints or perspectives should be connected with each other.
- Measures should be useful for setting goals, which are seen as realistic by those responsible for achieving them.

Importantly, the concept of performance measurement should be interpreted more widely than the concept of a performance measure. As Aaltonen et al. (1996, pp. 35–36) point out, measures comprise the visible and explicit part of a performance measurement system but the theories on the target of measurement and the theories on the measurement as such are equally important parts of a PM system. In other words, performance measures are *things* that are employed in the realization of performance measurement, but performance measurement can also take place without explicit measures. For instance, the sketching or the tentative defining of performance measures, the constructing of a PM system, or target and objective setting can be regarded as parts of performance measurement even with the absence of the very act of measurement and implemented measures.

In the context of product development, it is important to understand that there is a delay between the actual work and its outcome. Because many dimensions of product development performance are related to the outcomes, the measurement of product development performance is a longitudinal task. It is not possible to get comprehensive quantitative or even qualitative data on the performance of a product before it has been in the market, delivered through the supply chain, and used by customers for a while. On the other hand, it is possible in the product development phase to set objectives for the basis of measures and design the measures that could be applied when the data on the performance becomes available. Assuming that product development is a continuous process in an organization and that the organization consistently produces new products, the performance measurement of product development is also a continuous process: it is not possible now to quantify the performance of products being developed at the moment but it is possible to do that for the products that have been developed in the past. Thus overall, the measurement of product development performance takes place continuously with a delay that is context and industry specific.

3.3. Product and New Product

A product is not only a physical artifact but rather also a "bundle of utilities" including the image associated with it, sales services, warranties and after sales services. In the context of product development, product could be seen as a representation of everything that the customer pays for (Jaakkola & Tunkelo, 1987, p. 11) Quite consistently, according to Ulrich and Eppinger, product is something sold by an organization to its customers (Ulrich & Eppinger, 1995, p. 2). Naturally, these definitions are rather broad by their nature but they nevertheless depict the extent of challenge that is related to product management in an organization.

If product is other than only a physical artifact, product development should also include other issues than only those that relate to the physical product. The whole "package," including services and various direct and indirect issues or effects associated with the product, should be also addressed within product development. These elements that constitute a comprehensive product can be categorized as follows (Berg et al., 2001):

(1) Physical product with its features and performance
(2) Package including the brand, price, quality, and design
(3) Product support including warranty, instructions for use, service, and maintenance

New product is a relative concept. Some companies regard products introduced less than three years earlier as new, whereas others use a respective figure of four or five. In certain markets however, a product's newness lasts no longer than a couple of weeks (fashion clothes, for example). Among other things, at least the maturity of the technologies applied and the characteristics of markets pursued affect the definition of newness. Indeed, it can be concluded that one figure ("a product is new if it has been introduced within the last three years") is not appropriate for all situations (Griffin & Page, 1996). It goes without saying that industries are different in terms of new product introduction pace and the length of product life cycle. Hence, the definition of "new product" has to be adapted to correspond to the characteristics of the industry. The detailed definition of a really new product by Song and Montoya-Weiss includes three conditions (Song & Montoya-Weiss, 1998, p. 126). A really new product is one that:

• is based on technology never employed in the industry before,
• has a significant impact on the whole industry,
• is the first of its kind and, thus, totally new to the market.

It goes without saying that really new products that fulfill these requirements are very rare. Conversely to a really new product, an incremental product does not involve new technology or is not targeted to new markets as the first of its kind. Rather, it involves "adaptation, refinement, and enhancement of existing products and/or production and delivery systems" (Song & Montoya-Weiss, 1998, p. 126). Thus, even an existing product that is marketed through a new delivery system can be regarded as an incremental new product on the basis of the previous definition. In that sense, actual new product development would not necessarily take place in the process of introducing incremental products (see e.g. Green et al., 1995; Moorman, 1995).

As there are many different types of new products, there are also many interpretations for the concept of success in NPD. For example, an inventive product might be regarded as successful if it ever reaches the market in the first place. That would not be, however, a very remarkable achievement if the product was merely incremental.

Despite their degree of newness, new products often include elements of innovation. The definition of innovation has sometimes been connected with the resources of an organization. It has been said that innovations reconfigure the firm's resources. Yet, it does not mean that the new product and innovations should happen "by accident" or lack a connection to the strategy of an organization (Dougherty, 1990). It has been argued that inconsistencies regarding the definitions of innovations[5] and the operationalization of the concept have essentially contributed to the lack of academic advancements concerning the R&D process of various types of innovations (Garcia & Calantone, 2002). Within the academia, the different types of innovations are identified mostly on an ad hoc basis, which has caused a certain "research myopia" in this field. According to Garcia and Calantone, innovation includes not only technology and product development but also marketing, production, and product adaptation. These characteristics distinguish innovation from simple invention, which does not necessarily ever proceed into production or marketing. An innovation "differs from an invention in that it provides economic value and is diffused to other parties beyond the discoverers" (Garcia & Calantone, 2002).

3.4. Product Development

According to Nihtilä, it is a challenge to define the concepts of product development and new product development. The development of a new product may range from minor modifications to an existing product carried out by a single individual to several years' full-time effort from hundreds of people (Nihtilä, 1996). For the purposes of this study, no distinction is made between *product development* and *new product development*. Product development, either connected with the prefix new or not, aims to create products that are new to some extent. Naturally, as discussed earlier, the newness of products may vary a lot from one product to another but this is not a phenomenon that would be subjected to closer examination. The framework or blueprint for NPD performance measurement, as such, is intended to be applicable within a variety of settings. It is only the detailed realization of measurement and the individual measures that are expected to be sensitive to the environment (including the newness of products, for example).

Clark and Fujimoto place product development into the spectrum between basic research and production. According to their interpretation, product development is a part of R&D that can be distinguished from basic research (Clark & Fujimoto,

1991, p. 169). It could also be said that product development is the bridge that aims to fill the gap between basic research and production. This interpretation is aptly depicted by the definition made by Ulrich and Eppinger:

> Product development is the set of activities beginning with the perception of a market opportunity and ending in the production, sale, and delivery of a product (Ulrich & Eppinger, 1995, p. 2).

According to Clark and Fujimoto (1991), new product development can be considered essentially a process during which the production phase and the consumption phase of the product life cycle are somehow simulated. In this respect, product development is intended to create information assets that are anticipated to represent the elements of the future consumption process. In this information creation context, according to Clark and Fujimoto, the ability of the product development team to simulate the target customers and their requirements is critical to the effectiveness of a product development effort. Clark and Fujimoto describe effective product development at a general level as follows (Clark & Fujimoto, 1991, p. 25):

> ... effective product development simulates future consumer experience accurately at a detailed level.

Hertenstein and Platt (2000) argue that NPD overlaps partly with R&D. However, the authors remark that NPD is different from R&D as various functional departments – also other than R&D – collaborate to design and develop new products for the markets. Hence, the authors consider R&D as a functional department whereas NPD would rather be an activity or a set of activities.

It would be possible to discuss the nuances of the definition basically forever. However, it is far more important to understand the role of product development in terms of its importance for the firm's financial success potential. Product development is an activity that largely determines the amount of costs that will be associated with a product. Traditionally, it has been claimed that up to 80–90% of the product cost are determined during product and production development (see for example Asiedu & Gu, 1998; Ax & Ask, 1995, p. 134; Raffish, 1991; Uusi-Rauva & Paranko, 1998). In addition, it is a given fact that in many industries the selling prices of the products cannot be affected by the firm. Hence, it is the success of product development that largely determines not only the product cost but also the firm profitability for the future.

Product development is an interdisciplinary activity that includes at least three major functions: marketing, design, and manufacturing (see for example Ulrich & Eppinger, 1995). When analyzing the stakeholders of new product development, it is important to acknowledge the role of research and development in respect to other departments of an organization. Overall, it can be said that a research and development organization or department provides services to other parties within the same organization (Hirons et al., 1998). Overall, collaboration with both internal and external stakeholders should be considered for product development. Hence, R&D can be seen as an open system that is involved in product innovation. Consistently with this, Nixon argues that there is very little completely objective or concrete about either the inputs or the outputs associated with research and development activities (Nixon, 1998, p. 334).

A generic product development process includes five distinct (but partially overlapping) phases (see for example Nihtilä, 1996): concept development, system-level design, detail design, testing and refinement, and production ramp-up (Ulrich & Eppinger, 1995). Also, it is important to recognize that product development (and its performance measurement), which can be divided into several more homogenous subsections, does not concern only a small portion of an enterprise but rather the whole organization. Six sets of general new product development (cross-functional) activities are presented by Song and Montoya-Weiss (1998, p. 126). These include strategic planning, idea development and screening, business and market opportunity analysis, technical development, product testing, and product commercialization. Song and Montoya-Weiss have, however, found that while these activities describe the fundamental process of new product development, there is an essential variance across projects in terms of the details that are related to each set of activities. In this study, research is excluded from the definition of product development if it does not aim to produce commercial products. On the other hand, design is regarded not as a distinct phase of R&D but as one element of product development.

The process of research and new product development – from ideas to economic outcomes – can be depicted also as a system that consists of a number of subsystems. The inputs include people, ideas, different facilities, and funds. The processing system is the research and development itself, which turns the inputs into outputs including patents, new products, new processes, facts, or new knowledge. The receiving system comprises the consumers – both internal and external – of development outputs. Outcomes are those accomplishments of research and development that have value to the organization, including issues like sales volume of new products, cost reductions, market share, or preferable customer feedback concerning the products or services (Brown & Svenson, 1998) (Fig. 1).

The essence of effective product development process has been a popular topic in scientific literature (Repenning, 2001). Ulrich and Eppinger (1995) and Cooper (1996, 1997), for instance, have paid attention to defining a rigorous NPD process. Practice has proven, however, that many organizations have found it difficult to follow the defined processes. Repenning cites felicitously one engineer, when

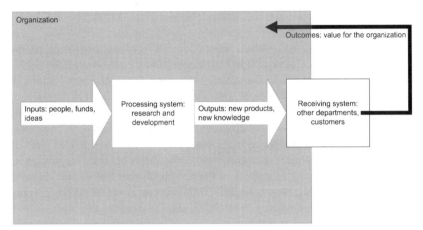

Fig. 1. System View of Product Development (Adapted from Brown & Svenson, 1998).

he describes his experiences with a newly implemented development process (Repenning, 2001, p. 285):

> The (new process) is a good one. Some day I'd like to work on a project that actually uses that.

One reason for this is a phenomenon called fire-fighting: an unplanned allocation of resources to solve problems that occur in late stages of the development cycle (Repenning, 2001). In practice, the process of innovation is often iterative. The iterative nature of innovation and product development means not only that certain problems have to be solved again and again but also that the emphasis of product development is dependable on the stage of the product's life cycle. During its life cycle, a product is likely to be subject to many types of innovations. In other words, innovations do not take place only in the product development phase. For instance at the beginning of the life cycle, the initial emphasis of the development may be on the product's general performance. Later, the main focus may be shifted to standardization or cost efficiency (see also Filson, 2002). The iterative nature of innovation results in a variety of different innovation types. The term "radical innovation" is typically associated with products at the early stages of their life cycle. In contrast, the term "incremental innovation" typically refers to a product that represents a more advanced stage of the life cycle (Garcia & Calantone, 2002). Although the border between incremental and innovative product development is not easy to draw, it can be said that the majority of industrial R&D investments are targeted to incremental product development activities. In terms of total money invested in product development, truly new products and new businesses are less emphasized (Jaakkola & Tunkelo, 1987).

3.5. Life Cycle

Life cycle orientation is to some extent a built-in characteristic of product development. However, to be able to fully understand the potential of the concept of life cycle for NPD management and measurement, different interpretations and perspectives of life cycle have to be discussed.

Dalén and Bolmsjö (1996), for example, point out that different components of a production system may have different life cycles. As a result, the estimation of life cycle costs of a product requires that a number of different life cycles can be identified. For instance, the employment cycle varies between employees and different machines differ in respect to the length of their life cycles. Also, the components of a product may have different life cycles from the product itself.

According to one definition, product life cycle is the period that starts with the initial product specification and ends with the withdrawal of the product from the marketplace. The life cycle is also characterized by a number of stages including research, development, introduction, maturity, decline, and abandonment (Player & Lacerda, 1999, p. 258). For the purposes of this study, this definition is, however, rather limited as it predominantly reflects the viewpoint of the producer. Seen from the perspectives of user, customer or society, it is hardly relevant to associate the withdrawal and end of life with each other. Especially regarding industrial goods with long life cycles, it is very likely that a product may continue its life even after the actual withdrawal.

The history of the concept of product life cycle dates back to the 1950s. However, the 1960s and 1970s witnessed the most impressive contributions regarding the definition and the utilization of the concept (Mercer, 1993). Perhaps the best-known critical review of the concept was published in 1976 (Dhalla & Yuspeh, 1976). Despite the general criticism targeted to the concept of PLC (see for example Grantham, 1997), inclusion of the concept of product life cycle provides additional dimensions for NPD performance measurement. According to Bauer and Fischer (2000, p. 704):

> Product life cycle theory, although suffering from a lack of generalization, is still an enduring framework in business. If this instrument is applied correctly and adapted to the specific empirical data set, it offers a large potential for analyzing the long-term economic performance of R&D activities.

It is suggested that the PLC concept, which was originally discussed in marketing theory and later utilized in analyzing and managing the environmental impacts of products, can also be useful in product development management and measurement. A part of this usefulness relates to the recognition of potential differences in product requirements that arise from different phases of PLC. From the NPD point of view this could be interpreted as indicating that the development work should rather focus on new product life cycles than on new products as such (Asiedu & Gu, 1998; Grossman, 2002).

A very important notice regards the dynamics of product life cycle. The traditional marketing view seems to imply that the PLC of a product is somehow a given period of time. However, this is often not the case. Grantham (1997) points out that if PLC is considered as given, it may result in self-fulfilling prophecy (that may also lead to overemphasis on new product development (Massey, 1999)). Therefore, product life cycle should not be considered as a passive phenomenon; rather, the PLC of virtually any product can be managed and affected. Also as suggested by Rink et al., it is worth acknowledging that PLC does not just happen with the passage of time; rather it is the result of the interaction between several companies' internal and external variables (Rink et al., 1999). As an example of an internal variable, Stadler (1991) addresses the issue of R&D dynamics in the product life cycle. He argues that it is possible to identify a generic pattern of R&D expenditure variations during the product life cycle for a successful entrepreneur (Stadler, 1991). Regarding the total effects of product development, it is important to recognize that products are developed not for a single moment of time but rather for a – shorter or longer – period, depending upon the specific industry and the type of product.

Marketing theory typically considers the life cycle curve that describes sales volume between product introduction and decline (see for example Rink et al., 1999) or (Magnan et al., 1999): the product life cycle depicts the sales of either product class, product form, or brand over its life. Environmental life cycle models have discussed phases that occur before, after, and during the period over which a customer applies the product (see for example Kane et al., 2000; Price & Coy, 2001). In R&D environment, a practical aim would be to identify the type of life cycle (including characteristic phases and corresponding product requirements) that is relevant in that particular environment. Several at least partly overlapping types of life cycles can be discussed that are associated with a new product or a product in general: first, there is product life cycle as seen and experienced by the customer; second, one can discuss product life cycle as perceived by the producer; third, life cycles of materials and components associated with the product can be analyzed separately. Further, each type of life cycle may consist of discrete phases that implicate different requirements for the product.

According to Dalén and Bolmsjö (1996), four phases comprise the life cycle for a production system. The first is called the concept and definition phase, the second is the acquisition phase, the third is labeled as the operation phase, and the fourth is the disposal phase. The end of the life cycle is defined as the moment of time when the costs of repair and maintenance increase to a level that is no longer profitable.

Hence, by interpreting the view of Dalén and Bolmsjö (1996), one could conclude that life cycle is defined as some kind of an "era of profitability." This seems to be consistent with the statement by Ryan and Riggs (1996) that a product should be marketed as long as it provides a return that minimizes opportunity costs. For a more comprehensive discussion concerning product deletion, see for example Harness (1998).

In the case of investment goods, the customer often utilizes the product for several years, which represents a substantial life cycle. Further, the period of interaction between the product and the customer can be divided into different phases that involve various requirements for the product. From the customer point of view, a product is tested for the first time when the customer is implementing it. General requirements associated with this might be, for instance, easiness of implementation, good instructions, or a logical interface. Another test – possibly the longest and the most significant one – is the phase of active use. General requirements associated with this phase include low maintenance and operations cost, product quality, and well-functioning customer support for the product. The final test might be the disposal of the product. During the last phase, quite different requirements, such as recyclability, may arise.

Product life cycle as seen by the producer is typically structured according to the development of sales. The generic PLC model implies the following successive life cycle phases: development, introduction, growth, maturity, and decline (Magnan et al., 1999; Massey, 1999; Prasad, 1997). Rink et al. (1999) depict product life cycle as a generalized model that describes the sales trend of a *narrowly defined* product from its market introduction to its removal. Furthermore, according to Rink et al. most products follow some kind of a life cycle curve. It is noted, however, that in some cases the seasonal patterns may override the PLC behavior of a product, resulting in a sales pattern that is different from the bell-shaped or S-curve presented in marketing textbooks. Overall, the requirements that arise from different life cycle phases may differ from each other. For instance in the introduction phase, it may be very important for the product to be able to awaken the interest of potential buyers by providing for example convincing technical specifications or industrial design. In the growth stage, the consistency between the product and the supply chain may be one of the most crucial issues, which would ensure a steady supply to the markets.

As one may conclude from the previous definitions, at the general level, the concept seems to be reasonably understandable and logically coherent. The concept of life cycle covers the various stages of the life of an entity representing its entire existence both as a whole (assembled, constructed) entity or as divided into parts that either will constitute or have constituted the very entity. However, depending on the perspective, PLC receives a number of meanings that differ from each other. Consistently, Prasad (1997), EPA (1993) and Mercer (1993) point out that the literature uses the term of life cycle rather loosely. One has to distinguish at least three different dimensions to look at the life cycle of a product:

(1) Product life cycle from the developer point of view
   (a) Level of individual product item: Provides a framework for the period and phases during which an individual product will be visible to its producer or developer. This view of PLC may imply life cycle phases such as development, production, sales, delivery, after sales (consisting of maintenance and spare part sales), disposal, or secondary use. For example, a cruise ship produced by a shipyard would be a fruitful subject to a life cycle analysis at this level. The ship is first designed as a response to individual customer needs and on the basis of an established concept of such a ship. After the ship is finished and delivered, the possible after sales business associated with the particular ship may constitute an additional phase to the life cycle. In addition, after the primary customer, the ship may be sold to a secondary owner.
   (b) Level of one product design: This is a typical aggregate marketing view that implies life cycle phases such as development, growth, maturity, and decline. The main focus of assessment may be on selling volume or cumulative profit impact. Depending on the purpose of the life cycle assessment, this view may also include life cycle phases analogous to 1a. For example, a certain cruise ship architecture representing a particular cruise ship concept would be a suitable unit of analysis in this respect. After its introduction, a particular architecture will live through an era during which it is capable of providing a competitive platform for individual customizations of marketable individual products. But gradually, due to, for instance, changing customer needs, increased competition, or renewed legislation the basic concept or architecture has to be changed.
(2) Product life cycle from the user point of view
   (c) Level of individual product item: An individual product would be the most likely basis for a user or for a customer to explore the life cycle of the product. This type of life cycle begins with the purchasing phase, after which the customer experiences some kind of a delivery and implementation phase. A learning process that is associated with an unfamiliar product may well constitute a phase of its own, after which the customer/user is likely to face a more stable stage of the life cycle, when the product is being utilized according to its primary purpose. This

mature phase may be followed by a phase that is characterized by an increased need for maintenance and renovation, and finally, the life of the product will end in a disposal of some kind. Basically any consumer product will follow an analogous life cycle, consider, for example, a pair of shoes or a car from the consumer point of view. Further, industrial products, such as paper machines or harvesters, would not make an exception.

(d) Level of one product design: The phases of the life cycle are quite similar to those assessed from the producer perspective. However, in this case, the life cycle normally begins with the product introduction, not with the design or development. Also, the user is not likely to emphasize the aggregate measures of life cycle such as the selling volume within a market. From the user point of view, the relative length of the individual product life cycle in respect to that of product design is far more interesting than the sales curve the product draws. Consider, for example, a set of china. The life cycle of individual item, as you know, may be rather unpredictable. An accidental dropping of a plate or bowl from a table may end the life of a product item. On the other hand, it may well be that the complete set of china survives a couple of generations in the family. Given the fragility of the product item, it is obvious that a long life cycle of the product design is perceived as valuable.

(3) Product life cycle from the environment/society point of view. This view covers the aspects that are related to the environmental and social impacts of a product. Also within this dimension, it would be appropriate to distinguish the levels of individual product and the product design. For instance, tobacco would be a beneficial example for a subject of environmental life cycle analysis. From the growing of tobacco plants to the increased risk for lung cancer (concerning both smokers and non-smokers), and further including harvesting the leafs, production and supply of the end product, the life cycle of tobacco covers a wide spectrum of issues both in terms of the time frame and the domains of effects related to the product.

3.6. Brief Synthesis of Core Concepts

Within the context of this study, *new product development performance measurement* is interpreted as the setting and articulating of the objectives for product development, the measurement of the outcomes of NPD, and the measurement of the variables associated with those outcomes that are present in a particular organizational environment. Product development (with or without the prefix new) is regarded as an activity that aims to develop and introduce products to the marketplace. Products – physical products and various services adjacent to them – represent the core outcomes of NPD through which a certain level of performance or certain objectives can be achieved. Performance measurement is interpreted here as the design of measurement frameworks and ideas as well as the construction of individual measures employed for these purposes.

No categorical distinction has been made between incremental or innovative products in terms of measuring the performance of their development. Inevitably, a developing company would be more familiar with the incremental products, which would enable better-grounded analyses regarding, for example, the requirements and life cycle of these products. However, the overall blueprint for measuring NPD performance is supposed to be applicable across a variety of settings.

Life cycle, or more specifically product life cycle, provides NPD performance measurement with a temporal frame that can be used for identifying and analyzing the requirements and goals that are associated with the developed products. The holistic view of product life cycle adopted for this study consists of the perspectives of producer/developer, customer/user, and society. Further, product life cycle can be identified – at least – on the levels of product class, product form, brand, design, and individual product item.

4. METHODOLOGY

4.1. Research Design

The methodological foundation of the study relies on conceptual analysis (Näsi, 1980, 1983) and on the case study approach (see e.g. Aaltio-Marjosola, 1999; Gummesson, 1993; Stake, 1995; Yin, 1994). The former is applied to construct a novel theoretical framework for supporting the performance measurement of new product development. This framework comprises the idea of "life cycle conscious" NPD performance measurement. The latter aims to provide the study with sufficient empirical background which would permit – on the basis of the conceptual analysis – the refinement and reflection of the constructed theoretical framework within a number of industrial settings. The case studies were focused to provide data on product life cycles and their distinct phases as well as on the requirements associated with life cycle phases within different industries.

As a research approach, conceptual research is generally applied for constructing conceptual frameworks or systems. As Olkkonen (1994) remarks, the developed conceptual framework may either be totally new or improved from a prior version. NPD performance measurement as such is a topic that has been widely and profoundly discussed; however, with few exceptions (see e.g. Brown & Svenson, 1998; Foster et al., 1985a, b; Krogh et al., 1988; Patterson, 1983), product life cycle has not been seriously taken into account in NPD performance measurement solutions (Meyer et al., 1997). Hence, the concept of product life cycle would provide fruitful ground for conceptual analysis that could enrich present measurement ideas regarding new product development.

The conducted case study includes six cases – six companies – that represent three different industries. However, the sample[6] for the study is reasonably homogeneous in as much as all the case companies are manufacturers of physical investment goods. The empirical data have been obtained mainly by using semi-structured interviews ($n = 13$). A product development manager or director was interviewed in each case; in addition, representatives from purchasing, after sales, manufacturing, sales and marketing were interviewed in one case company. Also, observations and other data sources such as direct observations, company presentations and archival data have been employed.

The questions that were employed in the interviews focused on the following main issues:

- The nature of product development in the case company.
- The general importance of a new product for the business of the case company.
- The length of product life cycles.
- The distinct phases of product life cycles and typical features of them: a picture of a good process/product as interpreted at different stages of life cycle.
- Product life cycle phases seen from the perspective of different corporate functions.

In order to respond to the validity challenges presented by Yin (1994), the interviewing process in all the cases followed a four-phase procedure (quite analogously to the procedure proposed by Goffin & New, 2001, p. 283): agreement on the interviews, conducting the actual interviews, writing a preliminary manuscript from the interview and feedback round. The agreements were made by phone, but the interviews were conducted person-to-person. In each case, after the researcher had finished the manuscript on the basis of the interview (within a couple of days after the company visit), the manuscript was sent to the company for a check-up and refinement. The feedback round enabled the inclusion of a variety of opinions from the company (other than that of interviewee) because the interviewee was instructed to circulate the interview manuscript among the key persons of the company to test the ideas and to reach a reasonable degree of consensus. In fact, at least some feedback was obtained from all the cases. After this feedback round, the analysis of the cases, including both within-case and cross-case analyses (see e.g. Eisenhardt, 1989), was performed.

4.2. *Generalizability and Validation of Results*

Applied sciences face a number of problems both at the beginning and at the end of the research process (Näsi, 1980b, p. 41). According to Näsi, the studies seldom resemble the realistic planning and decision-making situations (see also Kerssens-van Drongelen, 2001) and, in addition, significant questions arise when verifying and validating the research results. Qualitative research emphasizes deep understanding and explaining in the local context, as Alasuutari (1999, p. 55) portrays it. In a case study, the goal is not to generalize; rather the real business of a case study is particularization (Stake, 1995, p. 8). According to Stake (1995), Yin (1994) and Alasuutari (1999), actual (statistical) generalizations are completely the reserve of traditional survey studies.

By applying the principles of qualitative research, the problem of generalizability can be approached and solved at least to some degree. Qualitative research denies the dominance of statistical generalizations; yet qualitative methods are widely used, especially in social sciences. Qualitative research is applied to phenomena whose existence and therefore also the generalizability of the phenomena themselves cannot be questioned (Alasuutari, 1999, p. 237). If the principles of qualitative research are applied to conceptual research, the ability to define the population in which the developed conceptual framework would work becomes crucial. In other words, the researcher must be able to define the characteristics of an environment in which the framework would work. This is the foundation of contextual generalization (Lukka & Kasanen, 1995). Statistical generalization, such as that the framework would work in 70% of Finnish companies, is not required and not even expected to be given. The definition of the population, however, must be sufficiently exact so that the construction will work in every environment fulfilling the set preconditions. If this is not the case, the definition of the population needs to be changed. Furthermore, it has to be noticed that the researcher defines the population and therefore it is not necessarily related, for example, to a certain business.

Defining the population is closely related to the idea presented within the constructive research approach that the framework most likely should work in a "similar organization" (see for example Kasanen et al., 1991; Lyly-Yrjänäinen, 2003). The problem of the researcher is to define exactly what that "similar organization" is. Traditionally, this has been done by describing the operating environment of the case company at a detailed level, but the generalizability itself has rarely been commented on. The definition of population can be seen as a more advanced analysis compared to the description of the operating environment, and it will give at least some sort of understanding regarding the generalizability of the results.

Also according to Aaltio-Marjosola (1999), case study does not seek to generalize like survey research does (statistical or empirical generalization). However, in trying to gain understanding and to profoundly interpret particular cases within their real-life contexts, case study actually tries to identify the internal mechanisms and to organize the cause-effect-relationships of the cases in such a way that is rather similar to the traditional perception on generalization. In this respect, the amount of data is not crucial; rather, it is the soundness and sustainability of the inference that counts. Furthermore, Eskola and Suoranta (2001) suggest that instead of generalizability, qualitative research focuses on transferability of the findings: whether this inference can also be applied to different settings. Importantly, Aaltio-Marjosola (1999) suggests that the generalization cannot be the one and only purpose for scientific work. Sometimes, when issues are discussed in a very general level the actual content of the discussion gets very thin. The phenomenon becomes so general that it loses its contact with reality. Also Stake (1995) suggests that, first and foremost, a case study aims to catch "the complexity of a single case." Cases are not primarily studied for the purpose of understanding other cases. In general, two essential characteristics of qualitative research include orientation away from cause and effect explanation and holistic treatment of issues (Stake, 1995). Case study can be used as a feasible research instrument in this context.

In summary, the problem of generalizability can be solved fairly well using the arguments of qualitative research. However, validation and verification of the constructed framework may constitute another challenge. In the case of measurements, reliability refers to the exactness of the measurements, and validity, on the other hand, refers to the ability of the measure to measure the phenomena it is supposed to be measuring (see for example Niiniluoto, 1997, p. 187). However, according to McKinnon (1988), validity and reliability may be described at a broader level in respect to their applicability to research in general. According to her, validity is concerned with the question of whether the researcher is studying exactly the phenomenon he or she is claiming to study, neither more nor less, while reliability is concerned with whether the gathered data can be trusted.

According to Yin, reliability is concerned with the repeatability of the research. If someone else had gathered the data or formed the conclusions from the same information, he or she should have ended up with the same conclusions as well. To ensure validity[7] in case studies, Yin (1994, p. 33) proposes a number of tactics associated with construct, internal, and external validity. In short, construct validity is promoted by using multiple sources of evidence, by establishing a chain of evidence, and by having the key informants to review the draft case study report. Internal validity is built by doing pattern matching, explanation building, and by conducting a time-series analysis whenever possible. External validity can be improved by conducting several case studies, that is, by following replication logic in case studies.

In the conceptual research approach, construct validity could be seen to mean that the conceptual framework and its internal elements suit well the application in mind (very analogously to constructive research, see for example Lyly-Yrjänäinen, 2003). The tactics for improving the construct validity presented by Yin seem to be usable also in the conceptual research approach. The information required in forming the framework should be gathered from different sources and it is worth the trouble to allow a number of experts to comment on the framework and the ideas behind it. Careful and detailed description of the process will give the reader access to the logic in the creation process of the framework, thus maintaining the chain of evidence. Equally important when considering the chain of evidence is the preservation of the original documents created during the research process.

The purpose of internal validity is to rule out different types of disturbing factors affecting the research results. In that context, pattern matching means that empirical results are compared to the estimate or forecast created on the basis of theory. This has been done in this study as well, although internal validity is mainly a concern of causal studies (Yin, 1994). The researcher, however, must be aware of the four general threats to validity and reliability in a field study (McKinnon, 1988): observer-caused effects, observer bias, data access limitations, and the complexities and limitations of the human mind. The threats to internal validity of new product performance studies are mainly caused by the fact that it is difficult to develop rigorous experimental controls for the studies due to the fact that the researcher has to infer the relationship between a determinant of success and the performance either by using subjective interpretation or by relying on self-reported respondent information (Montoya-Weiss & Calantone, 1994).

When trying to increase the external validity, that is generalizability, the implementation of the conceptual framework in a number of settings is naturally a key question. However, it is not always possible to test the constructed framework in a number of companies, which also supports the significance of defining the population and the boundaries for applicability with regard to the generalizability of the framework. The following table refers to the issues or problems addressed by Leonard-Barton (1990) concerning retrospective case studies. Since these issues are relevant in this study also, each of the issues is briefly reviewed or discussed in terms of the purpose and realization of this study (Table 1).

When evaluating the role of the different dimensions of validity with regard this study, it seems clear that the external validity has only a limited importance – as discussed above – in a case study such as this. Second, construct validity, which refers to the operationalization of the construct of interest, seems always important in a study. The use of multiple sources of evidence whenever possible has been

Table 1. Discussion on the Issues Addressed by Leonard-Barton (1990)
Regarding this Study.

Research Activities	Issue
1. Data gathering	
Efficiency	Semi-structured interview platform. The structure of the interviews was communicated to the respondents in advance.
Objectivity	Data triangulation whenever possible: multiple interviewees, company documentation, feedback round.
Pattern recognition	Information on product life cycles and their distinct phases cumulated along the interviews: this enabled a gradual recognition of issues regarding PLC.
2. Establishing validity	
External validity	External validity is promoted by the definition of population or target group in which the results (the constructed framework) are applicable. Generalizability, as such, is not regarded as a primary aim of this study.
Internal validity	Cause-effect relationships are not of primary interest here. Pattern matching as a method of analysis is still applied to some extent. (Internal validity is a concern only for causal studies (Yin, 1994)).
Construct validity	The use of multiple sources of evidence and multiple cases are the core means to secure construct validity. Also the feedback round with the interview manuscript was intended to improve the validity of the findings.

the main instrument for improving the construct validity of the study. However, internal validity constitutes some kind of a dilemma regarding this study. As Yin (1994) points out, internal validity is mainly a concern of causal case studies. This study is not regarded as a causal study. For example, the study does not seek to produce explanations for the observed product life cycles in case studies. On the other hand, it could be argued that reaching a good internal validity even in a non-causal study could be able to improve the construct validity of the study. This would be possible because good internal validity would better facilitate for example the evaluation of the internal relationships between the concepts utilized in the study. In a multiple case study, this would improve the consistency of the constructs across the cases.

5. LITERATURE REVIEW

Literature review is one of the main sources of data in conceptual research. The following sections comprise the core findings made within three branches of literature: performance measurement, new product development and its management and measurement, and product life cycle. On the basis of this, the initial framework and blueprint for multifaceted NPD performance measurement is constructed.

5.1. Performance Measurement

Progress, growth, and improvement are issues, which are generally accepted as worth pursuing. In the business context, certain tools are needed to support the pursuit. Among them, performance measurement can be utilized for illustrating the progress achieved during a period of time in respect to the goals of an organization specified by the measures (Ijiri, 1975). An organization without well-defined performance criteria, through which the performance of individuals and the organization may be evaluated, would find it hard to plan and control the operation as well as motivate the employees (Globerson, 1985).

5.1.1. Relevance of the Discussion Concerning Performance Measurement
Overall, performance measurement is not a fundamentally new topic. In fact, it is a topic that has been widely discussed both by researchers and practitioners. In that sense, it could be assumed that any further discussion on this topic would have little value for anybody. Indeed, Neely (1999) remarks:

> Given that the 'basic management techniques' have been used for so long and that business performance measurement is undoubtedly one of these techniques, then surely most organisations should have had well developed performance measurement systems in place for many years by now.

Hence, all the problems and challenges associated with performance measurement would be solved? Even the briefest examination of the academic literature and practitioners' experience would confirm that this is not the case. There is a considerable interest around the issues related to good performance measurement (examples include Bourne et al., 2000; Ellis & Curtis, 1995; Euske et al., 1998; Kald & Nilsson, 2000; Kaplan & Norton, 2001; Laitinen, 1998; Lynch & Cross, 1995; Maisel, 1992; Nanni & Dixon, 1992; Suomala & Kulmala, 2001).

One of the most fundamental challenges of good measurement is presented by Ijiri (1975): normally performance measurement is not able to indicate whether this progress has been a result of a set of good decisions or just produced by *good luck* (Ijiri, 1975, pp. 179–189). The influence of good (or bad) luck on performance measures is certainly inconvenient as measurement is not only a passive representation of real life phenomena but it is also an active agent that affects real life through its influence on the decision-maker. Although performance measurement has traditionally illustrated the consequences of the decisions of the entity but not necessarily the causes that led to these consequences, it is very important for a performance measurement system to be able to show the essential cause-effect relationships within the measured phenomena. Especially in the case of output measures, it is at least an imperative to discuss the variety of factors that might have an effect on the measure. Otherwise, the decision-maker is likely to make distorted judgments on the basis of performance measurement.

Unfortunately, despite the fact that the cause-effect relationships have received more attention lately, many actual effects of performance measurement still remain open. This is the case with, for instance, the balanced scorecard (see Kaplan & Norton, 1996a, b). Although BSC includes the idea of cause-effect identification and measurement, it is a fact, as Ittner and Larcker (2001) remark, that despite the widespread adoption of the BSC, there is little hard evidence that a company's performance can be improved by its use. Due to this, essential value could be produced by conducting more work to explore the possible effects of measurement practices.

Because some of the fundamental issues regarding performance measurement have been identified already some 30 years ago, the question remains, as Neely puts it, why now? Why have so many people become so interested in business performance measurement so recently? The reasons have been classified into seven domains, including (Neely, 1999):

- The changing nature of work: the portion of direct labor cost from the total cost of goods sold seems to be less than before due to the heavy automation investment in many industries. Therefore, cost allocation on the basis of the distribution of direct cost is not feasible.
- Increasing competition: In the pressure of often global or at least international competition, organizations seek to differentiate in terms of quality of service, flexibility, customization, or innovation. Competing on the basis of non-financial factors means that organizations need information on how well they are performing across a range of dimensions.
- Specific improvement initiatives: As a response to increased competition, many organizations have built on different improvement initiatives. TQM, as one example, relies heavily on performance measurement. Before an organization is able to improve its operations, before it is capable of focusing on continuous improvement actions, it has to establish where and why its current performance is unacceptable. Hence there is a need for performance measures.

At least one issue can be added to this list. Vivid academic and practical discussion around the topic has certainly acted as an autocatalysis: discussion has encouraged more discussion, which in turn has triggered even more discussion. Perhaps the performance measurement boom cannot be totally explained using rational arguments.

In spite of this, as Neely (1999) remarks, there are many background issues regarding performance measurement that are very topical at the moment. On the other hand, there are issues that seem to be topical across decades. For example, nearly 20 years ago Uusi-Rauva (1986) stated that in the firm level, the accounting function should more effectively than before focus on the management of various activities of the operating processes instead of being interested primarily in the control of the financial process. Further, Ijiri (1975) points out that:

> Accounting measurement may then be characterized as primarily economic performance measurement, although in the future this field may be extended to include the performance measurement of social goals or even engineering goals.

These remarks are still relevant. Studies on performance measurement practices have shown that financial measures still seem to dominate the measurement culture although non-financial issues are also regarded as important. For example, Andersin et al. (1994) and Laakso (1997) conducted a survey of performance measurement practices. The survey was carried out back to 1992 and the focus was on Finnish metal industry firms. The response rate remained somewhat low: 123 responses out of 1350 sent questionnaires (9.1%). Anyhow, the analysis of the survey results showed that short-term financial measures are dominant. On the opposite end, employee- or supply-chain related measures are quite rare. The most common measures, according to the studies were, respectively:

(1) General financial measures (ca. 24% of all reported measures)
(2) Efficiency/effectiveness, productivity (ca. 21%)
(3) Ability to deliver (ca. 11%)
(4) Quality (ca. 11%)
(5) Sales (ca. 10%)
(6) Inventories (ca. 8%)
(7) Customers (ca. 7%)

In contrast, Ittner and Larcker (2001) surveyed 148 firms to clarify the managerial perceptions regarding to what extent different performance categories (both financial and non-financial ones) are important drivers for the organization's long-term success. The five most important performance categories were, in the order of the perceived average importance: customer, quality, operational, employee, and finance. Ittner and Larcker further remark that the non-financial categories were highly correlated, meaning that the respondents regard these domains of performance as substitutes.

The quality of present performance measurement solutions seems to be a concern. Ittner and Larcker (2001) found that the body of research and literature generally maintains that the selection of performance measures is a function of three aspects: organization's competitive environment, strategy, and organizational design. However, according to authors, the performance effects of these choices remain rather uncertain despite the research efforts. Further, a major limitation identified by Ittner and Larcker relates to the unsatisfactory quality of performance measurement. The authors compared the practitioners' ratings on the importance of different performance dimensions with the ratings on quality (scale of 1–7, where 1 = not important/poor quality, and 7 = very important/high quality). As a result, they showed that there are vast differences between the perceived importance and the quality of the performance measures. For instance, in customer related measures the average rating for importance was as high as 5.5 whereas the average rating for the measurement quality was about 3.8 (Ittner & Larcker, 2001).

As a conclusion, versatile and multidimensional measurement is certainly not a "done deal." On the other hand, Otley reminds that it is not realistic to assume that the research on performance measurement would result in a totally coherent outline of a rational set of control mechanisms well suited to the purposes for which they are intended. This is because individual measures or components of control systems may approach this degree of rationality but it is unlikely that the total package of control measures that are in place at any point in time will possess such a degree of coherence (Otley, 1999). Nevertheless, ideas concerning effective measurement practices, measurement frameworks and systems, and even individual measures should be further developed. In addition, more evidence is needed regarding the bottom-line effects of PM. The modern business environment calls for good performance measurement for supporting good performance. As Neely, suggests there are four fundamental questions that research regarding business performance seeks to address (Neely, 1999):

(1) What are the determinants of business performance?
(2) How can business performance be measured?
(3) How to decide which performance measures to adopt?
(4) How can the performance measurement system be managed?

As far as the present state of performance measurement literature is concerned, no single question is fully resolved. Within one application area – NPD – the foundation of this study relies on question two above. This study seeks to contribute to the question of how performance can be measured in product development.

5.1.2. Requirements for Good Performance Measurement

Performance measurement (PM) is most typically seen as a process that is intended to track the goal attainment of an organization (Gooderham, 2001). Hence at a general level, the focus of performance measurement lies on the effectiveness and efficiency of the operations. As there seems to exist a general agreement on the main purpose of performance measurement, many authors have collected lessons or advice that have been perceived as important in terms of achieving the objectives set for PM. Good performance measurement is a multidimensional question. Consistently, a wide range of different criteria and frameworks are presented in the literature (Neely et al., 1995). Gooderham (2001), for example, emphasizes the importance of an established link between the strategy of the organization and the measures (to provide means to identify the high-priority actions). Also Lingle and Schiemann (1994) argue (quite analogously to, for instance Brown, 1995; Grady, 1991; Kaplan & Norton, 1993–1996; Keegan et al., 1991; McMann & Nanni, 1994; Wisner & Fawcett, 1991) that the measures should be strategically anchored. In other words, measurement should be closely linked with business the strategy of the organization being evaluated. Lingle and Schiemann (1994) also propose a test of validity for the measures in terms of this principle: one should be able to determine the business strategy of the organization on the basis of the measures it applies.

Slater et al. (1997), similarly to many others, argue that performance measurement should be based on the strategy of the organization. However, they present a framework for strategy-based PM by relying on three generic strategies (presented by Treacy & Wiersema, 1993, 1995), which are further supplemented by a fourth "generic" strategy. These four strategic options – product leadership, operational excellence, customer intimacy and brand champion – are associated with a particular set of performance measures that are seen as the most relevant in each setting. Also the contingency theory of management accounting suggests that the choice of appropriate control techniques depends on the circumstances surrounding a specific organization. Key contingent variables include the strategy and objectives an organization chooses to pursue. That is, different strategy and different organizational plans are likely to cause different control system configurations (Otley, 1999).

Understanding cause-and-effect relationships seems to be equally important to strategy connection. Although those cannot be predicted with utmost accuracy, it is still important to reveal the *assumptions* about the relationships (Gooderham, 2001). Specifically, it has been argued that good measures should exhibit a direct cause-effect relationship instead of correlation relationships (Fry & Cox, 1989) (see Anderson & Fornell, 1994, for comparison). As an example of this, Fry and Cox (1989) found that firms that actually achieved high customer satisfaction also enjoyed superior economic returns (see also Ittner & Larcker, 1998a, b). An annual one-point increase in customer satisfaction had a net present value of $7.48 million over five years for a typical firm in Sweden. Given the average net income ($65 million) of the study's sample, this represented a cumulative increase of 11.5%.

According to Gooderham (2001), discussions regarding the priorities are also vital. In practice, assigning weights for measures means discussing priorities, which is a substantially important – and subjective – step in creating PM systems since measures with low weights may be very important in terms of overall goal attainment but would not receive sufficient attention until it is too late. Kennerlay and Neely (2002) refer to a number of criteria that are attributable to effective performance measurement, including – in addition to the previously mentioned – the ability to reflect the company's external environment, customer requirements, and internal objectives that are perceived as important.

In addition to these, Globerson (1985) proposes that performance criteria or measures have to fulfill the following conditions: First, they have to be derived from the company's objectives so that they are well aligned with the overall objectives and intent of the firm. Overall, it is important to make sure that the purpose of the criteria and the measures are clear for everyone. Second, the measures should facilitate benchmarking; they should enable the comparison of organizations in the same business. Third, the measures and criteria should be determined through discussions with the people involved and they should be under the control of the evaluated organizational unit.[8]

Further, Globerson (1985) suggested that it is important to have the data collection and calculating methods as clear as possible. Finally, ratios are preferred to absolute numbers and objective measures are preferred to subjective measures (Globerson, 1985). In line with the objectivity requirement, it has been suggested that the measures should reflect the outcomes rather than the activities themselves (Gooderham, 2001) (in contrast, see for example Keegan et al., 1991). At least when the number of feasible measures is very limited, one should concentrate on the results rather than on the doing. On the other hand, if one only measures outcomes, measurement is likely to produce little information on the case-effect relationships present in that environment.

The demand for consistency in PM systems is among the most important requirements. Performance measurement stimulates action towards certain directions (see Chenhall, 1997). It has been argued that the consistency of measures and the measurement framework is therefore important: as Neely (1995) cites Mintzberg (1978):

> . . . it is only through the consistency action that strategies are realized.

Keegan et al. (1991) underscore that performance measures should comprise an integrated set. Comprehensive utilization of performance indicators has been discussed quite early also in Finland (see for example Uusi-Rauva, 1986, 1996). One famous example of this is the Balanced scorecard, which seems to be the most extensively discussed performance measurement construct of the 1990s. Since the introduction of the concept in 1992 (Kaplan & Norton), an extensive number of authors and organizations (see for example Wahlström, 1998) have applied the Balanced scorecard approach for performance measurement (see for example Constantinides & Shank, 1994; Hoffeecker & Goldenberg, 1994; Maisel, 1992; McWilliams, 1996). Analogously to the balanced scorecard approach, Provost and Leddick (1993) propose that by taking into account the various stakeholders of an organization – owners, employees, customers, and communities – when measuring performance, an organization is able to avoid too narrow a focus that would result from the reliance on a single perspective. Also Schneiderman (1996a, b) underscores that good measures should be linked with stakeholder satisfaction.

Epstein and Manzoni (1997) remind us that French companies have been using a tool analogous to the Balanced scorecard for over 50 years (starting as early as in the 1940s) – called "Tableau de bord" (TDB). The logic behind TDB is quite similar to that of BSC. First, the strategy of an organization forms the basis for the measurement system. Second, on the basis of strategy formulation, a number of critical success factors are derived from the strategy. Third, performance indicators are developed to respond to the identified critical success factors. Both BSC and TDB recognize that non-financial and financial indicators of performance are needed, and they are regarded as substitutes for each other. On the other hand, according to Epstein and Manzoni (1997), many applications of TDB have somewhat failed to sufficiently emphasize non-financial indicators and measures that are derived from the company's external environment, including customer-based measures. Furthermore, Epstein and Manzoni (1997) suggest that the Balanced scorecard may have succeeded better in initializing communication and discussion within the organization in which it has been applied. However, it remains open whether this observed difference is due to the nature of the tools or caused by the different cultures of the organizations that apply the tools.

The concepts of the Balanced scorecard and its "relatives" underscore the view that performance measurement of an organization should take into account a number of perspectives or viewpoints. Performance can be comprehensively measured when it is assessed simultaneously from several directions (Kaplan & Norton, 1992, 1993, 1996a, b; Pillai et al., 2002, p. 168).

Quite analogously, it has been pointed out that focusing only on cost and efficiency when evaluating an organization's performance is not enough. Too many performance measurement systems have narrow or uni-dimensional focus. Also Fry and Cox (1989) stressed that local measures should be used with extreme caution. However, the authors do not advocate the elimination of local performance measures but they recommend analyzing the impact of the local measures on the more important global measures such as long-run profit and market share. They also recommend synchronizing the measures from supplier to customer and from short term to long term. In other words, according to Fry and Cox, measurement should be both multi-dimensional and consistent as a whole. As a reflection of this, Flapper et al. established a concept of "consistent performance management system" (PMS) (Flapper et al., 1996). By that they mean a system that is able to cover all aspects of performance that are relevant for the existence of an organization as a whole. As a solution, the authors propose a method for the construction of performance measures or indicators consisting of three steps (Flapper et al., 1996): Step 1, defining performance indicators, a preliminary list of indicator candidates for each function of an organization; Step 2, defining relationships between performance indicators. To assist this phase, classifications of indicators are proposed as practical means; Step 3, setting target values, values that trigger different actions on the basis of performance measurement. In addition to these, Lingle and Schiemann (1994) stress the importance of creating a counter-balance between the selected measures (supported also, for instance, by Brown (1995)). This is because improvements in other areas may result in degradation in others. Increased sales, for example, may in some occasions reflect decreasing profitability or product quality.

In addition to good results, Kim and Mauborgne (1998) stress the importance of a fair process. Even when the outcome of the process is desirable, a fair processing has been found important in terms of accepting the result and of overall satisfaction. This "fairness" theme is certainly relevant in the context of constructing performance measures as well: if the performance measures are not regarded as fair enough, one cannot expect to reach full benefits from the utilization of the measures. In creating a fair process, Kim and Mauborgne (1998) underscore the importance of three issues: engagement, explanation, and expectation clarity. In the performance measurement context, engagement can be translated as involving those individuals in the performance measures' creation process whose performance will be tracked or who will utilize the final measurement system in their work. Explanation means that those involved will understand why the decisions are made the way they are. Expectation clarity refers to a state when everyone knows what the standards to be met are (as demanding as the standards may be). Performance objectives may be very challenging to reach but it is still important to communicate the common objectives in a homogenous way for everyone.

As one synthesis of the literature, Neely et al. provide a list of recommendations for the design of performance measures. The list consists of 22 points, including remarks such as (Neely et al., 1995):

- Measures should be simple to understand (see also Ittner & Larcker, 1998a, b).
- PM should reflect the business process, that is both the supplier and customer should be involved in the definition of the measure.
- Performance measures should relate to specific goals and targets (see also McMann & Nanni, 1994).
- PM should be relevant.

Importantly, Flapper et al. note that in order to have a consistent performance management system, more is required than a (consistent) performance measurement system (see also Kerssens-van Drongelen & Cook, 1997). As this is clearly the case, it is unfortunate that the authors do not provide any further comments that would specify the nature or form of that "more."

In addition to all the previous issues, modern performance measurement should also facilitate learning and help to anticipate potential success and failure well in advance to prevent unnecessary drain of resources. According to Otley, performance measurement is a major mechanism that can be used to explicate the set of means-end relationships that the organization has developed to attain its strategic intent. Performance measurement should not only facilitate single-loop learning on the basis of feedback it provides but also double-loop learning to improve the system in such a way that prevents the same dysfunctional behavior to occur again and again (Otley, 1999). Pillai et al. (2002, p. 168) summarize that PM should provide help for continuously revalidating those assumptions that are made in the past. This should be done in the light of the knowledge gained from the present projects. The idea is to learn and to consider the requirements for future success. Hence, the importance of an integrated approach that links various phases of the project life cycle is underlined. Lingle and Schiemann (1994) point out that it is important to secure responsiveness to change. The longer the lag between acts and consequences, the more difficult it is to manage the situation. This is why organizations need to consider leading indicators that are able to – if not predict – but at least demonstrate the effect of potential future events.

An important point made by Lingle and Schiemann (1994) is that the measurement system should achieve a strong signal-to-noise relationship. That is, the validity of measures should be one of the principal concerns. The true message of a measure should not be interfered with "background noise" that would make the information communicated by the measure more difficult to interpret. In line with this, Brown (1995) stresses the importance of minimizing extraneous information that is not representative.

An optimal realization of performance measurement seems to depend, among other things, on culture. Namely, it has been found out that the national culture affects the choices of desired performance measures. For instance, cultural differences have been experienced in respect to individual or team performance measure preferences (Awasthi et al., 1998). Firm size has also been mentioned as a contingency variable of performance measurement system design: On the basis of analyzing both the Balanced scorecard system (Kaplan & Norton, 1992) and the performance pyramid model (Lynch & Cross, 1995), Laitinen (1996) proposes his own model for integrated performance measurement, especially for small businesses. Laitinen underscores causal links between measures and a sufficient number of perspectives to ensure a comprehensive view of performance. Performance measurement applications for small businesses have also been discussed by Chow et al. (1997).

5.1.3. Inappropriate Performance Measurement

As Johnson and Kaplan (1987) argue, good management accounting systems cannot assure success, and poor management accounting systems do not lead to automatic failure. However, an efficient and effective system does contribute to the survival of an organization. A number of factors have been associated with poor PM.

The main reasons or the primary sources of inappropriateness of performance measurement are: short-termism, the lack of strategic focus, and local optimization (Neely et al., 1995). Further, another typical shortcoming is that the measures encourage minimization of variance rather than continuous improvement (see for example Bourne et al., 2000; Johnson & Kaplan, 1987; Lynch & Cross, 1995). In addition, to be appropriate the measures should not be totally internal but also externally focused (for example Kaplan & Norton, 1992). Consistently, too narrow a focus has been considered as a major limitation of many financial and non-financial performance measurement studies. Performance seen as a consequence of something is associated with a number of antecedents that are also interdependent. Thus, a rather comprehensive stance is needed to attain the goal of identifying the regime of performance. Only by studying a single factor or an antecedent it may not be possible to disclose the most essential characteristics of processes related to good performance. Ittner and Larcker (2001, p. 373), for example, remarked that the value of many studies on non-financial performance measurement is limited due to the fact that these studies examine only one of many potential non-financial value drivers. As a result, misleading inferences are somewhat inherent in these studies if non-financial measures are highly correlated or if different non-financial value drivers are substitutes or complements for each other.

Santos et al. (2002) propose that one reason for failing performance measurement – observed in many organizations – is the lack of understanding concerning the relationships between specific performance measures. Santos et al. note that both the identification of appropriate measures and the consideration of potential trade-offs between measures can be supported if the relationships between the measures are discussed and understood. Some conceptual tools for this purpose have been proposed in the literature, including strategy maps (see for example Kaplan & Norton, 1996a, b) However, Santos et al. suggest that quantitative simulation (supplementing qualitative modeling) can produce value for the assessment of relationships between measures.

Ijiri speaks for unambiguous performance measurement. He notes that a number of measures that would be ideal from the standpoint of accurately reflecting the degree of achievement toward the goals of an organization have to be ruled out because they are impractical. He suggests that there are three main ingredients for hard measures – measures that are constructed in such a way that it is difficult for people to disagree – including (Ijiri, 1975): First, the measurement process has to begin with verifiable facts. If the measurement is based on fiction, opinions, or hypotheses, it will invite disagreement. Especially, Argyris points out that performance evaluation on the individual level is one of the things that may initiate defensive reasoning within an organization, thus creating a powerful obstacle to learning. Performance evaluation at this level represents a situation when professionals are forced to assess their performance and behavior against some formal standard. Thus, especially when the evaluation produces unsatisfactory ratings, professionals tend to rely on defensive reasoning that focuses on the claimed shortcomings of the evaluation rather than their own behavior that might provide relevant explanations for the ratings (Argyris, 1991).

Second, according to Ijiri (1975), the measurement process has to be well specified in such a way that it enables all the stakeholders of measurement to judge if the measurement rules used for transforming the input into actual figures are justified or not. Third, the number of measurement rules applicable for a given situation should be restricted. This is necessary in order to be able to secure the consistency of the measurement system.

The ingredients presented by Ijiri (1975) seem to be well grounded and logical. However, regarding the first one, hypotheses or opinions cannot be totally avoided in measurement situations that are focused on future events. For instance in product development, measurement may employ sensitivity analyses and scenarios that are based on assumptions, opinions, and anticipations. In spite of the fact that they can be disagreed on, they can still be very useful for structuring and analyzing the potential impacts and effects of new products. If nothing more, even measures that are not founded on hard facts could be able to provide the organization with a common framework and language that helps to more effectively organize the activity being measured. In addition, even though the measurement may *begin* with assumptions it can proceed into facts. Again in the case of product development, the assumptions made at the initial stages can be verified later in the life cycle when more evidence regarding product performance, markets, and customers is available.

Ittner and Larcker (2001, p. 377) argue that the selection of performance measures should be made on the basis of value driver analysis. However, contrary to this need, many of the empirical studies in the field somewhat ignore the analysis of value drivers. According to the literature review by Ittner and Larcker (2001), many studies proceed directly from the organizational design, strategy, or technology choices to appropriate performance measures. A failure in identifying the core issues – such as value drivers – may lead to too large a number of performance measures, which in turn might constitute an organizational problem. First, management may find it difficult to effectively employ and benefit from information if its supply becomes too extensive. Second, information is a resource and all resources are associated with costs (Upchurch, 2002). Therefore, rather than a large amount of information as such, the high quality and appropriateness of information should be considered the primary objective.

5.1.4. Dynamics Associated with Performance Measurement

Palmer and Parker (2001) discuss the deterministic assumptions about the world on which, according to the authors, dominant performance measurement models are largely based. The authors argue that the physical world has a fundamental uncertainty – grounded in two properties: sensitive dependence on initial conditions ("butterfly effect") and the impossibility to measure without participation (measurement always affects the system) – at its core. Palmer and Parker (2001) address the question of what lessons can be drawn from this notion in terms of management and performance measurement systems. They argue that aggregation of measures – concentration on "significant few" – is more useful than the attempts to measure at an individual or detailed level.

Also Ittner and Larcker (1998a, b) underscore that a very diverse set of performance measures is likely to cause managers to spread their efforts over too many objectives, which would reduce the overall effectiveness of the performance measurement system due to an "information overload" and a lack of focus. This phenomenon is reported as a typical shortcoming in many balanced scorecard implementations (Ittner & Larcker, 1998a, b, pp. 226–227).

Palmer and Parker (2001) put forward that rather than trying to correlate inputs with certain outputs, it is more useful to aggregate individual elements to help to determine which inputs are linked to many more elements within an organization. Furthermore, according to the authors, such a focus on critical few can initiate spontaneous and valuable self-organization that will result in the system being better aligned with the environment.

In many cases, however, self-organization of measures would be too optimistic an assumption. For instance, Vaivio (1999) discussed the emergence of non-financial performance measures. Among other things, he showed how the non-financial measures became embedded into management processes. The study illustrated that the systemization and evolution of non-financial performance measurement at the firm level can be a disciplined and intended effort indeed. In Vaivio's study, the systemization process did not organize itself but it was driven by a key actor. In addition, it required collaboration that provided the sufficient functional expertise. Vaivio (1999) pointed out the role of non-financial measures as a vehicle for focused interactive control. With the assistance of measures, the search for relevant knowledge and the emergence of new solutions were kept within and forced into tolerable limits.

Also Kennerlay and Neely (2002) point out that performance measurement should be a dynamic phenomenon: the measures and the measurement system have to be modified as the circumstances change. However, as a number of drivers of change can be identified (that cause the change to be necessary), one may observe that also a number of barriers for the change exist. According to Kennerlay and Neely (2002), the effective management of a PM evolution requires considering the following lessons: the active use of PM system is a prerequisite for evolution, three interrelated elements of a PM system – individual measures, the set of measures, and the enabling infrastructure – should all be considered during the evolution process, and four stages of evolution that form a continuous cycle exist: use, reflect, modify, and deploy.

5.1.5. Financial vs. Nonfinancial Measurement

Eccles (1991) points out that ever since double-entry bookkeeping was invented in the fifteenth century, accountants have developed financial performance evaluation methods. As a result, these methods are relatively developed at the moment. Still, supplementing the argument made by Eccles (1991), a word of caution is necessary: despite the fact that the financial performance evaluation *methods* are rather well-developed, financial evaluation *practices* at a firm level are often unsatisfactory and sometimes unreliable and misleading.

Nevertheless, in contrast with the substantial efforts to measure financial performance, efforts to measure, for example, the innovation activity have been relatively modest. According to Eccles (1991), significant resources are needed to be able to place new non-financial measures on an equal footing with financial data measures. Because many critical success factors cannot be measured by using financial measures, companies have adopted non-financial performance measures to supplement the financial measures (see for example Fisher, 1992). Non-financial measures may include, for instance, measures of customer satisfaction, quality, innovation, flexibility, efficiency, and effectiveness (Brinker, 1997).

Overall, it could be argued that performance measurement should basically incorporate any financial or non-financial measure that is able to provide incremental information on the managerial effort (Ittner & Larcker, 1998a, b). This, however, should be done subject to its cost. Among many other relevant issues in this domain, the balance between financial and non-financial performance measurement is one of the topics that has received substantial attention in the literature. It is argued, for instance, that the heavy emphasis placed on financial measures is not consistent with their relative importance (Ittner & Larcker, 1998a, b, pp. 206–207). Despite the relative emphasis on different types of measures, the perceived importance of performance measurement nevertheless seems to be increasing over time (see for example Ittner & Larcker, 1998a, b, p. 207).

Taking into account that an organization applying non-financial measures would still simultaneously apply also financial measures, the question of the interpretation of figures produced by indicators is interesting. As McNair et al. (1990) ask: do financial and non-financial measures have to agree? According to the authors, the answer is twofold. If permanent changes have occurred, either in terms of capacity, methods, or costs, all the measures should be synchronized. If, on the other hand, the differences between financial and non-financial figures represent volume-based effects or phenomena that will smooth over longer run, a balance between measures is not necessary. McNair (2000) also argues that interpreting the financial and non-financial signals of the business is primarily a management issue instead of an accounting concern. This argument seems to be in line with the idea that performance measurement and management accounting are tools that should be utilized responsibly. Any tools can be used ineffectively or hazardously if necessary caution is not practiced.

Consistently, Drucker (1994) suggests that financial accounting, profit-loss statements, and balance sheets are an X-ray of an organization's skeleton. But he also argues that much as the diseases people most commonly die from, such as heart disease or cancer, cannot be avoided by X-ray diagnostics, an organizational failure does not register in the accountant's figures until the damage has been done. Hence, according to Drucker, organizations need various leading and lagging indicators to point out the directions in which the environment and the organization is likely to proceed.

The claim that non-financial performance measures are the leading indicators of a firm's financial performance is problematic at least to some extent. Namely, it is a typical challenge with non-financial performance measures to show that the financial consequences of initiatives related to non-financial issues actually impact financial performance (see for example Ittner & Larcker, 1998a, b, pp. 218–220). Well in line with this, the adopters of the Balanced scorecard approach tend to place a substantial emphasis on the financial measures (56% of weight, compared to 15% to customer measures and 12% to internal process measures) (Ittner & Larcker, 1998a, b, p. 221). As regards the fundamental effects of PM, Ittner and Larcker (1998a, b) recognize that performance consequences that can be observed in performance measurement applications may represent merely a Hawthorne[9] effect and specific measures may only have marginal importance.

Non-financial performance measurement tends to focus on issues that are easy to measure, despite their importance. Important issues are rarely measured if the measurement is perceived as very challenging (Stivers et al., 1998). There are also aspects of performance that are not measured, although they are perceived as important, because the measurement would distort the process being measured (Otley, 1999). Due to the reason that there are many intangible factors that affect the success of an organization but that are very difficult to explicitly and quantitatively measure, Rangone (1997) proposes a fuzzy linguistic framework for assessing and modeling the imprecision related to these factors. The fuzzy framework, according to (Rangone, 1997), allows a proper handling of uncertainty and ambiguity associated with intangible success factors.

As a branch of non-financial measurement, environmental performance measurement has been advocated, for instance, by arguing that business has an ecological and social impact in addition to an economic one. It is also reminded that the environmental management of a corporation is often good business. (see for example (Eckel et al., 1992; Lawrence & Cerf, 1995)). Environmental performance measures would include both the measures of inputs and outputs. Suggested input measures include expenditures on environmental matters and the existence of recycling programs or employee education. Output measures would include, for instance, the volume of materials processed by internal and waste recycling programs, the volume of waste material generated, and monetary value of damages to the natural and social environment (Eckel et al., 1992).

5.1.6. Summary
Given the extensiveness of the literature on performance measurement, it would not be totally feasible to summarize all the key findings only by using a few bullet points. However, the following list comprises the themes that seem to be repeated by many studies and concerning these, a reasonable consensus seems to exist.

- Measures and measurement systems should be constructed from top down: from the strategies and objectives to ensure consistency.

- Internal coherence of measurement is important.
- Measurement should facilitate learning, learning from past mistakes.
- Measurement should provide means for anticipating some future effects.
- Measures should focus on outcomes, results, and achievements.
- Comprehensiveness and multidimensionality: external orientation and the inclusion of several stakeholders is recommended.
- Cause-effect relationships should be identified.

5.2. New Product Development Management

Networking and supply chain integration have affected the role of product development in a value chain. Development is – even if actually carried out by one firm – not necessarily only the concern of a single firm within a value chain. When the effects of product development extend over the boundaries of a single firm, also the role of product development carried out by a single actor may change substantially: A modern view of research and development includes a perception according to which the customers think of the supplier's research as theirs (Miller, 1995). Also, the success of a company developing new products depends on the success of the entire value chain the company is part of. This is an especially important notion for the companies that develop and produce industrial products – that is products that can be regarded as investment goods. Hence, the objective to help to increase the performance of the customer companies is one of the most important ones for industrial NPD (Kärkkäinen et al., 2001). As a result, the challenges of product development seem to be even more versatile than before. For generating profits through product development, the need to understand the process of customer value creation, for example, is underscored in product development management.

Further, Lichtenberg (1990) advocated that to make appropriate R&D expenditure decisions, firms need reliable data on research and development. Indeed, according to Morbey (1988), statistical analysis of data on the sales growth, R&D spending, and profit growth of U.S. companies covering a ten-year period from 1976 to 1985 showed that there is a strong association between sales growth and spending on research and development. However, Morbey (1988) acknowledges that R&D spending – though very important – is only one of the factors that affect the sales growth. The effect can also vary from one market to another (Hall & Bagchi-Sen, 2002). Furthermore, no significant relationship was found between R&D intensity and profitability. Quite to the contrary, at an aggregate level (including the data of all industries) a negative association was found between these two variables. In other words, when profitability declined,

R&D intensity increased. Overall, the findings made by Morbey (1988) seem to suggest that to maintain its competitiveness, an organization has to invest in R&D in order to maintain or increase the sales volume. But for maintaining its profitability, however, a high R&D spending *per se* is not enough. Rather, the organization has to simultaneously master a variety of other disciplines as well.

5.2.1. Need and Role of NPD Performance Measurement

On a general level, the importance of R&D performance measurement seems obvious. It has been pointed out that the role of performance measurement in ensuring the success of a new product development project and in securing the project's usefulness to the organization is important. It has also been shown that performance measurement and the specific metrics utilized actually affect the performance achieved by NPD (Pillai et al., 2002). Overall, the potential contribution of management accounting to new product development is quite well acknowledged and demonstrated (see for example Uusi-Rauva & Paranko, 1998). In many cases, however, practice shows that many industrial companies have not been able to fully utilize the potential of management accounting to promote successful and cost effective product development. For instance, studying the role and the contribution of accountants in new product development has revealed that accounting is consistently ranked as the least important functional team member in cross-functional product development teams (Rabino, 2001). According to the evidence presented by Rabino (2001), accounting was the most likely member of the team to be disregarded. In his survey, 66% of respondents did not include accountants as product development team members at all. However, it is not clear to what extent the reluctance is based on an interpretation according to which accounting and bookkeeping are more or less the same thing. In other words, it could be possible that the reluctance is rather due to the notorious reputation of the accounting function than doubts regarding the usefulness of accounting or measurement information per se.

Among many other issues, the need for performance measurement is founded on the notion that product development is a function that has to be managed in a well-organized way:

> A 'strategy of hope' approach to R&D management has been replaced by a very systematic, disciplined one that emphasizes contribution to shareholder and customer value (Pearson et al., 2000).

The more difficult question is then what should be measured in the R&D context. Ellis argues that without objectively measuring the process of innovation,[10] one is not able to determine whether expenditures on R&D are beneficial or not. Both the desired outcomes and the inputs and R&D processes that contribute to these outcomes should be measured (Ellis, 1997, p. 3). Consistently, McLeod suggests several factors that should be taken into account when selecting R&D projects, including probability of success, time to first sales, profitability, and compatibility with the company's long-term plans (strategy). However, it is argued that there is little point in trying to give the factors any order of priority. According to McLeod, all these factors should be considered as a whole. The construction of numerical indices, struggling with figures, and scoring the projects is not seen as beneficial (McLeod, 1988, p. 254). Indeed, inasmuch as literature is rich with suggestions for measuring NPD, it seems reasonable to argue that performance measurement is no longer excluded from product development activities. Attempts have been made to establish measurement principles, systems, and individual measures for the research and development environment. To a great extent, however, the research focusing on product development performance measurement has not been able to produce effective and powerful practices and support to actually carry out the measurement in product development. For instance, a profound analysis of a proper construction process for NPD performance measures or for an NPD measurement system is virtually absent (Kerssens-van Drongelen & Bilderbeek, 1999). It has also been pointed out that in many cases information needs during the product development process are not matched by the supply of information (Batson, 1987). Further, it has been argued that there is a gap between the methods and approaches proposed in the literature, and the methods that are actually observed in practice (Kerssens-van Drongelen & Bilderbeek, 1999).

Despite the widely acknowledged need for performance measures in NPD, sometimes the act of measurement is thought to restrict and discourage creativity that is seen as a prerequisite for research and development. This kind of view implies that the management of the company should be content with *a faith* that the development actually produces value for the organization. Without measuring the activity, managers are thus expected to *believe* that the development of a new product is an economic investment. It has been stressed that this kind of naïve belief is not appropriate: R&D is not only expected to produce and develop new products and processes but also to show their value to the organization (Brown & Svenson, 1998). However, managing R&D strictly by measures can also be misleading if inferences are made too loosely. A promising project does not have to be a major success according to all R&D metrics. Partly because of the uncertainty associated with long-term future events affecting the success criteria of new product development, it sometimes might be necessary also to encourage those projects that are not in line with the selected R&D metrics. Abetti points out that the long-term payoff for R&D might require faith in the value of exploratory research (also), which allows more freedom to create than does applied research or development (Abetti, 2002). A multidimensional and structured set of metrics is likely to present the aspects of R&D in a form that enables managers to consider both the long-term and short-term effects of R&D for various stakeholders. Therefore, multidimensional measurement aims at reducing the risk of abandoning or promoting projects on too weak grounds. The findings made by Davis et al. (2001) are in line with this. Davis et al. noted that the probability of commercial success of a project is affected by a number of factors that should be considered when making R&D decisions. Further, the logic of multifaceted measurement is also supported by Cooper and Kleinschmidt (1995), who point out that new product performance is a multidimensional concept. Therefore, a single measure for NPD performance monitoring may not be enough (see also Griffin & Page, 1996).

5.2.2. What is Pursued: The Essence of NPD Success and Performance?

If an outcome-oriented definition of performance is adopted, the success and performance of new products can be perceived virtually as synonyms. NPD performance and success are multidimensional concepts that have received a number of different interpretations and definitions. The following summarizes both the explicit and implicit ones presented in the literature.

First, according to a very general definition, success is the degree to which the product met the firm's profit objectives for this product (Song & Montoya-Weiss, 1998). Second, Brown and Eisenhardt have collected and synthesized a wide body of new product development literature. They have identified three main streams of research: "rational plan" built on the studies by Myers and Marquis (1969), "communication web" originated by Allen (1971, 1977) at MIT, and finally, problem-solving by Imai and colleagues (1985). In each stream, the conception of new product development success seems to be slightly different. As the rational stream interprets success mainly as financial success consisting of, for example, profits, sales, and market share, the communication stream deals with success that is mostly perceptual by its nature: success is defined by a subjective team and management ratings. The problem solving stream concentrates on the operational success concerning more specific issues such as speed or productivity (Brown & Eisenhardt, 1995).

Gomes et al. (2003) explored the relationship between functional intra-organizational integration and new product performance under different conditions of new product project uncertainty. However, the definition of new product performance employed in their survey was a rather narrow one (but a very common one, too). The performance was measured by three budget-type measures:

- Time for development: launched before or after the anticipated time.
- Cost: project cost less or more than budgeted.
- Quality of end product: lower or higher quality than expected.

Taking into account that the authors used survey as their research instrument, the selected measures of success raise a number of questions. First, on the basis of mail survey it is very challenging to obtain reliable information about the real goals employed in respect to time, cost, and quality. Second, relying on the relative measures of success causes difficulties to determine whether a project had actually succeeded or had only attained the goals set for its development but nevertheless failed in the market. Finally, other end product-related aspects than perceived quality were not inquired. In effect, the success of the actual outcomes of NPD is left almost totally unexplored.

Also according to Terwiesch et al., generally discussed NPD performance dimensions have been illustrated through three perspectives (Terwiesch et al., 1998): development time, cost, and quality. Further, some studies such as the one by Brown and Eisenhardt (1995), have added a suggestion that relevant performance dimensions for product development cannot be generalized across different industries, that is, market contexts. Nevertheless, Terwiesch et al. made an interesting observation that *the effect of development performance on the business success was the most significant in slow-growth markets and in markets with long PLC's.* Also, the results showed that NPD performance has a more important role for explaining the profitability of dominant firms than that of firms with low market shares. (Terwiesch et al., 1998). In their study, product development performance was assessed by using five measures (Terwiesch et al., 1998):

- Market leadership: the percentage of significant product innovations that were first to market in the reported period.
- Technical product performance: self-assessed technical performance of the product related to competition.
- Product line freshness: percentage of sales from the products introduced within the previous three years.
- Innovation rate: product life cycle in years multiplied by the number of essential product line changes within the previous three years, further normalized as the relative deviation from the industry mean value.
- Development intensity: the number of development personnel for the product group in question divided by respective revenues.

Above all, NPD success seems to be a relative concept: Dougherty studied interpretative barriers to successful product innovation in large firms. Her study covered four successful cases, seven uncertain cases, and six cases that failed. Successful products were those that met or exceeded the expectations after their introduction. In contrast, failed products were those that were introduced but subsequently canceled. In the midst of these, uncertain products were not canceled but they did not quite meet the expectations (Dougherty, 1990, 1992). Griffin has analyzed product development cycle times of business-to-business products using absolute numbers. Among other things, she has investigated the relationship between the cycle times and product success. Griffin employed seven success measures – including, for instance, new product sales as a percentage of total sales and new product profits as a percentage of total profits – that covered three distinct success dimensions: overall success compared to competitors, success compared to the organization's objectives, and market or financial success (Griffin, 2002).

Shenhar et al. (2002) have established three success dimensions in their study, including: (1) meeting design goals; (2) benefits to customers; and (3) commercial success and future potential. These dimensions contain altogether 13 measures of success. However, the authors note that their study yielded a major insight that the list of project success factors is far from universal. In another study concentrating on the role of launch in NPD success, the concept of "success" was measured with relative market share, total sales, months to break even, and the size of the served market. In this study, Oakley found that in order to reach the full benefits of NPD, companies should set ambitious objectives for the product launch and place emphasis on the early introduction into foreign markets (Oakley, 1996).

Further, Cooper (1996) and Cooper and Kleinschmidt (1995) have identified 10 different measures, including the percentage of sales by new products, success rates, impact on the firm, and the overall profitability of the business's total new product efforts. In fact, provided that it is challenging to define the term success in the first place, it is interesting that the literature is full of more or less anecdotal statements regarding the probability of success. For instance, "about 60% of developed products actually will become a commercial success" (Cooper, 1985, p. 34).

In addition, the concept of product success can be extended over the primary product: Goffin remarks that among the many things a product's design influences, one of great importance is the issue of customer support requirements. Product support or after-sales service is important for many manufactures not only because it serves as a means to achieve financial benefits through lifetime support revenues that may be essentially higher than the initial product revenue, but also because it is vital for achieving customer satisfaction and competitive advantage (Goffin & New, 2001). Also, Lele (1986) notes that product design is a key factor that affects the efficiency and economics of customer support. Thus, there seems to be a need to also consider customer support during the NPD process. Goffin suggests that ignoring service issues – including for instance installation times, fault diagnosis times, field access times, repair costs, or user training times – in the development process might lead to products being difficult to repair, products which have high warranty and service costs (Goffin & New, 2001).

Further complicating the concept of success, the objectives of different stakeholders for the new product may occasionally be contradictory. For instance, Goffin and New (2001) has found that the primary objective of the manufacturing department may be to reduce assembly costs, which could be seen as an opposing objective for that of the after sales department. This is due to the perception that a product that is easy to manufacture might be difficult to repair at customers' sites.

Foster et al. (1985a, b) have provided a feasible approach to structure R&D performance. The authors distinguish between R&D return (the ratio of profits and investments), R&D productivity (the ratio of technical progress and R&D investment), and R&D yield (the ratio of profits and technical progress). It has been argued that productivity and yield may be rather independent. For example, a positive R&D productivity illustrates that technical progress is possible but for instance due to poor cost efficiency or overcapacity within the industry, the R&D yield may be negative. Quite similarly, according to Ernst and Ross (1993), the profit from R&D is a function of two variables: (1) R&D productivity, which relates to technical progress made for a given level of investment. (2) R&D yield, which is interpreted as the amount of profit made from the achieved technological progress. On the basis of this distinction, it can be pointed out that a company may have high R&D productivity but zero R&D yield, for instance, due to technology development that is not able to currently produce value for the customer. Using this framework for R&D performance, one may observe that R&D performance cannot be comprehensively evaluated on the basis of one variable but the evaluation should cover (at least) both the aspects of productivity and yield.

5.2.3. Drivers of Success and Performance

It is of interest to both practitioners and academics to pursuit drivers of good new product development performance. Given the rather significant spending on NPD activities across industries and research institutions, some indications concerning the drivers of successful product development would be necessary. Consistently, a rather extensive body of literature has focused on the drivers of NPD performance. Regarding this literature, it is important to recognize that models that are intended for selecting and screening product development projects include at least an implicit premise or assumption that successful projects can be identified in the development stage. That is, these models are based on a belief that a desirable profile for a project actually exists and that the profile is also reasonably capable of predicting the project's outcome (see for example Cooper, 1985, p. 37).

A good fit between the product and user need is one of the most fundamental issues facilitating success. Dougherty reminds that successful innovators – from the commercial point of view – understand the user needs better than their failed counterparts (Dougherty, 1990). It is an imperative that new products are relevant to the needs of the end user (Hirons et al., 1998). In the same spirit Cooper (1996) advocates the facilitators of success: (1) A high-quality new product process that is characterized by: up-front homework on predevelopment work, sharp and early product definition before the development actually started, based on the strong focus on the customer ("voice of the customer") throughout. (2) A clear and well-communicated new product strategy for the business unit that sets the objectives and describes the contribution of NPD to the overall corporate goal. Also recognizes the long-term nature of new product activities. (3) Adequate resources for NPD: sufficient budget and the necessary people available.

An even more comprehensive list was published three years later. Cooper identifies eight denominators of successful NPD. Levers, as Cooper calls them, that one can pull to heighten one's odds of success are (Cooper, 1999):

(1) Up-front homework before proceeding further from the idea stage
(2) Building in the voice of the customer
(3) Seeking differentiated and superior products
(4) Early and stable product definition before actual development
(5) Strong market launch
(6) Tough go/kill decision points
(7) Organizing around cross-functional project teams
(8) Building an international orientation into NPD process

In addition to the previous list, Cooper and Kleinschmidt have also stressed the importance of a well-defined new product strategy, adequate resources (needed people), and spending on NPD in an earlier study (Cooper & Kleinschmidt, 1996). Furthermore, Ottum and Moore have investigated the role of market information in new product success or failure in their study. They have shown that there is a strong relationship between market information processing and new product success. Ottum and Moore stress that effective market information processing requires not only good quality information gathering but also good effort in sharing and using that information (Ottum & Moore, 1997). However, to the extent of customer involvement in NPD there is also somewhat different evidence available. Namely, it is argued that there is no automatic short-term commercial benefit associated with customer partnering when compared to in-house development. Possible explanations for this – as the authors put it, "surprising lack of impact of partnering on new product performance" – may be that the risk-level or complexity differ between in-house and partnering projects or that the quality of collaboration happened to be poor in the sample partnerships. The authors also remind that in the long term, partnering may be important to gain access to customers or to elicit learning (Campbell & Cooper, 1999).

Zirger and Maidique conducted a study that analyzed the success or failure of 172 electronics products. Success was measured by financial terms: the more the product contributed to profitability, the more successful it was considered. They found five major issues that affect the success of a new product (Zirger & Maidique, 1990):

(1) Managerial excellence: Products are likely to succeed if they are planned and implemented well. This includes good coordination, proper monitoring, and efficient product champions that are able to nurture the project through development.
(2) New products should provide significant value to the customer: Value can take several forms. It can be related to superior technical performance, to lower price due to a cost efficient design, or it can be associated with a set of unique features.
(3) Strategic focus: Products that are based on the company's existing technological, marketing, or organizational competences should be preferred. However, without any ventures in new directions, the company will soon exhaust the potential of its present product lines.
(4) Management commitment: Without support from the management, the necessary resources for the development are not likely to be approved. To secure the support, it is suggested that the new product team should be able to clearly demonstrate the market need for the new product.
(5) Market environment: Products that are first to the market and experience little competition are likely to be successful.

Poolton and Barclay (1998) have collected a number of factors that are associated with the development success of new products. They have organized them into two classes: tactical and strategic. Tactical factors include, for instance, good communication (internal and external), innovation as a corporate-wide activity, high quality of management, key individuals, understanding user needs, and good after-sales service for the products. Strategic factors include, for instance, management support for innovation, long-term strategy with a focus on innovation, long-term commitment to major projects, and acceptance of risk. Davis et al. propose five factors of technical probability of success for R&D projects including: proprietary position, competencies and skills, complexity, access to external technology, and manufacturing capability. Further, they introduce six factors of commercial probability for success including: customer and market need; market and brand recognition; distribution channels; customer strength; raw materials supply; and environment, health and safety (Davis et al., 2001). Pinto and Slevin have identified ten factors that are critical to and predictive of success for R&D projects including project mission, top management support, client consultation, personnel, client acceptance, monitoring and feedback, and communication. The order of importance of these factors is further depending on the stage of the NPD project life cycle. The life cycle of the project is organized around four stages: conceptual, planning, execution, and termination (Pinto & Slevin, 1989) In addition, to further extend the list of success factors, the following factors having a statistically significant impact on the R&D success of related new products at 3M have been identified (Krogh et al., 1988):

- The competitive position of the business unit developing the product.
- The firm's product performance in relation to competition.
- Degree to which the technology being developed is related to the existing technical base of the firm.
- Degree to which the market of the product being developed is related to the existing business base of the firm.

In addition, provided that the success of a product is a temporal variable, also the factors affecting success have a temporal dimension. Clark and Fujimoto point out that inasmuch as many industrial products have long life cycles and companies' development actions can be considered a continuous process that results in products over a long period of time, customer satisfaction must extend over the long term. Clark and Fujimoto distinguish three factors that affect the ability of the product to satisfy customers (Clark & Fujimoto, 1991, p. 68):

(1) Total product quality (TPQ). The extent to which the product satisfies customer requirements. TPQ is built on both objective attributes such as, taking an example from the car industry, acceleration and fuel efficiency and subjective elements such as aesthetics, styling, or driving experience.
(2) Product development lead time. A measure of how quickly a company is able to move from concept to market. Lead time affects both the execution of the development and the acceptance of the design in the market.
(3) Productivity. The level of resources required to take the product development project from the concept phase to a commercial product. Productivity has at least a twofold effect on the performance. First, it has a direct (but sometimes relatively small) effect on the unit cost of the product. Second, it affects the firm ability to conduct a number of product development projects at a given level of development resources.

The effect of these three factors on competitiveness and customer satisfaction is seen as somewhat hierarchical. Long-term competitiveness is suggested as a function of total product quality and contributions that originate from other functions. Further, total product quality is connected to product development performance represented by lead time and productivity (Fig. 2).

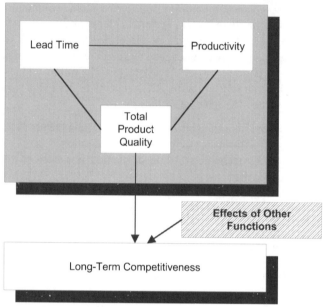

Fig. 2. Factors Associated with the Product Development Performance (Clark & Fujimoto, 1991).

Montoya-Weiss and Calantone (1994) studied 47 articles on new product success. All of these included commercial[11] measures of performance as a dependent variable describing new product performance. Only four studies were found to include technical success measures. Regarding the antecedents of success, eighteen factors were identified within the literature. These factors relate to four categories: market environment, new product strategy, development process execution, and organization. Montoya-Weiss and Calantone (1994) remind us that while there is some consistency as to which factors (determinants) are included in analyses, the typical set of factors employed within one study is too narrow (Table 2).

Analyzing unsuccessful projects may also reveal important lessons regarding factors that drive good performance. Whittaker studied information technology projects carried out in leading organizations in Canada. She found out that the most common reasons for a failing project were (Whittaker, 1999): Poor project planning in terms of inadequate planning and risk analysis, a weak business case in which organizational goals were not well aligned with the project, and the lack of support from the top management. Management support is an issue that is

Table 2. Determinants of Success Employed in Studies on New Product
Performance (Montoya-Weiss & Calantone, 1994).

Category	Factor
Strategic	Product advantage
	Technological synergy
	Company resources
	Strategy
	Marketing synergy
Development process	Proficiency of technical activities
	Proficiency of marketing activities
	Protocol
	Top management support
	Proficiency of pre-development activities
	Speed to market
	Financial business analysis
	Costs
Market environment	Market potential
	Market competitiveness
	Environment
Organizational	Internal/external relationships
	Organizational factors

often referred to and it was found to be important also in this study. Furthermore, Whittaker noted that 60% of the failed projects were planned to take less than a year to complete. It indicates that especially in the short projects the risks and requirements associated with the project are too easily underestimated (Whittaker, 1999).

As one may observe from the above, the findings of many studies on new product development performance read like a "fishing expedition." There are sometimes even too many variables associated with the success. Especially in the rational stream – that looks at NPD as an activity that is supposed to be based on rational planning and execution – it is common for a study to report 10–20 or more factors that contribute to success. Also, the research streams suffer from retrospective "sense making" of complex past processes that includes a host of different kinds of biases, myopia, and memory lapses. This is partly due to frequent use of single informants in those studies (Brown & Eisenhardt, 1995).

In contrast, there are also studies, which try to elaborate the mechanisms that are either connected to successful product development or actually lead to successful innovations. These studies often discuss a limited number of issues at a time but in doing so have the possibility to provide more in-depth understanding of cause-effect relationships present in product development. For instance, for successful innovation activity, Dougherty suggests that attention has to be paid on the effects of thought worlds – "a community of persons engaged in a certain domain of activity who have shared understanding about that activity" – and organizational routines. According to Dougherty, two aspects of thought worlds are relevant to product innovation: their "fund of knowledge" – what they know, and their "systems of meaning" – how they know (Dougherty, 1992). In new product development, departmental thought worlds could selectively filter information and ideas. Due to specialization, a certain thought world is likely to best understand some issues, but also to ignore information that might also be essential to the task. Therefore, thought worlds may disable an important link between the technological possibilities of a product and the market possibilities. thus limiting the comprehensive understanding. As Dougherty demonstrates, innovation is an interpretative process. The management of innovation must involve the management of interpretative schemes that shape how people make sense of their work. Collective action is required in the innovation process. To be able to overcome the possible interpretative barriers, three processes are suggested (Dougherty, 1992):

(1) Use the unique insights of each thought world: all must actively contribute to the design, and actively challenge each other.
(2) Develop collaborative mechanisms: interdisciplinary responsibility for focus groups, market research plans, and visits with users should, for instance, enhance collaboration.
(3) Develop an organizational context for collective actions: interactions should be based on appreciation and joint development; product definitions should be based on collective and first-order customer knowledge.

Indeed, there are many studies that emphasize the role of good internal communication and effective cross-functional cooperation in successful new product development (Elias et al., 2002). This notion has been reinforced by the study of Song et al. (1997) by stating that cooperation as an antecedent of NPD success is seen quite consistently within different functional departments such as marketing, R&D, and manufacturing.

> All critical organizational parties should take part in the NPD process from the beginning of the process (Song et al., 1997).

Also the role of top management is seen as very important in NPD. This is due to, among many other things, its significant control over the culture of cooperation (Song et al., 1997). However, the top management is not the only group that is of importance. It has been found that R&D and product development should not only concern and satisfy the needs of customers but also respond to the requirements of different stakeholders: such as employees, owners, suppliers, dealers and alliances (Miller, 1995). Identifying the stakeholders[12] of an R&D or a new product development project and analyzing[13] their interests supports better management of the projects. A systematic management of the stakeholder interests is underlined because of the rather generally acknowledged difficulty in R&D management to communicate the value of the development to sponsors and to other stakeholders who make decisions regarding the funding (Elias et al., 2002).

Despite the belief that the effects of cooperation are generally positive, cooperation does not seem to be equally important in all settings. Gomes et al. (2003), for instance, conclude that the degree of product innovativeness is one of the contingent variables explaining the nature of the relationship between intra-organizational collaboration and new product performance. According to Gomes et al. (2003), collaboration is the most relevant and effective in the case of high product innovativeness. In addition, Ancona and Caldwell provide more contingent variables regarding the benefits of collaboration. They have investigated the effect of the composition of the new product team on the performance. Performance has been interpreted as, for example, team efficiency, quality of technical innovations, ability to resolve conflicts, adherence to schedules, and adherence to budgets. They found that, although literature predicts that team diversity – in general – will have an impact on performance, certain distinct effects can be identified depending upon the type of diversity: The more heterogeneous the team in terms of tenure, the greater the clarity of the group's goals and priorities. This is, for one, associated with high team ratings of overall performance. On the other hand, rich external communication is associated with great functional diversity. The more external communication the team members have with other teams, the higher the managerial ratings concerning team innovation (Ancona & Caldwell, 1992). Further, it has been found that the product development team's stability increases the probability of product success in stable environments. However, in turbulent conditions, when reducing or eliminating pre-existing knowledge is sometimes needed for the sake of removing potential barriers to learning, team stability does not play such an important role. These findings have been made on the basis of defining success as meeting or exceeding expectations regarding sales volume, profits, market share, and some subjective criteria (Akgün & Lynn, 2002).

Further depicting the role of cooperation, Kessler et al. found that external sourcing – using external ideas to prompt learning – within the product development process has significant effects on the speed of innovation and on the creation of competitive advantage. Further, these impacts were found to be contingent on the stage of the product development process. In contrast with externally generated ideas, internal sourcing – when it takes place at the early stage of the innovation process – provides the development team members with a good basis to work together in a committed way to secure the successful completion of the project. In addition, outsourcing seems to increase the completion times of projects, especially when it takes place in the technology development phase (Kessler et al., 2000).

There are some attempts to connect the NPD success with the way to organize the new product development project (Larson & Gobeli, 1988). Larson and Gobeli found that there is no single best way to organize an NPD project. Project team, project matrix, and balanced matrix demonstrated roughly equal success rates.[14] However, functional matrix and functional organization are suggested to be less effective than the other forms.

Time is one of the contingent variables that are regarded as important for new product development success (see for example Anthony & McKay, 1992). At the same time, it seems to be a rather common misconception that a short new product cycle time is strongly connected to good new product success. Griffin demonstrated the lack of such a connection in a study that employed seven success measures, including financial ones. She notes, however, that the short development time might be otherwise beneficial to an organization, for instance, by providing the firm with a possibility to reduce development costs or by providing the personnel with an opportunity to participate in more new product projects during their career with the firm (Griffin, 2002). In contrast, a study by Lynn et al. has illustrated a positive correlation between development speed and new product success. However, they had not employed absolute measures either concerning the speed or the success. Speed had been measured by asking about the perceptions of management regarding, for instance, the timeliness of launch, the overall time-to-market, and the performance compared to an industrial norm. The concept of success was also a multi-item construct relying on managerial perceptions (Lynn et al., 1999). Further, to comprehensively understand the effect of NPD cycle time on product success, one should also consider the issue of market growth. For instance, Lynch and Cross (1995, p. 108), cite an analysis of McKinsey & Co showing that late commercialization has a significant impact on the life cycle profit of the product. In summary, similar to the behavior of several other factors in new product development, speed or cycle time – faster product development – alone is not able to secure high performance and success (Ittner & Larcker, 1997). It has also been pointed out that the impact of speed to market on new product performance has not been studied extensively enough (Montoya-Weiss & Calantone, 1994).

Clark and Fujimoto argue that *integrity* is the factor that differentiates successful innovators from those that tend to fail. As a measure of integrity concerning industrial customers, it is proposed that new products should mesh with existing components in a system or production process. More specifically, Clark and Fujimoto divide the integrity into two components: internal and external. Internal integrity refers to the consistency between a product's function and its structure. As a means to achieve internal consistency, they advocate cross-functional coordination within the company and with the suppliers. In contrast, external integrity is interpreted as the consistency between a product's performance and the customers' expectations (Clark & Fujimoto, 1990).

Inventions (new products) can also be viewed as results from the combination of components, either physical things or ideas, in new and useful ways (Fleming & Sorensen, 2001). Rather interesting findings can be made at this level. By drawing on the data of the U.S. Patent Office covering over 200 years of innovation history, Fleming and Sorenson have concluded that even though using interdependent components – in contrast to modular designs – in product designs makes innovation much more uncertain and difficult, it often results in breakthrough products. They put forth that highly modular designs make product development more predictable indeed, but many companies use modularization techniques to an extent where they actually undermine the innovation process by unnecessarily reducing the opportunities for more radical advances (Fleming & Sorensen, 2001). To some degree consistently, Firth and Narayanan studied 459 new product introductions during a five-year period in altogether 18 large firms. They found out that firms emphasizing market innovativeness in their new products achieved higher returns (operationalized by using measures such as ROI, return on investment) compared to those of less innovative firms. Surprisingly, the innovative organizations gained the advantage without a simultaneous rise in the risk level (Firth & Narayanan, 1996). In contrast, the analysis of a number of successful and unsuccessful R&D programs at 3M has revealed that the programs that are related to "maintenance of existing business" have the highest odds to succeed, whereas the programs that pertain to the creation of totally new business are the most likely to fail (Krogh et al., 1988). Regarding the totally new products, the uniqueness or newness to the world of the developed product and the firm's competitive position in the closest industry have been identified as having the most significant effect on the success (Krogh et al., 1988). Between these two, the probability of the success of programs focusing on new products that are well connected to the existing business of the firm depends on the target of the program: success is achieved more often with those programs that pursue high sales targets than with those that are aimed at smaller ones (Krogh et al., 1988). Further, Hultink et al. have studied the new product selling performance as one dimension of success. The main focus was on the determinants of success and, indeed, a number of factors positively correlated with the selling performance were identified including, for instance, an experienced sales force responsible for selling the product, market familiarity, and product familiarity. "New to the firm" and "new to the market" products were found to be negatively correlated with new product selling performance (Hultink et al., 2000).

Overall, it seems clear that no single recipe for success can be given. Success depends on the nature of the market, individual customer preferences, the maturity of the technology, or the degree of innovativeness, for example. As regards the product development practices, "one size does not fit all." Too generic approaches for product development management and measurement are restricting the possibilities for practitioners to implement them into action. According to Poolton and Barclay, it is more appropriate to adjust the product development practices on the basis of the type of product than to suggest a generic approach (Poolton & Barclay, 1998). Well in line with this, the performance measures could be attached specifically to the product being developed: the product would be the focal point when NPD measures are being developed. In practice, this would require the systematic and comprehensive assessment of the anticipated product life cycle and its phases.

The success factors of new product development may also be contingent upon the firm size. For instance, Ledwith (2000) has found that small firms have somewhat different success factors than large firms. Souder and Jenssen, for one, have studied successful new product development practices on a cross-cultural basis between Scandinavia and the U.S. As a conclusion, they implicate that some core NPD management principles may be common to all cultures, whereas others have to be adjusted to cultural variations (Souder & Jenssen, 1999). It should be noted, however, that in the process of linking antecedents and outcomes (NPD success or failure) Souder and Jenssen have interpreted NPD success only as the commercial success of the outcome. Further, Hultink et al. have concentrated on one of the antecedents, namely product launch decisions and the launch support program, to understand new product success (Hultink et al., 1999). However, in their study it also remains unclear to some extent what is actually meant by "success" and "failure." Further, the study by Song and Montoya-Weiss underscores clear differences in the determinants of success for really new and incremental products. The authors note that there might exist a basic skeleton of a new product development process that is mainly applicable across different development conditions, but the process is to be applied differently depending on the product innovativeness and type. The findings of the study produce several interesting insights (Song & Montoya-Weiss, 1998). First, insufficient emphasis seems to be placed on product commercialization activities. This holds true for both really new and incremental products. The findings, however, suggest that proficient execution of product commercialization activities is an equally important requirement for the success of both types of new products. Second, a significant gap has been found between current and best practices regarding the relative emphasis on strategic planning activities. The level of proficiency in strategic planning activities is relatively low for really new products. In contrast, for incremental products the mean level of proficiency in this domain seems to be relatively high. Yet this seems to be exactly the opposite order to what is really needed for success. Really new products would benefit from greater emphasis on strategic planning. This planning would be able to give some boundary guidelines that help to cope with the uncertainty associated with the development of totally new products. In contrast, incremental products are merely hurt by excessive efforts in strategic planning. Regarding these products, strategic planning could be simplified by drawing on previous insights and successes.

> For really new products, customer needs are often not well-defined and competitor capabilities are often not clearly established. As a result, detailed market studies are not of great value and can be exorbitantly costly. Really new products will likely involve extensive consumer education and iterative learning from the market as customer requirements and technological capabilities co-evolve" (Song & Montoya-Weiss, 1998, p. 132).

The evidence by Song and Montoya-Weiss supports the finding that really new products consistently achieve higher levels of success compared with incremental products (Song & Montoya-Weiss, 1998, p. 132).

Whilst several decades of R&D studies have produced a good deal of data with respect to variables associated with the success and failure of new products, the research has not been able to resolve a practical problem: how should R&D be actually managed to promote high new product success rates? Poolton and Barclay conclude that managers are still relying on gut feeling regarding "best practice" in new product development. Analogously, research has tended to be theory-driven instead of being applications-based (Poolton & Barclay, 1998). Driva et al. conclude that in most cases companies do not measure the R&D activity very well but they are striving to find out how to do it effectively (Driva et al., 2000). In this respect, it seems fair to claim that a good deal of work to improve the efficiency of the interface between industrial R&D management and academic R&D research is still needed.

The nature of the management control system seems to be an important issue also in a sense that it itself affects the performance. When the new product performance is defined on the basis of subjective, self-reported measures, it is shown that the use of different measurement information (including cost-, time- and product design-related) is significantly related to performance. More specifically, better cost and product design information is positively associated with the performance but time information has a negative effect. Thus, a management control system's design is, as such, related to performance (Davila, 2000). This notion highlights the importance of paying proper attention to the design, composition, and use of any control system. Indeed, there is evidence available that the most successful organizations tend to use performance measurement in new product development more extensively than the firms whose performance is inferior (Griffin, 1997):

- 75.6% of the firms develop formal financial objectives against which the performance could be evaluated.
- The portion of best firms that employ formal financial criteria is slightly bigger than the respective portion of inferior firms. However, the difference between these two is not statistically significant.
- 63.2% of the best firms actually monitored the actual NPD performance against the formal criteria.
- Only 48% of inferior firms monitored the actual NPD performance against the formal criteria.

In addition, higher targets lead to better outcomes: according to the PDMA best practice study by Griffin, the best firms typically have higher expectations for the future new product development performance than the rest of the firms (Griffin, 1997).

Finally, it seems appropriate to conclude this section with a remark that deals with the importance of an overall pattern in contrast with the importance of details. After studying the car industry and the product development performance of a number of car manufacturing companies in the United States, in Japan, and in Europe in the 1980s Clark and Fujimoto conclude that a prerequisite for high-performance development seems to be consistency in the overall pattern of product development (Clark & Fujimoto, 1991, p. 306):

> No single capability, no one structural characteristic, no particular strategy, no specific process made the difference . . . Only when a company developed a consistent pattern across many variables in all areas did it achieve superior performance. It appears that to be effective in product development, an organization must do many things well in a consistent way, rather than do a few key things exceptionally well.

Quite consistently, it has been argued that achieving success requires a firm to have control over a number of disciplines simultaneously. Griffin (1997), for instance, reminds that benchmarking the best practices of new product development has revealed that the best-performing firms do not succeed by utilizing one NPD practice better than the others, but by using a number of practices and methods more effectively.

5.2.4. Performance Measurement Applications

5.2.4.1. Guidelines for measurement. Werner and Souder have studied the state of the art of measuring R&D performance. By conducting an extensive

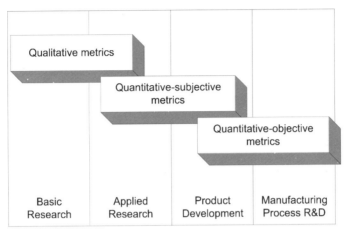

Basic Research   Applied Research   Product Development   Manufacturing Process R&D

Fig. 3. Preferred Approaches for R&D Measurement in Each Stage of the R&D Cycle (Adopted from Werner & Souder, 1997a, b, p. 40).

literature study, they have structured the present measurement techniques into three main categories on the basis of two dimensions (Werner & Souder, 1997a, b): First, measures can be either qualitative or quantitative and secondly, the measures are either based on objective information or on subjective judgments. Thus, quantitative-objective, quantitative-subjective, and qualitative-subjective classes of research and development performance measures are established. A qualitative-objective measure is regarded as a paradox, which is excluded from the analysis. In addition, integrated measures that combine the subjective and objective elements constitute a class of measures of their own. Indeed, according to Werner and Souder, some degree of integration between subjective and objective elements would produce the most effective measures for research and development. This is because the integration is likely to reduce biases and capable of taking advantage of multiple dimensions of excellence. Hence, to be able to capture the nature of a number of different research and development processes, integrated measures are often needed. Furthermore, taking into account the wide spectrum of issues that relate to different stages of the R&D cycle, different methods are preferred depending on the stage and its requirements (Fig. 3).

Further, Nixon has identified three main limitations of the literature on research and development performance measurement (Nixon, 1998). First, according to Nixon, behavioral and more qualitative factors that may influence the design and operation of performance measurement systems have not received enough attention. These factors include issues like styles of evaluation, organizational culture and climate, strategic management styles, cognitive styles of decision-makers, and belief systems. Second, the literature on the evaluation and measurement of development has to some extent neglected the management process of simultaneous new product development and the modern practices that organizations are being compelled to adopt to reduce costs, risks, or time-to-market. For instance, many companies are striving to guide product innovation and development so as to find a balance between the company's cash flow or profitability requirements and customers' purchase price and ownership cost needs. These challenges should receive more attention in the performance measurement literature. Third, the definitions of research and development (what activities are included, what are the inputs and outputs) leave an enormous scope for different judgments about these activities. As a result, it is a big challenge to define quantifiable measures for research and development or to allocate/assign costs to these activities. Considering the limitations in the literature, Nixon proposes that management accounting techniques could be applied to enhance and develop R&D performance measurement (Nixon, 1998).

One of the most important problems related to new product development success measurement is the issue of multidimensionality of product development outcomes (Griffin & Page, 1996, p. 479). At least three general dimensions can be presented (Griffin and Page, 1996, p.479): consumer-based, financial, and technical. Griffin and Page argue that these dimensions are independent of each other: "Achieving success with consumers is unrelated to whether a product produces profit for a firm." This seems to be, however, only partly true: one could achieve customer-based success without producing profits to the organization but is not very likely in a competitive market to be able to produce financial results without simultaneously succeeding with respect to the customer perspective. Nevertheless, as Griffin and Page point out, firms often have to settle with some kinds of compromises between these three success dimensions. A sacrifice in one level might be required in order to be able to reach success in another. Griffin and Page found that the most appropriate measures for new product success depend on the new product and business strategy of the organization (Griffin & Page, 1996). On the basis of simulated strategy scenarios that were assessed by new product professionals in order to identify the measures that would be the most appropriate for each strategy option, the authors concluded that for *new-to-the-world* products, customer satisfaction and customer acceptance were the most useful measures, in addition, meeting profit goals and internal rate of return and competitive advantage were seen as the most appropriate measures. The success of *new-to-the-company* products would be the most relevant to assess by using measures like profits, market share goals, competitive advantage, and customer satisfaction. For *product improvements* customer satisfaction, profits, and competitive advantage were regarded as the most appropriate measures of success. Regarding *cost reduction projects*, the measures of meeting profit margin goals and, once again, customer satisfaction, were seen as important. Utilizing four generic business strategy types originally presented by Miles and Snow (1978) (see for example Slater & Narver, 1993), namely prospector, analyzer, defender, and reactor, Griffin and Page identified that in addition to the new product strategy, the business strategy also affects the appropriate performance measures of new product success. Further, a particular set of measures always varies from company to company (Tipping et al., 1995). This is due to, for instance, different requirements in different industries and differences between competitive strategies between firms within a particular industry. Tipping et al. argue that one thing is still common to all measurement situations in R&D: to be able to comprehensively measure the performance, one has to adopt a holistic view (Tipping et al., 1995).

The need for multidimensional and multifaceted (including both financial and non-financial measures) measurement of NPD leads to an idea to employ some kind of balanced scorecard system for measurement. In fact, the Balanced scorecard has been identified as a suitable method for the performance analysis of new product development. According to Sandström, at least three benefits are associated with the utilization of the Balanced scorecard in product development: its future orientation, its clearness, and the ability of the BSC to capture multiple perspectives of performance. A prerequisite for the successful implementation of the BSC is the involvement of the designers (users, more generally) during the process of developing the measurement system (Sandström & Toivanen, 2002). Generally speaking, the involvement seems to be important since the R&D measurement should be consistent with the way the development is organized and planned. Hence, emphasis has to be put on the alignment of performance measures and the decision-making process (Pearson et al., 2000). Measures should not come "out of the blue," so to speak. Further, the alignment between the measurement system and decision-making process is a result of many issues. Five major parameters for research and development performance measurement systems and their design are identified by (Kerssens-van Drongelen & Cook, 1997). These include (see also Uusi-Rauva, 1996):

- The metrics or measures of performance themselves and the structure along which the measures are organized.
- The norms and standards against which the performance is determined.
- The techniques and methods employed in the measurement.
- The frequency and timing of reporting and measurement.
- The reporting format.

Besides the choices regarding the five basic parameters, a number of contingency factors are likely to influence the performance system design. For instance, the organizational level is affecting the measurement. Also, the nature of R&D – i.e. the position of the subject of measurement in the continuum from basic research to product development – and the type of industry are factors that affect the design of a performance measurement system (Kerssens-van Drongelen & Cook, 1997). However, although the contingency factors seem reasonable and valid as such, it is to some extent in doubt whether the contingency factors actually directly affect the performance measurement design or whether the factors just affect the choices made regarding the five basic parameters. Nevertheless, a number of issues shape the performance measurement system and its requirements. Interestingly, the authors found that the selection of measures was not as criticalan aspect of performance system design as it was anticipated to be. The least and most effective measurement systems included roughly the same set of indicators, which implies that the other design parameters are far more important than the metrics for the effective design of an NPD performance measurement system (Kerssens-van Drongelen & Bilderbeek, 1999).

One of the possible explanations relates to organizational climate: Krogh et al. have recognized the importance of the right atmosphere and attitudes for the success of R&D evaluation and assessment. They have argued that a constructive approach is most likely to truly support the R&D units being evaluated. Also, Krogh et al. support a practice that the recommendations that can be derived from the performance evaluations do not automatically lead to certain actions. In other words, although the performance of an R&D project or program would be evaluated as questionable, that would not result in automatic termination of the project. Hence, the primary aim of the R&D evaluation is not a straightforward screening of efforts, but rather the evaluation is targeted to support the planning and allocation of resources (Krogh et al., 1988). This view is underscored by the fact that in many cases NPD performance measurement has to be conducted on the basis of subjective assessments. If this is the case, one of the problems that have to be solved is the standardization of subjective opinions or responses. Davis et al. suggest anchored scales for the assessment of R&D efforts (Davis et al., 2001). According to them, an anchored scales-system is able to standardize the responses when multiple evaluators are conducting subjective assessment. An anchored scales-system consists of ordinal numeric indicators, each of which is associated with a set of words or phrases that help the evaluators to anchor their opinions. As an example, consider the assessment of raw material or key components supply related to a new product (Table 3).

The idea presented by Davis et al. conveys the logic that for each factor being assessed, one should determine a set of conditions or scenarios that would represent both the more desirable and undesirable conditions for the new product. Based on this, the project evaluation could be conducted also on a quantitative basis.

Table 3.   Example of Using Anchored Scales for NPD Assessment (Davis et al., 2001).

Anchor Point	Anchor Point Description
Anchored scale for raw material or key components supply	
5	Multiple suppliers; vendor relationships, with acceptable pricing, easily negotiated
4	Single, reliable source with stable contact
3	Currently producing, single supplier identified, but no commitment to supply
2	Supplier identified, willing to manufacture but currently is not
1	No known suppliers

Quantitative assessment would allow, for instance, numeric weighting of the factors if one has to be emphasized over another.

Theoretically, anchored scales seem like a feasible idea. However, in practice, the method raises a number of questions: First, it is likely to be rather challenging to determine a set of consistent and suitable descriptions for a number of factors. Second, it is nearly impossible to reach any commensurability within and across different factors as different descriptions reflect either more demanding or less demanding criteria for reaching a certain anchor point. Thirdly, even on the basis of written descriptions of the anchor scales, individual evaluators are likely to rely on their own interpretations, which to some extent jeopardize the sort of "pure standardization" that is pursued with this method.

Performance evaluation can be founded on the external customers' opinions. For instance, Hirons et al. (1998) propose external customer satisfaction as a measure of research and development management. On the other hand, Pearson et al. identify the "everything should begin with the customer" – thinking as one of the most popular management dogmas that is also well represented in the measurement of development activities, for instance, through an emphasis on customer satisfaction metrics (Pearson et al., 2000). At the same time, there is a consistent pattern in the failure of leading companies to stay on the cutting edge of their industry when a technological or market paradigm shift occurs. Hence, good management of R&D is characterized by the design of an evaluation process that focuses on weeding out the products and the technologies that do not properly address the customer needs (Pearson et al., 2000).

A word of caution has been added regarding the use of surrogate measures (such as number of patents or new products). A surrogate measure may fail to capture, for instance, the true relationship between technical progress and a number of selected variables (surrogates). Consider, for example, a surrogate measure like "the number of new products" at different stages of the technology life cycle: as technology matures, the rate of progress decreases inevitably. At the same time, however, the rate of new product introductions may remain constant (Foster et al., 1985a, b). Consistently, it has been argued, that the key performance indicators (KPIs) should reflect the achievement of the goals for the activities being measured rather than their outputs (O'Donnel & Duffy, 2002). Simultaneously, it has been argued that most of the measurement effort in recent decades has focused on the *output* of research and development. Hence, the true measurement of development *effectiveness*[15] has been practically absent (Szakonyi, 1994a, b, p. 29). O'Donnel and Duffy give an example (O'Donnel & Duffy 2002, pp. 1207–1208):

> . . . the number of drawings (output) is used to measure the performance of a draughting activity. This then changes the behaviour and output of the activity in order to achieve a seemingly high performance with respect to the metric. However, the goal of the activity is more likely to be to define the product's geometry to such a degree as to enable further analyses or product development. The KPIs should in fact reflect and support the goals of the activities and not their output. A more appropriate performance indicator in this example may be something like drawing usability, appropriateness or completeness. Such measures could be given by downstream activities and fed back to indicate the drawing activity's performance.

One of the common features of all performance measurement systems is that they include (at least implicit) assumptions concerning causes and effects (see for example Akgün & Lynn, 2002). On the other hand, practice has shown that revealing cause and effect assumptions (making them explicit) is very important in clarifying differences of opinion and settling conflicts that arise in discussions about strategy (Gooderham, 2001). Given the typically long time period between some causes and business effects, this is especially important in the R&D context. Further, important cause-effect relationships may be detected also at the level of management and measurement techniques (Lewis, 2001). For instance, according to Lewis' evidence, incremental innovations that are the most often associated with prescriptive project management techniques might increase the risk of restricting strategic resource (skills, knowledge and experiences of the development team) development. The risk is even more highlighted as the effectiveness of R&D is assessed against an arbitrary sense of "normal."[16] When constructing multidimensional R&D performance measurement, the possibilities to communicate the assumptions behind the metrics, and also behind the structure of the measurement framework, should be carefully considered.

Subjects or Topics for Measures. It has been argued that the diversity of R&D functions, including activities from basic research to product or process improvements, calls for a diverse set of measures to be able to completely cover the measurement need within these activities. In line with this, Brown and Gobeli have suggested a versatile R&D measurement practice. It would be organized around a concept of "top ten R&D productivity indicators" intended to capture the multidimensionality of R&D performance, including measures for (Brown & Gobeli, 1992):

- Resources
- Project management
- People management
- Planning
- New technology study and development
- Outputs
- Division results and outcomes

It is likely that no single approach for NPD performance measurement can be established. On the basis of a number of factors, performance measurement should be rather adapted to fit any particular context seen as relevant. It has been pointed out that different objectives require different types of measures (Schumann et al., 1995). As one typology, Schumann et al. propose a matrix the dimensions of which represent the external/internal focus of measurement and the timing (end-of-process vs. in-process) of it.[17] Schumann et al. suggest that internal end-of-process measurement would be mainly used for performance tracking purposes, and internal in-process measurement for technical productivity improvement purposes. On the other hand, external end-of-process measurement would allow competitor assessment while external end-of-process measurement facilitates the search for best practices. As regards the unit of analysis in performance measurement, Schumann et al. (1995) suggest four levels of aspects (see also Fig. 4):

- People: The professionals working in an organization and their technical vitality constitute the people category. Technical vitality refers to personal responsibility to ensure that the creative talents of individuals are used to promote change or development. It is about carrying out each activity "with excellence."
- Process: Gaining experience in the process can facilitate learning. This logic is related to a belief that when one gains more understanding on the factors associated with the desired outputs, these outputs are more likely to occur. Suggested process measures would result in understanding how the process is actually carried out. Hence, good process measures would act as a feedback mechanism with a certain amount of delay.
- Outputs: The primary output of research and development activities is information, technology, or products. As it is often very challenging to evaluate the value of information (a context-specific issue) Schumann et al. propose peer review as a means to overcome the challenge. Overall, when measuring the

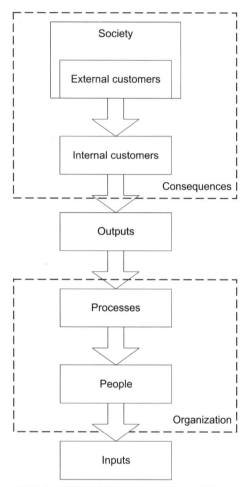

Fig. 4. Scheme of Market-Driven Measurement System (Schumann et al., 1995).

output, it is underscored that the customers and the competitors are those stakes that best define the quality standards of the output that should be reached.

- Consequences: The consequences can also be referred to as outcomes of research and development activities. In this respect, each stakeholder of R&D would require measures of its own because the outcomes can be evaluated from quite different perspectives. For example, although the needs of external customers may constitute the primary concern during the actual development work, in the pragmatic sense, satisfying the internal customer that provides the funding for the whole activity may be the most immediate need. Naturally, when the interests of different stakeholders do not conflict, balancing the measures of consequences across a number of stakeholders is not very problematic; unfortunately, this is not always the case.

Besides this, performance measures for new product development have been organized and classified in many ways. Naturally, one of the most general and typical classifications is based on the distinction between financial and non-financial indicators. Hertenstein and Platt have presented a more specified typology on the basis of this traditional classification for the measurement of design performance. Financial measures constitute one domain including measures such as revenue/sales, product cost, development costs, gross profit of the new product, sales to break-even, or the percentage of new product sales from the total sales. Non-financial measures are further divided into eight subgroups (Hertenstein & Platt, 2000):

(1) Timing measures
    (a) Time to market
    (b) Cycle time by phase
(2) Design effectiveness measures
    (a) Percentage of the first design meeting the needs
    (b) Team assessment of design effectiveness
(3) Design efficiency measures
    (a) Number of design modifications
    (b) Frequency of specification changes
(4) Customer satisfaction measures
    (a) Satisfaction concerning the product
    (b) Satisfaction concerning the ease of use
(5) Employee-rated measures
    (a) Employee morale
    (b) Team assessment of individual contributions
(6) Strategic measures
    (a) Achievement of specific strategic goals
    (b) The alignment of design with the company strategy
(7) Innovation measures
    (a) Number of patents
    (b) Number of new products developed
(8) Volume measures
    (a) Number of products in the pipeline
    (b) Number of products started

Many measures in the typology of Hertenstein and Platt (2000) are not very well operationalized. Especially the strategic measures are not really measures at all; rather they represent still somewhat ambiguous ideas regarding what could be measured in terms of strategy in new product development. Also from the new product performance point of view, it seems irrelevant to measure, for instance, employee morale or individual contribution. They may be seen as antecedents for the performance but they do not really indicate performance as such. The typology also includes some shortcomings regarding the hierarchy of the measures; for instance, in the category of customer satisfaction measures, satisfaction concerning the product and the satisfaction concerning the ease of use seem to be overlapping.

Furthermore, Szakonyi has constructed a framework for the evaluation of research and technology effectiveness. Effectiveness is defined as a function of, for instance, good R&D planning, identifying a market need for R&D, competent management of personnel, and good teamwork. The assessment of effectiveness is based on performance evaluation on ten activities, including for instance (Szakonyi, 1994a, b):

• Selecting R&D
• Planning and managing projects
• Transferring technology to manufacturing
• Fostering collaboration between R&D and finance
• Linking R&D to business planning
• Coordinating marketing and R&D

In each activity, the evaluation is carried out by utilizing a scale of six pre-determined levels of performance (Szakonyi, 1994a, b):

(1) Issue not recognize.
(2) Initial efforts are made towards addressing the issue.
(3) Right skills are in place.
(4) Appropriate methods are used.
(5) Responsibilities are clarified.
(6) Continuous improvement is underway.

One can easily derive from the previous description that the method proposed by Szakonyi is designed primarily for monitoring purposes and for both external and internal benchmarking, not for supporting the practical everyday management of development activities.

Tipping et al. (1995) stress that: "one cannot judge the value of an R&D organization to a corporation simply by looking at the new products it has produced recently, just as one cannot judge the value of a house by looking at the exterior brickwork." Instead, the authors propose a model called the "Technology value pyramid," TPV, for assessing this function. TPV aims to communicate that value creation is the primary driver of the overall business returns that can be derived from new products. The basis of TPV relies on a number of beliefs, including (Tipping et al., 1995):

- The R&D effort should defend and develop the value of the corporation.
- A linkage has to exist between R&D and corporate strategic aims.
- R&D has to sustain its capabilities to be able to produce relevant output in the long term.

The authors also propose a number of measures that can be used to operationalize the ideas of TPV. According to Tipping et al., TPV provides a holistic view on R&D and enables both prospective and retrospective measurement. However, the authors note that prospective measures should be used cautiously. The projections concerning the future will only be as good as the assumptions concerning the cause-effect relationships (Tipping et al., 1995).

Concrete Measures. Pillai et al. (2002) argue that R&D projects are difficult to measure properly due to the fact that they are inherently complex and uncertain. Furthermore, Pillai et al. suggest that to avoid poor overall NPD performance, each phase of product development should not be managed and measured separately but rather the measures of new product development should encompass the entire life cycle of the project. As a solution to this problem, the method or tool, Integrated Performance Index (IPI), that is suggested by Pillai et al. can be regarded as an attempt to link the key factors from each phase of R&D together. However, because IPI integrates several measured factors into one figure, the construct obviously suffers from the lack of ability to directly associate the measure with a real-life phenomenon that has actually affected the measure. Thus, it seems somewhat too complex to be widely adopted by the practitioners. The life cycle of a new product development project, according to Pillai et al. consists of three phases (Pillai et al., 2002):

(1) Project selection phase that mainly concerns screening, evaluation and selection of potential projects.
(2) Project execution phase that covers technology and product development and, further, performance demonstration.
(3) Implementation phase, which is related to the implementation of the project to the production, marketing, and sales.

However, one product development project or one new product is not the only possible unit of analysis in performance measurement. In this sense, it is important to acknowledge that measuring the performance of a single product development project is different from evaluating the performance of a portfolio of projects. This distinction is made, for instance by Nixon (1998), who argues that the differences between these two relate to different risk assessment requirements and a different emphasis on strategic dimensions. On the level of product family, Meyer at al propose two measures for NPD performance (Meyer et al., 1997):

(1) Product platform efficiency. It is interpreted as the degree to which a platform provides the possibility for the economic generation of follow-up products. Mathematically, the efficiency is defined as a simple ratio: Platform efficiency (E) = R&D costs for the derivative product/R&D costs for the platform version.
(2) Product platform effectiveness. It is defined as the degree to which the products relying on the same platform are able to produce revenue for the firm in relation to the costs associated with the development of those products. Mathematically, the effectiveness (L) is given by the ratio: L = cumulative sales of the products associated with a platform/cumulative costs of developing the platform and the products associated with it.

Coccia presents a methodology called *relev* for evaluating R&D performance. The method is based on a number of indices representing the principal activities that are carried out in the organization. Again, the method produces a single figure, a score that is to be used to rank several R&D organizations against each other. Thus, the relev method is mainly beneficial for an external evaluator and it is not primarily targeted at managerial purposes within a single firm (Coccia, 2001). Analogously, McGrath and Romeri propose an aggregate measure for monitoring the overall success of product development called R&D Effectiveness Index (EI) (McGrath & Romeri, 1994). The EI index combines the revenue from new products with the overall net profit and R&D investment. It is said to describe whether the returns from new products are greater than the respective costs. However, the authors are not able to demonstrate the actual validity of the measure. Furthermore, their logic contains features that have to be regarded as misleading, such as: "The profitability of new products is a result of how successful the products are in meeting the customer needs compared to competitive products" (McGrath & Romeri, 1994). It is self-evident that meeting the customer needs in respect to competitive products could be a driver of profitability, but a number of other factors, such as the direct manufacturing or material costs, affect the profitability far more directly.

Chiesa and Masella distinguish between performance measures that are to be used before the end of a development project (*t*) and after it. This distinction is made on the basis of a logic that the critical drivers of performance before *t* are intrinsic to R&D, but after *t* the performance is affected also by other functions. The first category, measures before the end-of-project, consists of measures in two domains: technical success measures and efficiency measures. Efficiency measures are further divided into subcategories of productivity and synergy measures, the measures of adherence to scheduling, and risk measures. The measures that focus on the period after project completion are said to concern mainly integration issues. Two broad domains of measures are established (Chiesa & Masella, 1996):

- Manufacturing integration
  - Time to market
  - Number of redesigns
  - Design performance
- Marketing integration
  - Number of new products, licenses, patents
  - percentage of sales and profit from new products
  - Customer satisfaction

Suitable measures have been organized on the basis of the chosen new product strategy of the company. Prospectors who pursue to be the first to the market would utilize measures such as (Griffin & Page, 1996):

- Percentage of profits from products $< n$ years old.
- Degree to which today's products lead to future opportunities.
- Percentage of sales from products $< n$ years old.

Analyzers who are seldom first to the market but are able to respond quickly and effectively to produce fairly innovative products are likely to utilize measures like (Griffin & Page, 1996):

- Degree to which products fit business strategy.
- Development program ROI.
- Success/failure rate.
- Percentage of profits from products $< n$ years old.

Defenders attempt to maintain or secure a rather stable niche and to provide high quality or superior service. For defenders, the following measures are appropriate (Griffin & Page, 1996):

- Development program ROI.
- Degree to which products fit business strategy.

Reactors are less active operators in the markets and tend to respond only if they are forced to do so. For them, the suggested measures are (Griffin & Page, 1996):

- Development program ROI.
- Success/failure rate.

- Degree to which products fit business strategy.
- Subjective overall program success.

The strategy-based measures proposed by Griffin and Page (1996) are clearly upper-level measures. They primarily illustrate the overall success of product development but tell little about the success of individual products and causes related to possible successes or failures.

Some, although rare, proposed measures of product development comprise the life cycle dimension of outcomes. For instance, Brown and Svenson (1998), have suggested the net present cash flows during product life cycle to development cost as a measure of product development. Demonstrating a kind of life cycle orientation, Curtis has analyzed the relationship between a product's lifetime revenues and the duration of the development cycle (Curtis, 1994). On the basis of his analysis, Curtis suggests that companies should be cautious in compressing their product development cycles. This is because, as Curtis argues, a point will occur at which further development cycle reduction may not add to a product's life cycle revenues due to, for example, an inability to cover the incremental costs of acceleration through higher prices (Curtis, 1994). On the other hand, according to Johnson and Kaplan (1987), traditional accounting methods are not suitable for organizations that are characterized by short product life cycles and high importance of research and development (Johnson & Kaplan, 1987).

Despite the practical problems with accounting measures, regarding the financial objectives of research and new product development, there is a number of different dimensions or perspectives that need to be acknowledged. From the financial and management accounting point of view, Nixon underscores the importance of three different measures (Nixon, 1998, pp. 340–341):

(1) The total development cost. The total costs include all the costs that can be either directly or indirectly assigned to the development project including consulting, testing, and overheads.
(2) Direct costs of the new product/service, that is, what the costs associated with the production of the new product are.
(3) Operating costs. These refer to costs that the customer incurs when using the product for its purpose.

Importantly, the interactions between these three types of costs are very complex. Hence, Nixon underscores the importance of close collaboration between engineers, R&D team, manufacturing, component supplier and customer, and financial controller in order to be able to finalize the product development in a way that balances the different cost requirements. Especially the role of the financial controller is very crucial in assisting the designers to evaluate the effect of different design possibilities and alternatives on the cost of producing and operating the product. On the basis of an extensive and longitudinal case study, Nixon summarizes the importance of different cost targets in product development: "Increasingly, producers must look beyond their competitors and focus on the competitive environment of their customers. In the case of CCM Ltd. the purchase price [of the new machine] is far less significant for its customers than the operating cost" (Nixon, 1998, p. 343). Furthermore, this finding seems to be consistent across different industries (for example Jokioinen, 2003).

The fact that the literature is full of suggestions concerning measures and measurement system designs could indicate that it is possible to identify a suitable set of measures for every setting. This view, however, is misleading. Above all, measures and measurement systems should not be regarded as static constructs; rather, measurement is a dynamic phenomenon that should be adapted to changing conditions and requirements.

> Once measures are made they should not be regarded as the answers. Instead, they need to be continually reviewed and refined (Driva et al., 2000, p. 156).

For instance, Nixon has found that the process of evolution regarding a product development project is essentially about uncertainty reduction and consensus building within the organization. The better the consensus, the more resources can be assigned to the development. There is typically a "gestation period" before significant resources are committed to development. This is quite consistent with the ideas presented by (Matthews, 1991). Hence, when considering the role of performance measurement in new product development, it is necessary to analyze the needs that cover the entire cycle of development. During high uncertainty, the requirements for performance measurement are likely to differ from those that are related to stages of relatively low uncertainty in the later stages of development (Nixon, 1998). In other words, a performance measurement system, in practice, may be an iterative process that cannot be totally separated from the basic nature of the design and development process. Thus, as the information and criteria associated with product development in general evolves from the more soft or general towards the more specific and reliable, the performance measurement system also evolves. In the later stages of development, more objective and explicit data are required. A performance measurement system should then produce information that is more structured and organized and that can be directly used as a decision-making criterion (Nixon, 1998).

5.2.5. *Other Managerial Constructs*
A good number of suggestions – that directly or indirectly relate to performance measurement – for managing product development performance and success can

be found from the literature. Ransley and Rogers (1994), for example, identified seven best practices of research and development concerning which a consensus seems to exist. These include: (1) A clear technology strategy that relies on a common vocabulary (such as time frame, approach, and risk) and that is understood widely across functions; (2) rigorous program and project management including analytical tools are used in balancing and assessing R&D programs; (3) identified core technologies that are also integrated into long-term development plans; (4) effectiveness meaning that the results are measured against technology and business objectives; (5) external awareness including a systematic process for monitoring external threats and opportunities through a number of stakeholders; (6) technology transfer across functions through, for instance, cross-disciplinary teams; and (7) effective and careful personnel recruitment and education. For facilitating these purposes, however not equally focused regarding all these seven mentioned, a number of tools and techniques exist. One of the most well-known R&D management constructs is presented by Cooper (1996): the Stage-gate system. A Third-generation stage-gate system consists of five stages (preliminary investigation, detailed investigation, development, testing and validation, full production, and market launch) and of five gates (go/kill decision points) that control the process.Delano et al. indicate that Quality Function Deployment (QFD) is able to provide many benefits for an organization during the product development process (see also Akao, 1990; Pullman et al., 2002). These would include tight focus on the customer and customer requirements, good communication, and effective teamwork across the developing organization (Delano et al., 2000): "Decision making requires the ability to gather and communicate information and to perform different types of analysis" (Delano et al., 2000, p. 606). QFD, among other possible techniques, is able to provide tools to support decision-making in the R&D environment. Further, more generic techniques have also been discussed. Poh et al. have compared several R&D evaluation or selection techniques including scoring method, AHP, decision tree technique, economic analysis, and cost-benefit analysis. The comparison was carried out by using the AHP technique. The criteria deployed in the comparison included aspects such as the ability of the method to cope with multiple objectives (typical in the NPD environment), simplicity, data availability, and cost. On the basis of this comparison, the authors conclude that the scoring method would be the most favorable method for evaluating R&D projects. The strength of the scoring method seems to be in its ability to deal with multiple criteria and in its simplicity (Poh et al., 2001).

In addition to valuing development projects, options-based analysis for R&D projects has been presented as an alternative to more traditional discounted cash flow (DCF) techniques. The justification for options-based approaches is underscored by a view that an R&D project is actually an initial investment that creates future follow-on commercial opportunities (Herath & Park, 1999). On the contrary, traditional DCF methods are seen as unable to correctly value the projects because the total economic value of these investments includes an option value that is associated with the future opportunity to commercialize (Herath & Park, 1999, p. 2). Further, risk assessment is closely connected to option-based approaches. Davis argues that a robust product development process should somehow make the risks associated with it understandable and measurable. The risks, as Davis has perceived them, are further divided into market risk, technical risk, and user risk. He proposes a construct called NPVR, which is based on the traditional net present value calculation supplemented with a risk evaluation. The risks are operationalized in the NPV calculations by using market research and questioning and further, heuristically interpreting the information gathered (Davis, 2002).

Cooper has developed the NewProd model for separating probable successful projects from probable losers. He remarks that project selection is pivotal to effective risk reduction in product development. A scoring model could be a valuable tool in screening proposals. According to the NewProd model, product superiority/quality, market need, growth and size, and product scope are the factors that have the strongest impact on the probability of success (Cooper, 1985). Hollander has reported the potential of the Genesis model for project assessment. His study is based on Cooper's NewProd studies. The objective of both of these models is to provide support for the product development team, especially for "go or no go" decisions. The Genesis model is focused on development projects and teams. The question is: Does the team have the necessary resources and skills and how is the product positioned in respect to markets and competitors' products? (Hollander, 2000).

Slevin and Pinto (1986) have proposed a framework for estimating or anticipating project management success. The framework is called the project implementation profile (PIP). The authors have identified ten success factors, including for instance project mission, top management support, client consultation, communication, and troubleshooting, which are related to a project's success. By studying 82 successful projects, Slevin and Pinto have provided a reference score scale for each success factor that enables benchmarking a certain project performance with the success profiles of known successful projects. (For instance, regarding the factor of communication, the 0th percentile of 12 points refers to the fact that none of the studied success projects scored less than 12 points, and the 100th percentile of 99 indicates that the full score of 100 was not achieved by any project.) If a project's performance in the case of any factor is below the 50th percentile, one should – according to Slevin and Pinto – devote extra attention to that factor to improve the odds of success.

Kim and Oh have noted that economic compensation or a reward system is a good tool for motivating the personnel working in research and development. However, to be able to employ such a system, the organization has to establish a fair and an effective means to measure the performance of its development activities. From the performance measurement point of view, at least two questions have to be answered properly: (1) Who should measure the performance of R&D workers? (2) What criteria should be employed to measure the performance? The former question implies that performance measurement is not totally neutral activity in respect to the subject of measurement. Therefore, the one who is responsible for the measurement has to be carefully selected. The latter question suggests – at least implicitly – that attention has to be paid to the resolution of the question: How do we actually define the R&D performance? Kim and Oh put forth four broad sets of criteria that could be utilized in evaluating R&D engineers' and scientists' performance (Kim & Oh, 2002):

(1) Market-oriented including public relationship building, social activity such as lectures and spreading information, and commercial profit.
(2) R&D project-specific including technological complexity and the duration of the R&D project.
(3) R&D researcher's technological attributes including personal technical expertise, the number of publications such as books or papers, and the number of patents.
(4) R&D researcher's behavioral attributes including mentoring for junior researchers, leadership, the ability to get things done, and efforts for teamwork building.

Kim and Oh have shown that there exists a strong correlation between R&D personnel's job satisfaction and their satisfaction with the performance measurement system employed. Thus, it seems important to carefully design and implement the measures that are employed for tracking the employees' performance. In practice, a measurement system that relies on the inputs from the employees themselves, their peer reviewers, and external customers is perceived as more fair and better than one relying only on the inputs from R&D project directors and top executives. Furthermore, the results of the survey indicate that an ideal R&D performance measurement system – according to the R&D workers – would emphasise measures that are based on the behavioral criteria such as teamwork building abilities or leadership for the R&D organization (Kim & Oh, 2002).

Managing costs is an important part of managing the profitability of new products. Costs can be assessed at least from the perspectives of customer and manufacturer. From the customer point of view, it has been suggested that cost of ownership is a key issue in business-to-business markets (Goffin & New, 2001), which should be considered in product development. If the product development process lacks rigorous control over product design, many product features may be added to the product specification in response to sub-segment requests without a thorough consideration of the total effects of these additions (Rabino, 2001). In line with this, it is suggested that launching a new product to the market on the basis of qualitative market study is very risky in contrast with relying on a more quantitative one. According to Howley, this is because qualitative market research is likely to lead to undesirable bias for the development process (Howley, 1990). As a form of rigorous control, target costing is one of the possible applications (Ansari et al., 1997; Cooper & Slagmulder, 1999a, b; Dutton & Marx, 1999; Fisher, 1995; Horvath et al., 1998; IMA, 1998a, b; Kato & Boer, 1995; Tanaka, 1993). Benefits associated with the practice of target costing during the product development process imply that assigning specific cost targets for product developers should result in favorable financial outcomes. That is, the employment of explicit cost targets during the product development would lead to lower costs of the developed product than, for instance, relying on a general objective to strive for low product cost. This notion has been basically supported by (Everaert & Bruggeman, 2002). However, they add that target costing only has a positive effect on the new product when employees can afford to work relaxed (Everaert & Bruggeman, 2002, pp. 1349–1350). This reminds of something that is almost self-evident regarding all managerial tools: it is not only the tool itself but the way it is used that determines the success of the application.

Cost estimation can be regarded as one means to conduct financial assessment within product development. Generally, cost estimation is employed in order to be able to predict costs such as labor or material over time on the basis of some data on cost drivers. Smith and Mason argue that cost estimation is an important activity that relates to a number of decisions concerning, for instance, engineering or business in general (Smith & Mason, 1997). The estimation of the costs of a new product is a typical managerial challenge in new product development. At least two appropriate approaches have been introduced that can be employed when estimating new product costs:

(1) Using an analogy with other, already existing, products produced either by the firm itself or by competitors.
(2) Through parametric models, that can relate a representative number of parameters of the product to the cost of the product.

Activity based management (ABM, see e.g. ICMS Inc., 1992; Kaplan, 1992; Ness et al., 2001; Pryor, 1998), that is based mainly on information produced by activity based costing (ABC, see for example Cokins, 1999; Cooper, 1990a, b; Cooper & Kaplan, 1988; Cooper & Slagmulder, 1999a, b; Hardy & Hubbard,

1992; Innes & Mitchell, 1995; Johnson et al., 1991; Jones & Dugdale, 2002; Krumwiede, 1998; Lahikainen & Paranko, 2001; Lukka & Granlund, 2002; Mecimore & Bell, 1995; Ness & Cuzuzza, 1995; Turney & Stratton, 1992; Zeller et al., 2001) has been mentioned as a methodology that can be applied to research and development activities. According to Maccarrone (1998), ABM would be a helpful tool regarding a number of issues including the evaluation of economic benefits that can be gained through re-design of processes, the evaluation of product life-cycle costs or budgeting and controlling of product development activities. More specifically, Maccarrone (1998) suggests that using the ABM methodology in the cost estimation process of a new product can reinforce, and integrate, both approaches. This is because ABM enables a detailed analysis of differences between the new and the existing products. The costs of new products can be analyzed as combinations of activities that are carried out in the various processes of a firm. Activities consumed by the products are thus seen as the parameters that affect the cost of the product. Hence, a parametric approach – that relies on analogies between new and existing products – for the cost estimation of new products consists of two main building blocks: (1) On the basis of activity based costing a firm is able to know the unit costs of activities; and (2) On the basis of analogies with and anticipated differences between new and existing products in terms of activity consumption, a firm can assess the amount of activities the product will require. By combining these two pieces of information, a cost estimate for a new product can be established.

5.2.6. Life Cycle Oriented Measurement
In striking contrast with the popularity of the topics of performance measurement and new product development management, product life cycle has been discussed to a very limited extent in the context of new product development performance measurement. For example, the number of journal articles that have explicitly addressed the issue is as low as less than ten. Still, life cycle orientation seems to be to some degree a built-in characteristic of product development. As Tipping et al. (1995) notes, R&D has to be able to sustain its capability to produce useful output over the long term. Furthermore, life cycle concerns in NPD performance measurement should be well aligned with the overall "broadening" trend in project management. As Fangel (1993) argues, the applications of project management have changed substantially during recent decades. One of the identified trends is the shift of focus from the period from contracting until commissioning towards handling the entire life cycle. A product's performance can be viewed as an aggregate measure that is not established on the basis of a moment of time but rather as a function of time over its entire life cycle. Moreover, field service or after sales service related to – or wrapped around – the physical product is one of

the elements that affect the customer's perception of the product. It is worth noting that – in addition to providing a source of revenue for the manufacturer – the service function also provides the company with a possibility to gather feedback on product performance and information on customer preferences (Hull & Cox, 1994).

Some evidence has been presented implicating that the characteristics of product life cycles have an impact on the relevant design of NPD performance measurement systems. Terwiesch et al. (1998) emphasize the importance of analyzing the characteristics of the industry when designing new product development performance measurement. The authors argue that although a universally valid relationship between new product development performance and business performance (success) may exist, the relevant NPD performance measures seem to depend on the industry in which a firm operates. The market context that can be derived from the industry includes three dimensions: market share, market growth, and external stability that refers to the average length of product life cycle (PLC) in the market.

Also, the relevant measures of NPD performance seem to be time-dependent. For instance, Hultink found that measures perceived as important at the beginning of the product life cycle differ from those seen as the most important later in the PLC. Product performance-related measures were regarded as the most important in the short term; that is, at the beginning of the life cycle, whereas financial aspects and customer-related measures gain importance towards the end of the life cycle (Hultink & Robben, 1995). It was concluded by Griffin and Page (1996) that either the most relevant and useful measures of success change during the product life cycle, or there is a need to obtain different measures at different points of time. As the idea presented by Griffin and Page is merely a hypothesis, it seems consistent to argue that the life cycle stage affects the optimal set of performance measures. Consistently, also Foster et al. (1985a, b) remark that the relevant performance measures vary over time due to changing customer needs. According to Foster et al. (1985a, b) the fact that customer need is a temporal variable is rarely fully acknowledged. The authors argue that the profound understanding of customer needs can be reached on the basis of two analyses. First, it has to be understood what the customer values now. Second, an understanding should be obtained regarding what the customer will likely value in the future.

The overall characteristics of an effective measurement system for product development have received significant attention in the literature (Davis et al., 2001; Kerssens-van Drongelen & Bilderbeek, 1999; Nixon, 1998; Schumann et al., 1995; Szakonyi, 1994a, b). Brown and Svenson (1998), for instance, suggest several issues. First, according to them, the focus should be on external measures rather than on internal measures. Internal measurement might be a valuable quality control tool, but for evaluation purposes external measures are more valid and important. This could be partly seen as implying stakeholder-oriented performance measurement. An important part of developing a feasible and effective PM system for new product development is to identify the stakeholders involved, to understand their needs, and to agree upon them (see for example Tipping et al., 1995). Also, it would be necessary to integrate the stakeholders into the process of developing a new product, because this allows the effective use of both leading and lagging indicators of performance. It should also be noted that different stakeholders have different interests, which means that the important measures for one group of stakeholders would be secondary for another. Furthermore, it is not only the fundamental interests that differ between stakeholders but also the preferred time frame may be different. Therefore, the measurement should allow different stakeholders to address their particular period of interest for measuring the development activity. Despite the possible conflict of interests between stakeholders, Tipping et al. (1995) stress the importance of communicating the interconnectedness between the factors measured.

Second, Brown and Svenson (1998) state that outputs and outcomes should be measured instead of behavior. This focus implies that as long as the outcomes are desirable, the individuals should have the possibility to select the most appropriate means to achieve them. Outcomes should be measured along the three basic dimensions: quality, quantity, and cost. Essentially, the two points made are well in line with the idea presented by Foster et al. (1985a, b) that the measures should track the performance as the customer sees it. In other words, the measure ought to relate to benefits that the customer experiences when using the new product (Kerssens-van Drongelen & Bilderbeek, 1999). This conclusion regarding the essential measurement focus can also be made from a rather different perspective. Namely, when Kortge and Okonkwo discussed the role of marketing strategy in new product development, they noted that one of the most essential activities of the marketing manager is participating in the development of new products that meet customer demands and attain the objectives of the company (Kortge & Okonkwo, 1992).

Further, Brown and Svenson (1998) argue that only the valuable accomplishments should be measured. Curiosities, even though they might be easy to quantify, should not be of interest. An example of a curiosity could be the number of citations in a technical journal or the number of new products per se. Brown and Svenson (1998) also suggest keeping the measurement system as simple as possible. In addition, they advocate using indices that comprise several aspects of performance rather than separate indices for each dimension of performance. As a rule of thumb, six to eight key indices is recommended. Finally, according to Brown and Svenson (1998), the measurement system should be kept as objective as possible. Quite similarly, Foster et al. (1985a, b) advocate the use of technical measures (such as tensile strength or yield). When it is not possible to totally avoid subjectivity, then it should be at least minimized. For instance, when the impact of a certain development output is in question, the evaluation should be based on an assessment by a stakeholder rather than on an opinion of the R&D manager. Brown and Svenson (1998) have also proposed some measures which explicitly involve the life cycle dimension of outcomes. For instance, they suggested the net present cash flows of the PLC compared to development cost as a measure of product development. On the other hand, Krogh et al. (1988, p. 11) propose an R&D program evaluation that is carried out on the basis of nine wide factors that cover both the technical and business aspects of development. Among the proposed measures, the measure of financial potential, which includes anticipation of future sales and profits associated with the product, represents life cycle-oriented performance measurement. However, Patterson (1983) provides perhaps the most crystallized example of life cycle-oriented PM by reporting the performance evaluation practices at Alcoa Laboratories. The evaluation of R&D at Alcoa relies on projections of future economic benefits produced by new products or innovations. First, different functions of the organization collaborate to establish the magnitude of potential new product-related economic benefits, which can take several forms including cost reduction, sales advantage, capital avoidance, capacity expansion, or knowledge. Second, the series of benefits (within a limited time horizon of 15 years) is converted to a present value by using a discounting factor (corresponding to a standard NPV calculation). Third, to measure the benefit ratio within the organization, the discounted benefits of implemented innovations are proportioned to respective expenditures. Obviously, as Patterson (1983) points out, this ratio varies quite heavily on a temporal basis.

Cordero (1990) presents a framework for the comprehensive evaluation of a firm's innovation performance. According to his model (and analogously to the ideas presented by Krogh, 1998), to obtain overall performance evaluation, one has to measure both commercial and technical performance. Moreover, performance could be tracked on the levels of firm, business unit, or function. During the early stages of product life cycle, it is recommended that the performance measures should focus on estimations and help in the evaluation of alternatives. At the later stages, the measurement focus would shift to recording the realized outputs (Fig. 5).

Meyer et al. (1997) approach the problem of short-termism in NPD measurement by suggesting measures for product families and platforms as opposed to measures for single projects or products. A successful product platform can be considered a long-term investment as it provides the possibility to launch a number of follow-on products that are based on the same architecture. Further, Osawa et al. (2002) have

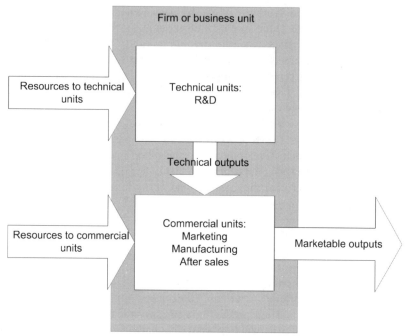

Fig. 5. Model of Comprehensive Innovation Performance Measurement (Adapted from Cordero, 1990, p. 186).

presented a conceptual model for evaluating industrial R&D projects. In a way, they have also grasped a life cycle dimension of new product development as they have adopted a five-year period for the financial appraisal. The method of Osawa and Murakami is still quite subjective and heuristic, since it relies heavily on the project manager's projections regarding the product. The authors note, however, that the main advantage of the method is that it provides project managers with a platform to discuss and reach consensus with the project's stakeholders. Second, the utilization of the method accumulates quantitative data within the organization that can be exploited when assessing development projects in the future (Osawa & Murakami, 2002).

5.2.7. Use of Performance Measures and Measurement in Product Development

The overall observation in the literature seems to be that the measurement of product development is not as developed as it probably should be. Compared to many other application areas, such as manufacturing, performance measurement in product development is rather poorly developed (O'Donnel & Duffy, 2002, p. 1199).

When measuring the effectiveness of research and development, one should aim to demonstrate the organization's performance in this critical dimension of new product development and to point out the means to improve it in the future. Somewhat in contrast with this, the measures of NPD in many companies suffer from short-termism and an overemphasis on single projects or products. A very typical measure of product development assesses the variance between a project's plan and actual outcome along the dimensions of cost and time (Meyer et al., 1997, p. 89).

Driva et al. have conducted a survey on the usage of performance measures in product development both in Europe and the USA. They received some 150 replies from European and American companies. The results show that the five most common performance measures are (Driva et al., 2000, pp. 151–152):

- total cost of the project (71% of the companies employed)
- on-time delivery of the development project (60%)
- actual project cost compared to budgeted cost (60%)
- actual vs. target time for the project completion (58%)
- lead time to market (57%)

Furthermore, 51% of the surveyed companies employed some kind of a projected profitability analysis. However, 18% of those not employing it at the moment wanted to use it in the future. Overall, it is highly interesting that none of the five most important measures actually concern the outcomes and effects of product development.

According to a survey, 50% of companies use performance indicators that are related to product performance including broad aspects such as quality, technical performance, development cost, production cost, and unit cost of the product (Hyland et al., 2002). According to the same study, approximately 60% of the companies monitor the profits generated by the product innovation activity. Hyland et al. also conclude that, apparently, many companies are much more involved in establishing an innovation process than actually trying to improve it. Thus, the potential of performance measures in improving and developing activities or processes is not fully utilized (Hyland et al., 2002). As a piece of data from 20 years ago, Meyer cites a study by Schainblatt (1982) who found that 59% of the studied firms did not measure the R&D activity at all. Further, as little as 20% of the studied firms carried out comparisons of R&D costs and commercial outcomes on a quantitative basis (Meyer et al., 1997, p. 89). More recently according to Kerssens-van Drongelen and Bilderbeek (1999), a survey among Dutch companies revealed that 80% of the companies that had some kind of R&D activities measured product development at least in some manner. While it is difficult to list the comprehensive reasons for these observations, Nixon points out one by putting forth that:

The measurement of R&D productivity and effectiveness has received relatively little attention in the management control and accounting literatures (Nixon, 1998, p. 330).

On the other hand, it has been recognized that management is generally unsatisfied with the present R&D measurement approaches presented in the literature (Pearson et al., 2000, p. 357). Nevertheless, it is a fact that many companies do not utilize explicit measurement of new product development performance at all and that, overall, comprehensive and consistent measures are still in their infancy (Driva et al., 2000, p. 158). However, it has been found that those companies that do useexplicit measurement often deploy both financial and non-financial measurement. Further, according to Hertenstein and Platt, NPD managers are generally not satisfied with the performance measurement of new product development. Also, the link between the measurement and corporate strategy seems to be weak in many cases despite the fact that a number of managers stress the importance of measuring the strategy alignment of product development (Hertenstein & Platt, 2000).

Werner and Souder studied the differences between U.S. and German practices of R&D performance measurement. They found out that both the perceptions on the usefulness of the measures and the fundamental philosophy related to performance measurement in these countries were different from each other (Werner & Souder, 1997a, b). German managers did not show any particular trust on performance measures. Particularly output measures were distrusted, whereas input measures were employed more often. U.S. managers, on the other hand, relied mostly on measures like the number of patents, financial measures such as rate-of-return, or quality assessments. The authors underscore, as a lesson from the cross-cultural study, that research and development measures cannot be selected "in a vacuum"; rather, performance measurement needs to be adapted to the organization in a such way that the measures are consistent with the particular organizational culture and philosophy. Hence, the greatest effectiveness through measures is only achieved when they become an integral part of the firm's research and development system (Werner & Souder, 1997a, b).

By using four case studies, Davila has shown the diversity that exists among the use of management control systems in new product development. Depending on the project characteristics, the role of control systems seems to vary. Prototyping, for instance, is likely to partially replace management control systems when technology is the main source of uncertainty. In contrast, when uncertainty is mostly due to the market of the project scope, management control systems are seen as vehicles to reduce uncertainty rather than to monitor and control. Thus, on the basis of this evidence, the information perspective – the role of measures in producing relevant information for the decision-making process – is supported.

(Davila, 2000) Davila's study also pointed out the relative importance of non-financial measures:

> ... project managers rely on non-financial performance measurement much more than they do on financial ones. This finding suggests that researching management control systems in new product development cannot be restricted to traditional accounting measures, but needs to encompass a broader set of measures. This is so because managers work with the implicit assumption that good performance in non-financials will drive good financial performance (Davila, 2000).

Consistently with this, it has also been argued that NPD managers might want to increase the emphasis on non-financial measures and, simultaneously, decrease the emphasis on financial ones. The rationale for this would be the difficulty to separate the financial results of NPD from those of other functions (Hertenstein & Platt, 2000). In other words, non-financial measures are expected to, better than financial ones, capture the specific contribution of NPD to the company objectives.

The lack of measures per se is not a problem. Meyer has found some 75 different measures of research and development in the literature. On the basis of analyzing them, he criticizes the existing performance measures of R&D. He argues that the actual impact of these various measures is questionable due to a number of aspects, including (Meyer et al., 1997):

(1) The measures are not able to provide help for the management to understand the long-term dynamics of evolving product lines.
(2) The measures do not provide understanding concerning the leverage that the underlying product architecture, that is product platform,[18] can provide in derivative products (products that can be derived from or based on a platform).

One of the reasons for poor measurement may the one presented by Szakonyi. He points out that the collaboration between R&D and finance is quite underdeveloped. He found that the lack of collaboration between these parties can be regarded as one of the most dramatic shortcomings of R&D effectiveness (Szakonyi, 1994a, b, p. 53). According to Szakonyi, an average R&D department has not recognized the benefits associated with the collaboration between R&D and finance. Hence, they lie on the first level A. The column "Points" in the table refers to the scoring used in the evaluation method of R&D effectiveness (Szakonyi, 1994a, b). On the other hand, it can be asked whether the non-financial measurement of product development, for example, should be a responsibility of financial department at all (Table 4).

According to Nixon (1998), the exclusion of accountants from the NPD teams can be due to the perception that accounting has traditionally placed on control rather than on constructive planning. On the other hand, the accounting function itself has not traditionally been very keen on participating in product development

Table 4. Present State of Collaboration Between R&D and Finance (Szakonyi, 1994a, b, p. 53).

Performance Level	Description	Points
Level A (Not recognized)	R&D department does not recognize how poor its relations with the finance or accounting department are	0
Level B (Initial efforts)	R&D managers are interested in working better with finance, but lack knowledge about the financial affairs of the company	1
Level C (Skills)	Understands financial matters, but lacks methods for determining the financial benefits of R&D	2
Level D (Methods)	Economic analysts work closely with R&D people, but there are disagreements about involvement and responsibilities	3
Level E (Responsibilities)	A finance person is transferred to R&D to serve as a bridge with finance, but company's accounting procedures short-change benefits of technology	4
Level F (Continuous improvements)	R&D managers have option of discussing with finance managers how economic analyses of technology are conducted if it looks like strategic benefits of technology are neglected.	5

in the first place, which has resulted in underdeveloped applications of management accounting information in product development.

5.2.8. NPD and Learning

The knowledge-based view of the firm is an approach that addresses questions such as "How to understand the learning process of the firm?" or "How to manage the knowledge base of an organization?" (see for example Grant, 1996; Nonaka, 1994.) From the knowledge point of view, the success of the firm depends on how well it is able to (Kessler et al., 2000):

(1) Enhance its own knowledge-base by creating or obtaining knowledge from various sources.
(2) Integrate the numerous knowledge areas effectively within the firm.
(3) Apply the knowledge to develop successful new products or to improve the existing products.

Thus, learning is an essential part of product development. Yet, it has been demonstrated that people do not really know how to learn effectively (Argyris, 1991). According to Argyris, many skilled and educated people are quite good at single-loop learning but, in contrast, they fail to properly conduct double-loop learning. In other words, these skilled people tend to succeed in what they normally do – in the things they are educated for. But ironically, since they quite rarely experience a failure they often lack the ability to learn from the mistakes: "their ability to learn shuts down precisely at the moment they need it the most" (Argyris, 1991, p. 100). Defensive reasoning has been identified as a major antecedent for the deficiency of the professionals in double-loop learning. Argyris points out that effective double-loop learning necessitates a reflection of how people think. The cognitive rules and reasoning that are employed to design and implement one's actions have to be exposed. By this exposure, defensive reasoning that blocks learning can be identified and perhaps gradually replaced (Argyris, 1991).

Organizational learning can be discussed in the knowledge-creation framework. Perhaps the most well-known authors who have studied the knowledge creation process are Nonaka and Takeuchi, who have, among others, presented a model that describes the knowledge conversion from individual tacit knowledge to organizational knowledge (1995). As seen in the context of knowledge creation, the concept of product development success receives one additional interpretation: R&D activities can be perceived as successful when they enable or generate valuable knowledge building. This seems to be reasonably well in line with Lewis' (Lewis, 2001) notion that NPD can be seen as a specific illustration of organizational learning. Lewis has created a model that defines the elements and their basic interaction of organizational competence. According to Lewis' definition:

> organisational competencies are those combinations of organisational resources and processes (including NPD) that together underpin sustainable competitive advantage for a specific firm competing in a particular product/service market.

Lewis argues that the interaction between resources and processes is not uni-dimensional: resources create value when they are utilized in processes, which in turn helps to create new or extend existing resources. In NPD this means that skilled resources is not only one of the prerequisites of a good NPD process but the good process itself generates valuable information, knowledge, or experience – that is resources. Another definition is presented by Drejer and Riis (1999) who view competencies as a system of human beings, using technology in an organized way and under the influence of a culture to create output that yields a competitive advantage for the firm. Both of the definitions are essentially similar: both perceive competencies as systems to some extent – action and interaction are strongly present, and both link competencies tightly with the creation of competitive advantage. Competencies are not just any abilities to respond to "random" demands but rather building blocks for the firm's competitive advantage. Lehtonen (2002) has listed several different parties that an organization can utilize when striving to increase or develop its competencies including customers (networking), subcontractors, competitors, and educational institutions. He also postulates that sometimes the only available method for competence building is to invest in the firm's own product development. Interestingly however, Lehtonen has made a notion that in the case environment he studied, competence building has not been a really intentional nor a target-oriented activity. On the basis of this case, Lehtonen suggests that instead of the expression "knowledge is built" one should rather use the more passive expression "knowledge is grown" when the knowledge creation process cannot be examined as an intentional activity. Happonen (2001), for one, concluded that a product development project is not a closed entity, whose results are communicated only after the project completion. In contrast, it is typical that knowledge transfer takes place already during the actual development project.

5.2.9. Summary

New product development management seems to be a popular topic that has attracted both academics and practitioners. Within the overall subject, the performance measurement of product development has also inspired many insights. Regarding this theme, the above section primarily reviewed four streams of literature: (1) One that discusses performance measurement and related applications as such. (2) One that explores the application and utilization of performance measurement in companies. (3) One that discusses on the interpretation of new product success and performance. (4) One that seeks antecedents of success and tries to identify mechanisms associated with successful product development. The following list comprises some of the key findings made on the basis of the literature:

- The changing role of product development: increased investments, networking, R&D cooperation.
- Product development should be founded on a clear understanding of customer value: how the customers create value in their processes.
- The importance of NPD performance measurement has been underscored.
- Measurement should be simultaneously relatively simple and comprehensive.
- Dangers related to too straightforward measurement have been pointed out.
- Need for multifaceted measurement has been identified, but there is a very limited number of practical solutions available.
- The construction process of the PM system needs more support.
- The utilization of performance measurement in practice is not very well developed.
- NPD is one vehicle for organizational learning and measurement should also support learning.
- Success is both stakeholder- and context-specific issue.

- Success is very often assessed in relative terms.
- Success is a temporal variable.
- Many cause-effect-relationships have been established regarding the antecedents and consequences of success.
- Product life cycle is one contingent variable of PM system's design.
- Life cycle-oriented measurement has been discussed to a very limited extent.
- Life cycle would provide a feasible foundation for PM:
  - Comprehensiveness: different stakeholders, a longer time frame, and different requirements are represented.
  - Outcome orientation: the "total effects" of a product.

5.3. Product Life Cycle and Life Cycle Management

What is frequently lacking for management discussion is an adequate set of options about the future, and the means to measure them (Miller, 1995).

5.3.1. Applicability of the Concept

Life cycle is an applicable concept regarding many issues. Overall, life cycle models imply that the needs and requirements associated with products and technologies (or even entire industries) have an evolutionary character. In other words, products and technologies are seen as dynamic phenomena whose requirements evolve as a function of time. The requirements that are important in early stages of life cycle become less vital when a product or technology reaches the later stages of its life cycle. Massey (1999) lists a number of different purposes, which have been mentioned to benefit from the PLC concept. It has been proposed in the literature that product life cycle would be a useful framework to determine appropriate business strategies (see for example Anderson & Zeithaml, 1984, pp. 21–22; Rink et al., 1999) and it could be applied in some marketing problems – such as marketing planning. Also, it has been suggested that a potential area would be forecasting the sales of new products. For instance, Nelson (1992) has analyzed the product demand of engineered metals such as steel, aluminium and titanium by employing the product life cycle concept.

Magnan et al. (1999) have studied the applicability of the PLC concept for developing or selecting the most appropriate manufacturing strategy or practice for products. A number of different manufacturing practices were analyzed regarding which life cycle phase would be the most appropriate for utilizing a particular manufacturing practice. In fact, on the basis of the survey, a variety of different practices were found suitable for the design, introduction, growth, and maturity stages. However, the respondents did not see many manufacturing practices as relevant within the decline stage. This notion implies that the end of the life cycle still receives little attention from the practitioners. Overall, it was confirmed by this survey that firms with products in different life cycle stages employ different manufacturing practices and emphasize different kinds of strategies. Overall, according to the survey of 500 manufacturing managers by Magnan et al. (1999), the PLC concept was used by most firms, although at a somewhat moderate level.

Anderson and Zeithaml (1984) stress the potential of the product life cycle concept in the long-term assessment of business impacts. They note that the decision-makers may, for instance, in many industries face high product development costs and investment requirements when developing and launching new products. If this is the case, according to Anderson and Zeithaml, the business has to determine or project the implications of various operating modes for profits over time. Also, it would be relevant in these circumstances to carefully assess the feasibility and profitability of market share gains through the development activities. Anderson and Zeithaml (1984) describe two main methods to proactively benefit from the product life cycle concept:

(1) Especially growth businesses should consider the implications of their perceived objectives and strategies for the later stages of product life cycle. The analysis would be based on projections of anticipated market conditions and, on the other hand, the assessment of competitors' strategies.
(2) Business management should evaluate the evolutionary development of the market. This comprises continuous evaluation of the company's position in the market and implementation of strategies that enable proper responses to changing conditions.

General support for the idea that life cycle and its phases can be used to structure different requirements and patterns of action can be found from literature. For instance, a study by Moores and Yuen (2001) adopted a life cycle perspective to study management accounting systems and their formality that organizations employ in different stages of life cycle. According to the study, firms in the growth phase pay particular attention to increasing the formality of their management accounting systems.

Werker (2003) refers to a generally agreed relationship that market performance, innovation, and competition depend on the maturity of markets. The level of maturity can be usually described as a function of competition: new markets are typically associated with competition between several firms, whereas mature markets would be dominated by fewer firms. However, all the real-life situations do not correspond to this definition (consider, for instance, the food industry).

Weisenfeld et al. (2001) discussed the differences between forms of collaboration and, especially, the suitability of a collaboration profile for a particular phase of technology life cycle. According to Weisenfeld et al. (2001, p. 99), two collaboration profiles that have validity in high-tech areas are industrial platforms and virtual companies. Industrial platforms should be especially suited for the early phases of technology life cycle since they can be used to promote technology transfer by setting up an infrastructure for technology development. At the commercialization stage, virtual companies are recommended as a means to master the management of competencies and market orientation. These findings are, however, made on the basis of a limited number of interviews, thus limiting the validity of these generalizations.

Among other things, the concept of product life cycle has been employed in cost management (Ansari et al., 1997). Life cycle costing (LCC) is founded on the notion that the majority of costs associated with a product could be other than initial: maintenance, replacement, and finance. For instance, over 60% of the total costs of a typical office building consist of maintenance, operations, energy consumption, and replacement (Dell'Isola, 1997). Furthermore, life cycle has been adopted as a structure for organizing many organizational issues. For example, Sherman and Olsen (1996) investigated the relationship between various dimensions of organizational climate and performance across the life cycle stages of an R&D project. van den Ende (2003), for one, has showed that the service product life cycle affects the choice of the governance mode of development projects. His analysis is made on the basis of distinguishing between the mature and fluid phases of life cycle. Hart and Tzokas (2000) analyzed the marketing mix decisions related to product launch over product-market life cycle. In addition to product life cycle, technology life cycles, project life cycles, and industrial life cycles have been discussed. For instance, despite the fact that the recognition of project life cycle phases may be difficult, it has been argued that the description and analysis of life cycle as a collection of discrete phases can help to understand the logic and phenomena related to the project and its life cycle (Vartiainen et al., 1999). However, in spite of the numerous possible applications of the life cycle concept, product life cycle is the main interest of this study.

5.3.2. NPD Management and Life Cycle
So far, it has been made clear that new product development management is a crucial issue for successful business. The life cycle management of a product, on the other hand, seems to be among the issues that should be considered within effective NPD management. For instance, Westkämper et al. (2001) define life cycle management (LCM) as an approach that considers the entire product life cycle in order to optimize the interaction between product design and its life cycle

activities. On the other hand, Clifford (1965) identified two functions for LCM, one of them being very different from the function identified by Westkämper et al. (2001). Namely, the second function referred to controlling the *product mix* in terms of life cycle stages represented. Further, it has been reminded that product development should not merely translate an identified need into a description of a product but should rather ensure that the design is compatible with the elements across the product's life cycle including performance, effectiveness, producibility, reliability, maintainability, quality, and cost (Asiedu & Gu, 1998, pp. 884–885).

Profitability can be best nurtured with sound decisions during the early stages of product life cycle (Prasad, 1997). It has been pointed out that if careless decisions are made during the early stages of product development, the process is continuously in a fire-fighting mode: all the things cannot be resolved because there is always something urgent going on. Hence, Prasad underscores the importance of careful definition and design phases of product development. Through thorough and rigorous initial development, later redesign phases can be avoided. Prahad gives an example that covers two shipyards: one of them put emphasis on early definition when developing the first vessel for a customer, while the other somewhat neglected the initial phase. As a result, when another similar order was placed, the latter company had to put significant effort into redesigning the initial concept (Fig. 6).

Wyland (1998) suggests that the capabilities of a product can – and need to – be tracked throughout the supply chain. Furthermore, the tracking can be extended to cover the entire life cycle of a product. Hence, according to Wyland, the full life cycle management of a product is cradle-to-grave management of the product

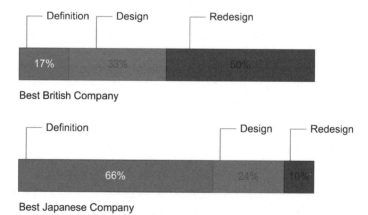

Fig. 6. Distribution of Product Development Efforts (Prasad, 1997, p. 94).

as it progresses through the logistics pipelines. As many different types of data are inherently involved in product life cycle management, some causal data is also likely to be obtained.

At the product level, both the lifetime, the expenditures associated with it, and all the revenues have to be assessed in the LCM process. Bauer and Fischer stress the importance of product life cycle for the long-term profitability of new products (Bauer & Fischer, 2000). They have shown that to economically cover the R&D investments of a late-mover pharmaceutical product, the product life cycle needs to reach a sales maximum as early as in the first years after the product launch. This result relies on studied life cycle patterns of pharmaceutical products and the typical R&D costs, marketing expenses, capital costs, and product cost structure associated with them.

Overall, the importance of total life cycle management seems to be increasing as Westkämper et al. (2001, p. 677) point out:

> In future times, the designers and manufacturers of manufacturing systems will have an increasing responsibility in developing systems and devices appropriate or adequate to the demands of the whole life cycle. The complete development process is of utmost importance for the future product.

The first reason for this is pointed out by many authors: product development influences a large portion of the total costs of a product (see for example Asiedu & Gu, 1998; Uusi-Rauva & Paranko, 1998). The second reason is the paradigm shift (especially in the industrial context) regarding the essence of "merchandise." Traditionally, producers of investment goods have sold machines or manufacturing lines, for example. Increasingly, however, these manufacturers perceive themselves as "solution providers" or "value/benefit providers." In other words, a manufacturer will not only deliver a system but will also operate and maintain the system. In effect, the manufacturer's responsibility for the product and/or service increases, which leads to the increasing importance of life cycle performance seen from the manufacturer's perspective (Westkämper et al., 2001).

Product life cycle and product development are dynamically inter-connected issues:

> The win-win of joint life-cycle planning is that both the company and the suppliers can smoothly move from one product generation to the next. The company is able to optimize time-to-market, while both the company and the supplier benefit from better capacity utilization and reduced total inventories and obsolescence (Hoover et al., 2001, p. 143).

Harness et al. (1998) remark that the life cycle management of a product also includes the question of product deletion. As a part of the deletion process, one should be able to identify when a product ceases to fulfil its rationale for existence. To better understand the logic of product deletion, the authors have identified a number of factors that create the need for ending the life of the product. They found that the deletion process may be lead by external, customer-based, strategy-based, or operationally-based factors. Hence, these issues of product deletion add one aspect to the discussion concerning the nature of product life cycle. That is, product life cycle is predominantly a dependable variable that can be *partly* affected by the company and its actions. External factors that may lead to product deletion cannot always be anticipated or affected.

Successful innovations may require close collaboration between suppliers and customers. Collaboration serves not only as a means to identify needs that are communicated by the customers but also as a means to familiarize with the customer's industrial environment. Athaide et al. (1996) stress that the collaboration should not only take place during the development or early commercialization but should rather be a continuous process that goes on also after product installation and implementation. Product development, for instance, works closely with the customer during the customization process. This kind of collaboration requires a clear understanding of the customer's needs, which may not be attained without long-term interaction. Athaide et al. (1996) found that the quality of interactions between product development and customer affect the buyers' satisfaction and future purchase intentions. Also, interaction may facilitate that product development could be able to identify opportunities (such as desired product enhancements that may serve as a foundation for future generations of the product) along the product life cycle as they arise. If the supplier is familiar with the trajectories present in the customer's industry, he will be able to anticipate rising needs via, for instance, modified products.

The performance of a product through its life cycle has been mentioned as a predominantly qualitative measure of R&D productivity (Brown & Gobeli, 1992). Also, the economic life cycle of the product is commonly used as a (implicit) basis for economic analysis in product development. In fact, anticipating a product's economic life is a prerequisite for using discounted cash flow techniques, such as net present value (NPV). However, life cycle-based information is often applied in a very straightforward manner, not considering – for instance – the different stages of the life cycle and their characteristics. For example, when testing an option-based approach for R&D project valuation Herath and Park (1999, p. 22) note: "... operations continue at the current level over an economic life of eight years. We can then obtain the required gross values using the present value formula of an equal payment series." In this example, it is obvious that the life cycle is not more than a numerical parameter for one formula in the value calculation process.

On the other hand, opposite examples can also be found in the literature. There are several authors who have applied the concept of life cycle to various management themes. For instance, the concept of life cycle has provided value when positioning products in the market. Grantham (1997) reports a story of a small software producer that employed the PLC concept when competing against Microsoft. This small producer noticed that its product would be more suitable than that of Microsoft's for the majority of users with older computers unwilling to update their systems. By positioning the product in the later stages of the life cycle, the producer found the niche that was the most suitable for it.

The recognition of important and less important activities and tasks of product development has to be based on the analysis of the product life cycle. Maccarone argues that a number of product development activities may apparently not add value if only the product development process is considered. However, these activities may be of fundamental importance to reach a certain target level of market performance. Hence, the analysis of activities and the identification of value-adding activities has to be made with respect to all the stages of the life cycle of a product (Maccarrone, 1998, p. 150).

Further, especially at successful product introductions, demand exceeds supply. Therefore, preparing for demand is an essential issue in life cycle management. In network relationships, sharing of aggregate volumes (concerning also ramp-up and ramp-down plans) for the whole life cycle is a key activity in joint life cycle management (Hoover et al., 2001, pp. 143–144). Consistently, Kurawarwala and Matsuo (1998) point out that a total sales estimate covering the entire life cycle of a product and sales estimations for a shorter period would be valuable for many companies. The reasons for this include the length of lead times of major components (in some cases a component's lead time may cover a large portion of the product's entire cycle), volatility in the prices of components, and, especially at the beginning of a life cycle, the lack of *de facto* sales history. However, Kurawarwala and Matsuo (1998) remind that the availability of data on *prior similar* products may act as a surrogate for the scarcity of data on any particular product. As the authors point out, the complete sales history and volume of a number of preceding products is typically available. On the basis of this, forecasts regarding future products can be produced.

Ryan and Riggs (1996) discuss the levels of different activities during the life cycle of a product. They recognize that the workload of various functions or activities depends on the life cycle stage. In fact, Ryan and Riggs have refined the traditional life cycle model. They have established a so-called five-element product wave, whose elements are design engineering, process engineering, product marketing, production, and end-of life activities. Illustrating the varying activity levels, according to Ryan and Riggs, a number of waves occur during the entire product life cycle. The first one is associated with the design of the first version of the product, the next wave with the second upgrade, and so on. Ryan and Riggs point out that the varying activity levels are a direct consequence of product introductions and redesigns that primarily have to be based on company strategy, core capabilities, and the state of the competitive environment. As an example of key activity, product innovation is often considered to take place only within the product development phase of the product life cycle. However, in terms of the innovation activity, the other phases of the life cycle are important as well. The other phases are not only essential due to the fact that they may provide product developers with information that is useful for feeding next-generation product development projects, but they can also provide opportunities for product innovation within a single product life cycle (Boer et al., 2001).

Customer support is one of the issues that should be considered in comprehensive life cycle-oriented NPD. Goffin (1998) argues that to increase the likelihood of customer satisfaction, a firm has to consider the product's support requirements already during the design stage in new product development. Support, as Goffin (1998) sees it, may take different forms, including: installation, documentation, field service, user training and product upgrades. The important role of support is generally agreed on (see for example Lele, 1986, 1997; Suomala et al., 2002a, b): effective product support will, for instance, increase customer satisfaction, provide competitive advantage, and serve as a source of revenue (Goffin, 1998, p. 43). Considering that product design has a strong influence on support (Lele, 1986), the measurement of support-related aspects is rather underdeveloped. In a survey covering responses from 66 companies, Goffin (1998) identified sixteen measures that were engaged to track product support during product design. According to Goffin (1998), these measures, if used in combination, offer a means for evaluating support requirements at the design stage more comprehensively than is currently often the case (Table 5).

Also Cohen and Whang (1997) put forth that managerial decision-making should focus on the profitability of the product over its entire life cycle rather than on the profitability of a single purchase transaction or on the profitability per a certain period of time. The authors note that the life cycle perspective is relevant and applicable for service industries as well. Also, regarding both product and services industries, it is not uncommon for companies to sell their products or services at a loss in order to gain profits from the after sales period. Indeed, a number of observations suggest that in many industries – including electronics, communication, machine construction, and car industry – the after sales period is very essential both in terms of total product revenues and, especially, generated profits (Suomala et al., 2002a, b). Cohen and Whang argue that in many industries, the profit margin of after sales service provided and the margin of service part sales exceeds the profit margin on the sale of the product itself.

Table 5. Identified Support Measures (Adopted from Goffin, 1998, p. 49).

Support Aspect	Design Stage Measure	Notes
Installation	Time required (Human) resource/skill level Material/equipment required	Some companies used mean-time-to-install as a goal
User training	Time to train the user Trainer's skill level	Only 20% of respondents applied
Maintenance	Mean-time-between-maintenance Human resource Time per maintenance Material/equipment required	Evaluated by 44% but none of the respondents used all the measures
Repair	Failure rate Fault diagnosis time Mean-time-to-repair (MTTR) (Human) resource required	Failure rate and MTTR were the most common measures of all
Upgrades	Time required (Human) resource required Material/equipment required	

5.3.3. Other than Producer-Based Views on PLC

When assessing the interface between a product design and environment, the concept of product life cycle plays an important role. It is increasingly important to consider all aspects of the impacts of a product on its environment. Concerning the attributes of new products including functionality, time to market, profitability, reliability, safety, and cost of ownership, the life cycle perspective is viable to apply to each of them. Functionality, for instance, receives different interpretations along the life cycle. The comprehensive effect of time-to-market, for one, on the profitability depends on the length of product life cycle. The cost-of-ownership, on the other hand, may differ from one life cycle phase to another. Due to this, it is a question of emphasis whether certain product parameters that affect the ownership costs receive more attention than the others (Pringle, 2001).

A lot of valuable work regarding the life cycle assessment of products has been done with an environmental focus or emphasis on environmental issues. These include studies that – despite their specific environmental emphasis – are still quite generic at the level of their fundamental logic concerning the life cycle impacts of the products. Hence, these studies have potential to extend their analyses over a number of aspects in addition to those directly related to environmental impacts (see Kumaran et al., 2001; Leastadius & Karlson, 2001). For instance, Kane et al. (2000), propose a stepwise life cycle engineering and assessment methodology for large made-to-order products (LMTO products). One of the requirements of the methodology is that it is possible to produce an estimation of the environmental impact of a product over its entire life cycle. The estimation often relies on measures that can be derived either from primary or secondary principles of clean design. Clean design refers to a number of both primary and secondary principles that can be regarded as – at least – indirect measures of life cycle impacts of products. The primary principles include (Kane et al., 2000, p. 177):

- Dematerialization, that is, using less material.
- Substitution, that is, use materials with less harmful waste products.
- Use external sources of energy, that is, solar/wind/tidal or bio fuels.

The secondary principles include:

- Use recycled material.
- Use recyclable material.
- Energy efficiency.
- Use biodegradable materials.
- Extend life span of products.

For the actual assessment of material flows and their effect on the environment one approach is provided by the ISO 14040 standard. The life cycle assessment (LCA) approach described in ISO 14040 is structured around four stages of analysis. The first stage sets the scope for the analysis. In other words, during the first stage, the boundaries for the system being assessed are defined. The second stage comprises an "inventory analysis," which means that all the material and energy flows that occur along the life cycle are determined. The third stage, impact assessment, determines the contribution of the predetermined energy and material flows to certain environmental effects. In the fourth stage, by using sensitivity analysis and subjective weighting, the actual environmental effects are combined and summarized to produce a holistic view. Kumaran et al. (2001) add one dimension to LCA, namely the identification of life cycle stages. It constitutes a basis for the entire analysis and may be seen as a part of setting the scope for LCA (see Kane, 2000). Furthermore, Kumaran et al. (2001) point out that life cycle impact analysis does not necessarily seek to quantify the specific impacts associated with a process or a product, it rather attempts to establish a link or connection between the potential impacts and the product (and its characteristics).

Cohen and Whang (1997) have developed a life cycle model that considers the product's life and its stages from the owner or user point of view to support the consideration of trade-off between profit from product sales and from after sales services. The after sales profit can be seen as a function of after sales service and its quality. Consistently with this, Cohen and Whang point out that after sales service quality can be regarded as one of the design and development decisions. Hence, it is implied that the tasks of product development could be extended to explicitly cover the entire life cycle of the product. "From product development toward product life cycle development."

Price and Coy (2001) have described the life cycle management (LCM) process at the 3M company. The LCM process addresses the general idea that the scope of a manufacturer's environmental responsibility extends to cover not only manufacturing and raw material supply but also the period of customer use and disposal. The example of 3M LCM shows that the environmental life cycle concerns are rather directly connected to competitive viewpoints. Namely, the two main objectives for LCM at 3M are, firstly, to identify the sources of competitive advantage that are based on the exemplary life cycle performance of a product and, secondly, to manage the environmental risks and resource consumption throughout the life cycle. Methodologically the life cycle management process, which is closely interlinked with the product commercialization process, relies on qualitative analysis. In addition, it is underscored that as a support to this qualitative process, more quantitative methods, such as life cycle assessment, could be beneficial. In a more detailed level, the LCM process can be described as a sequence of six discrete stages:

(1) A complete LCM screen that aims to identify how a product can be adapted to gain the largest environmental, health, and safety (EHS) advantages. Typically, this review is carried out in the concept design phase for a new product.
(2) Gathering of preliminary information concerning all the aspects of the product being developed. A number of scoping questions are employed at this phase. These questions include: What functions are included in the analysis? What is the typical use pattern for the product?
(3) Developing charts on energy and raw material consumption and EHS exposures along the different life cycle stages.
(4) Complete the LCM matrix, which comprises the sequence of relevant life cycle stages and, respectively, the qualitative assessment of EHS issues at each stage of the life cycle.
(5) and (6) Assess the product advantages and disadvantages using a predetermined coding (+ for EHS opportunity and ? for risks, for instance).

5.3.4. Life Cycle Costs

The notion that virtually all the material and energy flows that occur within a product life cycle have an economic value leads to the idea of life cycle cost (LCC) of the product (Kane et al., 2000). Woodward (1997) defines the LCC for

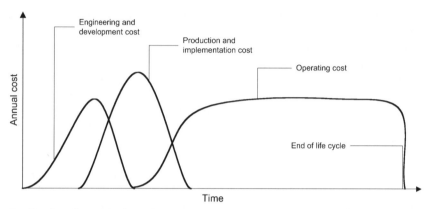

Fig. 7.   Cost Categorization Along Product Life Cycle (Adapted from Woodward, 1997, p. 336).

an item as:

The sum of all funds expended in support of the item from its conception and fabrication through its operation to the end if its useful life.

Or in other words, as Kumaran et al. (2001) formulate, the life cycle cost analysis is to provide a framework for calculating the total costs of design, development, production, use, and disposal of the product. Hence, LCC does not clearly represent either the developer's or user's point of view. Rather, LCC looks at the life cycle just as the product itself "experiences" it.

Building the cost structure so as to identify the potential cost trade-offs is one of the essential elements of LCC. Woodward (1997) points out that while alternative cost structures could be proposed, the required depth and breadth of the analysis mainly determines the appropriate structure. A typical three-category structure is depicted in Fig. 7.

A variety of methods have been established to identify and calculate the life cycle costs of a product. The models described in the literature feature a number of dimensions that may benefit from the life cycle cost assessment,[19] including development of cost breakdown structures (CBS's), generation of cost estimates, total cost determination, and sensitivity analysis. (see for example Asiedu & Gu, 1998; Dalén & Bolmsjö, 1996; Emblemsvåg, 2001; Kumaran et al., 2001; Woodward, 1997) For instance, Emblemsvåg (2001) argues that as organizations become increasingly aware of both environmental costs and customer service costs, the costs of the entire life cycle become very important to assess. In conducting the life cycle cost analysis, Emblemsvåg stresses the handling of uncertainty (see also Badri et al., 1997, for the utilization of simulation in dealing with R&D project's

uncertainty). Because uncertainty is more or less inherent in product development and related forecasting, uncertainty has to be included in LCC. The activity-based LCC that Emblemsvåg advocates utilizes Monte Carlo[20] simulations to handle uncertainty. The construction process of activity-based LCC consists of five main phases (Emblemsvåg, 2001, pp. 19–22):

(1) Create an activity hierarchy and network, which is supposed to describe the activities that take place during the product's life-span.
(2) Identify the resources.
(3) Identify both the resource and the activity drivers.
(4) Identify the relationships between the (activity) drivers and design parameters.
(5) Calculate the costs, energy consumption, and waste generation of the consumption of activities.

Comprehensively, the life cycle costs of a product can be organized on the basis of product life cycle stages and different stakeholders included in the analysis (see Table 6).

As an example of a specific LCC application, Dalén and Bolmsjö (1996) have proposed life cycle-based costing for labor factor analysis. They have utilized life cycle thinking in estimating the total costs for an employee over the whole employment cycle. The analysis is made on the basis of three cost factors:

(1) Employment costs consisting of recruitment, education, and training-related issues.
(2) Operational costs that reflect the salaries and related overheads.

Table 6. Product Life Cycle Costs (Adapted from Asiedu & Gu, 1998; Perera et al., 1999).

Phase	Manufacturer	User	Society
Product development/design	Market recognition, product development	–	–
Production	Raw material, labor, processing, energy	–	Waste, pollution, health damage
Distribution	Transport, inventory, damages	Transport, damages	–
Usage	Warranty, service	Energy, maintenance, breakdown	Pollution, health damage
Disposal and recycling	Recycling, disposal	Disposal dues	Pollution, health damage

(3) Work environmental costs that include the costs of absenteeism, rehabilitation, and pensions.

According to Dalén and Bolmsjö (1996), the life cycle costs of an employee behave analogously to those of a production system. That is, if the costs are plotted as a function of time, the curve will look like a bathtub: At the first stage (acquisition phase) the costs are relatively high mainly due to the costs associated with the employment (analogously to the costs of purchase, installation, and projecting in the case of a production system). Within the second phase (operation phase), the costs are first decreasing to find an equilibrium. In the employment cycle, salaries and overheads mainly comprise the operational costs. Finally at the third stage, the work environmental costs will rise resulting in an increase in the total costs. In the case of a production system, the increasing costs in the final stage often relate to repairs and disruptions.

A presupposition that consumers – or industrial customers – are rational and that they make efficient selections to maximize their wealth is an interesting issue with regard to life cycle costing. For instance, decisions related to life cycle costs include temporal elements. Hence, to be in a position to make efficient decisions, taking into account the life cycle effects, customers are required to cope with two kinds of cost elements: those related to purchase and those that are connected with use and maintenance. The ability of customers to make efficient decisions that are based on total life cycle costs is analyzed for instance by Liebermann and Ungar (2002). They found out that, generally, consumers cope rather well with LCC situations. However, recent studies have shown that industrial investments decisions are seldom based on life cycle costs (Järvinen et al., 2004).

Kane et al. (2000, p. 181) have found that discounting economic values associated with future events is perhaps not as problem-free as one might expect. Kane et al. argue that sometimes discounting may conflict with the idea of life cycle consciousness: "There is, however, a dichotomy between discounting and sustainable development. Using a private-sector discount rate (typically 20–25%) reduces most costs in the intergenerational time frame (20 years) to a negligible level, diminishing the importance of such future issues as decommissioning." As one solution, Kane et al. propose variable rate discounting that utilizes a hyperbolic function to calculate the discounting factor (VDF):

$$\text{VDF} = \frac{1}{(1 + rt)},$$

where r is the discount rate and t is time.

Whereas constant discounting factor is given by:

$$DF = \frac{1}{(1+r)^t}$$

According to Kane, it is even suggested that the variable rate discounting is actually closer to public's time preference for money than constant rate discounting (Kane et al., 2000).

5.3.5. Length of Life Cycle

The profits from a product or service have to be earned during its economic life cycle. Therefore, an important consideration that also restricts the product development process and the practices employed is the relation between the product development lead time and the length of the product's entire life cycle. If the development phase is relatively long compared with the entire life cycle, the efficiency of the development process gains importance. On the other hand, when the development phase is relatively short compared to the length of the entire life cycle, the efficiency of the development phase might not be a primary concern. In the former case, any practices (including utilization of performance measurement techniques) that require a lot of effort and resources and are time-consuming are more likely to be a burden for the life cycle profitability. This is because rapid product development is a prerequisite for the economic life cycle of a product. In the latter case, an effort taken – even a time-consuming one – in the product development phase is more likely to produce sufficient economic returns later in the life cycle. Especially in consumer markets, product development lead time is one of the most important competitive factors (Prasad, 1997). Consistently with this, in many companies the actual development costs are rather small (10–20%) compared to the total cost of product, and the changes made during the development phase are relatively cost effective compared with those made in later phases (Prasad, 1997, p. 95; Sievänen et al., 2001).

It has often been pointed out that the product life cycles are shortening on the average or that short life cycles are becoming increasingly common (see for instance Kurawarwala & Matsuo, 1998; Ryan & Riggs, 1996). This not necessarily the whole truth: As a clear majority of authors argue that the product life cycles are generally getting shorter, some evidence has been found to support the opposite view. According to Bayus (1994) for example, no clear empirical support exists for shrinking life cycles either at the level of industries, product categories, or product models. Furthermore, limiting the credibility of the shortening life cycle-argument to some extent, it is also noteworthy that this same argument has been constantly used for decades. For instance, already Clifford (1965) stated that life cycles are getting shorter. Instead of over-simplifying the issue too much, it would be more realistic to say that the length of life cycles differs across industries and very long life cycles exist as well. For instance, it has been noted that the length of product lifetime in many industries exceeds 10 years and it is not even uncommon to have product lifetime longer than 20 years (Goffin & New, 2001, p. 285; Suomala et al., 2002a, b).

Despite the length, forecasting the life of an asset has a major influence on the life cycle analysis. But how to anticipate the length of life of a product? Woodward (1997) refers to five possible determinants of an asset's life expectancy:

- Functional life, which represents the period over which the need for the product is anticipated.
- Physical life, the period that the product may be expected to last physically.
- Technological life, which refers to the period after which technical obsolescence occurs (due to technically superior alternative).
- Economic life, which corresponds to the period after which economic obsolescence occurs along the emergence of a lower cost alternative.
- Social and legal life, which represents the period over which human desire and/or legal requirements do not require replacement.

Uncertainty is an inherent element of life cycle analysis and life cycle cost analysis. Therefore, (see for example Jiang & Zhang, 2003), included elements and system costs within these analyses are typically represented by statistical distributions. Kane et al. (2000, p. 184), for one, underscore that it is a particularly challenging task to predict the life cycle of a product. Therefore, it is important for a methodology concerning life cycle assessment to allow the application of several potential life cycles. The occurrence of each alternative life cycle can be anticipated with some degree of probability.

Bauer and Fischer (2000) have conducted a time-series analysis on the sales data of pharmaceuticals to determine the long-term economic behavior of such products. As a part of the study, they have identified an international classification of product life cycles for pharmaceuticals. They ended up with three different life cycle patterns for pharmaceuticals that represent the real-life clusters of life cycles describing the sales patterns of new products in this industry (see Fig. 8).

It has been found out that the shape of the life cycle depends on the degree of innovativeness: the first movers and late movers seem to behave differently in terms of sales volume development. The first movers typically witness a long growth period toward the peak of the life cycle, while the late movers usually proceed more rapidly into the point of the highest sales volume of their life cycle. Further, one might observe that, according to Bauer and Fischer, the PLC describes the phases of a product from its introduction to the market until its withdrawal. Hence, this definition is based on the market presence of the product

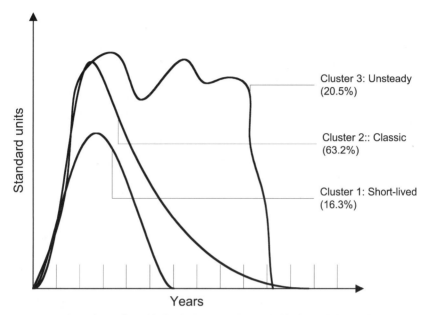

Fig. 8. Alternative Life Cycle Patterns (Bauer & Fischer, 2000, p. 709).

and the development phase of the product, for instance, is not considered as a life cycle phase of its own. This approach is quite natural and appropriate if the primary aim of the life cycle assessment is on the sales behavior of the product.

Curtis (1994) argues that a major determinant of product life is the ease of service and maintenance. According to him, many products are discarded because the costs of maintenance become too high compared to the perceived product value. Contrary to practices observed by Curtis (1994), to ensure the greatest influence the aspects of service, disassembly, and recycling have to be considered in the early stages of product design. It is proposed that these considerations can be made in conjunction with the design for assembly (DFA) analysis. By using the DFA structure, it is possible, for instance, to determine a disassembly sequence for a certain service task. Together with cost estimations related to service parts, one is able to assess the serviceability of the product to a certain extent.

5.3.6. Technology Life Cycle
Product life cycle can also be analyzed within a broader framework of technology life cycle. The framework of technology life cycle refers to an idea that technologies

evolve – analogous to products – through a number of phases or stages whose characters are different from each other. First, a technology is created or developed, after which it will witness some kind of an introduction to the market. If it is able to demonstrate value to some extent, it will exhibit a wider adoption and application phase. Eventually, as more competitive new technologies are introduced, the technology life cycle will reach its end and the technology is replaced. It is argued that different technology life cycle phases have different kinds of characteristic features. For example, rapid innovation accompanies the early stages of technology life cycle. On the other hand, the importance of process innovation becomes more evident as the technology matures. Also, it is suggested that as technology gets more mature, the uncertainties and limitations related to technology decline enabling the standardization of products and processes.

Hence, relying on the concept of technology life cycle and its ideas about varying requirements, products that represent different technology life cycle phases should be managed with a different kind of emphasis. As the success criteria for a product differs from phase to phase, the products should demonstrate different qualities to be able to succeed. For instance, products that are essentially based on new technology (technology in the early stages of its life cycle) are likely to be able to demonstrate competitiveness in the market if they are merely technologically progressive and innovative. This is consistent with an observation made by Rhyne (1996), according to which technological genius or creativity may be a basis for success during the early stages of life cycle. In addition, technological quality in the early stages may also mask other organizational shortfalls to some degree. However, to be able to be competitive, products whose technological core is relatively mature have to meet different criteria related to, for example, cost efficiency and effectiveness.

The concept of the technology S-curve (Fig. 9) is one of the models that have been presented to illustrate the nature of technology evolution during its life cycle. According to the concept, small or marginal improvements on a product's performance will require a relatively large development effort during the early stages of technology development. As the technology becomes more familiar and utilized in a variety of products, the improvements in performance can be achieved by a smaller effort. Finally, as the technology approaches its limits, the improvements in performance become increasingly difficult to obtain. However, although major breakthroughs are difficult to achieve towards the end of the life cycle, a series of incremental improvements may result in significant overall performance gain (Rhyne, 1996).

Meldrum (1995) reminds that the technology and market life do not necessarily go hand in hand: although the technology may have reached its maturity, the market

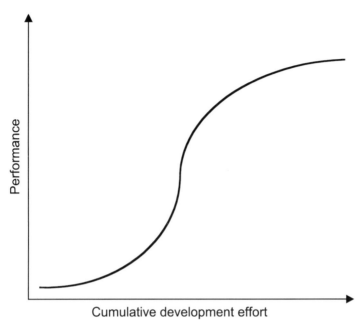

Fig. 9. Technology S-Curve (Adapted from Meldrum, 1995, p. 51).

may not still be very mature. Alleged that technologies develop according to an S-curve, it is possible to provide an explanation for the impression that product life cycles seem short in high-tech markets. It may be that short product life cycles result from the fact that the technologies become easier to develop (Meldrum, 1995). Of course, it is sometimes very difficult to determine whether a product is high-tech or a new technology product by its nature. Meldrum (1995) depicts this problem: "The worlds of automobiles and copiers both provide good examples of products which utilize a whole range of advanced and old technologies. Some of these will be regarded as high-tech, others will not. It is, therefore, difficult to differentiate between high-tech and non high-tech products purely in terms of the technology they incorporate." In fact, Meldrum suggests that the customers and the suppliers are those who essentially determine whether a product is regarded as high-tech or not.

Further, the S-curve illustrates that product development faces different situations along the technology life cycle. Products that are based on emerging technology will probably require large investments to reach substantial performance improvements. Hence, at this point, product development-based strategies would be rather restricted or at least expensive. At the later stages, however, when moderate development efforts result in essential performance improvements, rightly timed product development efforts become an important means to produce competitive advantage (Meldrum, 1995). Lessons on successful innovations made during the mature phase of technology life cycle include (Rhyne, 1996):

- The technology is not enough per se, it should also be used effectively. This calls for co-operation that covers both sales, customer service, financial department, and production.
- The technology is rarely too mature to be further developed and invested in. Small or even marginal improvements can make a difference.
- Look outside the organization. The best solutions for the problems in hand may be found somewhere else.

5.3.7. Measurement Issues

Rink et al. (1999) point out that the financial management of a firm must consider, for instance, the profitability of a new product investment along the different life cycle stages. A product may seem unprofitable at the introduction stage, but it may actually provide the organization with an option to invest further to enter a new market. As a result, the product will turn profitable in the growth and maturity phases. According to this example, the financial management of the firm has to pay attention at the introduction stage to correctly value the options that are associated with the possible future investments and profits from the succeeding phases of the product life cycle. Another product life cycle-related issue for management is the balance (or lack of it) between life cycle phases represented by the company's present product portfolio. In terms of risk management and sufficient and continuous cash flow, it is advisable to have active products in different life cycle phases.

Hayes and Wheelwright (1979a, b) have connected product life cycle with (manufacturing) process life cycle arguing that a change in either one of the dimensions should be accompanied by a change in the other one, too. According to Hayes and Wheelwright, just as a product evolves through a number of life cycle phases, the production process should be adapted accordingly. The authors argue that the process evolution typically begins with a state that is characterized by high flexibility and low cost efficiency. Towards the end of the product life cycle, the process becomes more standardized and automated. When measuring the performance of such processes, these characteristics should be taken into account. However, despite its ideological appeal, the linking between process and product life cycle remains questionable. Hayes and Wheelwright do not – in addition to some anecdotal issues – provide empirical support for the general idea. The idea that one particular type of production process would be more suitable for a certain type of product than for another seems logical per se. However, the validity of the idea that product evolution is accompanied with simultaneous process evolution is more doubtful. Above all, it is in clear contrast with many real-life cases in which the production process, once it is established, remains rather stable along the life cycle. This is especially true at the level of brands and even product forms. However, at the level of product classes, the connection between product and process evolution would be more applicable.

A study by Richardson and Gordon (1980) is one of the few that focus on the relationship between the product life cycle concept and performance measurement. Interestingly however, the total concept of PLC (and its general validity) is argued to be less central to the discussion presented by the authors. Richardson and Gordon identify that many products do not follow a standard life cycle pattern that consists of a sequence of a number of discrete stages, but rather, a wide range of life cycle patterns – from short-term fads to virtually everlasting commodities – exists. Hence, the precise form or life cycle behavior is not the key. The key is the finding that different life cycle stages merely exist and that the appropriate measures differ from stage to stage. Richardson and Gordon (1980) have studied performance measurement practices across the product life cycle stages in fifteen Canadian manufacturing companies. They propose that life cycle would be a suitable framework for establishing performance measures for manufacturing organizations. As a rationale for their study, Richardson and Gordon mention that too little attention has been paid to the changes in the criteria for evaluating a manufacturer's performance over the product life cycle. The underlying logic behind the dynamic performance measurement along the PLC is that the critical tasks of manufacturing change as a product moves through its life cycle (see for example Hayes & Wheelwright, 1979a, b). As the critical tasks change, the appropriate performance measurement is also different from one stage to another. According to Richardson and Gordon (1980), measures that focus on innovation, responsiveness, and flexibility should be the most appropriate early in the life cycle. At the growth stage, measures that indicate ability to deliver gain importance, including indicators for capacity growth and utilization rates. At the mature stage, productivity and cost efficiency measures should be the most important. The observed industrial practices, however, differed quite clearly from those derived theoretically: firms did not measure performance in terms of life cycle. Instead, most measures were typically designed for or appropriate for mature products only.

To summarize, Richardson and Gordon (1980) suggest that the evaluation of performance should consider both product life cycle and operating strategy. Furthermore, the measurement should identify or support the prioritization of different performance areas. In other words, the measurement should be able to answer to what is critical for the firm and what is not.

Malmi et al. (2002, p. 25) have also connected performance measurement and the life cycle concept. However, they discuss organizational life cycle rather than product life cycle. The nature, focus, and emphasis of performance measures depend upon the situation – or the stage of corporate life cycle – of the organization. Typical measures for the organizations in an intensive growth phase include several measures that indicate the growth of sales. On the other hand, organizations that are in the middle of a mature and stable phase of their life cycle – constituting a majority of all organizations – tend to emphasize the measures of profitability. Further, towards the end of corporate life cycle the measures of cash flow gain more importance (Malmi et al., 2002, p. 25).

5.3.8. Critical Remarks
Polli and Cook (1969) were among the first to investigate the validity of the product life cycle concept. Despite the criticism that the concept has received more lately, Polli and Cook (1969) conclude that the life cycle model is valid in many common market situations. Furthermore, they add that the fit of the product life cycle model is the most importantly depending on the definition of the product used. The life cycle model was found to be more appropriate in product form analysis than at the level of product class.

According to Bauer and Fischer (2000), there are many problems unsolved with the PLC concept:

- Definition of metrics to trace life cycle phase transition.
- The choice of proper level of aggregation (product class, product form, brand).
- Empirical generalization of the PLC.

Also Massey argues that a number of problems have been identified with the PLC concept. Among them, there is an empirically observed phenomenon called second life: a product "refuses" to die despite a general belief that it is the decline stage. Also, automatic strategy implications on the basis of the life cycle phase are found to be rather problematic: extreme caution is needed when determining an appropriate strategy for a product based on a life cycle phase. This is because, for example, a product may look like it is entering the decline stage, whilst it actually just suffers from a temporary sales decline due to other factors than the life cycle phase (Massey, 1999).

For instance, at the level of product classes, many commodities such as Scotch whisky or French perfumes have lived a prosperous maturity stage for centuries. If a commodity serves to satisfy a kind of basic need, its life may be extended virtually endlessly (Dhalla & Yuspeh, 1976). It has even been argued that:

It is a tautology that products are created and later die (Mercer, 1993).

However, Bauer and Fischer (2000) note that the existence of the product life cycle per se is not a question. This seems to be in contrast with the criticism the concept has received. Bauer and Fischer (2000) provide some insight regarding the focal points of criticism. First, there is a traditional ideal of PLC that is typically presented in marketing textbooks: product life cycle is depicted as a symmetrical bell-shaped curve. Inevitably, this kind of assumption on sales development is too restrictive and it is not capable of corresponding to empirical diversity. Second, a number of questions that are highly relevant for the practitioners are unsolved. These include: the length of the phases, the length of PLC in itself, unknown forces that moderate the variables in PLC's, influence of product newness, or order of entry on PLC.

Do the issues brought up within the PLC criticism actually jeopardize the applicability of the concept? No single answer can be given. To be able to approach the question, it is necessary to assess in detail the context within which the PLC concept is applied. In this context, product development measurement, the validity of the PLC concept is not an issue as such. For the purposes of measurement there is no reason to expect that a product would follow a smooth bell-shaped life cycle model. The key is to understand that the product will eventually go through various life cycle stages that can be associated with a number of distinct requirements. As a summary, the identified problems of the generic life cycle model include (see for example Dhalla & Yuspeh, 1976; Grantham, 1997):

- PLC is a self-fulfilling prophecy.
- Stages of the life cycle may vary in terms of length and behavior.
- Products may reincarnate or PLC's can be extended by means of marketing or design/engineering.
- It is difficult to determine at what stage the product actually is.
- Planning period of many organizations does not match the whole life cycle but rather a small part of it.
- PLC has lead to over-emphasis of new product introductions at the cost of neglecting older brands.
- In PLC analysis the definition of the concept of "product" is left ambiguous. It is unclear whether PLC refers to product class, product form, or brand. Dhalla and Yuspeh (1976) note, however, that the product form is thought of in most cases when referred to a "product" in the PLC context.
- Although it has been generally questioned that the product life cycle can be validated at any level (Dhalla & Yuspeh, 1976, p. 103), the smallest validity of PLC is recorded at the level of brands: most market leaders for example in 1970s are still market leaders (see Mercer, 1993).

Concerning these problems, the most significant ones in terms of the realization of measurement seem to be the difficulty to determine at what stage the product actually is and the possible ambiguity of the concept of new product.

5.3.9. Summary

As a brief summary, a number of issues can be raised on the basis of both the criticism and support that the concept of PLC has received:

- PLC should not be regarded as a deterministic concept but a more existentialistic one: PLC does not determine the appropriate strategies but the appropriate strategies are able to affect PLC (Massey, 1999, p. 305), (Tellis & Crawford, 1981 in Massey, 1999). That is, PLC is essentially a dependent variable – not an independent one – that can be affected by a number of means including those of falling under the broad categories of new product development and marketing.
- PLC would be a good framework for proactive rather than reactive management. For instance, in the spirit of "Lamarckism" (see Massey, 1999), one should look at the most important attributes, which can be passed to future product generations. And also vice versa, the product management should identify those product attributes that are not required in a particular environment.
- Combination of the concept of product life cycle and the Lamarckian model of product evolution could be a fruitful basis for product innovations. The Lamarckian model of evolution implies active marketing research and a systematic approach to new product development (see the previous point).
- Product life cycle receives a number of interpretations depending on the selected viewpoint and the level of assessment. The marketing view that considers the life cycles of product forms, product classes, and brands is only one of them. The customer perspective of the life cycle is also able to provide the manufacturer with proliferant insights into product management.
- From the financial management point of view, the length of PLC is one of the most essential parameters. It determines the window of opportunity for gaining profits through the product. However, similar to PLC at a general level, it is important to perceive the length of life cycle also as a variable rather than as a constant.
- Product life cycle can be structured in meaningful ways depending on the selected interpretation. Structuring may comprise dividing the life cycle into discrete phases that constitute the sequence referred to as the entire life cycle. The discrete phases may be associated with a number of features, requirements, or circumstances that are characteristic of a certain life cycle phase. Further, it is not necessary to structure the life cycle around discrete phases, but it is possible to depict a life cycle also as an evolutionary trajectory. This view is actually

consistent with the real-life situation: a product does not jump from one stage to another, rather it evolves gradually as the environment changes.

Despite the fact that some of the product requirements are somewhat life cycle phase-specific, general requirements for product life cycle can be identified as well. An essential one is a product's profitability: an evident financial objective is that the cumulative profit from a product should be positive. Otherwise, in the business sense, the product's justification is questionable. However, even in this case, the product could produce some positive implications, for instance, by promoting organizational learning or providing the firm with a catalyst for important developments in the organization. To summarize, due to the nature of life cycle phases and the associated requirements, the quality and nature of R&D outcome cannot be determined only by assessing the direct output of a product development project or program or by evaluating the experiences of the first customers. If a set of multifaceted measures for new product development is pursued, product life cycles and their distinct phases should be carefully analyzed to be able to set comprehensive objectives for R&D activity.

6. THE TENTATIVE FRAMEWORK: MULTIFACETED NPD MEASUREMENT

This section includes a discussion that aims to conclude and summarize the issues raised by the literature review on NPD management, performance measurement and life cycle management. On the basis of this, a conceptual framework for life cycle-conscious performance measurement (LCCM) in the product development context is proposed.

6.1. Summary of Relevant Literature

Research and development, or more specifically new product development, should be able to positively contribute to the future success of an organization. However, it has also been argued that product-centered strategy provides only a limited insight into the process by which the strategy of a firm is able to contribute to its future success (see for example Fowler et al., 2000; Hamel, 1996; Hamel & Prahalad, 1994). Two different approaches for the future success of an organization include product-centered strategy and competence-based strategy. The fundamental difference between these two is that while product-centered strategy focuses on products and (minor) improvements on them, competence-based strategy focuses on the capabilities[21] that underlie the firm's ability to create successful products (see for example Prahalad & Hamel, 1990). Fowler et al. (2000) distinguish between three types of competencies: technological, market-driven, and integration competencies.

However, in terms of competence development new products and NPD are important components. Fowler et al. (2000) argue that new product development activities combine the organization's current competencies in marketing with its current technological competencies to create commercially viable products. Further, if the strategy of an organization emphasizes competencies over products, the product development-related investments are likely to focus on how to optimally build on and extend the current competencies to develop competitive products on a longer term. This view of competence-based product development is in line with the life cycle-conscious new product development. As Fowler et al. (2000) note, it is very unusual the present competencies of a firm correspond directly to the needs that have been identified in product development. When organizations employ the knowledge integration process necessary to develop a new product, they actually engage in a process of problem solving in which they have to develop new capabilities to solve various unanticipated problems. This process implies the need for new capabilities and thus acts as a primary driver of new competencies.

Hence, a careful assessment and anticipation of product life cycles and an organization of products' lives on the basis of a number of phases that are associated with different requirements could be one of the means to support the long-term competence development of a firm. Orientation towards future requirements using the product life cycle concept encourages or even enforces the firm to consider the developments that are required in the long term to be able to stay competitive or to increase competitiveness.

Fowler et al. (2000) note that the measurement of competencies is difficult. This observation is based on the idea that competencies are dynamic and intangible. However, despite the difficulty, Fowler et al. propose a number of measures for both market-driven, technological, and integration competencies. The measures proposed (for instance, measures such as "spending per customer," "on-time delivery," or "number of competitors serving this customer" for market-driven competencies, and measures such as "product profitability," "percent of sales from new products," or "number of competitors delivering similar products" for integration competencies) raise a question of what is the primary purpose for measuring competencies. If it is indeed as difficult to define proper metrics for competencies as the previous examples illustrate, it could be questionable to establish any explicit metrics at all. The measures that are proposed can be regarded as surrogate and ambiguous at best. At least regarding the measures used as an example, the general validity is a major concern. For instance, it should be a minimum requirement for the measurement of competencies to distinguish between the actual capability and the driver of a capability.

Instead of focusing on distinct metrics or measures, this study suggests that the overall framework for new product development performance measurement – the blueprint for life cycle-conscious PM – should also provide support for competence development and sustainable product development. Life cycle orientation in constructing performance measures facilitates the identification of requirements that need to be fulfilled in the long term. Combining the requirements derived from the needs of the different stakeholders of product development and the requirements associated with the whole life cycle of the product broadens the view on NPD performance and enables versatile and multidimensional target setting. While the measurement framework thus also supports long-term competence development, it does not advocate explicit measures for issues that cannot be properly measured. The identification of an important objective may be sometimes enough for directing attention towards issues that need to be further developed. In other words, an explicit measure is not an imperative of management.

The idea and the presented framework for multifaceted and life cycle-conscious performance measurement of product development relies heavily on the literatures on performance measurement, new product development management, and life cycle. These bodies of literature are all rather extensive. The key findings, however, provide the foundation for the measurement framework presented in this chapter.

Above all, the literature on performance measurement includes observations that are common to measurement systems in general. First, measures and measurement systems are not independent structures. Consistently with this, the construction of measures and measurement systems should be somehow anchored to wider frameworks such as organizational goals and schemes. Therefore, it has been commonly suggested that measures should be constructed or derived from the top down. A good alignment between the measurement system and organizational strategies and objectives would ensure the consistency (or external validity) of measurement. Second, in addition to external consistency, the measurement system should not include severe internal conflicts. It has been stressed that the internal coherence of measurement is important. Different measures should probably convey a reasonably consistent message for the decision-makers and utilizers if any real effect is desired. The identification of cause-effect relationships is a part of the process for ensuring the internal coherence of a measurement system. A cause-effect relationship can be identified, for instance, by analyzing past or present experiences and/or by employing specific tools such as strategy maps or cause-effect diagrams. Third, although the measurement of leading indicators – or causes if you like – has gained interest, it has been argued that in most cases measurement should focus on the outcomes, results, and achievements.

Nevertheless, they are the primary objects for the measurement: if we are not able to properly identify the outcomes of our actions, there is little point in trying to identify a number of causes for outcomes we are not able to prove. Fourth, virtually all the measurement frameworks presented in the literature share the interest of comprehensiveness. Balanced scorecards, performance pyramids, or prisms illustrate that performance is a multidimensional subject that calls for comprehensive measurement. Consistently with this, simultaneous internal and external orientation and the inclusion of several stakeholders characterize the frameworks presented in the literature. Furthermore, as regards the purpose of measurement, it has been reminded that it should enable learning, for instance by facilitating learning from past mistakes. Complementing this, measurement should also provide a means for anticipating some future effects. The identification of leading indicators and determinants of success is part of this but sensitivity analyses and scenarios are needed, as well.

The literature of NPD management indicates a good number of findings. First, product development should be founded on a clear understanding of customer value. More specifically, it should be understood how the customers create value in their processes. All the product characteristics do not relate to customer value. Understanding customer value creation enables product development to focus on issues that are perceived as the most important and valuable. Second, in general, the importance of NPD performance measurement has been underscored by many studies. Performance measurement has been recognized as a means to improve the effectiveness of product development and a number of more specific purposes for measurement have been identified. To be effective, measurement should be simultaneously relatively simple and comprehensive. In other words, too sophisticated a measurement system will not likely be implemented and actively used. On the other hand, the dangers related to too straightforward measurement have also been pointed out. This is important since measures can be very powerful tools for directing efforts towards a certain direction. It can be regarded as a paradox: the need for comprehensive measurement has been identified, but there is a very limited number of practical solutions available and especially, it has been argued that the utilization of performance measurement in practice is not very well developed.

Third, the fact that product development success (or performance) is both a stakeholder- and context-specific issue makes measurement very challenging. In practice, success is very often assessed in relative terms, for example by comparing the achievements to prior expectations. Also, it has been remarked that success is a temporal variable. Success receives different interpretations depending on the life cycle phase, for example. Despite the dilemma of success, many cause-effect-relationships have been established regarding the antecedents and consequences of success.

Fourth, life cycle-oriented measurement has been discussed to a very limited extent within the NPD performance measurement literature. On the other hand, it can be concluded from the literature that product life cycle is one contingent variable of a PM system's design. The concept of product life cycle implicates at least two issues that are important for performance measurement: (1) Comprehensiveness; it facilitates the inclusion of different stakeholders, a longer time frame and different phase-specific requirements. (2) Outcome orientation: the analysis of the whole PLC is able to depict the "total effects" of a product.

The literature on product life cycle can be summarized briefly as follows. First, PLC should not be regarded as a deterministic concept but a more existentialistic one. That is, PLC is essentially a dependent variable – not an independent one. It can be affected by a number of means including those that fall under the broad categories of new product development and marketing. Second, it has been suggested that PLC would be a good framework for proactive management rather than for reactive management. The concept of life cycle can be employed for identifying those product attributes that are (or are not) required in a particular environment. Third, product life cycle is not a homogenous concept but it receives a number of interpretations depending on the selected viewpoint and the level of assessment. The marketing view that considers the life cycles of product forms, product classes, and brands is only one of them. The customer perspective of life cycle is also able to provide the manufacturer with fruitful insights into product management. Fourth, from the financial management point of view, the length of product life cycle is one of the most essential parameters. It determines the window of opportunity for gaining profits through the product. However, similar to PLC at a general level, it is important to perceive the length of life cycle also as a variable rather than as a constant. Finally, PLC can be structured in a number of ways depending on the selected interpretation. Structuring may be interpreted as dividing the life cycle into discrete phases that constitute the sequence referred to as the entire life cycle. The discrete phases may be associated with a number of features, requirements, or circumstances that are characteristic of a certain life cycle phase. Further, it is not the only possibility to structure the life cycle on the basis of discrete phases, but it is possible to depict the life cycle also as an evolutionary trajectory. This view is consistent with the real-life phenomenon: a product does not jump from one stage to another; rather, it evolves gradually.

To conclude, life cycle – seen from one perspective or simultaneously from several perspectives – would have potential to serve as the overall framework for constructing performance measures. The effects of new products are time-dependent and comprehensive effects cannot be found unless a longer time frame is considered. This indicates the importance of proactive life cycle phase-specific analysis that should be extended to cover the whole anticipated life cycle.

Proactive analysis can later be supplemented with a reactive one as data on the life cycle cumulates. In addition, the stakeholders (and success interpretations associated with them) should also be carefully considered in NPD to identify the comprehensive objectives for a new product and possibly conflicting interests. Outcome orientation, for one, indicates that NPD performance measurement should not only mean the measurement of the product development process but it should also track the actual achievements that will not be realized until customers have gained experiences from using the product. The identification of cause-effect –relationships and antecedents of success would also be important for continuous NPD management.

6.2. Life Cycle-Conscious NPD PM of Industrial Products

Figure 10 summarizes the idea of life cycle-conscious product development and provides a framework for constructing and evaluating the performance measures of new product development. The figure depicts three interpretations of the concept of life cycle consciousness in the context of product development performance measurement. The interpretations are not suggested as mutually exclusive; rather, they are intended to supplement each other. However, depending on the type of product and the market, the relative relevance of the interpretations may vary. That is, all the interpretations are not necessarily equally relevant or important in different environments.

According to the first interpretation, new product development is an activity that takes place primarily at the beginning of the product life cycle. Further, the entire life cycle of the product can be divided into smaller, and relatively homogenous, blocks that represent life cycle stages or phases that a product experiences during its life. Each phase includes a number of characteristics that can be translated into process or product requirements. As these requirements are collected together, the multifaceted set of product requirements can be formulated. Hence, the identification of distinct life cycle phases and associated product requirements constitutes a foundation for an NPD target-setting process for performance measurement. In this procedure, it is not necessary to restrict the possibly versatile interpretations of the concept of product life cycle. That is, product life cycle can either be evaluated from the perspective of customer, producer, or society – or these can be used in combination to be able to depict the product's life even more comprehensively. Further, the emphasis on and importance of a distinct life cycle phase can be determined, for instance, by evaluating the duration of the phases or the costs associated with them, or by assessing the workload of various corporate functions over the entire life cycle.

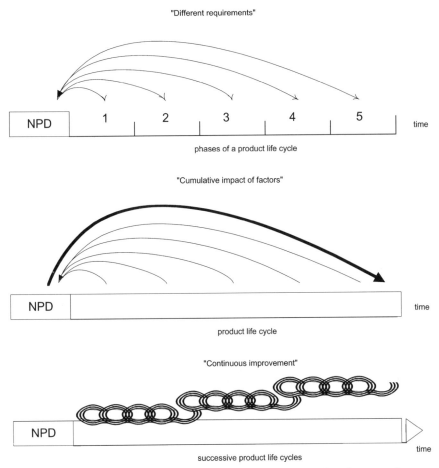

Fig. 10. Life Cycle and Challenges of Product Development: Three Interpretations.

If the customer's perspective is adopted as the basis for the assessment, a thorough understanding of the customer's process and value creation is needed to be able to identify objectives and measures for distinct life cycle phases. The assessment could be founded on profits, costs, or other (non-financial) issues that the customer experiences during the identified life cycle phases. Regarding industrial investment products, producers are typically rather familiar with the customers' processes, at least at a general level. In that sense, constructing performance measures on the basis of the product life cycle phases experienced by the customers should be feasible in most cases.

Naturally, the more detailed a description and quantification of the life cycle is pursued, the more effort and additional inquiries or customer/market studies are needed.

If the producer perspective is adopted as the basis, very little external information is likely to be needed. In the case of evolutionary product development, the producer could mainly lean on the life cycle analysis of previous or present products to understand the life cycle phases and associated requirements. If the product development includes revolutionary elements or if the product being developed is very different from the previous products of the producer, other means are likely to be employed. For example, benchmarking could provide analogies that would be useful for identifying life cycle patterns.

In addition to the identification of requirements, the first interpretation can also be useful for assessing the impacts of product development decisions. It can be argued that the effects of certain product development decisions relate to certain product life cycle phases more than to some others. To be able to assess the feasibility of product development decisions, this is an important point that should be considered as well.

According to the second interpretation, new product development is still regarded as an activity that takes place primarily at the beginning of the product life cycle. However, life cycle is not seen as a collection of distinct phases associated with a number of requirements; rather, it represents a continuum of time. The importance of this view is underscored by the fact that many industrial products still have very long life cycles. Hence, when developing these kinds of products, the developing company to a great extent determines its financial success potential for a long time (see e.g. Uusi-Rauva & Paranko, 1998). If the cumulative impact of a new product is not fully and carefully assessed, the financial possibilities and risks of the product remain ambiguous.

From the financial point of view, this interpretation of product life cycle can be addressed by applying investment calculations such as NPV or ROI (taking into account the appropriate discount rate) during product development. However, it is worth remembering that both the profitability of the product and the profitability of the after sales business associated with the product affect the financial success and constitute the total profitability of the product. Investment calculations should be based on well-grounded scenarios regarding the duration of life cycle and the cost structure of product as well as on the activity consumption of the developed product. Development investments besides the initial NPD effort should also be included in calculations.

If the second interpretation is assessed from the customer point of view, issues such as total cost of ownership (TCO) could be addressed. Inevitably, the customer has an interest in minimizing the life cycle costs and maximizing the life cycle revenues associated with a product. Hence, the costs that the customer experiences during the life cycle of a product could be perceived as a key objective for product development. Established methods or managerial practices such as target costing (Ansari et al., 1997; Cooper & Slagmulder, 1997; Dutton & Marx, 1999) and life cycle costing (Emblemsvåg, 2001; Kaplan & Atkinson, 1998; Keoleian & Menerey, 1993; Woodward, 1997) include the financial elements that are needed for life cycle conscious NPD management. However, life cycle provides companies also with a framework for weighting and organizing non-financial measures of success. Consider, for instance, the need for maintenance and availability of spare parts as a success measure of a new truck. Depending on the nature and duration of the life cycle experienced by the primary customer, this success measure receives different emphasis. If the primary customer uses the truck for 20 years, the maintenance is one of the key issues; however, if the customer buys a new one after every five years, the issue is probably not as important. Of course, one might argue that maintenance costs will be reflected in the resale value of the product after five years. However, there is somewhat contradictory evidence available concerning the consumers' ability to cope with LCC data when making investment decisions (Hutton & Wilkie, 1980; Liebermann & Ungar, 2002). A recent study showed that life cycle costs have a negligible effect on the investment decisions in the railway industry (Järvinen et al., 2004).

The third interpretation implies that product development is an activity that takes place both at the beginning of the product life cycle and during it. In fact, in many cases, it is virtually impossible to determine where one life cycle ends and where another begins. Sequential product generations may include a number of mutual components and features, which makes it difficult to separate distinct product life cycles; rather, the concepts of product family life cycle or product platform life cycle may be more appropriate in some cases. Even within the life cycle of a single product, innovations may take place not only at the beginning but also towards the end of life. Hence, performance measurement of product development should acknowledge that the challenges and requirements of product development are connected with the innovation continuum. Consequently, product development performance or success receives different interpretations depending on the point of life cycle. At the beginning, it might be enough to obtain a few positive reference customers, while towards the end competitive products are likely to increase the pressure for better performance. Further, one of the key objectives – a continuous challenge – of product development during product life cycle is to ensure that viable products are sufficiently updated and kept competitive. On the other hand, as the product becomes more mature, the more data on the product's technical and market performance will be available. This data would provide guidance for the further development of the product.

Regarding all the previous interpretations, performance measurement of product development is interested in and intended to grasp outcomes and effects that will become materialized not until after a period of time. Inevitably, this poses a challenge for the very act of measurement. However, a few solutions are available:

- One could measure now issues that are expected to have an impact on future effects. This implies the identification of cause-effect chains. For instance, the use of recurrent materials (percentage of all materials included in a product) can be perceived as an indicator that is primarily related to the recyclability of the product and the final stages of its life cycle, but that be quantified already at the product development stage.
- One could postpone the actual measurement of issues that will be relevant in the future, but set targets for them now. For instance, customer satisfaction cannot be found until the product has been applied for a certain period of time; however, a target level for satisfaction can be set in the development phase. This may guide the product development into the desired direction.
- One could focus on issues that will be relevant in the future on the basis of anticipated effects and values. Scenarios and sensitivity analyses can be applied to demonstrate, for instance, the preferences between alternative product designs. For example, if after sales profitability is a major concern, the total profitability of a product can be simulated by anticipating the need and sales margin of spare parts. Different scenarios can be used to reveal the sensitivity of total profitability, depending on spare part consumption.

6.3. Stakeholder-Oriented Performance Measurement

6.3.1. Performance Dimensions

Fundamentally, stakeholder theory comprises the idea that a company or organization has stakeholders. On this account, stakeholder theory of the organization has several connections also to new product development and its performance measurement. As noted by Donaldson and Preston (1995), descriptive use, instrumental use, and normative use of stakeholder theory are the three interrelated but rather distinct aspects that comprise the entire theory.

First, descriptive use refers to situations where stakeholder theory is applied to describe or explain specific corporate characteristics and behavior. For example, stakeholder theory has been used to describe the nature of the firm, the way managers or board members think about managing, and relevant interests present in corporate activities. The argumentation used in the literature to justify the descriptive use of stakeholder theory typically attempts to show that the concepts and ideas represented in the theory correspond to the observed reality (Donaldson & Preston, 1995). In new product development, the identification of customers and suppliers and their interests as well as the identification of society-based requirements typically correspond to the descriptive use of stakeholder theory.

Second, instrumental use of stakeholder theory seeks to identify the possible connections between stakeholder management and the attainment of corporate goals. Studies in this domain have attempted to generate implications that stakeholder theory serves as a catalyst for corporate goals equal to or better than possible rival approaches. The instrumental justification often relies on the evidence of the connection between stakeholder thinking and corporate performance (Donaldson & Preston, 1995). The domain of NPD performance literature that investigates the relationship between different antecedents and consequences of new product success, for instance, represents this approach. That is, a study that investigates the relationship between performance and society or customer need anticipation, at least implicitly relies on the instrumental purpose of stakeholder theory.

Third, the normative essence of the theory considers issues that relate to the function of the organization. Within the normative approach, philosophical and moral guidelines for the operation and corporate management are identified and formulated. According to Donaldson and Preston (1995) normative aspects comprise the core of stakeholder theory. The justification of the normative approach typically appeals to fundamental concepts behind stakeholder theory such as individual right, group right, or "social contract" (Donaldson & Preston, 1995). Approaches to product development research that are colored by normative stakeholder theory can also be found. For example, studies that refer to environmental concerns or sustainable growth principles have a normative flavor.

It is argued that the key stakeholders of product development can be typified into four classes: company shareholders (owners), customers and utilizers of products/services (users), the developing organization, which may be comprised of internal and external actors (product development, R&D), and the supply chain that facilitates the realization of the product including internal and external supply chain members. The perspectives of these stakeholders related to the (new) product are depicted in Fig. 11. Relevant questions and objectives for each stakeholder group would include, for example:

- *Customer view*: how well (for example compared with competitors' products) does the product respond to the customer need, is the quality sufficient, what are the operating costs, is appropriate after sales support available?

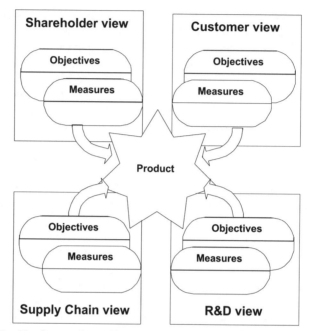

Fig. 11. Perspectives of Key Stakeholders of Product Development.

- *Shareholder view*: does R&D and product development produce profitable business, is the growth rate of the business acceptable, what is the competitive position?
- *R&D view*: deployment of strategic resources, competence development, and learning.
- *Supply chain view*: cost efficiency, time to market, design for assembly or manufacture, availability of appropriate sales, and delivery channel/feasibility of the product from the supply chain point of view.

It is maintained that the supply chain view should be interpreted rather widely. Supply chain includes not only external actors such as suppliers or distributors, but also internal actors such as manufacturing, sales, and purchases.

Each stakeholder has a number of objectives regarding the new product or the product being developed. Some of the objectives may be mutual to all stakeholders whereas others are more stakeholder-specific. For example, product safety could be a concern for all the stakeholders. On the other hand, manufacturing investments needed for the new product are not a primary issue of interest for the customer but they could be one of the most important concerns for the shareholders. Of course, it goes almost without saying that also the customer will experience the high manufacturing investments through higher costs associated with the product.

Considering the objectives of different stakeholders, the overall success of a new product can be multifacetedly defined using the framework depicted in Fig. 11. A successful product will basically fulfill the objectives derived from all the perspectives. Naturally, the emphasis on each perspective or view does not have to be equal. For a given product, for example the supply chain view could be less important compared to the other three stakeholder perspectives.

6.3.2. Combining Stakeholders and Life Cycle Requirements

To finalize the life cycle-conscious measurement framework, Fig. 12 illustrates the idea of connecting life cycle phases and the requirements or objectives of different stakeholders into one framework.

In this example, life cycle is depicted as the typical marketing life cycle seen by the producer. In this view, life cycle is comprised of introduction stage, growth stage, maturity stage, and decline stage. However, any life cycle model could be adopted as a basis for this synthesis. Analogously, life cycle could be organized on the basis of phases experienced by the customer: purchase, implementation, active use, maintenance, disposal, and secondary use, for example. In addition, the concept of life cycle can be combined with the four perspectives even without any life cycle phases at all.

Primarily related to the first interpretation of life cycle consciousness, multifaceted objectives for the product can be derived as depicted in the figure. As mentioned, the first phase is to identify the particular life cycle model and the phases associated with it. Second, the four perspectives to the product will be assessed separately in each phase of the life cycle: What objectives are related to the shareholder view in the introduction phase? What objectives are related to the product development view in the introduction phase? What objectives are related to the customer view in the introduction phase? What objectives are related to the supply chain view in the introduction phase? This sequence will be repeated regarding all the phases of the life cycle. It is important to acknowledge that it may be possible that all the perspectives or views have no significance in every phase. In other words, it could be possible that, for example, only the shareholder view, the supply chain view and the customer view are considered in the growth phase.

Third, the objectives that were identified for each stakeholder and for each life cycle phase will be collected and reflected back to product development. Hence, a tentative set of objectives for a product has been achieved. This includes also the identification of determinants that can be associated with the identified objectives.

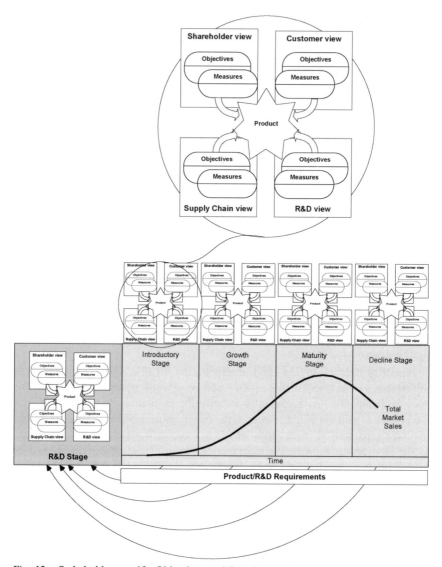

Fig. 12. Stakeholder-specific Objectives and Requirements can be Associated with Life Cycle Phases.

In other words, it should be considered by which means the identified objectives can be fulfilled. In practice, this set of objectives and cause-effect chains may contain issues that seem to be conflicting or internally ambiguous. However, to be able to rationally discuss and prioritize the objectives, a multifaceted set of tentative objectives are needed. Through selection and the elimination of secondary objectives, the more compressed set of final objectives can be reached.

Fourth, on the basis of prioritized and selected objectives, the process of creating and constructing measures can be initiated. However, as discussed above, it is not necessary to establish a measure for every objective. Taking into account the difficulties that are related to future-oriented measurement, the construction of the measures should be carried out cautiously. In many cases, the existence of the explicit objective can motivate and direct the efforts into issues that are important provided that the life cycle of the product has certain identified characteristics.

According to the second interpretation, rather than a collection of phases, product life cycle is a continuum of time. During that continuum, various factors contribute to the cumulative effects of a product. Combining this life cycle view with the perspectives presented in Fig. 11 results in an idea that those cumulative effects can be assessed at least from the perspectives of shareholders, customer, supply chain, and R&D. From the customer point of view, it would be important to acknowledge, for instance, how certain product development decisions affect the investment costs or operating costs experienced by the customer or which design parameters contribute to the value a customer creates by using the product. From the shareholder point of view, it is naturally important to make sure that the cumulative profits (caused by the product and by the after sales business connected with it) are maximized. This example implicates not only rigorous profitability and cost management related to product design, but also a proper spare part strategy that creates profitable spare parts sales.

Further, from the product development or R&D point of view, the goals consistent with the second interpretation would include, for instance, effective competence and capability development during the whole product life cycle. The life cycle provides the product development with a possibility to learn from the customer experiences. The development of the next product can be at least partly built on the observations made during the previous product's life cycle. Finally, the supply chain perspective may include objectives that are similar to those identified in the shareholder perspective. Others may include the length of supplier commitment (external supply chain) related to the product, or the estimated production investments related to the product (internal supply chain).

It is important to observe that the performance achieved with respect to one perspective may be independent of the performance achieved in another. Consider, for instance, the material cost of a product experienced by the producer. It is quite possible that the value of the product seen from the perspective of the customer does not depend upon the cost reduction of a certain component if the total quality of the product does not correlate with the cost of a single component (which is quite often the case). On the other hand, performance seen from one perspective may relate to the performance seen from another. Consider, for example, a situation in which a feature is added to a product to increase the value of the product for a customer. The additional feature also causes increased material costs as well as increased assembly costs, which lead to lower relative profitability due to an intensive competition allowing only a marginal selling price increase.

The third interpretation acknowledges that distinct product life cycles may be difficult to identify in some cases. Products can be continuously developed, which implicates a product's life cycle is not a clear-cut period but rather a part of continuous evolution. Connecting this observation with the perspectives of the presented stakeholders leads to many performance targets or objectives for product development. From the customer point of view, it could be worth pursuing that the products of the following generations are at least partially compatible. Consider, for example, the compatibility of auxiliary equipment or spare parts associated with the product or a situation in which the product is not an independent unit but rather a part of a larger production system of the customer. From the manufacturing point of view, component commonality across successive product generations – for instance – could be an important objective.

Overall, the combination of the four stakeholder perspectives and the third life cycle interpretation implicates that the performance targets – just like the products being developed – can be perceived as a long continuum. The performance measurement of product development could be founded on the idea of continuous improvement: the performance of a new product should be – at least with regard to some perspective – better than the performance of an older product.

7. EMPIRICAL RESULTS

This section comprises the key empirical findings made in the study. As discussed earlier, the empirical part of the study consists of a case study of six companies. The case study seeks to produce insights into product life cycles in different companies (common and uncommon issues across companies) and thus in this context, multiple cases are primarily selected for enabling either literal or theoretical replication of observations. The selection of cases is purposeful in a sense that all the cases are reasonably homogenous: they all are middle-sized or large manufacturers of industrial investment goods. Also the concept of product life cycle was expected to be relevant one way or another in each case: especially in machine construction, the life cycles of products are relatively long including an after sales phase. Being the main unit of analysis, the relevance of life cycle is certainly necessary. On the other hand, the cases were selected in such a way that within the specified boundaries the cases would also differ in terms of size, products, and environment.

7.1. Case Study Results

This section presents the main findings made in the case study of six companies. The section begins with brief within-case descriptions and ends with a cross-case analysis. First, the nature of product development and the perceived importance of a new product in each case company are briefly discussed. Second, the length of product life cycles, the distinct phases of PLCs, and their characteristics are discussed. Third, on the basis of the two issues just mentioned, requirements for a good process or product as interpreted at different stages of life cycle are considered. The companies represent three broad industries: metal and machine manufacturing, material and component manufacturing in electronics, and equipment manufacturing (electronics). The products supplied by these companies – despite their vast difference in character and size – can all be regarded as physical investment goods.

Especially in the within-case section, the findings of the case study are reported without intentional interpretation by the researcher, if possible. This means that the observations made in the interviews and collected by using the companies' product development and life cycle documentation are reported without inferences concerning the causes and effects or motives behind the statements. In other words, the study focuses primarily on the *perceptions* of the companies regarding their product life cycles. In fact, it is possible that the "true" life cycles differ from the perceptions to some extent, but this has not been the interest of the study (quite consistently with the naturalistic perception of science, see for example Hammersley & Atkinson, 1995). Also, since the case section relies on company-specific terms and discourse, it is possible that some of the terms used are not totally consistent across cases. For example, it can be that the term "cross-functional" refers to collaboration between R&D, manufacturing, and purchase in another setting while in other setting it refers to the collaboration between marketing, R&D, and manufacturing.

7.1.1. Case A
Company A is a middle-sized Finnish subsidiary of an international corporation. It has less than 250 employees. The products include machinery and equipment

used in many industries and environments. The industrial sector of Company A is metal industry and machine manufacturing.

The role of new product is said to be remarkably important. Products are continuously developed, which means that both evolutionary and revolutionary elements are present in product development. To a great extent, large global competitors set the pace for new product development and product introductions. As a result, the customers are used to a certain new product introduction pace.

At the general level, the characteristics of product life cycle in Company A can be described as follows:

- The product life cycle is relatively long (approximately five to ten years + the after sales phase), in which the significance of after sales and spare part business is high.
- The length of product life cycle from the customer point of view is approximately 25 years. Even over 30 years is not exceptional.
- Across the company's product line, PLCs are rather homogenous. The length is typically inversely proportional to the physical size of the product.

Seven life cycle phases were identified in Company A. It is important to acknowledge that they are not completely distinct but partly overlapping (especially as regards after sales). The identified life cycle phases primarily implicate the view of the producer. The following phases and tasks comprise the life cycle, respectively:

(1) New product opportunity study
   - Market analysis
   - Tentative product specification
(2) New product development
   - Product development, prototypes, testing
   - Manufacturing implementation
   - Marketing and manufacturing launch
(3) Active production
   - "Learning by doing"
   - Education
   - Strong marketing effort
(4) Production shutdown
   - Typically initiated by new product launch
   - Possible subcontracting
   - Serving secondary customers/markets

(5) End of production
   • On the basis of profitability analysis, if available
   • Somewhat unclear criteria
(6) After sales
   • Spare parts and service
(7) End of product
   • Rarely happens

Respectively, the primary responsibility and the workload distribution of corporate functions were perceived as follows (Question 7c: Which corporate functions are primarily employed in life cycle phases?):

• Initial phases, opportunity identification
   • Top management
   • Marketing
• NPD
   • Cross-functional
• Active phase
   • Manufacturing
   • Sales and marketing
• Later phases
   • Manufacturing
   • Purchases

7.1.2. Case B

Company B is a business unit of a large and leading global manufacturer and supplier of process industry production systems, machines, and equipment in its field. The whole company has over 10,000 employees. The industrial sector of Company B is metal industry and machine manufacturing.

The objective of Company B is to be a technology leader in its field, which underscores the importance of innovativeness regarding key products. A clear majority of product development represents evolution. Revolutionary products are perceived as those that are new for the markets and customers. The evolutionary character of NPD is illustrated in the distribution of new products in terms of their newness (year 2001):

• 40% were product upgrades and improvements
• 40% were new for the company
• 20% were new for the market

At the general level, the characteristics of product life cycle in Company B can be described as follows:

- Product life cycle is relatively long (approximately 15–25 years for a platform and five years for a product + the after sales phase). The importance of after sales service is high.
- The length of product life cycle from the customer point of view is approximately 10–15 years.
- Across the company's product line, PLCs are rather homogenous. The lengths are the shortest in areas that are characterized by rapid technology development due to customers' process improvement.

Six life cycle phases were identified in Company B. Also in this case, the phases are not completely distinct but partly overlapping. The identified life cycle phases primarily implicate the view of the producer. The following phases and tasks comprise the life cycle, respectively:

(1) Draft and concept phase + product development
  - The continuum from idea to concept
  - From concept to product
  - Prototypes, laboratory tests
(2) Market launch
  - Primary segment definition
  - Sales arguments development
(3) Production development/redesign
  - Design for manufacturability
(4) Product maturation
  - Increasing number of delivery projects
  - Strong competition
(5) New product generation using the old platform
  - Redesign and improvement on the basis of the present platform and concept
(6) Product fades out
  - The technology becomes uncompetitive
  - Too strong competitors

Respectively, the primary responsibility and the workload distribution of corporate functions were perceived as follows (Question 7c: Which corporate functions are primarily employed in life cycle phases?):

- Initial phases
  - Product development
  - Sales and marketing

- Production development
  - Manufacturing
  - Cross-functional team
  - External partners
  Later phases
  - Manufacturing
  - Delivery projects
  - Service
- New generation
  - New product development

7.1.3. Case C

Company C is a business unit of a large international Finnish corporation. The company has over 2,000 employees altogether. The products include vehicles and systems used in special applications. The industrial sector of Company C is metal industry and machine manufacturing.

The fact that the number of customers is somewhat limited characterizes the operational environment of Company C. Hence; a new product typically represents a response to evolved customer needs. New products are also seen as a means to improve cost efficiency and manufacturability. Product evolution is continuous, revolutions that are associated with essential technological leaps take place maybe once in a decade.

At the general level, the characteristics of product life cycle in Company C can be described as follows:

Product life cycle is relatively long (approximately 20–30 years including the after sales phase). The importance of after sales and spare part business is high and these phases comprise roughly one half of the life cycle.

- The next-generation product is typically initiated and developed in the middle of the life cycle of the previous product.
- The length of product life cycle from the customer point of view is approximately 20–30 years.
- Across the company's product line, PLCs are rather homogenous. The length of component life cycle can be very different from that of end product.

Seven life cycle phases were identified in Company C. It is important to acknowledge that they are not completely distinct but partly overlapping (especially as regards after sales). The identified life cycle phases primarily implicate the view of the producer. The following phases and tasks comprise the life cycle, respectively:

(1) Market and concept study
   • Cross-functional cooperation
   • Customer involvement
(2) Product development
   • Development, prototypes
   • Customer involvement
(3) Launch and the first customer delivery
   • Includes lots of engineering
   • Integrated project teams
   • Customer representation
(4) Customer deliveries and versions
   • Same as previous
   • Includes also service development
(5) Product support
   • Education
   • Product information distribution
   • On-site support
(6) Product renovation and modernization
   • Major upgrade
(7) End of product support
   • Exact end somewhat ambiguous

Respectively, the primary responsibility and the workload distribution of corporate functions were perceived as follows (Question 7c: Which corporate functions are primarily employed in life cycle phases?):

• Initial phases
   • Marketing
   • Product development
• Customer deliveries
   • Manufacturing
   • Product support
• Support and renovation
   • Product support
   • Product development

7.1.4. Case D

Company D is a large Finnish subsidiary of a leading global corporation in its field. The Finnish company employs over 400 people. The products include machines and special application vehicles. The industrial sector of company D is metal industry and machine manufacturing.

New products are seen as a means to improve sales, profitability, and the level of technology. Product evolution takes place continuously, but there is also room for revolutions due to the fact that the technology life cycle has not reached maturity: the products of the company have a relatively short history dating back to 1950s.

At the general level, the characteristics of product life cycle in Company D can be described as follows:

- The product life cycle is relatively long (the active phase is approximately 10 years). In addition, the importance of the after sales phase and spare part business is high. The length of the after sales phase may be almost 15 years.
- The length of product life cycle from the user point of view is approximately 15 years. The first user employs the product for about five years, after which follows the period of secondary users. The last five years do not typically result in any spare part sales.
- The concept of product life cycle will receive a different interpretation as the paradigm shift (selling a physical product vs. selling performance or output) takes place or becomes more obvious.

Six life cycle phases were identified in Company D. The life cycle phases are not completely distinct but rather partly overlapping (especially as regards after sales). The identified life cycle phases primarily implicate the view of the producer. The following phases and tasks comprise the life cycle, respectively:

(1) Concept development
    - Technical testing of an idea
    - May not proceed
(2) Business case study
    - Economical assessment
    - Investment calculations
(3) Product development
    - Finalized concept
    - Concurrent development process
(4) Market launch
    - Implementation throughout the organization
(5) Active production
    - Stable phase
    - Minor modifications and evolution
(6) After sales
    - "Spare part support never ends"

Respectively, the primary responsibility and the workload distribution of corporate functions were perceived as follows (Question 7c: Which corporate functions are primarily employed in life cycle phases?):

- Concept development
  - Product development, R&D
- Business study
  - Cross-functional
  - Manufacturing not included
- Product development and launch
  - Cross-functional
  - Manufacturing
  - Purchase
  - Quality
- Active phase
  - Manufacturing
  - Product development: minor refinements
- After sales
  - Service

7.1.5. Case E

Company E is a middle-sized Finnish subsidiary of an international corporation. The Finnish subsidiary employs less than 250 people. The products include materials and components used in many applications and environments. The industrial sector of Company E is electronics, and more specifically, component manufacturing.

The role of new products is to generate turnover and to improve profitability. Consistently with this, better manufacturability is also a key objective. The role of product revolutions has decreased during the last seven years, which is in fact the time that the company has been in business. Today, a majority of product development is comprised of product evolution that aims to improve efficiency.

At the general level, the characteristics of product life cycle in Company E can be described as follows:

- Product life cycle is shorter than in the previous cases (the active phase is approximately five to ten years). The fundamental issue is the lack of an after sales phase. It is not applicable because the company is a component producer whose products do not require actual after sales support.
- The length of product life cycle from the user point of view is difficult to estimate. This is because it depends heavily on the particular application. Many system

products in which the components are employed are utilized for about 10 to 15 years.

- The life cycles of different products are not quite homogenous but the product line can be divided into two parts in terms of the nature of their life cycle.

Six life cycle phases were identified in Company E. The identified life cycle phases primarily implicate the view of the producer and they are quite strongly focused on the beginning of product life. The following phases and tasks comprise the life cycle, respectively:

(1) Concept development
  - Market and technology (existing technologies) analysis
  - Risk assessment
(2) Development plan and decision
  - Project plan
  - Project initiation
  - Product specification
(3) Product and process development
  - Development
  - Alpha tests
(4) Pilot product
  - Beta tests
  - Manufacturing launch
(5) Market launch
  - First sales
(6) End of life
  - Stable phase
  - Active manufacturing and sales

Respectively, the primary responsibility and the workload distribution of corporate functions were perceived as follows (Question 7c: Which corporate functions are primarily employed in life cycle phases?):

- Concept development
  - Marketing
  - Product development (minor role)
- Development plan
  - Management of various functions
- Development and pilots
  - Product development
  - Gradually manufacturing

- End of life
  - Manufacturing
  - Sales

7.1.6. Case F

Company F is a large Finnish subsidiary of an international corporation. The number of employees in Finland is over 500. The products of Company F include equipment and systems used in special applications. The industrial sector would be electronics, and more specifically, equipment manufacturing.

Concerning the role of product development, it has a significant strategic emphasis. The fundamental rule is that the performance of a new product should always exceed that of its predecessor. Revolutionary steps in product development are taken approximately every five years. However, in the future the frequency will probably increase. In addition, product evolution takes place continuously.

At the general level, the characteristics of product life cycle in Company F can be described as follows:

- The length of product life cycle is about five years but it is getting shorter and will probably decrease to three or four years (the active phase). In addition to this, after sales extends the life by seven years, which is the length of the spare part availability guarantee.
- The length of product life cycle from the user point of view depends on the customer segment. Two main segments exist and within these, typical life cycles are about four years and ten years.
- The life cycles of different products are rather homogenous.

Six life cycle phases were identified in Company F. The identified life cycle phases primarily implicate the view of the producer. The phases are perceived as rather distinct so they do not overlap each other. The following phases and tasks comprise the life cycle, respectively:

(1) Product development
  - Strong effort to create a new product platform
(2) Platform launch and start
  - "Completing the tails of product development"
  - Marketing launch
  - Further development, "year models"
(3) Steady supply
  - Focus on sales and manufacturing

(4) Facelift and (re)focus
  - Product improvements
  - Boosting the profitability
  - Possible subcontracting
(5) Harvest
  - End of development
  - Price competition
(6) End of product
  - On the basis of the volume of orders

Respectively, the primary responsibility and the workload distribution of corporate functions were perceived as follows (Question 7c: Which corporate functions are primarily employed in life cycle phases?):

- Product development and platform launch
  - NPD
  - Marketing
  - Manufacturing
  - "Learning phase"
- Steady phase
  - Manufacturing
- Facelift
  - Product development
  - Marketing
- Harvest and the end
  - Manufacturing

7.1.7. Cross-Case Comparison

Table 7 includes a brief summary and descriptions of the cases regarding the role of new product and overall characteristics of the companies. The first two columns contain mainly public information, but the third column summarizes the opinions of interviewees in each company regarding the nature of NPD and the role of a new product. Companies A, B, C, and D represent metal industry and machine manufacturing. Companies E and F are connected with electronics; one focuses on components and materials, while the other is primarily an equipment supplier. In terms of size, small companies are not represented; two companies are middle-sized,[22] while four are clearly large. All the companies are at least partly located in Finland, but all of them also have international or global operations.

Regarding the nature of product development, an inevitable observation is that products are developed rather continuously. That is, product development does not only take place at the beginning of a product's life cycle; rather, the

Table 7. Description and Comparison of Cases.

	Description of Company	Industry	Role of New Product
Company A	Middle-sized (less than 250 employees) Finnish subsidiary of international corporation. Products include machinery and equipment used in many industries and environments.	Metal industry/ Machine manufacturing	Role of new product is remarkably important. Products are continuously developed, both evolutionary and revolutionary elements are present. Large global competitors set the pace for new product introductions. As a result, customers are used to a certain new product introduction pace.
Company B	Business unit of large (over 10,000 employees) and leading global manufacturer and supplier of process industry production systems, machines, and equipment in its field.	Metal industry/ Machine manufacturing	Company's objective is to be a technology leader, which underscores the importance of innovativeness regarding key products. A clear majority of product development represents evolution. Revolutionary products are those new for the markets and customers.
Company C	Business unit of large international Finnish corporation (over 2,000 employees). Products include vehicles and systems used in special applications.	Metal industry/ Machine manufacturing	Number of customers is somewhat limited. Hence, a new product typically represents a response to evolved customer needs. New products are also seen as a means to improve cost efficiency and manufacturability. Product evolution is continuous, revolutions take place maybe once in a decade.
Company D	Large (over 400 employees) Finnish subsidiary of leading global corporation in its field. Products include machines and vehicles.	Metal industry/ Machine manufacturing	New products are seen as a means to improve sales, profitability, and the level of technology. Product evolution takes place continuously, but there is also room for revolutions due to the fact that the technology life cycle has not reached maturity.
Company E	Middle-sized (less than 250 employees) Finnish subsidiary of international corporation. Products include materials components used in many applications and environments.	Electronics/ Component manufacturing	New products generate turnover and profitability. Better manufacturability is also a key objective. The role of product revolutions has decreased during the last seven years, which is the time that the company has been in business. Today, product development equals evolution that aims to improve efficiency.
Company F	Large (over 500 employees) Finnish subsidiary of international corporation. Products include equipment and systems used in special applications.	Electronics/ Equipment manufacturing	Product development has significant strategic emphasis. New product performance should always exceed that of its predecessor. Revolutionary steps are taken every five years. However, in the future the frequency will probably increase. In addition, product evolution takes place continuously.

companies set objectives in order to improve products in a more evolutionary manner. It would be very unusual for a product to stay competitive for several years without small or bigger evolutionary steps during its active life. On the other hand, all interviewees perceived that product development includes also revolutionary elements. However, one should observe that the interpretation of the term "revolutionary" in machine manufacturing is different from the interpretation of the same term in electronics. Relatively small steps of progress represent a revolution in machine manufacturing, which is a mature business. Instead, relatively rapid progress is seen as evolution in the manufacturing of electronic components. The phase of technology life cycle explains this difference.

Quite as expected, all the companies regard the role of a new product as important. The importance is founded on the fact that new products are expected to improve profitability through more optimal manufacturability (lower costs) or the ability to set higher prices on the basis of improved performance. On the other hand, depending on the corporate function represented by the interviewee, different emphasis could be observed. Indeed, it seems quite natural that product development managers emphasize the role of NPD, whereas marketing directors – for instance – underscore the impact of sales and marketing on the success of the company. However, objective measures, such as R&D investments compared to net sales, show that all the investigated companies invest in R&D more than an average Finnish firm.[23]

Table 8 depicts the product life cycle phases as perceived by the six companies. The six rightmost columns comprise the phases that were mentioned by the interviewees. The first column, in contrast, summarizes more generic life cycle phases that seem to fit all case companies.

Although all the identified life cycles have their own characteristics, they include also some similarities. First, they are all seen from the perspective of the producer or supplier – not from that of the customer. When structuring the life cycles of their products, some companies tend to emphasize the beginning of the life cycle (e.g. company E: more detailed description of initial phases), while others perceive the end of life on a more detailed level (e.g. company A). It is important to notice that all the metal industry companies (A–D) perceive after sales or service as important. Company B, however, forms something of an exception because it does not explicitly mention after sales as a distinct phase. This is founded on the fact that the company sees its product as a sum of physical product and service. Hence, after sales service is regarded as an inherent part of the product. Further, companies E and F have not explicitly identified an after sales phase. In case of company E, this is simply because the components and materials supplied by the company do not require maintenance, as such. On the contrary, company F indeed *has* an after sales period (guaranteed seven years after the end of production), but it was not

Table 8. Identified Product Life Cycle Phases Grouped According to Generic Life Cycle Phases.

Generic	Company A	Company B	Company C	Company D	Company E	Company F
Feasibility studies/ preliminary phases	New product opportunity study		Market and concept study	Concept development / Business case study	Concept development / Development plan and decision	Concept development
Product development	New product development	Draft and concept phase + product development	Product development	Product development	Product and process development	Product development
Market launch		Market launch	Launch and the first customer delivery	Market launch	Pilot product / Market launch	Platform launch and start
Active phase	Active production	Production development/ redesign	Customer deliveries and versions	Active production	End of life	Steady supply
Support, maintenance and further development		Product maturation	Product support	After sales		Facelift and (re)focus
		New product generation using old platform	Product renovation and modernization			Harvest
End-of-life phases	Production shutdown / End of production / After sales / End of product	Product fades out	End of product support			End of product

Table 9. Length of Product Life Cycle (Producer View).

Phase No.	Company A	Company B	Company C	Company D	Company E	Company F
1	0.5	3.0	1.5	0.5	0.0	2.0
2	1.0	1.5	1.5	0.2	0.2	2.0
3	5.0	3.0	2.5	2.0	1.5	2.0
4	3.0	7.0	5.0	0.0	0.8	1.0
5	0.0	0.0	25.0	10.0	0.0	2.0
6	20.0	4.0	0.0	15.0	7.5	1.0
7	0.0		1.5			
Total	29.5	18.5	37.0	27.7	10.0	10.0

mentioned – for some reason – during this part of the interview. The recognition of the after sales phase as a part of the product life cycle, especially in the metal industry and machine manufacturing, is partly related to a belief according to which new product sales is not nearly as profitable as the after sales. Therefore, from the profitability point of view, many companies representing this industry try to focus on the after sales phase when managing and improving the total profitability of a product. Thus, considering the financial success of new product, a profitable after sales phase is a necessary element of PLC.

In terms of length, the product life cycles (see Table 9) reported by the companies vary between 10 years (company E and company F, after sales not included) and 37 years (company C). It should be noted that when the after sales phase is included, it may partly overlap with the manufacturing phase. Hence, the true length (in terms of time) is somewhat shorter. The single longest phase is typically after sales or support: between 7 years (company F) and 25–30 years (company C). The length of after sales exceeds 20 years also in companies A and D. It is important to observe that the companies engaged in the after sales of products typically experience very long product life cycles. A 30-year-old product may consume the company's resources through spare part inquiries or through different kinds of technical consultation. This resource consumption has a monetary effect, which should also be considered in performance measurement.

Table 10 summarizes the requirements associated with life cycle phases. The observations and findings that were made in each company are not reported separately. Rather, the findings are presented at an aggregate level. This is feasible due to the fact that the interviewees had something of a consensus regarding the identified requirements. It can be said that the views of different companies were both overlapping and supplemented each other.

According to the interviewees, a crucial issue in the beginning is the correct identification of customer needs. Feasibility studies may also include setting

Table 10.   Requirements for a Good or Successful Product and the Process
Associated with it Organized on the Basis of Generic Life Cycle Phases.

Generic	Summary of All Companies
Feasibility studies/preliminary phases	Correct and accurate identification of customer needs is important: "With this, we cannot afford to fail." Setting the target cost is also essential. The product and the competencies of NPD should be consistent.
Product development	On the basis of the previous phase, the aim is to obtain the defined technical specifications. Achievement of technical objectives related to product and product development lead time are key issues. Life cycle costs of the product should be considered. Other objectives include fluent start for actual product development, achievement of development budget and schedule targets, sufficient product quality and profit margin.
Market launch	Good start with the sales. Sufficient number of customer deliveries. Emphasis is on customer and product development perspectives. Small number of product modifications and versions. Customers are aware of the new product. It is about "redeeming the promises given at the beginning."
Active phase	Emphasis on financial perspective: product cost, product profitability, cost effective purchases. Good product quality. In addition, manufacturability (fluent manufacturing launch) and easiness of assembly are important. Consistency of the product with the entire supply chain. A key measure is the success of tailored customer versions. It is important to reach the target cost level set for the product. After a short delay, more evidence on the ability of the product to respond to customer needs will be obtained.
Support, maintenance, and further development	Earning through the product. Emphasis is on the financial perspective. The roles of product development, the customer, and marketing gain importance. Rather analogous to the product development phase. Availability of service and spare parts. A technically capable and viable product is a core objective. As a rule of thumb: "If it is rather quiet, everything has probably gone well." Only at the end of product life cycle is a final closing of the "accounts" regarding the product possible. Increased sales (measures by volume). "Successful demand peak." Efficient and effective after sales support. Availability of material and items for manufacturing.
End-of-life phases	The objective, from the customer point of view, is to reach a sufficient level of continuity. The ability to respond to the needs of the customer. In addition, meeting profitability targets is essential. From the financial point of view: unprofitable products have to be removed. A clear product deletion would be a good objective. Rapid and effective spare part sales, delivery and maintenance service. Cost effective and profitable customer service.

a target level for product cost. This will guide the further stages of product development and help to determine whether the product is feasible in the first place. In addition, it has been pointed out that it is important to ensure a reasonable coherence between product development competences and product requirements. Therefore, as a part of PM, competence evaluation could be utilized in the early phases of the product development process. However, the requirements identified in the product development phase mainly imply traditional measures of NPD success and performance such as product development lead time or the achievement of development budget targets. Furthermore, one company explicitly suggests that life cycle cost should be assessed and controlled during this phase. On the other hand, practical applications of life cycle costing suffer from inconsistent methods, concepts, and practices in companies, so there is need for development in this area (see also Järvinen et al., 2004). The need for effective life cycle costing is highlighted in companies associated with long product life cycles and high relative importance of the after sales phase.

The third phase, market launch, implies issues such as fluent start of sales of new product and gaining of positive reference customers. Customer awareness regarding the new product and a small number of product modifications are also perceived as important measures of the launch phase. It has to be stressed that some areas of business – such as paper machine manufacturing – are very dependent on reference customers. Paper machine manufacturers perceive their industry as a reference business due to the fact that it is virtually impossible to sell new products without proper references. This makes the introduction of a new product very challenging: at least one customer would be needed before the first one.

The active phase of life cycle underscores the importance of traditional financial success measures. Product cost, profitability and cost effectiveness in general are considered key issues. In addition, product quality and the suitability of the product for the supply chain could be a feasible measure of success. Customization is an important feature of business in industrial investment goods manufacturing (see e.g. Suomala et al., 2002a, b). This is also the case regarding the companies A, B, C, and D. The comprehensive recognition of the financial effects of customization requires not only product profitability measures but also measures for identifying the profitability difference between customers. In addition, the active phase of product life cycle provides companies with the possibility to evaluate their progress in the learning curve concerning, for instance, direct manufacturing costs. Setting cost and time based targets in the product development phase has little value unless the achievement of those targets is at least occasionally controlled.

The last two phases emphasize profitability and good earnings through the product on the one hand and availability of components on the other hand.

Many companies maintain that these later stages provide firms with valuable possibilities to improve demand by upgrading and enhancing the performance of a product or by reducing product cost. The quality and effectiveness of after sales service becomes important as well. True financial success of a product cannot be calculated without knowing the profit impact of the after sales phase. Unfortunately, companies have very limited abilities to connect spare part sales to a particular product due to the fact that a spare part item may work with several end products. Hence, total profitability calculation requires updated product structures and effective product data management systems throughout the life cycle. Further, one company suggests that a reasonable continuity has to be reached in order to satisfy the needs of customers. This remark relates to the fact that successive product life cycles, no matter how distinct, comprise a continuum from the supplier company's and customer's point of view. During one end product's life cycle, several generations of components or subassemblies are often required, which is especially important for a component manufacturer. To cope with this situation, compatibility issues such as the standardization of interfaces become essential.

Overall, what does the case study contribute to the theoretical part of the study? The tentative framework for connecting NPD PM and product life cycle that was founded on the literature study included three different conjectures regarding the relationship between product development and product life cycle:

(1) Product life cycle as an assemblage of discrete phases and requirements. The objectives and success measures of NPD could be derived by identifying these phase-specific requirements taking into account the relevant stakeholders.
(2) Product life cycle as a continuum of time. The objectives and the interpretations of success of product development could be determined on the basis of the anticipated cumulative impacts of products and the identification of their determinants.
(3) Emphasis on the fact that product life cycle is a dependent variable that is affected by product development and by a number of other actors inside and outside the company. Challenges and performance standards evolve during PLC.

The relevance of and justification for the first conjecture is founded on the fact that – despite some critical remarks – product life cycle is a viable concept that provides us with an acceptable model of reality. Companies perceive that their products have life cycles and that the life cycles include distinct phases and respective requirements. The case study confirmed that companies did not find it difficult to name product life cycle phases. Even more importantly, it was perceived that life cycle phases are associated with specific requirements that vary during the product life cycle. The first conjecture receives support also from the literature (Hultink & Robben, 1995); (Foster et al., 1985a, b; Griffin & Page, 1996).

As the case study points out, many companies face substantial challenges due to the fact that the life cycles, including after sales or service, are quite long. This is also shown in the literature (see for example Goffin, 1998, p. 43; Lele, 1986, 1997; Suomala et al., 2002a, b). Profitability, to a great extent, depends not only on the physical product but increasingly also on after sales business and service function. Life cycle costing is one of the means that can be applied to grasp the cumulative effects of products and product life cycles. Overall, as Fangel (1993) argues, handling the entire life cycle becomes more important. This underscores the relevance of the second conjecture.

The justification for the third conjecture is founded on the observation made in case studies that products are subjects for continuous evolution. Product development takes place both in the beginning of and during the life cycle. Therefore, performance measures should adapt themselves to ever-changing challenges and requirements. The nature of product development work is not a constant (see for example Grantham, 1997; Ryan & Riggs, 1996); rather, the development work and the process of setting performance standards are different when, for instance, revolutionary or evolutionary innovations are concerned.

All the conjectures seem to be in line with the present trend, according to which companies, instead of supplying physical products, increasingly emphasize their role as system providers or even performance providers. Hence, the question of what is a product and what is a product's life cycle becomes even more challenging. Further, companies are likely to face increasing pressure for firmer and more systematized life cycle management of products – whatever they are.

7.1.8. Summary

- Product life cycle seems to be a feasible concept in different industries for identifying tasks and issues related to a particular product.
- Distinct (but partly overlapping) life cycle phases were identified in all the cases.
- For the respondents, it seemed to be feasible to identify a number of characteristics for each phase. Among other things, the workload of different corporate functions can be utilized as a basis for structuring the life cycle.
- Product requirements for each phase were also identified. The requirements seem to differ from phase to phase. Some companies understand the importance of managing the whole life cycle of a product.
- The length of product life cycle in the case companies is often extensive, especially due to long after sales phases.

8. CONCLUSIONS AND IMPLICATIONS

8.1. Discussion of Results

The discussion of the results is feasible to build on the established research questions and objectives. The study includes two research questions that will be first discussed.

> A. Multifaceted performance measurement and the concept of product life cycle- conscious new product development: What would be the potential role of product life cycle in new product development performance measurement and management?

Life cycle or product life cycle is able to provide NPD performance measurement with a temporal frame that facilitates multifaceted measurement. Life cycle is a multidimensional concept that includes several perspectives and interpretations. These can be perceived as mutually complementary. For managerial purposes and for performance measurement construction, life cycle can be organized, for instance, on the basis of the phases that the customer experiences when utilizing the product. In addition, a different life cycle perception can be obtained when the product life cycle and its phases are assessed from the manufacturer's or society's point of view. The most comprehensive requirements for a product can be revealed when all the different views are taken into account.

The study does not argue that multifaceted performance measurement can only be realized through life cycle consciousness. It is quite likely that also other measurement ideas could have been produced on the basis of the analysis of the PM doctrine, ideas which would be able to provide some answers for the problems encountered within new product development performance measurement. However, it is argued that the proposed framework is well in line both with the identified NPD measurement problems and with the general guidelines discussed regarding the feasible and appropriate measurement of organizational activities.

> B. How would it be possible and expedient to organize the measurement of (new) product development performance taking into account the challenges and requirements that arise from the product life cycle and its discrete phases?

The study proposed three interpretations for synthesizing NPD performance measurement and the concept of life cycle. These are not mutually exclusive but they rather support each other. The essence of the first conjecture is that a life cycle is an assemblage of life cycle phases and that the phases are associated with a number of requirements that should be observed in product development. Product development is seen as an activity that is mainly carried out at the beginning of the product life cycle. The phase-specific requirements can be useful when determining the objectives for product development but they can also be applied when anticipating the effects of certain product development decisions concerning, for instance, the product's parameters. Performance measurement that is founded on the first conjecture requires systematic identification of PLC phases and product requirements from the different stakeholders' point of view. Importantly, it is possible that the requirements are partly contradictory, which means that the realization of PM requires also prioritization of objectives and stakeholders.

The second conjecture or interpretation suggests that PLC can be perceived as a continuum of time. Product development, which takes place at the beginning of the life cycle, determines the success potential of an organization for a long time. As shown in the case study, the lengths of product life cycles in many industries are extensive, especially when all the impacts are considered. NPD performance measurement that is consistent with the second conjecture requires long-term measures of success, such as the ones based on the whole life cycle costs experienced by different stakeholders or the ones that focus on the long-term profitability of the product. These would include measures not only for the profitability of the physical product but also for indirect services associated with it.

According to the third conjecture, product development is an activity that is more or less continuous in an organization. Product development takes place at the beginning of the PLC but companies are also required to practice product development during life cycles. Rarely would products stay competitive unless they were continuously improved during their lives. From the product development management point of view, this implies that it is imperative to practice continuous improvement and make sure that the capabilities gradually develop. On the other hand, evolutionary product development can be founded on explicit customers' or other stakeholders' experiences, which may help to allocate resources to the right issues. Performance measurement consistent with the third conjecture is focused on the explication of continuous improvement and the capability development that takes place. It should also rely on the data gained from the real-life experiences related to the product. Overall, the third conjecture suggests that if it is difficult to distinguish a separate product life cycle, the long-term nature of product development effects can be reflected by the measurement that seeks to identify improvements made through the gradual development of products and product platforms.

Regarding the three objectives set for this study, a number of observations can be made. The following comprises the main results that can be associated with the objectives, respectively:

I. To structure and analyze the concept of product life cycle in the context of new product development. This objective includes answering the question of what elements comprise product life cycle and identifying the different types of life cycles relevant regarding NPD performance measurement.

The concept of life cycle has been discussed both separately and connected with a number of managerial themes. It was found that the validity of PLC has been occasionally questioned but that the concept still seems to an expedient tool for organizing the long-term requirements for a product. The case study was founded on the product life cycle seen from the perspective of the producer. Important phases across the case companies included: development phase, introduction or implementation phase, active phase or steady phase, and, very often, also an after sales or maintenance phase.

II. To establish and analyze the concept of life cycle-conscious NPD performance measurement. This includes identifying the various requirements for performance measurement that are founded on the characteristics of life cycle.

The literature study and the case study were employed to fulfill this objective. As discussed earlier, the analysis produced three conjectures that were based on different interpretations of life cycle and the role of product development. It was also pointed out that the product should not only be assessed from the manufacturer point of view but that life cycle may have quite different meanings – but very useful meanings regarding performance measurement – if it is seen from the customer point of view. (Consider, for instance, the life cycle of a chocolate bar from the customer and from the manufacturer point of view.)

III. To build a construct or a conceptual model that connects product life cycle with new product development performance measurement. The construct should take into account the different stakeholders of the product and the interpretations regarding the product life cycle. As a result, the conceptual model should provide a multifaceted framework for measuring NPD performance.

The proposed framework was discussed in Chapter 5. The extensive literature study was conducted first to ensure a good alignment between the proposed framework and the guidelines set in the literature and second, to demonstrate the lack of such multifaceted blueprint in the doctrine.

8.2. Contribution of the Study

The literature suggested that the performance measurement of product development is not as effective as it should be. Despite the efforts from the managerial or practical side and from the academic side, the "performance measurement community" has not been able to resolve the challenges of NPD PM. New ideas and suggestions have been welcomed to overcome the problems, for instance, associated with the construction process of a PM system, the short-term focus of measurement, and the lack of outcome orientation.

Consistently with these shortcomings, the primary contribution of the study is the proposed multifaceted framework for measuring product development. It is meant to be applicable in the product development phase in the process of considering issues that are important given a particular product. The framework facilitates the analytical selection of objectives for constructing measures and can enable finding a balance for the measurement system. Overall, it connects two streams of literature: PLC and NPD PM.

Case study findings can be seen not only as a part of this primary contribution but also as an independent contribution in itself. The six case studies produced evidence concerning the *perceived* nature of industrial PLC. It was shown that distinct life cycle phases and the requirements associated with the phases can be identified within a number of settings. The case studies also showed the applicability of the framework at least within some industrial environments.

8.3. Managerial Implications

The study suggests that product life cycle is a key contingency variable of performance measurement in the product development context and it should be considered in NPD performance measurement system design. Management control systems can be seen as mechanisms that are intended to provide managers with information that is perceived as important in developing and maintaining viable patterns of behavior. Life cycle-oriented or -conscious performance measurement of new product development is in line with the contingency theory of management accounting, which suggests that the choice of appropriate control techniques depends on the circumstances surrounding a specific organization. Key contingent variables include the strategy and objectives an organization chooses to pursue: that is, different strategies and different organizational plans are likely to cause different control system configurations (Otley, 1999, pp. 365–366).

As a whole, the study indicates that there are several ways in which NPD performance measurement would benefit from the concept of product life cycle. First, life cycle orientation would provide companies with an expedient framework for constructing the performance measures of NPD. The framework is likely to reduce the short-termism typically associated with NPD performance measurement, when the long-term effects of new products and requirements that arise from the later stages of PLC are considered a foundation for performance measures.

In addition, life cycle could provide help for weighting the criteria and the measures utilized in NPD on the basis of the relative importance of the distinct PLC phases and the requirements associated with them. Further, a comprehensive framework such as PLC would help in finding a balance for the measurement system and in directing sufficient attention towards the comprehensive effects of new products.

Finally, measures – no matter how sophisticated or comprehensive they are – only provide information for improving something. Effective measurement requires an appropriate system that takes into account the characteristics of the particular environments. But above all, effective measurement requires the right attitudes and motivation to actually utilize the information provided by the system and energy to improve and continuously develop the measurement system to better reflect the challenges faced in the business.

8.4. Limitations of the Study and Guidelines for Further Research

The case study of the six companies and the interviewees provide only a limited empirical context within which the ideas presented in this study seem to apply. This allows no statistical generalizations. Naturally, the study did not seek to produce statistical generalizations but rather contextual ones. The case studies were not able to provide data on the true life cycles of the products but rather on the perceptions regarding the product life cycles in these companies. This is not, however, a fundamental problem. The actual implementation of the measurement framework can and will produce more reliable data on the actual life cycles and the issues related to them.

Overall, the limitations of the study can be discussed in the dimensions of validity and reliability. Validity can be further divided into external validity, internal validity, and construct validity.

Despite the fact that the primary aim of the study has not been to produce generalizations, it is appropriate to discuss the generality of the results of this study, Overall, the generalizability or the external validity of case studies (that is, case studies of multiple cases) relies on replication logic. On the other hand, the generalizability of qualitative research relies on contextual generalization. The case studies provided the study with a (replicated) context within which the results (the LCCM framework) are relevant. The study is mainly focused on industrial companies that produce industrial investment goods. In terms of size, middle-sized and large companies have been dealt with. Above all, the case studies featured certain issues that define the boundaries for generalizing the results:

- The ability to identify and structure the product life cycle.
- The extensive length of PLC.
- The continuous evolution of products.

Construct validity was promoted by using multiple sources of evidence in the case studies. The interviewees' opinions were triangulated by using other documents and evidence that were available. These included technology reports, life cycle management models, and data gained by direct observation (two companies). In addition, the interview memos were circulated among the studied companies. In data analysis and composition, the process relied partly on the expertise of two researchers.

As pointed out by Yin (1994), internal validity is a concern of causal studies. This is not one of those. In other words, the purpose of this study was not to find cause-effect links within the cases that would explain certain investigated phenomena. As regards the case studies, the units of analyses were associated with the concept of life cycle. The researcher did not try to explain why the life cycles were what they were but he was to investigate whether it is possible to overall identify PLCs, life cycle phases, and requirements.

Reliability refers to the ability to repeat the same research process using the same material. Taking into account that the majority of the study has been conceptual, the question of reliability in this sense is interesting to answer. In my opinion, it is not very likely that another researcher would have ended up with exactly the same conclusions and frameworks. However, the phases of the research and the documentation were prepared with such rigor that the same researcher would not end up with totally different conclusions if the material was revisited. Finally, with conceptual research, it is somewhat unclear whether it is the repeatability of the research process or the applicability and reliability of the given framework that is the major point of interest.

The practical limitations of the study include some issues. The lack of the ability to rely on historical data regarding life cycles may make it very difficult to actually practice the LCCM proposed in this study. If the life cycle cannot be anticipated, it could be very challenging to place any objectives or measures on the basis of life cycle requirements. Thus, the LCCM framework is likely to be the most applicable in those environments that are characterized by the feasibility of reasonable life cycle anticipation. Also, if different measures were employed in different parts of a life cycle, one of the practical challenges would be the difficulty to identify a shift into a particular phase. As shown in the literature, life cycles may take different forms and the sales pattern, for instance, cannot be straightforwardly used as a basis for life cycle analysis. In addition, the proposed LCCM could lead to too heavy a procedure for some companies. The systematic way to construct measures that is advocated by the framework means that the construction process may require considerable effort if all the relevant stakeholders, life cycle interpretations, and life cycle phases are analyzed within the process. Finally, to support the practical implementation process, more practical ideas concerning, for instance, the actual measures will be needed.

Future research could be focused at least on the following themes: First, specific measures that would support the presented blueprint should be constructed and tested in different organizations. Conceptual research approach or constructive research approach would be suitable methods regarding this theme. Second, quantitative evidence on the product life cycles in metal industry should be collected. This can be done either by survey research or by in-depth case studies. Third, implementation of the measurement framework in an organization that practices product development would provide more information concerning the feasibility and applicability of the framework in a real-life situation. The appropriate research strategy for this could be action research or constructive research.

NOTES

1. A product concept is an approximate description of the technology, working principles, and form of the product. It is a concise description of how the product will satisfy the customers' needs (Ulrich & Eppinger, 1995).

2. As far as a company's management is concerned, a major dilemma in the management of research and development is that the number of potential research, development, and design projects is greater than it is possible to carry out. The limited resources and skills compel managers to select projects from those proposed. A comprehensive description of different selection methods is presented (for example) by Martino (1995).

3. See Hannula and Suomala (1997) and Hannula (1999).

4. Ellis and Curtis (1995) divide customers into three subcategories: consumers/end users, distribution chain customers, and downstream internal operations within the company.

5. Innovation: the introduction of something new, a new idea, method, or device [Merriam-Webster, 2002 #696] or new idea, method, or device; the act of creating a new product or process. The act includes invention as well as the work required to bring an idea or concept into final form (PDMA, 2002).

6. According to Yin (1994), it is not totally appropriate to use the term "sample" in case studies as the purpose of the case study is not to produce statistical generalizations.

7. Emory (1985) defines validity in general as: "The extent to which differences found with a measuring tool reflect true differences among those being tested."

8. "For any performance measurement system to work, the measures must be reported back to those that have the ability to affect them" (Frigo & Krumwiede, 1998, p. 2).

9. The Hawthorne effect (known also as the reactivity effect) refers to the phenomenon that subjects in an experiment behave differently when they know they are being observed. This can threaten the external validity of an experiment. The phenomenon is called the Hawthorne effect because of a study conducted in the Western Electric Company's Hawthorne plant in Illinois in the late 1930s. This study was conducted to measure the effects of certain factors such as lighting on worker's productivity. The researchers varied the conditions at the Hawthorne plant and compared that plant's productivity with another plant. (see for example http://www.ugrad.cs.ubc.ca/~cs444/revised-gloss-stud.shtml or http://www.sociologyessentials-2nded.nelson.com/glossary3.html).

10. Innovation can be defined as an application of new or different approaches or methods or technologies to meet organizational goals (Schroeder et al., 1989).

11. Both financial success measures and market share attainment measures were considered as commercial measures of performance.

12. The concept of "stakeholder" dates back to 1963 in management literature. According to Elias et al, the concept appeared in a memorandum at the Stanford Research Institute. According to that definition, stakeholders were seen as groups whose support is elemental for the existence of an organization. In other words, a firm is not likely to survive without the support of the stakeholders (Elias et al., 2002).

13. Three levels of stakeholder analysis include rational, process, and transactional (Elias et al., 2002):

- rational level: an understanding regarding who the stakeholders are and what their perceived stakes are;
- process level: an understanding of how the organization either implicitly or explicitly manages its relationship with the stakeholders;
- transactional level: understanding the set of transactions and bargains between the organization and its stakeholders.

14. See Larson and Gobeli (1988, pp. 181–182) for detailed descriptions of the different project structures.

15. This view of effectiveness is quite interesting when compared with that of, for instance, O'Donnel's (O'Donnel & Duffy, 2002). Traditionally, effectiveness is seen as closely connected with output, although output and effectiveness have also essential differences. One of the biggest differences is that effectiveness is a context-specific concept, whereas the concept of output is unrelated to any particular context.

16. Lewis uses the claim *"this type of project should cost this much"* as a typical example of an "arbitrary sense of normal."

17. Chiesa and Masella (1996) employs a similar classification but introduces also an additional category for the timing, namely ex-ante measurement that can be utilized when the input resources or the skills of an organization are evaluated.

18. A product platform is the technological foundation of a product family. "A platform is the physical implementation of a technical design that serves as the base architecture for a series of derivative products" (Meyer et al., 1997, p. 90).

19. However, a study by Leastadius and Karlson (2001) reports that the use of life cycle assessment (LCA) techniques in product development is still underdeveloped. By using ABB as a case, they conclude that the current benefits from life cycle assessments are still quite modest due to the low integration of these methods with operational activities. In

contrast with this, they found out that LCA is expected to be a valuable tool in the future and that it will stay in the toolbox of practitioners.

20. Monte Carlo simulation is a numerical approximation method used in mathematics, statistics, and operations research to resolve problems by the use of random sampling. The behavior of a system is simulated by feeding in values of the system variables, and repeating the operation over different sets of values so as to explore the system under a variety of conditions. http://www.manningaffordability.com/s&tweb/PUBS/Man_Mach/annexi.html.

21. Competencies and capabilities can be used as synonyms (Fowler et al., 2000).

22. According to the guidelines set by the EU Commission, turnover of less than 50 MEUR and the number of employees less than 250.

23. An average Finnish firm invests about 1.3% of their net sales in R&D (2002).

REFERENCES

Aaltio-Marjosola, I. (1999). Case-tutkimus metodisena lähestymistapana. *Metodix*, 2000.

Aaltonen, P., Koivula, A., Pankakoski, M., Teikari, V., & Ventä, M. (1996). *Tiimistä toimeen: Kuinka kirkastat tiimin tavoitteet ja luot mittariston sekä palautejärjestelmän.* Espoo, Teknillinen korkeakoulu.

Abetti, P. A. (2002). From science to technology to products and profits. Superconductivity at General Electric and intermagnetics general (1960–1990). *Journal of Business Venturing, 17*, 83–98.

Akao, Y. (Ed.) (1990). *Quality function deployment.* Productivity Press.

Akgün, A. E., & Lynn, G. S. (2002). Antecedents and consequences of team stability on new product development performance. *Journal of Engineering and Technology Management, 19*, 263–286.

Alasuutari, P. (1999). *Laadullinen tutkimus.* Tampere, Vastapaino.

Ancona, D. G., & Caldwell, D. F. (1992). Demography and design: Predictors of new product team performance. *Organization Science, 3*(3), 321–341.

Andersin, H., Karjalainen, J., & Laakso, T. (1994). *Suoritusten mittaus ohjausvälineenä.* Helsinki, MET.

Anderson, C. R., & Zeithaml, C. P. (1984). Stage of the product life cycle, business strategy, and business performance. *Academy of Management Journal, 2*(1), 5–24.

Anderson, E. W., & Fornell, C. (1994). Customer satisfaction, market share, and profitability: Findings from Sweden. *Journal of Marketing, 58*(3), 53–66.

Ansari, S. L., Bell, J. E., Cypher, J. H., Dears, P. H., Dutton, J. J., Ferguson, M. D., Hallin, K., Marx, C. A., Ross, C. G., & Zampino, P. A. (1997). *Target costing: The next frontier in strategic cost management.* Chicago, IL: Irwin.

Anthony, M. T., & McKay, J. (1992). Balancing the product development process: Achieving product and cycle-time excellence in high-technology industries. *Journal of Product Innovation Management, 9*, 140–147.

Argyris, C. (1991). Teaching smart people how to learn. *Harvard Business Review* (May–June), 99–109.

Asiedu, Y., & Gu, P. (1998). Product life cycle cost analysis: State of the art review. *International Journal of Production Research, 36*(4), 883–908.

Athaide, G. A., Meyers, P. W., & Wilemon, D. L. (1996). Seller-buyer interactions during the commercialization of technological process innovations. *Journal of Product Innovation Management, 13*, 406–421.

Awasthi, V. N., Chow, C. W., & Wu, A. (1998). Performance measure and resource expenditure choices in a teamwork environment: The effects of national culture. *Management Accounting Research*, *9*, 119–138.

Ax, C., & Ask, U. (1995). *Cost management*. Studentlitteratur.

Badri, M. A., Mortagy, A., Davis, D., & Davis, D. (1997). Effective analysis and planning of R&D stages: A simulation approach. *International Journal of Project Management*, *15*(6), 351–358.

Batson, R. G. (1987). Characteristics of R&D management which influence information needs. *IEEE Transactions on Engineering Management*, *34*(3), 178–183.

Batty, J. (1988). *Accounting for research and development*. Aldershot: Gower.

Bauer, H. H., & Fischer, M. (2000). Product life cycle patterns for pharmaceuticals and their impact on R&D profitability of late mover products. *International Business Review*, *9*, 703–725.

Bayus, B. L. (1994). Are product life cycles really getting shorter? *Journal of Product Innovation Management*, *11*(4), 300–308.

Berg, P., Leivo, V., Pihjalamaa, J., & Leinonen, M. (2001). *Tuotekehitystoiminnan laadun ja kypsyyden arviointi*. MET.

Boer, H., Caffyn, S., Corso, M., Coughlan, P., Gieskes, J., Magnusson, M., Pavesi, S., & Ronchi, S. (2001). Knowledge and continuous innovation. The CIMA methodology. *International Journal of Operations & Production Management*, *21*(4).

Bourne, M., Mills, J., Wilcox, M., Neely, A., & Platts, K. (2000). Designing, implementing and updating performance measurement systems. *International Journal of Operations & Production Management*, *20*(7), 754–771.

Brinker, B. J. (Ed.) (1997). *Emerging practices in cost management: Performance measurement*. Emerging Practices in Cost Management. Boston, WG&L/RIA Group.

Brown, K. K. (1995). Strategic performance measurements. *Florida CPA Today*, 28–30.

Brown, M. G., & Svenson, R. A. (1998). Measuring R&D productivity. *Research Technology Management*, *41*(6), 30–36.

Brown, S. L., & Eisenhardt, K. M. (1995). Product development: Past research, present findings, and future directions. *Academy of Management Review*, *20*(2), 343–378.

Brown, W. B., & Gobeli, D. (1992). Observations on the measurement of R&D productivity: A case study. *IEEE Transactions on Engineering Management*, *39*(4), 325–331.

Campbell, A. J., & Cooper, R. G. (1999). Do customer partnerships improve new product success rates? *Industrial Marketing Management*, *28*, 507–519.

Chenhall, R. H. (1997). Reliance on manufacturing performance measures, total quality management and organizational performance. *Management Accounting Research*, *8*, 187–206.

Chiesa, V., & Masella, C. (1996). Searching for an effective measure of R&D performance. *Management Decision*, *34*(7), 49–57.

Chow, C. W., Haddad, K. M., & Williamson, J. E. (1997). Applying the balanced scorecard to small companies. *Management Accounting*, *1997* (August), 21–27.

Clark, K. B., & Fujimoto, T. (1990). The power of product integrity. *Harvard Business Review* (November–December), 107–118.

Clark, K. B., & Fujimoto, T. (1991). *Product development performance. Strategy, organization, and management in the world auto industry*. Boston: Harvard Business School Press.

Clifford, D. K. (1965). Managing the product life cycle. *Management Review* (June), 34–38.

Coccia, M. (2001). A basic model for evaluating R&D performance: Theory and application in Italy. *R&D Management*, *31*(4), 453–464.

Cohen, M. A., & Whang, S. (1997). Competing in product and service: A product life-cycle model. *Management Science*, *43*(4), 535–545.

Cokins, G. (1999). *Why is traditional accounting failing quality managers? Activity-based costing is the solution.* Quality Congress. ASQC . . . Annual Quality Congress Proceedings, Milwaukee, ASQC.

Constantinides, K., & Shank, J. K. (1994). Matching accounting to strategy: One mill's experience. *Management Accounting, 1994* (September), 32–36.

Cooper, R. (1990a). ABC: A need, not an option. *Accountancy* (September), 86–88.

Cooper, R. (1990b). Explicating the logic of ABC. *Emerging Practices in Cost Management* (pp. L6-1–L6-5). B. Brinker, J. Boston, Warren, Gorham & Lamont.

Cooper, R., & Kaplan, S. (1988). Measure costs right: Make the right decisions. *Harvard Business Review, 66*(5), 96–103.

Cooper, R., & Slagmulder, R. (1997). *Target costing and value engineering* (379 pp.). Portland: Productivity Press.

Cooper, R., & Slagmulder, R. (1999a). Designing ABC systems for strategic costing and operational improvement. *Strategic Finance, 81*(2), 18–20.

Cooper, R., & Slagmulder, R. (1999b). Develop profitable new products with target costing. *Sloan Management Review* (Summer), 23–33.

Cooper, R. G. (1985). Selecting winning new product projects: Using the NewProd system. *Journal of Product Innovation Management* (2), 34–44.

Cooper, R. G. (1996). Overhauling the new product process. *Industrial Marketing Management, 25,* 465–482.

Cooper, R. G. (1997). *Winning at new products. Accelerating the process from idea to launch.* Addison-Wesley Publishing Company.

Cooper, R. G. (1999). The invisible success factors in product innovation. *Journal of Product Innovation Management, 16,* 115–133.

Cooper, R. G., & Kleinschmidt, E. J. (1995). Benchmarking the firm's critical success factors in new product development. *Journal of Product Innovation Management, 1995*(12), 374–391.

Cooper, R. G., & Kleinschmidt, E. J. (1996). Winning businesses in product development. *Research Technology Management* (July/August), 18–30.

Cordero, R. (1990). The measurement of innovation performance in the firm: An overview. *Research Policy, 19,* 185–192.

Curtis, C. C. (1994). Nonfinancial performance measures in product development. *Journal of Cost Management* (Fall), 18–26.

Curtis, M. (1994). Designing for the future. *World Class Design to Manufacture, 1*(4), 46–48.

Dalén, P., & Bolmsjö, G. S. (1996). Life-cycle cost analysis of the labor factor. *International Journal of Production Economics, 46–47,* 459–467.

Davila, T. (2000). An empirical study on the drivers of management control system's design in new product development. *Accounting, Organizations and Society, 25,* 383–409.

Davis, C. R. (2002). Calculated risk: A framework for evaluating product development. *MIT Sloan Management Review* (Summer), 71–77.

Davis, J., Fusfeld, A., Scriven, E., & Tritle, G. (2001). Determining a projects's probability of success. *Research Technology Management, 2001*(May–June), 51–57.

De Bono, E. (1991). *Minä olen oikeassa, sinä väärässä.* Juva, WSOY.

Delano, G., Parnell, G. S., Smith, C., & Vance, M. (2000). Quality function deployment and decision analysis. An R&D case study. *International Journal of Operations & Production Management, 20*(5), 591–609.

Dell'Isola, A. (1997). *Value engineering: Practical applications for design, construction, maintenance and operations.* Kingston, RS Means Co.

Dhalla, N. K., & Yuspeh, S. (1976). Forget the product life cycle concept! *Harvard Business Review* (January–February), 102–112.

Donaldson, T., & Preston, L. E. (1995). The stakeholder theory of the corporation: Concepts, evidence, and implications. *Academy of Management Review, 20*(1), 85–91.

Dougherty, D. (1990). Understanding new markets for new products. *Strategic Management Journal, 11*, 59–78.

Dougherty, D. (1992). Interpretive barriers to successful product innovation in large firms. *Organization Science, 3*(2), 179–202.

Drejer, A., & Riis, J. O. (1999). Competence development and technology. How learning and technology can be meaningfully integrated. *Technovation, 19*, 631–644.

Driva, H., Pawar, K. S., & Menon, U. (2000). Measuring product development performance in manufacturing organisations. *International Journal of Production Economics, 63*, 147–159.

Drucker, P. F. (1994). We need to measure, not count. *Drucker Management, 1994*(Fall), 2–4.

Dutton, J. J., & Marx, C. A. (1999). Target costing. *Handbook of Cost Management* (D2-1–D2-26). J. B. Edwards. Boston, Warren, Gorham & Lamont.

Eccles, R. G. (1991). The performance measurement manifesto. *Harvard Business Review, 1991*, 131–137.

Eckel, L., Fisher, K., & Russel, G. (1992). Environmental performance measurement. *CMA, 1992*, 16–23.

EIRMA (1985). Evaluation of R&D output. Paris, European Industrial Research Management Institute: 67.

EIRMA (1995). Evaluation of R&D projects. Paris, European Industrial Research Management Association: 101.

Eisenhardt, K. M. (1989). Building theories from case study research. *Academy of Management Review, 14*(4), 532–550.

Elias, A. A., Cavana, R. Y., & Jackson, L. S. (2002). Stakeholder analysis for R&D project management. *R&D Management, 32*(4), 301–310.

Ellis, L. (1997). *Evaluation of R&D processes: Effectiveness through measurements*. Boston: Artech House.

Ellis, L. W., & Curtis, C. C. (1995). Measuring customer satisfaction. *Research Technology Management, 38*(5), 45–56.

Eloranta, E., & Räisänen, J. (1986). *Ohjattavuusanalyysi. Tutkimus tuotannon ja sen ohjauksen kehittämisestä Suomessa.* Helsinki, SITRA.

Emblemsvåg, J. (2001). Activity-based life-cycle costing. *Managerial Auditing Journal, 16*(1), 17–27.

Emory, W. C. (1985). *Business research methods.* Homewood: Richard D. Irwin.

EPA (1993). *Life cycle design guidance manual – Environmental requirements and the product system* (p. 181). Washington, National Pollution Prevention Center, University of Michigan.

Epstein, M. J., & Manzoni, J.-F. (1997). The balanced scorecard and tableau de bord: Translating strategy into action. *Management Accounting, 1997*(August), 28–36.

Ernst, R., & Ross, D. N. (1993). The delta force approach to balancing long-run performance. *Business Horizons, 1993*(May–June), 4–10.

Eskola, J., & Suoranta, J. (2001). *Johdatus laadulliseen tutkimukseen.* Jyväskylä, Vastapaino.

Euske, K. J., Frause, N., Peck, T., Rosenstiel, B., & Schreck, S. (1998). *Service process measurement: Breaking the code.* Bedford, CAM-I.

Everaert, P., & Bruggeman, W. (2002). Cost targets and time pressure during new product development. *International Journal of Operations & Production Management, 22*(12), 1339–1353.

Fangel, M. (1993). The broadening of project management. *International Journal of Project Management*, *11*(2), 72.

Filson, D. (2002). Product and process innovations in the life cycle of an industry. *Journal of Economic Behavior & Organization*, *49*, 97–112.

Firth, R. W., & Narayanan, V. K. (1996). New product strategies of large, dominant product manufacturing firms: An exploratory analysis. *Journal of Product Innovation Management*, *13*, 334–347.

Fisher, J. (1992). Use of nonfinancial performance measures. *Journal of Cost Management*, *1992*(Spring), 31–38.

Fisher, J. (1995). Implementing target costing. *Journal of Cost Management*, *9*(2), 50–59.

Flapper, S. D. P., Fortuin, L., & Stoop, P. P. M. (1996). Towards consistent performance management systems. *International Journal of Operations & Production Management*, *16*(7), 27–37.

Fleming, L., & Sorensen, O. (2001). The dangers of modularity. *Harvard Business Review* (September), 20–21.

Fogelholm, J., & Karjalainen, J. (2001). *Tuotantotoiminnan mittaaminen*. Vantaa, WSOY.

Foster, R. N., Linden, L. H., Whiteley, R. L., & Kantrow, A. M. (1985a). Improving the return on R&D: I. *Research Technology Management* (January–February), 12–17.

Foster, R. N., Linden, L. H., Whiteley, R. L., & Kantrow, A. M. (1985b). Improving the return on R&D: II. *Research Technology Management* (March–April), 13–22.

Fowler, S. W., King, A. W., Marsh, S. J., & Victor, B. (2000). Beyond products: New strategic imperatives for developing competencies in dynamic environments. *Journal of Engineering Technology Management*, *17*, 357–377.

Frigo, M. L., & Krumwiede, K. (1998). Cost management group survey on performance measurement: Tips on implementing the balanced scorecard approach, IMA.

Fry, T. D., & Cox, J. F. (1989). Manufacturing performance: Local vs. global measures. *Production and Inventory Management Journal*, *30*(2), 52–56.

Garcia, R., & Calantone, R. (2002). A critical look at technological innovation typology and innovativeness terminology: A literature review. *The Journal of Product Innovation Management*, *19*, 110–132.

Globerson, S. (1985). Issues in developing a performance criteria system for an organization. *International Journal of Production Research*, *23*(4), 639–646.

Goffin, K. (1998). Evaluating customer support during new product development – An exploratory study. *Journal of Product Innovation Management*, *15*, 42–56.

Goffin, K., & New, C. (2001). Customer support and new product development. *International Journal of Operations and Production Management*, *21*(3), 275–301.

Gomes, J. F. S., de Weerd-Nederhof, P. C., Pearson, A. W., & Cunha, M. P. (2003). Is more always better? An exploration of the differential effects of functional integration on performance in new product development. *Technovation*, *23*, 185–191.

Gooderham, G. (2001). The top 10 lessons of implementing performance management systems. *Journal of Cost Management*, *2001*(January/February), 29–33.

Grady, M. W. (1991). Performance measurement: Implementing strategy. *Management Accounting*, *1991*, 49–53.

Grant, R. M. (1996). Prospering in dynamically-competitive environments: Organizational capability as knowledge integration. *Organization Science*, *7*(4), 375–387.

Grantham, L. M. (1997). The validity of the product life cycle in the high-tech industry. *Marketing Intelligence & Planning*, *15*(1), 4–10.

Green, D. H., Barclay, D. W., & Ryans, A. B. (1995). Entry strategy and long term performance: Conceptualization and empirical examination. *Journal of Marketing, 59*(4), 1–16.

Griffin, A. (1997). PDMA research on new product development practices: Updating trends and benchmarking best practices. *Journal of Product Innovation Management* (14), 429–458.

Griffin, A. (2002). Product development cycle time for business-to-business products. *Industrial Marketing Management, 31,* 291–304.

Griffin, A., & Page, A. L. (1996). PDMA success measurement project: Recommended measures for product development success and failure. *Journal of Product Innovation Management* (13), 478–496.

Grossman (2002). Managing product life. *Strategic Decision, 18*(8), 25–28.

Grönfors, T. (1996). *Performance management: The effects of paradigms, underlying theory and intrinsic processes.* Espoo, Facile Publishing.

Hall, L. A., & Bagchi-Sen, S. (2002). A study of R&D, innovation, and business performance in the Canadian biotechnology industry. *Technovation, 22,* 231–244.

Hamel, G. (1996). Strategy as a revolution. *Harvard Business Review* (July–August), 69–82.

Hamel, G., & Prahalad, C. K. (1994). *Competing for the future.* Boston: Harvard Business School Press.

Hammersley, M., & Atkinson, P. (1995). *Ethnography. Principles in practice.* London: Routledge.

Hannula, M. (1999). Expedient total productivity measurement. *Industrial Engineering and Management* (p. 179). Tampere: Tampere University of Technology.

Hannula, M., & Suomala, P. (1997). *Tuottavuuden kehittämisen esteet pirkanmaalaisissa pkt-yrityksissä.* Tampere: Tampereen teknillinen korkeakoulu.

Happonen, H. (2001). Framework for integrating knowledge and process dimensions of a product development system: A Theoretical and empirical study in the field of modern process automation. *Automation and Control Institute* (p. 188). Tampere: Tampere University of Technology.

Hardy, J. W., & Hubbard, E. D. (1992). ABC: Revisiting the basics. *CMA Magazine* (November), 24–28.

Harness, D. R., Marr, N. E., & Goy, T. (1998). The identification of weak products revisited. *Journal of Product and Brand Management, 7*(4), 319–335.

Hart, S. (1993). Dimensions of success in new product development: An exploratory investigation. *Journal of Marketing Management, 1993*(9), 23–41.

Hart, S., & Tzokas, N. (2000). New product launch mix in growth and mature product markets. *Benchmarking: An International Journal, 7*(5), 389–405.

Hayes, R. H., & Wheelwright, S. C. (1979a). The dynamics of process-product life cycles. *Harvard Business Review* (March–April), 127–136.

Hayes, R. H., & Wheelwright, S. C. (1979b). Link manufacturing process and product life cycles. *Harvard Business Review, 57*(1), 133–140.

Herath, H. S. B., & Park, C. S. (1999). Economic Analysis of R&D Projects: An Options Approach. *The Engineering Economist, 44*(1), 1–35.

Hertenstein, J. H., & Platt, M. B. (2000). Performance measures and management control in new product development. *Accounting Horizons, 14*(3), 303–323.

Hirons, E., Simon, A., & Simon, C. (1998). External customer satisfaction as a performance measure of the management of a research and development department. *International Journal of Quality & Reliability Management, 15*(8/9), 969–987.

Hoffeecker, J., & Goldenberg, C. (1994). Using the balanced scorecard to develop companywide performance measures. *Journal of Cost Management, 1994,* 5–17.

Hollander, J. (2000). *Genesis, a product assessment instrument used during the product development process*. 7th International Product Development Management Conference, Leuven, Belgium, EIASM.

Hoover, W. E., Eloranta, E., Holmström, J., & Huttunen, K. (2001). *Managing the demand-supply chain. Value innovations for customer satisfaction*. Wiley.

Horvath, P., Gleich, R., & Schmidt, S. (1998). Linking target costing to ABC and a U.S. automotive supplier. *Journal of Cost Management, 12*(2), 16–24.

Howley, M. (1990). Criteria for success in new product development for consumer goods: A comparative study. *European Journal of Marketing, 24*(4), 55–60.

Hull, D. L., & Cox, J. F. (1994). The field service function in the electronics industry: Providing a link between customers and production/marketing. *International Journal of Production Economics, 37*, 115–126.

Hultink, E. J., Atuahene-Gima, K., & Lebbink, I. (2000). Determinants of new product selling performance: An empirical examination in The Netherlands. *European Journal of Innovation Management, 3*(1), 27–34.

Hultink, E. J., Hart, S., Robben, H. S. J., & Griffin, A. (1999). Launch decisions and new product success: An empirical comparison of consumer and industrial products. *Journal of Product Innovation Management, 17*, 5–23.

Hultink, E. J., & Robben, H. S. J. (1995). Measuring new product success: The difference that time perspective makes. *Journal of Product Innovation Management, 1995* (12).

Hutton, R. B., & Wilkie, W. L. (1980). Life cycle cost: A new form of consumer information. *Journal of Consumer Research, 6*(March), 349–360.

Hyland, P., Gieskes, J., & Sloan, T. (2002). *Performance measurement and product innovation*. Continuous Innovation in Business Processes and Networks, Helsinki University of Technology, Espoo, Finland.

ICMS Inc. (1992). *Activity dictionary. A comprehensive reference tool for ABM and ABC*.

Ijiri, Y. (1975). *Theory of accounting measurement*. Sarasota, American Accounting Association.

IMA (1998a). *Practices and techniques: Tools and techniques for implementing integrated performance measurement systems* (p. 54). Montvale, Institute of Management Accountants.

IMA (1998b). *Tools and techniques for implementing target costing* (p. 46). Montvale, Institute of Management Accountants.

Innes, J., & Mitchell, F. (1995). ABC: A follow-up survey of CIMA members. *Management Accounting, 73*(7), 50–51.

IRI (2000). R&D facts 2000, Industrial Research Institute.

Ittner, C. D., & Larcker, D. F. (1997). Product development cycle time and organizational performance. *Journal of Marketing Research, 34*(February), 13–23.

Ittner, C. D., & Larcker, D. F. (1998a). Are nonfinancial measures leading indicators of financial performance? An analysis of customer satisfaction. *Journal of Accounting Research, 36*, 1–35.

Ittner, C. D., & Larcker, D. F. (1998b). Innovations in performance measurement: Trends and research implications. *Journal of Management Accounting Research, 10*(6), 205–238.

Ittner, C. D., & Larcker, D. F. (2001). Assessing empirical research in managerial accounting: A value-based management perspective. *Journal of Accounting and Economics, 32*, 349–410.

Jaakkola, J., & Tunkelo, E. (1987). *Tuotekehitys – ideoista markkinoille*. Espoo, Weilin+Göös.

Jackson, T. W., & Spurlock, J. M. (1966). *Research and development management*. Homewood, IL: Dow Jones-Irwin.

Järvinen, A., Suomala, P., & Paranko, J. (2004). *Elinkaarilaskennan nykytila raideliikenteen toimitusketjussa* (34 pp.). Tampere: Tampereen teknillinen yliopisto.

Jiang, R., & Zhang, P. J. (2003). Required characteristics of statistical distribution models for life cycle cost estimation. *International Journal of Production Economics, 83*, 185–194.

Johnson, H. T., & Kaplan, R. S. (1987). *Relevance lost: The rise and fall of management accounting.* Boston: Harvard Business School Press.

Johnson, H. T., Vance, T. P., & Player, R. S. (1991). Pitfalls in using ABC cost-driver information to manage operating costs. *Corporate Controller* (Jan/Feb), 26–32.

Jokioinen (2003). Interview: Important design parameters in paper machine industry.

Jones, C. T., & Dugdale, D. (2002). The ABC bandwagon and the juggernaut of modernity. *Accounting, Organizations and Society, 27*, 121–163.

Kald, M., & Nilsson, F. (2000). Performance measurement at nordic companies. *European Management Journal, 18*(1), 113–127.

Kane, G., Stoyell, J. L., Howarth, C. R., Norman, P., & Vaughan, R. (2000). A stepwise life cycle engineering methodology for the clean design of large made to order products. *Journal of Engineering Design, 11*(2), 175–189.

Kaplan, R. S. (1992). From ABC to ABM. *Management Accounting*, 54–57.

Kaplan, R. S., & Atkinson, A. A. (1998). *Advanced management accounting* (3rd ed., 798 pp.). Upper Saddle River: Prentice-Hall.

Kaplan, R. S., & Norton, D. P. (1992). The balanced scorecard – measures that drive performance. *Harvard Business Review, 1992*(January–February), 71–79.

Kaplan, R. S., & Norton, D. P. (1993). Putting the balanced scorecard to work. *Harvard Business Review* (September–October), 134–147.

Kaplan, R. S., & Norton, D. P. (1996a). *The balanced scorecard. Translating strategy into action.* Boston: Harvard Business School Press.

Kaplan, R. S., & Norton, D. P. (1996b). Using the balanced scorecard as a strategic management system. *Harvard Business Review, 74*(1), 11.

Kaplan, R. S., & Norton, D. P. (2001). Transforming the balanced scorecard from performance measurement to strategic management: Part I. *Accounting Horizons, 15*(1), 87–104.

Kärkkäinen, H., Piippo, P., & Tuominen, M. (2001). Ten tools for customer-driven product development in industrial companies. *International Journal of Production Economics, 69*, 161–176.

Kasanen, E., Lukka, K., & Siitonen, A. (1991). Konstruktiivinen tutkimusote liiketaloustieteessä. *Liiketaloudellinen Aikakauskirja* (3), 301–327.

Kato, Y., & Boer, G. (1995). Target costing: An integrative management process. *Journal of Cost Management, 9*(1), 39–51.

Keegan, D. P., Jones, C. R., & Eiler, R. G. (1991). To implement your strategies, change your measures. *Price Waterhouse Review, 1991*(1), 29–38.

Kennerlay, M., & Neely, A. (2002). A framework of the factors affecting the evolution of performance measurement systems. *International Journal of Operations and Production Management, 22*(11), 1222–1245.

Keoleian, G. A., & Menerey, D. (1993). *Life cycle design guidance manual – Environmental requirements and the product system* (181 pp.). Environmental Protection Agency, National Pollution Prevention Center, University of Michigan.

Kerssens-van Drongelen, I. C. (2001). The iterative theory-building process: Rationale, principles and evaluation. *Management Decision, 39*(7), 503–512.

Kerssens-van Drongelen, I. C., & Bilderbeek, J. (1999). R&D performance measurement: More than choosing a set of metrics. *R&D Management, 29*(1), 35–46.

Kerssens-van Drongelen, K., & Cook, A. (1997). Design principles for the development of measurement systems for research and development processes. *R&D Management, 27*(4), 345–357.

Kessler, E. H., Bierly, P. E., & Gopalakrishnan, S. (2000). Internal vs. external learning in new product development: Effects on speed, costs and competitive advantage. *R&D Management, 30*(3), 213–223.

Kim, B., & Oh, H. (2002). An effective R&D performance measurement system: Survey of Korean R&D researchers. *Omega: The International Journal of Management Science, 30*, 19–31.

Kim, C. W., & Mauborgne, R. (1998). Oikeudenmukainen prosessi: Johtaminen tietotaloudessa. *Yritystalous*, 28–39.

Kortge, G. D., & Okonkwo, P. A. (1992). Linking marketing strategy to new-product development. *Journal of Education for Business, 68*(1), 21–26.

Krogh, L. C., Prager, J. H., Sorensen, D. P., & Tomlinson, J. D. (1988). How 3M evaluates its R&D programs. *Research Technology Management* (November–December), 10–14.

Krumwiede, K. R. (1998). ABC: Why it's tried and how it succeeds. *Management Accounting (IMA-USA)* (April), 32–38.

Kumaran, D. S., Ong, S. K., Tan, R. B. H., N. A. Y. C., (2001). Environmental life cycle cost analysis of products. *Environmental Management and Health, 12*(3), 260–276.

Kurawarwala, A. A., & Matsuo, H. (1998). Product growth models for medium-term forecasting of short life cycle products. *Technological Forecasting and Social Change, 57*, 169–196.

Laakso, T. (1997). *Performance evaluation and process interventions: A method for business process development*. Espoo, Finnish Academy of Technology.

Lahikainen, T., & Paranko, J. (2001). *Easy method for assigning activities to products – an application of ABC*. 5th International Seminar on Manufacturing Accounting Research, Pisa, Italy, EIASM.

Laitinen, E. K. (1996). *Framework for small business performance measurement*. Vaasa, Vaasan yliopisto.

Laitinen, E. K. (1998). *Yritystoiminnan uudet mittarit*. Helsinki, Kauppakaari.

Larson, E. W., & Gobeli, D. H. (1988). Organizing for product development projects. *Journal of Product Innovation Management* (5), 180–190.

Lawrence, J. E., & Cerf, D. (1995). Management and reporting of environmental liabilities. *Management Accounting, 1995*(August), 48–54.

Leastadius, S., & Karlson, L. (2001). Eco-efficient products and services through LCA in R&D/design. *Environmental Management and Health, 12*(2), 181–190.

Ledwith, A. (2000). Management of new product development in small electronics firms. *Journal of European Industrial Training, 24*, 137–148.

Lehtonen, T. J. (2002). Organisaation osaamisen strateginen hallinta. *Kasvatustieteiden tiedekunta*. Tampere, Tampereen yliopisto.

Lele, M. M. (1986). How service needs influence product strategy. *Sloan Management Review* (Fall), 63–70.

Lele, M. M. (1997). After-sales service – necessary evil or strategic opportunity? *Managing Service Quality, 7*(3), 141–145.

Leonard-Barton, D. (1990). A dual methodology for case studies. In: G. P. Huber & A. H. Van de Ven (Eds), *Longitudinal Field Research Methods. Studying Processes of Organizational Change* (p. 373). Thousand Oaks: Sage.

Lewis, M. A. (2001). Success, failure and organisational competence: A case study of the new product development process. *Journal of Engineering Technology Management, 18*, 185–206.

Lichtenberg, F. R. (1990). Issues in measuring industrial R&D. *Research Policy, 19*, 157–163.

Liebermann, Y., & Ungar, M. (2002). Efficiency of customer intertemporal choice under life cycle cost conditions. *Journal of Economic Psychology, 23*, 729–748.

Lingle, J. H., & Schiemann, W. A. (1994). Is data scatter subverting your strategy? *Management Review, 1994*, 53–58.

Lukka, K., & Granlund, M. (2002). The fragmented communication structure within the accounting academia: The case of activity-based costing research genres. *Accounting, Organizations and Society, 27*(1–2), 165–190.

Lukka, K., & Kasanen, E. (1995). The problem of generalizability: Anecdotes and evidence in accounting research. *Accounting, Auditing & Accountability Journal, 8*(5), 71–90.

Lyly-Yrjänäinen, J. (2003). *Applying a product portfolio in activity assignment* (p. 107). Tampere: Tampere University of Technology.

Lynch, R., & Cross, K. (1995). *Measure up! How to measure corporate performance*. USA: Blackwell.

Lynn, G. S., Abel, K. D., Valentine, W. S., & Wright, R. C. (1999). Key factors in increasing speed to market and improving new product success. *Industrial Marketing Management, 28*, 319–326.

Maccarrone, P. (1998). Activity-based management and the product development process. *European Journal of Innovation Management, 1*(3), 148–156.

Magnan, G. M., Fawcett, S. E., & Birou, L. M. (1999). Benchmarking manufacturing practice using the product life cycle. *Benchmarking: An International Journal, 6*(3), 239–253.

Maisel, L. S. (1992). Performance measurement: The balanced scorecard approach. *Journal of Cost Management, 6*(2), 6.

Malmi, T., Peltola, J., & Toivanen, J. (2002). *Balanced scorecard. Rakenna ja sovella tehokkaasti.* Helsinki, Kauppakaari.

Martino, J. P. (1995). *R&D project selection*. New York: Wiley.

Massey, G. R. (1999). Product evolution: A Darwinian or Lamarckian phenomenon. *Journal of Product and Brand Management, 8*(4), 301–318.

Matthews, W. H. (1991). Kissing technological frogs: Managing technology as a strategic resource. *European Management Journal, 9*(2), 145–148.

McGrath, M. M., & Romeri, M. N. (1994). The R&D effectiveness index: A metric for product development performance. *Journal of Product Innovation Management, 11*(3), 213–220.

McKinnon, J. (1988). Reliability and validity in field research: Some strategies and tactics. *Accounting, Auditing & Accountability Journal, 1*(1), 34–54.

McLeod, T. (1988). *The management of research, development and design in industry*. Aldershot: Gower Technical Press.

McMann, P., & Nanni, A. J. (1994). Is your company really measuring performance? *Management Accounting, 1994*(November), 55–58.

McNair, C. (2000). *Value quest: Driving profit and performance by integrating strategic management processes*. Bedford, CAM-I.

McNair, C. J. L., Richard, L., & Cross, K. F. (1990). Do financial and nonfinancial performance measures have to agree? *Management Accounting, 72*(5), 7.

McWilliams, B. (1996). The measure of success. *Across the Board, 1996*, 16–20.

Mecimore, C. D., & Bell, T. (1995). Are we ready for fourth-generation ABC? *Management Accounting, 76*(7), 22–26.

Meldrum, M. J. (1995). Marketing high-tech products: The emerging themes. *European Journal of Marketing, 29*(10), 45–58.

Mercer, D. (1993). A two-decade test of product life cycle theory. *British Journal of Management, 4*, 269–274.

Meyer, M. H., Tertzakian, P., & Utterback, J. M. (1997). Metrics for managing research and development in the context of the product family. *Management Science, 43*(1), 88–111.

Miller, W. L. (1995). A broader mission for R&D. *Research Technology Management, 38*(6), 24–36.

Montoya-Weiss, M. M., & Calantone, R. (1994). Determinants of new product performance: A review and meta-analysis. *Journal of Product Innovation Management, 11*, 397–417.

Moores, K., & Yuen, S. (2001). Management accounting systems and organizational configuration: A life-cycle perspective. *Accounting, Organizations and Society, 26*, 351–389.

Moorman, C. (1995). Organizational market information processes: Cultural antecedents and new product outcomes. *Journal of Marketing Research, 32*(3), 318–335.

Morbey, G. K. (1988). R&D: Its relationship to company performance. *Journal of Product Innovation Management, 5*, 191–200.

Morbey, G. K., & Reithner, R. M. (1990). How R&D affects sales growth, productivity and profitability. *Research Technology Management* (May–June), 11–14.

Nanni, J. A. J., & Dixon, R. J. (1992). Integrated performance measurement: Management accounting to support the new manufacturing .... *Journal of Management Accounting Research, 4*(Fall), 19.

Näsi, J. (1980). Ajatuksia käsiteanalyysistä ja sen käytöstä yrityksen taloustieteessä. Tampere, Tampereen yliopiston Yrityksen taloustieteen ja yksityisoikeuden laitos: 41.

Neely, A. (1999). The performance measurement revolution: Why now and what next? *International Journal of Operations & Production Management, 19*(2), 205–228.

Neely, A., Gregory, M., & Platts, K. (1995). Performance measurement system design: A literature review and research agenda. *International Journal of Operations & Production Management, 15*(4), 80–116.

Neilimo, K., & Uusi-Rauva, E. (1999). *Johdon laskentatoimi.* Helsinki, Edita.

Nelson, E. (1992). The product life cycle of engineered metals: A comparative analysis of the application of product life cycle theory. *The Journal of Business and Industrial Marketing, 7*(2).

Ness, J. A., & Cuzuzza, T. G. (1995). Tapping the full potential of ABC. *Harvard Business Review, 73*(4), 130–139.

Ness, J. A., Schroeck, M. J., Letendre, R. A., & Douglas, W. J. (2001). The role of ABM in measuring customer value. *Strategic Finance* (March), 32–37.

Nihtilä, J. (1996). Integration mechanism in new product development. *Department of Industrial Management* (p. 162). Hensinki: Helsinki University of Technology.

Niiniluoto, I. (1997). *Johdatus tieteenfilosofiaan. Käsitteen- ja teorianmuodostus.* Keuruu, Otava.

Nixon, B. (1998). Research and development performance measurement: A case study. *Management Accounting Research, 9*, 329–355.

Nonaka, I. (1994). A dynamic theory of organizational knowledge creation. *Organization Science, 5*(1), 14–37.

Oakley, P. (1996). High-tech NPD success through faster overseas launch. *European Journal of Marketing, 30*(8), 75–91.

O'Donnel, F. J., & Duffy, A. H. B. (2002). Modelling design development performance. *International Journal of Operations and Production Management, 22*(11), 1198–1221.

Ojanen, V., Kärkkäinen, H., Piippo, P., & Tuominen, M. (1998). *Supporting the selection of performance measures for R&D at company level.* Lappeenranta, Lappeenrannan teknillinen korkeakoulu.

Olkkonen, T. (1994). *Johdatus teollisuustalouden tutkimustyöhön* (2nd ed., No. 152, 143 pp.). Report, Helsinki University of Technology, Industrial Economics and Industrial Psychology. Espoo: Helsinki University of Technology.

Olve, N.-G., Roy, J., & Wetter, M. (1999). *Performance drivers: A practical guide to using the balanced scorecard.* Chichester: Wiley.

Ormala, E. (1986). *Analysing and supporting R&D project evaluation: An applied systems analytic approach* (p. 118). Espoo, Helsinki University of Technology.

Osawa, Y., & Murakami, M. (2002). Development and application of a new methodology of evaluating industrial R&D projects. *R&D Management, 32*(1), 79–85.

Otley, D. (1999). Performance management: A framework for management control systems research. *Management Accounting Research, 10*, 363–382.

Ottum, B. D., & Moore, W. L. (1997). The role of market information in new product success/failure. *Journal of Product Innovation Management, 14*, 258–273.

Palmer, E., & Parker, D. (2001). Understanding performance measurement systems using physical science uncertainty principles. *International Journal of Operations and Production Management, 21*(7), 981–999.

Patterson, W. C. (1983). Evaluating R&D performance at Alcoa Laboratories. *Research Technology Management* (March–April), 23–27.

PDMA (2002). PDMA handbook of new product development: Glossary of new product development terms, PDMA.

Pearson, A. W., Nixon, W. A., & Kerssens-van Drongelen, I. C. (2000). R&D as a business – what are the implications for performance measurement? *R&D Management, 30*(4), 355–366.

Perera, H. S. C., Nagarur, N., & Tabucanon, M. T. (1999). Component part standardization: A way to reduce the life-cycle costs of products. *International Journal of Production Economics, 60–61*, 109–116.

Pillai, A. S., Joshi, A., & Rao, K. S. (2002). Performance measurement of R&D projects in a multi-project, concurrent engineering environment. *International Journal of Project Management, 20*, 165–177.

Pinto, J. K., & Slevin, D. P. (1989). Critical success factors in R&D projects. *Research Technology Management* (January–February), 31–35.

Player, S., & Lacerda, R. (Eds) (1999). *Arthur Andersen's global lessons in activity-based management.* Wiley Cost Management Series: Wiley.

Poh, K. L., Ang, B. W., & Bai, F. (2001). A comparative analysis of R&D evaluation methods. *R&D Management, 31*(1), 63–75.

Polli, R., & Cook, V. (1969). Validity of the product life cycle. *The Journal of Business, 42*(4), 385–400.

Poolton, J., & Barclay, I. (1998). New product development from past research to future applications. *Industrial Marketing Management, 27*, 197–212.

Prahalad, C., & Hamel, G. (1990). The core competence of the corporation. *Harvard Business Review, 68*(May/June), 79–91.

Prasad, B. (1997). Re-engineering life-cycle management of products to achieve global success in the changing marketplace. *Industrial Management & Data Systems, 97*(3), 90–98.

Price, E. E., & Coy, D. R. (2001). Life cycle management at 3M. A practical approach. *Environmental Management and Health, 12*(3), 254–259.

Pringle, P. (2001). The life cycle process. *Manufacturing Engineer* (December), 284–287.

Provost, L., & Leddick, S. (1993). How to take multiple measures to get a complete picture of organizational performance. *National Productivity Review, 1993*(Autumn), 477–490.

Pryor, T. (1998). *Pryor convictions: 31 insights into ABM.* Arlington, ICMS.

Pullman, M., Moore, W., & Wardell, D. (2002). A comparison of quality function deployment and conjoint analysis in new product design. *The Journal of Product Innovation Management, 19*, 354–364.

Rabino, S. (2001). The accountant's contribution to product development teams – a case study. *Journal of Engineering and Technology Management, 18*, 73–90.

Raffish, N. (1991). How much does that product really cost? *Management Accounting* (March), 36–39.

Rangone, A. (1997). Linking organizational effectiveness, key success factors and performance measures: An analytical framework. *Management Accounting Research, 8*, 207–219.

Ransley, D. L., & Rogers, J. L. (1994). A consensus on best R&D practices. *Research Technology Management* (March/April), 19–26.

Repenning, N. P. (2001). Understanding fire fighting in new product development. *The Journal of Product Innovation Management, 18*, 285–300.

Rhyne, L. C. (1996). Product development in the late stages of a technology life cycle: Lessons from the America's Cup 1995. *Journal of Product and Brand Management, 5*(2), 55–67.

Richardson, P. R., & Gordon, J. R. M. (1980). Measuring total manufacturing performance. *Sloan Management Review* (Winter), 47–58.

Riistama, V., & Jyrkkiö, E. (1991). *Operatiivinen laskentatoimi: Perusteet ja hyväksikäyttö.* Espoo, Weilin + Göös.

Rink, D. R., Roden, D. M., & Fox, H. W. (1999). Financial management and planning with the product life cycle concept. *Business Horizons* (September–October), 65–72.

Rouhiainen, P. (1997). *Managing new product development project implementation in metal industry* (p. 293). Tampere: Tampere University of Technology.

Rummler, G. A., & Brache, A. P. (1995). *Improving performance. How to manage the white space on the organization chart.* San Francisco: Jossey-Bass.

Ryan, C., & Riggs, W. E. (1996). Redefining the product life cycle: The five-element product wave. *Business Horizons, 39*(5), 33–41.

Sandström, J., & Toivanen, J. (2002). The problem of managing product development engineers: Can the balanced scorecard be an answer? *International Journal of Production Economics, 78*(1), 79–90.

Santos, S. P., Belton, V., & Howick, S. (2002). Adding value to performance measurement by using system dynamics and multicriteria analysis. *International Journal of Operations and Production Management, 22*(11), 1246–1272.

Schneiderman, A. M. (1996a). Metrics for the order fulfillment process (Part I). In: B. J. Brinker (Ed.), *Emerging Practices in Cost Management. Performance Measurement.* Boston, WG&L/RIA Group. 1997, K3-1–K3-13.

Schneiderman, A. M. (1996b). Metrics for the order fulfillment process (Part II). In: B. J. Brinker (Ed.), *Emerging Practices in Cost Management. Performance Measurement.* Boston, WG&L/RIA Group. 1997: K4-1–K4-12.

Schroeder, R., Scudder, L. G. D., & Elm, E. (1989). Innovation in manufacturing. *Journal of Operations Management, 8*(1), 1–15.

Schumann, P. A., Ransley, D. L., & Prestwood, D. C. (1995). Measuring R&D performance. *Research Technology Management, 38*(3), 45–55.

Sharman, P. (1995). How to implement performance measurement in your organization. *CMA*, 33–37.

Shenhar, A. J., Tishler, A., Dvir, D., Lipovetsky, S., & Lechter, T. (2002). Refining the search for project success factors: A multivariate, typological approach. *R&D Management, 32*(2), 111–126.

Sherman, J. D., & Olsen, E. A. (1996). Stages in the project life cycle in R&D organizations and the differing relationships between organizational climate and performance. *The Journal of High Technology Management Research, 7*(1), 79–90.

Sievänen, M., Suomala, P., & Paranko, J. (2001). *Activity-based costing and product profitability.* 5th International Seminar on Manufacturing Accounting Research, Pisa, Italy.

Slater, S. F., & Narver, J. C. (1993). Product-market strategy and performance: An analysis of the Miles and Snow strategy types. *European Journal of Marketing, 27*(10), 33–51.

Slater, S. F., Olson, E. M., & Venkateshwar, K. R. (1997). Strategy-based performance measurement. *Business Horizons* (July–August), 37–43.

Slevin, D. P., & Pinto, J. K. (1986). The project implementation profile: New tool for project managers. *Project Management Journal* (September), 57–71.

Smith, A. E., & Mason, A. K. (1997). Cost estimation predictive modeling: Regression vs. neural network. *The Engineering Economist, 42*(2), 137–161.

Song, X. M., & Montoya-Weiss, M. M. (1998). Critical development activities for really new vs. incremental products. *Journal of Product Innovation Management, 15*, 124–135.

Song, X. M., Montoya-Weiss, M. M., & Schmidt, J. B. (1997). Antecedents and consequences of cross-functional cooperation: A comparison of R&D, manufacturing, and marketing perspectives. *Journal of Product Innovation Management, 14*, 35–47.

Souder, W. E., & Jenssen, S. A. (1999). Management practices influencing new product success and failure in the United States and Scandinavia: A cross-cultural comparative study. *Journal of Product Innovation Management, 16*, 183–203.

Stadler, M. (1991). R&D dynamics in the product life cycle. *Journal of Evolutionary Economics* (1), 293–305.

Stake, R. E. (1995). *The art of case study research.* London, Sage.

Stivers, B. P., Covin, T. J., Green, H., & Smalt, S. W. (1998). How nonfinancial performance measures are used. *Management Accounting* (February), 44–49.

Suomala, P., & Kulmala, H. I. (2001). *Performance measurement in supply networks.* 24th EAA Annual Congress, Athens, Greece.

Suomala, P., Sievänen, M., & Paranko, J. (2002a). Customization of capital goods – implications for after sales. In: C. Rautenstrauch, R. Seelmann-Eggebert & K. Turowski (Eds), *Moving into Mass Customization – Information Systems and Management Principles* (pp. 231–248). Springer.

Suomala, P., Sievänen, M., & Paranko, J. (2002b). The effects of customization on spare part business: A case study in the metal industry. *International Journal of Production Economics, 79*(1), 57–66.

Szakonyi, R. (1994a). Measuring R&D effectiveness – I. *Research Technology Management* (March–April), 27–32.

Szakonyi, R. (1994b). Measuring R&D effectiveness – II. *Research Technology Management* (May–June), 44–55.

Tanaka, T. (1993). Target costing at Toyota. *Journal of Cost Management, 7*(1), 4–11.

Terwiesch, C., Loch, C., & Niederkofler, M. (1998). When product development performance makes a difference: A statistical analysis in the electronics industry. *Journal of Product Innovation Management, 15*, 3–15.

Thomson, K. (1995). The benefits of measuring customer satisfaction. *CMA*, 32–36.

Tipping, J. W., Zeffren, E., & Fusfeld, A. R. (1995). Assessing the value of your technology. *Research Technology Management, 38*(5).

Treacy, M., & Wiersema, F. (1993). Customer intimacy and other value disciplines. *Harvard Business Review* (January–February), 84–93.

Treacy, M., & Wiersema, F. (1995). *The discipline of market leaders: Choose your customers, narrow your focus, dominate your market.* Reading: Perseus Books.

Turney, P. B. B., & Stratton, A. J. (1992). Using ABC to support continuous improvement. *Management Accounting, 74*(3), 46–50.

Ulrich, K. T., & Eppinger, S. D. (1995). *Product design and development.* New York, NY: McGraw-Hill.

Upchurch, A. (2002). *Cost accounting – Principles and practice.* Prentice-Hall.

Uusi-Rauva, E. (1986). *Yrityksen ohjauksen tunnuslukujärjestelmä.* Helsinki, Tuottavuuskeskus ry.

Uusi-Rauva, E. (1996). *Ohjauksen tunnusluvut ja suoritusten mittaus*. Tampere: Tampereen teknillinen korkeakoulu.

Uusi-Rauva, E., & Paranko, J. (1998). *Kustannuslaskenta ja tuotekehityksen tarpeet*. Tampere: TTKK/Teollisuustalous.

Vaivio, J. (1999). Exploring a 'non-financial' accounting change. *Management Accounting Research*, *10*, 409–437.

van den Ende, J. (2003). Modes of governance of new service development for mobile networks. A life cycle perspective. *Research Policy*, 1–18.

Vartiainen, M., Rantamäki, T., Hakonen, M., & Simola, A. (1999). *Tuotekehityksen palkitseminen*. Helsinki, Metalliteollisuuden kustannus.

Wahlström, K. (1998). Suomessa kehitetty balanced scorecard – mittaristo. *Yritystalous* (1), 53–57.

Weisenfeld, U., Reeves, J. C., & Hunck-Meiswinkel, A. (2001). Technology management and collaboration profile: Virtual companies and industrial platforms in the high-tech biotechnology industries. *R&D Management*, *31*(1), 91–100.

Werker, C. (2003). Innovation, market performance, and competition: Lessons from a product life cycle model. *Technovation*, *23*(4), 281–290.

Werner, B. M., & Souder, W. E. (1997a). Measuring R&D performance – state of the art. *Research Technology Management*, *40*(2), 34–42.

Werner, B. M., & Souder, W. E. (1997b). Measuring R&D performance – U.S. and German practices. *Research Technology Management*, *40*(3), 28–32.

Westkämper, E., Niemann, J., & Dauensteiner, A. (2001). Economic and ecological aspects in product life cycle evaluation. *Proc Instn Mech Engineers*, *215*, 673–681.

Whittaker, B. (1999). What went wrong? Unsuccessful information technology projects. *Information Management & Computer Security*, *7*(1), 23–29.

Wisner, J. D., & Fawcett, S. E. (1991). Linking firm strategy to operating decisions through performance measurement. *Production and Inventory Management Journal* (3/4), 5–11.

Woodward, D. G. (1997). Life cycle costing-theory, information acquisition and application. *International Journal of Project Management*, *15*(6), 335–344.

Wyland, D. W. (1998). Keep your product in play: Introducing full life-cycle management. *Chain Store Age* (September), 186.

Yin, R. K. (1994). *Case study research: Design and methods*. Newbury Park, CA: Sage.

Zeller, T. L., Kublank, D. R., & Makris, P. G. (2001). Uses ABC to succeed. *Strategic Finance* (March), 25–31.

Zif, J., & McCarthy, D. J. (1997). The R&D cycle: The influence of product and process R&D on short-term ROI. *IEEE Transactions on Engineering Management*, *44*(2), 114–122.

Zirger, B. J., & Maidique, M. A. (1990). A model of new product development: An empirical test. *Management Science*, *36*(7), 867–883.

BARRIERS TO STRATEGIC INNOVATION IN INDUSTRIAL MARKETS

Koen Vandenbempt and Paul Matthyssens

ABSTRACT

This report examines strategic innovation efforts of companies in an industry displaying traits of maturity. Strategic innovation efforts intend to create superior customer value and competitive advantage. Realizing the full benefits of these efforts necessitates that companies change their view on existing relationships in the supply chain of the industry under consideration. Based on case study research in nine installation companies in the Dutch electro technical industry, we conclude that a mismatch between intended strategies and the dominant logic of these companies (and their business partners) impedes strategic innovation efforts. We thus identify barriers to strategic innovation. This report suggests strategy options that have the potential to overcome these barriers and relate these options to managerial mindsets and cognitions with respect to competitive strategy, organization and network relationships.

1. INTRODUCTION

Existing literature on competitive strategy stresses the importance of strategic innovation as a crucial means to create competitive advantage (Baden-Fuller & Pitt, 1996; Baden-Fuller & Stopford, 1994; Govindarajan & Trimble, 2004; Johnston

Managing Product Innovation
Advances in Business Marketing and Purchasing, Volume 13, 701–723
© 2005 Published by Elsevier Ltd.
ISSN: 1069-0964/doi:10.1016/S1069-0964(04)13005-6

& Douglas Bate, 2003) and superior customer value (Gale, 1994; Payne & Holt, 2001) and/or to beat the commodity magnet (Rangan & Bowman, 1995; Sawhney et al., 2004). Strategic innovation refers to a situation in which companies achieve a high level of success when attacking an established industry leader (Markides, 1997, 1998), and thereby create a competitive advantage. The essence of strategic innovation is the creation of new superior customer value. This can be done with or without new technologies or recombinations of existing technology. In order to study the essence of strategic innovation, we opt for a research context where innovation based on new technology breakthrough is practically non-existent (see also section "the research context").

The literature on strategy and business-to-business marketing discusses the fact that strategies of firms are "embedded" in the surrounding network (Dyer & Singh, 1998; Madhavan, Koka & Prescott, 1998; Nohria & Eccles, 1992; Ritter, 1999). In order to understand the nature and the dynamics of competitive advantage, a network perspective is needed (Madhavan et al., 1998). The structure of an industry network plays an important role in the value creation process (Kothandaram & Wilson, 2001) and, therefore, networks have a significant impact on both firm performance and industry evolution. A business network as a collection of external relationships provides access to key resources, such as information, raw materials, technology and markets. Ford et al. (2003) and Gemünden, Ritter and Walter (1997) among others describe companies as interdependent units engaged in different relationships, which are characterized by activity links, resources ties, and actor bonds. Managers are thus stimulated to expand their views on products and markets by adopting a network perspective. According to this literature, each company is embedded in complex webs of relationships (both direct and indirect). Such networks have their own dynamics. As emphasized by Ford (1997), the "state of the network and the direction of its evolution is the result of the actions and motivations of many different companies, some acting alone and some together" (p. 14).

Although the interaction/network approach is already an important research perspective (see for instance, Möller & Halinen, 1999), additional research needs to be undertaken. Turnbull, Ford and Cunningham (1996) argue that "our continuing work is to try to understand *the patterns of meanings and the beliefs* which guide managers in their interactions with others in the increasingly complex networks in which they operate" (p. 59; emphasis added). Although theoretical contributions state that no firm can afford to be a self-contained island anymore and that learning through relationships is crucial in the competitive battle for customers (Ford, Gadde, Hakansson & Snehota, 2003; Möller & Halinen, 1999), the question remains how companies can actually implement the suggestions advanced in the literature.

By combining the strategy and the business-to-business literature, we postulate that strategic innovation, and thus the continuous creation of competitive advantage, requires that companies must change their views on the relationships with other parties in the supply chain and the management of these relationships. Consequently, this report examines how strategic innovation efforts are contingent upon the managerial cognition of the ties within a given industry. Consequently, studying barriers that prevent managers from changing their views on network relationships is paramount. As an example of the importance of barriers to strategic innovation in a business-to-business setting, the concept of the e-wall (Kalakota, Oliva & Donath, 1999). Incumbents face this e-wall while adapting their business models to the new realities of the electronic marketplace. The barriers consist of legacy systems, contracts, incentives, physical property, corporate cultures, diverse organizational barriers, relationships with current business partners and established patterns of thinking.

Within the strategy literature, the concept of "barriers" has received considerable attention. However, the focus was more on the mere identifications of factors inhibiting new entrants ("barriers to entry") or companies of another strategic group ("mobility barriers," "resource positioning barriers") to attack the market position of incumbents in an industry (see for instance Barney, 1996 for an overview). We want to further elaborate the concept of barriers by: (1) discussing how identified barriers relate to managerial cognition and (2) focusing on the process aspects of the formation of barriers.

To do this, we proceed along the following outline. In the next section, we further develop our problem statement and derive research questions. Next, the industry under study is described. Third, we elaborate on the applied research methodology. Fourth, the results of our empirical study are presented. Finally, managerial conclusions are drawn and an agenda for further research is proposed.

2. PROBLEM STATEMENT AND RESEARCH QUESTIONS

In this empirically grounded research, we start by studying strategic innovation efforts. By focusing on a key level (the electro technical installation companies, see further) of the supply chain of the Dutch electro technical industry, we offer insights in barriers that prevent companies from creating superior customer value and competitive advantage. As discussed in detail below, the research process consists of different phases. We first describe how companies are positioned in the market place and how they are embedded in the industry network. Next, we evaluate their strategic innovation efforts and relate this to managerial cognition.

This leads to the identification of barriers to strategic innovation. The report then suggests ways by which companies can overcome these barriers.

Given the above, consider the following research questions:

(1) Which barriers withhold managers from adapting their competitive strategy and improving their overall market position?
(2) Which strategies overcome these barriers and what is the impact of these strategies on the management of relationships?
(3) How can a network perspective enable managers to overcome barriers to strategic innovation?

By addressing these research questions, this paper aims at: (1) further bridging the gap between the strategy literature and the business-to-business marketing literature; (2) applying and further elaborating a methodology which allows a multilevel theory to be built by integrating the micro domain's focus on individuals and groups with the macro domain's focus on organizations, environment, and strategy (Klein, Tosi, & Cannella, 1999); and (3) giving insight into the "mechanics" of strategic innovation.

3. THE RESEARCH CONTEXT

The research context of this study is the Dutch Electro Technical industry. This industry consists of a chain of companies that are linked to each other by logistical flows of physical products and immaterial flows of support services and information. Participants include producers of electro technical products (such as, Philips, ABB, GE, Alcatel), wholesalers (such as, Hagemeyer Holland, Technische Unie), installation companies (such as Stork Technical Services, Fabricom/GTI, Croon Elektrotechniek, Imtech) and end users (industrial applications, government, institutional markets, construction industry). The market is highly competitive with many contenders at all levels of the chain (see Fig. 1).

We focus on the level of the electro technical installation companies. In the Netherlands, about 3,000 installation companies offer employment to more than 60,000 people. Installers use a wide array of electro technical installation materials and components (more than 80,000 articles) ranging from high tech and complex products to low tech commodities. The service installers offer, however, is very standardized and is relatively "low-tech" oriented.

The sector is highly fragmented with a great variety of the companies, ranging from very small family owned shops (76% of the companies has less than 10 employees) to very professional "cluster" companies combining and integrating many smaller companies. Empirical evidence shows that companies have a hard

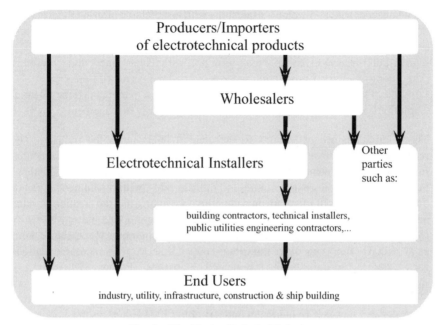

Fig. 1. The Electro Technical Industry.

time differentiating their product offerings from one another. In fact, they tend to offer more a capacity to solve electro technical problems than a clearly defined product or service offering.

This industry displays traits of *maturity* for more than a decade. This is mirrored by fierce price competition, low service/product-differentiation and a common approach to the market. Moreover, incumbent installation companies are facing increasing competition from firms in adjacent industries, such as pure industrial automation companies and ICT-software firms. These characteristics and tendencies have provoked growing unrest in the market. Installation companies are searching for ways to achieve above average profit (the average profit margin after tax is about 2.5%). Diverse and scattered initiatives have been undertaken to stimulate cooperation by different parties within the electro technical industry. Some selected examples are illustrative:

- a number of installation companies are building a common platform for electronic ordering and product information connecting three levels of the supply chain: producers of the materials and components, wholesalers, and installers;

- a wholesaler tries to develop partnerships with installers by offering them loyalty plans (with consumer-like bonus schemes when buying specific components and materials), extra services, etc.;
- an installer tries to establish a long-term link with its customers and a producer in order to monitor a production process over a long period of time.
- Installers try to offer integral service concepts such as "park management" (total solutions for office management on one site) or energy management.

These initiatives are exceptions to the general behavior in the industry. The recommendations advanced in the literature discussed above are not implemented in this industry. We want to further investigate the reasons why the behavior of these installation companies is not in line, and often at odds, with recommendations of the different strands of literature on competitive advantage and the creation of value adding bonds. We already mentioned recent developments in the strategy literature (for instance, Markides, 1997) and business marketing literature (for instance, Ford et al., 2003). But even older contributions, such as Porter's recommendations for strategies to cope with fragmented industries (Porter, 1980) are not implemented.

Recent literature shows many suggestions on how to create strategic innovation or strategic renewal. Govindarajan and Trimble (2004) pinpoint the importance of fast learning. Sawhney, Balasubramanian and Krishnan (2004) suggest using a tool – the service opportunity matrix – in a world of commoditized products in order to turn companies' product offerings into service offerings. Prahalad and Ramaswamy (2003, 2004) suggest to personalize experiences (rather than standard products) co-created with customers and other network partners. Kampas (2003) shows that a combination of "business innovation genes" consisting of commodity-marketing, lean production and aggressive deal-making, must replace "product innovation genes" when technology ages. This study tries to uncover the reasons why in reality (and especially in this industry) the above recommendations seem so hard to realize.

4. METHOD

This report focuses on the study of barriers to strategic innovation efforts and how companies can overcome these barriers. A qualitative research methodology, case study research, was chosen as a useful logic of discovery. This choice was based on the following considerations. First, the purpose of the research is to explore the complex concept of strategic innovation in its natural setting. Referring to our concise literature review and the overview of the industry under study, the typical way of researching is difficult to execute (existing theories, formulation of hypotheses, data collection and analysis, testing of hypotheses). We need to better understand the specific nature of different concepts and constructs (such as barriers to strategic innovation). Some authors state explicitly that under these circumstances, the problem statement is still in a context of discovery (Hunt, 1991) and that case study research is appropriate (Yin, 1994). Secondly, our research project is based on the epistemological premises that organizations and their environments are socially constructed and thus that managers enact their environments (Starbuck, 1982; Weick, 1979). We thus need a methodology that enables us to study managerial cognitions and changes in these cognitions (Hodgkinson, 1997). Hence, our research design must provide information on processes of preferences formation and changes in cognition (Vaughan, 1998). Again, this refers to the fact that concepts/constructs are embedded in their natural context and should be studied as such. The need and the usefulness of interpretative research methodologies is discussed at length in the recent literature, see for instance, the special issue on interpretative research methodologies in the *Journal of Business & Industrial Marketing*, 2003 18 (6/7).

The research design, data collection, and analysis process are structured following the recommendations of Eisenhardt (1989) and Yin (1994) in order to secure methodological rigor (specification of research issues, sampling, measurement of constructs, multiple data sources and triangulation). Especially, addressing theory development in the field of dyads within business networks, Anderson, Håkansson, and Johanson (1994) have referred to qualitative field research such as field-depth interviews and case studies as playing an essential part in refining the construct definitions and elaborating the content domains of each construct. They argue for detailed case studies. The use of case study research provides us with contextualized data and descriptions of a complex reality, which is needed to understand existing theoretical concepts in context.

4.1. Research Design

Studying different aspects of barriers to strategic innovation requires a research design that focuses on *process data*. The reasons are at least twofold. First, we must reveal how the companies under study actually behave in the industry. Merely reporting *intended strategies* is not enough; we must also reveal the *dominant logic* of those companies (see for instance, Prahalad & Bettis, 1986; Spender, 1989). Second, studying both intended strategy and dominant logic implies that we have access to multiple respondents. Both concepts have an important collective dimension (Hodgkinson, 1997).

Given the above considerations, the applied research design displays the following characteristics. First, the overall methodological design is based on the comparative multiple case study research as advanced by Eisenhardt (1989) and Yin (1994). In total nine case studies (electro technical installation companies) were included in the research project. These companies were selected using theoretical sampling (Yin, 1994). Second, since we are interested in extracting the actual perceptions of managers with respect to strategic innovation efforts, unobtrusive measures (Webb & Weick, 1979) were important means of organizational inquiry. For example, we use the competitive strategy to reveal how each company was making sense of events and tendencies within the industry. Third, our data collection and analysis processes are highly iterative in nature. Theory building is the result of inductive as well as deductive analysis. In this way, the mid-range theory is not developed from scratch (as in grounded theory) but from combining data with existing theories. Orton (1997) refers to this methodological position as *iterative-grounded theory*. Dubois and Gadde (2002) refer to this process as "systematic combining" and applied this methodology in a study of outsourcing networks. Worthwhile is also to note that we used qualitative (in-depth interviews) as well as quantitative data (questionnaires filled out by the members of the management team per case study) as data sources. In summary, our multiple-case study method aimed at constructing cognitive maps of how organizations make sense of what is happening. In this way, we actually got access to the dominant logic of these companies and we used these maps to identify barriers to strategic innovation and their impact on business networks.

4.2. Data Collection and Data Analysis

Table 1 includes nine ET-installers contributing to our empirical database. In all nine cases, we used the same data collection protocol. Eventually, we crafted detailed case stories from eight of the original nine selected companies. The empirical data obtained from 1 company (case Iota) were not "restructured" in a case story, since data triangulation was not possible. For each case study, the primary data sources were (1) semi structured in-depth interviews; (2) questionnaires and (3) discussions of intermediate results (Table 1). Other data sources, such as field observation and secondary information (expert reports, company financial data, industry studies,...) were only used for triangulation purposes.

Given our problem statement and our epistemological premises (social construction of reality), semi structured in-depth interviews were the main data sources. The advantage of this type of data collection is that the researcher

Table 1. Description of the Cases and Data Sources.

Company	Size (No. of People Employed)	Number of Regional Offices (Affiliates)	Number of in-Depth Interviews	Number of Questionnaires	Discussions of Intermediate Results
Alpha	> 600	Many and national coverage	4	11	3
Beta	> 600	Many and national coverage	5	9	2
Gamma	> 600	Many and national coverage	5	18	3
Delta	> 100, < 600	One	5	12	3
Epsilon	> 100, < 600	One	4	5	2
Zeta	> 100, < 600	One	5	4	2
Eta	< 100	One	4	3	2
Theta	< 100	One	5	4	2
Iota	< 100	One	3 (only with the CEO)	1	–

has direct access to facts, perceptions, judgments, ideas and the language of the participants (Coopey et al., 1998; Silverman, 1993). In order to construct a comparable empirical database for all cases, several interview rounds were held. The interview system was as follows: the next interview round in one company only started when the previous interview round was finished in all participating companies. Such a protocol permits additional topics to be added to the interview guides, thus improving internal validity and construct validity. The respondents for the first two interview rounds were the CEO's of the participating companies. The next interview rounds were held with members of the management team, project managers, and office managers. All interviews were taped and transcribed. Interviews lasted between 1 and 3 hours. To minimize interview biases, consecutive interviews with the same respondents started with a discussion of the main conclusion drawn form the previous interview. Triangulation was further realized by studying press releases, published interviews, sector studies, annual reports and so on. As multiple respondents were needed in order to detect the dominant logic of the companies involved, questionnaires were filled out by the members of the management team. Combining the data contained in the interviews with the results of the questionnaires, we could construct cognitive maps per each case study. Besides written materials, three wholesalers and two producers were interviewed to gain further insight concerning relevant network players.

The iterative nature of our research couples data collection to data analysis and vice versa. This means that numerous iterations were made between data gathering and extant theories in order to come to insights with respect to the barriers to strategic innovation. In other words, the result of the analysis from the first round of data collection was the input for the second round of data collection. Our insights in the barriers to strategic innovation grew gradually. The main trust of this process was the description and subsequent analysis of: (1) intended strategies of each of the case studies and (2) the dominant logic of each of the case studies. In most cases, intended strategies could be revealed using existing company information. The majority of companies have formulated a corporate vision and mission statements in which intended competitive strategies are described. For other cases, the semi-structured interviews and the questionnaires were used. For the analysis of the dominant logic, a more complex discovery process was necessary. As said before the dominant logic of a company can be studied by looking at the actual competitive behavior in the market and the customer value creation approach taken. In order to reveal the dominant logic for each case study, we analyzed and coded the collected empirical database (see section data collection) using a model of competitive advantage. The model of competitive advantage used (Matthyssens & Vandenbempt, 1998) reflects the insights of extant competitive strategy literature (e.g. Foss, 1996) that brings together both outside-in views of strategy (e.g. Porter, 1980) and inside-out views of strategy (e.g. Wernerfelt, 1984). This model makes a distinction between the value proposition (strategic intent) and the value drivers (for instance, assets, processes and systems, and culture, human resources and organization).

The next step was the confrontation of the intended strategy of each case study with its dominant logic. This led to the identification of barriers to strategic innovation efforts, and ways to overcome these barriers.

5. FINDINGS

We report our findings in the following way. First, we discuss strategic innovation efforts and derive barriers that withhold companies from realizing the intended strategic innovation. Secondly, we advance a strategy typology based on the creation of different types of superior customer value for this industry. This strategy typology is positioned as a tool to overcome the identified barriers. Next, we relate this typology to the management of relationships within the supply chain. Finally, we discuss how a network perspective can help managers to overcome the identified barriers to strategic innovation.

Table 2.   Consistency Issues: Strategic Intent vs. Rationality.

Company	Intended Strategies Main Focus on . . .	Rationality of the Company
Alpha	Integral service provider	No deviation from the dominant industry recipe (DIR)
Beta	Integral service provider	No deviation from the DIR
Gamma	Integral service provider	No deviation from the DIR
Delta	Focus on specific markets	Small deviation from the DIR
Epsilon	Integral service provider	No deviation from the DIR
Zeta	Focus on specific markets	No deviation from the DIR
Eta	Focus on special markets/projects	No deviation from the DIR
Theta	Integral service provider	No deviation from the DIR

5.1. Strategic Innovation Efforts and Related Barriers

Most companies in the electro technical installation industry are initiating efforts to improve their market positioning. Lack of consistency between the strategic innovation efforts (the intended strategies) and the prevailing dominant logic of the company (the rationality of the company) is the main problem noticed (using the constructed empirical case study data). This consistency problem becomes apparent by confronting the intended strategies of the eight companies with their actual competitive behavior in the market (the value creation approach).

Table 2 summarizes the findings. With respect to the intended strategies, we discovered two main focuses. The first group of companies (Alpha, Beta, Gamma, Epsilon, Theta) has the clear intention of becoming an integral service provider; the second group of companies (Delta, Zeta, Eta) focuses more on developing a niche strategy in specialized markets/projects. What is important is that both intended strategies (integral service provider and niche strategy) are considered in the industry as the way to successful differentiation from the competition. With respect to the rationality of the company, we even discover fewer differences between the case companies. In most cases, the actual behavior of the company is on the efficient execution of pre-defined installation work (we have above referred to this behavior as "low-tech installation capacity"). Building further on these findings and using the work of Spender (1989), we can conclude that this industry not only displays traits of maturity and commodization but is also characterized by a dominant industry recipe, focused on efficient project management of physical installation work. Table 2 indicates whether or not the rationality of each company is deviant from this dominant industry recipe (DIR).

We see that all eight cases reveal almost the *same* intended strategies and dominant logic. Differences were visible, but the lack of consistency was in all cases present (except for Delta). As such, very few differences in the actual competitive behavior of electro technical installation companies are revealed. Table 3 elaborates on the observed lack of consistency by discussing the generalized interpretations of both the strategic intent and the dominant logic. Based on this, we derive barriers that prevent these companies to change their actual market behaviors.

Table 3 shows that the case companies understand that "something has to change" and even have an idea of the "right" approach (see strategic intent). "Right" should be interpreted as an approach that creates customer value. However, the dominant logic of these case studies is not in line with the strategic intent, which causes inconsistency in efforts to change their market strategies. We identify the main reasons for this inconsistency as *barriers to strategic innovation* (see, Table 3). A following observation is that these barriers have a cognitive as well as structural dimension. The cognitive dimension refers to the ingrained mental models of managers (see also Kim & Mauborgne, 1999) and to an outdated

Table 3. Generalized Findings on Strategic Intent, Dominant Logic and Barriers.

Construct	Findings
Strategic Intent (intended strategic innovation efforts)	Installers intend to offer an integral/total solution to the customer or to become specialists in niche markets. Offering "customer value" in the form of a knowledge-based problem solution and a proactive market approach are frequently mentioned intentions. They define more clearly either the specialized fields or sub markets where they want to realize the above. They also refer to the intent to be involved from project conception to the actual realization of the project. Extended cooperation with other companies is seen as an adequate way to upgrade ones own expertise and potential to deliver customer value.
Dominant Logic (actual value creating approaches)	The dominant logic of these companies consists of a reactive, project-based approach and a dominance of technical problem solving for all customer problems. Consequently, they are only paid to build/construct "what others have designed" (see above: efficient execution of pre-defined installation work). Also, the actual competitive behavior focuses too much on existing customers and lacks a conceptual way of thinking.
Identified Barriers	Overall, the following barriers are responsible for the identified gaps between strategic intent and the dominant logic: traditional working culture in the industry and companies (reactive, technical dominance, price-dominated marketing) and local rationality by the (many) regional offices and project managers.

perception of cause and effect relationships that hinders strategic innovation (see also Baden-Fuller & Stopford, 1994). The structural dimension implies that the cognitive barriers are embedded in the structure and the routines (see also Henderson & Clark, 1990), and the culture of the companies involved. In this way, these barriers become also "resource-positioning" or "mobility" barriers.

5.2. Strategic Innovation: Value Creating Strategies

Following the perceived lack of consistency in strategic innovation efforts, we put forward the following question: how can companies overcome the identified barriers? As a first step to answering this question, consider different types of customer value. A functional strategy typology is advanced based on the constructed empirical database, discussions between the authors, and consultations with knowledgeable experts. This typology identifies the strategy options and their implications on the organization of electro technical installation companies. Comparing the strategic intent (see Table 2) of the companies with the de-commodization strategies proposed by Mathur (1984), Rangan (1995) and to the well-know generic value creation strategies of Porter (1980), we come up with three generic strategy options for installation companies. As will be discussed further, the strategy options are internally consistent: they are focused on delivering one type of customer value proposition. Table 4 displays three strategy options and their main characteristics along three dimensions that were identified.

These three dimensions reflect the three fundamental choices installers face while re-defining their competitive strategic positioning.

- *Choice 1*: **The width of technical knowledge.**
  This refers to the number of technical areas the company masters. When the focus is small, the company is active in only one technical field such as safety installations, industrial automation or ICT networks. A broad width implies that a company wants to offer more than one area of technical expertise.
- *Choice 2*: **The degree of service providing.**
  With a limited degree of service providing, the installer only focuses on the actual execution of an installation project. With a high degree of service providing, the installer carries out activities ranging from design and conception (the definition of the technical installation project) to maintenance and upgrading of existing installation.
- *Choice 3*: **The external focus.**
  A customer base can be approached on a one by one project basis. Optimization is sought with one project/customer. The other possibility is that customers are approached using concepts. In that case, product solutions are based on the

Table 4. Strategy Options and Strategy Dimensions.

Strategy Options	Strategy Dimensions		
	Width of Technical Knowledge	Degree of Service Providing	External Focus of the Installer
Capacity installer	Broad (many expertises) or narrow (focused on one technical domain)	Limited: mostly the factual realization of technical installation projects ('execution')	• Reactive project based
The specialist	Very narrow but in-depth knowledge	Very high: from the conception of technical installation projects to the maintenance activities	Can be: • Project-based • Segment-based (even the development of concepts)
Integral service provider (ISP)	Very broad	Very high: from the conception of technical installation projects to the maintenance activities	Can be: • Project-based • Segment-based (even the development of concepts for niche markets)

similar needs of the identified segments, within safety systems for financial institutions, assistance/surveillance systems for care and medical institutions. The former approach is reactive, the latter proactive.

As Table 4 indicates, the combination of the three dimensions leads to three types of strategy options. These options are "internally consistent" displaying a fit between the customer value proposition (strategic intent) and the value drivers (dominant logic or actual customer value creating approaches).

- Type 1: The Capacity Installer (CI)
  This installation company focuses in a clear and straightforward way on the execution of installation projects. The work is rather limited in the degree of service providing. Important value drivers for this strategic position to be viable and successful are strict cost containment and competitive pricing, excellent cost calculation and management, fast and flexible execution of projects, a "cost leadership" culture, project management and planning skills, a fair level of technicality on some (narrow CI) or many (broad CI) skill fields. Case companies Gamma, Epsilon & Theta are close to this type and should adapt their strategic intent and rationality accordingly.
- Type 2: The Specialist
  A specialist tries to offer superior value in a narrow, often complex field. The specialist offers a complete solution to the customer from (co-)design to execution and often follow-up activities (e.g. installation of a data and telematics network). The specialist needs the following value drivers: in-depth knowledge of the specialization field, consultative "selling approach," full sensing of the customer activity cycle, integration of solution in customer operations, product innovation and upgrading, and expert systems. Case companies Delta, Zeta & Eta are close to this type.
- Type 3: The Integral Service Provider (ISP)
  The ISP can take two forms depending on its external focus (project/reactive vs. concepts/proactive). In any case, ISPs will go for a *system integrator* role, offering the customer a complete, integrated and customized solution. They have defined and developed the solution, take responsibility for the realization (i.e. they will frequently outsource part of this "low level" work) and take care of the follow up. The following value drivers are key: multidisciplinary technical knowledge and skills, knowledge and sensing of customer needs, ability to realize from genesis to nemesis complex projects, knowledge and project database and expert systems, optimal communication among personnel, efficient realization (or skills to outsource in an efficient way), top project management, market sensing and customer linking and advanced learning. Case companies Alpha & Beta are close to this type and should especially further

adapt the rationality of their respective companies in order to reflect the strategic intent.

5.3. Impact on the Management of Relationships

The perceived lack of consistency in strategic innovation efforts by companies within the industry under study also has effects on the management of their relationships. We already noticed that adaptations of the network structure are rather embryonic and haphazard with diverse initiatives and mixed results. A more focused relationship management must occur for the strategic innovation efforts to succeed. Using the strategy typology, we can now further define how companies can overcome the identified barriers (see Table 3) and thus improve their market positioning. To do this, we formulate, in Table 5, the alleged implications of the three strategy options for the management of relationships. We distinguish between vertical and horizontal relationships.

As Table 5 indicates, by coupling strategy options to the management of relationships, the "typically" haphazard view on relationships within the electro technical industry can be overcome. Each strategic option has a consistent view on managing relationships within the supply chain. Consequently, based on this, managers have a more clear idea how they can adapt their relationship structure in order to facilitate strategic innovation.

5.4. A Network Perspective as a Driver to Overcome Barriers

From discussing the strategy options and the implication on the management of relationships within the industry under study, this industry offers an interesting setting for observing partnering and networking. However, a caveat should be formulated here. So far, the low profit margins that were described above have stifled most innovation initiatives.

Building strategic partnerships and developing long term strategy development are consequently not the rule in the industry. Lack of consistency, mirrored by antagonistic dyadic buying attitudes and short-term opportunism has prevailed so far. Managers of the installation companies are thus confronted with the following paradox. On the one hand, some managers feel that strategic innovation can only be realized when tough strategic choices (in terms of activities pursued) are made and partnerships are established. On the other hand, the fear of choice and the reaction of others in the industry paralyze. This leads to postponement of choice, scattered initiatives, limited focus and commitment, and even less freedom of choice afterwards.

Table 5. Impact of the Strategy Options on the Management of Relationships.

Strategy Option	Type of Relations		
	Upward Vertical	Downward Vertical	Horizontal
Capacity organization	• antagonistic purchasing attitude for standard electro technical components • joint cost reduction programs with select suppliers (many specific, differentiated components)	• some traditional relationship management: "PR" and "networking style" (see also section "Research Context")	• occasional outsourcing of work in case of shortage of installing personnel • outsourcing relations for non-ET specific work to "fixed" partners
Specialist	• thorough relationship with a few suppliers • occasional input in new product development of suppliers possible • continuous one-way learning relation (e.g. use of suppliers training and demo facilities)	• some limited cooperation with customer during quick scan and order cycle • some maintenance and/or upgrading (i.e. life time relationship management)	• good long term relations with more general installers (CI, ISP) required as they might subcontract specialist tasks
Integral service provider	• co-development with innovative suppliers • intense relationship with suppliers of smart and complex subsystems (two way learning) • relation with wholesaler for one stop shopping of standard components	• intense, long term and open relationship with customers (in house suppliers) • joint improvement projects and trust-building services	• long term relations with some smaller capacity installers to whom regular low level tasks are outsourced/subcontracted • building of intense partnerships with specialized companies and engineering offices

A network perspective on the electro technical supply chain can help managers to overcome the identified barriers. To do so, we advance a "remodeled" supply chain of this industry into a hybrid task structure. The above implies for electro technical installation companies four role models with diverse tasks and network positions.

- Quadrant I
  Given the central position of the electro technical installation company in the network (and the close contact with end-users), the focus is on becoming an integral service provider and developing partnerships with suppliers and buyers accordingly (see Table 4).

- Quadrant II
  Advisors and engineering companies act as project managers and pre-specify solutions to customers. As such, installers are confronted with pre-set specifications leading to price competition. Traditional partnerships should be developed to new relationships with these "intelligent intermediaries." Electro technical installers should focus on becoming a capacity installer or a specialist (see Table 4).

- Quadrant III
  New types of "customers" originate in the industry such as (a) big building contractors and infrastructure companies offering "complete" projects, (b) the installation and maintenance divisions of public utilities which often are forced to offer their services inside as well as outside of their company in a more competitive mode and (c) even technical installation companies with capacity shortages while "managing" big projects. For the ET-installer the three groups (a)–(c) are new types of customers, which are knowledgeable and critical, thereby emphasizing competitive pricing. Group (c) implies the extra challenge of dealing with the same company as a competitor in quadrant I and as a customer in quadrant III. An installer in this position should consider becoming a capacity installer or a specialist.

- Quadrant IV
  Mainly for specialties (e.g. security networks, lighting for offices, telecom networks) and for high tech components, producers might consult, design, and install at the end users' premises. The installer might get some lower-level "outsourced" tasks from these suppliers. Just like group (c) in quadrant III, this situation might lead to tension. For instance, the same company in its role of supplier might be approached in an aggressive mode by the purchasing department in the traditional chain (quadrant I) while at the same time must be dealt with as a customer in quadrant IV. Often, only an innovation towards a capacity installer will pay off (Fig. 2).

Using the network perspective, companies can begin their strategic innovation efforts by determining their actual position in the supply chain: what is the main task

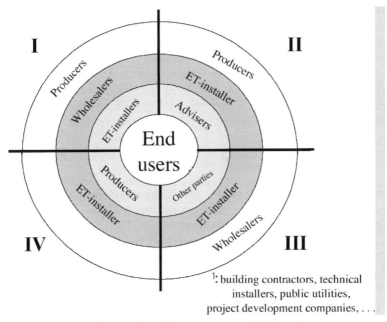

I

II

Producers

Producers

Wholesalers

ET-installer

ET-installers

Advisers

End
users

Producers

Other parties

ET-installer

ET-installer

Wholesalers

IV

III

[1]: building contractors, technical
installers, public utilities,
project development companies, . . .

Fig. 2. The Hybrid Task Structure of ET-Installers.

they have to carry out in the market? What kind of value do they deliver? Answering these questions is the first step in determining the future strategic direction. Redesigning structures and routines by changing ingrained mental models can thus be induced by adopting this network perspective. In this way barriers (Table 3) are overcome and strategic innovation efforts will be more successful.

The conclusion that strategy innovation requires a re-conceptualization of existing relationships is in line with Ford's contention that strategy formulation in business markets often implies a re-definition of working relations with existing partners rather than the initiation of new ones. This is also in line with Prahalad and Ramaswamy's (2003, 2004) idea of co-creation and with the learning perspective from Crossan and Berdrow (2003) and Govindarajan and Trimble (2004).

6. RECOMMENDATIONS FOR MANAGERS AND AREAS FOR FUTURE RESEARCH

In an industry characterized by commodization and intense rivalry such as the Dutch electro technical installation industry, cost and price remain key parameters limiting strategic degrees of freedom and thought. Consequently, companies tend to converge around unquestioned managerial mindsets (Baden-Fuller & Stopford, 1994). Strategic innovation, although widely recognized as being necessary and even urgent, is blocked by ingrained mental models that are embedded in the structure and the routines of companies. Changing partnerships and relationships are confrontational and opportunistic at best. Traditional vertical relations in the supply chain are short term and adversarial (price pressure, tactical multiple sourcing, parallel and non-transparent channels, etc). Most of the time, horizontal partnerships are developed in a haphazard and opportunistic way.

6.1. Recommendations

Analyzing data from nine case studies identifies barriers that prevent companies from successfully implementing strategic innovation efforts. We constructed a strategy typology aimed at delivering customer value. This typology and its strategy options relate to the management of the network ties in the supply chain under study. From this discussion, as illustrated in Table 5, different strategy options imply different types of relations. Partnerships play at least four different roles in the process of successfully implementing strategic innovation efforts:

(1) *To strengthen the necessary value drivers of each value strategy.* For instance, a specialist performs better if backed by few top high tech suppliers that are willing to invest in permanently updating the skill base of the specialist, provide continuously improved electro technical products etc. Another example is that of innovative ordering, logistics, and cost monitoring systems for a capacity installer to be provided by vertical partners and systems suppliers. For an integral service provider (ISP) on the other hand, co-operation with consultants and providers of expert and knowledge systems is of uttermost interest.

(2) *To overcome cognitive barriers to strategic innovation.* For instance, an ISP needs to combine and master so many techniques and technologies that close partnerships with customers and experts are needed. It is widely accepted in the industry that no company can excel in all technical expertise areas.

(3) *To use as a change agent.* Partnership on a single project may be used as a case example. The message to the industry and the local personnel is that cooperation can yield better results than the dominant antagonistic logic.

(4) *To occasionally or regularly compensate for shortcomings in the capacity of the installation company* while safeguarding the quality. As such, a capacity installer might chose for a limited set of certified subcontractors to temporarily assign execution tasks to, rather than via a competing bidding approach each time the problem arises.

6.2. Avenues for Further Research

This study uses a qualitative methodology. As such, we stress mainly internal and construct validity, thereby downplaying external generalizations. However, this approach enables a deep understanding of managerial preferences and cognitions regarding strategic innovation efforts. In this way, our research is in line the methodological position that concepts are always embedded in context and that they can only be studied as such (Pettigrew, 1992; Vaughan, 1998). Within such a perspective, the changing role of relationships and networks in strategic innovation processes need further research attention. This entails studying the relation among managerial cognition and perception on the one hand and organizational changes, competitive strategy (and customer value), supply chain relationships on the other hand. More longitudinal and case based research efforts are necessary in order to fully grasp the complexity of the phenomenon. Future research must further stress multilevel theory building. Klein et al. (1999) argues that multilevel theory building, linking for instance changes in managerial cognition on a micro level to conditions for optimal learning in networks on a macro level of inquiry, is needed in order to advance understanding in theory and practice. The issues raised and discussed in this paper serve as an invitation.

REFERENCES

Anderson, J. C., Håkansson, & Johanson, J. (1994). Dyadic business relationships within a business network context. *Journal of Marketing, 58*, 1–15.

Baden-Fuller, C., & Pitt, M. (1996). *Strategic innovation*. London: Routledge.

Baden-Fuller, C., & Stopford, J. M. (1994). *Rejuvenating the mature business*. Boston, MA: Harvard Business School Press.

Barney, J. (1996). *Gaining and sustaining competitive advantage*. Reading, MA: Addison-Wesley.

Coopey, J., Keegan, O., & Emler, N. (1998). Managers' innovation and the structuration of innovation. *Journal of Management Studies, 35*(3), 263–284.

Crossan, M. M., & Berdrow, I. (2003). Organizational learning and strategic renewal. *Strategic Management Journal, 24*(11), 1087–1105.

Dubois, A., & Gadde, L.-E. (2002). Systematic combining: An abductive approach to case research. *Journal of Business Research, 55*, 553–560.

Dyer, J., & Singh, H. (1998). The relational view: Cooperative strategy and sources of interorganizational competitive advantage. *Academy of Management Review, 23*(4), 660–679.

Eisenhardt, K. M. (1989). Building theories from case study research. *Academy of Management Review, 14*(4), 532–550.

Ford, D. (1997). *Understanding business markets*. London: Dryden.

Ford, D., Gadde, L.-E., Hakansson, H., & Snehota, I. (2003). *Managing business relationships*. Chichester: Wiley.

Foss, N. J. (1996). Research in strategy, economics and Michael Porter. *Journal of Management Studies*, *33*(1), 1–24.

Gale, B. T. (1994). *Managing customer value. Creating quality & service that customers can see*. New York, NY: Free Press.

Gemünden, H. G., Ritter, T., & Walter, A. (Eds) (1997). *Relationships and networks in international markets*. Oxford: Pergamon.

Govindarajan, V., & Trimble, C. (2004). Strategic innovation, and the science of learning. *Sloan Management Review*, *45*(Winter), 67–75.

Henderson, R. M., & Clark, K. (1990). Architectural innovation: The reconfiguration of existing product technologies and the failure of established firms. *Administrative Science Quarterly*, *35*, 9–30.

Hodgkinson, G. P. (1997). The cognitive analysis of competitive structures. A review and critique. *Human Relations*, *50*(6), 525–551.

Hunt, S. D. (1991). *Modern marketing theory. Critical issues in the philosophy of marketing science*. Cincinnati: South-Western Publishing.

Johnston, R. E., & Douglas Bate, J. (2003). *The power of strategy innovation*. New York: AMACOM.

Kalakota, R., Oliva, R. A., & Donath, B. (1999). Move over, e-commerce. *Marketing Management* (Fall), 23–32.

Kampas, P. J. (2003). Shifting cultural gears in technology-driven industries. *Sloan Management Review*, *44*(1), 41–48.

Kim, W. C., & Mauborgne, R. (1999). Creating new market space. *Harvard Business Review* (January–February), 83–93.

Klein, K. J., Tosi, H., & Cannella, A. A. (1999). Multilevel theory building. Benefits, barriers and new developments. *Academy of Management Review*, *24*, 243–248.

Kothandaram, P., & Wilson, D. T. (2001). The future of competition. *Industrial Marketing Management*, *30*(4), 379–389.

Madhavan, R., Koka, B. R., & Prescott, K. E. (1998). Networks in transition: How industry events (re)shape interfirm relationships. *Strategic Management Journal*, *19*, 439–459.

Markides, C. (1997). Strategic innovation. *Sloan Management Review* (Spring), 9–23.

Markides, C. (1998). Strategic innovation in established companies. *Sloan Management Review* (Spring) 31–42.

Mathur, S. S. (1984). Competitive industrial marketing strategies. *Long Range Planning*, *17*(4), 102–109.

Matthyssens, P., & Vandenbempt, K. (1998). Creating competitive advantages for industrial services. *Journal of Business and Industrial Marketing*, *13*(4/5), 339–355.

Möller, K., & Halinen, A. (1999). Business relationships and networks: Managerial challenges of network era. *Industrial Marketing Management*, *28*, 413–427.

Nohria, N., & Eccles, R. (1992). *Networks and organizations: Structure, form and action*. Boston, MA: Harvard Business School Press.

Orton, J. D. (1997). From inductive to iterative grounded theory: Zipping the gap between process theory and process data. *Scandinavian Journal of Management*, *13*(4), 419–438.

Payne, A., & Holt, S. (2001). Diagnosing customer value: Integrating the value process and relationship marketing. *British Journal of Management*, *12*(2), 159–182.

Pettigrew, A. (1992). The character and the significance of process research. *Strategic Management Journal*, *13*(Special Issue Winter), 5–16.

Porter, M. E. (1980). *Competitive strategy. Techniques of analyzing industries and competitors*. New York, NY: Free Press.

Prahalad, C. K., & Bettis, R. A. (1986). The dominant logic: A new linkage between diversity and performance. *Strategic Management Journal, 7,* 485–501.

Prahalad, C. K., & Ramaswamy, V. (2003). The new frontier of experience innovation. *Sloan Management Review, 44*(4), 12–18.

Prahalad, C. K., & Ramaswamy, V. (2004). *The future of competition.* Boston: Harvard Business School Press.

Rangan, K., & Bowman, G. T. (1995). Beating the commodity magnet. In: K. Rangan, B. P. Shapiro & R. T. Moriarty (Eds), *Business Marketing Strategy. Concepts and Applications* (pp. 137–151). Irwin, Chicago.

Ritter, T. (1999). The networking company. Antecedents for coping with relationships and networks effectively. *Industrial Marketing Management, 28,* 467–479.

Sawhney, M., Balasubramanian, S., & Krishnan, V. V. (2004). Creating growth with services. *Sloan Management Review, 45*(Winter), 34–43.

Silverman, D. (1993). *Interpreting qualitative data: Methods for analysing talk, text and interaction.* London: Sage.

Spender, J.-C. (1989). *Industry recipes. The nature and sources of managerial judgement.* Oxford: Basil Blackwell.

Starbuck, W. H. (1982). Congealing oil: Inventing ideologies to justify ideologies out. *Journal of Management Studies, 19*(1), 3–27.

Turnbull, P., Ford, D., & Cunningham, M. (1996). Interaction, relationship and networks in business markets: An evolving perspective. *Journal of Business and Industrial Marketing, 11*(3/4), 44–52.

Vaughan, D. (1998). Rational choice, situated action, and the social control of organizations. *Law & Society Review, 32*(1), 23–61.

Webb, E., & Weick, K. E. (1979). Unobstrusive measures in organizational theory: A reminder. *Administrative Science Quarterly, 24,* 650–659.

Weick, K. E. (1979). *The social psychology of organizing* (2nd ed.). New York, NY: McGraw-Hill.

Wernerfelt, B. (1984). A resource-based view of the firm. *Strategic Management Journal, 5,* 171–180.

Yin, R. K. (1994). *Case study research: Design and methods.* Thousand Oaks: Sage.

UPSTREAM AND DIRECT INFLUENCES ON NEW PRODUCT PERFORMANCE IN EUROPEAN HIGH-TECH INDUSTRIAL FIRMS

Arch G. Woodside, Günter Specht, Hans Mühlbacher and Clas Wahlbin

ABSTRACT

This paper examines three issues. First, do multiple possible paths to high versus low new product performance (NPP) occur among European, high-tech, industrial manufacturing firms? Second, what are the upstream influences on high NPP? For example, what background factors affect the levels of the KSFs? Third, do consistent country-level differences occur among Austrian, German, and Swedish executives in their evaluations of antecedents and high-tech NPP? To probe these issues, a total of 771 chief operating officers and project managers participated in face-to-face long interviews (McCracken, 1988) covering 241 less and 264 more successful than average industrial NPD projects. The empirical findings support the propositions that: (1) multiple paths lead to high versus low NPP; (2) unique antecedent variables affect the KSFs for high NPP; and (3) for several upstream and direct influences, consistent national differences occur among executives' assessments of NPP. A key implication of the study for NPD executives is to recognize the possibility of alternative paths leading to successful NPD.

Managing Product Innovation
Advances in Business Marketing and Purchasing, Volume 13, 725–780
Copyright © 2005 by Elsevier Ltd.
All rights of reproduction in any form reserved
ISSN: 1069-0964/doi:10.1016/S1069-0964(04)13006-8

1. INTRODUCTION

Theoretically and empirically this paper examines three issues. First, do multiple possible paths to high versus low new product performance (NPP) occur among European, high-tech, industrial manufacturing firms? While several NPP researchers identify key success factors (KSFs) for high performance (e.g. Cooper, 1998; Hart, 1993; Montoya-Weiss & Calantone, 1994; Panne, van Beers & Kleinknecht, 2003), their reviews and empirical studies demonstrate that certain independent variables labeled KSFs associate positively with high versus low NPP – high NPP occurs for a number of launches in the absence of one or more KSFs. However, each of the identified KSFs is neither necessary nor sufficient for high NPP; a number of cases occur in the empirical studies that these studies report showing the high NPP occurs in the absence of one or more specific KSFs.

Recognizing that certain path combinations of environmental conditions, strategic actions, and risk factors lead to high versus low NPP likely represents taking a useful step beyond thinking in terms of identifying KSFs. Certain paths or combinations of environmental conditions – management actions – risk factors likely lead to high NPP and other paths or combinations likely lead to low NPP. From an empirical positivist perspective, proposing moderating and interaction effects among independent variables influencing NPP reflects such causal path thinking (e.g. see Song & Parry, 1997). From a case study interpretive perspective, specific sequences of actions-events leading to NPD success versus failure reflects such causal path thinking (e.g. see Christensen, 2001; Dougherty, 1992; Tellis & Golder, 2000). Such case study research of action-event sequences is the primary focus of the comparative method (see Ragin, 1987).

From an empirical positivist perspective, this paper asks and empirical probes the question: what alternative paths take us to NPD success versus failure? The theoretical and empirical work here supports and goes beyond the previous path analysis report by Song and Parry (1997) – unlike Song and Parry the present report examines environmental conditions as precursors, rather than as moderators to new product "positional advantage" (see Song & Parry, 1997); the study here examines the possibility of multiple direct and indirect paths from environmental variables to NPP. Song and Parry (1997) report findings from mail surveys of 788 Japanese and 612 U.S. project managers; the study here reports findings from personal, face-to-face interviews ($n = 768$) for 502 more and less successful NPD projects in high-tech industrial firms in three European countries: Austria ($n = 167$ projects), Germany ($n = 246$ projects), and Sweden ($n = 91$ projects).

Second, what are the upstream influences on high NPP? For example, what background factors affect the levels of the KSFs? While prior work (Cooper, 1998) finds substantial positive relationships among KSFs, far less empirical work is available on the antecedents to the KSFs.

Third, do consistent country-level differences occur among Austrian, German, and Swedish executives in their evaluations of antecedents and high-tech NPP? Even though all three nations are well established members of the EU and have advanced high-tech industrial manufacturing sectors, subtleties in the "thought worlds" (Dougherty, 1992) likely occur when executives in these three nations describe the decision process, actions, and environments for highly successful and less successful new product launches. The empirical findings from face-to-face surveys of 768 executives support the propositions that: (1) multiple paths lead to high versus low NPP; (2) unique antecedent variables affect the KSFs for high NPP; and (3) for a few variables only, consistent national differences occur among executives' assessments of NPP.

There are many types of new products. Their novelty can be defined on at least two dimensions (Cooper, 1995):

(1) New to the company, in the sense that the firm has never made or sold this type of product before, but other firms might have.
(2) New to the market; the product is the first of its kind on the market.

Development of new products is crucial for a company to maintain a competitive advantage (Cooper, 1995; Cooper & Kleinschmidt, 1995b; Zinkhan & Pereira, 1994). Cooper emphasizes the importance of innovations and their proportion on corporate profits:

> New products have a similar impact on corporate profits. In the period 1976–1981 new products contributed 22% of corporate profits. This had grown to 33% for the next five-year period (1981–1986). By 1995, it was estimated, the figure would rise to 46%. That is, profits from new products accounted for almost half of corporate profits (Cooper, 1995, p. 462).

Cooper's (1998) later analysis of the "cornerstones of [new product] performance" emphasizes Von Braun's (1997) view that rapidly changing technologies, heightened competition, and dynamic customer needs and wants are rendering existing products obsolete at an ever increasing pace: product life cycles are becoming shorter. Cooper (1998, p. 1) emphasizes, "The message to senior management is simple: *either innovate or die!*" Using historical analysis of the performance impacts of new products launched using new technology platforms competing against established products using currently dominating technologies, Tellis and Golder (2000) and Christensen (1997) confirm Cooper's innovate or die prophecy.

Tellis and Golder (2002) provide circumstantial evidence of Ansoff's (1984, p. 329) wisdom, "Success breeds failure . . . the historical success model becomes the major obstacle to the firm's adaptation to the new reality." Following several years, often decades, of high performance from manufacturing and marketing products based on a currently dominating technology, inertia builds up and leads to failure to embrace new technology product platforms and subsequent death of the strategic business unit (SBU), and possibly the entire enterprise (see Christensen, 1997 for detailed examples).

These advances in NPD theory and empirical findings are the rationales for the continuing study of the antecedents to new product performance (NPP). While most of the focus on the NPD performance literature is on identifying key success factors (KSFs) and environmental factors (for reviews, see Montoya-Weiss & Calantone, 1994; van der Panne, van Beers & Kleinknecht, 2003), this paper offers a system dynamics perspective on NPP. A systems view offers the advantages of: (1) proposing multiple routes to high and low NPP; (2) recognizing that no one factor is necessary or sufficient for achieving high performance and thereby allows for high NPP in the absence of a KSF; (3) advocating a contingency versus a deterministic approach to modeling high and low NPP.

2. A SYSTEM DYNAMICS MODEL OF NEW PRODUCT PERFORMANCE AND SUCCESS

Figure 1 summarizes a system dynamic view of NPP. All variables except one, (A) external environment, are endogenous in this model – each variable has both antecedents and consequences. The arrow from box H (success) to box B (strategy/activities) illustrates success having a negative influence on innovation strategy and activities (hypothesis 6 among a set of hypotheses discussed below), that is, success reduces innovativeness due to inertia (see Christensen, 1997; Tellis & Golder, 2000).

Note that H6 is a negative, balancing, relationship (see Sterman, 2000). Because increases or growth can not be the only outcome for performance and relationships of all cycles in a system, all system dynamic models need to reflect at least one negative endogenous relationship. Also, H6 reflects Ansoff's (1987) prediction and empirical findings from historical analysis.

H6 is the one hypothesis that is not examined further in the present report. This paper proposes H6, a feedback loop, for theoretical completeness. The focus here is on theoretically and empirically examining the one-directional relationships from box A, external environment, to box H, success. Because this study does not include data on the dynamics of NPD (e.g. over five or ten years) and relies on survey data, the model excludes feedback loops that are likely to occur among variables between several boxes in Fig. 1.

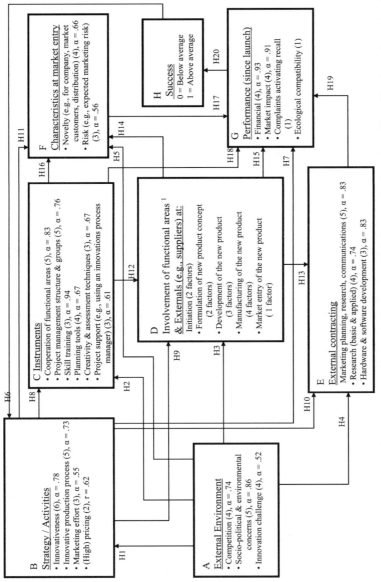

Fig. 1. Theoretical Framework for Upstream and Direct Influences on New Product Performance. *Note*: Number of question items shown in parentheses; α = coefficient alpha. Figure 1 excludes variables with low reliabilities (α < 0.50). [1] Involvement of functional areas and externals varied by stage in NPD (number of factors identified by stage).

2.1. External Environment

As Fig. 1 shows, increases in external environment activity serves to increase upstream factors that eventually affect NPP levels. A firm's executives are likely to become aware of higher versus lower levels of environment activities. Such heightened awareness leads to increases in a firm's innovativeness and marketing effort (H1) and stimulates greater use of instruments used for innovative behavior (H2). Heightened external environment activity is likely to increase discussion and involvement about NPD across functional areas (H3), as well as the possibility of using external contracting (H4).

Several NPD literature reviews (e.g. Montoya-Weiss & Calantone, 1994; Soni, Lilien & Wind, 1993; van der Panne et al., 2003) identify substantial direct external environment effects on: (1) innovativeness; (2) NPP; and (3) a substantial moderating influence of external factors on the effects of "positional advantage of product differentiation" (i.e. higher quality, more innovative product resulting from NPD compared to competitors) on NPP. Song and Parry (1997) report this third (moderating) influence of external factors on executives' beliefs about the quality of the new product versus competitors' products. Soni et al. (1993) report that low industry concentration and a high degree of rivalry influence innovativeness positively.

Note that Fig. 1 includes only three external environment factors in box A: level of competition; socio-political environmental concerns, and innovative challenge. However, empirically the study examines seven factors. The survey items used to measure the three factors in Fig. 1 all met reliability criteria and the factor-weighted sum-scored for these three constructs were used in empirically estimating the model. The data for the other four factors were not included in the estimating the model.

2.2. Strategy/Activities

The model includes the hypotheses that increases in innovative strategy and activities increases the instruments (i.e. tools) relating to innovative behavior (H8); involvement of several functional areas at several stages in the NPD process (H9); external contracting (H10); the level of novelty and risk taken at market entry (H11); as well as having a direct effect on NPP (H7). Figure 1 shows five factors in box B for strategy/activities.

The literature provides extensive support for the basic proposition that increases in NPD strategic planning and activities affects the quality of the implemented NPD process (Song & Parry, 1997) as well as directly influencing NPP (e.g. Cooper,

1998). Zinkhan and Pereira (1994) provide a historical overview of marketing strategy. They especially emphasize the crucial role of marketing strategy for successful new product development.

Many studies focus on how the strategy planning can make a difference. Hart and Banbury (1994) offer a review of prior research. They point out that, with a few exceptions, research on the linkage between strategy-making processes and firm performance adopts an econometric perspective. They strongly support the theory that firms committing to substantial strategy planning show high levels of performance. Firms that combine high levels of competence in multiple modes of strategy appear to be the best performers. After the strategy making process, the strategy has to be implemented. Nath and Sudharshan (1994) emphasize the importance of the planned and implemented strategy coherence at different firm management levels. Such coherence is defined as the underlying fit or consistency between a firm's strategies formulated by the top management and implementation by the functional levels. Nath and Sudharshan (1994) group corporations by their strategic statement and looked for the similarities in their planned and implemented decision patterns. In their findings, this measure of coherence relates positively to performance.

2.3. Instruments

The NPP model shows that the increase in use of NPD tools requires greater versus less involvement of functional areas in the firm (H12); affects the configuration of the new product at market entry (H16); and has a direct effect on the level of NPP (H18). For example, Cooper (1998) confirms that increases in the quality of project teams (an instruments factor) have a positive impact on new product profitability.

2.4. Involvement of Functional Areas

(H14) Increases in involvement of functional areas (box D) affects risk and novelty in the NPD (box F). Bringing more functional areas into the NPD process increases the opportunity of changing new product design resulting in either increases or decreases in novelty and risk because of demands made and tradeoffs required to satisfy the multiple parties. Dougherty (1992) provides telling evidence of how the clashes of multiple functional "thought worlds" affects the outcomes of NPD processes.

(H15) Increasing involvement of functional areas serves to increase NPP. Diversity of multiple functional viewpoints results in debugging problems and consequently provides superior product performance that result in increases in NPP. This view is a translation of the old saw, "two heads are better than one" for achieving superior NPD solutions.

2.5. External Contracting, Box E in Fig. 1

(H19) Increasing use of external contracting increases NPP. Rationale: external contractors provide specialized expertise and provide efficiencies that otherwise are difficult to achieve. Also, the empirical literature provides evidence of a positive relationship between using external contractors and NPP (see Montoya-Weiss & Calantone, 1994).

2.6. Characteristics at Market Entry, Box F in Fig. 1

Novelty and risk are two characteristics examined at market entry. H17a predicts that increases in novelty affect NPP positively. The historical analyses by Tellis and Golder (2000) indicates that radically different new products are more profitable that imitative NPD.

H17b predicts that increases in risk affect NPP negatively. Risk includes expected marketing risk; technical complexity of the product; customers' problems in using the product.

2.7. New Product Performance, Box G in Fig. 1

H20 predicts that different factors of NPP relate to global measures of success in varying strengths. The NPD literature identifies more than one NPP construct (e.g. see Cooper, 1998; Hart, 1993; Song & Parry, 1997). Song and Parry (1997) examine separate models for predicting three different indicators of NPP: relative profitability, relative sales, and relative market share. Their survey includes four questions to measure relative profitability via an 11-point scale. For example, "How successful was this product from an overall profitability standpoint? (0 = A great financial failure . . . 10 = A great financial success, i.e. far exceeded our minimum acceptable profitability criteria." Their survey includes three items to measure relative sales and three items to measure relative market share. While their findings (Table 3 in Song & Parry, 1997, p. 10) do not indicate systematic differences in the predicted influences on NPP, testing for such possibilities provides nuance in understanding possible causes of NPP.

Figure 1 includes four NPP constructs: financial, market impact, quality (i.e. low number of customer problems), and ecological compatibility. What are the relative strengths of these different NPP measurements in affecting executives' global assessment of new product success? Few executives might be willing to agree explicitly that profitability alone drives their overall assessment of success. The present study provides explicit evidence of NPD project executives' implicit assessments of how measures of NPP relate to their global assessments of new product success.

The exclusive use of financial measures for measuring NPP is often criticized (e.g. Aaker, 1988; Hart, 1993). However, most of the non-financial measures likely associate positively with future financial success. Hart (1993) considers three separate factors of performance:

- Factor 1 comprises by "beating competition technologically," "beating the competition market" and "technological breakthrough."
- Factor 2 includes "reduced production costs/beating the competition on price," "meeting objectives" and "opening new markets."
- Factor 3 features high loadings of "beating the competition to market," "profit generation/return on investment" and "meeting objectives."

Cooper and Kleinschmidt (1987) offer a related yet unique, set of three dimensions of performance in their investigation. These dimensions include:

- Financial Performance: captures the overall financial success of the product. This dimension is comprised of relative profits and sales, meeting profit and sales objectives, profitability level, and payback period.
- Opportunity Window: portrays the degree to which the new product opened up new opportunities to the firm in terms of a new category of products and a new market area for the firm.
- Market Impact: describes the impact of the product in both domestic and foreign markets – domestic market share and foreign market share – and to a lesser extent, relative sales and meeting sales and profit objectives (Cooper & Kleinschmidt, 1987, p. 216).

The dichotomy between profit and market share is examined as one of the important interrelations within these dimensions of performance. Cooper and Kleinschmidt (1987, 1995a) sort them into separate dimensions and Hart (1993) reports that sales and profit are not significantly related. On the other hand, she (Hart, 1993, p. 34) writes, "Clearly, sales and profits cannot be assumed to be 'alternative indicators,' although judging by the nonchalance with which either appear to have been selected by past researchers, perhaps such an assumption has been at work."

3. NEW PRODUCT DEVELOPMENT PROCESS

During a new product development-project different functional areas of the company and externals are involved. Their involvement has an impact on the new product performance (Doyle et al., 1993; Hagedoorn & Schakenraad, 1994; Kalwani et al., 1995; Shaw, 1995). Specht (1995) explains the specific importance of the interfaces between functional areas. To cope with increased quality and flexibility requirements, the interfaces need nurturing.

Hagedorn and Schakenraad (1994) measure the effect of strategic partnering between firms for the development of new products. They find a strong tendency for the intensity of strategic partnering to increase with the size of the firm. However, strategic partnering can be used to attract, rather than to generate technological knowledge.

Booz-Allen and Hamilton (1982) categorize the new product development process into five stages: idea generation; business analysis; development; testing and validation; and commercialization. Booz-Allen and Hamilton (1982) analyze these phases and break down the expenditures for each of them.

3.1. Idea Generation

This stage reflects the generation of the idea of the new product. Ideas arrive from outside and inside the firm. Cooper (1995) distinguishes common external sources of ideas and internal sources of ideas. Idea generation can be proactive (e.g. as a result of activities such as brainstorming techniques) and reactive (ideas are sent in by employees or by customers). Ideas emerge as "technology push" (where a technical innovation opens up new possibilities) or "market pull" (where a customer need is identified and solutions are sought). Ideas identified as poor and expected to be not successful will be sorted out. In this stage, only 35% of all the money spent on idea generation goes to successful products (Booz-Allen & Hamilton, 1982).

3.2. Business Analysis

Cooper (1995) describes this second stage as "the critical homework phase." The second stage defines the new product and a detailed product specification is be set up. The target market and the marketing strategy should be also set up and an early financial analysis be completed.

To verify the perspectives of a new product, detailed market research and concept tests with customers should be accomplished, this includes a competitive analysis. This results in pricing estimations and affects the turnover and spending expectations.

All this seems to form a critical phase to separate winners from losers. If executed well, this "homework" can save money that would have been spend in the development of unsuccessful products (Cooper, 1995). Surprisingly, Booz-Allen and Hamilton (1982) find that only 6% of the money that firms spend on product innovations goes to this stage.

3.3. Development

In the development stage the product defined by stage two will be translated into reality. Therefore this phase tends to be dominated by technical work, executed by scientists, engineers, software writers or other technical professionals (Cooper, 1995). Market research continues in this phase. Early prototype products are tested and the customer's feedback should be taken into consideration in the development of the new product. The highest proportion of money is spent in this stage according to Booz-Allen and Hamilton (1982).

3.4. Testing and Validation

Stage four is where the product and its marketing are tested and validated. This has an effect on the design of the production process which should be tested during this phase to prove and debug the manufacturing methods and to confirm costs and throughputs.

In-house tests could be executed, which are typically technical and are undertaken in controlled settings (Cooper, 1995). Customer test, which test the ability of the product to last in the "real world" follow the technical examination. The testing and validation could proceed with a simulated test market. Potential customers could be exposed to the product. Their feedback is useful for future improvements.

3.5. Commercialization

The commercialization stage includes the startup of a full-scale production and the market launch. Involved in this process should be advertisement, promotion and all marketing related activities. This phase accounts by far for the most money in the new product development process. A total of 43% is spent for the commercialization; most of the projects do not reach this final stage, therefore only 26% of all company spending on innovation is given to this stage (Booz-Allen & Hamilton, 1982).

4. IMPACT OF PRODUCT QUALITY ON PERFORMANCE

Product superiority separates winners from losers more often than any other single factor (Cooper, 1995). Cooper and Kleinschmidt (1995b, p. 454) advocate: "The rule is simple: if you can't get advantage, then don't play!" Products that have real product advantages (high quality, high value for money, superior to competitive products in meeting customer needs) are considered to be successful (Cooper & Kleinschmidt, 1995a). Occasionally, the question occurs, whether it is more important to be first to the market, or to take more time and enter the market with a better product. Indeed it is more important for the company to know about the customers' needs and to provide a superior product rather than to be first to the market (Cooper & Kleinschmidt, 1995a).

Therefore in many industries, competition mainly rests on claims of technical superiority by one company over another (Friar, 1995). However, if a company applies product innovation to differentiate itself to the competitors, the customer should be able to recognize this. Friar (1995) tested the product performance dimension as to customer ability to perceive differences. His conclusion is that customers do not identify the product differentiation as manufacturers thought it was there.

Opposed to Britain and the U.S., the marketing strategy of German companies seeks a competitive advantage through product quality and reliability (Shaw, 1993). Doyle et al. (1993) report a difference in the managers' self-evaluation of the competitive advantage and positioning of German and U.S. companies:

> The U.S. companies believed their competitive advantage to be the superior quality and performance of their products. [...] Meanwhile the German manufacturers, who have a reputation for producing quality goods appeared to be more conservative in their estimation of their product quality but believed they could command a premium price for their better engineered products (Doyle et al., 1993, p. 387).

5. INVOLVEMENT OF THE TOP MANAGEMENT AND THE IMPACT ON PERFORMANCE

The support of top management is considered to be necessary to get the product to the market. Top management can cut through the organizational bureaucracy and speed up the process as a "behind the scene operator" (Cooper, 1995). This is especially important in large industrial companies. Lee and Na (1994) report a high positive relation between the support of top management to the new product team and technical performance. Furthermore, they found out that this support does not significant increase if the products innovativeness is radical. The restriction of their study is the limitation on technical performance only.

6. INVOLVEMENT OF CUSTOMERS AND SUPPLIERS AND THE IMPACT ON PERFORMANCE

Customer integration is found by Cooper and Kleinschmidt (1995a) to be another crucial ingredient of new product's success. Their findings recommend involving customers in every stage of the new product development process – beginning with idea generation. As Kalwani and Narayandas (1995, p. 3) explain, "... existing customers can be sources of new product ideas, test sites for new product development, and also serve as showcase accounts." They report that suppliers in long-term relationships with selected customers are able to achieve a higher level of performance over time opposed to firms that are not engaged in such relationships. Customer involvement is also crucial to explore the needs and the wants of the market, for example, to define the product quality.

The involvement of suppliers has become of pressing importance in the 21st Century. During the 1990s a lot of companies cut back the number of suppliers they use and demanded higher quality from those they kept. Xerox cut the number of suppliers by 90%, Motorola by 70% and Digital Equipment by 67% (Emshwiller, 1991). They concentrated on a few selected suppliers to achieve a stronger competitive position. Nevertheless, the involvement of suppliers in the new product development process is much less examined than the engagement of customers.

7. MARKET ORIENTATION AND ITS EFFECT ON PERFORMANCE

Market Orientation – the generation of appropriate market intelligence pertaining to current and future customer needs, and the relative abilities of competitive entities to satisfy these needs; the integration and dissemination of such intelligence across departments; and the coordinated design and execution of the organization's strategic response to market opportunities (Deng & Dart, 1994, p. 726).

Market orientation is considered to be one of the most important factors of success. Deng and Dart (1994) consider how to measure this factor. They offer a four-component market orientation construct for further research: Customer orientation, competitor orientation, interfunctional coordination and profit orientation.

Dougherty (1990) provides a model suggesting that three cycles of market knowledge creation operate simultaneously: departmental, interdepartmental, and organizational. Within each of these cycles market knowledge is defined and selected and finally established in the routine interactions of the organization. German companies are found to be more market orientated and have clearer marketing objectives, strategies and plans than their Anglo-American counterparts (Doyle et al., 1993). A strong market orientation is also necessary when the project is still a concept. During this phase, heavy reliance is usually placed on intention surveys to forecast sales (Armstrong, 1995).

In contrast, Zinkhan and Pereira (1994) found no evidence by reviewing the literature that "marketing orientation" always leads to the optimum new product development strategy.

8. TYPE OF NEW SOLUTION AND THE IMPACT ON PERFORMANCE

New products can be distinguished by their degree of novelty to the company, to the market or both (Cooper, 1995). Radical versus incremental innovation is another major characteristic of new products. Its effect on NPP was investigated in some studies (Banbury et al., 1995; Cooper & Kleinschmidt, 1995a; Lee et al., 1994; Soni et al., 1993).

Cooper and Kleinschmidt (1995a, p. 324) ask, "Should the firm opt for developing highly innovative products, the first of their kind, or should it be a follower, content to develop 'me too' products, essentially copies of competitive ones?" Their answer is clear: A more innovative strategy is the more successful. They conclude that product innovativeness is positively connected to five out of seven performance measures they used: success rates, profitability rating, market share, impact on the firm and technical success rating.

Soni et al. (1993) hypothesize that: (1) more innovative firms perform better in terms of sales growth and profitability than less innovative firms; and that (2) firms producing mainly radical innovations perform better than firms producing mainly imitative innovations. Due to insufficient data they were not able to test the second hypothesis, but the first was supported.

Banbury and Mitchell (1995) defend the idea that incremental product innovation is a critically competitive factor in established industries. They report that the market share is greater, the more times a firm is among the first to introduce important incremental innovations to the market.

9. EXTERNAL ENVIRONMENT

Examining the external environment at the beginning of the innovation project is one goal of this study. The categories demand, competition, suppliers, technology, and other environment represent the items focusing on external environment. Responses to all items were made using seven-point scales (very few to very much; very low to very strong or very high; not existing to very strong; very stable to very turbulent). Seven factors are singled out:

* competition,
* socio-political and environmental concerns,
* innovation challenge,
* demand predictability,
* suppliers' competition,
* employees, and
* behavior of market players.

Competition captures the rivalry in the market. This construct portrays the number of competitors, the intensity of competition, competition in the field of quality, and price competition. Coefficient alpha equals 0.74 for this factor for the four items.

Socio-Political and Environmental Concerns characterizes politics, effect of law, effect of the state and ecology. Additionally, ecological competition is part of this factor, although, the loading score only 0.53. Coefficient alpha equals 0.68 for this factor for the five items.

Innovation Challenge describes how fast the technological evolution was paced, what role innovation plays in terms of competition, how receivable customers are for new product releases, and how demand will develop in the future. This innovation challenge construct contains the variables: technology change ratio, innovation competition, openness for novelties, and development of demand. The latter two load 0.52 each. Cronbach coefficient α barely surpasses the arbitrary cutoff (coefficient $\alpha = 0.50$).

Demand Predictability portrays the possibility to forecast demand, the stability of demand's progress, and the number of prospective customers. Coefficient α does not exceed the arbitrary cutoff.

Suppliers' Competition explains the situation on the procurement side. The variables are number of suppliers and intensity of competition among suppliers. Both items load with more than 0.7 on this factor and are highly correlated ($r = 0.49$).

Employees and their social environment are another driving force in the firm's environment. The factor is characterized by the variables power of employees and social environment. These two items are significantly correlated ($r = 0.42$, $p < 0.01$).

Behavior of Market Players features the similarity (or difference) of actions within groups, buyers and competitors. The two variables are not correlated significantly ($r = 0.25$). This factor was not considered in further analysis.

10. ARE THESE FINDINGS RELEVANT?

Many studies tried to find the factors in the new product development which drive success. Most of them formulated some dos and don'ts for managers.

Do practitioners agree with these findings? Calantone et al. (1995) assess the extent to which product practitioners agree with fundamental principles of product development and management compiled from the academic literature. Their studies show a very high level of agreement with practically all principles, suggests that what academic researchers do is relevant and that their recommendations are not out of the "ivory tower."

11. FIELD METHOD

The empirical study was carried out in the context of the international research project "Effectiveness and Efficiency of Research and Development" ($E^2R\&D$). Academics in five countries – Austria, China, Germany, Hungary, and Sweden – agreed to participate.

- The original goals of the study centered on comparing NPD industrial behavior cross-nationally. However, since data for the study were collected for only three of the nations and because the effect sizes for national influences are small and infrequent, the findings focus mainly on the NPD industrial behavior and NPP for three nations combined.

11.1. Survey Instruments

Data were collected through face-to-face interviews using standardized questionnaires. The questionnaires, jointly developed within the research team, include mostly closed-end, seven-point questions. For validation, single questions were revised after the first versions of the questionnaires had been tested in trial-interviews.

The first draft of the questionnaire had been more comprehensive than the final version. During the pretests, it became obvious that the number of questions required too much effort for respondents to complete. Therefore some questions had been eliminated. Specific activities during the various phases of the innovation process were least interesting to the researchers at that date. As a result, the items concerning this topic had been deleted.

The questionnaires were first written and edited in German. Subsequently, they were translated in Swedish, Hungarian, and Chinese. The Swedish versions were written by a team member with bilingual knowledge in both languages, German and Swedish. The project teams in Hungary and China never completely translated and tested the survey instrument and, unfortunately, this part of the study was abandoned.

11.2. Samples

Data collection was completed in three industrial developed countries in Europe: Austria, Germany, and Sweden. Companies in these countries are, along with U.S. American and Japanese firms, the driving force in terms of high technology innovation.

The three industries approached – machinery, electric, and electronic industry – manufactured five different types of products:

- installations (consisting of mechanic elements, electrical elements and construction),
- systems for automatic control (incl. electronic data processing systems),
- single machines and equipment (not linked, stand alone),
- components and parts from suppliers (finished product, to be installed in or assembled to other single machines or equipment, system or installation without a remarkable machining or processing), and
- input materials (semi-finished products, raw and auxiliary material, and fuel).

Target product type had been technical product innovations. Therefore, machinery, electric and electronic industry was approached because technical oriented products – oppose to consume and service products – play a major role in their product line. Furthermore, the initiating research team has had the most experience in these industries, due to earlier studies.

All contacted companies employed more than 200 employees with a minimum of 50 employees working for the observed business unit. A maximum of three business units per company was allowed to interview.

In consideration of these premises, the selection of contacted companies respected certain quotas. These quotas were designed to reflect the proportion of company sizes in each branch of the determined entire population. This guaranteed

Table 1. Number of Employees of Observed SBUs.

Number of Employees (Proportion of Cases)	All (%)	Austria (%)	Germany (%)	Sweden (%)
Less than 200	16.9	30.1	10.2	11.0
200–499	38.4	38.7	33.6	50.5
500–999	20.1	20.9	20.1	18.7
1000–4999	20.5	9.2	29.5	16.5
5000–9999	3.2	0	5.7	2.2
10000 and more	1.0	1.2	0.8	1.1
Total	100	100	100	100

a certain representative of the results. Selection within the specific clusters was at random.

Data collection was completed over a six month period. A total of 92 Austrian, 126 German, and 48 Swedish business units is included. Table 1 displays the proportions of the number of employees of the strategic business unit by country.

Three interviews with three different executives were attempted in each firm:

• one interview with the top manager of the SBU, responsible for new product development;
• one interview with an executive managing an innovation project experiencing more than average success;
• one interview with an executive managing an innovation project experiencing less than average success.

However, in seven small companies with limited staff it was allowed that one person answered for both projects, the less and the more successful. In all cases, at least two interviews per business unit were completed.

In 266 business units 502 product innovations were analyzed. Table 2 provides more details.

Table 2. Frequencies of Interviews by Executive Position and by Country.

Population	All	Austria	Germany	Sweden
Number of top managers interviewed	266	92	126	48
Number of innovation project managers interviewed				
Project less successful than average	241	78	119	44
Project more successful than average	264	89	124	47
Total projects	502	167	246	91

To obtain a realistic evaluation of the new products' performance only product innovations launched at least one year prior to the survey were considered. The majority of product launches in this study took place between two years prior to the interviews. Most of the products were still on the market when the study was carried out. However, 12% had been withdrawn according to disappointing performance.

11.3. Procedure of Data Selection

Data were collected in two steps. First, a chief operating officer (COO) of the unit was interviewed was contacted by mail, followed by telephone, and finally by personal visit. Among other questions he or she was requested to name two projects within the unit: one project enjoying more than average, the other less than average success. In step two the responsible project managers were contacted to obtain more detailed information about the specific projects and to validate the responses to common questions answered by the COO and the senior project managers.

Two different types of questionnaires were applied. The different levels of authority of top manager and innovation project managers were respected. Aspects of both the SBU as a whole and the innovation project had been observed. The questionnaires for the less and more successful project were identical.

The interviewed managers were asked to choose the response option which they perceive best characterized their situation. This "self-reporting" approach has been acknowledged as an appropriate method (Harrigan, 1983; Huber & Power, 1985; Snow & Hambrick, 1980).

The effective cooperation and completion rates among firms initially contacted were very high in all three countries: 86% in Austria ($n = 105$ firms contacted); 81% in Germany ($n = 156$ firms contacted); and 94% in Sweden ($n = 51$ firms contacted). The high completion rates are likely due substantially to meeting face-to-face with each respondent and first gaining agreement to participate in the study from the COO in the respective firms.

The project managers were encouraged to consult available documents and colleagues while completing the survey. Questions, if any, were answered by the interviewer while the respondent completed the survey. To insure for high expertise in answering questions, each interviewer attended two or more earlier interviews with another interviewer before conducting one-on-one interviews. The survey responses were checked for completeness before concluding each interview meeting.

11.4. Statistical Analysis

The statistical analysis was executed with SPSS for Windows – Release 6.1.2. Additional calculations were completed with Microsoft Excel Version 5.0.

Means, standard deviation and variance analysis (F-test, ω^2) were calculated for all variables by country. Factor analyses were run for each block of the theoretical framework. Varimax rotation was applied. For the factors in this report all eigenvalues exceed 1.0. For verification of the internal consistency Cronbach Alphas have been computed. Factors with coefficient alphas less than 0.5 have not been taken into account for further analysis. Two-item factors have been excluded when the correlation coefficient was less than 0.30.

For more relevant results new variables were defined. The new factor value was the sum of weighted scores of all factor items. In case of negative loading the item scale was inverted.

Multiple regressions were run to explore dependencies between the sectors. Independent variables were all factors in sectors with theoretical links pointing on the sector containing the dependent variable. Factors were entered stepwise to the multiple regression equations.

12. LIMITATIONS

As every empirical study the following findings underlie certain restrictions. Although a wide range of industries and product types were examined it is not said that the results can be applied for different branches. Industries producing business-to-business goods might have comparable characteristics when their technical products have a similar relevance in terms of production as well as marketing.

This study focuses on the differences and similarities among the three countries. An analysis of the data per product type per country is not possible due to insufficient data. Consolidating the data cross-nationally within major product types would provide satisfactory data set sizes. However, this study was not undertaken.

Cultural differences could be considered as a violation of consistency because of the managers' self assessment. Also, questions could have been misinterpreted in different countries, even between Austria and Germany, both using the German questionnaire. The initiating research team examined this problem by applying variance analysis (including multiple mean comparisons), factor, and cluster analysis. Consequently, no difference between Austrian and German answers was detected while Swedish answers differ significantly.

This might be due to cultural bias or misinterpretation of the questions. Haire et al. (1966) point out that thinking and performing of managers with a different cultural background varies. However, it is more influenced by their adherence to a specific trade group than by the culture of their country.

With one exception (extent of external contracting of basic research for Sweden) the number of answers was sufficient for all statistical analysis applied in this study. A total of eight records with a high number of missing codes was deleted. Other records had been eliminated because the market entry was less than one year before data collection or the product was never launched.

The study focuses more on the functional areas and externals involved during phases of the new product development process instead of detailed activities within these areas. Therefore, a direct comparison of our findings with other models in the roles played by different functions in NPD is not advisable.

The use of seven-point scales and self-reporting surveys always pose limitations. Hart (1993, p. 35) compares the use of direct measures of numerical estimates of performance with "indirect" relative questioning and she concludes that the indirect approach "... yields a picture consistent with a direct measurement. Furthermore, the experience of the authors may well be more fruitful in accessing data." However, respondents' answers about a NPD process and NPP can never been assumed to be completely accurate; additional data should be collected using triangulation methods (e.g. asking questions, direct observation via case studies, and examining written/electronic documents and physical evidence) whenever possible. The present study benefits from having at least two persons confirm the direction of performance (more and less successful than average) for each NPD process examined.

13. FINDINGS FOR CONCEPTS IN THE NPD AND NPP MODEL

13.1. Conceptual Framework: The Factors of the Seven Global Dimensions

The conceptual framework consists of seven global dimensions all leading to the ultimate dimension, the managers' perceptions of success. These seven dimensions, whether key success factors or moderators, were examined through different questions with up to 36 items per sector. The involvement of functional areas and externals represents five stages, from initiation to market entry, including 18 variables each stage. Initially this model contains 217 variables in total. Using factor analysis for data reduction, up to eight factors were extracted in each sector. Involvement of functional areas and externals plays an extraordinary role, featuring five factors per stage.

First we explain the key success factors, External Environment and Strategy/Activities, and then describe the moderators – Instruments, Involvement, External Contracting, Characteristics at Market Entry, and Performance Ratios.

Cronbach coefficient alphas were computed for all factors. A factor featuring a coefficient alpha less than 0.5 did not enter later considerations but was explained in this paper. A total of 27 of the 37 remaining constructs showed high internal consistency (coefficient $\alpha \geq 0.65$).

13.2. Strategy and Activities

Cooper and Kleinschmidt (1995a) describe strategy as one driving factor of success. The three areas, R&D, Marketing, and Production had been observed. Both product and non-product advantages have been singled out as factors of this sector:

- Innovation strategy,
- Production process,
- Production type,
- Marketing,
- Pricing,
- Cooperation,
- Technical orientation, and
- Target market.

Innovation strategy describes whether the company acts as technological leader or follower, the emphasis on product innovations, and whether the SBU follows a path of small or large innovation steps. This innovation factor also portrays the first-to-market/market follower strategy, and the emphasis on product individuality as well as on patentability. The factor includes six survey items including low/high emphasis on product innovations; the firm being a technological follower versus leader; taking small versus large innovative steps; low versus high emphasis on patentability; emphasizing product individuality or not; being a market follower or first-to-market. Coefficient alpha was 0.78 for this factor for these six items.

Production process captures all items related to the manufacturing procedure. It contains type of production means, production technology, type of operation, emphasis on production process innovation, and production volume.

Production type focuses more on the product aspect within the production. It comprises the degree of product standardization, type of production, and production size.

Coefficient α scored -0.33. Five different product categories – from job-produced installations to large-series manufactured components – were examined in this survey. None of these categories was significantly more (or less) successful than the others. The production type factor is not taken into account in later research.

Marketing captures promotion, product range, and the total amount of the marketing budget. Promotion is limited on the support of market entry through communication.

Pricing exhibits another aspect of marketing strategy. Both variables contained in this construct, price level at market entry and in the post entry phase, load extremely high (0.82 and 0.78 respectively) and are highly correlated ($r = 0.62$).

Cooperation with externals describes the joint activities with other companies. The factor reflects the autonomous respectively joint venture policy in the fields of R&D as well as marketing.

With a loading of 0.50, the orientation of R&D towards product license sales was entered, too. This cooperation strategy missed the coefficient α cutoff exiguously. It was not considered in later examinations.

Technical orientation opposed to marketing or cost oriented policy is portrayed by this factor. It evaluates technology versus market orientation in R&D and technical versus cost oriented investment in means of production. The two variables are barely correlated ($r = 0.23$); therefore the factor was not entered in further equations.

Target Market captures to what extent the SBU operates on the various market segments and whether it is domestic or international oriented. The addition of the third variable, type of procurement of production means (internal development/buy-in) disturbs the consistency of the target market construct (Cronbach $\alpha = 0.32$).

13.3. Instruments

Managers use tools and instruments to achieve their goals. Eight dimensions have been extracted to describe the former 35 items:

- Cooperation of functional areas,
- Project management,
- Skills training,
- Planning tools,

- Creativity and assessment techniques,
- Project support,
- Conflict culture, and
- Conflict solving procedure.

Cooperation of functional areas is displayed by how members of different areas communicate with each other and work together. The cooperation construct merges the variables:

- motivation or incentive system to encourage early informal communication,
- cooperation and coordination of the relevant functional areas,
- obligation to achieve harmony between the relevant functional areas, and
- emphasis of an integration concept within the company philosophy or the company mission.

Project management portrays the way the project was guided. Project linked steering groups, project linked advisory groups, permanent steering committees, moderators for group work, and project groups were the options.

Skill training in contact- and team skills, discussion skills and willingness, and conflict management form this construct. All three variables load extremely high (0.86 and above) and the factor scores a coefficient α of 0.94.

Planning tools help to layout a process. Network planning, bar charts, mile stone plans, and manuals for innovation projects were captured in this planning tools factor.

Creativity and assessment techniques are necessary to generate evaluate new ideas. Beside the two variables, creativity techniques and assessment techniques, a third item – audits, with auditors independent from the project team – contributes to this construct.

Project support captures how the innovation project was promoted, either via work force or systems. The Project Support factor describes the extent to which an innovation process manager was employed, the use of an innovation supporting information system, and the emphasis on the autonomy of the innovation-/venture-units.

Conflict culture portrays the precautions taken to prevent negative impacts on the project outcome arising from conflicts. The factor merges the variables voluntary problem-solving groups, selection of personnel with productive conflict management potential, and swapping of personnel. The coefficient α scores 0.48, the factor was not considered in later research.

Conflict solving procedures explains mechanism to ease distress emerging from conflicts. The specific procedures are involvement of top management in conflict solving, internal company conciliation board or referee, and talking to immediate superior when conflicts arise. Cronbach α scores 0.48, the factor was not taken into account for further examinations.

13.4. Involvement of Functional Areas and Externals

Functional departments implement the strategies and carry out the activities set by the top management. In some cases externals participate in this process, either hired by the company or on a voluntarily basis.

Five stages had been examined: project initiation, product formulation, development, production, and market entry. Each phase was observed separately. The factors found for each stage were mostly congruent with those found for the other stages. However, loadings and coefficient alphas varied.

The variable "Other State Institutions" was created to measure the involvement of state institutions other than universities because almost all universities in the three observed countries are state run.

13.4.1. Initiation

Internal departments are those functional areas where no (or only little) contact to the market is expected. These departments are during the initiation stage: procurement/purchasing, controlling, financial department, human resources development, production, and quality assurance. The internal department factor provides high internal consistency (coefficient $\alpha = 0.85$).

External research comprises organizations like universities, other state institutions, commercial research institutes, and marketing research firms.

Marketing and market features the market forces. The company's marketing and distribution department, customer, and competitor form this factor. Internal consistency did not fulfill the arbitrary requirements; the Marketing and Market factor was not considered in later research.

External consultants represent those externals who are not researching. The involvement of suppliers and consultancy firms is merged in this construct, but the two variables are not correlated satisfactory ($r = 0.20$).

Top management and R&D compose an independent factor. However, they were not correlated satisfactory ($r = 0.15$) either.

13.4.2. Formulation

Internal departments in the formulation stage are extended by the suppliers. The new variable enjoys a factor loading of 0.50 and was therefore entered in the internal departments construct.

External research is enlarged with the variable involvement of inventors. One variable, commercial research institutes dropped out of this external research factor.

Marketing and management features a factor reflecting the engagement of top management, marketing department, and external consultancy firms. Coefficient α scored 0.40, internal consistency was not given.

Market is now representing the involvement of customers and competitors in the formulation phase. The two variables are not related strong enough, the market factor is not taken into account in later equations.

Research and development is a single item factor featuring the involvement of the R&D department only. The factor loading of this variable is 0.72.

13.4.3. Development

The Internal departments factor of previous stages is now split into two independent constructs, production and internal resources.

Production captures all areas and external involved in the production process. The involvement of procurement/purchasing, production, quality assurance, and suppliers are merged in the production factor.

Internal resources combine these internal departments which provide resources for the company. This internal resource factor includes the engagement of the financial department, human resources development, and controlling.

External research at the development stage is indifferent from the external research factor in the phase of formulation.

Marketing and market differs during the phase of development from the initiation stage in so far as customers were not included in this factor. Only the involvement of the marketing department and competitors is merged in the Marketing and Market factor. The two variables are not strongly correlated, further application is rejected.

Research and development here is extended with the involvement of commercial research institutes. The engagement of the two groups is not correlated at all. The R&D (development phase) factor is not included in later considerations.

13.4.4. Production

Externals are a combination of two earlier factors: External Research and Market. It describes the involvement of universities, other state institutions, commercial research institutes, marketing research firms, customers, and competitors. The internal consistency is high (coefficient $\alpha = 0.72$).

Internal departments capture the involvement of the same functional areas as in the initiation phase (production, controlling, quality assurance, financial department, and human resources development). The engagement of the procurement/purchasing department is measured through the procurement factor.

Marketing and management is extended by the involvement of the research and development department. This marketing and management construct surpassed the internal consistency cutoff exiguously.

Procurement features the involvement of all groups engaged in the procurement process: procurement/purchasing department, suppliers, and external consultancy firms.

13.4.5. Market Entry

Five factors have been disclosed for this stage. Only one – Internal Departments – shows high internal consistency. The others were not considered in further research.

Internal departments exhibit the involvement of all groups listed for internal departments at formulation stage.

External research describes the engagement of marketing research firms, external consultancies, and commercial research institutes.

Research and development at market entry is not limited on input from within the company. The R&D factor features the involvement of R&D/engineering department, other state institutions, and inventors.

Market contains the involvement of customers and competitors, exactly as during the formulation phase.

Marketing and management is composed of the engagement of the marketing and distribution department as well as the top management.

13.5. External Contracts

The three factors found contain all twelve variables related to this question. High internal consistency characterized the factors (coefficient $\alpha > 0.70$ on all constructs) and 9 out of 12 variables load high (0.75 and above).

Marketing research, planning, and communication illustrate the marketing sector. The four variables marketing research in early as well as later stages of the innovation process, marketing planning, and market communication at market entry stage achieve all loadings of 0.78 and above. The fifth item, production techniques, does not seem to fit at first sight (loading = 0.58) but it is correlated ($r > 0.27$) with all other four variables.

Research is also contracted externally. Basic research and applied research are scoring higher loadings than adaptation of product to specific customer needs and process development.

Hard- and software development is the last category of external contracts. It was not specified whether the development concerned production means or the product itself. This factor contains development of hardware, development of software, and joint development of hard- and software.

13.6. Characteristics at Market Entry

The evaluation of the product at market entry might effect managers' perception of the product's success. Two characteristics have been found, novelty of the product and risk for the company. However, both factors are not highly internal consistent (coefficient $\alpha = 0.66$ and 0.56 respectively).

Novelty describes the output of the innovation process. The degree of novelty to the company, for the market, for distribution and sales, and of the customers to the company is part of the novelty construct.

Risk is the downside of innovation. It is expressed through the customers' problem in using the product, the technical complexity of the product, and the expected marketing risk.

13.7. Performance Factors

Performance measures are often applied to capture the different facets of success. This study captured two questions on performance. One featuring the performance since market launch related to the expectations, containing eight variables. The other question evaluated the economical success.

The two different scales (both 7 point; much poorer/much better than expected versus very low/very high) applied in the questions might limit the results. Running the factor analysis with and without entering the economical success variable led to the conclusion that factor loadings as well as coefficient alphas improved with entering the additional variable.

Four performance ratios were extracted: financial performance, market impact, quality, and ecological compatibility. The latter two are single item factors with eigenvalues scoring less than 1.0. A two factor model did not separate the measures clearly.

Financial Performance describes the overall financial success of the product. It includes profit or contribution margin, economical performance, payback period for R&D cost, and sales.

Market Impact captures the effect of the product in the markets. This performance construct contains number of new customers, global market share, domestic market share, and sales.

Quality is the number of complaints activating a product recall. This one item scores an extremely high loading (0.95). Performance information was collected from much worse-to-much better than average on this item.

Ecological compatibility, another single item factor (loading $= 0.98$), measures the unanimity of the product with its ecological environment.

14. TESTING THE CONCEPTUAL FRAMEWORK: THE RELATIONS BETWEEN THE SECTORS

According to the hypothesis in the theoretical framework, multiple regressions were run to confirm the stated hypothesis. Figure 2 provides an overview over the findings. Figure 2 displays the results of all regressions run within the model.

14.1. Strategy and Activities

The key strategy factors in the empirical framework are innovation, production process, marketing, and pricing. Those excluded did not fulfill the internal consistency criteria.

The independent variables influencing strategy and activities derive from the external environment sector: Competition, socio-political and environmental concerns, and innovation challenge. Strategies not only depending on external environment but they are set by executives. Therefore, they are mainly autonomous which explains the low scores for the goodness of fit of the regressions run.

14.1.1. Innovation

Innovation strategies and activities relate with innovation challenge, competition, and socio-political and environmental concerns.

It is unsurprising that innovation challenge – external influences like the technical change ratio, innovation competition, and the customers' openness for novelties – accelerates innovation strategies. A high technological change ratio and strong innovation competition encourage producers to apply a leader strategy (Fierman, 1995), in technology as well as in the market. Customers open for novelties abet a high emphasis on product innovations and on patentability, and large innovation steps. Innovation challenge has the strongest impact on innovation ($\beta = 0.35, p < 0.0001$).

Strong effects of law and of the state and the importance of ecological interests lead to a high factor. This results in a positive impact on value for socio-political and environmental concerns innovation strategies. Companies are forced to come up with new solutions to meet the requirements set by the state and society. However, the influence is not as important as the other two factors ($\beta = 0.12, p < 0.01$).

Surprisingly competition has a negative effect on innovation strategies. In an environment characterized by a high intensity of competition – in the field of

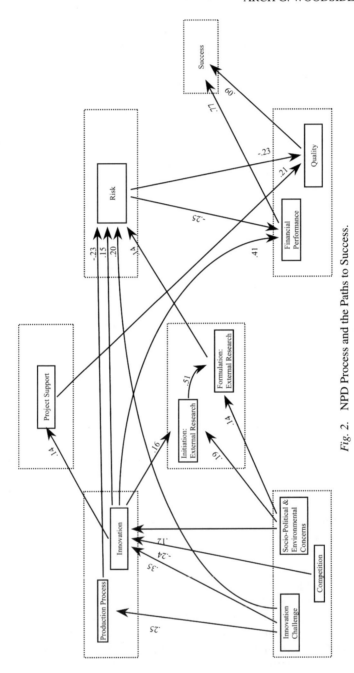

Fig. 2. NPD Process and the Paths to Success.

quality and/or price – innovation steps are kept small, and product individuality is not emphasized ($\beta = -0.24, p < 0.0001$). The company is more likely to follow an incremental product innovation strategy (Banburry & Mitchell, 1995). With these three factors, the regression achieves an adjusted R^2 of 0.16.

14.1.2. Production Process

Innovation challenge is the only factor significant in the regression equation ($\beta = 0.25, p < 0.0001$) for predicting production process. A high technological change ratio and a strong technology competition lead to the selection of specialized production means and to the emphasis on production process innovations (Tilton, 1995).

On the other hand, it is understandable that the production process is designed largely independent from external conditions resulting in a low goodness of fit for the regression equation (adjusted $R^2 = 0.06$).

14.1.3. Marketing

Product life cycles are short when technological change ratio is high and competition is technology driven. Markets characterized by short product life cycles require a higher marketing budget and more communication support during market. Thus, innovation challenge has a positive influence on marketing activities ($\beta = 0.19, p < 0.0001$). However, the influence is not to strong; adjusted R^2 counts 0.03. Table 3 includes this model.

14.1.4. Pricing

The competition factor has a strong impact on pricing ($\beta = -0.16, p < 0.001$). As expected, an intense price competition disables a company to maintain high prices. On the other hand, higher prices can be accomplished when demand is increasing and customers are open for novelties. Therefore, innovation challenge has a positive effect on pricing strategy ($\beta = 0.15, p < 0.005$). A high technological change ratio supports high prices at least at market entry. As would be expecting by an individual level analysis of the data, pricing strategy is not explained substantially by this regression model (adjusted $R^2 = 0.04$).

14.2. Instruments

The factors cooperation amongst functional areas, project management, project support, skill training, planning tools, creativity and assessment techniques, conflict culture, and conflict solving procedure form this sector. Strategy and activities and the external environment influence the application of these instruments. Note

Table 3. Beta Scores and Adjusted R^2.

BETA SCORES AND ADJUSTED R2	DEPENDENT VARIABLE	Strategy / Activities				Instruments						Involvement in Initiation		Involvement in Formulation			Involvement in Development			Involvement in Production					in Market Entry	External Contracts			Characteristics at Market Entry		Performance Ratios				
INDEPENDENT VARIABLE*		Innovation	Production Process	Marketing	Pricing	Cooperation of Functional Areas	Project Management	SkillTraining	Planning Tools	Creativity & Assesment Techniques	Project Support	Internal Departments	External Research	Internal Departments	External Research	R & D	Production	Internal Resources	External Research	Externals	Internal Departments	Management, Marketing, and R&D	Procurement	Inventors	Internal Departments	Marketing	Research	Hard- and Software Development	Novelty	Risk	Financial Performance	Market Impact	Quality	Ecological Compatibility	More or less successful than average
External Environment	Competition	-.24			-.16					.14				.09																					
	Socio-Political & Environmental concerns	.12					.10		.21	.20		.11	.19		.14			.11																	
	Innovation Challenge	.35	.25	.19	.15	.14			.12													.13						.18		.20					
	Demand Predictability						.16																												
	Suppliers' Competition							.15				.12													.09			.21							
Strategy / Activities	Innovation					.11	.21	.26	.11	.24	.14		.16			.16					.11	.12							.34	.15	.41	.15		.31	
	Production Process											.18						.09			.14		.11			.15				-.23		.23			
	Marketing					.13	.13			.10							.09																		
	Pricing																								.07										
Instruments	Cooperation of Functional Areas											.19						.08		.10	.12				.11										
	Project Management													.16					.09				.24												
	SkillTraining																																		
	Planning Tools																																		
	Creativity & Assesment Techniques																																		
	Project Support																																.21	.41	
Involvement in Initiation	Internal Departments													.65																					
	External Research														.51																				
Involvement in Formulation	Internal Departments																.62	.58								.13									
	External Research																		.79							.33			.14	.14					
	R & D																																		
Involvement in Development	Production																				.22	.14	.38												
	Internal Resources																				.46	.14					.19								
	External Research																			.52		.12	.11	.59			.40								
Involvement in Production	Externals																								.31										
	Internal Departments																								.29										
	Management, Marketing, and R & D																								.10										
	Procurement																								.20			.17							
	Inventors																																		
Characteristics at Market Entry	Novelty																																		
	Risk																														-.25		-.23		
Performance Ratios	Financial Performance																																		.77
	Market Impact																																		
	Quality																																		.09
	Ecological Compatibility																																		
	Adjusted R^2	.16	.06	.03	.04	.06	.11	.09	.08	.15	.02	.10	.06	.49	.31	.02	.41	.42	.65	.28	.48	.13	.30	.35	.47	.15	.21	.10	.14	.12	.16	.08	.07	.27	.66

* Sectors "Involvement in Market Entry" and "External Contracts" had not been entered in any equation.

for example in Table 3 how innovation strategy influences all the instruments variables. The overall influence of strategy is gradually stronger because more strategy/activities variables enter in the regressions compare to the external environment variables. The b scores tend to be higher, too. See Table 3 for details.

14.2.1. Cooperation Amongst Functional Areas

Innovation and marketing strategies as well as the external based innovation challenge have an impact on the selection of tools applicable to enhance cooperation among functional areas.

An innovation oriented corporation relies on cooperation, informal information, and coordination of functional departments. Motivational and/or incentive systems to encourage communication and cooperation help creating a creative atmosphere. In such an atmosphere a strategy perusing large innovation steps with a high emphasis on product innovations and patentability is more likely to succeed. Therefore the revealed relation between innovation strategy and cooperation tools is rational ($\beta = 0.11, p < 0.05$).

For the same reasons the strongest impact on cooperation instruments is executed by the external Innovation Challenge factor ($\beta = 0.14, p < 0.01$).

A marketing strategy with a broad product range requires more communication and cooperation amongst functional areas. An extended use of cooperation encouraging instruments derives from this strategy ($\beta = 0.13, p < 0.05$). With these three factors in the equation, the adjusted R^2 scores at 0.06.

14.2.2. Project Organization

Strategies concerning innovation and marketing, socio-political and environmental concerns, and the suppliers' competition are the determinants of the use of project management tools (adjusted $R^2 = 0.11$).

Innovation strategy has the strongest impact ($\beta = 0.21, p < 0.0001$). By using permanent or project linked steering committees the project team is focusing on the main issues of the project and is not following sidetracks.

A stronger emphasis on marketing strategy encourages project management ($\beta = 0.13, p < 0.01$) as steering or advisory groups have a better overview over the broader product range. A bigger marketing budget stresses the importance of controlling. Steering groups are the first to create controlling because of their close link to the project.

From the external environment, an increased supplier competition ($\beta = 0.16, p < 0.05$) and high socio-political concerns ($\beta = 0.16, p < 0.001$) result in a higher use of the instruments comprising project organization. Both factors display a more complex environment, the company responds with the tools comprised in project organization.

14.2.3. Skill Training

Training contact and team skills, discussion skills and willingness, and conflict management supports cooperation and communication within the project team and amongst functional areas. A cooperative and communicative environment is the soil for high innovativeness. Corporations following an innovation strategy train their employees' skills (Rhyne, 1994) ($\beta = 0.26, p < 0.001$).

In companies where employees have more power skill training are applied more often ($\beta = 0.15, p < 0.01$). Employees' power can either derive because the firm is stressing the worth and welfare of their employees or it is founded in the legal system accomplish by unions.

14.2.4. Planning Tools

Planning tools are employed by companies following an innovation strategy, in an environment with strong socio-political concerns, and in a market characterized by technological challenge. An innovation driven corporation uses planning instruments to achieve the strategy of large innovation steps (product innovation, patentability) and being first to market ($\beta = 0.11, p < 0.05$). Employing network planning, bar charts, or milestone plans help to keep deadlines and speed up the project's process.

The same reasons hold true for the positive influence of innovation challenge on the extent to which planning tools are applied ($\beta = 0.12, p < 0.05$). The socio-political and environmental concerns have a positive impact on the use of planning instruments ($\beta = 0.21, p < 0.0001$) in so far as strong effects of law and state require well defined procedures. Manuals for innovation projects, network planning, and milestone plans support the definition of structured procedures.

14.2.5. Creativity and Assessment Techniques

Innovation and marketing strategies, socio-political and environmental concerns, and competition determine the extent tools to enforce creativity and assessment techniques are used.

A company pursuing an Innovation strategy depends on new ideas and original solutions. Creativity techniques can encourage those outcomes. Assessing the output leads to an accelerated realization of generated ideas or the early termination of the innovation project. In the latter case resources are reallocated to strengthen the development of other projects. Emphasizing innovation strategy enhances the extent to which creativity and assessment techniques are utilized ($\beta = 0.24$, $p < 0.0001$).

The importance of marketing in a company's strategy has a positive impact on the use of creativity and assessment methods, too ($\beta = 0.10, p < 0.05$). Creativity is required to activate potential customers and to communicate product benefits at market entry. A broad product range leads to more assessments about the product's strategic decisions (Cespedes, 1988).

Strong competition influences the employment of creativity and assessment tools positively ($\beta = 0.14$, $p < 0.01$). In a high competitive market the company has to distinguish its product from competition. Creative solutions and well audited plans assist to achieve this goal.

The socio-political and environmental concerns effect the application of creativity and assessment instruments ($\beta = 0.20$, $p < 0.0001$). Solutions have to be found to meet regulations. Creativity is one ingredient to come up with answers to the defined problems. Additional research is needed to evaluate whether or not the requirements are fulfilled.

14.2.6. Project Support

Project support – the emphasis on autonomy of the innovation unit, employment of an innovation process manager, and the use of an information system – is influenced by the competitive environment only ($\beta = 0.14$, $p < 0.01$). However, the quality of the regression model is very low (adj. $R^2 = 0.02$). This indicates that competition is not the only factor determining the way the innovation project is supported. Other factors than competition were not entered in the regression equation. Therefore, different determinants than those concluded in the framework explain project support.

14.3. Involvement of Functional Areas and Externals

We examine the existence of influences from the external environment (H3), strategy/activities (H9), and instruments (H12) on the involvement of functional areas and externals for each of the five different stages. All factors which exceed the internal consistency criteria of the external environment and the strategy/activities enter in the regression models. The factors of the instruments have been selected manually. We expect the factors cooperation of functional areas and project management to have an impact on the involvement sector. They directly influence the project organization and the way the functional areas are working together. The remaining six factors are not expected to influence the involvement and have been sorted out in order to get stronger results.

The remaining factors in our empirical framework are the involvement of internal departments and the involvement of external research. The other factors did not meet the internal consistency criteria.

14.3.1. Internal Departments

The higher the power of employees and the more stable the social environment is, the more intensive are the internal departments involved in the initiation of a new product ($\beta = 0.12$, $p < 0.05$). A new product project can cause doubts and opportunities for the employees. If the power of the employees is high, they are more often able to influence and moderate the early stage of a new project. If the employees have less power, than they are less involved and perhaps the decisions are made by the corporate management (Blanchard, 1995).

Another determinant of internal department involvement from the external environment is socio-political and environmental concerns. The stronger the effect of law and the higher the ecological concern, the more the internal departments are involved ($\beta = 0.11$, $p < 0.05$). If a company has to consider legal aspects, the internal departments have to be more involved in the initiation of the project. They have to find a way how to handle these ecological concerns and how to fulfill the legal requirements.

The production process factor of the strategy sector influences the involvement, too ($\beta = 0.18$, $p < 0.001$). A highly specialized and innovative production leads to higher involvement of the internal departments. The production, as well as procurement/purchasing and quality assurance have to be involved in the innovation process to respond to the high importance of the production process strategy.

Most of the items comprising the production process factor are highly significant for more or less successful projects in Austria and Germany. In Sweden this difference is not significant.

A high use of instruments to encourage cooperation results in a high involvement of internal departments ($\beta = 0.19$, $p < 0.0001$). If the company uses instruments to encourage cooperation between the functional areas, the internal departments are getting more information and can give statements to the new product ideas. Especially the use of information technologies increases the power to employees (Stuart, 1995).

Overall, the explained multiple regression achieves an adjusted R^2 of 0.10, this is comparably low, but still an acceptable value if we consider the high number of records. This view is underlined by the high significance ($p < 0.0001$) of the F-test.

When the importance of this factor is compared for more and less successful projects, we can see that especially the involvement of quality assurance makes a difference. This is clearly identified for the Swedish dataset, where the difference is significant at the 0.05-level.

14.3.2. External Research

The strongest impact in the regression is caused by the socio-political and environmental concerns factor in the external environment ($\beta = 0.19$, $p < 0.001$).

This supports our hypothesis, that the company responds strong effects by law and state, strong ecological concerns, and turbulent competition with contracting external research. This enables the company to cope with changes and strong regulations for the new product (e.g. product safety).

In the same way the innovation factor from the strategy/activities sector influences the involvement of externals. The more a company emphasizes innovation within its strategy, the higher the involvement of external research ($\beta = 0.16$, $p < 0.01$). Universities and other research institutes often act as "knowledge suppliers" (van Rossum & Cabo, 1995).

The whole model for the involvement of external research during the phase of product initiation has a relatively weak adjusted R^2 level of 0.06 ($p < 0.0001$).

14.3.3. Formulation

In the formulation phase, the factors internal departments, external research and research and development exceed the internal consistency criteria.

Internal Departments. As explained in the hypothesis, the involvement of the factors is expected to depend mainly on the involvement of the same factor in the phase before. Therefore we entered the discussed factors from the initiation phase into the regression. As predicted, we found a strong relation between the intensity of involvement of the internal departments in the phase of initiation and the phase of formulation ($\beta = 0.65, p < 0.0001$).

The involvement of internal departments also depends on the instruments used for the project management ($\beta = 0.16$, $p < 0.0001$). Steering committees and project groups are composed with employees of different departments (Durand, 1995). If these instruments are used, the internal departments contribute higher in this phase than without them. Anand (1993) undines this point; he finds cross level teams enhance communication and cooperation among different company levels.

Another factor included is the competition ($\beta = 0.09, p < 0.05$). Competition increases the cost pressure (Coy, 1993; Lineback, 1994) and therefore the internal departments are more involved in the process to control the financial aspects. With these three factors in the equation, the regression scores an adjusted R^2 of 0.49 and is highly significant ($p < 0.0001$).

External Research. The external research factor during formulation phase depends mainly on the involvement of external research during project initiation. Even as the composition of the external research factor gradually changed, the b scores high and is highly significant ($\beta = 0.51, p < 0.0001$).

The factor still depends on the socio-political and environmental concerns factor of the external environment. The help from external researchers is still needed; the product has to be improved after early evaluations. Nevertheless, the b scores gradually lower ($\beta = 0.14, p < 0.01$). The adjusted R^2 is 0.31 ($p < 0.0001$).

14.3.4. Research and Development

A high emphasize on an innovation strategy increases the involvement of the R&D during the formulation ($\beta = 0.16$, $p < 0.01$). If a company is following a strategy to be the technological leader and to be innovative, than the company has to involve the R&D department more in the formulation of the new product to find new solutions or to develop new technologies. With only this one item the adjusted R^2 is quite low at 0.02 ($p < 0.01$).

14.4. Development

In the phase of development, three factors have been identified and fulfilled the internal consistency criteria: production, internal resources and external research.

14.4.1. Production

The production factor is identified for the first time during this development. Before the departments forming the production factor were included in the internal departments factor. Therefore the regression shows a relation to the internal departments factor during the formulation ($\beta = 0.62$, $p < 0.0001$). This finding illustrates that the intensity of the involvement depends on the one in the phase before.

The second factor influencing the involvement of production is the marketing factor in the strategy and activities sector ($\beta = 0.09, p < 0.05$). This finding seems to be surprising on the first view. If we look on the correlation between the items of both factors, we see a significant correlation ($p < 0.01$) between market entry not/intensively supported by market entry and all the items forming the production factor. To support the market entry intensively by communication, the functional areas forming the production factor, have to be stronger involved. The regression reaches an adjusted R^2 of 0.41 ($p < 0.0001$).

14.4.2. Internal Resources

The factor includes controlling, finance and human resources. These departments have been part of the internal departments factor in the phase before. The involvement of internal departments during formulation influences the internal resources factor strongly ($\beta = 0.58$, $p < 0.0001$).

The more relevant the socio-political and environmental concerns in the external environment, the more are internal resources involved ($\beta = 0.11, p < 0.01$). The company has to cope with effects of law and state, this is already explained before.

Another influence is coming from the production process factor of the strategy sector. An innovative production process strategy leads to a higher involvement of the internal resources during the development ($\beta = 0.09$, $p < 0.05$). The production process has to be controlled and the finance department has to check the financing of the production. This increases if the project follows a strategy of innovative production technologies, large-series-type production and/or specialized production means.

A high use of instruments to encourage the cooperation of functional areas leads to a higher involvement of internal resources, too ($\beta = 0.08$, $p < 0.05$). The internal resources are higher involved through these instruments, because they get information and can contribute to the development process. The adjusted R^2 for the regression is 0.42 and the regression is highly significant ($p < 0.0001$).

14.4.3. External Research
Again, this factor mainly depends on the same factor in the phase before. The external research factor in formulation determines the factor in the development ($\beta = 0.79$, $p < 0.0001$).

The second factor select by the regression is project management. If the project is organized in project groups and linked to steering or advisory groups or permanent steering committees, the external research factor is scoring higher ($\beta = 0.09$, $p < 0.01$). Steering committees and especially advisory groups are comprised of employees of different departments and externals (Durand, 1995). These steering committees are installed for the whole new product process; hence the externals are still in the committee during the development to advice the company. These steering committees therefore increase the involvement of externals for more than just the initiation and formulation. With these two factors the regression achieves a quite high adjusted R^2 of 0.65 ($p < 0.0001$).

14.5. Production

All factors of the production phase exceeded the internal consistency criteria. The five factors are: externals; internal departments; management, marketing and R&D; procurement; and inventors.

14.5.1. Externals
The involvement of externals depends on the involvement of the external research factor during development ($\beta = 0.52$, $p < 0.0001$). Another influence has the cooperation strategy ($\beta = 0.10$, $p < 0.0001$). The cooperation within the company is displayed in the external relations, too. The regression achieves an adjusted R^2 of 0.28 at a $p < 0.0001$.

14.5.2. Internal Departments

During the production phase the factor internal departments includes production and financial related departments, which were separated in two different factors during the development phase. Therefore internal departments is influenced by the production factor ($\beta = 0.22$, $p < 0.0001$) and internal resources ($\beta = 0.46$, $p < 0.0001$).

The production process strategy has an impact on the internal departments, too ($\beta = 0.14$, $p < 0.001$). A specialized, large series production and a high emphasis on production process innovation require a more intense involvement of the internal departments (incl. production and quality control) in the production phase.

Analogously the innovation strategy influences a higher involvement of the internal departments ($\beta = 0.11$, $p < 0.01$). The strategy to develop innovative product and to be the technological leader in the market results in higher requirements for the departments comprising the internal departments factor.

The instruments used to encourage cooperation within the company are causing a higher involvement, too ($\beta = 0.12$, $p < 0.01$). This relationship is consistent through all the examined phases and was explained before. Altogether, the regression has an adjusted R^2 of 0.48 and is also highly significant ($p < 0.0001$).

14.5.3. Management, Marketing and Research and Development

The three functional areas combined in production are the "innovators" of the company. The support of the corporate management is considered to be necessary to get the product to the market (Cooper, 1995) and marketing is often the source of a new idea as the marketing is connected to the customer (Kalwani & Narayandas, 1995).

R&D has to develop the new product idea and to search for new technologies. Therefore it is not surprising that this factor is depending on the innovation challenge factor in the external environment ($\beta = 0.13$, $p < 0.05$) and the innovation strategy ($\beta = 0.12$, $p < 0.05$).

More complex is the dependence on the preceding phase. The involvement of management, marketing and R&D does not depend on the factors which included these areas during development stage. It depends on production ($\beta = 0.14$, $p < 0.01$), internal resources ($\beta = 0.14$, $p < 0.05$) and external research ($\beta = 0.12$, $p < 0.05$).

As hypothesized, we expected no constantly high involvement of the corporate management during the process (H22). We interpret these relationships as an answer on the facts that are given from the mentioned three factors during the development phase. Information is gathered from the production related departments, the internal resources and the external researchers. During the production phase, the management, in cooperation with marketing and R&D has to evaluate these information and to decide what to do. The regression for the management, marketing and R&D factor has a relatively low adjusted R^2 of 0.13, but is still highly significant ($p < 0.0001$).

14.5.4. Procurement

The factor procurement includes procurement/purchasing, suppliers and external consultants. It depends on the factors production ($\beta = 0.38$, $p < 0.0001$) and external research ($\beta = 0.11$, $p < 0.05$) of the development phase. The procurement was included in the production factor of the development phase. Both relations are supporting our hypothesis about the dependence of the involvement of one factor on the involvement of the equivalent factor in the stage before.

The production process strategy influences this factor, too ($\beta = 0.11, p < 0.05$). The support of the procurement and supplier is needed to fulfill the strategy of a specialized, large series production and innovative production technology. Bandyopadhyay and Jayaram (1995) support this finding; they examine the implementing of just-in-time production and the contribution of the procurement.

The project management factor of the instruments sector influences the involvement of the procurement during the production ($\beta = 0.24$, $p < 0.0001$). Project groups including different functional departments, therefore the procurement/purchase and the external consultants are more involved. The regression achieves an adjusted R^2 of 0.30 ($p < 0.0001$).

14.5.5. Inventors

The fifth factor in the phase of production is solely comprised by the inventors. The involvement of the inventors depends only on the external research factor during the development ($\beta = 0.59$, $p < 0.0001$). This relation was expected; during development stage, inventors are included in the external research factor. With only this one factor the regression still achieves an adjusted R^2 of 0.35 and a high significance ($p < 0.0001$).

14.6. Market Entry

During the phase of market entry, there is only one factor exceeding the internal consistency criteria: internal departments. All factors except the inventors of the production phase determine the involvement of the internal departments during the market entry. Externals factor ($\beta = 0.31, p < 0.0001$) has the strongest influence, followed by the internal departments ($\beta = 0.29$, $p < 0.0001$). Lower effects are coming from the procurement factor ($\beta = 0.20, p < 0.0001$) and the management, marketing and R&D factor ($\beta = 0.10$, $p < 0.05$). This finding supports the hypothesis that the relations between phase four and five are more complex (H24) and can not be explained easily.

The stronger the suppliers' competition in the external environment, the more are the internal departments involved ($\beta = 0.09, p < 0.05$). Looking on the correlation among the items comprising the factors, we see that especially a high number of suppliers influence higher involvement of the internals: to coordinate and control this high number of suppliers, the areas comprising the internals factor are needed.

Pricing strategy influences the involvement of internal departments, too ($\beta = 0.07, p < 0.05$). To achieve high prices in the market, the product quality has to be outstanding. Therefore production, controlling, and quality assurance have to be involved higher.

If instruments to encourage the cooperation among the company are used the involvement of the internal departments increases ($\beta = 0.11, p < 0.01$). This was found in the other phases, too. The adjusted R^2 for the regression is 0.47 ($p < 0.0001$).

14.7. External Contracting

Companies place external orders in the fields of marketing, research, and hard- and software development. Input variables are production process related strategy, innovation challenge and employees within the external environment, the involvement of internal departments and external research during formulation and development phase, and the engagement of procurement at production stage.

14.7.1. Marketing

Strategy and the involvement of functional areas and externals at formulation stage affect the extent to which external marketing is contracted. A high involvement of external research during formulation is reflected by a high extent of external contracts in marketing ($\beta = 0.33, p < 0.0001$).

The engagement of internal departments has a positive effect on external contracted marketing services, too ($\beta = 0.13, p < 0.05$). One reason is that departments like controlling or finance insist on market research in that early stage of the innovation process to minimize the economic risk. The alternative to marketing research conducted by the marketing department is outsourcing.

Production process strategy has an impact on the extent to which marketing research is ordered externally ($\beta = 0.15, p < 0.01$). Innovative, highly specialized production means are expensive and represent a great risk. More information can reduce the risk.

14.7.2. Research

The involvement of functional areas and externals during the development phase determines the amount of external contracting of research (adj. $R^2 = 0.21$). Intensively involved internal resources – like controlling, financial department, and human resources development – predominate research orders ($\beta = 0.19$, $p < 0.01$).

The engagement of external research in development – the independent variable – is comprised by universities, other state institutions, marketing research firms, and inventors. Contracts include basic and applied research, process development, and product adaptation ($\beta = 0.40, p < 0.0001$).

14.7.3. Hard- and Software Development

Hard- and software development is influenced by innovation challenge and suppliers' competition of the external environment. A high innovation challenge leads to external contracting in hard- and software development ($\beta = 0.18$, $p < 0.01$). To maintain the company's position in an innovation challenge environment, the company has to prove if the soft- and hardware can be developed at the same quality as externals it could do.

Additionally a high suppliers' competition leads the company to contract the hard- and software development to externals ($\beta = 0.21$, $p < 0.01$) and the involvement of procurement in production ($\beta = 0.17, p < 0.05$). The adjusted R^2 scores relatively low at 0.10, this could explain why the last two factors are entered in the equation.

14.8. Characteristics at Market Entry

At market launch the project outcome was evaluated. Novelty and risk are the two observed characteristics. Strategy, external environment, and the involvement of external research during the formulation phase determine the product's evaluation.

14.8.1. Novelty

The external environment was believed to play a crucial role in managers' perception of product's characteristics (H5). After running the regression, innovation challenge was selected to have a significant impact on the degree of novelty. However, innovation challenge is correlated with innovation strategy, another input variable. We believe that the external environment is not causing novelty directly, but effects the evaluation through strategy.

A policy of being the market and/or technology leader and the successful transposition undoubtedly leads to a high degree of novelty–novelty for the market and/or for the company. If product innovations or product individuality are strongly emphasized the originality for distribution and sales might be high as well. Innovation strategy is the key factor for characterizing the product as novelty ($\beta = 0.34, p < 0.0001$).

Research executed by universities, other state institutions, and inventors brings new ideas in the company. It is free of old-fashioned ways of thinking and is performed on an advanced theoretical level. The intensity to which external research was employed effects the degree of novelty positively ($\beta = 0.14$, $p < 0.01$).

14.8.2. Risk

Innovation challenge ($\beta = 0.20$, $p < 0.01$) and an innovative strategy increases the risk factor ($\beta = 0.15$, $p < 0.01$). Large innovation step and high product individuality enlarge the technical complexity of the product. Customers have more problems in using the product when it is the first of its kind on the market. Market and/or technology leader expect a higher marketing risk as they have to communicate the product's benefits to the potential customer.

Surprisingly external research during formulation phase increases the risk evaluation, too ($\beta = 0.14$, $p < 0.01$). On the other hand, companies applying large-series production and flow operation were expecting a lower marketing risk at market entry ($\beta = -0.23, p < 0.0001$).

14.9. Performance Ratios

Financial performance, market impact, quality, and ecological compatibility are the measures of performance. Input variables are strategy/activities, instruments, involvement of functional areas and externals, external contracting and characteristics at market entry. The strategy sector plays a dominating role in the prediction of performance, whereas involvement and external contracting factors does not appear in any of the equations.

14.9.1. Financial Performance

Innovation strategy is the dominating factor in predicting financial performance ($\beta = 0.41, p < 0.0001$). This finding concurs with the results of Soni et al. (1993) and Cooper and Kleinschmidt (1995a) that product innovation relates positively with profitability.

The perceived risk at market entry has a negative effect on the financial achievement of the product ($\beta = -0.25$, $p < 0.05$). A higher marketing risk as well as customers' problems in using the product decreases sales and economic performance and prolongs the payback period for R&D cost.

14.9.2. Market Impact

A strong emphasis on product innovation attracts new customer and increases market share. Technology leader and first to market strategies have a positive impact on market share, too. Overall, innovation strategy enlarges market impact ($\beta = 0.15, p < 0.01$).

Large-series production combined with an innovative production technology premises higher sales. Production process strategy focusing on innovation and large scale is positively linked to market impact ($\beta = 0.23, p < 0.0001$).

Other determinants of market share (as price and the quality of a distribution network) have been disclosed in former literature. Their absence might explain the low goodness of fit (adjusted $R^2 = 0.08$).

14.9.3. Quality

The number of customer complaints and the number of events customer claimed a product recall based on a guarantee contract successfully is explainable through the risk perceived at market launch and the project support provided during the development process. For these two factors, the adjusted R^2 is quite low at 0.07.

Customers' problems in using the product are obviously mirrored in the number of complaints. Complaining customers are not satisfied with the product's performance; their expectations are not fulfilled. Therefore, the risk factor has a negative influence on quality measure ($\beta = -0.23, p < 0.05$).

Applying the appropriate tools can help to improve quality. The employment of an innovation process manager and the intensive use of an innovation-supporting information system keep the project team up to date. Well executed project support leads to higher quality ($\beta = 0.21, p < 0.05$).

14.9.4. Ecological Compatibility

Innovation strategy and project support manifest the project's outcome in ecological concerns (adjusted $R^2 = 0.27$). In an environment, where ecological consciousness is a key issue, product innovation takes ecological concerns into account. Technological leadership can also reflect the leading position in environmental technology. An emphasized Innovation strategy leads to ecologically compatible products ($\beta = 0.31, p < 0.001$).

An innovation-supporting information system can provide data on the latest development on the ecological sector as well. Innovation process managers can easily keep track that the development process is not leaving out ecological requirements. Applying the project support instrument improves the product's ecological compatibility ($\beta = 0.41, p < 0.0001$).

14.9.5. Success

The overall perception of success is best explainable with two performance ratios: financial performance and quality. The goodness of fit scores highest of all regressions within this framework (adjusted $R^2 = 0.66$).

Financial performance – capturing sales, profit margin, payback period for R&D cost, and economic performance measured versus the objectives in these category – dominates over the quality factor (β's: 0.77 and 0.09 respectively). Nonetheless, most of the performance measures that Cooper and Kleinschmidt (1995a) and Hart (1993) identify are included in these two factors.

15. COUNTRY LEVEL COMPARISONS

Figure 3 provides country level comparisons of average responses for three measures of NPP for NPD projects judged less and more successful by senior executives and the project managers. While the analysis may seem to confirm the obvious – performance associates with success – the results provide construct validity for the questions asked and indicate that all three NPP measures strongly associate with the two levels of success.

Note the consistency in the NPP average differences among the three countries. Swedish executives consistently report lower performance differences for the two levels of success compared to the Austrian and German executives. This national culture finding shows up consistently across all factors with only one exception (see panel C in Fig. 5).

In part Fig. 4 supports the findings discussed from the regression analyses of the influence of strategy/activities on success. Figure 4 illustrates the higher average scores for product innovativeness versus production process innovation and marketing as NPD strategy/activities. Note again in Fig. 4 how the average differences for low versus high success among Swedish executives are lower consistently compared to the Austrian and German executives.

Possibly the lower differences for the Swedish executives reflects underlying national culture values of Sweden compared to Austria and Germany (see Hofstede, 2001). For example, Hofstede (2001) reports low power distance index (PDI) scores for Sweden compared to Austrian and German PDI scores. Swedish executives and Swedish lifestyle particularly value harmony, equality, and balance as the following quote illustrates:

> Swedish companies place a strong emphasis on teamwork and tend to be less hierarchical than elsewhere. Each individual is valued so they feel they're contributing. While there's still a strong feeling of social harmony and equality in Sweden, entrepreneurship has flourished over the past 15 years or so, particularly in areas such as IT. (Statement by Greg Geiselhart (2004),

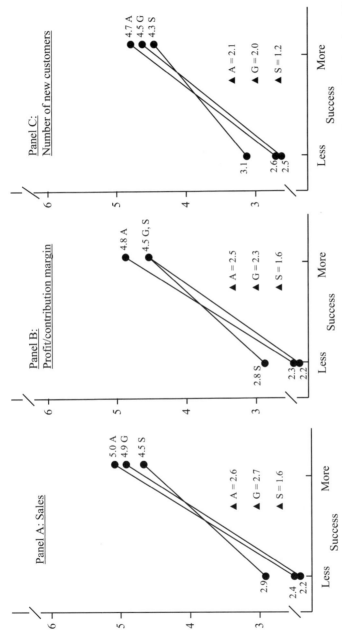

Fig. 3. Assessment of Performance Measures for Low and High NPP Projects. *Note:* A = Austria; G = Germany; S = Sweden. All differences for evaluating projects with less versus more than average NPP are significant ($p < 0.0000$) with substantial effect sizes ($\omega^2 > 0.20$). While the evaluations by country interactions are not statistically significant, the pattern is consistent: the more versus less performance differences are larger among the Austrian and German executives versus the Swedish executives for all four factors and nine measures of performance (Fig. 3 shows 3 measures for 2 of the 4 factors).

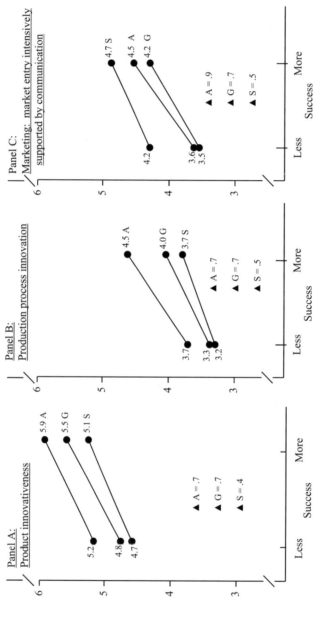

Fig. 4. Assessment of Strategy Activities in NPD for Low and High NPP Projects. *Note:* For the Austrian (A) and German (G) averages, all differences for evaluating projects with more versus less than average NPP are significant ($p < 0.001$) with small effect sizes ($\omega^2 > 0.04$). The differences for the Swedish averages are not significant statistically. While the evaluations by country interactions are not statistically significant, the pattern is consistent: the more versus less performance differences are larger among the Austrian and German executives versus the Swedish executives for all eight factors and all measures of strategy activities (Fig. 4 shows 3 measures – one each for 3 of the 8 factors).

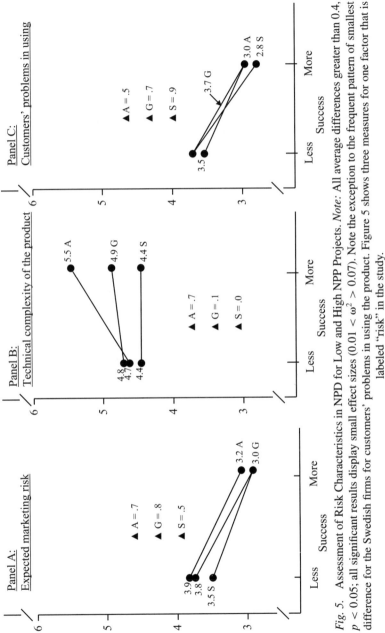

Fig. 5. Assessment of Risk Characteristics in NPD for Low and High NPP Projects. *Note:* All average differences greater than 0.4, $p < 0.05$; all significant results display small effect sizes ($0.01 < \omega^2 > 0.07$). Note the exception to the frequent pattern of smallest difference for the Swedish firms for customers' problems in using the product. Figure 5 shows three measures for one factor that is labeled "risk" in the study.

Marketing Manager, Telematics Valley, Sweden, who moved from Minneapolis, Minnesota (USA), to Sweden in 1990; itsweden.com/speakers.)

In a study (Globe, 2004) of 18,000 executives in middle management positions in 62 countries for nine cultural values, Swedish executives had the lowest average score (3.4) on assertiveness and German and Austrian executives had the highest average scores, 4.6 and 4.7 respectively. Consequently, Swedish executives may be less prone to report values as extreme for antecedents for less versus more successful new products than their Austrian and German counterparts.

Figure 5 includes the average scores for the three questions of the risk variable for each of the three countries for less and more success new products. Note the usefulness of examining the averages for individual items in the survey. Rather low marketing risk relates to high success as seen by the project managers in all three countries. High versus low technical complexity associates with high success only among the Austrian executives. See Fig. 5 for further details.

16. CONCLUSION

Understanding the antecedents and predicting more versus less success for new product performance requires more than ranking KSFs. For high-tech, new industrial products, modeling the system of relationships among NPD strategy and actions and NPP is a useful step toward modeling the system dynamics of how high versus low success occurs. Dependencies between external environment and company internal variables exist and these dependencies relates strongly to the project's success. Almost all hypotheses are supported.

The framework shows the three layers: key success factors, moderators, and project evaluation. External environment as one of the key factors has not only a direct and strong impact on the company's strategy and activities (H1) and the instruments used (H2). External environment affects the involvement of functional areas and externals (H3) as well as external contracting (H4) and the product assessment at market launch (H5). Additionally, external environment has an indirect impact on performance ratios through strategy and activities.

A useful view for increasing sense making of NPD processes is to consider strategy and activities as upstream influences leading eventually to NPP via interfunctional and external involvement and via affecting risk. Also, a strong influence on instruments was detected (H8). The impacts on involvement (H9) and evaluation at market launch (H11) is less intensive but still important. The strongest direct effect of a strategy variable on NPP links innovativeness to financial performance (supporting H7).

Three moderators in the framework are supported empirically: instruments, involvement of functional areas, and external contracting. The findings indicate important but subtle influence of these moderators. Three of five links hypothesized were not confirmed. The instruments used have no impact on the characteristics of the product (H16). A higher intensity of involvement of functional areas and externals is not leading to better performance (H15). And the extent of external contracting is indifferent to performance, too (H19).

The influence of instruments on performance was validated (H18). Compared to the impact of strategy and external environment the influence was rather weak. Same applies to the effect of involvement on product characteristics (H14).

Figure 2 provides a comprehension look at paths to more versus less success. Figure 2 presents a parsimonious view of 11 upstream and direct factors relating to success. Care should be taken not to view only these 11 factors to be necessary or sufficient antecedents for success. Because of substantial relationships (multi-colinearity) among variables antecedent to success, additional models only somewhat more modest in explanatory ability can be identified. However, the view of NPD associating with NPP and success is particularly useful for generalizing executives' networks of beliefs relating to new high-tech industrial product strategies and outcomes.

Innovation strategy has the strongest impact. It is influenced by the innovation challenge, a measure for innovation competition, technological change, and customers' openness for novelties. Competition has a negative impact on innovation strategy. Innovation steps are smaller and product innovation is less emphasized when more competitors wrestle intensively for market share.

Socio-political and environmental concerns play a less important role when innovation strategy is set up. This is not surprising as many regulations concerning technology are in effect in Europe. Environmental groups are very powerful and exert their influence.

Strategy and activities stressing innovation in the production process are leading to success, too. Compared to innovation strategy, their impact is far less strong. The application of innovative production technology and specialized production means is promoted by the external innovation challenge.

The influence of external environment is not limited on strategy. The socio-political and environmental concerns have an impact on the involvement of functional areas and externals. Especially external research at initiation and formulation stage is employed when the pressure is high. This engagement leads to a higher risk at market entry. Additionally, innovation challenge is increasing the risk measure. This characteristic captures hazards like customers' problems in using the product, technical complexity, and the expected marketing risk.

The characteristics at market entry are only partly influenced by the external environment and involvement of external research. This sector within the measurement layer is mainly affected by strategy. A policy stressing innovation increases the risk factor. Furthermore, risk is affected by the innovation challenge.

The second measurement sector comprises the performance ratios. Strategy and product characteristics at market entry affect this sector. Financial performance is determined by the innovation strategy and activities and the risk factor. The strategy impact is far stronger than the threat originated in the risk. Innovation strategy and risk affect quality, too. However, the strategy does not influence quality directly. It affects project support first. This instrument captures the emphasis on the autonomy of the innovation unit and the employment of an innovation process manager. Additionally, the use of innovation-supporting information system is included. Companies focusing on innovation widely employ these instruments. The result is a better product quality. These two performance ratios – financial performance and quality – were measured against the company's expectations. Together they form the executives' perceptions of success.

17. IMPLICATIONS AND RECOMMENDATIONS

This study examines the NPD process, where factors in every sector are identified and their impacts on success are measured. Financial performance and quality are the two performance ratios managers have in mind when they think about success. What actions help reach high financial performance and maintain high quality?

17.1. Innovative Thinking and Actions

Successful project management follows an innovative approach. Being the technological leader with individual products enables the company to protect their innovations through patents. This leadership results in high financial performance.

17.2. Supporting the New Project Team

To execute an innovation strategy project supporting tools are necessary. Innovation strategy itself does not lead to higher quality. Through applying project supporting instruments the strategy is transformed into high quality.

Information systems are providing facts about the product progress from other involved areas. The systems also provide the results and characteristics of previous projects. With these facts the project participants are better informed and able to recognize their specific problems in the "big picture." The additional information and the recognition of the project's environment are crucial for a well designed product.

Employing an innovation process manager enforces a more overall approach. This manger is responsible for bringing the project members together and increasing the consistency of their undertaken activities. Therefore the application of the project support instruments leads to higher quality.

17.3. Minimizing Risk

The downside of innovation is risk. The project management has to be conscious about that. The risk factor is multidimensional featuring marketing risk as well as a high technical complexity of the product followed by customers' problems to use it. These risks jeopardize the financial success and the quality of the product.

The contradiction of the innovation strategy now becomes obvious: to follow an innovative strategy increases financial performance – on the other hand it also increases the risk.

17.4. How to be Innovative Without Increasing the Risk?

The innovative product strategy has to be complemented by an innovative production strategy. Technical complexity can be reduced by using innovative technology. New technology enables the company to find new and more primitive solutions. The result is a consistent innovation strategy with reduced risk.

18. RECOMMENDATIONS FOR FUTURE RESEARCH

This study describes the impact of the innovation strategy on performance. For further research we recommend to examine the results for alternative complete strategies. This could be accomplished by clustering the data sets by their followed strategy and observing the achievement within the performance ratios as well as the differences in influencing the other sectors of the framework.

Furthermore factors outside the framework influencing the sectors should be uncovered. These factors should be included and their impact should be examined. We especially expect outside factors to influence strategy. Determinants of the external environment should be uncovered, too. We expect a strong cultural dependence.

A cross-cultural study, perhaps observing Europe, North America, and Asia, is recommended. Examining the impacts of the different cultures on the performance of high-tech new product innovations deserves attention in research in industrial marketing strategy.

ACKNOWLEDGMENTS

The authors gratefully acknowledging the efforts of the research team in completing the study that this paper describes; members of the team include: Hans Donnert, Martin Fark, Goran Lindstrom, Ralph M. Pfeffer, Dieter Schoenknecht, Roland Sjostrom, and Sabine Watzlik.

REFERENCES

Aaker, D. A. (1988). *Strategic market management*. New York: Wiley.
Anand, K. N. (1993). Eliminating shop-floor defects with cross-level teamwork. *Quality Progress, 26*, 45–47.
Armstrong, J. S. (1995). Sales forecasting. In: M. J. Baker (Ed.), *Companion Encyclopedia of Marketing* (pp. 378–393). London and New York: Routledge.
Banbury, C. M., & Mitchell, W. (1995). The effect of introducing important incremental innovations on market share and business survival. *Strategic Management Journal, 16*, 161–182.
Bandyopadhyay, J. K., & Jayaram, M. J. (1995). Implementing just-in-time production and procurement. *International Journal of Management, 12*, 83–90.
Blanchard, K. (1995). Points of power. *Executive Excellence, 12*(3), 11–12.
Booz-Allen & Hamilton (1982). *New product management for the 1980s*. New York: Booz-Allen & Hamilton Inc.
Calantone, R. J., Vickery, S. K., & Dröge, C. (1995). Principles of new product management: Exploring the beliefs of product practitioners. *Journal of Product Innovation Management, 12*, 235–247.
Cespedes, F. V. (1988). Channel management is general management. *California Management Review, 31*, 98–120.
Christensen, C. M. (1997). *The innovator's dilemma*. Cambridge: Harvard Business School Press.
Cooper, R. G. (1995). New product development. In: M. J. Baker (Ed.), *Companion Encyclopedia of Marketing* (pp. 462–479). London and New York: Routledge.
Cooper, R. (1998). Benchmarking new product performance: Results of the best practices study. *European Management Journal, 16*, 1–17.
Cooper, R. G., & Kleinschmidt, E. J. (1987). Success factors in product innovation. *Industrial Marketing Management, 16*, 215–223.
Cooper, R. G., & Kleinschmidt, E. J. (1995a). New product performance: Keys to success, profitability, profitability & cycle time reduction. *Journal of Marketing Management, 11*, 315–337.
Cooper, R. G., & Kleinschmidt, E. J. (1995b). Performance typologies of new product projects. *Industrial Marketing Management, 24*, 439–456.
Coy, P. (1993, June 28). In the labs, the fight to spend less, get more. *Business Week* (3325), 102–127.

Deng, S., & Dart, J. (1994). Measuring market orientation: A multi-factor, multi-item approach. *Journal of Marketing Management, 10,* 725–742.

Dougherty, D. (1990). Understanding new markets for new products. *Strategic Management Journal, 11,* 59–78.

Dougherty, D. (1992). Interpretive barriers to successful product innovation in large firms. *Organizational Science, 3,* 179–202.

Doyle, P., Shaw, V., & Wong, V. (1993). International competition in the UK machine tool market. *Journal of Marketing Management, 9,* 383–391.

Durand, T. (1995). Concurrent engineering and interfunctional project groups. *International Journal of Technology Management, 10,* 67–78.

Emshwiller, J. R. (1991). Suppliers struggle to improve quality as big firms slash their vendor rolls. *Wall Street Journal* (August 16), B1–B2.

Fierman, J. (1995). When genteel rivals become mortal enemies. *Fortune, 131,* 90–100.

Friar, J. H. (1995). Competitive advantage through product performance innovation in a competitive market. *Journal of Product Innovation Management, 12,* 33–42.

Geiselhart, G. (2004). Sweden's high quality of life- three foreign managers give their views. http://www.itsweden.com/speakers/main.aspx?id=12&pageid=125.

Globe (2004). Cultural acumen for the global manager. Mumbai, India: Larsen & Toubro (ccd@lth.ltindia.com) at http://www.larsentoubro.com/students_portal/news02.asp.

Hagedoorn, J., & Schakenraad, J. (1994). The effect of strategic technology alliances on company performance. *Strategic Management Journal, 15,* 291–309.

Haire, M., Ghiselli, E. E., & Porter, L. W. (1966). *Managerial thinking: An international study.* New York: McGraw-Hill.

Harrigan, K. R. (1983). Research methodologies for contingency approaches to business strategy. *Academy of Management Review, 8,* 398–405.

Hart, S., & Banbury, C. (1994). How strategy-making processes can make a difference. *Strategic Management Journal, 15,* 251–269.

Hart, S. N. (1993). Dimensions of success in new product development: An exploratory investigation. *Journal of Marketing Management, 9,* 23–41.

Hofstede, G. (2001). *Culture's consequence.* Thousand Oaks, CA: Sage.

Huber, G. P., & Power, D. J. (1985). Retrospective reports of strategic level managers: Guidelines for increasing their accuracy. *Strategic Management Journal, 6,* 171–180.

Kalwani, M. U., & Narayandas, N. (1995). Long-term manufacturer-supplier relationships: Do they pay off for supplier firms? *Journal of Marketing, 59,* 1–16.

Lee, M., & Na, D. (1994). Determinants of technical success in product development when innovative radicalness is considered. *Journal of Product Innovation Management, 11,* 62–68.

Lineback, J. R. (1994). Pressure builds for lower cost MPU testers. *Electronic Business Buyer, 20,* 30–32.

Montoya-Weiss, M., & Calantone, R. (1994). Determinants of new product performance: A review and meta-analysis. *Journal of Product Innovation Management, 11,* 397–417.

Nath, D., & Sudharshan, D. (1994). Measuring strategy coherence through patterns of strategic choices. *Strategic Management Journal, 15,* 43–60.

Ragin, C. C. (1987). *The comparative method.* Berkeley: California University Press.

Rhyne, L. (1994). Product development with a new technology: Lessons from the America's Cup. *Journal of Product & Brand Management, 3,* 39–50.

Shaw, V. (1995). Successful marketing strategies: A study of British and German companies in the machine tool market. *Industrial Marketing Management, 24,* 329–339.

Snow, C. C., & Hambrick, D. C. (1980). Measuring organizational strategies: Some theoretical and methodological problems. *Academy of Management Review, 5*, 527–538.

Song, X. M., & Parry, M. E. (1997). A cross-national comparative study of new product development processes: Japan and the United States. *Journal of Marketing, 61*, 1–18.

Soni, P. K., Lilien, G., & Wilson, D. T. (1993). Industrial innovation and firm performance: A re-conceptualization and exploratory structural equation analysis. *International Journal of Research in Marketing, 10*, 365–380.

Specht, G. (1995). Schnittstellenmanagement. In: B. O. Tietz, R. Köhler & J. Zentes (Eds), *Handwörterbuch des Marketing* (2nd ed., pp. 2266–2276). Stuttgart, Germany: Schäffer-Poeschel Verlag.

Sterman, J. (2000). *Business dynamics*. Boston: McGraw-Hill/Irwin.

Stuart, A. (1995). Can you spare some change? *CIO Conference Supplement* (February 1), 3–4.

Tilton, H. (1995). Intermediates '95: Photoactives add capacity. *Chemical Marketing Reporter, 248*, SR11–SR14.

van Rossum, W., & Cabo, P. G. (1995). The contribution of research institutes in eureka projects. *International Journal of Technology Management, 10*, 853–866.

Zinkhan, G. M., & Pereira, A. (1994). An overview of marketing strategy and planning. *International Journal of Research in Marketing, 11*, 185–218.